ATHEISM

A Philosophical Justification

A·T·H·E·I·S·M

A Philosophical Justification

MICHAEL MARTIN

TEMPLE UNIVERSITY PRESS

Philadelphia

Temple University Press, Philadelphia 19122
Copyright © 1990 by Temple University.   All rights reserved
Published 1990
Printed in the United States of America

The paper used in this publication meets the minimum requirements of
American National Standard for Information Sciences—Permanence of Paper
for Printed Library Materials, ANSI Z39.48-1984

Library of Congress Cataloging-in-Publication Data

Martin, Michael, 1932 Feb. 3–
    Atheism : a philosophical justification / Michael Martin.
       p.   cm.
    Bibliography: p.
    Includes index.
    ISBN 0-87722-642-3 (alk. paper)
    1. Atheism   I. Title
BL2747.3.M3313   1990
211'.8—dc20

                                                                    89-33121
                                                                    CIP

In memory of Louis Young

CONTENTS

PART II ◊ POSITIVE ATHEISM

11. The Justification of Positive Atheism: Some Preliminaries

12. Divine Attributes and Incoherence

13. Atheistic Teleological Arguments

14. The Argument from Evil

15. The Free Will Defense

16. Natural Evil

17. Soul Making Theodicy

PREFACE

This book is dedicated to the person who had the greatest influence on my disbelief in God, my step-grandfather, Louis Young. Lou—I always called him that—was a self-educated man. Although Lou had only a fourth-grade education he read highbrow nonfiction books, wrote letters that were published in the Cincinnati newspapers, and attended lectures on a wide variety of topics. All this greatly impressed my mother and father, who considered Lou to be *very* smart and intellectual.

Even as a young child I had many talks with Lou about God. He was an atheist with a definite metaphysical turn of mind, and I recall vividly his saying, "It is difficult to understand how something could be uncaused; but it is also difficult to understand how a chain of causes could go on forever." This was heady stuff for a young boy, and it no doubt influenced not only my later views but even my choice of profession. There were few careers besides philosophy in which one was paid for pursuing the sorts of questions that Lou asked. Lou's influence was particularly strong since my parents had only the vaguest religious convictions, were never members of a church, and gave me no religious instruction. His influence remained with me all through my childhood in Cincinnati, my service in the Marine Corps, my brief stint at the U.S. Naval Academy, my college days in Arizona, and my years in graduate school at Harvard.

Growing up as an atheist in a Catholic lower-middle-class neighborhood in Cincinnati was not as difficult as one might suppose. When the subject of God came up in our childhood conversations and I expressed my atheistic views, they were not greeted with scorn. Whether this was the result of my friends' respect for my fighting prowess or their natural religious tolerance, I do not know. Although I was a quiet, introspective boy and kept to myself a great deal of the time, I was big and strong for my age and was considered a good fighter by my peers.

Nevertheless, even as a child I was aware that my atheism was not something I should advertise. I realized that most people believed in God and suspected the worst of atheists. Indeed, I vividly recall the day in the third grade when I revealed to a sympathetic guidance counselor that I was an atheist. This confession to a stranger was such a traumatic and emotional experience that I broke out in hives a quarter of an hour later and had to be sent home.

When I joined the Marines at age seventeen I had to declare which religious denomination I belonged to: Catholic, Protestant, Jew. Since there was no category for nonbelievers I arbitrarily chose Protestant. Fortunately, the Marine Corps did not seem to care what one said, and there was no pressure to attend church. Indeed, I never set foot inside a church until I was 19 and, for a brief time, a midshipman at the U.S. Naval Academy, where I was compelled to attend chapel. Once I learned the system I began to peel off into the bushes as we marched to chapel on Sunday morning, and then walk back to my room and sleep. It is fortunate that I soon resigned, for eventually I would have been caught.

When I started studying philosophy as an undergraduate in Arizona, the refutations of the classical arguments for the existence of God held great fascination for me. I realized for the first time that the questions I had heard Lou Young ask when I was a small boy had been discussed by famous religious skeptics and that atheistic thought had a long history and many brilliant advocates. However, as I pursued my graduate education in philosophy at Harvard I specialized in the philosophy of science, not the philosophy of religion. The former seemed vital and fresh, the latter dead and uninteresting. It seemed to me quite clear in the light of the evidence that disbelief in God was more justified than belief. So the question of God's existence seemed closed, while questions about the justification of induction, the existence of theoretical entities in science, and the incommensurability of scientific theories were open. I have changed my mind about this, primarily because of the recent resurgence of interest in the philosophy of religion. Although I have not changed my opinion that disbelief in God is more justified than belief, as I explain in the Introduction, recent philosophical arguments for theism make it necessary to reassess and reformulate the case for atheism.

Besides Lou Young, many atheists and critics of religion have influenced my thought. Of the philosophical greats, David Hume certainly stands out. Bertrand Russell's famous essay "Why I Am Not a Christian" also had a great effect on me. In recent years J. L. Mackie, Michael Scriven, Kai Nielsen, Wallace Matson, Richard Robinson, Paul Kurtz, Edward Madden, Peter Hare, Antony Flew, Walter Kaufman, Ernest

Nagel, and Paul Edwards have all influenced my thinking about religion. I am grateful for their inspiration.

This book would not have been finished without the help of my wife, Jane. Although she had philosophical work of her own to do, she unselfishly read the manuscript in its entirety and made invaluable suggestions concerning style and substance. I would also like to thank Jane Cullen, my editor, who encouraged me and gave me her moral support and wise advice. In addition, I am grateful to two anonymous readers whose suggestions improved the manuscript.

Finally, I would like to thank the editors and publishers who have given me permission to incorporate the following essays into this book:

"Swinburne's Inductive Cosmological Argument," *The Heythrop Journal*, 27, 1986, pp. 151–162; incorporated by permission of *The Heythrop Journal*.

"Reichenbach on Natural Evil," *Religious Studies*, 24, 1988, pp. 91–99; "The Principle of Credulity," *Religious Studies*, 22, 1986, pp. 79–93; "Pascal's Wager as an Argument for Not Believing in God," *Religious Studies*, 19, 1983, pp. 57–64; "Theological Statements, Phenomenalistic Language, and Confirmation," *Religious Studies*, 14, 1978, pp. 217–221; incorporated by permission of *Religious Studies* and Cambridge University Press.

"Does The Evidence Confirm Theism More Than Naturalism?" *International Journal for Philosophy of Religion*, 16, 1984, pp. 257–262; copyright © 1984 by Martinus Nijhoff Publishers, Dordrecht, Boston, Lancaster, and incorporated by permission of Kluwer Academic Publishers.

Newton, Massachusetts
July 1989

Introduction

The Scope of Nonbelief

Nonbelief in the existence of God is a worldwide phenomenon with a long and distinguished history.[1] For example, philosophers of the ancient world such as Epicurus and Lucretius were nonbelievers,[2] and leading thinkers of the Enlightenment such as Baron d'Holbach and Diderot were professed atheists.[3] Even in the Middle Ages there were skeptical and naturalistic currents of thought.[4] Expressions of nonbelief are found, moreover, in the literature of the Western world: in the writings of Mark Twain and Upton Sinclair; Shelley, Byron, and Thomas Hardy; Jean-Paul Sartre; and Turgenev.[5] Today, nonbelievers are found from the Netherlands to New Zealand, from Canada to China, from Spain to South America.[6]

The number of nonbelievers in the world today is surprisingly large. *The World Christian Encyclopedia*, perhaps the most comprehensive source of religious statistics available, estimated in 1982 that by 1985 there would be about 210 million atheists and 805 million agnostics in the world.[7] This means that about 21 percent of the world's population consists of nonbelievers. Moreover, this figure does not include members of religions such as Jainism that involve no belief in God. Since this calculation is based in part on public opinion polls and on governmental, church, and business statistics, as well as on other data,[8] there is good reason, furthermore, to suppose that the actual number of nonbelievers is much greater. In many countries there is social pressure against expression of nonbelief in God.[9] In addition, the yes–no format of typical surveys is likely to result in the recording of responses of unbelief only by hardened atheists.[10] Nonetheless, even the typical yes–no format shows that in some countries the percentage of nonbelievers is surprisingly high. For example, to the question "Do you believe in God or a universal spirit?" 56 percent of the people in Japan either answered no or were uncertain; in Scandinavia the figure was 35 percent, in West Germany 28 percent, in France 28 percent, and in the United Kingdom 24 percent.[11]

Public opinion surveys in the United States using a typical yes–no format indicate that over a 30-year period (1944–1975), 2 percent to 6

percent of the population were nonbelievers.[12] Supposing the population
to be approximately 226 million, this means that in the United States
alone, between 4.52 and 13.56 million people in that period did not
believe in God. Studies where more flexible responses have been allowed
suggest that the number of nonbelievers in the United States is much
higher than this. For example, in one survey only 68 percent of the
sample agreed strongly with the assertion, "I believe in the existence of
God as I define Him."[13]

Given the large number of nonbelievers, it is not surprising that atheistic societies, periodicals, and conferences exist across the world.[14] Despite
its extent and history, however, at least in the United States atheism
remains almost invisible. While the opinions of religious leaders are
sought by the media on the various moral and social issues of the day,
those atheist leaders such as Madelyn Murray O'Hair and Paul Kurtz are
ignored. In fact, atheists are considered so suspect that a presidential
candidate who was an avowed atheist would have little chance of being
elected. Theistic religion today has the spotlight.

A Brief Defense of Atheism Against Some Common Criticisms

Why is atheism so invisible? One reason is that atheists and atheism have
a negative image not only in the popular mind but even in sophisticated
intellectual circles. Not only is atheism a false view, it is said, but atheists
are immoral, atheistic morality is impossible, and life is absurd or meaningless or worthless if atheism is true. The most important criticism—
that atheism is false—is answered in the chapters to follow. Several objections to atheism that fall outside the book's main argument are examined
here. I first consider theistic attacks on the moral character of atheists;
then the allegation that it is impossible to have an adequate morality
without belief in God; and, finally, the claim that life is meaningless,
absurd, or without value if God does not exist. Although I cannot possibly
cover all the criticisms that have ever been made against atheism, I have
tried to include the ones that are historically most important and the
ones that are most commonly raised by believers.

CRITICISMS OF THE MORAL CHARACTER OF ATHEISTS

Historically, atheists have been attacked for flaws in their moral character: It has often been alleged that they cannot be honest and truthful.
For example, in 1724 Richard Bentley, an English Christian apologist,
maintained that "no atheist as such can be a true friend, an affectionate
relation, or a loyal subject."[15] John Locke, famous for his advocacy of

religious tolerance, maintained in *A Letter Concerning Tolerance*, "promises, covenants, and oaths, which are the bonds of human society, can have no effect on an atheist."[16] Locke's belief was enshrined in legal rules that prevented atheists from testifying in court. For example, until the passage of the Evidence Amendment Act of 1869, atheists in England were considered incompetent to give evidence in a court of law.[17] Similar legal restrictions were found in the United States. For instance, in 1856 one Ira Aldrich was disqualified as a witness in an Illinois case after he testified that he did not believe in a God that "punishes people for perjury, either in this world or any other,"[18] and as late as 1871 the Supreme Court of Tennessee maintained:

> The man who has the hardihood to avow that he does not believe in God, shows a recklessness of moral character and utter want of moral sensibility, such as very little entitles him to be *heard or believed* in a court of justice in a country designated as Christian.[19]

Although this view is no longer enshrined in our laws, many religious people still hold the opinion that religious belief is closely related to moral action. But is there any reason to suppose that religious belief and morality are intimately associated?

To answer this question, a number of different theses need to be distinguished. Someone holding the view that religion and morality are connected might be maintaining that belief in God is a necessary condition for having a high moral character. This thesis can be stated as follows:

(1) It is impossible to have a high moral character without belief in God.

That person might, however, simply be arguing that, although it is possible to have a high moral character without belief in God, such a state of affairs is unlikely. This thesis can be formulated thus:

(2) It is more probable than not that a person without a belief in God will not have a high moral character.

Or our critic of the moral character of atheists may be maintaining that people who do not believe in God are less likely to have a high moral character than people who do. Consider:

(3) It is more probable that a person without a belief in God will not have a high moral character than that a person with a belief in God will.

Now, it seems clear that thesis (1) is false. Jainists are atheists, yet they follow a strict ethical code that forbids injuring any living creature.[20]

David Hume has been described as the saintly infidel;[21] Percy Shelley, who was an atheist, has been described as driven by principles and high ideals, and his life has been characterized as one of generosity and integrity.[22] A theist might of course disagree with these judgments, but then one must ask if he or she is using the sentence "X is a person of high moral character" in such a way that it entails "X believes in God." If so, then no possible evidence could refute (1). However, since this is surely not the way the expression "high moral character" is normally understood, the onus to say what possible evidence could refute (1) is on the theist.

What about thesis (2)? It entails that most atheists do not have high moral characters. Whether or not this is true I do not know. It must be understood, however, that an atheist could readily admit the truth of (2). He or she could maintain that high moral character is a rare trait, one that is distributed at approximately the same low rate of frequency among theists and atheists alike. That is, the atheist could argue that in addition to (2) the following thesis is true:

(2') It is more probable than not that a person with a belief in God will not have a high moral character.

Is (2') correct? If it is, then (3) must be mistaken. Is it? The empirical research is vast and difficult to interpret. Certainly some studies suggest that religion may have little to do with criminal activity,[23] delinquency,[24] and humanitarian behavior[25] and that, statistically speaking, atheists are morally at least as well off as theists. For example, a review by Gorsuch and Aleshire of the empirical research up to 1974 on the relationship between Christian belief and ethnic prejudice indicated that moderately active church members were more prejudiced than highly active members and that highly active members were as tolerant as nonmembers. This review concluded that "holding a strong value position which allowed one to stand outside the value tradition of society at large was crucial in adopting a nonprejudiced position and was typical of nonreligious and highly religious people."[26] Thus Gorsuch and Aleshire suggest that, at least as far as ethnic tolerance is concerned, nonbelievers are just as moral as the most devout religious believers and more moral than the less devout believers. Although reviews such as this one are suggestive, at the present time there does not seem to be any clear and definite evidence showing (3) to be false. On the other hand, there is no clear and definite evidence that supports (3). Thus the truth of (3) cannot at present be conclusively determined. However, one can say that in the light of available evidence, (3) seems dubious.

For the sake of argument, let us assume that (3) is true. One still cannot immediately leap to the conclusion that there is a causal relation between nonbelief in God and low moral character. After all, atheists might have other traits that causally account for the supposed differential rate of high moral character between them and theists.

At the present time this is of course pure speculation. We do not even know *if* (3) is true, let alone, if it is, *why* it is. Without better evidence than we have now, the criticism that atheism has an adverse influence on moral character is unwarranted.

ATHEISTIC MORALITY

The above criticism maintained that low moral character was associated with atheism. However, critics of atheism might maintain that although atheists might be no less moral than believers, they have no justification for being so. The problem with atheism, then, is not that atheists have lower moral character than theists but that they can offer no plausible rationale for their moral actions.

One common criticism of atheism is that without God there are no moral obligations and no moral prohibitions. Every action whatsoever is morally permitted. But then, there is no such thing as right or wrong moral action. In other words, if there is no God, moral anarchy will prevail in theory if not in practice. If God does not exist, people may well be kind and compassionate. However, they will have no *obligation* to be kind and compassionate, and nothing will deter them from being cruel and inhumane.

This criticism can be formulated as follows:

(4) If atheism is true, then moral anarchy is true.

But what does moral anarchy mean? Let us understand moral anarchy in such a way that it entails:

(5) For any action A, it is morally permitted that A.

Alternatively, the criticism can be construed as making a much less serious charge against atheism: that if atheism is true, then there are no absolute moral principles; that morality based on an atheistic foundation would be relative. This thesis can be stated as follows:

(6) If atheism is true, then there are no absolute moral statements.

Another way to state the thesis is as follows:

(6′) If atheism is true, then all ethical statements are relative.

What does it mean to say that a moral statement is absolute? On one construal, an absolute moral statement is one in which the analysis of moral statements contains no egocentric expression—that is, no expression whose meaning varies systematically with the speaker as do personal pronouns (I, you), the corresponding possessive adjectives (my, your), words that refer directly but relatively to spatial and temporal location (this, that, here, now, past, present).[27] Let us call this construal of an absolute moral statement the *no-egocentric-term analysis*. To illustrate, consider the following analyses of the expression "is morally obligatory."

(a) p is morally obligatory = p is considered morally correct in this culture.
(b) p is morally obligatory = Bringing about p brings about the greatest good for the greatest number.
(c) p is morally obligatory = p is strongly approved of by me.
(d) p is morally obligatory = p is commanded by God.
(e) p is morally obligatory = If there were an ideal observer, that observer would contemplate p with a feeling of approval.

Now, the analysis of sentences (a) and (c) contains the egocentric terms "this" and "me" respectively. On the other hand, the analysis of (b), (d), and (e) contain no egocentric terms. On this construal, then, an ethical statement such as "Taking care of your children is morally obligatory" is an absolute moral statement when "is morally obligatory" is used in the sense of (b) or (d) or (e). If "is morally obligatory" is used in the sense of (a) or (c), it is a relative moral statement.

The no-egocentric-term analysis of ethical absolutism is in terms of the meaning of ethical expressions. But another analysis of ethical absolutism is possible. We sometimes think of ethical absolutism in methodological terms: Ethical absolutism is true if there would be agreement on what ethical statements are either justified or unjustified. This agreement would be achieved by some unique rational ethical methodology—let us call it methodology M—used in conjunction with unlimited factual knowledge. Ethical relativism would be true if ethical absolutism was false; that is, if M when combined with unlimited factual knowledge would sometimes result in the justification of conflicting ethical statements. On this construal, to say that a moral statement is absolute means:

An ethical statement S is absolute IFF either S or ~S, but not both, would be justified in terms of methodology M when used in conjunction with unlimited factual knowledge.

On this interpretation it does not follow that if an ethical statement is relative, then both S and ~S would be true. S and ~S could not both be true, since they contradict one another. But both S and ~S could be justified by M when used in conjunction with unlimited factual knowledge.[28] Let us call this construal of an absolute moral statement the *unique justification analysis.*

There is still another construal of ethical absolutism. As we have seen, the unique justification analysis assumes a unique rational method. It may be argued that there is no unique rational method of ethical evaluation. The view that there is a unique rational method we call *methodological ethical absolutism,* and the view that there is no unique rational method we call *methodological ethical relativism.* (In (6') above we were discussing nonmethodological ethical relativism, since the ethical relativism at issue was not about ethical method but about ethical statements justified by some unique rational method.) The critics of atheism may maintain:

(7) If atheism is true, then methodological ethical absolutism is false.

It is important to see that methodological ethical relativism is compatible with complete agreement on all ethical matters and methodological ethical absolutism is compatible with wide-spread disagreement. On the one hand, ethical agreement may not be based on using the same rational method, since the agreement may be purely accidental. On the other hand, wide disagreement may be the result of not applying the method or at least not applying it long enough, or it may result from nonmethodological relativism. In the latter case, one unique rational method may justify many conflicting moral statements. How likely this possibility is, is another question.

What can we say about these charges against atheism? Let us consider (4) first. An ethical theory called the divine command theory holds that what is morally obligatory, forbidden, or permitted is construed in terms of what God commands or fails to command.[29] In some of its versions this theory entails moral anarchy if God does not exist. For example, on one version of this theory the following analysis of "morally permitted" is offered:

(f) It is morally permitted that p = It is not the case that God commands that ~p.

On this construal, if God did not exist, everything would be permitted. Thus if one embraced this theory, thesis (4) would be justified.

However, there is good reason to reject analysis (f) even if one believes in God. First, there is an obvious semantic problem. (f) does not seem to be what many people mean by "morally permitted." But suppose we do not assume that the meaning of "morally permitted" can be analyzed in terms of what God does not command.[30] Suppose we assume only that:

(g) It is necessary that for all p it is morally permitted that p IFF it
     is not the case that God commands that ~p.

This means that in any possible worlds where p is morally permitted, it
is not the case that God commands ~p and conversely.

Although this version of the divine command theory does not have
the semantic problem of (f), it has others. First, there is a moral problem.
Presumably, (g) is meant to capture the idea that p is morally permitted
because it is not the case that God commands that ~p and not the reverse.
However, it is difficult to see how this can be captured unless we assume
that God has no essential moral nature. But if this is assumed, then in
some possible worlds it is not the case that God commands that it not be
the case that people be cruel for its own sake. But this seems morally
repugnant to many people, and attempts by theists to justify such implications of their view are unpersuasive.[31]

There is also an epistemological problem: How can we know what
God commands? How, in particular, can one separate what are genuine
commands of God from what are only apparent commands? This problem is serious for several reasons. First of all, there are a number of
apparent sources of God's revelations to humans. In the Western tradition alone there is the Bible, the Koran, the Book of Mormon, and the
teachings of Reverend Moon and many lesser known religious figures.
Clearly it is impossible to follow the alleged commands found in all these
books and issued by all the people claiming to speak for God, since they
are in conflict. Furthermore, even within a single religious tradition—
say, Christianity—the same alleged command of God is interpreted in
different ways. For example, the command "Thou shalt not kill" is said
by some Christians to entail pacifism and by others not to, by some to
justify abolishing the death penalty and by others not to. What *is* the
correct interpretation of the command? In addition, some apparent commands seem to many modern religious people, even those within this
tradition, to be morally questionable. The Old Testament forbids male
homosexual relations. The New Testament forbids divorce except for
infidelity. Must modern Christians follow these apparent commands although they conflict with some of their deeply held moral judgments?

Finally, there is a conceptual problem. The notion of a command is
ambiguous in that it is sometimes considered a certain kind of speech act
and sometimes the content of this speech act. Thus the content of the
command to close the door is conveyed by an imperative sentence "Close
the door" and is the result of a speech act involving an utterance of those
words on a certain occasion. This ambiguity holds in religious contexts
too. The content of the command not to kill is conveyed by the imperative
sentence "Thou shalt not kill" and is presumably the result of a speech

act involving the utterance of those words. But this creates a certain problem. If one interprets God as a nonspatial, nontemporal being without a body, what sense can one make of God's performing a speech act? Such a being would seem incapable of an act that assumes, if not a body, at least some spatial and temporal point of origin. The only sense one can make of a divine command is to understand God in a nontranscendent way as a being operating within space and time. But even this concession may not be enough, for it is unclear how a being within time and space could fail to have a body or how such a being could issue commands. The existence of a voice issuing commands seems to presume some physical vocal apparatus; golden letters written in the sky would seem to presuppose some physical writing appendage. However, this understanding of God assumes an anthropomorphism rejected by sophisticated theologians today. Moreover, since this anthropomorphic god is a being operating within time and space, it is subject to empirical investigation. Unfortunately, the available evidence no more supports the hypothesis of its existence than it supports the hypothesis that Santa Claus exists. The advocate of the divine command theory is thus presented with a dilemma. If God is transcendent, the notion of divine command seems difficult to understand. If God is construed in anthropomorphic terms, the concept of divine command makes sense but the hypothesis that God exists becomes very improbable.

Moreover, moral anarchy would *not* follow from all forms of this theory. For example, on another version of the divine command theory—the hypothetical divine command theory—the following is offered as an analysis of "morally permitted":

It is morally permitted that p = It is not the case that if there were a God, God would command that ~p.

This analysis of "morally permitted" does not entail moral anarchy if God does not exist. Therefore, on this theory, (4) would not be justified. Thus (4) is justified only if one accepts one form of an implausible ethical theory.

What about (6), the claim that if atheism is true, there are not absolute moral statements, or the equivalent claim (6') that if atheism is true, then all ethical statements are relative? These claims are also incorrect. Consider first the no-egocentric-term analysis. Ethical statements that use "is morally obligatory" in the senses of analyses (b) and (e) are just as absolute as ethical statements that use "is morally obligatory" in the sense of analysis (d). Yet analyses (b) and (e) are compatible with not believing in God.

It may be argued that (b) and (d) have many problems and are implausible as analyses of "is morally obligatory." I am not attempting here to enter into the controversy over which analysis of ethical terms, if any, is correct. However, three points should be made. First, whether (b) and (d) are adequate analyses is controversial. It has been by no means established that they are inadequate. However, as we have seen, the divine command theory has serious problems. So if the two absolute analyses considered above have problems, the divine command theory may have problems that are just as serious. Third, analyses (b) and (e) are by no means the only absolute analyses that do not presume the existence of God. The theistic critic of a morality that does not presume God's existence must show that all these analyses are faulty.

What about the unique justification analysis? According to some well-known theorists who have proposed a rational ethical method to evaluate moral statements—a method that does not presume any belief in God—few, if any, moral statements are likely to turn out to be relative. For example, William Frankena maintains that in ethical deliberation we should be fully informed, conceptually clear, impartial, and willing to universalize our ethical principles. He says:

> It is . . . extremely difficult to show that people's basic ethical and value judgments would still be different even if they were fully enlightened, conceptually clear, shared the same factual beliefs, and were taking the same point of view. To show this, one would have to find clear cases in which all of these conditions are fulfilled and people still differ. Cultural anthropologists do not show us such cases; in all of their cases, there are differences in conceptual understanding and factual belief. Even when one takes two people in the same culture one cannot be sure that all of the necessary conditions are fulfilled. I conclude, therefore, that meta-ethical relativism [the view that two conflicting basic ethical judgments may be equally correct] has not been proved and, hence, that we need not, in our ethical and value judgments, give up the claim that they are objective in the sense that they will be sustained by a review by all those who are free, clear headed, fully informed, and who take the point of view in question.[32]

Richard Brandt argues for the qualified attitude method, which is very similar to the one recommended by Frankena. Brandt, like Frankena, also maintains that it is very difficult to show that in using this method, a moral statement and its contradictory would both be justified. Unlike Frankena, however, Brandt seems to believe that there is at least one case where the evidence suggests that a moral statement is relative.[33] However, he argues that such cases may be rare:

> Thus, ethical relativism may be true, in the sense that there are *some* cases of conflicting ethical judgments that are equally valid; but it would be a mistake to take it as a truth with pervasive scope. Relativism as an emphasis

is misleading, because it draws our attention away from the central identities, from widespread agreement on the items we care most about. Furthermore, the actual agreement on the central things suggest the possibility that, with better understanding of the facts, the scope of the agreement would be much wider.[34]

We may conclude that even if there are conflicting ethical statements that are equally justified by some rational method—a claim that has not been proven—the scope of the disagreement may be very small.

Is there one unique rational method of ethical deliberation that does not presume God? Or is (7) true? Answering this question in any detail is beyond the scope of this book. However, two brief points can be made. One point is that there have been several impressive attempts to develop such methodology.[35] A critic of atheism who advances (7) must show that all these attempts are unsuccessful. The other point is that although the divine command theory purports to provide an absolute analysis of ethical discourse, in practice it does not. Although one is supposed to follow the commands of God, there is wide disagreement over what God commands, and there seems to be no rational method to reconcile these disagreements. So if it turns out that there is no unique rational method in ethics if God does not exist, it does not follow that there is one *in practice* if God does exist and if one accepts the divine command theory.

So far I have argued that acceptance of atheism does not entail moral anarchy and that several varieties of ethical absolutism are compatible with atheism. I have also maintained that if it turns out that an ethics without God is relativistic, the relativism might be quite tolerable. Furthermore, I have stressed that any problems that one finds with atheistic ethics should always be put in perspective by comparing these with the enormous problems connected with the divine command theory.

There is one final thing that must be said here. Even if all the criticisms of the moral implications of atheism were true—which they are not—this would not show that atheism is false. Fortunately, we need not choose between an atheism justified by the evidence but with more undesirable ethical implications than theism, and a theism not justified by the evidence with less undesirable ethical implications than atheism. Atheism, as I have shown, has no more undesirable ethical implications than theism. As we shall see, atheism, not theism, is justified by the evidence.

ATHEISM AND THE MEANINGLESSNESS, ABSURDITY, AND VALUE OF HUMAN LIFE

Another common criticism of atheism is that if there is no God, life has no meaning or value. Atheism, it is said, is committed to a bleak, pessimistic view of human existence. Such a view has been expressed by believers and nonbelievers alike. Thus William James, a believer, maintained that "old age has the last word: a purely naturalistic look at life, however enthusiastically it may begin, is sure to end in sadness,"[36] while G. L. Romanes, a nineteenth-century biologist and nonbeliever, confessed at the end of *A Candid Examination of Theism* that "with this virtual denial of God, the universe has lost to me its soul of loveliness."[37] Other nonbelievers have also expressed deeply pessimistic attitudes. For example, Bertrand Russell argued that "all the labors of the ages, all the devotion, all the inspiration, all the noonday brightness of human genius, are destined to extinction in the vast death of the solar system, and the whole temple of man's achievement must inevitably be buried beneath the debris of a universe in ruins."[38]

One problem in evaluating this criticism is that it is not easy to understand. What does it mean to say that life has no meaning? that life has no value? In addition to the issue of what exactly the critics mean, it is unclear what arguments they have to justify their criticisms. Perhaps they have none and are merely expressing a mood that has no rational basis. We can approach our problem by noting certain implications that seem to follow from a commonly accepted naturalistic and scientific view of the world. It is to this view of the world that critics seem to be implicitly appealing when they attempt to derive pessimistic implications from atheism.

It is commonly accepted that if a naturalistic view of the world is true, then all of the following are true:

(1) There is no cosmic purpose.
(2) Each human life is finite.
(3) Human life in general is finite.

The acceptance of (1) seems to be entailed by the acceptance of naturalism. This acceptance rules out not only belief in a personal theistic God but also belief in an impersonal purpose that guides our destiny. In contrast, (2) and (3) are not entailed by naturalism per se. However, they seem overwhelmingly probable in the light of our present scientific evidence. Given these three premises, the critic of atheism attempts to derive conclusions such as the following:

(4) Human life is meaningless.
(5) Human life is absurd.
(6) Human life is worthless.

The question is, given the facts described in (1), (2), and (3), are the pessimistic conclusions of (4), (5), and (6) justified?

The first thing to note before we attempt to answer this question is that atheism per se is not committed to the naturalistic world view of science that entails (1), (2), and (3). Some of the nontheistic religions—for example, Jainism—deny (1), (2), and (3). One can be an atheist and believe in the immortality of the individual soul and in a grand cosmic plan of salvation.[39] Thus only certain kinds of atheism can plausibly be accused of having pessimistic implications.

The second thing to note is that if pessimistic conclusions do follow from a naturalistic atheism, this does not show that such an atheism is false. This is not to say that the practical implications of a theory have no relevance in theory choice. However, as I argue in Chapter 1, although practical implications might play some role in theory choice, their role should be very limited. There is a presumption that practical considerations should play no role in theory choice and there is a presumption, if practical considerations do play a role, that they should be used only when nonpractical considerations cannot decide. Since, as we shall see, there are good nonpractical reasons for belief in atheism, there is a presumption that belief in atheism should not be based on whether it has pessimistic implications. Thus a rational person might regret that a view so well justified by the evidence has pessimistic implications, but one should not abandon it simply for these reasons. If pessimism is justified by the evidence, then we must be pessimistic. If we are optimistic when pessimism is justified, we are irrational.

The final thing to note is that unless they are supplemented by other premises, (1), (2), and (3) do not entail (4), (5), and (6). Although we may be able to reconstruct arguments that do justify the pessimistic conclusions of (4), (5), and (6), we must look carefully at the additional premises used in them, for unless these are true, the arguments fail. Let us attempt to reconstruct some of the arguments that seem to be explicitly or implicitly involved here.

The Meaninglessness of Human Life
Perhaps one of most important arguments used to show that life is meaningless is what might be called the argument from cosmic purpose, which can be stated as follows:

(1) If there is no cosmic purpose, then human life in general has no meaning (purpose).
(2) There is no cosmic purpose.

---

(3) Therefore, human life in general has no meaning (purpose).
(4) If human life in general has no meaning (purpose), then individual human lives have no meaning (purpose).

---

(5) Therefore, individual human lives have no meaning (purpose).

The crucial term in this argument is "meaning." Granted, it is reasonable to suppose that in this context "meaning" and "purpose" have approximately the same connotation. However, as commentators have made clear, "purpose" is ambiguous.[40] The term is sometimes used to refer to the function that an object was created to perform and is sometimes used to refer to a person's reason for doing certain things. Once this ambiguity is made clear, the above argument is seen to rest on an equivocation.

Let us call the former the *created function* sense of purpose. According to this sense, one may say that the purpose of an automobile is to provide transportation or that the purpose of a hammer is to drive nails. Clearly what is meant here is that providing transportation is the function an automobile was created to serve, that driving nails is the function a hammer was created to serve. But if God does not exist, then human beings do not have a creator and hence do not have a purpose in the created function sense. In this sense, then, statement (3) of the above argument is correct. Furthermore, the created function sense of purpose is what seems to be meant in the first occurrence of the term in premise (4).

Consider now what may be called the *reason* sense of the term "purpose." When we say that some person has a purpose for doing something, in this sense we only mean that he or she has some reason for the action. It seems reasonable to identify the second occurrence of the term in (4) with the reason sense of purpose. If so, then (4) is incorrect. We can see this if we reformulate (4) so that the ambiguity is made clear.

(4′) If human life in general has no created function, then individual humans have no reasons for their actions.

Clearly (4′) is false. Humans usually do have reasons for their actions, even actions that involve long-term commitment and a life's work. The truth of (4′) has nothing to do with there being any cosmic purpose or even with whether humans believe that there is some cosmic purpose. In particular, it has nothing to do with whether humans are created by God.

Perhaps a slightly different argument is intended, however. One might admit that people do give reasons for their actions and yet maintain that, for life to have meaning, the reasons they give must be justified. It might be argued that they are not and could not be justified if there is no God; that if there is no cosmic purpose, the reasons humans give are arbitrary and must be so. This argument from arbitrary justification can be stated as follows:

(1) If there is no cosmic purpose, there is no justification for the reasons humans have for their actions.

(2) If there is no justification for the reasons humans have for their actions, the reasons humans have for their actions are arbitrary.

(3) There is no cosmic purpose.

---

(4) Therefore, the reasons humans have for their actions are arbitrary.

What does it mean to say that there is no justification for the reasons that human beings give for their actions? Presumably, that no matter what reason a person gives to justify an action, it is not better than any other reason that could be given. On this interpretation, it is difficult to see how premise (1) of the argument from arbitrary justification is to be maintained. If there is no cosmic purpose, some reasons for one's actions would still be better than others. Implicitly the argument from arbitrary justification might be relying on reasoning similar to that which was criticized earlier in this chapter; namely, that if there is no God, moral anarchy is the correct moral position. Such reasoning is even less plausible here than it was in the context in which we initially encountered it. As we have seen, atheism does not entail moral anarchy. Supposing that it did, it would not follow that *all* reasons are arbitrary. It would simply show that all *ethical* reasons are arbitrary. Thus if any action was morally permitted, not wanting to experience pain would still be a better reason for not putting your hand on a red hot stove than for going to the moon. Moreover, if atheism did not entail moral anarchy, then ethical reasons would not be arbitrary; some would be better than others in justifying a particular action. For example, under normal circumstances, not causing a sentient being needless pain would be a better moral reason for not torturing a kitten than not being conducive to humankind's intellectual growth. Even if some form of ethical relativism is true, ethical reasons would not be arbitrary; their correctness would simply be relative.

The Absurdity of Human Life

Closely related to the idea that life is meaningless is the idea that life is absurd. What does it mean to say this? Perhaps it means no more than that life is meaningless in the ways we have already analyzed. If so, no new evaluation of the position is needed. But another interpretation is possible. Albert Camus[41] maintained that the absurdity of human existence is a function of two things: the expectations of human beings and the reality that they find. Human beings expect to live in a world that is rational and unified. What they find is a world that is neither rational nor unified. This tension between expectation and reality generates the absurdity of existence. For many people this absurdity is too much to bear; some try to escape by physical suicide and some commit what Camus calls philosophical suicide, in which by a leap of religious faith one assumes, despite the evidence, that the universe is rational and unified. Camus argues that such escapes are dishonest and unauthentic.

One must live one's life with the full realization that human existence is absurd, in defiance of the universe to which one is unreconciled.

Although atheists may approve of Camus's opposition to religious leaps of faith, they should not let his claim that human existence is absurd go unexamined. Putting aside Camus's recommendations on how one should live one's life in the face of the absurdity of human existence, the crucial question is: Is Camus's argument for the absurdity of human existence sound? This is the argument from tension, which can be formulated this way:

(1) If humans expect the universe to be rational and unified and find neither rationality nor unity in the universe, then human existence is absurd.

(2) Humans expect the universe to be rational and unified.

(3) Humans find neither rationality nor unity in the universe.

_____

(4) Therefore, human existence is absurd.

One may wish to quarrel over the use of the term "absurd" in premise (1). Calling the tension between the alleged expectations of human beings and the alleged irrationality of the world "absurd" does little to add to the clarity of the position. But let this point pass. The crucial premises are (2) and (3). Premise (2) does not seem to be true in the way that Camus intended, and although premise (3) is true in Camus's sense, it is trivial. Who ever claimed that the universe is rational or unified in the senses Camus seems to have in mind? Consider, for example, what he says:

> If man realized that the universe like him can love and suffer, he would be reconciled. If thought discovered in the shimmering mirrors of phenomena eternal relations capable of summing them up and summing themselves up in a single principle, then would be seen an intellectual joy of which the myth of the blessed would be but a ridiculous imitation. That nostalgia for unity, that appetite for the absolute illustrates the essential impulse of the human drama. But the fact of that nostalgia's existence does not imply that it is to be immediately satisfied. For if, bridging the gulf that separates desire from conquest, we assert with Parmenides the reality of the One (whatever it may be), we fall into the ridiculous contradiction of a mind that asserts total unity and proves by its assertion its own difference and the diversity it claimed to resolve.[42]

Camus seems to be suggesting at least three different respects in which the universe disappoints human expectation. First, the universe disappoints human expectation because it is not a sentient creature that can love and suffer. Furthermore, we cannot sum up all we discover about reality in a single principle. And finally, we want the universe to be a

Parmenidian One and yet we notice that our minds are not part of the One.

Who has these expectations? Certainly not modern-day scientists; they do not expect the universe to be any of the things Camus claims humans expect. An ideal of the unity of science is sometimes suggested as a heuristic principle of science, and physicists continue to search for a unified theory of the physical sciences. Yet no scientist supposes that everything could be summed up in a single principle or that the unity they seek is like the Parmenidian One, let alone that the universe is irrational unless it loves and suffers. Moreover, if scientists did expect any of these things of the universe, their expectations would surely be unwarranted. Although it may not be logically impossible for the universe to have the properties that Camus says humans demand, it is at least physically impossible and in any case is completely unnecessary for scientific inquiry.

We may conclude that if humans demand or should demand what Camus says, there would indeed be a tension in human existence. But humans do not and should not.

Now, Thomas Nagel has a different argument for the absurdity of human existence.[43] Arguing that a philosophical sense of absurdity comes from the "collision between the seriousness with which we take our lives and the perpetual possibility of regarding everything about which we are serious or arbitrary, or open to doubt,"[44] Nagel maintains that although as human beings we take our lives seriously, it is possible to take another vantage point outside of our selves. Unlike animals and inanimate things we can transcend our own limited perspective and see our lives *sub specie aeternitatis*. From this perspective, Nagel says, all we do appears to be arbitrary. Yet our ability to take this perspective does not disengage us from life, and "there lies the absurdity: not in the fact that such an external view can be taken of us, but in the fact that we ourselves can take it without ceasing to be the persons whose ultimate concerns are so coolly regarded."[45] Nagel argues that it is futile to try to escape this position by taking some wider perspective that may give our lives meaning. In particular, he doubts whether belief in God and His cosmic purpose can eliminate the sense of the absurd. If we can step back from the purposes of individual life and doubt their point, it is possible to step back from the kingdom and glory of God and doubt its point as well: "What makes doubt inescapable with regard to the limited aim of the individual also makes it inescapable with regard to any larger purpose that encourages the sense that life is meaningless."[46]

Unlike Camus, Nagel does not recommend a heroic defiance of the universe in the face of this absurdity. This sort of dramatic response, Nagel says, fails to appreciate the "cosmic unimportance of the situation."

Further: "If *sub specie aeternitatis* there is no reason to believe that anything matters, then that does not matter either, and we can approach our absurd lives with irony instead of heroism or despair."[47]

This *argument from sub specie aeternitatis* can be stated as follows:

(1) When we view our life *sub specie aeternitatis*, our goals, aspirations, and the like seem arbitrary.

(2) If our goals, aspirations, and the like seem arbitrary and we do not disengage from life, then our life is absurd.

(3) We do sometimes view our life *sub specie aeternitatis*.

(4) We do not disengage from life.

---

(5) Therefore, our life is absurd.

This argument, even if sound, gives no comfort to theists. For suppose that God exists and that His purpose in creating the universe and life was X. Nagel maintains that if we look at our life and X *sub specie aeternitatis*, our life in relation to X seems arbitrary. So, if our life is absurd in an atheistic world, according to Nagel, it is equally absurd in a theistic one.

Is the argument sound? One problem with it is that premises (1) and (3) merely established that our goals and aspirations *seem* arbitrary only from a peculiar point of view that we take of our life in certain reflective moments. Perhaps it may seem to us in these reflective moments as if we are viewing our life *sub specie aeternitatis*. But we clearly are not—only an omniscient being could do this—and the perspective that we take should not be dignified in these terms. We are merely looking at our life from another point of view from which our goals and aspirations have no importance. But why should one suppose that this point of view should be taken seriously? To make this clear and to reflect the true state of affairs, premises (1) and (2) should be replaced by the following:

(1′) When we view our life from what seems like *sub specie aeternitatis*, our goals, aspirations, and the like seem arbitrary.

(2′) If our goals, aspirations, and the like seem arbitrary from what seems like *sub specie aeternitatis* and we do not disengage from life, then our life seems absurd from what seems like *sub specie aeternitatis*.

Given (1′) and (2′), we can derive:

(5′) Therefore, our life seems absurd from what seems like *sub specie aeternitatis*.

Without further argument it is difficult to see why we should take the appearances specified in (2′) and (5′) seriously. Things may appear to us in all sorts of ways and from a variety of apparent perspectives. For example, mystics claim that in what seems like the perspective of the absolute, everything, including their lives, appears in complete harmony. If we take what they say to reflect reality, then it is difficult to take Nagel's vision of the absurdity of existence as reflecting reality. To only some of these ways in which things appear to us and to only some of our apparent perspectives do we give serious consideration. In the present case, why should we give such consideration to this apparent perspective and to the apparent reality shown from this perspective? In a sense, Nagel admits that how things appear from what seems like *sub specie aeternitatis* is unimportant and should not be taken seriously. Thus he says that a vision of our life *sub specie aeternitatis* has no practical implications, that because of it we should not change our way of life in any way. For example, both suicide and heroic defiance would be unwarranted. After our vision of the absurdity of life, we simply approach our life with irony. However, it is hard to see why even irony would be an appropriate response to this absurdity unless there was some reason to suppose that this perspective was a reliable one and, consequently, that the appearance of absurdity had some claim to truth. Yet this is precisely what has not been established.[48]

It must be concluded that if Nagel is correct, human life is absurd from both an atheistic and a theistic point of view. However, he has yet to show the validity of the perspective from which the judgment of the absurdity of human life is made.

The Value of Human Life

So far we have seen that arguments for the meaninglessness of life and the absurdity of human existence either fail or do not differentiate between atheism and theism. However, critics of atheism maintain that without God, human life is not only meaningless and absurd but without value. What does it mean to say that something has value? Any definition is bound to be controversial, but one plausible account would be this: X is valuable for person P if, and only if, were P rational, fully informed, and unbiased, P would desire X. This account allows that what is valuable may vary from person to person, since not all rational, fully informed, unbiased people may desire the same thing. On the other hand, it is also compatible with complete agreement among such persons. But the question remains as to what it would mean, given this account, to say that P's life as a whole is valuable. One plausible suggestion is: Life L of P is valuable as a whole for P IFF, if P were rational, fully informed, and unbiased, then P would by and large desire L.

Using the above account of value, let us consider several arguments for the worthlessness of human existence. Some critics of atheism maintain that, without God and the immortality that He provides, human existence has no value. This argument from finiteness can be reconstructed as follows:

(1) If human existence is not of definite duration, then it is worthless.
(2) Human existence is not of definite duration.

(3) Therefore, human existence is worthless.

Here the problem is surely premise (1). It is difficult to see why one should believe it. Of course, it is possible for an individual to judge his or her life as worthless. If we are rational, we judge a person's life, including our own, as valuable or worthless in terms of considerations such as the accomplishments, the efforts toward achieving certain worthwhile goals, and the moral style of the person's daily activities. However, the same sort of considerations that enable us to judge some lives as worthless enable us to judge other lives as having value. These considerations are not based on the length of the life. A relatively short life may have been of great value, whereas a long one may have been worthless. If there were immortal beings, they might lead worthless or worthwhile lives. One could not determine this simply from knowing that they were immortal.

Another argument given for the worthlessness of life is based on the transitory nature of human achievements. The attitude that motivates this argument was well expressed by Bertrand Russell in the quotation cited earlier, expressing profound regret that even the greatest achievements of humankind in art, literature, technology, and science will someday vanish from the universe. As an argument against atheism the assumption implicit in this sentiment must be that unless the fruits of human civilization last forever (at least in cultural memory), they are worthless. Consider then the argument from the transitory nature of things:

(1) Unless the cultural and intellectual accomplishments of humankind in literature, art, technology, and science last forever, they are worthless.
(2) All the cultural and intellectual accomplishments of humankind in literature, art, technology, and science will someday perish.

(3) Therefore, the cultural and intellectual accomplishments of humankind in literature, art, technology, and science are worthless.
(4) If the cultural and intellectual accomplishments of humankind

in literature, art, technology, and science are worthless, then human life itself is worthless.

(5) Therefore, human life itself is worthless.

Premises (1) and (4) constitute two major problems with this argument. It is hard to see how premise (1) can be maintained. The worth of literature, art, technology, science, and culture is surely not eternal. They serve various purposes, and when these purposes are no longer possible, they cease to have any value and may indeed become worthless. Premise (1) assumes that in order for something to have positive worth in one context, it must have worth in all contexts. Nothing could be further from the truth. Such a view not only is false but in certain cases makes little sense. For example, with "the vast death of the solar system," to use Russell's phrase, the notion of something having worth would have no meaning. However, it would not follow from this that before this vast death, certain things did not have worth.

The second problem with the argument is premise (4). I see no reason to suppose that if the cultural and intellectual accomplishments of X are worthless, then X's life is worthless. A mother who has raised intelligent, healthy, morally upright children, a doctor whose life has been devoted to caring for the indigent, a teacher who has spent a lifetime teaching pupils to be just and compassionate—each may have accomplished little from a cultural or intellectual point of view, but each has led a worthwhile life nevertheless. The worthwhileness of a person's life is also a function of its beneficial effect on family, friends, and community. Thus the worth of a life should not be identified with cultural and intellectual accomplishments.

I conclude that unless better arguments are produced, there is no support for the thesis that if there is no God, human life is meaningless, absurd, and worthless, while if there is God, human life is meaningful, worthwhile, and not absurd.

CONCLUSION

We have seen that some important criticisms of atheism are incorrect. In particular, there is no good reason to suppose that atheists are of a lower moral character than theists. Even if there were reason to suppose this, it would not show that having no belief in God was the cause. Atheism does not entail moral anarchy unless we adopt one version of an implausible metaethical position. In several senses of the term "moral relativity," atheism does not entail moral relativity. Even if an atheistic ethics did involve some form of ethical relativity, the agreement among rational, fully informed, and unbiased moral agents might be considerable and might compare quite favorably with the lack of agreement among theists. Finally, there is no good reason to suppose that life is meaningless, absurd, or worthless if God does not exist; or, if there *is* good reason, there is no more reason to suppose it is meaningless, absurd, or worthless if God does not exist than if He does.

Purpose

The aim of this book is not to make atheism a popular belief or even to overcome its invisibility. My object is not utopian. It is merely to provide good reasons for being an atheist. Atheism is defended and justified. I present a comprehensive critique of the arguments for the existence of God and a defense of arguments against the existence of God, showing in detail their relevance to atheism. In order to accomplish this I concentrate on arguments and counterarguments in British–American analytic philosophy today that deal with questions of God's existence. My object is to show that atheism is a rational position and that belief in God is not. I am quite aware that theistic beliefs are not always based on reason. My claim is that they should be.[49] I confine my efforts to showing the irrationality of belief in the existence of the Hebrew–Christian God, a personal being who is omniscient, omnipotent, and completely good and who created heaven and earth. I do this for the simple reason that the debates between atheists and believers in our society have been for the most part over whether such a being exists.

Atheists have often attacked the traditional arguments for the existence of God and have developed arguments to show that God does not exist. In this sense the project of this book is not new. However, the field of philosophy of religion has been rejuvenated in recent years. Contemporary theistic philosophers have developed new arguments and new approaches, which need to be examined. Traditional atheistic positions and arguments then must be reevaluated and reassessed in the light of these new ideas. For example, using concepts from confirmation theory and inductive logic, Richard Swinburne has recently defended probabilistic versions of the traditional arguments for the existence of God.[50] Using notions from foundationalist epistemology, Alvin Plantinga has maintained that belief in God is basic, so it is rational to hold it without support.[51] Moreover, theists have attempted to reply to atheistic arguments for the nonexistence of God. For instance, Plantinga has recently criticized the argument from evil, using a sophisticated version of the free will defense based on possible world semantics.[52] In this book I analyze and reconstruct these new arguments and approaches and answer the theists' replies. In addition, this work provides a needed comprehensive statement and defense of atheism that pulls together criticisms scattered throughout atheistic literature. Some of the most interesting and important arguments for atheism and criticisms of arguments for the existence of God are to be found in recent journal articles. These are brought together here. To be sure, there are books that have defended atheism. Unfortunately, some of these, such as George Smith's *Atheism: The Case Against God,*[53] argue forcefully for atheism but do not consider recent philosophical arguments and approaches and thus lack contemporary philosophical relevance. Other philosophically sophisticated works, such as J. L. Mackie's *The Miracle of Theism,* criticize recent theistic arguments and defend arguments for the nonexistence of God but barely mention atheism.[54] I avoid both of these problems. Thus although the present study builds on the arguments of great religious skeptics and atheists of the past such as David Hume and distinguished atheists of the present such as Antony Flew, Kai Nielsen, and Richard Robinson, it goes beyond them.

Since I concentrate on theoretical problems found in the literature of analytic philosophy of religion, I ignore certain issues that traditionally atheists have been concerned with and some approaches that many atheists have used. In particular, I do not discuss here either atheistic existentialism,[55] in which the traditional arguments for and against the existence of God are not considered,[56] or atheistic Marxism, in which the nonexistence of God is taken for granted and belief in God is seen simply as a delusion that has no function except to blind us to the irrationalities of the system of production.[57] Furthermore, although I have briefly considered some theoretical ethical questions connected with theism and atheism, I omit various practical ethical issues that have traditionally concerned atheism. Ernest Nagel once remarked that historically "atheism has been, and indeed continues to be, a form of social and political protest, directed as much against institutional religion as against theistic doctrine. Atheism has been, in effect, a moral revulsion against the undoubted abuses of the secular power exercised by religious leaders and religious institutions."[58] Except for the briefest mention in the Conclusion, I do not consider issues of church and state here despite their tremendous practical importance.[59] Finally, although I have defended atheism against charges of moral anarchy and moral relativism earlier in this introduction, I do not work out the details of an atheistic morality.[60]

This book has limitations not only from an atheistic point of view, but from a general philosophical one as well. Although I argue that atheistic belief is rational and justified and that theism is not, no extended theory of rationality or justification is given. No doubt the few general comments I do make about these topics are controversial. I do not believe that they would be any less so, however, if they were embedded in some larger epistemological theory. Indeed, it seems to me that any attempt to justify them by subsuming them under a larger theory would be premature, given the controversial state of general epistemological theories. It is far better, in my view, to develop certain middle-level principles of justification that are in accord with our ordinary and scientific rational practice and to argue for atheism in terms of these than to justify atheism in terms of some larger and more controversial theory. In fact, if one had to wait for the availability of a general theory of rationality and justification that is free from problems and widely accepted before judging that some belief was irrational, a judgment might never be made. Moreover, although I use inductive arguments in this work, I provide no general account of inductive arguments. I appeal to common rational practices regardless of how their details are construed by inductive logicians. Although I am sympathetic with some general theories of justification, the coherence theory in particular, I leave their defense to others. Indeed, since this book's basic quarrel is with one version of foundationalism, I can with complete consistency accept other versions of foundationalism.

This book is divided into two parts. In Part I, I defend negative atheism, the position of not believing that a theistic God exists. In so doing I consider what is involved in justifying negative atheism (Chapter 1). I then argue that a good case can be made for the cognitive meaninglessness of religious utterances (Chapter 2). However, I argue that even if religious utterances are cognitively meaningful, religious beliefs are not based on good reasons. Next the classical arguments for the existence of God are shown to be unsound (Chapters 3 to 5). I then argue that religious experience cannot provide a basis for religious belief (Chapter 6). I show that the argument from miracles is invalid (Chapter 7). I refute several minor arguments for God (Chapter 8). I undermine some well known practical arguments for belief in God (Chapter 9). Finally, I argue, religious beliefs can neither be founded on faith nor be basic beliefs (Chapter 10).

In Part II, a justification is provided for positive atheism, the position of disbelieving that the theistic God exists. I consider first what is involved in such a justification (Chapter 11). I then show that the concept of the theistic God is incoherent (Chapter 12). I argue that the teleological argument for God can be turned against theism and made to provide an inductive argument for the nonexistence of God (Chapter 13), and I defend in general terms an inductive argument from evil against recent criticisms of it (Chapter 14). The best known theodicies and also some minor ones are refuted (Chapters 15 and 18).

In the book's Conclusion I consider what would and would not follow if my main arguments were widely accepted. In the Appendix I define atheism and distinguish it from other isms and movements.

PART I

Negative Atheism

CHAPTER 1

The Justification of Negative Atheism: Some Preliminaries

What must be shown in order to support negative atheism with respect to the existence of the Christian–Hebraic God? How does one justify the view that one ought not to believe in an all-good, all-powerful, all-knowing God who created the universe? Must anything be shown? Is the burden of proof really on theists to provide reasons for their belief? What sort of reasons must theists provide to support their case and must atheists undermine to establish their own? Is it sufficient that theists provide reasons showing that belief in God is beneficial to them? Or it is necessary that they provide reasons showing that belief in God is true? Do atheists who demand that theists provide reasons showing that their belief in God is true assume an unacceptable objectivist epistemology? In this chapter these preliminary questions are addressed in order to set the stage for the arguments that follow.

A Presumption of Atheism

In "The Presumption of Atheism"[1] Antony Flew maintains that the burden of proof is on the believer: "Until and unless some such grounds [for claims of knowledge of God] are produced we have literally no reason at all for believing; and in that situation the only reasonable posture must be that of either the negative atheist or the agnostic."[2] It may be argued that in the chapters that follow I have things backward. I argue that negative atheism is not justified until it is shown that God talk is cognitively meaningless or, if God talk is cognitively meaningful, that the reasons for believing in God are inadequate. Does not this way of arguing the case for negative atheism put the burden of proof on the wrong group? Atheists, it might be argued, should not be required to show that religious language is meaningless and the reasons for believing in God are inadequate. The burden of proof instead should be on believers, since negative atheists are not making any claims to knowledge and the believers are.

This objection to my way of arguing my case for negative atheism is misplaced. I have chosen to remain neutral on whether there is a presumption in favor of atheism; for even if there is, theists have put forth reasons for believing that religious language is cognitively meaningful; and they have given arguments that an all-good, all-powerful, and all-knowing being exists. Negative atheists must show that these reasons and arguments are inadequate. To be sure, if theists had never given reasons for supposing that God talk is meaningful or that God exists, perhaps negative atheists would not have to produce refutations to be secure in their nonbelief. But this is not the case. Thus even if Flew is right about the burden of proof, this does not affect to any significant extent what negative atheists must do. They must undermine reasons and arguments produced by theists before their position is secure. If they need not make the first move, they must make the second.

The Ethics of Belief

The thesis that without adequate reason one should not believe that an all-good, all-powerful, and all-knowing being exists has been interpreted as a special case of the more general thesis that without adequate reason one should not believe anything.[3] This general thesis can be given a broad or narrow interpretation. In the broad interpretation we can understand that good reason for believing something is true includes reasons that make the belief likely as well as ones that benefit the believer and others. Let us call the first sort *epistemic reasons* and an argument based on these an epistemic argument. Let us call the second sort *beneficial reasons* and an argument based on these a beneficial argument. Beneficial reasons can, in turn, be either moral or prudential. In "The Will to Believe" William James argued that in very special circumstances it is permissible to believe for beneficial reasons. More recently, Roderick Chisholm has also adopted the broad interpretation. Other philosophers argue that one should base one's belief on epistemic reasons. In other words, they accept a narrow interpretation according to which the only reasons are epistemic ones.

A hypothetical example should make the distinction between epistemic and beneficial reasons clear. Let us suppose the available evidence indicates that the Mormon religion is very probably based on a hoax perpetuated by Joseph Smith. If good reasons are interpreted narrowly as purely epistemic ones, then clearly no one, including present-day Mormons, should believe that the doctrines of the Mormon religion are true. But let us suppose that reasons are understood broadly. In this case, some advocates of the use of beneficial reasons might argue that at least Mormons should continue to believe, for example, on the grounds that from a utilitarian point of view there are significant benefits to Mormons to believe Mormon doctrines.

It could be argued from a more inclusive utilitarian perspective, however, that the decision to base belief on beneficial reasons is problematic. Maintaining one's belief in the light of clearly negative evidence because of the benefits that result could have a profound effect on one's entire belief system. Indeed, in order to keep a system of beliefs intact in the face of negative evidence, it may be necessary to change other beliefs in the system that in turn have profound and damaging psychological effects. Moreover, if change in a belief system is allowed when there is a clearly worthwhile social goal, it could set a precedent for change when there is no obvious and immediate social benefit. Further, one person's example might induce others to maintain or change their beliefs for the slightest whim or the most selfish motive.

It is perhaps because of the potentially dangerous implications of believing for beneficial rather than epistemic reasons that some philosophers have argued that it is always morally wrong to believe in anything unless one has adequate epistemic reasons. W. K. Clifford, in "The Ethics of Belief,"[4] argues that "it is wrong always, everywhere, and for anyone, to believe anything on insufficient evidence." Clifford maintains that believing on insufficient evidence has a variety of harmful consequences: It corrupts our character, undermines public confidence, leads to irresponsible action, and fosters self-deception. Although Clifford's fears may have been exaggerated, there is surely a great deal of truth in what he says: There are indeed great dangers in believing something because it is beneficial to do so. Although basing your belief on what is beneficial to you and others is not necessarily morally wrong, as apparently Clifford thinks, there are certainly moral dangers in doing so, and as a general social policy it should be avoided. Moreover, Clifford overlooks an important point. His argument for using purely epistemic reasons is itself a moral one. Thus, ironically, his reason for not using beneficial reasons in justifying belief is apparently based on one type of beneficial reason: the undesirable *moral* consequences of doing so.

In addition, Clifford should have argued that there is an independent *epistemological* duty to base one's beliefs on purely epistemic reasons. If one does not base one's beliefs on purely epistemic reasons, one is epistemologically irresponsible. To be sure, under some circumstances this epistemological duty may have to give way to moral considerations, and at times there should be what Lorraine Code calls a "teleological suspension of the epistemic."[5] But this does not mean that there is not an epistemological duty that must be outweighed by moral considerations. Although Clifford gives strong *moral* reasons why in general this suspension is impermissible, he does not consider the initial *epistemological* duty that these reasons must outweigh.

Some philosophers who do not take as strong a stand as Clifford have attempted to circumscribe carefully when belief based on beneficial reasons is morally permissible. However, it is not completely clear that they, any more than Clifford, clearly separate the epistemic and moral duties. Roderick Chisholm for one, in arguing against Clifford, maintains that a proposition is innocent until proved guilty; that is, it is unreasonable for us to believe a proposition only when we have adequate evidence for the contradictory of the proposition.[6] Chisholm's view is compatible with the thesis that it is not unreasonable to believe a proposition on the basis of beneficial reasons if there is no adequate evidence for the contradictory. This idea rules out appeals to beneficial reasons for believing that p only if the epistemic reasons support believing that ~p. In our hypothetical example, Chisholm's requirement would prevent Mormons from believing that Mormon doctrines are true on the basis of the benefits of believing them only if the evidence supports the proposition that they are false. Since by hypothesis there is such evidence, Chisholm's requirement would entail that Mormons give up their belief that their doctrines are true. On the other hand, if we change the example and suppose there is no adequate evidence indicating that Mormon doctrine is false, then Mormons could believe their doctrines are true if it was beneficial to do so. William James, whose views are discussed at length in Chapter 9, also put restrictions on the use of beneficial reasons. Certainly he would not advocate that Mormons continue to believe their doctrines if the evidence indicated that they are probably false; he would agree with Chisholm that believing that p was true on the basis of beneficial reasons is not permissible when the evidence supports ~p.

However, it is unclear if Chisholm recognizes an independent epistemological obligation to believe on the basis of purely epistemic reasons. Is he saying that it is *epistemologically* or *morally* permissible for someone to believe p if there is no adequate evidence for ~p? On one plausible interpretation he could be saying that although there is an *epistemological* duty to believe that p on the basis of purely epistemic reasons, it is *morally* permissible to believe p on beneficial grounds only if there is no epistemic reason to believe ~p.

No matter how Chisholm's suggestion is interpreted, it may be too restrictive in one respect and not restrictive enough in another. It may demon hypothesis seriously, then instead of claiming that belief in God can be rational, one would have to say that no belief at all is rational. Even belief in an external world, in other minds, and in the past becomes questionable and problematic, given this hypothesis. Surely, acceptance of the Cartesian evil demon argument or of similar considerations cannot lead to the rationality of religious belief in any normal sense of the term "rationality." It can only lead to the most profound skepticism concerning the rationality of all beliefs. Indeed, if the evil demon hypothesis were true, paradoxically it would seem to entail that we could never be justified in thinking that it was.

Second, it is difficult to see how theists in particular could accept the view that there could be no connection between evidence and truth. For if God is all-good, all-powerful, and all-knowing, why would He systematically deceive us into thinking that there is a connection or allow an evil demon to do so? Although it may be barely conceivable that an evil demon could deceive us, the idea that God does or would allow an evil demon to do so surely verges on incoherence.

Third, even if belief in God is compatible with rejection of objective knowledge, the skeptical arguments that lead to this rejection are so controversial[12] that it seems ill-advised for theists like Kvanvig to attempt to support their position indirectly by accepting them. At the very least a refutation of these criticisms of the skeptical arguments is needed. None is provided by Kvanvig.

Fourth, what possible reason could one have to consider seriously either the evil demon hypothesis or similar ones? It cannot be to save theism from the charge of being irrational, for given the evil demon hypothesis, unless one radically alters the meaning of "rational belief," no belief is justified. There is no more evidence supporting this hypothesis than the alternative one that there is a close connection between evidence and truth. What is more, the alternative hypothesis surely is much simpler than the evil demon hypothesis. Therefore, on grounds of simplicity alone the evil demon hypothesis should not be seriously considered.[13] In addition, the evil demon hypothesis has a low initial probability. Given the possibility that an evil demon could have any of an infinite number of purposes and motives, it is unlikely that it would have and continue to have precisely those purposes and motives that would explain what we experience.[14] Furthermore, the evil demon hypothesis does not give a plausible account of human survival. If there is no connection between evidence and truth, it is difficult to see how the human race has survived to date. We base the actions that we need to perform in order to survive on what we believe is true, and we believe this latter on the evidence. But then, if there were no connection between truth and evidence, our survival would be a mystery.[15] In addition, the

be too restrictive in that it may undermine certain important social relationships that one wants to preserve. For example, on moral grounds it may be reasonable up to a point to believe that one's friend is truthful even when there is adequate evidence for believing otherwise.[7] At the same time the suggestion may not be morally restrictive enough in actual practice. Psychologically it may be difficult for the average person who is blind to negative evidence against his or her own views to distinguish a situation in which the evidence is against a proposition he or she believe from a situation in which it is not. Given this blindness, it may be all too easy for the person to claim that it is permissible to believe p on beneficial reasons because there are no adequate epistemic reasons to believe ~p. Thus in application Chisholm's principle could lead to some of the morally undesirable consequences that worried Clifford.[8]

Nevertheless, both Clifford and Chisholm have a point. Given the moral dangers of believing for purely beneficial reasons pointed out by Clifford and the independent epistemological duty to base one's beliefs on purely epistemic reasons that he did not recognize, there is a strong presumption that in justifying belief one should only use epistemic reasons. Let us call this the presumption of the primacy of epistemic reasons. So Clifford was at least partially correct. Further, because of the independent epistemological duty to base one's beliefs on purely epistemic reasons and the need to guard against the moral dangers of believing for beneficial reasons, there is a strong presumption that if beneficial reasons are used to justify p, the available epistemic reasons should not justify ~p. In one special case, beneficial reasons can be used to decide whether to believe p or ~p when there are equally strong epistemic reasons for p and ~p. Let us call this the presumption of the purely supplementary role of beneficial reasons. So Chisholm was partially correct as well.

It should be noted that both presumptions allow that in special circumstances it is morally permissible for people to believe something because of beneficial reasons and without adequate epistemic reasons and that in *very* special circumstances it is morally permissible for people to believe something for beneficial reasons even when there are strong epistemic reasons to believe the opposite.[9] Clearly, however, candidates for these special circumstances must be scrutinized *very* carefully in terms of both the likely benefits that will result from belief in terms of beneficial reasons and the possible long-term adverse effects on society, its institutions, and human personality and character.

How do these presumptions affect atheism in the sense of nonbelief in the Christian–Hebraic God? On what kind of reasons should belief or nonbelief in a good, all-powerful, all-knowing being be based? There is a presumption that these should be based on epistemic reasons. There is a presumption that they should be based on beneficial reasons only if the issue cannot be decided by epistemic reasons. Although there may be very special and unusual circumstances that defeat these presumptions, the candidates for circumstances that do so must be examined with great care. Let us consider some possible cases.

An obvious special circumstance that would defeat our presumptions is the imminent danger of a great disaster because one did or did not believe. Suppose you are an atheist and are kidnapped by a religious maniac with access to nuclear weapons who will kill you and blow up New York City, London, Paris, and Tokyo unless you accept God. You have good reason to suppose that if you undergo two months of rigorous religious indoctrination, you will accept God. To make the case crystal clear, let us suppose that few people will know of your conversion, that the fanatic will die in three months, that he has no disciples to carry on his work, and that the effects of the indoctrination will disappear in four months. Presumably in such a case there would be good reason for submitting to the religious indoctrination. Even the most militant atheist would admit that under this circumstance, refusing to convert would serve no purpose—indeed, would be an act of insanity.

An analogous case can be constructed for not believing in God on beneficial grounds. You, a theist, are kidnapped by a maniac with access to nuclear weapons who will kill you and blow up New York City, London, Paris, and Tokyo unless you give up your belief in God. You have good reason to suppose that you will cease to believe in God if you undergo two months of rigorous atheistic indoctrination. To make the case crystal clear, let us suppose that few people will know of your conversion, that the maniac will die in three months, that he has no disciples to carry on his work, and that the effects of the indoctrination will wear off in four months. In such a case too there would be good reason for submitting to the atheistic indoctrination.

Let us now consider a more realistic case in which the question is whether beneficial reasons for believing in God should count. On her deathbed Mrs. Smith, an 89-year-old atheist and former Catholic, is not completely reconciled to the possibility of there being no afterlife and, as a consequence, of not seeing her dead husband after her own death. Her last few days will be more content and happy if she believes that God exists and that she will soon see her husband. It is clear that her mental state is such that with only a little encouragement from a priest she will embrace her old faith once again. Should she ask for a priest to visit her? The answer may seem obvious, but it is not until many questions are resolved. For example, given her present situation, is she competent to make the choice? Will this case set a precedent for other cases? Will other people know of her return to the fold and be encouraged to do the same?

In order to simplify the case, let us assume that there are no more epistemic reasons to believe than not to believe that there is a God and an afterlife, that her return to Catholicism would set no precedent, that she has only a few days to live, that she would be much happier if she did believe, that few people would ever know about her return, and that her choice to return was competent, rational, and uncoerced. We may conclude that under these assumptions she should send for a priest. But these are big assumptions to make and cannot be assumed as a matter of course.

It may be asked: If we grant the presumption of the primacy of epistemic reasons and the presumption of the purely supplementary role of beneficial reasons, is there not still a presumption that, in those rare cases where it is legitimate to use beneficial reasons to decide what to believe or not to believe, belief in God is to be preferred? A detailed answer is given to this question in Chapter 9, where we examine two of the most famous attempts to base belief in God on beneficial reasons: Pascal's wager and William James's argument in "The Will to Believe."

The Evil Demon and Objectivist Epistemology

It may be objected that in our statement of what needs to be shown to establish that negative atheism is true, we are assuming something that we cannot assume; that in adopting a presumption that only epistemic reasons should be used, we are supposing that there is a close connection between having adequate epistemic reasons and truth. In particular, Jonathan Kvanvig has claimed that advocates of objectivist epistemology must assume that proposition p is more likely to be true if proposition e is true and is evidence for proposition p than if e were not true.[10] But this assumption is mistaken, Kvanvig argues, since it "runs afoul of Cartesian evil demon considerations."[11] According to this argument there is a possible world containing an evil demon who deceives inhabitants about the truth of what they believe. In this possible world there is no close relation between the evidence that people have for a proposition and the truth of the proposition, although it seems as if there is. Since a world with such a deceiving evil demon would be indistinguishable from one without it, there could be no reason to suppose that our world does not have such a demon and, consequently, no reason to suppose that our evidence has any close relation to truth. Once it is seen that this basic assumption of a close connection between evidence and truth is questionable, the argument proceeds, one can develop a more pragmatic and subjective approach to epistemic warrant according to which it is rational to believe in God although there is no adequate evidence.

What can one say about this argument? First, if one takes the evil

evil demon hypothesis is usually formulated in a way that is not falsifiable; in other words, there is no empirical evidence that could refute it. If there is a connection between testability and factual meaning, as in Chapter 2 I argue there is, then such a hypothesis is not genuine at all, for it asserts no factual claim. Thus on the standard scientific criteria of simplicity, explanatory power, and testability the evil demon thesis has no claim to serious consideration.[16]

Fifth, the alternative view has absurd implications. Consider the following subjectivist account of justified belief proposed by Kvanvig as an alternative to the standard objectivist account:[17]

> S is justified in believing p if (i) there is a general human tendency to believe p when e; (ii) it is acceptable for S that e is evidence for p; (iii) S believes p on e without ground for doubt; and (iv) e.

According to this view there is a natural human tendency to believe on the basis of certain evidence that God exists, just as there is a natural tendency for people to make inductive inferences on the basis of past constant conjunctions.[18] For example, there is a natural human tendency when "contemplating the majesty of mountains, the starry heavens, or the beauty of a flower" to respond with a belief in God.[19] Further, the circumstances that prompt this response are normally accepted by persons with a belief in God as evidence for their belief, and they normally are without grounds for doubt since, for example, they may accept nothing as counting against their belief in God.[20]

Now, one may well question whether there is a natural tendency to believe in God or whether the tendency is based on cultural and social training. If there were such a natural tendency, one would expect belief in God to be statistically uniform in different cultures. However, it varies widely across cultures.[21]

More important, if there is a natural tendency to believe in God, one can argue equally well that there is a natural tendency to believe in occult explanations. Furthermore, this belief is justified in terms of Kvanvig's theory. However, this is a *reductio* of Kvanvig's theory, since we have excellent reason to suppose that such occult explanations are not true.

We know, for example, that people tend to explain things that they cannot understand by postulating ghosts, ancient astronauts, extrasensory perception, psychic powers, and the like.[22] In most instances this tendency seems to be prompted by a circumstance such as Uri Geller's appearance on television apparently doing feats of psychokinesis. Thus condition (i) of Kvanvig's theory is met. It is certainly acceptable to the typical occult believer that the circumstances that prompt the occult beliefs is evidence for them. Thus condition (ii) is met. Further, for many occult believers their beliefs are without ground of doubt in the sense of that term employed here, since they accept nothing as counting against their beliefs although there may be overwhelming evidence that in the very cases prompting the beliefs a fraud was committed. For example, the evidence is rather clear that Geller's TV feats of seeming psychokinesis were done by sleight of hand,[23] and yet many people refused to accept this evidence. Thus condition (iii) is met. Suppose Geller again appears on TV and this prompts belief in occult explanations of his feats. Then condition (iv) is met. Thus on Kvanvig's subjectivist account of justified belief, believers in occult explanations of Geller's powers would meet all Kvanvig's conditions and thus would be justified in their beliefs. Other examples could be given in which, according to Kvanvig's account, people would be justified in believing in explanations in terms of ghosts and little green aliens although strong objective evidence showed that fraud and deception prompted the beliefs. Surely this suggests that something is seriously wrong with Kvanvig's account of justification.

Conclusion

I have remained neutral on the question of whether there is a presumption in favor of negative atheism. Since theists have given reasons for their belief, negative atheists must refute these to be secure in their position. But what sorts of reasons are relevant? I have argued that there is a presumption that belief in God should be based on epistemic reasons and a presumption that beneficial reasons for believing in God should have only a supplementary role. Assuming that God talk is meaningful, the first order of business in defending negative atheism is to undermine the epistemic reasons that have been offered by theists. But suppose that the conditions are met for using beneficial reasons. The second order of business in defending negative atheism would be to undermine these reasons. I have rejected the argument that, in establishing negative atheism in the way that I propose, I will be assuming an unacceptable objectivist theory of knowledge. The arguments against such a theory are weak and the proposed alternative to it unacceptable.

I just said *assuming* that God talk is cognitively meaningful, the first order of business in defending negative atheism is to undermine the epistemic reasons offered by theists. But this assumption we cannot make. Indeed, I argue in the next chapter that religious language is cognitively meaningless. If this argument is successful, negative atheism is established and there is no need for negative atheists to undermine the reasons that theists give for belief in God. Let us suppose I am mistaken, however, and that God talk is cognitively meaningful. If so, theists must give reasons for their belief in God. I show in the chapters that follow that no such reasons are available. In Chapters 3 through 5, I show that the classical traditional arguments for the existence of God fail to provide good epistemic reasons for belief. In Chapters 6 through 8, I show that other arguments also fail to provide such reasons. In Chapter 9, I consider some classical beneficial arguments for the existence of God and argue that they do not in general provide good reason for belief in those cases where I have allowed that their use is normally appropriate. However, theists might argue that belief in God does not need either epistemic or beneficial grounds. Belief in God, they might say, is basic or should be based on faith, not reason. In Chapter 10, I argue against this view.

Although the part of my argument that involves undermining the reasons given for belief in theism is by far the most extensive and detailed, it is not conclusive. It might be the case that a new argument will be developed that could support a belief in an all-good, all-powerful, all-knowing being. This possibility seems unlikely, however. To be sure, philosophers and theologians still are developing arguments for the existence of such a being, but these seem to be merely subtle variants of arguments that have been around for centuries, and they add little to the standard reasons. It seems unlikely, then, that future philosophers and theologians will develop anything but more variants of the old reasons.

Nevertheless, although a conclusive case cannot be made for negative atheism, if a good case can be made for supposing that belief in God should be based on reason and that all the available reasons for believing in an all-good, all-powerful, and all-knowing being are inadequate, negative atheism in the narrow sense will be justified as much as it can be in relation to our present knowledge. If we have good grounds for supposing that all available reasons for believing in an all-good, all-powerful, and all-knowing being are inadequate when such reasons are needed for justified belief, then people would be justified in having no belief that such a being exists.

CHAPTER 2

The Meaningfulness of
Religious Language

Overview of the Problem

Religious people use language to talk about God. However, there are such fundamental differences between this use and our everyday use that the question arises even for religious believers as to whether God talk is meaningful.

In the first place, when terms like "is loving," "is forgiving," and "brings about" are applied to God, they seem to mean something very different from what they mean when they are applied to human beings. For example, when we speak of a mother as being loving, we are referring in part to her behavior, and in particular the way she responds to her children. When we say that Jones brought about a fire, we are referring to certain of his bodily actions, such as his carelessly throwing a match onto a pile of paper. But when we say God is loving or God brought about a miracle, we cannot be referring to the behavior or bodily action of God, for He has no body.

Moreover, when we speak of a mother as being loving toward her children, there can be evidence that would and should induce us to withdraw our assertion. If a mother were systematically to torture her children, deprive them of food, and plot to kill them, we would have grounds for saying that she is not loving. Indeed, a person who insisted on saying, despite this evidence, that she was loving would be accused of not understanding what loving means or of misusing language. However, religious people speak of God as loving His creatures no matter how much natural evil there is in the world and no matter what the evidence. Yet it would seem that God, an all-powerful being, could prevent this evil.

Furthermore, the claim that Jones brought about the fire would have to be withdrawn if Jones could not have acted so as to bring it about. A person who continues to claim that Jones brought about the fire while admitting that his claim is not based on any evidence of Jones's actions, and who would continue to make this claim no matter what negative evidence was produced, would be said not to understand plain English. Yet the claims of religious believers that God produced miracles are usually made despite negative evidence and indeed may continue to be made despite all possible negative evidence.

In the second place, the use of the term "God" itself raises fundamental problems. It is difficult to understand the logical status of the term "God." It functions differently from proper names, definite descriptions, and other types of terms that it might be thought to be assimilated to. Indeed, there is no coherent and consistent scheme that can cope with its varied and inconsistent uses. It has been argued, for example, that "God" cannot be considered a proper name, since asking what it refers to makes no sense. The very notion of referring assumes some temporal or spatial or spatial–temporal scheme, and God is an entity that is supposed to be "outside of space and time."[1]

The view that the meaningfulness of God talk is problematic is not new. David Hume maintained that the only legitimate propositions are those of matters of fact and those of the relations of ideas; that is, what we would today call synthetic *a posteriori* and analytic *a priori* propositions. In a well-known passage in the *Enquiry* he declares:

> If we take in our hands any volume; of divinity or school metaphysics, for instance; let us ask, *Does it contain any abstract reasoning concerning quantity or number?* No. *Does it contain any experimental reasoning concerning matters of fact and existence?* No. Commit it then to the flames, for it can contain nothing but sophistry and illusion.[2]

Since sentences about God express neither statements of experimental reasoning concerning matters of fact and existence nor statements about the relations of ideas, the volumes that contain them should, according to Hume, be committed to the flames. Moreover, many atheists of the past have denied that the concept of God had any meaning. For example, Charles Bradlaugh, a well-known nineteenth-century atheistic orator and writer, argued: "The Atheist does not say 'There is no God,' but he says: 'I know not what you mean by God; I am without the idea of God; the word "God" is to me a sound conveying no clear or distinct affirmation.' "[3]

The most sustained attack on the meaningfulness of religious language came in the twentieth century with the rise of logical positivism. Wanting to eliminate what they considered to be meaningless discourse from philosophy and to establish philosophy on a sound empirical and logical basis, logical positivists proposed the following theory of meaning:

(1) A statement has factual meaning if and only if it is empirically verifiable.
(2) A statement has formal meaning if and only if it is analytic or self-contradictory.
(3) A statement has cognitive or literal meaning if and only if it has either formal meaning or factual meaning.
(4) A statement has cognitive or literal meaning if and only if it is either true or false.

Since statements about God and other such metaphysical entities were not considered either to be verifiable even in principle or to be analytic or self-contradictory, they were declared factually meaningless by the logical positivists.

There were various responses to this attack on the factual meaninglessness of religious language. Some religious believers took it very seriously and attempted to meet it head-on by arguing that religious statements are in principle capable of empirical verification. They argued that religious statements are factually meaningful in terms of the logical positivists' own verifiability criterion. Others sympathetic to religion maintained that the logical positivists were correct that religious discourse is not factually meaningful, since it is not capable of empirical verification, and they proceeded to give a noncognitive interpretation of it.[4] They argued that although religious language cannot be used to assert or deny the existence of any transcendent being, it plays other roles in our language; for example, it expresses some moral points of view by means of parables. However, the most common reaction to the logical positivist attack was to reject the verifiability theory of meaning. On this strategy, although religious statements did not meet the logical positivist criterion of verifiability, this did not show that religious statements were factually meaningless. The problem was with the verifiability theory itself and not with religious language.

Two problems plagued the positivist theory right from the start. To many critics the above analysis of meaning seemed arbitrary. They said that there was no good reason why anyone should accept this theory. Without adequate justification, the argument ran, the theory could not be used to eliminate religious or metaphysical discourse as meaningless. Furthermore, the positivists were unable to formulate a precise criterion of empirical verifiability that did the job expected of it: to eliminate metaphysical and theological statements as factually meaningless and yet to allow the statements of science as factually meaningful. As the criterion was formulated in positivist writings, either the criterion was too broad and allowed any sentence at all—even clearly nonsensical ones—to become factually meaningful, or else it was too restrictive and eliminated as meaningless the quite legitimate statements of theoretical science. On the too liberal formulations, religious sentences such as "God exists" became factually meaningful, as did clearly nonsense sentences such as "Glub is gurb." On the too restrictive formulations, statements of theoretic science such as "Electrons exist" became factually meaningless.

It is perhaps in part for these reasons that the verifiability theory is currently out of favor with philosophers of religion. Even many leading atheists no longer take it seriously. Thus J. L. Mackie in *The Miracle of Theism* takes it for granted that any verifiability theory of meaning entailing that statements about the existence of God be literally meaningless is "highly implausible."[5] Most leading theistic philosophers of religion believe that the theory has been shown to be completely inadequate. For example, Alvin Plantinga devoted 12 pages to refuting the theory in *God and Other Minds*,[6] but later in *God, Freedom, and Evil* he dismisses it in one paragraph,[7] citing as his reasons for rejecting the theory precisely the ones given here.

Nevertheless, a few philosophers of religion still take the theory seriously. Kai Nielsen, an atheist who is perhaps the best known defender of the verifiability theory in contemporary philosophy of religion, has devoted several books to defending the thesis that religious language is factually meaningless because it is not verifiable in principle.[8] And Richard Swinburne, a theist, has recently attempted a detailed refutation of the verifiability theory of meaning.[9]

In this chapter I argue that despite the widespread contention that the verifiability theory of meaning has been shown to be mistaken, it can be defended against the standard criticisms and is plausible in its own right. If I am correct, then a prima facie case can be made that a large part of religious language is factually meaningless. The implications of this thesis for atheism are clear. If talk of God is factually meaningless, then the sentence "God does not exist" is just as factually meaningless as the sentence "God exists." Consequently, negative atheism is justified: If belief in God is factually meaningless, then having no such belief is justified. However, positive atheism is refuted; if belief in the nonexistence of God is also factually meaningless, then such a belief is unjustified.

Incoherence and Meaninglessness

Before we consider the thesis that religious language is factually meaningless, it is important to be clear on the distinction between incoherence and meaninglessness. Sometimes the term "incoherent" is used synonymously with "meaningless"; sometimes the term "incoherent" is used to refer to sentences that express statements entailing a contradiction; sometimes it is used in a broad sense to refer either to sentences that are meaningless or to ones expressing statements that entail a contradiction. Religious language can be incoherent in any of these three senses. In order to avoid ambiguity here I use the term "incoherent" to refer only to sentences expressing statements that entail a contradiction; I do not call meaningless sentences incoherent.

Some examples make this distinction and my usage clear. Consider the following:

(1) Jones is a married bachelor.
(2) Jones is gluberfied.
(3) Jones big impossible.

The statement expressed by (1) is incoherent in the sense that, provided one gives the expressions "married" and "bachelor" their usual meaning, it entails a contradiction. (2) and (3) are not incoherent in our terms; they are meaningless. (3) is meaningless since it does not have the syntax of a sentence and, as it would normally be interpreted, does not express something that is true or false. Although all the words in (3) are meaningful, they are strung together in a way that makes no sense. In contrast, the syntax of (2) is acceptable. Yet (2) as well as (3) is meaningless, for "gluberfied" is a nonsense term that has no semantic rules governing its use. Consequently, (3) as well as (2) does not express anything that could be true or false. Since what is expressed by a sentence could be true or false, (2) and (3) do not express statements. However, (1) expresses a statement that is necessarily false.

Now, it should be noted that a sentence can express some particular statement in one context and in a different context express no statement at all. For example, consider the use of (2) in two different contexts. In the first, the term "gluberfied" is a purely nonsense term; hence (2) does not express a statement. In this context (2) is meaningless. In the second context the term "gluberfied" means the same as "married bachelor"; hence (2) expresses an inconsistent statement. In this context (2) is incoherent. But what presumably cannot be the case is that in the same context a sentence is meaningless and yet expresses a statement that is incoherent in the sense that it entails a contradiction.

One sentence might express a statement in one religious context and no statement in another. In one context the sentence "God exists" may not express a statement and in another context it may express a statement that entails a contradiction. The same religious sentence cannot express an incoherent statement in one context and in the same context be factually meaningless.

Nielsen's Critique of God Talk

Kai Nielsen[10] is the best known advocate of the thesis that talk about God is in an important sense meaningless. Although Nielsen is strongly influenced by the logical positivists' verifiability theory of meaning, his argument is much more sophisticated than the positivists' and much more in tune with the subtleties of religious discourse. Thus in order to see if the verifiability theory of meaning can be defended, we can do no better than to turn to Nielsen's writings.

Nielsen first attempts to clear the ground by clarifying his thesis and by showing that certain typical ways of arguing that religious discourse is meaningful will not stand critical scrutiny.

First, Nielsen does not maintain that all religious discourse is factually meaningless. For example, he says that the unsophisticated discourse of believers in an anthropomorphic God is not meaningless; it is merely false. Consider the view that God is a large and powerful spatial–temporal entity that resides somewhere high in the sky. A sentence expressing this is not factually meaningless. We understand what it means and, according to Nielsen, know in the light of the evidence that the statement it expresses is false. What troubles Nielsen is the discourse of the sophisticated believer who says, for example, that God transcends space and time, has no body, and yet performs actions that affect things in space and time. He maintains that this sort of discourse is factually meaningless and therefore neither true nor false.

Nielsen does not say that religious discourse is meaningless in all senses. In particular, he does not deny that religious expressions have a use in our language or that one can make inferences on the basis of these expressions. Thus the sentence

(4) God has no body and yet acts in the world

is clearly not meaningless in the sense that

(5) God is gluberfied

or

(6) God big impossible

or

(7) Goo Foo is gluberfied

is meaningless.

Terms such as "God," "has a body," "acts," and "in the world," unlike "Goo Foo" and "is gluberfied," have uses in our language. Furthermore, (4) has no syntactical irregularities. In addition, "God" has a fixed syntax, making possible certain logical inferences from (4). For example, from (4) it follows that

(4′) It is possible for God to act without a body

and

(4″) God does not have eyes and ears

Nielsen insists, however, that none of this shows that statements like (4) are factually meaningful; that is, that they are either true or false. In the first place, following Paul Edwards[11] he maintains that the mere fact that one can make an inference from some sentence does not show that it is factually meaningful. For example, from

(8) Box sleeps more rapidly than Cox

it follows that

(9) Cox sleeps more slowly than Box

But it is generally agreed that (8) and (9) are meaningless sentences. Further, as (8) illustrates the fact that a sentence has an unproblematic syntax does not entail that it is factually meaningful.

Moreover, it does not follow that just because an expression has a use in our language it has factual meaning. Nielsen vigorously attacks the view he calls Wittgensteinian fideism—the notion that every so-called form of life has its own language game with its own rules and logic and that one cannot critically evaluate a language game from the outside. On this view, it is a serious mistake for a philosopher of religion to impose some external standard of meaning on religious discourse, for such discourse is acceptable as it stands. According to Wittgensteinian fideism, the job of a philosopher of religion is not to evaluate the discourse of a form of life but to clarify its logic and to eliminate confusions caused by misusing the language of this form of life. Against this view Nielsen maintains:

> There is no "religious language" or "scientific language." There is rather the international notation of mathematics and logic; and English, French, Spanish and the like. In short, "religious discourse" and "scientific discourse" are part of the same overall conceptual structure. Moreover, in that conceptual structure there is a large amount of discourse, which is neither religious nor scientific, that is constantly being utilized by both the religious man and the scientist when they make religious and scientific claims. In short, they share a number of key categories.[12]

Given this common conceptual structure and shared categories, Nielsen argues, it is possible to evaluate the meaningfulness of some part of the structure, such as the language of religion, and maintain that it is factually meaningless. Thus there seems to be nothing inconsistent in saying, "X is an ongoing but irrational form of life," even though Wittgensteinian fideism entails that there is. Wittgensteinian fideism, Nielsen maintains, is committed to an absurd form of relativism: that every form of life is autonomous, can be evaluated on its own terms, and cannot be criticized from the outside. But this relativism, Nielsen argues, has absurd consequences. For example, it entails that the forms of life associated with belief in magic and fairies cannot be criticized from the outside. "By now, by people," he says, "working from the inside, the entire practice, the entire form of life, has come to be rejected as incoherent."[13] Yet at one time magic talk and fairy talk had a use in our language. If we reject the absurd implications of this form of relativism and admit that the form of life associated with fairies and magic should be rejected also, then, Nielsen maintains, it is possible that the form associated with God should be as well. God talk has a use but may still be factually meaningless.

So far, as I have presented Nielsen's position, he argues that it does not follow that just because certain expressions have a use in our language or have unproblematic syntax, they are factually meaningful. Thus God talk may be factually meaningless despite the fact that it has a use in our language and has unproblematic syntax. However, Nielsen must do much more to establish his case. First, he must explain why we should think that God talk is meaningless. Second, even if he provides some reason to suppose that God talk is meaningless, since he attempts to defend the verifiability theory of meaning, he must argue that religious language is meaningless because it is not verifiable in principle. Let us consider his answers.

Nielsen maintains that in order to understand a factual statement one must have some idea about what counts for or against it; indeed, this is simply part of what it means to understand a statement.[14] That this is so can, he thinks, be shown by actual examples. Consider clear cases of sentences that do not express statements—for example, "Colors speak faster than the speed of light," "Physics is more mobile than chemistry," "Close the door," "I promise to pay you ten dollars." We have no idea of what evidence in principle would count for or against these sentences. Nielsen challenges critics of the verifiability of meaning to come up with one example of "an utterance that would quite unequivocally be generally accepted as a statement of fact that is not so confirmable or infirmable." Thus, the verifiability theory matches our intuitions in clear cases of what is factually meaningful and what is not.

But why should we suppose that religious utterances are not clear cases of meaningful utterances? Nielsen maintains that we can legitimately suppose there is something amiss in religious language because many religious practitioners suppose there is. Often, he says, religious believers themselves have doubts whether any of their religious beliefs are true or false.[15] This is not because of some externally imposed theory of factual meaning that they have accepted. He urges that the difficulty is intrinsic to sophisticated nonanthropomorphic God talk, with its references to an infinite nonspatial entity, a disembodied spirit that acts in the world, and the like. Ordinary thoughtful religious people are puzzled to know what to make of this talk. And their puzzlement may not be completely relieved by knowing the uses of these expressions in religious discourse or the logical inferences that can be made from statements containing these terms.

Nielsen can be understood as approaching the problem in this way. Let us refer to the clear cases of factually meaningful and factually meaningless utterances as linguistic data E. As we have seen, the verifiability theory matches our intuitions with respect to E. Thus the theory can be understood as providing a clear criterion of factual meaningfulness. However, once this criterion has gained support from E, it can be used to decide the more controversial cases. Given the fact, acknowledged even by many religious believers, that it is unclear whether in speaking of God one is asserting any statements at all, one may wish a clear criterion of factual significance. The verifiability theory provides this criterion.

One notices that puzzling, putative religious statements are compatible with any conceivable empirical evidence. For example, one putative and yet extremely puzzling statement is that an infinite nonspatial entity exists. Yet there can be no conceivable evidence that would count for or against such a claim. Nielsen argues that this is true of other puzzling and yet putative factual statements found in religious discourse. Thus the theory provides a clear criterion for distinguishing the putative religious statements that are factually meaningful from the putative religious statements that are not. So the theory explains why some religious discourse has seemed problematic to many people and gives us a criterion to decide borderline cases. Nielsen puts it this way:

> Noting these linguistic facts, a philosopher can suggest, as a criterion for factual intelligibility, confirmation/disconfirmation in principle. This is not an arbitrary suggestion and it would, if it were adopted, not be an arbitrary entrance requirement, for it brings out procedures which are actually employed in deciding whether a statement is indeed factual. It makes explicit an implicit practice. Moreover, there is a rational point to setting up such a requirement, given the truth of what I have just asserted. The point is this: if we have such a requirement, it can be used in deciding on borderline and disputed cases. Where certain utterances are allegedly bits of fact-stating discourse yet function in radically different ways than our paradigms of fact-stating discourse, we have good grounds for questioning

their factual intelligibility. My criterion makes explicit just what it is that makes a bit of discourse fact-stating discourse.[16]

Given this account of how the verifiability theory of meaning should function with respect to religious discourse, there is nothing question-begging about the proposal to use it.

Furthermore, given this understanding of the verifiability criterion, an objection that has been raised against Nielsen's theory can be answered. George Mavrodes has argued that it would be logically impossible to determine whether some evidence E verifies some putative statement p unless one already knows what p means. Consequently, it would be logically impossible to determine whether p was meaningful by first determining whether E could verify p.[17] However, as we have seen, Nielsen does not propose his criterion as a general theory of meaning or even as a theory of cognitive meaning. Verifiability in principle is proposed only as a criterion of *factual* meaning; that is, as a criterion of what sentences express statements. Thus Nielsen maintains that his criterion is used to *"demarcate within the class of meaningful sentences those that are used to make factual statements."*[18] So it is not logically impossible to apply the criterion. For example, since one has some prior understanding of what some putative statement p means, one can use the criterion to determine whether p is really a statement; that is, whether p is either true or false. One does this by determining whether any evidence would count for or against p.

I conclude that the claim that the use of the verifiability theory in religious contexts is arbitrary and begs the question has not been shown to be true and that there is in fact good reason to adopt this theory.

So far Nielsen has answered one of the traditional questions raised against the logical positivists' criterion of meaning—namely, that the use of this criterion is arbitrary and question-begging. But what about the other problem? As I pointed out above, critics have maintained that the logical positivists have failed to state a criterion of verifiability that both allows the statements of theoretical science and excludes the intuitively puzzling putative statements of sophisticated religious believers. Nielsen argues that once one is clear on how in general the verifiability criterion is to be understood, the problems of certain formulations of the criterion can be ignored.

Using a formulation of the verifiability theory based on Antony Flew's well known "Theology and Falsification,"[19] Nielsen maintains that in order to be factually meaningful, religious propositions "must be confirmable or infirmable in principle by nonreligious, straightforward, empirical statements." He holds that a statement is not confirmable or infirmable "unless at least some conceivable, empirically determinate state of affairs would count against its truth and some at least conceivable, empirically determinate state of affairs would count for its truth."[20] Furthermore, although he does not say this explicitly, Nielsen seems to suppose that if two statements are either confirmable or infirmable to the same extent by the same evidence, they have the same factual meaning.

Nielsen's formulation can be explicated as follows:

(P_1) For any statement S, S is factually meaningful if and only if there is at least some observational statement O that could count for or against S.

(P_2) For any statement S_1 and any statement S_2, S_1 has the same factual meaning as S_2 if and only if the same observational sentences that count for or against S_1 also count for or against S_2 and conversely and to the same degree.

Using this formulation, Nielsen can show how some standard criticisms of the principle fail—for example, those of Alvin Plantinga.[21] For example, it has been argued that

(10) There is a pink unicorn

and

(11) All crows are black

and

(12) Every democracy has some Fascists

are ruled out as meaningless by various formulations of the verifiability principle, although these sentences are factually meaningful. Thus the principle of verifiability is too restrictive. For example, (10) is ruled out by any principle that requires the possibility of decisive falsifiability; (11) is ruled out by any principle that requires the possibility of decisive confirmability; (12) is ruled out by any principle that requires the possibility of either decisive falsifiability or decisive confirmability. But on Nielsen's (P_1) neither (10), (11), nor (12) is ruled out since there are some observational statements that would count for or against them. Thus he can maintain that the verifiability of meaning, correctly understood, is not too restrictive.

But what about the opposite problem? Does the principle allow more than it is supposed to? Some, but by no means all, theists have argued that the existence of love, a concern for social justice, religious experience, and so on counts for the existence of God and that the existence of pain, suffering, and other evil counts against the existence of God. If so, would not a sentence such as "God governs the world" meet Nielsen's criterion? Nielsen argues that it would not. He says:

If "God governs the world" did have such significance, it would have to have a different empirical content than does "It is not the case that God governs the world" or "God does not govern the world." . . . But this is not the case for "God governs the world" and the like. Note that the non-believer might very well accept the believer's claim about human love, a sense of the numinous, a concern for social justice and the incidence of commitment to human solidarity and still not see how this gives us grounds for believing in God.[22]

One can interpret Nielsen's point in the following way. Let S be the observation sentence describing the existence of social justice and other facts that a believer may use to support theism (H). Nielsen can be understood as maintaining that H is no better confirmed relative to S than is its negation ~H. By (P$_2$) H would have the same factual meaning as ~H. But if H and ~H have the same factual meaning, H and ~H have no factual meaning. For if H and ~H were factually meaningful, they would be either true or false. But if H were true, ~H would be false and conversely. However, if H and ~H have the same factual meaning, then H and ~H could not have different truth values.[23] Thus it makes no sense to suppose that H and ~H have some factual meaning and have the same factual meaning. To put it in another way, if H and ~H have the same factual meaning, then neither one has factual meaning.

Still, it may be argued that the problem of allowing some clearly meaningless sentences as meaningful has not been solved by Nielsen's criterion. Although his criterion is not too restrictive, it may be argued that it is not restrictive enough since it allows clear cases of nonsensical statements to be meaningful. Consider:

(13) It is not the case that all crows are black.

(13) is factually meaningful by (P$_1$). But it may be argued that if (13) is factually meaningful by (P$_1$), then so is

(14) Either it is not the case that all crows are black or God is gluberfied,

which follows deductively from (13). Indeed, it is plausible to suppose, it may be said, that any logical consequence of a confirmable statement is itself confirmable. But if this is allowed, then given (14) and

(15) All crows are black

we can deductively infer:

(16) God is gluberfied.

But since (16) deductively follows from confirmable statements and hence from factually meaningful statements, it will be argued that (16) is confirmable and factually meaningful. However, since for (16) one could substitute any statement at all in the above argument, one could show that any sentences at all are meaningful. But this is absurd. Thus it can be maintained that Nielsen has failed to show that his criterion is not too liberal in allowing for any sentence whatsoever to be meaningful.

Although Nielsen does not explicitly consider this sort of problem, others have suggested ways to handle it. Wesley Salmon, for example, has argued that one may admit that a factually meaningful sentence can have factually meaningless components.[24] Thus he sees no problem in allowing that (14) is factually meaningful. Of course, as Salmon points out, such a view conflicts with the standard interpretation of the propositional calculus in which compound sentences must have component sentences that are true or false. Consequently, on this view it would be impossible to have compound sentences with components that are neither true nor false. But, Salmon maintains, the propositional calculus view of this matter lacks intuitive support: In ordinary language it is common for compound sentences to have components that have no factual meaning. One would normally suppose that the compound sentence "Today is Sunday and gerb is blub" is a meaningful sentence although one of its components is meaningless.

Salmon is surely correct. In addition, it is implausible to suppose that one bit of nonsense should cause the larger linguistic unit of which it is a part to be meaningless. But how do Salmon's ideas prevent us from deriving (16) and claiming that it is factually meaningful? He shows how it is possible to construct rules for eliminating factually meaningless components of compound sentences in ordinary language. Given those rules, one could say that (14) has the same meaning as (13). Consequently, one of the arguments given above:

(A) It is not the case that all crows are black

Therefore, either it is not the case that all crows are black or God is gluberfied

is reduced to

(B) It is not the case that all crows are black

Therefore, it is not the case that all crows are black

where the factually meaningless component of the conclusion is eliminated. The intuitive validity of (A) is thus preserved in the reduced version (B). The rule used to eliminate one component of the conclusion in (A) has its justification in terms of (P_2) since, according to (P_2), the sentence "Either it is not the case that all crows are black or God is gluberfied" has the same factual meaning as "It is not the case that all crows are black."

However, in the second argument it is not possible to preserve the validity since the conclusion is factually meaningless. Thus the argument:

(C) Either it is not the case that all crows are black or God is gluberfied.
All crows are black

Therefore, God is gluberfied

is reduced to

(D) It is not the case that all crows are black.
All crows are black.

It would not be possible to derive "God is gluberfied" on the grounds that this sentence appears as a component of a meaningful sentence in the premises of (C) and anything that follows from meaningful sentences is meaningful, since in the reduced version of the premises in (D) no such component appears.[25] Again, the rule used to justify the reduction of the sentence "Either it is not the case that all crows are black or God is gluberfied" to "It is not the case that all crows are black" is justified by (P_2) since, according to (P_2), both sentences have the same factual meaning. In this way Salmon demonstrates the failure of one common attempt to show that the verifiability theory of meaning is too liberal.

But there is another way that one might attempt to show that (P_1) is too liberal. Consider the sentence:

(17) God is gluberfied, and if God is gluberfied, then this rose is red.

It may be argued that since (17) is confirmed and hence factually meaningful, and since (17) entails

(18) This rose is red

and (17) is confirmed by the direct observation of this rose, (17) is indirectly confirmed. Furthermore, since (17) entails

(5) God is gluberfied

and whatever follows from a confirmed statement is confirmed, one would have to say that (5) is confirmed and hence is factually meaningful. We have already seen one technique for handling the undesirable inference by (17) to (5)—namely, eliminating the meaningless components of compound sentences by certain rules justified by (P_2). Using the rules suggested by Salmon, (17) would reduce to (18), and consequently we could not infer (5).

It might be thought that a case has been made that (17) is confirmed by means of (18) and hence that (17) is factually meaningful. Would not one be begging the question to suppose that certain components of (17) should be eliminated by Salmon's rule as meaningless? Since there are no redundant components in (17) and it is involved in the derivation of (18), (17) as a whole seems to be confirmed and hence meaningful by the confirmation of (18). Salmon argues, however, that this supposition is based on a widely held but incorrect view of inductive inference according to which induction is the converse of deduction. The thesis that the confirmation of (18) confirms (17) is based on this mistaken converse-of-deduction view that if H deductively implies I, then the confirmation of I inductively supports H. Salmon shows that many of the problems concerning the verifiability theory of meaning noted in the philosophical literature, including Alonzo Church's widely cited critique of A. J. Ayer's formulation of the theory,[26] depends on this mistaken view of induction. And he goes on to show how a more adequate specification of the relations of induction and confirmation can eliminate the sort of examples typically brought up by critics.

Salmon's efforts at meeting the problems raised by the critics are only a beginning since at the present time we do not have a sufficiently worked out theory of confirmation. It is important, therefore, to realize that the problem is *not* with the inadequacy of the verifiability theory of meaning, explicated in terms of confirmation and disconfirmation relations, but with the inadequacy of the confirmation theory used to explicate these relations. Salmon puts it this way:

> It is of the greatest importance to distinguish between the problem of explicating cognitive meaningfulness and the problem of explicating empirical verifiability. The problem of the meaning criterion is the problem of the propriety or desirability of explicating cognitive meaningfulness in terms of empirical verifiability. Leaving this problem entirely aside, there remains the problem of explicating empirical verifiability. This latter problem is surely an extremely important and fundamental one whether or not a verifiability criterion of meaning is adopted.[27]

Yet it is not necessary to have a completely worked out theory of confirmation or induction to realize that typical alleged counterexamples to the verifiability theory of meaning only end up showing that an inadequate view of confirmation has been assumed. Indeed, I know of no clearly agreed upon case in which a sentence is not confirmable and yet is considered factually meaningful or in which a sentence is confirmable and is not considered factually meaningful. For example, although few would agree that all the components of (17) are meaningful, few would suppose that (17) is confirmed by the evidence that confirms (18). Conversely, although few would deny that (10), (11), and (12) are factually meaningful, few would also deny that it is in principle possible to confirm or disconfirm them—that is, that some conceivable evidence would count for or against them.

I conclude that a strong prima facie case can be made for the thesis that if some theistic language is not confirmable or disconfirmable, it is factually meaningless; the standard traditional criticisms against the verifiability of meaning can be met, and there is independent reason to embrace such a theory since it can account for linguistic data concerning meaningfulness. Therefore, although a complete defense of this criterion needs a developed theory of meaning, there is a good prima facie reason to adopt this criterion even now.

Swinburne's Defense

So far I have defended the verifiability theory in a general way against standard traditional objections. However, I have not considered the critique of this theory presented by Richard Swinburne in *The Coherence of Theism*. It is important to do so, for not only is Swinburne's critique the most detailed to appear in recent years, but it raises some novel objections to the theory and does not rest on common misunderstandings. If his critique is shown to be inadequate, it will not only strengthen the case of the verifiability criterion but strengthen the case for the meaninglessness of religious discourse, since an essential part of Swinburne's defense of the meaningfulness of religious discourse is his critique of the verifiability criterion of meaning.

Swinburne's Critique of the Weak Verificationist Principle

To his credit, Swinburne does not focus on what he calls the strong verificationist principles, which make the factual meaningfulness of a sentence depend on whether the sentence is capable of being conclusively confirmed or conclusively disconfirmed. These strong principles, he points out, have been abandoned. The question he will investigate, he says, is whether a weak verificationist principle, in terms of less than conclusive confirmation or disconfirmation, is a plausible criterion for synthetic propositions. Fortunately Swinburne, unlike many other critics of the verificationist principle, does not take seriously the problems involved in giving a precise formulation of it. He argues that "whether or not any simple general account can be given of [criteria for when one statement confirms another], that has no tendency to cast doubt on the applicability of the weak verificationist principle itself. So long as we can recognize when one statement confirms another (as of course we often can) we can apply the principle."[28]

The first criticism that Swinburne advances is that even if the principle were true, it would "not be of great value in sorting out factual statements from others,"[29] for it relies on the notion of an observational statement. The principle states that a sentence is factually meaningful if an observational statement reporting an observation that would tend to confirm or disconfirm the sentence can be made "in principle." Now, an observation can be made in principle if it makes sense to make it—that is, if it is coherent or logically possible to suppose it can be made. However, Swinburne argues that there is no more agreement over what statements report observable, logically possible states of affairs than over what states of affairs themselves are logically possible in general. He maintains that everything from heaven to the end of the world has been claimed to be observable and that it would be arbitrary to limit observation to the so-called sensory properties, such as round, red, and hard. Philosophers have admitted, he says, that there is no simple and obvious limit to what can be observed. For example, one can observe bacteria under a microscope and the moons of Jupiter through a telescope. There is no easy way of determining which of these claims are mistaken. He therefore concludes that any attempt to prove that it is impossible to observe some state of affairs A will be a proof, by means other than the weak verificationist principle, that state of affairs A itself is impossible. He concludes:

> So although men may be agreed *by and large* about what statements are observation-statements, I see no reason to suppose that the degree of consensus is vastly greater here than over which statements are factual. And if this is so, the weak verificationist principle is not going to be of great help in clearing up the latter.[30]

The second difficulty Swinburne finds with the verificationist principle is that in order to show that a putative statement is not factually meaningful, one must show that it is neither confirmable nor disconfirmable by any observational statement. But since we do not "have before us a catalogue of types of observation-statement which we can run over quickly to see whether they have any confirmation relations to some given statement," we may make a mistake in concluding that the putative statement is not confirmable or disconfirmable by any observational statement.[31]

In addition to these problems in the application of the principle, Swinburne argues that he knows of only two arguments that can be given to support its truth, both of which are unsound. The first is that "if we consider any statement that we judge to be factual, we find that it is confirmable or disconfirmable through observation."[32] However, he says there are plenty of examples of statements that "*some* people judge to be factual which are not apparently confirmable or disconfirmable through observation."[33] He cites the following as examples:

(p₁) There is a being, like men in his behavior, physiology, and history, who nevertheless has no thoughts, feelings, or sensations.

(p₂) Some of the toys that to all appearances stay in the toy cupboard while people are asleep and no one is watching actually get up and dance in the middle of the night and then go back to the cupboard, leaving no trace of their activity.

Since some philosophers would consider (p₁) and (p₂) as factually meaningful and some would not, Swinburne concludes that one cannot appeal to examples of statements to support the principle.

The second argument Swinburne cites that may be used to support the principle is that one could not understand a factual claim unless one "knew what it would be like to observe it to hold or knew which observations would count for or against it."[34] But according to Swinburne, a premise of this argument is false. One can understand the statement "once upon a time, before there were men or other rational creatures, the earth was covered by sea" without having any idea of what geological evidence would count for or against the statement.[35] He says that "we understand a factual claim if we understand the words which occur in the sentence which expresses it, and if they are combined in a grammatical pattern of which we understand the significance."[36] So we can understand the "once upon a time" statement since we understand the words in it and its grammatical pattern.

EVALUATION OF SWINBURNE'S CRITIQUE

Swinburne concludes that "the arguments for the weak verificationist principle do not work."[37] Before we agree, let us consider his criticism of the arguments used to establish the truth of the principle and then his argument that the principle, even if true, cannot be applied.

Swinburne's first argument basically seems to be that since *some* people disagree over whether *some* examples of putative statements are factually meaningful, one cannot appeal to *any* examples to support this principle. But this is a non sequitur. He may be correct that putative statements such as (p₁) and (p₂) have been claimed by some to be factually meaningful while others have claimed the opposite, but from this it does not follow that no examples can be adduced to show that the principle is plausible.

Indeed, it seems clear that Swinburne does not understand how defenders of the principle have appealed to examples. As we have seen, they argue that the principle matches our intuitions in clear cases of both factually meaningful statements and meaningless sentences. These clear cases provide support for the principle,[38] and the principle, in turn, enables us to decide unclear cases. Defenders need not claim that there is agreement about all cases or that controversial cases can be used to support the principle. They can argue, however, that the principle gives an account of some area of discourse that is considered puzzling, not just by philosophers but by ordinary people. As we have seen, Nielsen maintains that the puzzlement many religious believers experience in trying to understand some religious language is explained by the theory of verifiability in that the puzzling cases of putative religious statements are not confirmable or disconfirmable while the nonpuzzling cases of religious statements are confirmable or disconfirmable. In the light of this use of examples, Swinburne's criticism from the mere existence of controversial examples seems irrelevant.

Furthermore, Swinburne's examples (p_1) and (p_2) seem ill-chosen. It is completely unclear why he thinks (p_2) is not confirmable or disconfirmable in principle, given that if one were present in the room, one could see whether or not the toys danced. Swinburne seems to have forgotten that the verifiability theory only demands observation in principle, so it need only be conceivable that an observation could be made, not that it be made. The fact that people are asleep when the toys are supposed to dance is thus irrelevant to the issue of confirmability.

Although (p_1) appears to be a more difficult case for the verificationist principle, in fact it is not. For the question is not, as Swinburne implies, whether (p_1) is conclusively confirmable or disconfirmable or is confirmable in the light of present evidence or technology but whether there is some conceivable evidence that would count for or against it. There surely is such evidence. For example, there could be telepathic evidence. Suppose the hypothesis that Smith has mental telepathy is well confirmed by the available evidence. If so, we would have good reason to suppose that Smith could know without behavioral clues what are people's thoughts, feelings and sensations. Suppose Smith maintains that Jones, who is like a human being in behavior, physiology, and history, has no thoughts, feelings, or sensations. Surely this would confirm (p_1), while the continued failure of Smith to locate a being who looks and acts exactly like a human being but who has no thoughts, feelings, and sensations would disconfirm it.

What about Swinburne's criticism of the second argument—namely, that one cannot understand without knowing what evidence would count for or against it. Despite what defenders of the principle say, he maintains one can understand a statement without knowing what evidence would count for or against it. An example of such a statement is: "Once upon a time, before there were men or other rational creatures, the earth was covered by sea" (N). One can understand N, he says, without having any idea of "what geological evidence would count for or against it." However, the question is not whether one can *understand* N without having any idea of what *geological* evidence would count for or against it. The crucial question is whether N *could be true or false* without our having any idea of what *conceivable* evidence, geological or otherwise, would count for or against it. Swinburne does not even attempt to answer this question. One would suppose that for many people the most obvious conceivable evidence for N would be observations of a hypothetical observer traveling around the earth billions of years ago from, say, several thousand feet in space. N would be disconfirmed if, for example, such an observer had seen land—an island, perhaps—and it would be confirmed if he or she had not seen land despite continued looking. It is not implausible to suppose that because there is such conceivable evidence, N is either true or false.

There seems to be no justification for Swinburne's claim that we can understand the factual significance of a statement so long as we "understand the words which occur in the sentence which expresses it and if they are combined in a grammatical pattern of which we understand the significance," even if we don't know what would confirm or disconfirm it. Consider, for example: "Once upon a time, before there was space and natural numbers, sleep was kibitzed by absolute freedom" (M). Surely, M is factually unintelligible; that is, it is neither true nor false, yet one can understand every word in it as well as the significance of the grammatical pattern. There must be more to understanding the factual significance of a sentence than Swinburne supposes. Nothing Swinburne says rules out the possibility that this more is understanding how to confirm or disconfirm it. Moreover, as we have seen from Nielsen's work, the verifiability theory can account for our clear linguistic intuitions of sentences that express statements and sentences that do not. The present examples support this theory. N is factually intelligible and either confirmable or disconfirmable in principle, while M is factually unintelligible and is not.

I conclude that Swinburne's criticisms of the arguments that he claims are used to support the principle of verifiability do not undermine the principle. However, as we have seen, Swinburne also maintains that the principle, even if true, would not be helpful in separating out factually meaningful from factually meaningless sentences. This is so, he says, because there are two problems in the application of the principle.

One problem Swinburne discusses is that in order to show that a

putative statement is factually meaningless one must show that it is neither confirmable nor disconfirmable by any observational sentence. But
since we do not "have before us a catalogue of types of observation-
statement which we can run over quickly to see whether they have any
confirmation relation to some given statement," we may make a mistake
in concluding that the putative statement is not confirmable of disconfirmable by any observational statement.

This criticism assumes that because a mistake is possible, the application of the principle would be seriously affected. But even if one does
have a catalogue of the kind Swinburne mentions, mistakes can always
be made in the application of *any* principle. This in itself, then, is hardly
ground for supposing that a principle is not useful. To make his case,
Swinburne must show that mistakes in application would be so common
that the verification principle would serve no useful purpose. The mere
possibility of mistake shows nothing.

The other problem Swinburne mentions in the application of the
verification principle is the lack of agreement over what sentences that
express statements can report observable, logically possible states of affairs. He maintains that it would be arbitrary to limit observation to so-
called sensory properties—red, round, smooth—and that philosophers
have admitted that there is no simple and obvious limit to what can be
observed. From this he concludes that there is no more agreement over
what putative statements are observable than over what ones are factually
meaningful. Consequently, a criterion of factual meaningfulness in terms
of confirmation or disconfirmation by observational statements is un-
helpful.

Now, Swinburne is certainly correct that many states of affairs have
been claimed to be observable and that, in recent years, philosophers
have generally agreed that there are no *a priori* limits on what can be
observed. But granting this does not commit one to Swinburne's conclusion that the principle of verifiability is not helpful in separating factually
meaningful sentences from ones that are not. Clearly one must choose a
particular observational language, and this choice should not be arbitrary.

Consider the religious context. In the first place, in applying the
verifiability theory to this context there is good reason to rule out certain
types of allegedly observational sentences. Some religious terms—for
example, the term "God" when it refers to an infinite nonspatial entity—
are considered problematic even by many religious believers themselves.
For this reason, observational reports should not contain such terms.
This does not mean that observational reports cannot be rediscovered in
a nonproblematic way—that is, by replacing "God" with some other term.
Consider the following two observational reports of someone who claims

to have had a religious experience. Let us assume that "God" in (O_1) is supposed to refer to an infinite nonspatial being.

(O_1) The son of God raised the dead

would not be permitted as an observational statement since it contains the problematic term "God," but the redescription of (O_1),

(O_2) A man bathed in a golden light raised the dead,

would. With this sort of observational statement excluded, it is likely that many of the most controversial observational statements in religious contexts will be eliminated.

In the second place, the question of what can be observed is itself an empirical question. Although there may be no *a priori* limits on what can be observed, in the light of our present evidence there are *a posteriori* limits. Thus any reference to observation in a formulation of the principle of verifiability must be understood to refer to observations that it would be possible, in the light of our present evidence, for an appropriately situated observer to make, even though such an observer could not be so situated at the present time. Given our present evidence, an ordinary observer traveling several thousand feet above the surface of the earth billions of years ago could have observed whether the earth was covered by water. On the other hand, given our present evidence, an ordinary observer traveling several million miles above the surface of the earth billions of years ago could not have observed whether the earth was covered by water without the aid of a telescope. Again, in the light of our present evidence an ordinary observer properly situated—say, standing ten yards away—could observe that a man who was bathed in golden light raised the dead, but such an observer situated in the same spatial position and at the same moment of time could not observe that the man was the son of an omnipotent being or born of a virgin. To be sure, these restrictions are tentative and subject to change as our evidence changes. For example, we might discover that men who are born in strange ways have a unique voice or unique mannerisms. With this knowledge we might wish to change our judgment about what it is possible to observe.

Given these restrictions there is surely more agreement over what is possible to observe than over what is factually meaningful. Furthermore, these restrictions seem perfectly reasonable and nonarbitrary. It would be absurd to allow problematic language that is embedded in observational statements to show that this same problematic language is meaningful. This would be like using a prima facie invalid argument to prove an argument valid. Furthermore, to restrict what is possible to observe to what is possible according to our best available evidence is merely good sense.

The Choice of an Observational Language

I agree with Swinburne that to limit observations to so-called sensory qualities is too restrictive. But whether the observational language one should adopt should be a physicalistic one or a phenomenalistic language of appearances remains an open question. If a phenomenalistic language is adopted, there are several types,[39] each with its own advantages and disadvantages, and there seems to be no conclusive reason to choose one over another in all contexts and for all purposes.

If one adopts a physicalistic observational language, the man referred to in (O_2) would be an entity located in the physical world and observable to all observers in the same situation and with the same background. Using this sort of observational language, (O_2) is intersubjectively verifiable. However, for certain purposes one might want to adopt a first-person phenomenalistic language in which O_2 would be understood to mean:

(O'_2) I seemed to see a man bathed in golden light who raised the dead.

This statement would purport to describe how things are appearing to me—that is, my subjective experiences—rather than how they really are.

An observational language could also be a language of the experiences of human beings and other organisms. On this interpretation, (O_2) would refer to the subjective experiences of some particular human being or other organism. For example, (O_2) might be understood to mean:

(O''_2) Mr. Jones seemed to see a man bathed in golden light who raised the dead.

Finally, an observational language might be a language of the subjective experience of some beings but not necessarily human beings or organisms. Understood in this way, (O_2) becomes:

(O'''_2) Someone seemed to see a man bathed in golden light who raised the dead.

This sort of observational language has been called existential quantified phenomenalistic language.[40]

In all these types of observational language the two restrictions mentioned above would apply, although it would be much more difficult to apply the second restriction to phenomenalistic languages than to physicalistic ones. For example, when we use a physicalistic observational language, in the light of our present evidence it is not too difficult to tell whether some normal observer on the earth's surface could, without an optical instrument, observe a fly walking on the surface of the moon. All the evidence suggests that this is impossible. But it is much harder to determine, in the light of our present evidence, whether without an optical instrument it could seem to human beings on the earth's surface that a fly was walking on the surface of the moon. Moreover, it is difficult to see how one could tell, in the light of our present evidence, how things could appear to beings that were neither humans nor organisms or even whether the idea of such beings makes much sense.[41]

Attempts to Show the Confirmability
of Theological Statements

So far we have seen that a verifiability criterion of meaning can be defended against both traditional objections and the recent objections of Swinburne. However, some thinkers have accepted the challenge of the verifiability principle and have attempted to show that seemingly problematic religious sentences are confirmable or disconfirmable, at least relative to certain observational languages, and hence are factually meaningful after all. This is an attempt to meet the verifications on their own terms. In this section I consider some of these attempts.

TOOLEY AND AN EXISTENTIAL QUANTIFIED PHENOMENALISTIC OBSERVATIONAL LANGUAGE

Michael Tooley[42] has argued that theological statements can be confirmed relative to an existential quantified phenomenalistic observational language. Consequently, he maintains, the verificationist challenge to theological statements—that in order to be significant they must be confirmable—can be answered. Tooley's argument, however, has serious problems.

Tooley suggests what he calls a constructability criterion of factual significance. On this criterion a sentence is cognitively meaningful if and only if it stands in a confirmation relation to basic observation sentences. Furthermore, any two sentences have the same factual significance if and only if any observational statements that confirm the one sentence also confirm the other to the same degree. An empirical sentence is a sentence that can be constructed from the basic observational sentences by means of truth functions, quantifiers, and other logical apparatus; or it is introduced in terms of basic observational sentences by means of confirmation function. Given a confirmation function that specifies the degree of confirmation of any set of basic observational sentences, it is possible to construct from, or introduce in terms of, the basic observational sentences some sentence that, in terms of each set of basic observational sentences, contains precisely the degree of confirmation that the function associates with that particular set. It follows that for any factually meaningful sentence S it must be possible to construct or introduce some empirical sentence E that has the same degree of confirmation as S. Thus if the sentence "God exists" is factually meaningful, it must be possible to construct or introduce some empirical sentence E that has the same degree of confirmation as "God exists."

However, according to Tooley, this is impossible given the usual understanding of "God" and the typical kind of observational language. Statements about God, he says, are "experientially transcendent." By this he means that they "could not be analyzed in terms of statements about the physical world or about experiences (actual or conditional) of human beings or embodied perceivers."[43] Given a physicalistic observational language, theological statements would not be significant. Nor would theological statements be significant if the basic observational language was in terms of the experiences of humans or other embodied beings. Any attempt to construct or introduce theological statements on the basis of this sort of observational language would fail. This is because such statements are by definition about experientially transcendent entities, and statements about experientially transcendent entities cannot be constructed from an observational language in terms of the experience of humans and other embodied beings, nor can they be confirmed relative to such a language. If anyone claims to have constructed theological statements in terms of this sort of basic observational language or to have confirmed them relative to this language, then we can be assured that the constructed or introduced statements cannot have the sort of reference they are intended to have; they would not be experientially transcendent.

However, if existentially quantified phenomenalistic observational language is used, says Tooley, the situation changes. Then there is no assumption that the experiences are of human beings or other embodied creatures. According to Tooley, given a language in which sentences of this type are found, the verificationist challenge can be met. Although the verification of theological statements would be beyond human experience, they would then be confirmable and consequently would have cognitive significance.

Tooley's argument seems to depend on an assumption that is never made explicit:

(a) Theological statements either can be constructed from existentially quantified phenomenalistic statements or can be confirmed relative to these statements.

It is important to notice that (a) is not entailed by anything in Tooley's account of theological statements or in his account of an existentially quantified phenomenalistic observational language. Further, the truth of (a) is certainly not obvious; thus before one embraces (a) certain problems have to be met.

On Tooley's view, God is omnipotent, omniscient, eternal, and incorporeal. But then, it is implausible to suppose that statements about God could be constructed from statements about the experiences of disembodied finite beings or could be confirmed relative to such experiences.[44] It would seem that the only experiential statements that could be used to construct or confirm statements about God would be ones about the experiences of an infinite being, the experiences of God Himself. However, the idea that statements about God are constructible or confirmable from statements about God's experience has problems. In the first place, it is unclear that God has experience in the intended sense. Tooley seems to identify experiences with having certain sensations, being appeared to, and so on. But it is not obvious that God's experiences would be of this sort since these experiences seem temporally locatable; that is, they happen at a particular time. Assuming that statements about God are constructible or confirmable from temporally specifiable statements of experiences, they themselves would presumably be temporal. But this seems to conflict with what many theologians consider to be God's atemporal nature.

Even if this problem were overcome, the issue of the sort of experience that would be relevant for the construction or confirmation would remain. Without begging the question of God's existence one would have to specify the confirmatory experiences hypothetically: If there were a being who was all-knowing, all-good, and so on, then statements about this being's experience could be used to construct or confirm theological statements. However, this construal faces two difficulties. First, the condition specifying the relevant experience is couched in theological terms. Consequently, the relevant experiences that confirm theological statements could not be specified without *already* supposing that theological statements are factually significant. Second, we must presuppose that the predicates that define God—all-knowing, all-good, and so on—are not in conflict. If they are, it would be logically impossible for there to be a confirming experience. However, the coherence of the concept of God is debatable. Indeed, as we shall see, there is good reason to suppose that under certain plausible interpretations the concept of God entails a contradiction.

Now, it might be argued that it is a mistake to maintain that theological statements could not be constructed from statements specifying the experience of finite disembodied beings. Although Tooley does not explicitly say so, from what he says in another context[45] one may suppose that he would wish to argue that such a construction is possible. Tooley also

considers another possible observational language: a first-person phenomenalistic one that would describe the experiences of a (finite) person:
oneself. Given this language there is, according to Tooley, one theological
sentence that is factually significant: "I am God." This is presumably
because "I am God" could be constructed from sentences in a first-
person phenomenalistic language or could be confirmable relative to this
language.

However, given that God is an infinite and transcendent being, it is
certainly not clear how statements about my experiences could confirm "I
am God," and Tooley never indicates how such confirmation is possible.
Surely any attempted confirmation could be challenged in the same way
that he suggests the confirmation of theological statements in terms of
physicalistic language could be. The resulting "theological" statement
could not have the sort of referent it was intended to have, for it was
intended to refer to a being that not only was experientially transcendent
but is infinite in power, knowledge, and so on.

But surely it may be suggested that, given my experiences, I could at
least disconfirm "I am God." Since I experience my body and my mistakes, I have evidence that I am corporeal and not all-knowing. However,
as the verifiability theory is usually formulated, for a statement to be
factually significant it is also necessary to specify what possible evidence
would confirm it as well as disconfirm it. But then, it is not at all clear
what evidence would confirm that I am a transcendent infinite being. For
example, what experience could I have that would confirm that I am an
infinite and not merely an extremely powerful finite being?

I must conclude that Tooley has not shown that a first-person phenomenalistic language enables one to construct or confirm theological statements. Consequently, no theological statement has been shown in his
own terms to be factually significant. The same point applies to his
contention that theological statements are confirmable and hence significant relative to an existential quantified phenomenalistic language.

John Hick and Eschatological Verification

One of the most interesting attempts to meet the verificationist challenge
is an argument of John Hick.[46] Hick argues that although no observations
in this life could confirm the statement "God exists" (G) more than its
negation, one could imagine postmortem observations that would. This
Hick calls *eschatological verification*. The possibility of these observations
shows that the difference between a Christian and an atheist is not merely
one of attitudes or of different ways of looking at the world. There are
genuine factual differences in what they believe. Although Hick argues
that Christian theism can be confirmed by postmortem experience, he

maintains that it cannot be disconfirmed. He says that Christian theism may be false but "*that* it is false can never be a fact which anyone has experientially verified."[47]

The sort of postmortem experiences that Hick maintains would confirm that the Christian God exists take place in what he calls a resurrected world to "resurrected beings." This resurrected world is not in physical space, although it is in space. An object in this nonphysical space is not situated at any distance or in any direction from any object in physical space. Although this space might have properties that are "manifestly incompatible with its being a region of physical space,"[48] this is not essential. If this space is not manifestly incompatible with physical space, there will be no direct way for the resurrected beings who inhabit it to know that they are not in some remote part of physical space, such as on a planet in some far-off galaxy. Nevertheless, there will be indirect evidence—no radio communication, for example, or rocket travel between the resurrected world and ours.

Hick maintains that the resurrected beings who inhabit the resurrected world have the memories of the human beings who once lived in physical space. For example, the resurrected Mr. Jones might remember his life in Ohio, his marriage, even the last days before he died and was resurrected. Although the resurrected Mr. Jones would have a body that had the shape of his former physical body, it would not be composed of physical matter. Mr. Jones would know that what he is experiencing is a postmortem existence since he would recognize relatives, friends, and historically important persons, all of whom had died.

Hick admits that his account of postmortem existence does not so far provide confirmation of Christian theism. Indeed, as he points out:

> The atheist, in his resurrected body, and able to remember his life on earth, might say that the universe has turned out to be more complex, and perhaps more to be approved of, than he had realized. But the mere fact of survival, with a new body in a new environment, would not demonstrate to him that there is a God.[49]

However, he says one can conceive of two sorts of afterlife experience that would confirm Christian theism. The first is "an experience of the fulfillment of God's purpose for ourselves, as has been disclosed in Christian revelation." The second conjoins this experience "with an experience of communion with God as he has revealed himself in the person of Christ."[50]

With respect to the first sort of experience, Hick admits that it is impossible to give any specific details of what the fulfillment of God's purpose would be like and that we have only the vaguest notion of what to expect in a postmortem existence. Yet he says that we would be able to recognize the fulfillment of God's purpose in ourselves when it occurred. In some important ways, he points out, our situation with respect to the fulfillment of God's purpose in a postmortem existence is like that of children with respect to being grown up. They have only the vaguest idea of what being a grownup is like and yet, as they mature, are able to recognize when they have become grownups.

Hick argues that the second experience—communion with God as "he has made himself known to men in Christ"—is crucial for the verifiability of Christianity because it seems impossible to verify an experience of God directly. For example, how can one verify that a being one has encountered has an infinite amount of power? He believes this problem is solved in Christianity by the doctrine of the incarnation. Hick says: "An experience of the reign of the Son in the Kingdom of the Father would confirm the authority, and therefore, indirectly, the validity of Jesus' teaching concerning the character of God in his infinite transcendent nature."[51]

There are a number of problems with Hick's account of eschatological verification. First, his description of the resurrected world and the resurrected beings that inhabit it is very hard to make sense of. For example, it is completely unclear what nonphysical space is or how something could have the shape of a physical body but not be composed of physical matter. Unfortunately, Hick does nothing to clarify these ideas. On the verifiability theory of meaning—a theory that Hick seems to accept—if the sentences that describe this world and its inhabitants are to have any factual meaning, it is crucial to know how to verify claims such as that the resurrected Mr. Jones has a nonphysical body. Other difficulties with Hick's account aside, the description of the postmortem world and its inhabitants seems to be factually meaningless.[52]

Even if we waive this problem, the crucial difficulty with Hick's argument remains. Since Hick admits that an atheist might accept the possibility of a resurrected world, the key question is what experience could occur to a postmortem being in such a world that would count for Christian theism as against atheism. The two kinds of experiences suggested by Hick simply will not do.

As Nielsen has argued, Hick's description of the first sort of experience—"the experience of the fulfillment of God's purpose for ourselves, as has been disclosed in Christian revelation"—assumes that talk of God's purpose has a factual meaning.[53] But this is precisely what is at issue. Hick uses problematic theological language, such as "the fulfillment of God's purpose" to describe the experience that he believes will show that theological language meets the verifiability criterion. This, Nielsen argues, "is asking us to pull ourselves up by our own bootstraps."[54]

Furthermore, in Nielsen's view the analogy Hick makes between our understanding of God's purpose and a child's understanding of what it means to be an adult is faulty. "The child, as soon as he can recognize anything at all," Nielsen says, "sees adults around him and is constantly in their presence, but Hick has not shown us how we can have a like idea of what 'the divine purpose is' or what we mean by 'God.' "[55] One could, of course, attempt to describe the relevant experience in nontheological and unproblematic terms. For example, one could maintain that postmortem beings experience a profound sense of peace, fulfillment, and happiness. But such experience would not confirm Christian theism as opposed to alternative views.

The second sort of experience Hick suggests has the same problem. As Nielsen shows,[56] one can understand what experiences would confirm a postmortem encounter with Jesus where "Jesus" refers to a man. But it is completely unclear what experiences would confirm a postmortem encounter with Christ where "Christ" refers to the son of God. Again Hick uses problematic theological language—for example, "Christ"—to describe the experience that he believes will show that theological language meets the verifiability criterion. Thus he is again asking us to pull ourselves up by our own bootstraps.

One could of course describe possible postmortem experience in unproblematic terms. For example, one can imagine having an encounter in a postmortem existence with a wonderfully wise and good teacher called Jesus who preaches brotherly love, cures the sick and the blind, and rules with complete authority. But such experience would be compatible with views beside Christian theism, including atheism, and cannot confirm a hypothesis about the existence of a transcendent God.[57]

Although Hick attempts to answer Nielsen's criticism, his reply is inadequate.[58] Hick maintains that it is impossible to "state in full what it is for God to be real"[59] and that Nielsen is correct that the concept of eschatological verification does not enable us do this. However, he maintains that eschatological verification is not meant to do this. The postmortem experiences he has described are not meant to define God exhaustively but to "describe a situation in which it would be irrational for a human being to doubt the reality of God."[60] However, this is precisely what Hick has not done. On the one hand, if the postmortem experiences were to be described in problematic theological terms, no progress toward clarification would be made. On the other hand, if the experiences were to be described in nontheological terms, it is not clear that it would be irrational to doubt the reality of God. Hick's claim that he did not intend to exhaustively define God by specifying certain postmortem experiences is irrelevant to this issue.[61]

KAVKA AND ESCHATOLOGICAL FALSIFICATION

So far we have seen that Hick's claim that eschatological verification of Christian theism is possible is unsubstantiated. Hick maintains that, although eschatological verification is possible, eschatological falsification is not. Gregory Kavka has argued, however, that, despite what Hick believes, Christian theism can be disconfirmed by postmortem experiences.[62] It is important to examine Kavka's argument, for if Hick is incorrect that confirmation is possible, theism may still partially meet the verifiability criterion by being disconfirmable in principle.

Two points can be made against Kavka. First, if he is correct that postmortem experience can disconfirm theism, then premortem experiences have already disconfirmed it. Second, Kavka does not fully appreciate the problems involved in his account of disconfirming postmortem experiences.

Suppose resurrected beings found that the resurrected world was ruled by "a cruel devil-like creature called Satan," Kavka says, and that in this world, power lay in the hands of a resurrected Hitler, a resurrected Stalin, and other cohorts of Satan who "live 'lives' of luxury while making 'life' miserable for good people, especially the resurrected saints." Suppose further that the resurrected beings in this world learned that "Christianity was a cruel hoax devised by Satan and that the historical Christ was an agent sent by Satan to raise in good people false hopes of eternal salvation."[63] Given this postmortem experience, he argues, Christian theism would be disconfirmed since such experience would provide a good reason, although not a logically conclusive reason, to believe that the Christian God does not exist.

The first obvious response to Kavka is that the sort of experiences he says might occur in the resurrected world have *already* partially occurred in this world. Hitler, Stalin, and other evil men did have great power, and evil men do have great power today; these men have made life miserable for many good people and continue to do so. Furthermore, some Christians have maintained that Satan's influence is everywhere. Alvin Plantinga, for one, has claimed that Satan may be responsible for all the natural evil in this world.[64] In addition, historical scholarship may not indicate that Christianity is a cruel hoax, but it strongly suggests that its major claims—for example, that Jesus existed—are dubious.[65] If the possible *post*mortem experience indicated by Kavka would disconfirm the statement that the Christian God exists, one can only wonder why actual *pre*mortem experience has not already disconfirmed this statement, if perhaps to a lesser degree.

Conversely, if actual premortem experiences of moral and natural evil, the possibility that Satan is the cause of all natural evil, and historical evidence of the dubiousness of the claims of Christianity have not discon-firmed the statement that the Christian God exists, why should the sort of possible postmortem experience suggested by Kavka disconfirm this statement? Surely all the usual defenses used by theists against the prob-lem of evil would be available to resurrected theists in the resurrected world. If they work in the actual world, they would work in the resur-rected world; if they do not work in our world, they would not work in the resurrected world. For example, the free will defense would surely be used by resurrected theists to explain why God allows Satan and his cohorts to rule and make the lives of good people miserable in the resurrected world, just as theists attempt to use this defense to explain the existence of evil in our world. All the standard defenses used by Christian apologists in our world against any historical scholarship that tends to cast doubt on the truth of Christianity would be used against any evidence presented by Satan in the resurrected world that tended to indicate the same thing.

Equally damaging to Kavka's argument is that his description of the resurrected world is ambiguous. Under some interpretations, Kavka's account of postmortem disconfirmatory experiences uses problematic religious language and thus has exactly the same problem as Hick's account of postmortem confirmatory experiences. Under other interpre-tations, Kavka's account, although it does not use problematic religious language, seems irrelevant to the disconfirmation of the existence of a transcendent God.

The resurrected world, Kavka says, may be ruled by "a cruel devil-like creature called Satan." But how are we to understand this? On the usual interpretation of the terms, "devil" and "Satan" refer to a fallen angel who disobeyed God. Thus the meaning of "devil" and "Satan" is parasitic on the meaning of "God," so any problem with the factual significance of sentences such as "God exists" is inherited by sentences such as "Satan exists." But then, if we understand these terms in their standard senses, Nielsen's criticism of Hick applies to Kavka; he too is asking to pull ourselves up by our bootstraps. To be sure, Kavka speaks only of a "devil-like creature called Satan," which suggests that he wants to understand these terms in a nonstandard way. But what way is this? Perhaps the only thing he means is that the resurrected world is ruled by a cruel creature with horns and a tail and with powers and abilities far beyond those of human beings or their resurrected counterparts, and this creature's name is Satan. Understood in this way, it is unclear why the existence of such experience would pose any problem for the resurrected theists, who believe in a completely transcendent God. It may be surprising to such theists that this creature rules the resurrected world. But the theists may simply say that God works in mysterious ways, or that there may well be other resurrections to follow, in which Satan and his cohorts will not rule, or that if we could see the whole picture, we would understand.

Furthermore, according to Kavka, in the resurrected world Satan might teach that "the historical Christ" was an agent sent by him to raise in good people false hopes of eternal salvation. But how can we understand this use of the phrase "this historical Christ"? "Christ" is usually understood to refer to the son of God. Given this understanding, Kavka is using problematic religious language to describe postmortem experiences. But this description would be unacceptable as an observation report that could be used to disconfirm the putative statement that God exists. Suppose instead we understand "the historical Christ" to refer to the historical person, Jesus, who was supposed to have been born of a virgin and to have died on the cross. For many sophisticated Christians, to learn that this person was involved in a hoax perpetrated by some evil being would not disconfirm their belief in Christ or God. As is well known, sophisticated modern Christian theologians such as Barth, Bultman, Brunner, and Tillich have argued that Christianity has no essential interest in the Jesus of history but only in the Christ of faith.[66] Indeed, influenced by existential philosophy, Bultman reduced the Christ of the New Testament to the achievement of authentic selfhood. Whether Jesus ever lived, let alone whether he was involved in a hoax, was to him completely irrelevant to this interpretation of Christ.

If Kavka is correct that postmortem experience could disconfirm theism, we must conclude that theism has already been disconfirmed by premortem experience. On the other hand, theism can be understood in a way that would make the postmortem experience specified in Kavka irrelevant to its confirmation or disconfirmation. Construed in this way, theism is not factually significant.

CROMBIE AND RELIGIOUS PARABLES

In "The Possibility of Theological Statements," I. M. Crombie[67] argues that there are "certain factual beliefs that are fundamental to Christianity"[68] and that it is impossible to analyze Christianity completely in terms of moral or religious practices. However, by Crombie's own admission these factual beliefs are paradoxical, elusive, and anomalous. Thus the critic of the factual meaningfulness of religious statements has a strong prima facie case.

Crombie finds perplexities about the term "God." It seems to be a proper name but, he argues, it is not like any other such name since fixing its referent is difficult. It is not like the proper name "Tom" that refers to a real individual, since one can be acquainted with Tom, but one cannot be acquainted with God. In this respect it is more like the proper name "Titania," since one cannot be acquainted with a fictional character in the same sense that one can be acquainted with Tom. But in another respect it is not at all like "Titania," since "God" purports to refer to a real entity. Thus Crombie calls "God" an "improper proper name."[69]

Crombie also finds perplexities concerning what we say about God. He argues that the predicates that we apply to God—for example, "loves us," "made the world,"—are not used in their everyday senses. For example, in the ordinary sense of "loves us," not every situation counts as some person loving us. If a mother tortures and starves her children, this would count against her loving them. But in theological contexts nothing seems to be excluded; everything seems to counts as God loving us. Thus sentences that contain such predicates as "loving us" seem irrefutable in religious contexts. Given this, it is puzzling to know how religious statements can be true or false. To be sure, Crombie says, some statements about fictional characters, such as "Holmes sprang into a passing hansom," are true or false and yet are unrefutable. But this comparison is embarrassing to theists, Crombie says, since their statements purport to be nonfictional.

It would be a serious mistake, Crombie argues, to infer from this difference between statements about God and statements about ordinary individuals that statements about God are factually meaningless. Indeed, these anomalies may only show that God is unlike all other individuals and, consequently, that the formal properties of theological statements are unique. However, the theist cannot rest with this negative clue and must go on to show how the so-called reference-range of theological statements can be fixed.[70]

Consider first the term "God." How are we to understand this improper proper name? Crombie maintains that although the concept of the divine is in "one sense an empty notion," it is a concept that could fill certain deficiencies in our experiences that "could not be filled in by further experience or scientific theory-making; and its positive content is simply the idea of something (we know not what) which might supply these deficiencies."[71] Thus we are willing to entertain the notion of a divine being outside of space—a spirit—because "we are unwilling to accept with complete contentment the idea that we are ourselves normal spatial–tempora beings." Moreover, the concepts we need for an adequate description of human experience, such as loving, feeling, hoping, all have "a relative independence of space." So there is some justification in experience for speaking of God as a pure spirit.

But God is also supposed to be an infinite pure spirit. How do we understand this? Crombie admits that it is difficult to understand what is being said when we speak of an infinity in religious contexts, since it is clear that "infinity" is not being used in the precise mathematical sense. He says that referring to God as infinite comes close to the same thing as referring to Him as omnipotent, necessary, the creator of all things. But these terms do not have a precise meaning, and their theological use is only loosely and vaguely related to our ordinary use. Yet we have some grasp of their meaning.

Crombie offers the following analogy. Suppose you have written a sentence that you are dissatisfied with. The sentence is inelegant and does not express your meaning, yet the correct version of the sentence is not without meaning to you despite the fact that at the present time you cannot conceive what it stands for. You would recognize it if it came, and it would remove a specific dissatisfaction. In a similar way an infinite pure spirit has meaning for us. This expression stands "for the abstract conception of the possibility of the removal of certain intellectual dissatisfactions which we may feel about the universe of common experience."[72]

Crombie points out that even if we have some understanding of the term "God," we may have no understanding of the content of religious statements—that is, what the predicates that are attributed to God are supposed to mean. At this point in his discussion he appeals to the love of Christ and to biblical parables. For example, since Christ loved His fellows in the everyday sense of the word "love," we assume that the love of Christ, the son, is "an image" of the father's love. However, Crombie argues that although we do not know what it is an image of, we do not need to know since we believe that the image is faithful. The things we say of God are parables, he says; they are not literally true. But if you accept them as faithful parables, you will not be misled as to the nature of the underlying reality.

Thus according to Crombie we must believe that there is some analogy between God's love and human love. This is not to say that an analogy is used to give sense to "love" in theological contexts; rather we postulate the analogy because we believe the image portrayed in the parable to be faithful. Because of this postulated analogy Crombie allows that certain evidence tends to count against theological statements. Irremediably pointless suffering, for example, would count against the existence of a loving God; "the Christian therefore is committed to believing there is no such thing" although he will be "continually tortured by what he sees around him."[73]

What can one conclude about this attempt to show that theological statements have factual meaning? Unfortunately it is altogether unclear in what way, according to Crombie, statements about God are either confirmable or disconfirmable. His own statements are confusing, if not incoherent, on this point. As we have seen, he says (1) that in statements such as "God loves us" the term "loves us" is not used in its everyday sense since nothing could count against the statement. But as we have also seen, he says (2) that because of the analogy between God the father's love and Christ the son's love, irremediably pointless suffering would count against the existence of God. In addition he says (3) that Christians are committed to believing that there is no such suffering. (1) and (2) certainly seem prima facie incompatible. Furthermore, (3) is hard to reconcile with (2) unless we suppose that Christians have an irrational obligation to believe that Christianity is true even if it were to be refuted.

In order to understand Crombie's position, it is helpful to consider an earlier essay, "Theology and Falsification,"[74] in which he makes many of these same points but considers the testability of religious statements in greater detail. In that essay he says that suffering that was "utterly, eternally and irredeemably pointless" would count against statements such as "God loves us" but that one cannot design a crucial experiment since "we can never see all of the picture."[75] He also draws a distinction between (a) the demand that all statements of fact must be verifiable in the sense that there must not exist a rule of language that precludes testing and (b) the claim that, to fully understand a statement, an individual must know what a test of it would be like.

Crombie argues that (a) is a legitimate demand and maintains that theological statements meet it. There is no logical impossibility of testing religious statements, only a factual impossibility, he says. In this respect, the statement "God loves us" has the same status as "Caesar had mutton before he crossed the Rubicon." He suggests that postmortem experience would provide a test of "God loves us," although "we cannot return to report what we find."[76] With respect to (b) the situation is more complicated. We understand statements about God only by means of biblical parables.[77] Within a parable we suppose that the statement "God loves us" is like the statement "My father loves me." We do not suppose, of course, that we can actually test "God loves us" any more than we can actually test "Aristotle's father loved him," but the communication value of "God loves us" is derived from "My father loves me." Once we step outside the parable, Crombie says, we do not know what we mean. Yet we have faith that the parable applies and "that we shall one day see how."[78]

Although Crombie's remarks in "Theology and Falsification" are not explicitly incoherent in the way they seem to be in "The Possibility of Theological Statements," they do not, any more than his remarks in the later essay, answer the question of how theological statements are verifiable and hence factually meaningful. Crombie's proposal to use postmortem experience to combat the charge that theological statements are not verifiable in principle has all the problems of Hick's and Kavka's similar proposals as well as problems of its own. As we have seen, he maintains that utterly, eternally, and irremediably pointless suffering would count against the statement "God loves us," but that there can be no crucial test since one can never see all of the picture. But in no possible postmortem existence would one be able to see all of the picture. No matter how long one's postmortem existence, one would still not see things *sub specie aeternitatis*.[79] There are, then, crucial differences between "God loves us" and "Caesar had mutton before he crossed the Rubicon." Not only can one imagine what historical evidence would refute the statement about Caesar, but one can specify what an observer living at the time of Caesar would have had to observe in order to refute the statement. But it is difficult to see what experience, postmortem or otherwise, could show that some evil was *eternally* and irremediably pointless.[80]

Crombie's use of parables does not help solve the problem of whether theological statements have factual meaning. He admits that outside of the parable we do not know what we mean and must have faith that the parable applies or, as he says in his later essay, that "the image" of the parable is faithful. This appears to be just another way of saying that although it seems as though "God loves us" has no factual meaning, we must believe it does. This is clearly no argument that the statement has factual meaning; indeed, it seems like an admission that no argument is possible. In fact, it is hard to understand how one can believe that the parable is faithful unless one already is justified in assuming that statements about God are factually meaningful. In order to assume that parables are faithful, Crombie must assume that one can have faith in the religious authority of the Bible; that is, that the Bible is divinely inspired. However, such faith only seems possible if one is independently justified in assuming that the statement "The Bible is divinely inspired" has factual meaning. But this is precisely what is at issue.[81]

In "The Possibility of Theological Statements" Crombie's case is weakened further by the use of misleading analogies and bad arguments. He attempts, as we have seen, to show how one can have some understanding of the obscure expression "an Infinite Pure Spirit," arguing by analogy that one can have some understanding of the expression "the correct version of the sentence." He says that although in both cases one does not know precisely what one is referring to by these expressions, the use of such expressions is still justified. But as Nielsen points out, the analogy is completely misleading:

> From past experiences with other sentences, we do indeed know what it is like finally after a struggle to get the correct version of a sentence. . . . Only we do not know, in *this particular* case, what "the correct version of the sentence" refers to. . . . But, as Pierce once observed, universes are not as numerous as blackberries. In other cases, we have not been able to contrast

"a finite dependent universe" with "an infinite, non-dependent being." We have never been able with other cases of universes independently to identify or indicate such an "infinite being," so we do not understand what is supposedly referred to or pointed to by such terms.[82]

We must conclude that Crombie has not succeeded in showing that theological statements are confirmable or disconfirmable in principle or that such statements are factually meaningful.

Conclusion

I conclude that a case can be made that religious language is unverifiable and hence factually meaningless when it is used in a sophisticated and nonanthropomorphic way. First, the standard criticisms of the verifiability theory of meaning fail. Despite what critics charge, the use of the verifiability theory of meaning is not arbitrary, since it is justified by how well it accounts for certain linguistic data. Moreover, the theory can be formulated in a way that neither allows every sentence to be meaningful nor excludes the sentences of theoretical science as meaningless. Second, Swinburne's more recent criticisms of the theory also fail. Third, several attempts to show that religious sentences can be verifiable and hence factually meaningful are unsuccessful.

In the light of my argument, negative atheism is justified and positive atheism is not. The sentence "God exists" is not factually meaningful; that is, it is neither true nor false. Negative atheism is justified, since one can only believe that God exists if the sentence "God exists" is either true or false. Hence negative atheists are justified in not believing in God. However, positive atheism is not justified, since the sentence "God does not exist" is also factually meaningless; that is, it is neither true nor false. One can believe that God does not exist only if the sentence "God does not exist" is either true or false. Hence positive atheists are not justified in believing God does not exist.

However, there are two reasons why more needs to be said and why the argument cannot stop here. The thesis that the sentences "God exists" and "God does not exist" are factually meaningless is only prima facie justified. This is so because a commonly accepted and fully developed theory of meaning is not yet available. Until one is, we must rest content with a partial theory and a partial justification. This consideration tells strongly against negative atheists' relying exclusively on the verifiability theory to support their case. In addition, even this partial justification could be undermined. Negative atheists who use the verifiability theory to support their view would be wise to have a fall-back position in case their arguments for the theory are shown to be mistaken.

Because of these reasons I do not assume in the rest of the book that the sentences "God exists" and "God does not exist" are factually meaningless. Indeed, except for a few minor exceptions[83] I act as if talk about God is factually meaningful and develop the case for negative atheism on independent grounds. Moreover, since I assume in the following chapters that the sentence "God does not exist" is factually meaningful, positive atheism is not ruled out on the ground of meaning. In fact, a case for it is presented in Part II.

CHAPTER 3

The Ontological Argument

The ontological argument is an attempt to prove the existence of God by simply analyzing the concept of God. There is no appeal, as there is in the cosmological argument and the teleological argument, to premises about the world. The ontological argument is thus the paradigmatic *a priori* argument for the existence of God. Historically this argument has been used in various forms by St. Anselm, its originator, as well as by Descartes, Spinoza, and Leibniz.[1] Until recently, Kant's critique of the argument was thought to be decisive by most philosophers. But the argument has been revived in contemporary philosophy by Charles Hartshorne, Norman Malcolm, Carl Kordig, and Alvin Plantinga. The argument seems to have a peculiar fascination for philosophers and refuses to die.

It is impossible to discuss all the variants of the argument here. But a refutation of the original version and four contemporary versions should provide good grounds for supposing that all versions are unsound.

Anselm's Ontological Argument

The most famous version of the ontological argument is that of St. Anselm, the Archbishop of Canterbury (1033–1109), in *Proslogion* 2. Anselm's argument takes the form of a commentary on the words of the Psalmist: "The fool hath said in his heart 'There is no God.' "

> And so, Lord, do thou, who dost give understanding to faith, give me, so far as thou knowest it to be profitable, to understand that thou art as we believe, and that thou art that which we believe. And, indeed, we believe that thou art a being than which nothing greater can be conceived. Or is

79

there no such nature, since the fool hath said in his heart, there is no God? ... But, at any rate, this very fool, when he hears of this being of which I speak—a being than which nothing greater can be conceived—understands what he hears, and what he understands is in his understanding, although he does not understand it to exist.

For, it is one thing for any object to be in the understanding, and another to understand that the object exists. When a painter first conceives of what he will afterward perform, he has it in his understanding, but he does not yet understand it to be, because he has not yet performed it. But after he has made the painting, he both has it in his understanding, and he understands that it exists, because he has made it.

Hence, even the fool is convinced that something exists in the understanding, at least, than which nothing greater can be conceived. For when he hears this, he understands it. And whatever is understood, exists in the understanding. And assuredly that, than which nothing greater can be conceived, cannot exist in the understanding alone. For suppose it exists in the understanding alone: then it can be conceived to exist in reality; which is greater.

Therefore, if that, than which nothing greater can be conceived, exists in the understanding alone, the very being than which nothing greater can be conceived, is one, than which a greater can be conceived. But obviously this is impossible. Hence, there is no doubt that there exists a being, than which nothing greater can be conceived, and it exists both in the understanding and in reality.[2]

The argument proceeds as a *reductio ad absurdum* that purports to show that the fool has uttered a contradiction. It can be reformulated as follows: God is, by definition, a being such that no greater being can be conceived. Even the fool understands this is the meaning of "God." Consequently, such a being exists at least in the fool's understanding— that is, in the fool's mind. The fool, however, thinks that such a being exists only in his mind and in other minds, that it exists only as a mental object. But a greater being can be conceived that exists outside the fool's mind, in the real world. So the fool's thinking is incoherent; he thinks that he has conceived of a being such that no greater being can be conceived and that such a being exists only as a mental object. However, a being such that no greater being can be conceived must exist outside his mind, in the real world, thus contradicting his belief that God exists only as a mental object.

Clearly, one crucial assumption of this argument is that an entity is greater if it exists in reality than if it exists only as a mental object, merely something that someone is thinking about. This assumption can be and has been challenged. First, Kant questioned whether existence can be a property of an object.[3] If it cannot, then it can hardly be the case that, other things being equal, an existing object is greater than a nonexistent one. For it is plausible to suppose that a sufficient condition for entity A being greater than entity B is that A has all and only the properties that B has except that A has, in addition, a property P that makes A more valued or prized than B. On this account, a judgment that A is a greater entity than B, given that A is exactly the same as B, except that A exists and B does not, assumes that existence is a property of A. However, the assumption that existence is a property of objects is a very controversial one; and insofar as the ontological argument makes this assumption, it is not a clearly sound argument. Kant's point still has force:

> By whatever and by however many predicates we may think a thing—even if we completely determine it—we do not make the least addition to the thing when we further declare that this thing *is*. Otherwise, it would not be exactly the same thing that exists, but something more than we had thought in the concept; and we could not, therefore, say that the exact object of my concept exists.[4]

Defenders of the argument at least have to show that existence is indeed a property. Although it may be possible to do this, Anselm did not attempt to show it.

Even if it is granted that existence is a property, the ontological argument further assumes that existence adds to the greatness of a being. After all, it may be the case that existence, although a property of an object, does not affect its greatness; indeed, it may be the case that existence even detracts from the object's greatness. God is supposed to be a perfect being. This means that He is all-good, all-knowing, and all-powerful. The assumption that God does not exist does not seem to take away from His perfection, as would, for example, the assumption that He is not all-knowing. Anselm seems to be using "a being, than which nothing greater can be conceived" as roughly synonymous with "a perfect being." So even if one allows that existence is a property of objects, the lack of existence would not detract from the greatness of a being who was all-good, all-knowing, and all-powerful. Furthermore, existence does not add to the greatness or value of other entities; hence it is difficult to see why it should with God. As Norman Malcolm points out:

> The doctrine that existence is a perfection is remarkably queer. It makes sense and is true to say that my future house will be a better one if it is insulated than if it is not insulated; but what could it mean to say that it will be a better house if it exists than if it does not? My future child will be a better man if he is honest than if he is not; who would understand the saying that he will be a better man if he exists than if he does not?[5]

On the other hand, it may be suggested that as far as religious believers are concerned, the existence of God is something that is valued and prized. Without the existence of God, life would be meaningless and without value. But this argument rests on a confusion. The existence of God adds not to the perfection or greatness of God per se, but to the value of something else, for example, human existence. This point suggests that we should amend the statement made above, which said that a sufficient condition for entity A being greater than entity B is that A has all and only the properties that B has except that A has, in addition, a property P that makes A more valued or prized than B. In order to be more accurate one should change the last phrase to read "in addition, a property P that makes A more valued or prized intrinsically than B."

Indeed, it may be argued that unless some such qualification is made, the value of the existence of God may be relativized to certain groups. Critics of religion may argue that the existence of God is not a desirable state of affairs. They may contend that a nonexistent God should be prized and valued as a beautiful and inspiring myth, while the actual existence of God would bring more problems than it is worth. If God existed, it may be argued, humans would lose a large part of their freedom and autonomy; they would be burdened with guilt and sin; they would have to accept repugnant ontology; they would be faced with the difficult problem of knowing what He commanded and forbade. So unless one restricts the value of God's existence to what is intrinsically valuable, whether the existence of God is valuable will be contextually determined. But so restricted it is not at all clear that existence adds to the greatness of God.

Moreover, supposing that existence is an essential part of the intrinsic value of God, why could not one argue that existence is an essential part of the intrinsic evilness of a completely evil being? Such a being, let us suppose, is all-powerful, all-knowing, and completely evil. Let us call it the absolute evil one. An ontological proof of the absolute evil one would proceed as follows.[6] By definition, the absolute evil one is a being such that no more evil being can be conceived. Even the fool understands that this is the meaning of "the absolute evil one." Consequently, such a being exists at least in the fool's understanding—that is, in the fool's mind. The fool, however, thinks that such a being exists only in his mind and in other minds, that it exists only as a mental object. But a more evil being can be conceived that exists outside the fool's mind, in the real world. So the fool's thinking is incoherent; he thinks that he has conceived of a being such that no more evil being can be conceived and that such a being exists only as a mental object. However, a being such that no more evil being can be conceived must exist outside his mind, in the real world, thus contradicting his belief that the absolute evil one exists only as a mental object. Clearly something is wrong. One cannot prove the existence of both God and the absolute evil one, since they are mutually exclusive.

Along these same lines Gaunilo, a contemporary of Anselm, parodied the ontological argument by arguing that one could prove that a perfect island existed.[7] However, Anselm rejected Gaunilo's proof[8] as have contemporary proponents of the ontological argument. Unfortunately, Anselm's reply consists in little more than insisting that the reasoning used in the argument can only be applied to God. Charles Hartshorne, a contemporary philosopher, argues that Gaunilo's parody fails since it assumes that a necessarily existing island is a coherent notion.[9] But it is not, according to Hartshorne. By its very nature, says Hartshorne, an island is a contingent being, not a necessary being.

Plantinga also rejects the parody on the ground that it is not possible for such an island to exist. But Plantinga conceives of the island not as a necessarily existing island, but as one such that no greater island can be conceived of. He contends that the idea of a greatest island is similar to the idea of a largest number. This idea is incoherent since, no matter how large a number one picks, there could always be a larger one. In a similar way there could not be a greatest island since, no matter what island one conceives of, one could always conceive of a greater island.[10] For example, if one conceives of an island with 1,000 coconut trees, one could conceive of an island with twice as many. In Plantinga's terms, the qualities that make for greatness in islands have no *intrinsic maximum*. However, this is not true in the case of the greatest being that can be conceived of, since the greatness of a being is defined in terms of qualities that do have intrinsic maximums. For example, a being such that no greater being can be conceived of would be all-knowing. However, an all-knowing being is one that for any proposition p would know whether p was true or false.

Hartshorne's and Plantinga's critiques are not very telling.[11] We will consider later in this chapter whether Gaunilo's type of criticism can be applied to Hartshorne's own modal version of the ontological argument. For now it is only necessary to point out that not all forms of the ontological argument in all its forms presuppose the notion of necessary existence. Indeed, Anselm's argument in its most familiar form, the one introduced above, does not. Nor, as we shall see, does Plantinga's version.

Plantinga's critique fails because he assumes that the greatest conceivable island must have an unlimited number of entities such as coconut trees. But if one means by "the greatest conceivable island" a perfect island, it will not have an unlimited number of coconut trees but only the *right* number of coconut trees, whatever that may be. Too many coconut trees would spoil the perfection of the island. The same could be said of other properties, such as sunny days or pure water. Further, as we shall see when we come to Plantinga's version of the ontological argument, his own argument can be parodied without relying on the notion of greatness or an appeal to properties that have no intrinsic maximums. Plantinga's ontological argument can be used to show that it is rational to believe in the existence of a marvelous island (although not perhaps the greatest conceivable island) that has 360 sunny days per year, 10,000 coconut trees, a year-round temperature of 72 degrees, and a population that never grows old.

So by indicating that this mode of argument can lead to absurd results that proponents of the ontological argument can hardly accept, Gaunilo's parody can be used to undermine the ontological argument. The onus is then on the proponents of the ontological argument to show why the parody of the ontological argument should not be accepted while the ontological argument should be.

So far we have seen that the ontological argument of Anselm is based on two debatable assumptions: that existence is a property and that existence is an essential part of the intrinsic value of God. We have seen also that even if these assumptions are granted, one can give a parody of the ontological proof for the existence of God—namely, ontological proof for the existence of the absolute evil one. But the problem remains of where the argument goes wrong.

Mackie has suggested[12] that even if one grants that existence is a property and is part of the intrinsic greatness of God, the argument does not work. Anselm appears to suppose that the fool's concept is that of *a nonexisting being than which no greater being can be conceived,* where the entire italicized phrase represents the content of his concept. Given this concept and the assumption that existence is part of the intrinsic greatness of God, the fool does indeed contradict himself. However, the fool need not and should not conceptualize the situation in this way. The fool may simply have the concept of *a being such that no greater being can be conceived.* He does not include nonexistence within the concept, although he believes that the concept has no application in the real world. Viewed in this way, the fool does not contradict himself. But can the fool afford to admit that existence is part of the concept of a being such that no greater one can be conceived of? There is no reason why he cannot admit this, for he can still insist that such a concept has no application to reality.

To put this in a different way, the argument can be undermined by noting the following: Suppose the fool admits that existence is a property of an entity, that existence would add to the greatness of any being, and that God is a being such that no greater being can be conceived of. The fool could say definitionally that God exists in reality. Or to put it in still a different way, "God is nonexistent" would be a contradiction. But the fool would not be forced into admitting that God *in fact* exists in reality and not just in his understanding. He could insist that the following is not a contradiction: "It is not the case that God exists" or "There is no God."

To say something exists definitionally and not in fact means that by virtue of the way a certain concept is defined, existence is part of the concept. For example, one can define a Loch Ness monster as a large sea animal that inhabits Loch Ness and define a *real* Loch Ness monster as a Loch Ness monster that exists in reality. Such a creature would then exist definitionally, since existence would be part of the definition of a real Loch Ness monster. But whether a real Loch Ness monster *in fact* exists is another question. Further, it would be a contradiction to say that a real Loch Ness monster did not exist. But one would not be uttering a contradiction by saying: "It is not the case that a real Loch Ness monster exists" or "There is no real Loch Ness monster." Similarly, if the fool said that God exists definitionally but not in fact, he would in a way be acknowledging Anselm's point that God exists by definition while insisting that the concept that includes existence need not apply to the real world.[13]

Given the above diagnosis of the problem, I must conclude that Anselm's ontological argument as it is usually formulated is unsound and that it is difficult to see how it could be revived.

Malcolm's Ontological Argument

In a 1960 article in *The Philosophical Review* Norman Malcolm defended a version of the ontological argument that he attributes to Chapter 3 of St. Anselm's *Proslogion*.[14] According to Malcolm, Anselm developed two versions of the ontological argument. He rejects the one that we have just expounded and criticized for the familiar reason that existence cannot be considered a perfection in that it does not add to the greatness of an entity. Malcolm argues, however, that although Anselm may not have realized it, he developed a different version of the argument to which this objection does not apply and, indeed, that this version is sound. In this second version, unlike the first, the modal notions of necessity and impossibility play a crucial role, and the conclusion of the argument is not merely that God exists but that God necessarily exists. Malcolm summarizes the argument in this way:

> If God, a being greater than which cannot be conceived, does not exist then He cannot *come* into existence. For if He did He would either have been *caused* to come into existence or have *happened* to come into existence, and in either case He would be a limited being, which by our conception of Him He is not. Since He cannot come into existence, if He does not exist His existence is impossible. If He does exist He cannot have come into existence (for the reason given), nor can He cease to exist, for nothing could cause Him to cease to exist nor could it just happen that he ceased to exist. So if God exists His existence is necessary. Thus, God's existence

is either impossible or necessary. It can be the former only if the concept of such a being is self-contradictory or in some way logically absurd. Assuming this is not so, it follows that He necessarily exists.[15]

In order to understand this we must distinguish Malcolm's main argument from the ones supporting its premises. The main argument is this:

(1) If God does not exist, His existence is logically impossible.
(2) If God does exist, His existence is logically necessary.
(3) Hence, either God's existence is logically impossible or it is logically necessary.
(4) If God's existence is logically impossible, the concept of God is contradictory.
(5) The concept of God is not contradictory.
(6) Therefore God's existence is logically necessary.

Even before we evaluate the supporting arguments for the premises, serious problems are evident. Consider premise (5). Malcolm maintains that he knows of no general proof for the consistency of the concept of God[16] and that it is not in any case legitimate to demand such proof. He points out that there is no general proof that the concept of a material object is free from contradiction, yet it has "a place in the thinking and the lives of human beings."[17] The concept of God does as well, he says. But this answer is inadequate. Although there may be no general proof of the consistency of the concept of God, there have been many arguments purporting to show that the concept of God is incoherent. Several of these are considered here in Chapter 12. Malcolm makes no attempt to refute any of these, but if any of them are successful, premise (5) is then false, and instead of (6) one can derive the conclusion:

(6') Therefore, God's existence is logically impossible.

Further, Malcolm's second version of Anselm's argument can be parodied in the same way the first version was. Although islands are usually considered contingent entities, one could define a super island as a beautiful island paradise such that if it exists, it exists necessarily; and if it does not exist, its existence is impossible.[18] It would follow that the super island's existence is either logically impossible or logically necessary. It may be argued, moreover, that the concept of a super island is not contradictory, and hence a super island exists. Clearly this last step in the parody is the crucial one. For it would surely be argued by defenders of the ontological argument that a noncontingent island is incoherent, that an island is by its very nature dependent on other things for its existence, whereas a noncontingent being cannot be so dependent.

I will take up this problem when we evaluate Hartshorne's version of the ontological argument. For now it is sufficient to point out that by a perhaps less controversial parody of the argument one could also prove that a variant of the absolute evil one exists.[19] Let us define the super absolute evil one as a being having all the properties of the absolute evil one and in addition have the property that, if it exists, it exists necessarily; and if it does not exist, its existence is impossible. Since the concept of the super absolute evil one is not contradictory, the super absolute evil one necessarily exists. But since the super absolute evil one and God cannot both exist, one cannot accept both arguments. In this parody it cannot be objected that by its very nature the absolute evil one is dependent on other things and cannot therefore be noncontingent. As we have defined the absolute evil one, it has all the attributes of God except His moral ones.

When one examines the supporting arguments for some of the premises in Malcolm's main argument, further problems appear.[20] Let us assume initially that Malcolm means "logically necessary" and "logically impossible" to apply to propositions or statements. Thus when he says "God's existence is logically necessary" he intends that to be equivalent to "The proposition 'God exists' is logically necessary" or "N(God exists)." Given this interpretation, let us go back and look at Malcolm's argument.

Consider premise (1) where the phrase "logically impossible" refers to the following propositions:

(1') If God does not exist, N(God does not exist).

In the summary of the argument quoted above he seems to attempt to deduce premise (1') from another statement:

(a) N(God never has and never will come into existence).

But this inference is invalid. What follows is not (1') but

(1") N(If there is a time at which God does not exist, then there is no subsequent time at which He does exist).

It should be noted that (1") is compatible with the contingent existence of God—that is, with ~N(God exists) and ~N(God does not exist).

Malcolm purports to deduce premise (2) of the main argument, that is:

(2') If God exists, N(God exists)

from (a) and (b):

(b) N(God never has ceased to exist and never will).

But this inference is incorrect as well. What follows is not (2') but:

(2") N(If at any time God exists, then at every time God exists).

Elsewhere in his paper[21] Malcolm argues that the noncontingent nature of God follows from the necessary fact that God's existence is not dependent on anything and has neither beginning nor end. But again this inference is invalid. Neither (1') nor (2') follows from

(c) N(If God exists, then His existence is not dependent on any other being and He has neither beginning nor end).

That Malcolm is assuming that "logically necessary" and "logically impossible" apply to propositions and statements is a natural interpretation to make, and it seems to be supported by the text. If it is not the correct one, however, then what Malcolm does mean is completely unclear.[22] In any case, we are certainly justified in concluding that Malcolm's version of the ontological argument fails.

Hartshorne's Ontological Argument

Charles Hartshorne, who maintains that he had shown long before Malcolm[23] that Anselm had two forms of the ontological argument, a modal form that was sound and a nonmodal form that was not, has perhaps written more on the ontological argument than any other contemporary philosopher. In *The Logic of Perfection* Hartshorne states the modal form of the argument in this way,[24] where q = There is a perfect being, N = It is necessary (logically true) that, $\sim$ = It is not the case that, v = or, and p $\rightarrow$ q = p strictly implies q.

(1)	$q \rightarrow Nq$	Anselm's principle
(2)	$Nq \text{ v} \sim Nq$	excluded middle
(3)	$\sim Nq \rightarrow N\sim Nq$	Becker's postulate
(4)	$Nq \text{ v } N\sim Nq$	from (2) and (3)
(5)	$N\sim Nq \rightarrow N\sim q$	from (1)
(6)	$Nq \text{ v } N\sim q$	from (4) and (5)
(7)	$\sim N\sim q$	intuitive postulate
(8)	Nq	from (6) and (7)
(9)	$Nq \rightarrow q$	modal axiom
(10)	q	from (8) and (9)

Now, premise (1) is Anselm's assumption that perfection could not exist contingently. Premise (3) is a well-accepted postulate of modal logic that modal status is always necessary. Premise (5) can be derived from (1) using principles of modal logic. It says in effect that the necessary falsity of the consequence implies the antecedent; Hartshorne calls this a modal form of *modus tollens*. Premise (7) is the assumption that the existence of a perfect being is not impossible. Premise (9) is the modal axiom that if a proposition is necessarily true, it is true.

There seems to be little doubt that the argument is valid. The crucial question is whether the premises are true. Clearly the most important ones for our purposes are premises (1) and (7). On Hartshorne's view, (7) is hardest to justify. He recommends using one or more of the theistic proofs that he claims demonstrate that perfection must be at least possible. But this seems to have things backward. The theistic proofs *presume* that the concept of God is coherent; they cannot demonstrate it. Furthermore, as we mentioned above, there have been many attempts to show that the concept of God is incoherent. Before one can claim that it is coherent, one at least needs to show that these attempts failed. Hartshorne has not done this, and consequently premise (7) is unjustified. Moreover, since, as we shall soon see, some of these attempts are successful (see Chapter 12), not only is premise (7) unjustified, but there is good reason to suppose that it is false.

Premise (1) is also problematic. Hartshorne seems to mean by "it is necessary that q" that it is *logically* necessary that q. However, there does not seem to be any reason to suppose that, if a perfect being exists, the existence is logically necessary. As R. L. Purtill has argued:

> It seems to be contrary to our idea of logical necessity that whether or not a statement is logically necessary should be determined by the existence or nonexistence of something. If by "logically necessary statement" we mean "theorem of a logical system" or "tautology" or "analytic statement," it seems quite clear that the existence or nonexistence of something is irrelevant to the question of whether or not a statement is a theorem, or a tautology, or is analytic. Even if our idea of logical necessity is claimed to be wider than any of these notions, it seems unlikely that any plausible account of logical necessity would allow it to be dependent on existence.[25]

Hartshorne believes that one cannot use the logic of perfection to prove the existence of a perfect island, but his attempts to meet a Gaunilo type of objection are not successful. He argues that it is incoherent to suppose that an island could be perfect, since in order to be perfect it would have to be a noncontingent being. However, he says, an island by its very nature is contingent. In response to Hartshorne, could one not introduce the concept of a super island that, if it existed at all, would exist necessarily? Hartshorne maintains that the concept of a necessarily existing island is "self-inconsistent."[26] What is his basis for this judgment? He maintains that a contingent being must have ten properties,[27] among which are being causally dependent for its existence on something else and being good for some legitimate purpose only. His argument seems to be that an island by its very nature must have these properties and consequently could not be noncontingent.

The trouble with this reply is that in the case of some of the ten properties listed, it is certainly not obvious that an island could not conceivably have them. For example, why does an island have to be causally dependent on other things? Islands are in fact so dependent, but it does not seem impossible to imagine an island that is not. To be sure, if such an island were to exist in our world it would be a miracle, since its existence would be in conflict with many laws of nature. But it would not, for that reason, be conceptually incoherent. In the case of some of the other properties listed by Hartshorne, although it is true that an island by its very nature must have them, it is unclear why he supposes that they are only properties of contingent beings. For example, one may admit that even a perfect island is only good for some purposes. But why must a noncontingent being be good for *all* purposes?

It would also seem possible to "prove" the existence of the super absolute evil one by modal argument with a structure identical to Hartshorne's, the basic difference being in the interpretation of q. Statement q would now mean "A perfectly evil being exists." Since such a being would be all-knowing, all-powerful, uncreated, independent of everything else, and the cause of all contingent things, of the ten properties of a contingent being listed by Hartshorne it would lack only one: It would not be good for all legitimate purposes. But, as suggested above, it is unclear that this property has anything to do with noncontingency.

In an earlier work Hartshorne argued against an ontological proof of a perfect devil. Since the idea of a perfect devil has close similarities to our idea of the absolute evil one, it is important to consider his argument. He says:

> A perfect devil would have at the same time to be infinitely responsible for all that exists besides itself, and yet infinitely averse to all that exists. It would have to attend with unrivaled care and patience and fullness of realization to the lives of all other beings (which must depend for existence upon this care), and yet must hate all these things with matchless bitterness. It must savagely torture a cosmos every item of which is integral with its own being, united to it with a vivid intimacy such as we can dimly imagine. In short, whether a perfect God is sense or nonsense, a perfect devil is unequivocally nonsense, and it is of no import whether the nonsensical does or does not exist, since in any case it necessarily does not exist, and its existence would be nothing, even though a necessary nothing.[28]

It is a mystery why Hartshorne attributes conflicting properties to the perfect devil, but in any case they are not the properties of the absolute evil one. As I conceive of the absolute evil one, although it is responsible for the existence of all contingent creatures in the sense that it is the ultimate cause of them, this is compatible with its inflicting great evil on these creatures. Thus the absolute evil one is not in one sense, at least, averse to all that exists since the torture of its creatures is its goal. It must create contingent sentient beings in order to cause them pain and suffering. It does not attend to their lives with care and patience in any sense that implies moral concern. It only attends to them in the way a torturer attends to his victims. The cosmos is not integral with its own being, for the absolute evil one transcends the cosmos and intervenes in it only for its own evil purposes. Thus Hartshorne has not shown that the super absolute evil one is a nonsensical notion, a "necessary nothing." Until this is shown, I must conclude that the ontological proof of the super absolute evil one is sound if the ontological proof of God is.

Kordig's Ontological Argument

Carl Kordig has recently presented a deontic version of the ontological argument that has two stages.[29] The first stage of the argument can be informally stated as follows: What is deontically perfect ought to exist. Since God is perfect He ought to exist. But Kordig argues that what ought to exist can exist. So it is possible that God exists. Stated more formally, with g standing for "God exists," and O the deontic operator, and $\Diamond$ the modal operator designating possibility, the first stage of the argument is this.

(1) Og
(2) $Og \rightarrow \Diamond g$

(3) Hence $\Diamond g$

The first premise says that God ought to exist. The second premise says that if God ought to exist, it is possible that God exists. By *modus ponens* one concludes that it is possible that God exists.

Stated informally, the second stage of the argument is that since it was established in the first stage of the argument that the existence of God is possible, the existence of God is necessary. This is because God is not a contingent being. If it is possible that He exists, He must exist. It is formally stated, with $\Box$ the modal operator designating necessity, as follows:

(4) $\Diamond g$
(5) $\Diamond g \rightarrow \Box g$

(6) Hence $\Box g$

Premise (4), the conclusion of the first stage of the argument, says that the existence of God is possible. Premise (5) of the argument says that if the existence of God is possible, then the existence of God is necessary.

Given these two premises, one concludes by *modus ponens* that it is necessary that God exists.

Even if there were no problems with the first stage of the argument, there would be serious problems with the second stage, problems identical to the one in Malcolm's and Hartshorne's versions of the ontological argument. For example, although islands are usually considered contingent entities, one can introduce the idea of a super island, an island paradise that not only has wondrous health benefits and the right number of coconut trees, days of sunshine, and so on but also has unusual modal properties. For example, if the super island exists at all, its existence is necessary. Since the concept of a super island is not logically impossible, by *modus ponens* one can conclude that the super island necessarily exists. Where s stands for "A super island exists" the argument is this.

(4') $\Diamond$s
(5') $\Diamond$s $\rightarrow$ $\Box$s

(6') Hence $\Box$s

Now, it may be objected that the concept of a super island is incoherent and, consequently, that (4') is false. However, it is not at all obvious that there is anything any more incoherent about the concept of a super island than about the concept of God. As we argued above, such an island should not be considered analogous to the largest number, which clearly is an incoherent idea. Nor are the sort of considerations adduced by Hartshorne persuasive. In any case, at this point the first stage of Kordig's argument comes to our rescue. Even skeptics who doubt that a super island exists surely believe that it ought to exist. After all, as we have defined it, the blind and ill could be cured simply by being transported there. But if it ought to exist, then it is possible for it to exist. Stated more formally:

(1') Os
(2') Os $\rightarrow$ $\Diamond$s

(3') Hence $\Diamond$s

As Patrick Grim has shown, all manner of bizarre deontically perfect beings can be demonstrated by this argument.[30] It is also possible to demonstrate the existence of the super absolute evil one. Let e stand for "The super absolute evil one exists." The argument then proceeds as follows:

(1a) O~e
(2a) O~e $\rightarrow$ $\Diamond$e

(3a) Hence ◇e
(4a) ◇e
(5a) ◇e → □e

(6a) Hence □e

Stated informally, this says that the super absolute evil one ought not to exist. So the super absolute evil one is possible. Since the super absolute evil one is by definition not a contingent being and it is possible that it exists, it must exist.

It seems clear that Kordig's deontic version of the ontological argument is no more acceptable than the other versions we have examined.

Plantinga's Ontological Argument

Plantinga has argued for the existence of God using a version of the ontological argument based on the logic of possible worlds.[31] He defines the property of maximal greatness as entailing maximal excellence in every possible world, and he defines maximal excellence as entailing omniscience, omnipotence, and moral perfection in every possible world. A simplified statement of his argument can be constructed as follows:

(1)   There is a possible world where maximal greatness is exemplified.
(1a) There is some possible world in which there is a being that is maximally great. (From (1))
(2)   Necessarily, a being that is maximally great is maximally excellent in every possible world. (By definition)
(3)   Necessarily, a being that is maximally excellent in every possible world is omniscient, omnipotent, and morally perfect in every possible world. (By definition)
(4)   Therefore, there is in our world and in every world a being that is omniscient, omnipotent, and morally perfect. (From (1a), (2), and (3))

Plantinga does not believe that this argument is a conclusive demonstration of the existence of God, since premise (1) is not rationally established; it could be denied by rational people. On the other hand, he maintains that (1) is not contrary to reason. Thus he concludes that the argument establishes not the truth of the thesis but "its rational acceptability."[32]

There are a number of problems with this argument. For one thing, technical questions can be raised about the use of possible world semantics and modal logic in his proof. In particular, it may be wondered if the system of modal logic used in Plantinga's proof is appropriate[33] and if

Plantinga has provided adequate truth conditions for modal sentences.[34] We do not pursue these issues here, however, for there are more basic problems with the argument.

To begin with, Plantinga may well be mistaken that premise (1) is not contrary to reason. If, for example, omniscience, omnipotence, and moral perfection constitute an incoherent set of properties, as we shall soon see, then maximal greatness would be incoherent as well. Furthermore, one of Plantinga's arguments for supposing that the acceptance of premise (1) is not irrational is suspect. He compares (1) to Leibniz's Law:

> (LL) For any object x and y and property P, if x = y, then x has P if and only if y has P

and maintains that despite the fact that we have no proof of (LL) we are justified in accepting it. Similarly, Plantinga argues that despite the fact that we have no proof of (1) we are justified in accepting it.[35] However, it has been plausibly argued that the analogy between (LL) and (1) is weak. (LL) is a free English translation of a theorem of the first-order predicate calculus with identity, but (1) is not a translation of a theorem of any standard logic. Disputes about (LL) in the history of philosophy, unlike disputes about (1), seem to be metalinguistic and not over the truth value of (LL).[36]

In addition, Plantinga's argument can be parodied[37] by using an argument with the same form to show the rational acceptability of fairies, ghosts, unicorns, and all manner of strange creatures. One *reductio* of this mode of argument proceeds as follows: Let us define the property of being a special fairy so that it entails the property of being a fairy in every possible world. Let us define the property of being a fairy so that it entails the property of being a tiny woodland creature with magical powers in every possible world. Then:

> (1′) There is one possible world where the property of being a special fairy is exemplified.
>
> (1a′) There is one possible world where there is a special fairy. (From (1))
>
> (2′) Necessarily, a being that is a special fairy is a fairy in every possible world. (By definition)
>
> (3′) Necessarily, a being that is a fairy in every possible world is a tiny woodland creature with magical powers in every possible world. (By definition)
>
> (4′) Therefore, there is a tiny woodland creature with magical powers in our world and in every world.

Since premise (1′) is no more contrary to reason than premise (1), one must assume that the conclusion (6′) is rationally acceptable. In a similar way one can show that there are gremlins, leprechauns, and unicorns. Using a similar mode of argument one can show the rational acceptability of a marvelous island of the kind specified above. One defines the property of a special marvelous island in such a way that it entails being a marvelous island in all possible worlds. One defines a marvelous island as an island where one never grows old, where there are 10,000 coconut trees, and so forth.[38] Then one has as the first premise of the argument:

(1″) There is a possible world where the property of being a special marvelous island is exemplified.

Presumably, (1″) is not contrary to reason or, at least, no more contrary to reason than (1). The argument then proceeds in the way outlined above. One concludes that belief in a marvelous island is rationally acceptable. It can be shown as well that the absolute evil one exists in our world and every world. But, since the absolute evil one is omniscient, omnipotent, and completely evil, God and the absolute evil could not both exist.[39]

I must conclude that Plantinga's version of the ontological argument is no more successful than the others we have examined.[40]

Conclusion

Arthur Schopenhauer wrote, "Considered by daylight . . . and without prejudice, this famous Ontological Proof is really a charming joke."[41] One is tempted to agree. Yet, as we have seen, some well-known philosophers who have reputations as profound thinkers have taken it quite seriously. Given the problems with the argument outlined here, it is difficult to understand why they do.

CHAPTER 4

The Cosmological Argument

Just as the ontological argument has been used by many philosophers to prove the existence of God, so has the cosmological argument. Indeed, Plato, Aristotle, St. Thomas Aquinas, Descartes, and Leibniz among others have put forth versions of this argument. It also seems to be a popular argument among lay persons. If one were to ask the average person why he or she believes in God, the answer would probably be some simple version of the cosmological argument. In all its forms this is an argument that starts off with certain facts about the world and attempts to infer from them the existence of God. In other words, unlike the ontological argument, the cosmological argument has some premises based on empirical observation. Nevertheless, although some recent writers have constructed inductive-probabilistic versions of the cosmological argument, the traditional form the argument takes is deductive. It is impossible here to consider all versions of the cosmological argument. I consider two of St. Thomas Aquinas's five ways—perhaps the most famous classical statement of the deductive version of the argument—as well as three of the most sophisticated contemporary versions of the argument: William Craig's and Bruce Reichenbach's deductive formulations and Richard Swinburne's inductive formulation. The refutation of this representative sample of formulations of the argument should provide good grounds for thinking that all versions of the argument fail.

Traditional Deductive Cosmological Arguments

THE SIMPLE VERSION

In its simplest form the cosmological argument is this: Everything we know has a cause. But there cannot be an infinite regress of causes, so there must be a first cause. This first cause is God.

It is well to state the problems with this simple version of the argument, since, as we shall see, they are found in some of the more sophisticated versions as well. Perhaps the major problem with this version of the argument is that even if it is successful in demonstrating a first cause, this first cause is not necessarily God.[1] A first cause need not have the properties usually associated with God. For example, a first cause need not have great, let alone infinite, knowledge or goodness. A first cause could be an evil being or the universe itself. In itself this problem makes the argument quite useless as support for the view that God exists. However, it has at least one other equally serious problem.

The argument assumes that there cannot be an infinite sequence of causes, but it is unclear why this should be so. Experience does not reveal causal sequences that have a first cause, a cause that is not caused. So the idea that there can be no infinite sequences and that there must be a first cause, a cause without a cause, finds no support in experience. This is not to say that experience indicates an infinite sequence of causes. Rather, the presumption of the existence of a first cause seems to be a nonempirical assumption that some people see as obvious or self-evident. From a historical point of view, however, any appeal to obviousness or self-evidence must be regarded with suspicion, for many things that have been claimed to be self-evidently true—for example, the divine right of kings and the earth as the center of the universe—have turned out not to be true at all.

Further, we have no experience of infinite causal sequences, but we do know that there are infinite series, such as natural numbers. One wonders why, if there can be infinite sequences in mathematics, there could not be one in causality. No doubt there are crucial differences between causal and mathematical series; but without further arguments showing precisely what these are, there is no reason to think that there could not be an infinite regression of causes. Some recent defenders of the cosmological argument have offered just such arguments, and I examine these arguments later. But even if they are successful, in themselves they do not show that the first cause is God.

More Complex Versions

As I have said, major problems facing the simple version of the cosmological argument reemerge in more sophisticated versions as well. Consider, for example, Aquinas's belief that God's existence could be demonstrated by rational arguments. In the *Summa Theologiae* he presents five arguments—what he calls ways—that he believes demonstrate the existence of God.[2] The first three of his five ways are sophisticated versions of the simple cosmological argument presented alone. I consider ways two and three.

Aquinas states the second way as follows:

> The second way is based on the notion of efficient causation. In the observable world we discover an order of efficient causes, but no case is found, or ever could be found, of something efficiently causing itself. Such a thing would have to be prior to itself, which is impossible. Now it is impossible to go on forever in a series of efficient causes. For in every ordered series of efficient causes the first member of the series causes the intermediate member or members, which in turn cause the final member. If you eliminate a cause you eliminate its effect, so there will not be final or intermediate members in the series unless there is a first member. But if the series goes on forever, then there will be no first efficient cause; and so there will be no final effect and no intermediate efficient cause, which is obviously false. Therefore it is necessary to posit some first efficient cause, to which everyone gives the name "God."[3]

In this argument Aquinas attempts to show that there could not be an infinite series of efficient causes and consequently there must be a first cause. Although this notion of efficient cause is perhaps closer to our modern view of causality than the other Aristotelian concepts of cause he used, there are some important differences. An efficient cause of something, for Aristotle and Aquinas, is not a prior event but a substantial agent that brings about change. The paradigm cases of causation for an Aristotelian are heating and wetting. For example, if A heats B, then A produces heat in B; if A wets B, then A produces wetness in B. In general, if A Φs B, then A produces Φness in B. The priority of a cause need not be temporal; a cause is prior to its effects in the sense that the cause can exist without the effect but not conversely.[4]

It is important to realize that Aquinas's argument purports to establish a first cause that maintains the universe here and now. His second way is not concerned with establishing a first cause of the universe in the distant past. Indeed, he believed that one could not demonstrate by philosophical argument that the universe had a beginning in time, although he believed that it did. This belief was a matter of faith, something that was part of Christian dogma, not something that one could certify by reason. Thus he was not opposed on *philosophical* grounds to the universe's having no temporal beginning. As the above quotation makes clear, he believed that the here-and-now maintenance of the universe could not be understood in terms of an infinite causal series.

Two analogies can perhaps make the distinction between temporal and nontemporal causal sequences clear. Consider a series of falling dominos. It is analogous to a temporal causal sequence. Aquinas does not deny on philosophical grounds that infinite sequences of this sort can exist. But now consider a chain in which one link supports the next. There is no temporal sequence here. The sort of causal sequence that

Aquinas says cannot go on forever but must end in a first cause is analogous to this.

The same problems that plagued the simple version of the argument plague this more sophisticated version. The first cause, even if established, need not be God; and Aquinas gives no non-question-begging reason why there could not be a nontemporal infinite regress of causes.[5] This latter is an especially acute problem. Unless some relevant difference is shown between a temporal and a nontemporal infinite series, Aquinas's claim that an infinite temporal sequence cannot be shown to be impossible by philosophical argument seems indirectly to cast doubt on his claim that philosophical argument can show the impossibility of a nontemporal causal series.

In the third way Aquinas argues as follows:

> Some things we encounter have the possibility of being and not being, since we find them being generated and corrupted, and accordingly with the possibility of being and not being. Now it is impossible for all that there is to be like that; because what has the possibility of not being, at some time is not. If therefore every thing has the possibility of not being, at one time there was nothing. But if this were the case, there would be nothing even now, because what is not does not begin to be except through something which is; so if nothing was in being, it was impossible for anything to begin to be, and so there would still be nothing, which is obviously false. Not everything therefore has the possibility [of being and not being] but there must be something which is necessary. Now everything which is necessary either has a cause of its necessity outside itself, or it does not. Now it is not possible to go on for ever in a series of necessary beings which have a cause of their necessity, just as was shown in the case of efficient causes. So it is necessary to assume something which is necessary of itself, and has no cause of its necessity outside itself, but is rather the cause of necessity in other things, and this all men call God.[6]

To critically evaluate Aquinas's argument, it is useful to reformulate it in the following steps.

(1) Each existing thing is capable of not existing.
(2) What is true of each thing is true of everything (the totality).
(3) Therefore, everything could cease to exist.
(4) If everything could cease to exist, then it has already occurred.
(5) Therefore, everything has ceased to exist.
(6) If everything has already ceased to exist and there could not be something brought into existence by nothing, then nothing exists now.
(7) There could not be something brought into existence by nothing.

(8) Therefore, nothing exists now.

(9) But something does exist now.

(10) Therefore, premise (1) is false.

(11) Therefore, there must be some being that is not capable of not existing—that is, a necessary being.

(12) Every necessary being must have the cause of its necessity either outside itself or not.

(13) There cannot be an infinite series of necessary beings that have a cause of their necessity outside themselves.

(14) Therefore, there is a necessary being that does not have the cause of its own necessity outside itself and that is the cause of the necessity of other beings.

(15) Therefore, God exists.

Of the many problems with Aquinas's argument, the major one is similar to that facing the simple version of the cosmological argument considered above. Even if a necessary being is established, it need not be God, for the universe itself may be necessary. Thus the last step of the argument from (14) to (15) is unwarranted.

There are a number of particular problems with Aquinas's argument as well. In premise (2) the argument seems to commit the fallacy of composition. Just because each thing is capable of not existing, it is not obvious that the totality would be capable of not existing. Furthermore, premise (4) seems implausible in the extreme. There is no reason to suppose that just because something is capable of not existing, at some time this possibility has been realized.

In addition, the supposition in premise (7) that there could not be something brought into existence by nothing is by no means self-evident. At least, given the biblical authority of the book of Genesis, where God created the world out of nothing, it should not have seemed so to Aquinas. For if God could create the world out of nothing, one might suppose that something could be spontaneously generated out of nothing without God's help. Surely this is all step (7) is denying by the words "there could not be something brought into existence by nothing." Furthermore, recently proposed cosmological theories suggest that the universe may indeed have been generated from nothing. Although a critical evaluation of these recent theories is beyond the scope of this book, it is important to realize that such theories are being seriously discussed and debated by physicists, astronomers, and philosophers of science in respectable publications.[7] Moreover, step (13) has all the problems inherited from Aquinas's arguments that there could not be an infinite series of efficient causes.[8]

I must conclude, then, that these two deductive versions of the cosmological argument are unsound and therefore cannot be used to support a belief in God.[9]

Three Contemporary Defenses of the Cosmological Argument

In recent years William Craig, Bruce Reichenbach, and Richard Swinburne have developed versions of the cosmological argument. Craig and Reichenbach can be understood as presenting deductive forms of the argument, while Swinburne's cosmological argument is inductive. Although there are other contemporary versions of the cosmological argument, these are among the most sophisticated and well argued in contemporary philosophical theology. We can therefore be fairly sure that if these arguments are found to be unsound, those left unexamined here would also be found lacking.

CRAIG'S DEFENSE OF THE KALAM COSMOLOGICAL ARGUMENT

The Argument

William Craig has recently defended the Kalam cosmological argument,[10] a version of the cosmological argument originating in the work of the sixth-century Alexandrian philosophical commentator and Christian theologian Joannes Philoponos. He argued against Aristotle's proofs that the universe was eternal, and his argument was developed with greater subtlety by medieval Islamic theologians of the Kalam school. The argument was carried to the Christian world in the thirteenth century and became a source of great philosophical debate between Bonaventure, who supported it, and Aquinas, who opposed it.[11] Unlike the second way of Aquinas, the attempt is made in this version of the argument to demonstrate that the universe was created at a particular moment in time.

The basic argument Craig presents is as follows:

(1) Everything that begins to exist has a cause of its existence.
(2) The universe began to exist.
(3) Therefore, the universe has a cause of its existence.

According to Craig, the key premise in the argument is (2).[12] Craig argues that those who deny it presuppose the possibility of an actual, in contrast to a potential, infinity of events. According to Craig, critics of the argument must assure that the temporal regression of events has no beginning and thus that these events, stretching back forever in time, form an actual infinity. Craig maintains that the notion of actual infinity, even in the realm of pure mathematics, has paradoxical implications—for example, the number·of even numbers is the same as the number of natural numbers—and that some mathematicians (for example, intuitionists) have therefore rejected the notion of an actual infinity. He argues that as it is analyzed by Georg Cantor, although the notion of an actual infinity in the realm of number theory may form a consistent mathematical system, it "carries with it no ontological import for the existence of actual infinity in the real world." Indeed, he maintains that the supposition that there are actual infinities in the real world entails absurdities. Suppose, Craig says, there is a library with an infinite number of books:

> Suppose further that each book in the library has a number printed on its spine so as to create a one-to-one correspondence with the natural numbers. Because the collection is an actual infinity, this means that *every possible* natural number is printed on some book. Therefore, it would be impossible to add another book to this library. For what would be the number of the new book? Clearly there is no number to assign to it. . . . Therefore, there would be no number for the new book. But this is absurd, since entities that exist in reality can be numbered.[13]

According to Craig, not only does the notion of actual infinity have absurd implications, but it is also impossible to form an actual infinity by successive addition. In order to form a collection by successive addition, each item in the collection must be added sequentially. He maintains that a collection formed in this way cannot be an actual infinity, since no matter how many items have been added, one more item can be added. Since the events that constitute our world up to this point in time are a collection formed by successive addition, one event following after another, these events cannot constitute an actual infinity.[14]

In addition to these essentially *a priori* arguments, Craig believes that evidence from science supports the idea that the universe had a beginning. He maintains that the evidence from scientific cosmology supports the hypothesis that the universe had an absolute beginning about 15 billion years ago and that alternative hypotheses such as the steady state theory and the oscillating model of the universe are not as well supported.[15] He argues also that the second law of thermodynamics predicts that if the universe had existed for an infinite length of time, then it should have reached a state of maximum entropy; that is, all energy in it should have become evenly distributed. But clearly this has not happened. Hence the universe had a beginning.[16]

Craig believes that premise (1) of the argument does not need as elaborate a defense as premise (2): "the idea that anything, especially the whole universe, could pop into existence uncaused is so repugnant that most thinkers intuitively recognize that the universe's beginning to exist entirely uncaused out of nothing is incapable of sincere affirmation."[17] Nevertheless, he outlines two possible lines of support for (1). He claims that the empirical evidence is overwhelming for the proposition that everything that has a beginning has a cause. He also takes a Kantian approach, suggesting that it is plausible to suppose that causality is an *a priori* category of the human mind. In other words, causality is a precondition of thought.

It should be clear, however, even if the premises of Craig's argument are accepted: The only conclusion one can draw is that the universe has a cause. This need not be a person, let alone an all-knowing, all-powerful, all-good person. Craig freely admits that the Kalam cosmological argument he presents does not prove the existence of God.[18] But he believes that other considerations support his view that the cause of the universe is a person. Unfortunately, this aspect of his argument is very condensed and obscure.[19]

To prove his case, Craig relies on the principle of determination found in Islamic philosophy. According to this principle, "when two different states of affairs are equally possible and one results, this realization of one rather than the other must be the result of the action of a personal agent who freely chooses one rather than the other." If the universe was created at some particular moment in time, then the question arises as to why it was created at that moment and did not exist from eternity. One might suppose the universe's creation could be accounted for by an alternative to the explanation that it was the result of a choice of a personal agent. Following the teachings of some Islamic philosophers, Craig rejects all alternative explanations and maintains that if "a mechanical cause" existed from eternity, then so would the universe. But if such a cause did not exist from eternity, then the universe could not have come into existence at all. On the other hand, in a Newtonian view of absolute time, a personal agent might freely choose to create the universe at any moment of time and, alternately, on a relational view of time a personal agent could choose timelessly to create the universe and with it time itself. Craig, in fact, opts for this last alternative, arguing that the universe was created by a personal Creator "who exists changelessly and independently prior to creation and in time subsequent to creation."[20]

Evaluation

It should be obvious that Craig's conclusion that a single personal agent created the universe is a non sequitur. At most, this Kalam argument shows that some personal agent or agents created the universe. Craig cannot validly conclude that a single agent is the creator. On the contrary, for all he shows, there may have been trillions of personal agents involved in the creation.

Furthermore, Craig in one place goes further than assuming a personal agent and claims that "our whole universe was caused to exist by *something* beyond it and greater than it."[21] It is hard to see, however, why the creator or creators of the universe must be greater than the universe itself. Indeed, experience by no means uniformly supports the hypothesis that a creator is greater than its creation. Parents, for example, give birth to children who turn out to be greater than they are. Craig supplies no reason to suppose that the relation between the universe and its creator or creators would be any different.

Moreover, Craig also claims to have shown that the universe was created *ex nihilo*,[22] but again there seems to be nothing in his argument to justify this conclusion. According to his argument, the universe is not eternal but was created. From this it does not follow that the universe was not created out of something else. One possibility is that the creator or creators of the universe created it out of something that existed in some timeless realm. Another is that the material existed from eternity and that the creator or creators took this and formed the universe at a particular moment and, with it, causality and change. The sort of *a priori* arguments that Craig brings to bear against infinite causal sequences would not hold, for there is no causality operating with respect to the state of affairs that existed before the universe was created. Craig may have answers to these problems, but they are not presented explicitly in his book.

Craig's argument that the cause of the universe is the action of a personal agent or agents remains to be considered. Although it turns on the truth of the principle of determination—if there are two equally possible results and one occurs, the result must be explained in terms of the choice of a personal agent—he makes no serious attempt to defend this principle. Yet it is especially in need of defense, since it seems to find no uniform support in existence. In ordinary life and in science one would be ill-advised to appeal *always* to the choice of a personal agent to explain what happens when two events are equally likely and one occurs. For example, if heads come up in a flip of our unbiased coin, one would try to explain this event by causal factors operating on the coin, none of which might be the result of the choice of a personal agent or agents. It is unclear why the situation should be any different in cosmology. It is unclear also why a mechanical, nonpersonal cause could not have brought about the universe. Perhaps some nonpersonal causes are nontemporal and yet create events in time. Why these events are created at one moment rather than some other by these mechanical causes is surely no more mysterious than how a personal agent operating timelessly creates something at one moment rather than another.

So far nothing has been said about Craig's argument that the universe has a beginning in time. As we have seen, this has two aspects: First he presents *a priori* considerations that an actual infinity is impossible, and then he presents scientific evidence that the universe had an absolute beginning in time. Let us consider these in turn.

Craig's *a priori* arguments are unsound or show at most that actual infinities have odd properties.[23] This latter fact is well known, however, and shows nothing about whether it is logically impossible to have actual infinities in the real world. Craig admits that the concept of an actual infinity in pure mathematics is perfectly consistent. But he fails to show that there is anything logically inconsistent about an actual infinity existing in reality. Moreover, in some of his examples he even fails to show that there is some nonlogical absurdity.

Consider his example of the library with an infinite number of books. Craig maintains that since each book had a number on its spine, no new books could be added to the library. But this, he concludes, is absurd (presumably in some nonlogical sense), since "entities that exist in reality can be numbered." This argument is unsound, however, for books can be added and numbered by simply renumbering the books already in the library. The new books would then be given the numbers of old books—the books that had already been assigned numbers—and the old books would be assigned new numbers.[24]

Although it is condensed and enthymatic, Craig's argument that one cannot construct an actual infinity by successive addition can perhaps be reconstructed as follows:

(1) For any point, it is impossible to begin at that point and construct an actual infinity by successive addition.
(2) In order to construct an actual infinity by successive addition, it is necessary to begin at some point.

---

(3) Therefore, an actual infinity cannot be constructed by successive addition.

It should be clear that (2) begs the question, since there is an alternative—namely, that an actual infinity can be constructed by successive addition if the successive addition is beginningless. To suppose that an actual infinity cannot be constructed in this way is to assume exactly what is at issue.[25]

Craig's claim that scientific evidence can support the hypothesis that the universe had an *absolute* beginning is completely misguided. For to say that the universe had an absolute beginning would preclude any *scientific* investigation of this beginning. As Milton Munitz has argued:

> Science is grounded in the use of the Principle of Sufficient Reason and, therefore, always leaves open the possibility of finding the explanation of *any* event. To say there is some unique event marking the beginning of the universe for which no [scientific] explanation *can* be given, is to say something contrary to the method of science. It is for this reason . . . that any conception of the beginning of the universe, when defended under the aegis of some supposedly scientific cosmology, is an indefensible notion.[26]

Of course, given the present state of scientific theory there may be no scientific explanation of what came before the beginning of the universe. But the possibility cannot be excluded that further developments in science will provide answers. As Munitz argues:

> Even if there is reason to prefer a model whose account of the past history of the universe includes a reference to an event called in *that* theory "the origin of the universe," it does not exclude the possibility of finding some more refined theory, in which inference can be made to events even earlier than the one identified as "the beginning" in the theory of the coarser grain. The search for a more refined theory that would explain the event considered "the beginning of the universe" (in the cruder theory) would be part of the normal interest of science.[27]

Moreover, as I suggested above in evaluating Aquinas's argument, even if the universe has a beginning in time, in the light of recently proposed cosmological theories this beginning may be uncaused. Despite Craig's claim that theories postulating that the universe "could pop into existence uncaused" are incapable of "sincere affirmation," such similar theories are in fact being taken seriously by scientists.[28]

One can conclude that Craig's defense of the cosmological argument fails.

SWINBURNE'S INDUCTIVE COSMOLOGICAL ARGUMENT

In *The Existence of God* Richard Swinburne develops an untraditional version of the cosmological argument.[29] Unlike traditional approaches, which use deductive logic, Swinburne's inductive form of argument is based on considerations derived from confirmation theory and probability theory.

The Argument

Swinburne distinguishes between a C-inductive and a P-inductive argument.[30] In a good C-inductive argument a new piece of evidence raises the probability of a hypothesis as compared with its former likelihood. Thus where H is the hypothesis, E is the new evidence, K is the background knowledge, and $P(p/q)$ means p is probable relative to q, in a good C-inductive argument:

(1) $P(H/E\&K) > P(H/K)$

In a good P-inductive argument the evidence makes the hypothesis H more probable than its negation ~H.

(2) $P(H/E\&K) > P(\sim H/E\&K)$

Now, in order to have a good C-inductive argument, the probability of the new evidence relative to H and K must be higher than the probability relative to K. Thus according to Swinburne a necessary and sufficient condition for (1) to be true is the truth of (3).

(3) $P(E/H\&K) > P(E/K)$

so long as $P(H/K) > 0$. (3) in turn is equivalent to

(3') $P(E/H\&K) > P(E/\sim H\&K)$

Thus if E is more probable relative to H and K than it is to K alone, it is more probable relative to H and K than it is to $\sim$H and K.

These inductive distinctions are relevant to the version of the cosmological argument in which one argues from the existence of a complex universe to the probable existence of God. Let

E = A complex universe exists
H = God exists
K = Background knowledge

Then, according to Swinburne, although E is not very probable relative to K and H, it is more probable relative to K and H than to K alone or to $\sim$H and K. The basic idea is that on the assumption of God's existence (H plus background knowledge) we have an explanation of the existence of a complex universe, a type of explanation Swinburne calls personal. Personal explanations, he says, are different from causal scientific ones in that they appeal to rational agents, their intentions and their powers, and cannot be reduced to them. But on the assumption of the background knowledge alone, there is no explanation of the universe; its existence is mysterious, an unexplained brute fact.

If the existence of the universe is more probable relative to the existence of God plus background knowledge than to background knowledge alone, then condition (3) has been met and consequently condition (1) is true. The existence of God is more probable relative to the existence of the universe and background knowledge than relative to background knowledge alone. We have, then, a good C-inductive argument for the existence of God.

Toward the end of his book[31] Swinburne considers whether the weight of evidence provides a good P-inductive argument for theism; that is, whether H is more probable relative to evidence and background knowledge than its rivals. I do not consider this issue here, however. Instead, I show that Swinburne's claim to having provided a good C-inductive argument is mistaken.

The A Priori *Probability of a Complex Universe*
In order to judge if Swinburne has provided a good C-inductive argument for theism one must have some estimate of two probabilities:

P(E/H&K) and P(E/K). The latter probability, according to Swinburne, is based on nonempirical considerations—that is, on what one can estimate the probability to be *a priori*. Let us call P(E/K) the *a priori* probability. If the *a priori* probability of E is high, then P(E/H&K) will have to be even higher to be a good C-inductive argument.

In order to determine the *a priori* probability of a complex universe, it would seem that one would first have to have some estimate of the number of possible complex universes relative to the number of possible universes. But what is meant by a complex universe? One possible interpretation is that the universe is made up of more than one simple part. Suppose, for example, that there are only 20 possible simple universes consisting exclusively of one simple part. On the most complex level there is one possible complex universe made up of all the simple parts. But how many possible universes would there be altogether? Using the formula $2^n - 1$,[32] there would be 1,048,575 possible universes of all levels of complexity. So assuming that a complex universe means a universe with at least two simple parts, and assuming that 20 simple parts are used to generate these universes, there are 1,048,575 less 20, or 1,048,555 possible complex universes. In other words, there is an overwhelming majority of possible complex universes.

This knowledge by itself would not generate any estimate of the *a priori* probability of the existence of a complex universe, however, for two other things must be specified. First, although there are 1,048,575 *possible* universes, there might in fact be no universes at all. How is one to estimate the probability that there could be nothing at all? Second, how is one to distribute the probability over the 1,048,575 possibilities? Or to put it in a different way, if one considers the possibility of there being no universe at all, how does one distribute the probabilities over 1,048,575 + 1 or 1,048,576 possibilities? In particular, given these possibilities, how does one estimate their probability, assuming that one has no empirical evidence and is limited to logical and tautological truths? It should be noted that Swinburne gives us *no* clue as to how he estimates P(E/K), although he seems to think it is small.

On one interpretation the estimate is purely subjective.[33] If so, then P(E/K) will vary according to who is estimating the probabilities. Swinburne may believe it is fairly low, I may believe it is high, and so on. On this subjectivist interpretation Swinburne's arguments would be credible only for those who shared his subjective estimate, but this hardly seems the conclusion he desires.

The other interpretation appeals to the so-called principle of ignorance or insufficient reason, according to which one assumes that all possibilities are equally likely.[34] Although the traditional method, it has a basic problem, for depending on how one counts the possibilities, one gets contradictory results. This problem emerges in the application of the principles of ignorance to the present case.

If one considers the two possibilities that there is a universe or there is nothing, then the probability that there is some universe is 0.5. Given that the overwhelming majority of universes are complex (given 20 possible simple generating parts), the probability that the universe is complex is very, very near 0.5. If, on the other hand, one assumes that the nonexistence of any universe is one possibility in addition to the many, many possible universes, then the probability of the existence of some universe is 0.99999. And the probability of the existence of a complex universe, given that the vast majority are complex, is 0.99998. So depending on how one counts the possibilities, the probability of a complex universe is very near either 0.5 or 0.99998.

What is one to do in the face of this difficulty? One can say that estimating *a priori* probabilities by the principle of ignorance is out of the question, since it leads to a contradiction. However, this seems to leave us with the subjective way of estimating *a priori* probability, which does not provide the support that Swinburne needs or wants.

There is a way out. One can use the principle of ignorance in a conditional way and say that if the possibilities are analyzed in way W_1, then the *a priori* probability is p_1; but if they are analyzed in way W_2, then it is p_2, and so on. On this interpretation, there is no *a priori* probability per se but only an *a priori* probability relative to a certain analysis of possibilities. One can then compare these different *a priori* probabilities with P(E/H&K) relative to W_1 or W_2. As we shall see, the number of possibilities that are available to God will also depend on how one analyzes possibilities. So as long as one analyzes the two in the same way in estimating P(E/K) and P(E/H&K), there should be no serious problems generated by different estimates.

One might object at this point that our universe does not just have *some* degree of complexity; rather, it has a high degree of complexity. This is true, but there is no reason to suppose that our universe has the highest degree of complexity possible. One can imagine possible universes with much higher levels of complexity; for instance, ones where the mating of six distinct sexes is necessary to produce offspring, where human brains are more complex, or where no natural law can be expressed in simple mathematical formulae.

Furthermore, it may not be necessary for a universe to have the degree of complexity of even our universe in order to fulfill God's purposes as these are characterized by Swinburne. Arguing that there are good reasons why God should make a complex physical universe, he says that "such a physical universe can be beautiful, and that is good; and also it can be a theatre for finite agents to develop and make of it what they will."[35] But surely, universes of a much lower level of complexity than ours is capable of fulfilling could be beautiful and provide such a theater. For example, a universe with fewer galaxies, stars, and so on could be as beautiful as ours and provide a theater for human free will. After all, most stars in our universe are irrelevant to human purposes, and a universe with a billion fewer stars could hardly diminish the aesthetic glory of the night sky.

So there seems to be a wide range of complexity in universes in which God's plans could be fulfilled. The crucial question is whether this wide range makes up the majority of the possible universes. Let us specify as n the degree of complexity of any universe necessary to fulfill God's purposes. Then it is clear that no matter how high n is, given enough simple parts, the number of possible universes generated by these parts with n or more complexity will be very, very large relative to the total number of possible universes. Consider this simple example. Let us suppose that $n = 3$; that is, in order to fulfill God's purpose a universe must have at least three simple parts. Then if there are three simple parts that can be used to generate possible universes, approximately 0.14 of the possible universes will have at least three parts. If there are four simple parts, then 0.33 will have at least three parts. About 0.52 of all possible universes will have at least three parts if there are five simple parts used to generate the possible universes, and about 0.67 of all possible universes will have at least three parts if there are six simple generating parts, and so on.

All this suggests that no matter how high the degree of complexity specified, given enough simple parts, the overwhelming number of possible universes will have at least that degree of complexity. Since there would seem to be no limit to the number of possible simple parts, the vast majority of the possible universes will have at least n degree of complexity.

What does this mean in terms of assigning *a priori* probability? Using the procedure of assigning equal probabilities to the possibilities of there being some universe or there not being any universe, the *a priori* probability of there being a complex universe is very near 0.5. However, using the procedure of assigning equal probabilities to all possibilities, where the nonexistence of the universe is considered one possibility in addition to the existence of many, many possible universes, then the *a priori* probability of there being a complex universe is very near one.

The A Priori *Probability of God*

According to Swinburne, P(H/K) is higher than any of its rivals, since h is simpler than its rivals. On the other hand, the existence of the universe is complex in comparison with the existence of God. Because of its complexity, the existence of our universe is less probable relative to tautological background knowledge than is the existence of God relative to this knowledge.[36]

This way of stating the problem is misleading, for the question is not the probability of this particular complex universe but the probability of some universe or other at a certain level of complexity. This is how e should be understood. As we have seen, the *a priori* probability of e depends on how one analyzes the possibilities. On some analyses the probability is near one and on another it is near 0.5. The crucial question is whether $P(H/K)$ is higher than $P(E/K)$, given a similar analysis of possibilities.

Is Swinburne's analysis of the *a priori* probability of God's existence plausible? There are some reasons for doubt. The first thing to note about his thesis is that it is by no means clear why the simplest hypothesis should always be *a priori* the most probable, other things being equal. It is intuitively obvious, of course, why the scope of a hypothesis should always be relevant to the *a priori* probability of a hypothesis. "All Australian ravens are black" is *a priori* more probable than "All ravens are black." The hypothesis with a lesser scope is more probable *a priori* than the hypothesis with a broader one because it asserts less and therefore allows less room for error. But why should a simpler hypothesis always be more *a priori* probable than a less simple one of the same scope? Consider two hypotheses with the same scope: "All heavenly bodies travel in straight lines" and "All heavenly bodies travel in circles." The first hypothesis is generally regarded as being simpler than the second, but it is by no means clear that it is *a priori* more likely than the second.[37]

Our skepticism remains in particular cases of hypotheses about supernatural beings. Consider the following two hypotheses:

H_1 = An omnipotent, omniscient, completely free being exists.

H_2 = A supernatural being exists that has finite power to degree X, has finite knowledge to degree Y, and is free to degree Z.

Swinburne says that H_1 is simpler than H_2; hence H_1 is *a priori* more probable than H_2. There is, first of all, the conceptual problem of understanding H_1. The lingering possibility remains that the concept of an infinitely powerful, infinitely knowledgeable, completely free being contains an implicit contradiction despite Swinburne's attempt to show otherwise.[38] This possibility tells to a certain extent against the alleged superior probability of H_1 over H_2. Moreover, the reason that is usually given for the superior simplicity of H_1 over H_2 seems irrelevant to whether H_1 is *a priori* more probable than H_2. It is argued that any limitation that one would place on the power, knowledge, or freedom of a supernatural being would be arbitrary. Thus it may be asked why the being has power to finite degree x rather than to some other finite degree. However, just because an arbitrary limit is drawn it does not necessarily mean that the hypothesis in which it is drawn is *a priori* less probable than a hypothesis in which it is not. Are we really to believe that the hypothesis "All bodies travel at infinite speed" is *a priori* more likely than the hypothesis "All bodies travel at the speed of light" because an arbitrary limit is drawn in the latter case and not in the former?

The final problem is this: Consider a very large number of hypotheses $H_2, H_3, H_4 \ldots H_n$, postulating very powerful, very knowledgeable, very free, but finite beings. One can imagine these beings as having different degrees of power, knowledge, and freedom. Let us suppose:

H_1 is *a priori* more probable than H_2.
H_1 is *a priori* more probable than H_3.
H_1 is *a priori* more probable than H_4, etc.

It would still stretch credibility too far to suppose that where H_m = Either H_2 or H_3 or $H_4 \ldots$ or H_n:

H_1 is *a priori* more probable than H_m where n is a very large number.

In order to suppose this, one would have to suppose that the *a priori* probability of H_1 relative to any one particular hypothesis that postulates a finite supernatural being is overwhelming. For suppose that the *a priori* probability of $H_1 >$ the *a priori* probability of either H_2 or H_3 or $\ldots$ or H_n, where n = 1,000,000. (In order to simplify things let us suppose that H_1 or H_2 or H_3 or $\ldots$ or H_n are mutually exclusive and jointly exhaustive of the rivals of H_1, and that $H_2, H_3, H_4 \ldots H_n$ are equally likely.) Then if the probability of H_1 is 0.51, any given hypothesis about a finite being has a less than 0.0000005 *a priori* probability. This means that the *a priori* probability of the existence of God is approximately a million times more than the *a priori* probability of the existence of any particular finite being. If the number of possible finite beings was larger than a million—say, billion—then the *a priori* probability of God's existence would be about a billion times higher than the existence of any particular finite being. These implications seem incredible.

So far we have questioned Swinburne's assumption that, other things being equal, the simplest hypothesis is the most probable and, in particular, that the hypothesis that there exists an omnipotent, omniscient, and perfectly free being is *a priori* more probable than that there exists some finite but powerful being or beings. One factor I have not yet considered is that there might be no God or gods at all. Even if Swinburne is correct that theism is *a priori* more probable than the hypothesis that some powerful but finite being exists, it is not obvious that this is more probable than the hypothesis that there is no god at all. One could hardly claim it is simpler to suppose that God exists than to suppose that no supernatural being exists. Indeed, it might well be argued that it is simpler to suppose that there is no supernatural being. If so, then on Swinburne's own view, it is *a priori* more likely that there is no supernatural being than that there is at least one.

However, it is necessary to invoke this argument to show that Swinburne has a problem. Independent of any judgment about the simplicity of this hypothesis, consider the *a priori* probability of the hypothesis of there being no supernatural being. Let us first suppose that there are two basic possibilities: Either there is some supernatural being or there is not. Using the principle of ignorance, the *a priori* probability of there being some supernatural being is 0.5. Supposing that Swinburne is correct that the *a priori* probability of H_1 is greater than that of H_m, the probability of there being an omnipotent, omniscient, and perfectly free being will be greater than 0.25 but less than 0.5 unless the *a priori* probability of $H_m = 0$. Since there is no reason to suppose that the *a priori* probability of $H_m = 0$, the absolute maximum *a priori* probability H_1 can have is near 0.5.

Let us estimate the *a priori* probability of H_1 in a different way. Let us suppose that the probability of there being no supernatural being at all is simply one more alternative to H_1. Let us modify H_m to be a disjunctive statement exactly like H_m above except that it has one added disjunct: the hypothesis that there is no supernatural being at all. Let us call this modification $H_{m'}$ and let us assume as before that the *a priori* probability of H_1 is greater than the *a priori* probability of $H_{m'}$. Then the probability of H_1 would be greater than 0.5 but less than 1.0 unless the probability of $H_{m'}$ is 0. Since there is no reason to suppose that the probability of $H_{m'} = 0$, the maximum *a priori* probability of H_1 is near one.

This analysis provides no justification for supposing that $P(H/K) > P(E/K)$. For, as we have seen, depending on how one analyzes the possibilities, $P(E/K)$ is either near 1.0 or 0.5. It turns out, then, that even if one ignores the various problems in Swinburne's position, it still has to be shown that the *a priori* probability of H_1 is greater than that of E.

Finally, let us suppose for the sake of the argument that:

$$P(H/K) > P(E/K).$$

It still does not follow that

$$P(E/H\&K) > P(E/K).$$

After all,

$$P(H/K) > P(E/K)$$

may be true, and yet

$P(E/H\&K) = P(E/K)$.

In this case, despite the fact that the *a priori* probability of H would be greater than that of E, the addition of H to K would not increase the probability of E.

God's Reasons and Probability

According to Swinburne there are two reasons why $P(E/H\&K)$ may exceed $P(E/K)$. One is that $P(E/\sim H\&K)$ is very low because E cannot be explained in any other way and has the kind of complexity that makes it a very unlikely stopping point for explanation, at least in comparison with the simplicity of God. The other reason is that E is the kind of state that God can be expected to bring about or allow others to bring about more than other states.[39] Swinburne says that in the cosmological argument he is appealing to the first reason, not the second.

I have, however, adduced considerations that question Swinburne's view that the first reason applies to the cosmological argument. It has yet to be shown that $P(E/K)$ is lower than $P(H/K)$. Furthermore, as we have just seen, even if $P(E/K)$ were lower than $P(H/K)$ this would not establish that $P(E/H\&K) > P(E/K)$. Indeed, it is difficult to see how the first reason is capable of yielding $P(E/H\&K) > P(E/K)$ without appeal to the second reason. Unless one can assume that a complex universe is the sort of state God could be expected to bring about, the *a priori* probability of H or E is not relevant.

The question remains whether God might have reasons for creating a universe that would support the claim that $P(E/H\&K) > P(E/K)$. Swinburne admits there is no reason to suppose that God has overriding reasons for creating a complex universe rather than a simple universe or no universe at all. This seems to entail that God has *equally* good reasons to create a simple universe or no universe at all. After all, if God had stronger reasons for creating a complex universe than not, or had no reason for creating a simple universe or no universe, then it would seem that God had overriding reasons for creating a complex universe.

How does one translate considerations about reasons into probabilities? A natural strategy would be to use a principle of translation T:

T = If X has equally good reason to do act A_1 as to do act A_2, and X can do A_1 or A_2, then the probability of doing A_1 is equal to the probability of doing A_2.

Given T, one way of analyzing the situation with respect to God would be to say that there are two basic acts A_1 and A_2:

A_1 = Creating some universe
A_2 = Creating no universe.

Since God has equally good reason for doing A_1 or A_2, using principle T the probability of creating some universe is 50 percent. One might further argue that there are two possibilities within A_1, namely A'_1 and A''_1.

A'_1 = Creating a complex universe.
A''_1 = Creating a simple universe.

Then, using principle T, the probability of creating a complex universe is 0.25.

There are, of course, other ways of analyzing the situation. One might say that within A_1 there are a vast number of possible acts:

A'_1 = Creating possible universe U_1.
A''_1 = Creating possible universe U_2.
A'''_1 = Creating possible universe U_3; etc.

The vast majority of complex universes are compatible with God's plans. Using principle T, then the probability of creating some complex universe is near 0.5. Alternatively, one might count the possible acts in this way:

A_1 = Creating no universe.
A_2 = Creating possible universe U_1.
A_3 = Creating possible universe U_2; etc.

Given that there are an overwhelming majority of universes with a complexity sufficient to fulfill God's reason for wanting a complex universe, using principle T, the probability of God's creating a complex universe is near one.

So far we have found no way of analyzing the situation in which the *a priori* probability of there being a complex universe is less than the probability of there being a complex universe given the existence of God. The postulation of God does not seem to help increase the probability of a universe with a requisite degree of complexity.

The Second Version of the Argument
Swinburne presents another version of the cosmological argument. Consider that

E' = There exists some finite object.

In this case Swinburne says $P(E'/K) > P(E/K)$, since E' is less specific than E. Nevertheless, $P(E'/H\&K) > P(E'/K)$ because "only if God refused throughout endless time to create any object other than himself could there fail, if there is a God, to be a finite object."[40]

However, the second argument proceeds too quickly, for we have as yet no idea what the *a priori* probability of E' is. Once again we can specify the possibilities in various ways. Given the two possibilities—either there exists a finite object or there does not—and using the principal of ignorance, the *a priori* probability is 0.5. On the other hand, one could analyze the situation so that the various possibilities are as follows:

P_1 = There is no finite object
P_2 = There is finite object$_1$
P_3 = There is finite object$_2$
.
.
.
P_n = There is finite object$_{n-1}$

where $n-1$ is some very large number. In this case, if one uses the principle of ignorance, the probability of there being some finite object is very, very near one.

What, then, is $P(E'/H\&K)$? As before, much will depend on what God's reasons are for creating some finite object. According to Swinburne, God has no overriding reasons for creating any finite object: "Maybe God will leave things with God alone modifying his own states (and the succession of his own states would be a beautiful and so a good thing) and exercise his powers in that way."[41] This suggests that God has as good a reason to create a finite object as not to. As before, using principle T to translate equally good reasons into equal probabilities, the probability of God's creating some finite thing is either 0.5 or near 1.0, depending on how one analyzes God's possible acts.

Swinburne's statement quoted above that "only if God would refuse throughout endless time to create any object other than himself could there fail, if there is a God, to be a finite object" suggests a slightly different interpretation. Consider an infinitely long series of moments of time at each of which God can either create a finite object or not. Assuming that whether God creates a finite object or not at each moment in time is equally likely, since God has equally good reason to create a finite object or not (principle of translation T), the probability that at least one finite object will be created at some time converges toward one as a limit, as the number of moments of time increases without end.

By the same token, at any moment of time there are a *a priori* two possibilities: Either there exists a finite object or there does not. Using the principle of ignorance, there is a 50 percent chance of there being a finite object at each moment of time. So the probability that there will be some finite object approaches one, as a limit, as the number of moments of time increases without end.

A similar line of argument could be used to show that the probabilities of $P(E'/H\&K)$ and $P(E'/K)$ are the same if the possibilities for each moment of time were very numerous. For example:

P_1 = No object exists at moment X
P_2 = Object$_1$ exists at moment X
P_3 = Object$_2$ exists at moment X

.

.

.

P_n = Object$_{n-1}$ exists at moment X

where n is very large.

As we have seen, recourse to the comparative *a priori* probabilities of E' and H will not help establish

$$P(E'/H\&K) > P(E'/K).$$

For even if $P(E'/K) < P(H/K)$, the addition of H to K may not increase the probability of E'. However, Swinburne has yet to produce any argument showing that $P(E'/K) < P(H/K)$.

Conclusion
We have seen that Swinburne's inductive cosmological argument for the existence of God fails. However, one might well ask whether a variant of Swinburne's argument could be made to work. Although Swinburne argues that God does not have overriding reasons for creating a complex universe, others might argue that in fact God has such reasons. If so, then $P(E/H\&K) = 1$. But then, using the methods employed above to compute $P(E/K)$,

$$P(E/H\&K) > P(E/K)$$

Theistic critics of Swinburne might argue that he gives no good reason why God does not have overriding reasons to create a complex universe, except to say that he does not see that God does and that, on the traditional view of theism, God is under no necessity to create anything. But surely it might be said that there is not one traditional view of theism, and others might see the situation differently. So if one is willing to postulate that God has overwhelming reasons, so long as $P(H/K) > 0$, then a good C-inductive argument for the existence of God is not hard to come by. Thus a cosmological argument in the spirit of Swinburne can be constructed after all.

The trouble with this suggestion is that constructing good C-inductive arguments begins to look much too easy. For on this construal good C-inductive arguments can be constructed for all manner of hypotheses about strange beings who create the universe. One need only define a class of beings, such that a complex universe will be entailed if the hypothesis that postulates their existence is true. Then so long as the *a priori* probability of these hypotheses is not zero, we will have a good C-inductive argument for each of these hypotheses. Consider the super elephant hypothesis (H_2). This creature has the power, and an overriding reason, to create a complex universe. Then $P(E/H_2\&K) = 1$. Since $P(E/K)$ is less than one, we have a good C-inductive argument for H_2.

This suggests that this variant of Swinburne's argument would prove much more than theists have bargained for. The question, then, is not whether one can construct a good C-inductive argument but whether one can construct a good P-inductive argument for theism and its rivals. For a comparison of the probability of theism and its rivals, new and more subtle arguments must be devised. This variant of Swinburne's cosmological argument does not provide them.

REICHENBACH'S COSMOLOGICAL ARGUMENT

The Argument

Bruce Reichenbach in *The Cosmological Argument: A Reassessment*[42] attempts to demonstrate by *a priori* arguments that a necessary being exists. Making it clear that by "a necessary being" he does not mean a *logical* necessary being but rather a being that "is uncaused and independent of all else," he argues that if such a being exists, it cannot cease to exist. This means that "it can neither be brought into existence nor pass out of existence."[43] Reichenbach admits that even if his argument is successful, he has not demonstrated that God exists, for God has more attributes than the attribute of being a necessary being. For example, God has moral attributes of being perfectly good and is, at least in the Christian tradition, the maker of heaven and earth. Reichenbach thus correctly points out that traditional proponents of the cosmological argument have not been as careful as they should have been about what they can conclude if the argument is valid, and in that way they have wrongly claimed to have demonstrated God's existence. Nevertheless, he maintains that since there is no conflict being a necessary being's attributes and God's attributes, and since God as traditionally conceived of has all the attributes of a necessary being, it is probable that a necessary being and God are "one and the same."[44]

Reichenbach stresses that this correlation of the attributes of God with those of a necessary being is not part of the cosmological argument proper. Without this correlation and the probabilistic conclusion that seems to follow—that a necessary being and God are identical—much of the interest diminishes. What is Reichenbach's argument that a necessary being exists? The basic structure of the argument is as follows:

(1) A contingent being exists.
   (a) This contingent being is caused either (i) by itself or (ii) by another.
   (b) If it were caused by itself, it would have to precede itself in existence, which is impossible.

(2) Therefore, this contingent being (ii) is caused by another; that is, it depends on something else for its existence.

(3) That which causes (provides the sufficient reason for) the existence of any contingent being must be either (iii) another contingent being or (iv) a noncontingent (necessary) being.
   (c) If (iii), then this contingent cause must itself be caused by another, and so to infinity.

(4) Therefore, that which causes (provides the sufficient reason for) the existence of any contingent being must be either (v) an infinite series of contingent beings or (iv) a necessary being.

(5) An infinite series of contingent beings (v) is incapable of yielding a sufficient reason for the existence of any being.

(6) Therefore, a necessary being exists.

One objection that can be raised against this argument is that (1) assumes that contingent beings must be caused, whereas such beings might simply occur; some contingent beings might have no cause. To this objection Reichenbach replies that it is part of the essence of contingent beings to be caused.

> Existence does not belong to them as an essential feature of their nature, but rather as accidental to their essence. Only if their nature were such that, if they existed, they could not be nonexistent, would their existence be essential to their nature. But this is to be a necessary, not a contingent, being.[45]

Insisting that "that which has its existence as accidental to it must be dependent on something else for its existence,"[46] he argues that a contingent being is dependent on something else; that is, it must be caused by something else.

Moreover, Reichenbach says that the causal principle "is a basic principle of the universe." People have a strong tendency to assume that everything has a cause, he says: "The natural procedure of the intellect is to search for the causes of the effects or events with which the intellect is presented." Since causality is a basic category of the mind, he maintains, we must assume that the causal principle reflects reality, for "without such a belief, human intellectual endeavor becomes nothing more than a charade, a ghostly dance in the ethereal realm."[47]

Evaluation of the Argument

Reichenbach's replies to the criticisms that he raises against his own argument are inadequate. To begin with, as critics have argued, Reichenbach's first reply begs the question.[48] He assumes what must be proved: that all contingent beings must be caused. To be sure, in one sense of "accidental," that of being extraneous or adventitious, if the existence of contingent beings is accidental, it may be the case that some contingent beings exist for *no reason at all*, that they are not produced by themselves or by another. In particular, if Reichenbach is correct that the universe considered as a totality or whole is contingent, there may be no reason for its existence, although there may be reason for the existence of every event in the universe in terms of other events. Presumably Reichenbach is not using "accidental" in this sense, however. Rather, he seems to be using it in the Aristotelian sense in which an accident inheres in a substance. In this sense, accident is dependent on substance. So if, as seems likely, Reichenbach is assuming the Aristotelian sense of "accidental," he has already assumed what he is out to prove: that contingent beings are dependent on something else.[49]

Insofar as this interpretation is correct, Reichenbach is presupposing a particular metaphysics of essence and accident that is very controversial. It is quite obscure how the essence of anything is to be established and how disagreements over what the essence of something is are to be reconciled. Indeed, some theories of essence would be in conflict with Reichenbach's thesis that existence is not part of the essence of contingent things. Plantinga, for example, argues that if existence is a property, then everything in every world in which it exists has existence as part of its essence.[50] Thus not only does Reichenbach seem to beg the question, he relies upon the obscure and controversial notion of essence.

Reichenbach's second reply is also inadequate, for it is fallacious reasoning as well as wishful thinking to argue that if p were not true, our effort would be a charade; therefore, p is true. Yet Reichenbach's argument approaches this form. It may be that if the causal principle is not true, our efforts to find a cause may come to naught. But this is surely no reason to suppose that the causal principle is true. Moreover, Reichenbach's claim—that unless we believe everything has a cause our intellectual endeavors become nothing more than a charade—is surely an exaggeration and may even represent a serious misunderstanding of how the principle should be conceived. One can look upon the causal principle not as metaphysical truth to be believed but as a principle of inquiry that it is useful to follow. On this view, if we act *as if* the principle is true whether we believe it or not, then if there is a cause to be discovered we have a chance of discovering it. On the other hand, if we do not so act, we stand no chance. Considered in this way, one need have no particular belief about the universal truth of the causal principle in order to engage in scientific and other inquiries in which it is important.

Another problem with Reichenbach's argument is the assumption made in (3) and (4) and if one rules out contingent beings as the causes of other contingent beings, the only alternative is a single necessary being. Why could there not be a plurality of necessary beings,[51] each of which is not dependent on any other necessary being but causes or partially causes some or all contingent beings? One can conceive of the causal relations between these necessary beings and contingent beings in different ways. On one theory, the actions of all necessary beings would provide necessary and sufficient conditions for every contingent being. On this view the existence of all contingent beings would be overdetermined; that is, there would be multiple sufficient conditions for the existence of each contingent being. On another theory, the action of one necessary being is the only sufficient condition for the existence of some contingent beings, while the action of another necessary being is the only sufficient condition for the existence of other contingent beings. On still another theory, the action of no necessary being would be the sufficient condition for any contingent being, but the action of every necessary being would be *part* of a sufficient condition for the existence of every contingent being. Other theories are also conceivable.

Although he does not explicitly discuss multiple necessary beings, he claims that the necessary being that he believes his argument has demonstrated "is not dependent on anything else, it cannot be limited by another being. Hence, it must be a non-finite being."[52] This indicates that Reichenbach believes he has demonstrated the existence of an infinite being. So his answer to our objection might well be that since a necessary being is an infinite being, there can be at most one necessary being. However, this reply is problematic at best. We can assume that by "infinite being" Reichenbach at least means a being that is omnipotent. If so, the conclusion that a necessary being exists in Reichenbach's sense does not entail that in the usual sense of omnipotence an omnipotent being exists. We may recall that, according to Reichenbach, a necessary being is not a logically necessary being and also that although if it exists, it "cannot go out of existence," the "cannot" does not have the force of logical impossibility. It is rather unclear, however, what this kind of necessity amounts to. Reichenbach says only that it is not causal necessity, yet it is real as opposed to being based on verbal conventions.[53] From this it does not seem to follow that a necessary being has all the powers usually associated with omnipotence. For example, it does not follow that a necessary being can create anything, let alone the heavens and earth. Indeed, the only thing that seems to follow is that a necessary being must have the ability to prevent itself from being destroyed and to maintain its own existence. Reichenbach's argument tries to establish that a necessary being is the cause, either directly or indirectly, of all contingent beings. But even if he has established this, it does not seem to follow from the definition of a necessary being. Moreover, even if it does, it does not follow that a being that is the cause of all contingent beings is omnipotent. I must therefore conclude that Reichenbach has not shown that there is only one necessary being; in other words, his argument is compatible with the existence of multiple necessary beings. But this is a good reason for thinking that he is much farther away from proving the existence of God than he supposes. For even if his argument is successful, it is compatible with polytheism.

Supposing for the sake of argument that there is only one necessary being, where is it? Reichenbach assumes that the necessary being whose existence he believes he has demonstrated is distinct from the world. In effect, then, he appears to assume that he has refuted pantheism. One can challenge this assumption, however, by arguing that the totality of contingent beings may be a necessary being. If so, in order to explain the existence of any particular contingent beings, one need not go outside this totality. It may be argued that to infer that the totality of contingent beings is itself contingent on the contingency of things that make up this totality is to commit the fallacy of composition.

Maintaining that the fallacy of composition is committed whenever the universal premise "which expresses the argument from part to whole ... cannot be shown to be necessarily true," Reichenbach attempts to answer this objection in the following way.[54] The universal premise is:

$$(x) \ (y) \ [(xRy)(Px) \rightarrow Py]$$

where R stands for "relation of parts to whole" and P stands for "some property." Reichenbach argues that in the case where P = is contingent, this premise is necessarily true. He argues as follows:

> The totality of contingent beings is nothing more than the sum total of individual contingent things; it is nothing over and above these beings. Each individual being then, if it exists could conceivably not be. But what would occur if all these beings ceased to exist at the next moment, something which is distinctly possible since each is contingent? Obviously, if such were the case, the totality itself would cease to exist. For if the totality is the sum total of all its parts, and if there were no parts, then it would be impossible for the totality to exist. But if this is the case, it is perfectly conceivable that the totality could not exist. And if the totality could conceivably not exist,

then it too must be contingent. Therefore, if all parts of something are contingent, the totality likewise *must* be contingent; it could conceivably not exist.[55]

The first thing to notice about this argument is that Reichenbach seems to assume that if something is not contingent—that is, necessary—one cannot conceive that it does not exist. But this is *not* how he originally introduced the term "necessary" as applied to beings. A noncontingent being, according to Reichenbach, is one that, if it exists, cannot cease to exist. We can conceive of a noncontingent being in this sense not existing. Thus the nonexistence of God, who Reichenbach supposes is a necessary being, is conceivable. So the fact that one can conceive of the totality of contingent beings not existing is completely irrelevant to what Reichenbach must prove, which is that if the totality of contingent beings exist, it can cease to exist.

The second thing to notice about the argument is that Reichenbach begs the question when he says: "But what would occur if all these beings ceased to exist at the next moment, something which is distinctly possible since each is contingent?" Surely one of the crucial questions at issue is whether all individual beings could cease to exist at the same time. Just because each individual being could cease to exist, it does not follow that all could cease to exist at the same time. Again the issue is not whether this possibility is conceivable. Given the unclarity of what Reichenbach means by "can" and "cannot," one sees no way of inferring from the part to the whole on *a priori* grounds.

But let us grant for the sake of argument what we questioned above— namely, that Reichenbach has demonstrated that exactly one necessary being is distinct from the totality of contingent things. Is he correct in supposing that, given the established correlations between the attributes of a necessary being and God, the hypothesis that God exists is probable? In order to be clear on this matter we must distinguish between two interpretations of what Reichenbach could mean. He might mean that in the light of correlation (E), the hypothesis (H) that God exists is more probable than its opposite. In other words, $P(H/E) > P(\sim H/E)$. Alternatively, he might mean that in the light of correlation (E), the hypothesis that God exists is more probable than it was before this evidence was known. In other words, $P(H/E) > P(H)$.

Given the second interpretation, Reichenbach would be incorrect only if the probability of the hypothesis that God exists is either zero or one. The probability would be zero if the hypothesis that God exists is incoherent, since no evidence can raise the probability of an incoherent hypothesis. But even if one grants that the God hypothesis is coherent and that the probability of this hypothesis is raised by the correlation, this would not take us far. For in the light of the total evidence, the probability of the hypothesis may be very low. Furthermore, the correlation may raise the probability of alternative hypotheses as well—for example, that there exists a necessary being that is completely evil.

This brings us to the first interpretation of what Reichenbach might mean. Clearly the correlation of the attributes of a necessary being and the attributes of God does not make the probability of the hypothesis that God exists more probable than the contradictory hypothesis. After all, the correlations established are compatible with many rival hypotheses. Besides the alternative one of a completely evil necessary being, there is, for example, the alternative hypothesis of a necessary being that is neither completely good nor completely evil. Why should we not suppose that these rival hypotheses are more probable than the hypothesis that God exists?

Thus Reichenbach has not shown that, if one accepts his conclusion that a necessary being exists, and if the attributes of God are correlated with those of a necessary being, the probability of the hypothesis that God exists is higher than its rival or even that the probability has been raised to any significant extent.

Conclusion

Given the various problems with Reichenbach's argument, it is safe to say that not only has he failed to provide evidence making the existence of God more probable than not, but he has also failed to establish with any degree of certainty that a unique necessary being distinct from the world exists.

General Conclusion

It would be unwarranted to suppose that the cosmological argument has been shown to be unsound in any final way, for I have not covered all existing versions of the argument, and in any case new sound versions may yet be created. But our sampling of versions of this argument both ancient and contemporary should give some confidence that no existing one is sound. Furthermore, since the best philosophical minds down through history have failed to construct a sound version of the argument, it is unlikely that one will be constructed.

CHAPTER 5

The Teleological Argument

In this chapter I critically consider versions of the teleological argument—the so-called argument from design. This argument, unlike the ontological argument and like the cosmological argument, is based on empirical premises about the world. Indeed, as the teleological argument and cosmological argument have often been presented, there is no sharp distinction between them. Whether one classifies an argument as cosmological or teleological is somewhat arbitrary.

Background to the Teleological Argument

In traditional versions of this argument one infers from the evidence of design in the universe the conclusion that the universe was created by a designer. Thus the intricate workings of nature and of organisms, the complex interrelations of parts and wholes, the subtle connections between aspects of the world, all have been used as evidence to support the hypothesis that the universe was fashioned by some great intelligence.

The teleological argument has usually been construed as an argument from analogy: Since the universe is analogous to some human artifact that one knows to be designed, probably the universe itself is designed. This is the way the argument was developed by William Paley in his classic formulation[1] and by David Hume in his criticism of the argument in *Dialogues Concerning Natural Religion*.[2] Paley argued that just as we can infer that a watch found on a heath has a designer, so we can infer that the universe has a designer. "Every indication of contrivance, every manifestation of design, which existed in the watch, exists in the work of nature; with the difference, on the side of nature, of being greater and more, and that in a degree which exceeds all computation."[3] Cleanthes, who advocates this argument in Hume's dialogues, maintains that since the universe is like a great machine in that it exhibits "a curious adapting of means to ends,"[4] and since a machine is created by intelligence, so the universe must be created by some super intelligence, namely God.

The teleological argument is not always construed as an argument from analogy. Indeed, some versions of it, including ones considered in this chapter, do not take this form. In the pages to follow, the teleological arguments of F. R. Tennant, George Schlesinger, Richard Swinburne, and Richard Taylor are critically considered. These versions have been selected because they are among the strongest and most interesting to appear in this century and are far more sophisticated and powerful than traditional ones such as Paley's. Indeed, Tennant's version of the teleological argument has been called "probably the strongest presentation that has been written of this type of theistic reasoning."[5] If his version as well as others should fail, therefore, we should have some confidence that as yet unexamined ones will not succeed.

In the last chapter we saw that in all versions of the cosmological argument one begins with certain empirical facts about the world and attempts to infer the existence of God. The teleological argument proceeds in the same way. What then is the difference between the teleological argument and the cosmological argument? Unfortunately, there is little agreement among philosophers of religion.

One traditional way of characterizing the difference is that the cosmological argument starts from the mere fact that the universe exists or from very general features of it such as change or motion or causation, whereas the teleological argument starts from more particular features of the universe. Consider Schlesinger's argument[6] from the fact that the laws of nature governing the universe and the initial conditions in it are such that creatures capable of responding to the divine are permitted to exist. Starting from a rather particular feature of the universe, on the present account it would be classified as a teleological argument.

It should be noted, however, that Swinburne's teleological argument[7] starts from the fact that the universe exhibits a certain kind of order that he calls temporal. This is certainly a much more general feature of the universe than the one singled out by Schlesinger. Recall that in Swinburne's first version of the cosmological argument he started out from the existence of a complex universe. It is dubious that there is a great deal of difference in degree of generality between the universe's complexity and its temporal order; yet Swinburne himself considers one argument cosmological and the other teleological.

Antony Flew has proposed that a cosmological argument be considered an argument for God's existence that starts from the mere fact that some empirical entity exists.[8] This must be considered in large part a stipulative definition, however, for it seems to conflict with the way these terms are used in philosophy. On Flew's view, only Swinburne's second version would be a genuine cosmological argument. In fact, neither Swinburne's first version nor any of St. Thomas's arguments would be considered cosmological arguments. Because I know of no clear way to distinguish the two types of argument that will do justice to the present unclarities in the use of the two labels, I solve the problem here by accepting the classification that theists give of their own arguments. If they do not label their own arguments, I make a decision—perhaps an arbitrary one—about whether to classify their arguments as teleological or cosmological. Thus I classify Schlesinger's argument as teleological although he does not label it as such.

Hume's criticisms of the teleological argument in the *Dialogues Concerning Natural Religion* have often been taken to be decisive. Philo, who presumably is Hume's spokesman, raises many objections to the analogical reasoning used by Cleanthes. He argues that if the analogy were carried to its logical extreme, one would end up with conclusions not acceptable to the theist. For example, machines are usually made by many intelligent beings; hence some form of polytheism rather than monotheism would be warranted by the argument. Also, the beings who create machines have bodies, so God must have a body. If machines have imperfections, we have grounds for supposing that the creators are not perfect. So since the universe has imperfections, one should conclude that God is not perfect. Furthermore, Philo points out that the analogy of the universe to a machine is a weak one and that various other weak analogies are possible. The universe is like a plant in certain respects and like an organism in others. If we follow through on these analogies, we arrive at rather different conclusions than that the universe was created by divine intelligence.

In a recent critique of the analogical version of the argument, Wallace Matson has maintained that both traditional proponents such as Paley and critics such as Hume assume that "the properties according to which we judge whether or not some object is an artifact, are accurate adjustments of parts and the curious adapting of means to ends."[9] He argues that this assumption is false. In actual practice one distinguishes an artifact from a natural object by the evidence of the machinery and the materials from which the objects are made. Anthropologists, for example, decide whether something is a rock or a hand ax, not by determining if the object can serve a purpose, but by looking "for those peculiar marks left by flaking tools and not produced by the weather."[10] Consequently, the teleological argument rests on a false premise.

Schlesinger's, Swinburne's, and Taylor's basic arguments are not analogical in the traditional sense discussed by Hume. Consequently, Matson's critique of the traditional analogical version of the teleological argument does not apply. To be sure, Swinburne introduces analogical

considerations when he argues that polytheism is not as well supported
as monotheism by the temporal order. Moreover, although Taylor's is
not an argument *from* analogy, on at least one interpretation his argument *rests* on an analogy. Nevertheless, in order to refute his argument,
considerations that go beyond either Hume or Matson must be presented.

Tennant's Cosmic Teleology

THE STRUCTURE OF THE ARGUMENT

Unlike many other versions of the teleological argument, the one presented by Tennant in his two-volume *Philosophical Theology* (1930) does
not rely on particular instances of apparent design in nature. Admitting
that each separate instance of apparent design may be adequately
explained by naturalistic theories, he maintains that "the multitude of
interwoven adaptations by which the world is constituted a theatre of
life, intelligence, and morality, cannot reasonably be regarded as an
outcome of mechanism, or blind formative power, or of aught but pur-
posive intelligence."[11]

Tennant considers six kinds of adaptation found in nature:[12]

(1) *The intelligibility of the world to the human mind.* The world and
human minds are so related that the world is intelligible to our minds.
To the human mind the world is "more or less intelligible, in that it
happens to be more or less a cosmos, when conceivably it might have
been a self-subsistent and determinate 'chaos' in which similar events
never occurred, none recurred, universals have no place, relations no
fixity, things no nexus of determination, and 'real' categories no
foothold."[13]

(2) *The adaptation of living organisms to their environment.* Although this
may be explained by evolutionary theory by means of natural selection,
Tennant argues that the process of evolution itself needs to be explained.
The findings of evolutionary biology have caused the teleologist "to shift
his ground from special design in the products to directivity in the
process, and plan in the primary collocation."[14]

(3) *The ways in which the inorganic world is conducive to the emergence and
maintenance of human and animal life.* The universe is made of inorganic
matter and yet has produced life. He says that if there were countless
universes, we might expect life to arise by chance. But there is only one
universe: "Presumably the world is comparable to a single throw of a
dice. And common sense is not foolish in suspecting the dice to have
been loaded."[15]

(4) *The beauty of nature.* Tennant argues that "theistically regarded,
nature's beauty is of a piece with the world's intelligibility and its being

a theatre for moral life; and thus far the case for theism is strengthened by aesthetic considerations."[16]

(5) *The ways in which the world is conducive to the moral development of human beings.* For example, Tennant maintains that in order for humans to cope with the world, they must develop their intellect, and intellectual development is in turn necessary for moral development. Furthermore, the hardships of human existence develop moral virtues. Thus if we look at evolutionary process, not in terms of its origins, but in terms of what it has accomplished with regard to our moral development, "the whole process of nature is capable of being regarded as instrumental to the development of intelligent and moral creatures."[17]

(6) *The overall progressiveness of the evolutionary process.* Tennant argues that considered separately, the above five aspects of nature can be regarded naturalistically. However, when they are taken as a whole they indicate a cosmic purpose that has used nature for the making and development of human beings. He further asserts that the more we learn about the complex factors that had to obtain in order to make human existence possible, "the less reasonable or credible becomes the alternative theory of cumulative groundless coincidence."[18]

Although Tennant does not explicitly characterize his argument as being from analogy, he does suppose that it rests on an anthropocentric view of the world.[19] He claims to find in the universe evidence of intelligent design—what he calls cosmic teleology—and he argues that from the attributes of rationality, appreciation, self-determination, and morality found in a limited degree in human beings we can have some clues as to the nature of the designer, God. Small wonder that commentators on his work have interpreted him to be utilizing analogical reasoning.[20] Tennant makes clear that in his teleological argument for the existence of God he makes use of the same sort of reasoning that is the foundation of all scientific induction. This reasoning, he maintains, is probabilistic and ultimately rests on faith; it is based on "the alogical probability which is the guide of life."[21]

EVALUATION OF THE ARGUMENT

The Irrelevance of Tennant's Argument to Theism

What can be said about this grand scheme of cosmic teleology? The first thing is that, even if it is successful, by Tennant's own admission it falls short of showing the high probability of the existence of a theistic God. His cosmic teleology is compatible with polytheism. Thus Tennant says that "in appropriating the name 'God,' no premature assumption of monotheism is intended. What is claimed to have as yet been reasonably established is that cosmic purposing is embodied in this world."[22] Furthermore, he denies that the evidence he cites makes it probable that God is perfect and immutable in several of the senses of these terms that are attributed to God by traditional theologians. He argues that the only perfection that can be attributed to God is moral perfection and the only immutability that can be predicted by God is immutability of purpose. However, when he attempts to explain what he means by the "moral perfection" of God, he says that God's "moral nature is largely incomparable with ours"[23] and that in speaking of the moral perfection of God we are merely denying that God has certain imperfections, such as conflicting desires, found in human beings. On Tennant's view we do not seem to be asserting anything positive of God.[24]

In addition to these differences between the theistic God and Tennant's God, if "God" is the appropriate term to describe the force that he postulates to explain cosmic teleology, there is a striking difference between the traditional view and Tennant's view of what the design of God involves. On the traditional view, God had a design before He executed it, He used certain means to bring about the design, and He existed before the existence of the universe. But none of this is true on Tennant's view. Tennant says that "if we are to speak in terms of time . . . the world is coeval with God and is contingent on His determinate nature, inclusive of will."[25] On the other hand, some of the attributes of Tennant's God are attributes of the traditional God. For example, he seems to hold the traditional view that creation is *not* simply the rearrangement of preexisting material. Tennant's designer is thus a genuine creator and not just an architect.[26] Moreover, Tennant's God, like the traditional God, has no body.

Noninductive Conclusions

One can only wonder how some of these attributes are justified by analogical inference from the appearances of design in the universe. For example, it is difficult to understand how, by analogical inference, we arrive at the conclusion that there is a cosmic creator and not just a cosmic architect. As far as our experience is concerned, all created objects are made from preexisting material; the creator of any object exists prior to the object although not necessarily prior to the material from which the object is made. However, this is not Tennant's view of creation. Divinely created objects are not created out of preexisting material, and God does not exist prior to His creations. Indeed, Tennant admits that "the notion of creation . . . is not derivable from experience."[27]

As C. D. Broad, a contemporary of Tennant, has pointed out, this is a particularly awkward admission for Tennant, since he claims that all our concepts are of empirical origin.[28] It is to no avail to suggest, as Tennant does, that "the ultimate mystery of the origination of the world confronts all theories alike."[29] As Broad comments: "But surely the essence of Dr. Tennant's defense of Theism is that it does, and rival theories do not, give an intellectually satisfactory explanation of this mystery. And, if it involves the admittedly unintelligible notion of creation, it is an unintelligible hypothesis supported by a superficial analogy which dissolves away when exposed to critical reflexion."[30] Thus Tennant's views on the creation of the universe are not based on inductive inferences from experience and, indeed, seem to be in conflict with any probabilistic conclusions that could be drawn from experience.

As we have seen, Tennant admits that his notion of God is compatible with either monotheism or polytheism, and he holds that the evidence cannot decide between the two. However, as Hume pointed out long ago, surely polytheism is more justified than monotheism. We have no experience of one person working in isolation and constructing a very large and complex object. Large and complex objects in our experience are made by many people working in cooperation. Since the world is very large and complex, one should infer that probably it was made by many beings working together.

It is also difficult to see why, on the basis of the evidence and inductive inferences, Tennant is justified in inferring that God has no body. As far as our experience is concerned, everything that is made is made by some being with a body. The conclusion that God has no body thus conflicts with all our experience and can hardly be probable in light of the evidence.[31]

Problems with Tennant's Evidence of Design
What about the particular kinds of adaptation that Tennant cites as evidence of design? In general, they fail to impress. For example, Tennant rejects the idea that life might have arisen by chance. Although his argument is condensed, it seems to be something like the following.[32] The hypothesis that life arose by chance might be a plausible view if we had billions of universes. In one of these billions it would be likely that life could have arisen by chance. But we have only one universe. Hence the fact that life arose is extremely improbable. One problem with this argument is that, although there is only one universe, there are billions of planets in it. There is no reason to suppose that in the overwhelming majority of these, life did arise. But one could maintain that it is hardly surprising that life arose in at least one of these billions of planets, for it is likely that the right opportunities for life to arise are present in at least one of these planets.

But does this answer Tennant's question? Could it not be said that it is improbable that we would have a universe in which life arose anywhere? One answer that might be given is that we do not know whether it is improbable or not. Judgments about *a priori* probabilities in such cases are arbitrary, and we have no evidence in this case of any relevant empirical probabilities. On this view one must question the basis of Tennant's judgment that it is improbable that life arose by chance; his appeal to "the alogical probability which is the guide of life" is really to no avail. As Broad has noted, "Is there *any* sense of probability, mathematical or 'alogical,' in which meaning can be attached to the statement that the antecedent probability of one constitution of the world as a whole is greater than or equal to or less than that of any other? I very much doubt if there is."[33]

However, recent thinking in astrophysics seems to lend some support both to Tennant's contention that life in our universe is extremely improbable and to his anthropocentric view of the world.[34] According to one recent account:

> Contemporary astrophysicists are investigating the possibility that the existence of life, in particular human life, may set constraints upon the allowable conditions of the early universe. Arguments such as these involve what has come to be called the "Anthropic Principle." Although these efforts differ somewhat from one another in their underlying philosophical spirit, they converge upon one fact: in order for life to exist today, an incredibly restrictive set of demands must be met in the early universe.[35]

These demands include the expansion rate of the universe, the amount of matter in the universe, the gravitational constant, the strong force constant, the isotropic distribution of matter and radiation, the ratio of matter to antimatter, and the presence of stable elements heavier than helium.[36] When all these demands are met, life is possible; but, according to some present thinking, if any of them had been different, life as we know it would not have been possible.

We may ask two questions about this recent evidence and thinking in astrophysics. First, does use of the anthropic principle commit one to some cosmic purpose? Second, does the improbability of life in our universe support theism?

Now, it can be admitted that some scientists use the anthropic principle in an explicitly teleological way.[37] For example, some scientists argue that the universe is isotropic in order to produce intelligent human life. However, even this reasoning does not necessarily entail a commitment to some cosmic conscious purpose, but only to a functional analysis of the situation. For example, someone who says that the heart beats in order to circulate the blood does not necessarily imply a conscious purpose; the statement can mean merely that the function of the heart is to circulate blood. Similarly, one can understand a statement in astrophysics of the form "X is Y in order for W" in a functional way.[38]

Furthermore, it is possible to use the anthropic principle in a purely methodological way. For example, we can understand the statement "The universe is isotropic in order to produce intelligent life" to mean simply that the universe's being isotropic is a necessary condition for intelligent life.[39] Although here there is not even the suggestion of a functional analysis, there is obvious anthropomorphism in the sense that the focus of attention is on human life. However, this sense of anthropomorphism entails nothing about the metaphysical makeup of the universe and seems to be justified on heuristic grounds.[40]

Even if one accepts this recent evidence that the conditions necessary for life are extremely unlikely, it lends no particular support to theism. First, it is compatible with a number of alternative supernatural hypotheses. For example, the improbability of life may be the result of many gods or of impersonal creative forces.[41] Moreover, cosmologists have developed an alternative naturalistic explanatory model in terms of so-called world ensembles. They have conjectured that what we call our universe—our galaxy and the other galaxies—may be one among many alternative worlds or universes. The universe as a whole is composed of a vast number of such worlds or universes. The overwhelming majority of these are lifeless, since the requirements for life as we understand it are not met in them. However, given enough universes, it is very likely that in some of these the complex conditions necessary for life would be found. Thus Tennant may be wrong. There may well be billions of worlds, and life could well have arisen by chance in this world. Although there are problems with the various models of world ensembles,[42] it is certainly not obvious that they are more serious than the problems with theistic accounts.

I must conclude, therefore, that despite recent evidence from astrophysics that may seem to support Tennant, there is no justification for the belief that the improbability of life supports theism.

One can also afford to be skeptical of Tennant's account of the adaptation of organisms to their environment. As we have seen, he maintains that the findings of evolutionary biology have caused many religious believers to shift their ground from denying the findings of evolution to arguing that the entire process of evolution suggests design. Unfortunately, Tennant does not consider any evidence that might be used to argue for the thesis that evolution is directed; his discussion remains completely general and removed from any attempt to assess the claim that evolution has a direction. Furthermore, where the relevant evidence has been assessed by experts, no clear direction can be discerned.[43]

Tennant's argument from the beauty of nature also has problems. According to Tennant the purpose of beauty in nature is the realization of our moral and religious values.[44] This beauty saturates all the universe from the microscopic to the telescopic realms. Yet he also admits that it may be possible that human life exists in only one small region of an otherwise lifeless universe.[45] The difficulty is to understand the relevance of all this beauty to God's purpose. Almost all of it seems wasted and irrelevant to the realization of moral and religious values.

In addition to this problem, Tennant argues that almost all the products of human beings other than professed works of art (which make up a very small part of the products of human beings) are "aesthetically vile," while almost all aspects of nature are beautiful.[46] Using an argument from analogy, we should be led to suppose that nature, a product of God, would be ugly. Yet we find that it is beautiful. It would seem, therefore, that the evidence of beauty in nature should count *against* the hypothesis that it is designed.[47] However, Tennant argues that beauty in nature counts *for* the hypothesis that it is designed.

The aspect of Tennant's argument having to do with the moral development of human beings also has problems. Tennant maintains that the world is apparently designed to further the moral development of human beings; indeed, that because of the hardships that human beings must undergo, they develop moral character. As we shall see in Chapter 17, considerations of this kind have been used not only to provide evidence of design in the universe, but to justify the existence of evil. Evil, it has been claimed, is necessary to build souls. Some of the difficulties with this answer to the problem of evil are shared by this aspect of Tennant's argument from design.

To begin with, the hardships that human beings face are more than enough to build character. Thus an excess of character-building hardships is not explained by any theory postulating that the universe was designed for the development of moral character. Moreover, given the great power of God, it would seem that He could further the development of desirable moral traits in less painful and more efficient ways. All too often a person is crushed by the hardships of life, and character is not built at all. If making the world a place of pain and hardships is God's way of making souls, it does not seem to be working very well. In addition, tremendous pain was experienced by nonhuman animals before the coming of *Homo sapiens.* Since these nonhuman animals cannot develop moral character, what could the purpose have been? Finally, if hardship, pain, and suffering build character, it would seem to follow that we should not seek to eliminate them. Indeed, to further God's purpose we should perhaps actually increase them. Since this is absurd, there is something suspect about Tennant's proposal.[48]

Tennant argues that the evidence taken as a whole indicates a cosmic purpose that has used nature for the making and development of human beings. However, there are predictions from Tennant's theory that seem to be in conflict with the best available evidence. For example, most scientists maintain that, in the light of the available evidence, in the very distant future all life will be extinguished with the breakup of the solar system, including all human life. However, it is difficult to see why God would create human beings by the long process of biological evolution, and provide a vast cosmos as a theater for their moral and aesthetic development, and then destroy it. Tennant seems to grasp this problem but dismisses this prediction, saying that "speculations as to the ruin of a fragment of the universe, based on partial knowledge of a larger fragment of what, for all we know, may be possessed of power to make all things new, are too precarious to be considered exhaustive of the possibilities even as to our terrestrial home, let alone those of a future life."[49] Although he is no doubt correct that the prediction of the ruin of the universe may not be true, it is nonetheless probable in the light of our present evidence. Moreover, it is not probable, in the light of the evidence, that all things will be made new or we will exist in future life.

CONCLUSION

I must conclude that Tennant's argument is unsuccessful. Furthermore, even if it were successful, it would not establish the existence of the traditional theistic God.

Schlesinger's Teleological Argument

THE ARGUMENT

In *Religion and Scientific Method* (1977) Schlesinger treats theism as a scientific hypothesis. Evidence for and against this hypothesis is evaluated using what he takes to be the canons of scientific method. In particular, Schlesinger purports to show that if one follows the inductive practice that prevails in science, theism is inductively supported by universally acknowledged evidence.

Schlesinger's argument is based on what he claims is an elementary principle underlying scientific method. This principle P can be stated as follows:[50]

When a given piece of evidence E is more probable on H than H', then E confirms H more than H'.

According to Schlesinger, principle P "should appear very reasonable to everyone." It can be illustrated as follows: Let

H_1 = All ravens are black.
H_2 = 99 percent of all ravens are black.
E = Of the five ravens hitherto observed, all were black.

Since, according to Schlesinger:

$$p(E/H_1) > p(E/H_2)$$

then by principle P

E confirms H_1 more than H_2.

Schlesinger is quick to point out that just because evidence E confirms H more than H′, it does not mean that we should subscribe to H rather than H′, since the initial credibility of H′ may be higher than H.

According to Schlesinger, the application of principle P to the confirmation of theism is that it is a widely accepted fact that

> R: The laws of nature governing the universe and the initial conditions in it are such that creatures capable of responding to the divine are permitted to exist.[51]

Let T be the theistic hypothesis and N be the naturalistic hypothesis. Now, according to Schlesinger:

$$p(R,T) > p(R,N)$$

This, according to Schlesinger, is because if T is true, then R must be true. However, if N is true, then R may or may not be true. N is compatible with a universe in which no creatures could exist or, if they did exist, they would not be capable of responding to the divine. Consequently, by principle P, R confirms T more than N.

This is basically Schlesinger's argument as to why T is more confirmed than N. To be sure, using another elementary principle of scientific method, which he calls principle A, Schlesinger goes on to try to argue that T is better confirmed than alternatives to N. But he seems to believe it "not very crucial"[52] that he succeed with these additional arguments, for on his view, during the last few hundred years N and not these other alternative hypotheses has been taken to be the real threat to T.

CRITIQUE OF SCHLESINGER'S ARGUMENT

The Principle of Total Evidence

The first thing to notice about Schlesinger's argument is that even if T is confirmed more than N by R, this does not mean that one should subscribe to T rather than to N.[53] As I have noted, Schlesinger admits that the initial credibility of the hypothesis affects whether one should subscribe to the hypothesis. T may be less initially credible than N. Indeed, I show later in this book that the concept of God is inconsistent. If any of our arguments are unsuccessful, T is initially less credible than N, since T would have zero initial probability and N would have initial probability greater than zero. Significantly, Schlesinger does not attempt to refute any arguments purporting to show that the concept of God is inconsistent. Furthermore, even assuming the equal credibility of T and N, the question of whether T is confirmed more than N by the available evidence is not settled by showing that T is confirmed more than N by R. What needs to be assessed is whether T is more confirmed than N by the *total available evidence*. Schlesinger makes no attempt to do this.

To be sure, he attempts to answer the plausible objection that the existence of evil counts against T. But even if he is successful in this attempt, other evidence he does not consider may confirm N more than T, and this may cancel out any confirmation of T over N by R and any other evidence brought up by Schlesinger.

Theism and Its Various Versions

According to Schlesinger, if T is true, then R must be true. Now, no doubt one could construe T in such a way that this claim is true. However, as theism is usually understood, it is simply the belief that a personal God exists. So interpreted, theism is contrasted with both deism and polytheism. Thus the mere existence of a personal God does not necessitate R. In order to derive R from the existence of a personal God, one must assume that this personal God has particular desires and powers. For example, one must at least assume all of the following:

(1) God wants some of His creatures to respond to Him.
(2) God has the power to create laws that make it possible for some creatures to respond to Him.
(3) God does not have other wants that conflict with His desire to have some creatures respond to Him.

If one builds (1), (2), and (3) into the concept of a personal God, it may be possible to argue that T necessitates R. Put in a slightly different way, T per se does not necessitate R. What is true is that a particular version of T necessitates R. Let us call this version T*. No doubt Schlesinger assumes T*.

However, it is also possible to interpret N in such a way that N necessitates R. Let us call this version of N, N*. So construed, N* is no less confirmed by R than T* is. Thus if Schlesinger can interpret T as T*, so can a naturalist interpret N as N* so that R is necessitated. To be sure, a naturalist who would interpret N as N* would be going beyond N as it is usually understood. But a theist who interprets T as T* would be going beyond T as it is usually understood.

T* and Protective Laws

Let us grant that Schlesinger's understanding of T as T* is not idiosyncratic, and let us allow that N* is indeed an idiosyncratic understanding of N. Surely other implications can be drawn from T* that are not supported by the available evidence.

Consider laws that would protect human beings from natural disasters that in turn prevent the humans from responding to God. For example, supernovas, colliding comets, and similar events that are beyond the control of God's creatures may well prevent humans from responding to God, since the human race could become extinct because of these events. Consider, too, laws that would stop certain (perhaps fortuitous) events from preventing the evolutionary development of human beings. If these events, which are completely outside the powers of God's creatures, were not prevented, they could disrupt the evolutionary process and prevent the development of any creatures capable of responding to the divine.

Let us call these protective laws, and let us call the hypothesis that such protective laws do not exist in the universe R'. The evidence for R' is strong. There is every reason to think that there are no laws protecting the human race from extinction as a result of natural disaster and no laws protecting the evolutionary process that resulted in the human species from being brought to a halt. Indeed, Schlesinger himself refers to human beings as "precarious systems."[54]

However, since it is not unreasonable to suppose that R' is incompatible with T* and that R' is compatible with N, then

$$p(R',N) > p(R', T*).$$

Consequently, by principle P

R' confirms N more than T*.

Since R and R' pull in different directions in terms of their confirmation of T* over N, it is not implausible to suppose that the confirmatory powers of R and R' cancel each other out in terms of T*. So even if R confirms T* more than N when R' is taken into account, T* is not more confirmed than N.

The Reasonableness of Principle P
So far I have uncritically accepted principle P, the foundation of Schlesinger's argument. Without this principle, his argument that T is confirmed more than N does not succeed. We are told that it should appear to be very reasonable, but no argument is given for this claim, and it seems to be a dubious one in the light of the following counterexamples. Let

H_3 = All ravens are black because the devil made them black.
H_2 = 99 percent of all ravens are black.
E_1 = Of the five ravens hitherto observed, all were black.

Now, according to principle P, since

$$p(E_1,H_3) > p(E_1,H_2)$$

then E_1 confirms H_3 more than H_2. But this seems absurd.

Schlesinger might attempt to get around this problem by suggesting that strictly speaking E_1 does confirm H_3 more than H_2, but that H_3 should not be subscribed to since it has a lower initial credibility than H_2. But other counterexamples to principle P can be generated where this reply will not work. Let

H_4 = All ravens are black and some roses are red.

Surely there is nothing initially less credible about H_4 than about H_2. Nevertheless, since

$$p(E_1,H_4) > p(E_1,H_2)$$

then

E_1 confirms H_4 more than H_2.

But this seems absurd.

I must conclude that despite Schlesinger's assurances that principle P should appear very reasonable, it is not a reasonable principle and should be rejected.

CONCLUSION

Schlesinger's argument for the confirmation of theism over naturalism fails, and principle P on which it is based is unacceptable. But even if principle P were acceptable, the argument would not succeed, for other evidence that Schlesinger does not consider pulls in the other direction, thereby canceling out the confirmatory effect of the evidence he does cite. Further, granted principle P, it is not clear that theism as it is usually understood makes the evidence he cites more probable than naturalism. Consequently, he is not justified in concluding that the evidence he cites confirms theism more than naturalism. Finally, Schlesinger fails to refute arguments purporting to show that the initial credibility of theism is less than that of naturalism—in other words, arguments purporting to show that theism is incoherent and naturalism is not. He also fails to take into account the total available evidence relevant to the confirmation of theism and naturalism.

Swinburne's Teleological Argument

THE ARGUMENT

In *The Existence of God* (1979) Richard Swinburne advances a variety of arguments for the existence of God that use considerations from confirmation theory and inductive logic.[55] Although he maintains that none of these arguments is strong taken in isolation, their combined weight makes theism more probable than its rivals. As we have seen in

Chapter 4, Swinburne distinguishes two kinds of inductive arguments: C-inductive and P-inductive. A C-inductive argument attempts to show that a hypothesis H is more probable on the basis of certain evidence E and background evidence K than on K alone. A P-inductive argument attempts to show that a hypothesis H is more probable than ~H on the basis of E and K. Swinburne attempts to provide a good C-inductive teleological argument.

His version of the teleological argument differs in significant respects from both Tennant's and Schlesinger's. Swinburne introduces a distinction between types of order: regularities of co-presence or spatial order, such as a section of books in a library arranged in alphabetical order by author, and regularities of succession or temporal order, such as the behavior of bodies in accordance with the law of gravitation. Because of the few cases of spatial order relative to the universe as a whole, Swinburne believes that despite the fact that theists have usually based their arguments on spatial order, it is less risky to base a teleological argument on temporal order. Temporal order is found throughout the universe, for it is exhibited in all laws governing natural processes.

From the fact E of temporal order throughout the universe, Swinburne constructs the following C-inductive argument. Let H be the hypotheses that God created E. As we have seen from our discussion of Swinburne's cosmological argument, the hypothesis that God acted in a certain way is an example of a personal explanation that is fundamentally different from scientific explanations. According to Swinburne there could be no scientific explanation for E; E must be simply a brute fact. For either there are some fundamental laws of temporal order, laws that have no explanation in terms of some higher laws, or else there is an infinite series of laws of increasing generality. In the former case there is by definition no explanation of the fundamental laws; in the latter case there is no explanation of the series as a whole. The only rival explanation to H considered by Swinburne is H', the hypothesis that the order was created by a plurality of gods. But, Swinburne argues, polytheism is a less simple hypothesis than theism and hence *a priori* less probable. Furthermore, there are *a posteriori* arguments against H'. Arguing that if H' were true, we would expect to see different temporal orders in different parts of the universe just as we see different "workmanship in the different houses of a city,"[56] he claims that we do not see this. The same temporal order holds throughout the universe.

Critique of Swinburne's Teleological Argument

The A Priori *Probability of Temporal Order*

So far we have seen why Swinburne believes that E supports H more than H'. But Swinburne must also argue that

(1) $P(E,H\&K) > P(E,K)$.

For unless he can show this, he cannot show that

(2) $P(H,E\&K) > P(H,K)$

where K is the background knowledge that a complex universe exists.[57]

In order to estimate (1), however, one must know the *a priori* probability that the universe has a temporal order, given that there is a universe at all. Although he does not tell us how he arrives at such *a priori* probability judgments, Swinburne thinks that P(E,K) is small. Since the computation will be *a priori*, we can rely on the same sorts of considerations that were relevant to evaluating *a priori* probability in the cosmological argument. This in turn involves considerations of what the possibilities are.[58]

One way of estimating probabilities is by assuming that there are two possibilities, P_1 and P_2:

P_1 = There is no temporal order anywhere in the universe.
P_2 = There is temporal order somewhere in the universe.

Using the method of ignorance as a way of assigning probabilities to these two possibilities P_1 and P_2, there would be a 0.5 *a priori* probability of P_1 and a 0.5 *a priori* probability of P_2.

However, there are other ways of figuring the possibilities. For instance:

P'_1 = No temporal order exists anywhere in the universe.
P'_2 = Uniform temporal order exists everywhere in the universe.
P'_3 = Different regional temporal order exists in the universe, and no region has no temporal order.
P'_4 = Different regional temporal order exists in the universe, and some regions have no temporal order.
P'_5 = Some regions have no temporal order, but where there is temporal order, it is uniform.

These possibilities would be jointly exhaustive and mutually exclusive. On this construal, using the method of ignorance, the *a priori* probability of each of the five possibilities is 0.2. Other ways of analyzing the possibilities are also available, but we need not pursue these ways any further. It is important, however, to note that on some estimates the *a priori* probability of there being temporal order is not negligible. Thus on the last estimate there is 0.8 *a priori* probability that there is temporal order in at least some parts of the universe.

The Reasons to Create the Universe
According to Swinburne, given God's character, God has overriding reasons to create a universe with temporal order.[59] He has a reason to

create a beautiful universe, and beauty involves temporal order. Further-more, temporal order is necessary for intelligent creatures to gain knowl-edge and to learn, and God wants His creatures to do both. Thus God has two reasons for creating a universe with temporal order, ones Swinburne believes are conclusive. So that where

E = The universe has temporal order
H = God exists

and where K is background knowledge, then

$P(E, H\&K) = 1.0$

It is important to see that these two reasons do not provide a conclusive reason for God to create P_2' rather than the other possibilities. God's purpose could be fulfilled even if temporal order were found in our galaxy and not in other regions of space, for beauty could perhaps be achieved only in the region of the universe inhabited by humans. Further, humans could learn all they need to learn in vast regions of the galaxy where temporal order reigns. In fact, given these two reasons, the *a priori* probability that God would actualize P_2' is 0.25. So the probability of

$P(E, H\&K) = 0.25$

where E is the fact of uniform temporal order throughout the universe. However, as we have seen, on the same analysis of possibilities, the *a priori* probabilities are

$P(E, K) = 0.2$

So on this analysis, although $P(E, H\&K) > P(E, H)$, the difference between the two probabilities may not be as great as Swinburne supposes. This would also be true if we construed E to be evidence that there is some temporal order at least somewhere in the universe, rather than evidence that there is uniform temporal order throughout the universe. On this construal,

$P(E, K) = 0.8$

whereas

$P(E, H\&K) = 1.0$

so $P(E, H\&K) > P(E, K)$.

Theism vs. Polytheism
Is Swinburne correct that

(3) $P(H, E\&K) > P(H', E\&K)$

where H is the theistic hypothesis and H' is the polytheistic hypothesis? As we have seen, Swinburne gives two arguments for (3). First, H is simpler than H' and hence *a priori* more likely; second, it is *a posteriori* more probable that theism is true, since if polytheism were true one would expect to find different temporal orders in different parts of the universe. But one does not.

However, it is not true that if polytheism were true, one would expect different temporal orders in different regions of space.[60] Consider the analogy with human beings. Manufactured products are today usually made by several people acting in a cooperative manner. Yet the products from the same manufacturing company can be uniform. For example, a particular type of Ford automobile is made by many people working at a number of Ford factories, but this automobile is uniform in its makeup wherever it is found throughout the world. On the other hand, when only one person is involved in making something, there is sometimes much less uniformity. Thus a skilled cabinetmaker working alone may make different types of cabinets, perhaps no one type more than once. Even when the cabinetmaker produces the same type of cabinet several times, these cabinets can be much less uniform than the cabinets made by a furniture company where many people are involved in making any given cabinet. Thus if one takes the analogy seriously, since there is no reason to expect more uniformity in products made by one human than those made by many, there is no reason to expect more uniformity in temporal orders made by one god than those made by many.

Where one is speaking in particular about temporal order produced by human beings, the same thing is true. Perhaps the most common uniform temporal order known to be the result of intelligence found today is the sound of musical recordings. A uniform temporal order is exhibited each time a particular recording is played. But these temporal orders are surely the result of many intelligences working in cooperation. On the other hand, the sound created by the performance of the music of individual folk or popular musicians playing in concert is not uniform. There are changes of some minor nature each time a single musician plays or sings a particular piece.[61] Thus if we take the analogy seriously, since there is no reason to expect more temporal uniformity in products made by one human than those made by many, there is no reason to expect more uniformity in temporal orders made by one god than those made by many.

Indeed, I believe that if one found uniform order—either spatial or temporal—known to be the result of intelligence in many regions, one would have a stronger inductive ground for inferring that the uniformity was the result of a plurality of intelligences working in cooperation than that it was the result of a single intelligence. We have good reason to suppose from our experience that either temporal or spatial uniformity is more often the result of many individuals working in cooperation than the result of one individual working in isolation. So by analogy, if temporal order of lawful natural phenomena is the result of superintelligence, one should infer that uniform temporal order is probably the result of a plurality of superintelligences.

Still to be considered is Swinburne's argument that H is simpler than H' and consequently *a priori* more probable. As we saw in discussing Swinburne's cosmological argument, a simpler hypothesis is not necessarily the most probable. Moreover, any *a priori* advantage that H would enjoy over H' could be swamped by empirical evidence. As has just been pointed out, analogical inference gives better support to H' than to H. Whether this *a posteriori* support is enough to swamp the alleged *a priori* advantage is unclear, but nothing Swinburne has said shows otherwise.

Thus Swinburne's argument for theism over polytheism fails.

Does God Have Reasons for Not Creating Uniform Temporal Order?

Swinburne argues that God has conclusive reasons for creating a world with uniform temporal order throughout the universe. However, we have seen that at most Swinburne has shown that God has conclusive reasons for creating temporal uniformity in the region of space inhabited by human beings. The reasons provided by Swinburne provide no more specific conclusion.

But are there considerations to be adduced suggesting that if God exists, He would not have created uniform temporal order throughout the universe? I believe that there are. In several places in his book Swinburne argues that God wants to provide a world that builds human character, that enables humans to make moral choices. One would expect that so long as the change was not too radical, a world in which temporal order changes from region to region would provide exciting challenges and therefore build character in a way that the present world cannot. In our world, legal rules change from state to state and from country to country, and these changes provide variety and challenge for criminals and honest citizens alike. Consider a possible world, W_2, in which physical laws differ from place to place: where, for example, death results from poison in one region and not in another; where people live to the age of 300 in one region and die at age 30 in another, where sexual pleasure is many times more intense in one region than in another and is entirely absent in still others. W_2 would call for new challenges and decisions and would test our ability to cope in a way that the present world does not. If God really wanted to provide character-building challenges to humans, surely it is a world like W_2 that He would have created.

Further, there is good reason why God might have wanted to create a world with some regions of chaos where there is no uniformity of temporal change. These would not be regions where humans would normally live and die, but they would be useful nevertheless. First of all, they would provide a contrast with regions having uniform temporal order. Since Swinburne believes that uniformity is associated with beauty, regions of chaos would by contrast tend to accentuate the beauty of the uniform regions. In addition, they would teach humans to appreciate the uniformity of the world they live in. Moreover, regions of chaos would provide the ultimate test for adventurous souls who want to live life in a completely unpredictable way, for while they were in such regions, people would literally not know what to expect next. Finally, since for most people the regions of chaos would be dreaded, they would provide the civil authorities with a natural place of punishment. Instead of being sent to prison, people could be banished to the regions of chaos as the ultimate punishment.

So it is not at all clear that

$$P(E,H\&K) = 1$$

where E is the evidence for uniform temporal order throughout the various regions of the universe. Indeed, depending on how seriously one takes the reasons given above, $P(E,H\&K)$ may be significantly less than one.

However, as we have seen, the *a priori* probability of E, which is $P(E,K)$, ranges anywhere from 0.5 to 0.2 depending on how one analyzes the possibilities involved. Thus it is far from clear that

$$P(E,H\&K) > P(E,K).$$

The problem of whether $P(E,H\&K) > P(E,K)$ could easily be solved if one were interested in having a strong C-inductive argument for a supernatural being but not for the existence of God in particular. For one could imagine a being—call it the temporal order creator (TOC)—that was all-powerful and all-knowing and had as its basic motive creating uniform temporal order throughout the universe. Let us call the hypothesis that TOC exists H″. Then certainly

$$P(E, H''\&K) = 1.0$$

So it is easy enough to find a good C-inductive argument for some supernatural hypothesis. Indeed, there will be an indefinite number of hypotheses in which, if these hypotheses are true, there is a uniform temporal order throughout the universe. Consider, for example, the set of hypotheses such that any member of this set entails E. Unfortunately, H may not be a member of this set. As we saw in relation to Swinburne's cosmological argument, the question is not whether one can construct a good C-inductive argument but whether one can construct a good P-inductive argument. For this task, new and subtle reasoning is needed.

Conclusion

We can conclude that Swinburne is not successful in showing that the existence of God is probable on the basis of the temporal order in the universe.[62]

Taylor's Teleological Argument

The Argument

Richard Taylor in *Metaphysics* (1963) has developed a version of the teleological argument with what he calls a peculiarly rational twist, and he claims that it "has, moreover, been hardly more than dimly perceived by most who have considered the subject."[63] Although he introduces his basic idea by means of a simple example, his actual argument can be interpreted in several ways. Suppose, he says, you are riding in a railway coach and when you look out the window you see numerous small white stones scattered about on a hillside in a pattern resembling these letters: THE BRITISH RAILWAY WELCOMES YOU TO WALES. Although you realize that it is logically possible that this arrangement came about by chance, you would be justified in thinking that these stones were purposely arranged. It is possible, of course, that the stones could have rolled down the hill one by one over the centuries and formed this interesting pattern, but it is highly unlikely.

However, Taylor argues that *if* you conclude that the stones did form the pattern by chance, *then* it would be irrational for you to conclude, just on the basis of this arrangement of them, that you were entering Wales. Put in a different way, if this pattern happened by chance, then, Taylor says, this pattern cannot be taken as evidence that you are entering Wales.

What is the relevance of this example to the teleological argument for the existence of God? As Taylor sees it, our sense organs and brains and nervous system are "things of the most amazing and bewildering complexity and delicacy."[64] Moreover, he maintains that not much progress has been made by science in understanding how human beings perceive the world. Some of our perceptual organs, Taylor argues, resemble things that are designed by human beings. For example, the parts and structure of the eye closely resemble a camera. Yet the resemblance is superficial, for the eye does not take pictures but enables "its possessor to perceive and understand." He maintains that it is "sometimes almost irresistible, when considering such a thing as the eye, to suppose that, however it may have originated, it is constructed in that manner *in order* to enable its possessor to see."[65]

Now, it is possible to suppose that, as in the case of the pattern of stones on the hill, the human eye was an accidental and unintended result. Taylor points out that this is indeed the view of most biologists, who suppose that "if we apply the conceptions of chance mutations and variations, natural selection, and so on, then we can see how it is at least possible—perhaps even almost inevitable—that things of this sort should finally emerge, without any purpose behind them at all."[66] However, if we accept the account of evolutionary biology, then Taylor finds it difficult to see how we can rely on our sense organs and brains in the way that we do. He says:

> We, in fact, whether justifiably or not, *rely* on them for the discovery of things that we suppose to be true and which we suppose to exist quite independently of those organs themselves. We suppose, without even think-ing about it, that they reveal to us things that have nothing to do with themselves, their structure, or their origins. Just as we suppose that the stones on the hill told us that we were entering Wales—a fact having nothing to do with the stones themselves—so also we suppose that our senses in some manner "tell us" what is true, at least sometimes. The stones on the hill could, to be sure, have been an accident, in which case we cannot suppose that they really tell us anything at all. So also, our senses and all our faculties could be accidental in their origins, and in that case they do not really tell us anything either. But the fact remains, that we do trust them, without the slightest reflection on the matter.[67]

Taylor concludes that it would be irrational for anyone to claim *both* that his or her "sensory and cognitive faculties had a natural, nonpurposeful origin and *also* that they reveal some truth with respect to something other than themselves, something that is not merely inferred from them."[68] Yet he maintains that many people assume that their sensory and cognitive faculties are reliable and that the evolutionary account of the origin of their cognitive faculties is correct. According to Taylor, these people are irrational.

Taylor believes that his argument has only marginal relevance to establishing the existence of God. He maintains that his reflections are "consistent with ever so many views that are radically inconsistent with religion. They imply almost nothing with respect to any divine attributes, such as benevolence, and one could insist with some justification that even the word God, which is supposed to be a proper name of a personal being and not just a label attached to metaphysically inferred things, is out of place in them."[69]

One certainly could be an atheist and with perfect consistency embrace

Taylor's argument. What one could not do, if Taylor is correct, is maintain that evolutionary biology's account of the origin of our sensory and
cognitive organs or some other naturalistic account is correct and also
that one could know that, for example, the proofs of the existence of
God are wrong or that God does not exist. In order to claim to have this
knowledge, one would have to maintain that one's sensory and cognitive
faculties are reliable. However, this is exactly what one cannot do, on
Taylor's account, if one accepts, for example, the biological account of
the origin of our sensory and cognitive organs. To put it in a different
way, if Taylor is correct, one could not embrace evolutionary or other
naturalistic accounts of our sensory and cognitive faculties and yet claim
to be a rational atheist in the negative or positive or the broad or narrow
senses. Since many atheists do wish to embrace such naturalistic accounts
and yet claim to be rational and justified in their atheistic beliefs, Taylor's
argument has some bite. Consequently, although a refutation of his
argument is not necessary to the refutation of theism, it is indirectly
relevant to the defense of *one* type of atheism.

CRITICISM OF THE ARGUMENT

What can one say about Taylor's argument? As we shall see, much depends on exactly what one takes his argument to be. Jan Narveson,[70] for
example, agrees with what he takes to be the leading principle of Taylor's
argument: If one finds a certain pattern that appears to express a certain
piece of information, it would be irrational for anyone to suppose *both*
that what is seemingly expressed by the marks is true and also that the
marks appear as the result of nonpurposeful forces. This principle holds,
provided that the marks are the sole evidence for believing that what
they seem to say is true. Narveson agrees with this principle if one
understands the marks to *mean* something in the narrowest sense of the
term "mean." In this sense, to suppose that a thing means something is
to suppose that someone meant a statement that *has* that meaning. In this
sense, only intelligent beings mean something; things do not. Obviously,
given this narrow construal the principle must be true, since if some
marks mean something they could not be the result of nonpurposeful
forces and must be the result of the purposeful actions of intelligent
beings.
    There are, Narveson points out, ever "widening senses" of "mean."[71]
For example, a linguistic expression can mean something by virtue of the
rules of our language, even if no person explicitly intended the expression
to mean anything. There are also nonlinguistic uses of "mean." For instance, we might say that the dark clouds mean rain in a causal sense or that
the Grand Canyon means the grandeur of existence in an aesthetic sense.

In these wider senses of "mean," Narveson argues, Taylor's principle does not hold. Thus it would not be irrational for someone to suppose both that what is meant by dark clouds is rain and also that the dark clouds (the marks) are the result of nonpurposeful forces.

According to Narveson, although Taylor's argument is not from analogy, when he applies his principle to the organs of sense and cognition his argument rests on an analogy between the sense in which an arrangement of marks tells us or informs us of something and the sense in which our eyes or other organs tell us something. Narveson suggests that Taylor recognizes this to some extent in that, when he says that our sense organs tell us something, he puts quotation marks around "tell us." Narveson says that "while an arrangement of marks that forms a sentence in some language tells those who know the language whatever it says in one perfectly literal sense of 'tells,' the same is decidedly untrue of our eyes when we see something. It is the *size* of the gap between the two senses that I wish to point out here."[72]

Pointing out that when we get information from the marks of meaningful discourse, we must apprehend the arrangement of the marks, Narveson insists that when we "get information" from our eyes we do not have to first apprehend the characteristics of our eyes. Unlike the situation in Taylor's story where we have to know the pattern of rocks in order to know what the marks tell us, we do not need to know the structure of the human eye in order to have our eyes inform us. Narveson argues in addition that our eyes do not mean anything in the only sense in which Taylor's principle is valid: "That principle required that the things that are informing us of something be informing us in the sense of *saying* it, expressing it *in a language*."[73] He concludes that "this unexpected and striking twist of a once popular argument for the existence of a purposeful Creator succeeds no better than the original version it supplants."[74]

Although he has had ample opportunity to do so, to my knowledge Taylor has not answered Narveson's criticism.[75] Nevertheless, Taylor has at least one defender. Richard Creel, arguing that Narveson misunderstands Taylor's argument, has reformulated it to bring out more clearly what he takes to be its essential features.[76] According to Creel, Narveson mistakenly supposes that Taylor's example of the stones on the hillside is an essential part of his argument. Creel maintains, however, that this example is only an illustration to facilitate understanding and has nothing to do with Taylor's main argument. To be sure, says Creel, the example of stones on the hillside has to do with linguistic meaning, but Taylor's main argument has nothing to do with this. Consequently, Creel argues, Narveson's criticism is irrelevant, turning as it does on the assumption that linguistic meaning is involved in the deliverances of our sensory and cognitive faculties.

Creel maintains that it is nonlinguistic meaning that is involved in the deliverances of those faculties. He calls one type *natural meaning* and another type *metaphysical meaning*. An example of natural meaning is that dark clouds naturally mean rain. In cases of natural meaning, he says, if Y means X, then the relation between Y and X is observable. In cases of metaphysical meaning, if Y means X, then the relation between Y and X is not observable. Although Creel agrees with Narveson that the deliverances of our sensory and cognitive faculties do not tell us anything in a literal sense, the deliverances of these faculties are usually interpreted to refer to (metaphysically mean) a world independent of our faculties that transcends our sensory experience. There is no way to get outside our sense experience and determine whether it reveals the way the world really is. Taylor's argument, according to Creel, is simply that without the assumption that our faculties are designed by God to reveal this world, we would have no reason to believe that the evidence of our senses metaphysically means what we normally suppose it does. The supposition that the evidence of our senses refers to (metaphysically means) a world that is independent of us Creel calls epistemological realism.

According to Creel, Taylor's argument is in fact a version of Descartes's argument in the *Meditations* that unless there is a God, we cannot trust our senses; and if there is a God, we can. The difference between Taylor and Descartes, says Creel, is that Taylor, unlike Descartes, has no confidence that God can be rationally proved. Creel believes that "Taylor's way of putting the point removes it from logical dependence on the question of the existence of God, because his claim can be unpacked into a hypothetical."[77] According to Creel, Taylor's thesis comes to this:

(ER) A person's assertion of epistemological realism is rational IFF the person asserts that there is a God who designed our faculties of sense and cognition to reveal to us the existence and nature of an independently existing world.

This cannot be a completely correct interpretation of Taylor's views, however, since, as we have seen, Taylor maintains that his position implies nothing about divine attributes. In the spirit of Creel's interpretation, the following might be considered a more accurate rendering of Taylor's thesis:

(ER') A person's assertion of epistemological realism is rational IFF the person asserts that our faculties of sense and cognition are designed to reveal to us the existence and nature of an independently existing world.

(ER') is compatible with our faculties of sense and cognition being designed by an entity (or entities) with attributes very different from those of the traditional God.

However, even (ER') is not quite correct, for one can assert something and not have any grounds for the assertion. Thus we could assert that our faculties are designed to reveal the world and yet not be justified in this assertion. Consequently, we would have no basis for our belief that epistemological realism is true. Hence our assertion of epistemological realism would not be rational. In the light of this problem, (ER') can be further revised:

> (ER″) A person's assertion of epistemological realism is rational IFF the person is justified in asserting that our faculties of sense and cognition are designed to reveal to us the existence and nature of an independently existing world.

Let us suppose for the moment that (ER″) captures the essential aspects of Taylor's thesis. One basic problem with (ER″) is that it is difficult to see how one could be justified in asserting that our faculties of sense and cognition are designed to reveal the existence and nature of an independently existing external world. Arguments for some designer or designers are normally based on the evidence of our senses. Unless we are already justified in supposing our faculties of sense and cognition are reliable, it is hard to see how we can use such evidence to establish that there is any design in the world. But we cannot be so justified, according to (ER″), without its being rational to assert that epistemological realism is true. However, it is rational to assert the truth of epistemological realism only if we are justified in supposing that our sensory and cognitive faculties are designed. It would seem that unless we have some nonempirical way of justifying our belief that our sense and cognitive faculties are designed, it would not be rational to believe that epistemological realism is true. However, it is difficult to see how such nonempirical justification could be possible. The ontological argument, the paradigm of an *a priori* argument, is unsound. Furthermore, as we shall see, the use of religious faith cannot justify religious belief. I must conclude, then, that if (ER″) is the correct interpretation of Taylor's position, it would result in profound epistemological skepticism for those who embrace it. This is hardly an implication of his view that Taylor anticipated.

Let us try another interpretation. If we go back to Taylor's original formulation, his thesis can be interpreted simply to be about the consistency of two claims. He can be taken to be saying that if a person P claims that epistemological realism is true (R), then P cannot consistently claim that P's sensory and cognitive faculties are not designed to reveal the truth about the world (D). But if this is Taylor's thesis, it is surely mistaken. A naturalistic account of the reliability of our sensory and cognitive faculties may be wrong, but there is nothing inconsistent about it. Indeed, Taylor does not present the naturalistic account as inconsistent but only as one about which he has grave doubts.

This suggests a final interpretation of Taylor's elusive thesis. Perhaps in the end Taylor is saying only that a naturalistic account of what we take to be the reliability of our sensory and cognitive faculties does not provide as adequate an explanation of this assumed reliability as some explanation in terms of design. Unfortunately, Taylor really gives no extended argument to support this view. Indeed, what he says could hardly be considered an argument at all. He thus dismisses the evolutionary account of the reliability of our sensory and cognitive faculties as follows:

> It is sometimes said that the capacity to grasp truths has a decided value to the survival of an organism, and that our cognitive faculties have evolved, quite naturally, through the operation of this principle. This appears far-fetched, however, even if for no other reason than that man's capacity to understand what is true through reliance upon his senses and cognitive faculties, far exceeds what is needed for survival. One might as well say that the sign on the hill welcoming tourists to Wales originated over the course of ages purely by accident, and has been preserved by the utility it was found to possess. This is of course possible, but highly implausible.[78]

Taylor makes no effort to appraise the evidence for the evolutionary account of what appears as design in organisms versus the account provided by advocates of the religious hypothesis that organism are in fact designed,[79] and he seems to suppose wrongly that evolutionary theory is committed to the thesis that all the properties of evolved organisms are adaptive.[80] Nor does he critically consider any of the recent attempts to develop a naturalistic epistemology.[81] Without this sort of appraisal we can say at least that the thesis is not established that a theory in terms of design better explains the alleged reliability of our sensory and cognitive faculties than naturalism does.

CONCLUSION

I must conclude that under several interpretations, Taylor's argument is unsound. His argument does not establish that our sensory and cognitive faculties are designed, or that it is inconsistent to hold both that they are not designed and that they are reliable, or that the hypothesis of design is a better account of their reliability than the theory of evolutionary biology. We have also seen that one interpretation results in profound skepticism. Moreover, in none of these interpretations is there any support for the theistic God.

General Conclusion

In this chapter we have examined four of the strongest recent teleological arguments for the existence of God. None of them even comes close to showing that God exists. This does not mean, of course, that no existing arguments are successful or that no future arguments will be. However, since the arguments discussed here do represent some of the best efforts of the human mind to argue teleologically for the existence of God, it seems unlikely that other arguments of this type can succeed. Further, given the long record of failures of this type of argument, it is a reasonable inductive inference to conclude that future attempts will also fail.

CHAPTER 6

The Argument from Religious Experience

Religious Experience Defined

Down through the ages religious believers have had a variety of religious experiences and have used these to justify their belief in God. What is a religious experience? Although the notion is difficult to define, for my purpose here a religious experience is understood as an experience in which one senses the immediate presence of some supernatural entity.[1] But what does this involve?

As I am using the term "senses," if someone senses the immediate presence of some entity, this does *not* entail that it exists. It does entail that the person either believes or is inclined to believe that the entity exists, at least partly on the basis of the person's experience.[2] For example, if Jones senses the immediate presence of the angel Gabriel, this does not entail that the angel Gabriel exists, but it does entail that Jones believes or is inclined to believe that the angel Gabriel exists, at least in part on the basis of his experience. However, the entailment cannot be reversed. One may believe that an entity is present or be inclined to believe that it is present and yet not do so on the basis of one's religious experience if, for example, one's belief is based entirely on faith or indirect evidence. Furthermore, by "some supernatural entity" I mean to include more than God, in the sense of an all-good, all-knowing, all-powerful being. For example, one could sense the immediate presence of an angel or a finite god. In addition, by sensing the immediate presence of some supernatural being I do not mean to imply that the being whose immediate presence is sensed is experienced as distinct or separate from the person who is having the experience. I mean rather to include phenomena in which the person experiences a union or a merging with the divine.

Types of Religious Experience

There are several types of religious experience in the sense defined above. It is useful to consider Swinburne's classification of religious experience, which is one of most extensive and illuminating schemes to appear in recent literature.[3]

Type 1 One can experience an ordinary nonreligious object *as* a supernatural being—for example, a dove as an angel. The experience is of a public object, an object that ordinary observers would experience under normal conditions. For example, ordinary observers under normal conditions would experience the dove, although they would not experience it as an angel.

Type 2 One can experience some supernatural being that is a public object and use ordinary vocabulary to describe the experience. This experience would not be of some ordinary object *as* a supernatural being but of a supernatural being in its normal guise. Thus a person P can experience an angel in its normal guise as a beautiful being with wings, and the object of P's experience can be such that any ordinary observer would experience what P would experience under ordinary circumstances. For example, Joseph Smith, the founder of the Mormon Church, had an experience of the angel Moroni "standing in the air" by his bedside on September 21, 1823.[4] If we assume that any normal observer who had been in Joseph Smith's bedroom on the night of September 21, 1823, would have experienced the angel Moroni standing in the air near Smith's bed, then Smith's experience would be of type 2.

Type 3 This is like type 2 experiences except that the experience is not of a public object. One can experience some supernatural being in its standard guise, not some ordinary object as a supernatural being, and use ordinary vocabulary to describe the experience, although this being could not be experienced by ordinary observers under normal conditions. For example, if we suppose that an ordinary observer could not have experienced the angel Moroni in Joseph Smith's bedroom on the night of September 21, 1823, then Smith's experience would be of type 3.

Type 4 Another kind of experience entails sensations that are not describable by the normal vocabulary. Mystical experiences, for example, are sometimes so difficult to describe that the mystic is forced to use paradoxical and negative terms. Thus Dionysius the Aeropagite described the object of his experience in a purely negative way in the following passage.

> It is not immovable nor in motion, or at rest, and has no power, and is not power or light, and does not live, and is not life; nor is It personal essence, or eternity, or time; nor can It be grasped by the understanding, since It

is not knowledge or truth; nor is It kingship or wisdom; nor is It one, nor is It unity, nor is It Godhead or Goodness; nor is It a Spirit, as we understand the term, since it is not Sonship or Fatherhood; nor is It any other thing such as we or any other being can have knowledge of; nor does it belong to the category of nonexistence or that of existence.[5]

In the case of mystical experiences the object of experience is not a public object open to scrutiny by all normal observers. Thus Dionysius the Aeropagite is surely not claiming that the elusive "It" of his mystical experience is an object that could have been experienced by ordinary observers under ordinary conditions.

Type 5 The experience of a supernatural being can involve no sensations at all. A person may experience God and not claim to have had any particular sensations either of the typical sort or of some sort that is difficult to describe.[6] For example, it is likely that one of the experiences of St. Teresa of Avila, a Spanish nun of the sixteenth century, was of this kind, for she described it in this way:

> I was at prayer on a festival of the glorious Saint Peter when I saw Christ at my side—or, to put it better, I was conscious of Him, for neither with the eyes of the body nor with those of the soul did I see anything. I thought He was quite close to me and I saw that it was He Who, as I thought, was speaking to me.[7]

This last type of experience is also of a nonpublic object. Her nonsensory experience of Christ is not something that ordinary people could have had.

THE ARGUMENT IN BRIEF

Although religious experiences have been used to justify religious belief, such as belief in the existence of God, it is sometimes maintained that this use does not constitute an *argument* for the existence of God because when one senses the presence of God, no inference is involved. Religious belief based on religious experience, it is said, is like a perceptual belief of tables and chairs; because it is immediate and noninferential, it cannot be construed as being based on an argument. Consequently, there is no argument from religious experience.

However, the thesis that appeals to religious experience to justify religious belief does not constitute an argument is much less compelling than it may seem. Its apparent plausibility rests on a confusion between how a belief is arrived at—that is, the genesis of the belief—and how it is justified. For it may well be true that a person who arrives at his or her beliefs by means of religious experiences or ordinary perceptual experience does so without using inferences or arguments, but it is not obviously true that this person could justify those beliefs without using inferences or arguments.[8] For example, in order to be able to justify my spontaneous perceptual belief that there is a brown table in front of me, it would seem to be necessary in principle to be able to argue thus: Spontaneous beliefs of a certain sort occurring under certain conditions are usually true, and my belief that there is a brown table in front of me is of this sort and occurs under these conditions. Consequently, my belief is probably true.

More formally stated, the necessary justifying argument would go like this:

(1) Under certain conditions C_1, spontaneous perceptual beliefs of a certain kind K_1 are likely to be true.

(2) Condition C_1 obtains.

(3) My perceptual belief that there is a brown table in front of me is of kind K_1.

(4) Hence my perceptual belief that there is a brown table in front of me is likely to be true.

Furthermore, it might be necessary to give additional reasons to support the premises of the argument. Since reasons are necessary to justify even perceptual beliefs that arise without inference, religious beliefs that arise without inference would have to be justified by arguments as well.

Given that religious beliefs based on religious experiences need to be justified by an argument, what kind would be appropriate? I suggest that the following sort is basic to justifying belief in God on the basis of religious experience:

(1′) Under certain conditions C_1, religious beliefs of type K_1—that is, beliefs generated by religious experience—are likely to be true.

(2′) Condition C_1 obtains.

(3′) My religious belief that God exists is of type K_1.

(4′) Hence my religious belief that God exists is likely to be true.

EVALUATION OF THE ARGUMENT

Clearly the crucial premise of the argument is premise (1′). What reason can we have for supposing that religious beliefs generated by certain types of religious experiences under certain conditions are likely to be true? One general problem with the several types of experience considered above is that they are concerned with nonpublic objects. In order for us to suppose that beliefs generated by these experiences are likely to be true, we must assume that each experience is caused by a reality external to the person who is having it, a reality that does not cause

ordinary persons to experience something similar. Let us call this supposition the external cause Hypothesis (H_1).

The problem arising in relation to premise ($1'$) is that there is a rival
hypothesis. One might suppose that a person's religious experience is
caused not by some external reality but by the workings of the person's
own mind. On this theory, a religious experience would have an origin
similar to that of delusion and delirium. But then religious experience
would have no objective import and would not be trustworthy at all. Let
us call this the psychological hypothesis (H_2).

Which hypothesis should be accepted? Consider first the reasons why
we do not use the external cause hypothesis (H_1) to explain the experiences that result from the use of certain drugs, from mental illness, and
from going without sleep for long periods of time. Why could not one
argue that these experiences are caused by some external reality and that
they provide evidence of the nature of such a reality? It may be suggested
that when one takes certain drugs, has a mental illness, or goes without
sleep the mind is opened to this reality and ordinary perception is unable
to make contact with it. Certainly, people who have such experiences
often interpret them as experiences of objects external to their minds.
We have good reasons to suppose, however, that such an interpretation
is mistaken and thus good reason not to use (H_1) to explain these experiences. Why? The primary reason is that experiences induced by drugs,
alcohol, sleep deprivation, and mental illness tell no uniform or coherent
story of a supposed external reality that one can experience only in these
extraordinary ways.

The situation could be different. Imagine a possible world where there
is a part of reality that can only be known by taking so-called reality
drugs. In this world, reality drug–induced experiences would tell a coherent story. Not only would the descriptions of each experience be coherent, but the descriptions of the experiences of different people would
tend to be consistent with one another, one person's experiences in a
drug-induced state corroborating the experiences of another. When
there was a lack of corroboration, one would have a plausible account as
to why there was a discrepancy. For example, it might be known that the
experiences of a person who did not take enough of the reality drug
would be untrustworthy. Moreover, if a person's descriptions of the
experience made no sense, there would be a ready explanation; for
instance, the person might not be properly trained to describe such
experiences. Indeed, there might be independent reason to suppose that
the incoherent descriptions could be translated into coherent terms. In
this possible world the external cause hypothesis might well be the best
explanation of these drug-induced experiences. So it would make good
sense to say that in such a world, taking the reality drugs opens the mind

to be acted upon by an external reality that cannot be known in other ways.

Clearly, this possible world is not ours. Drug-induced experiences tell no uniform story; indeed, sometimes the description of a drug-induced experience makes no sense at all. We have no plausible theory to account for the discrepancies and have no ready explanation of this incoherence and no reason to suppose that some suggested coherent translation captures the meaning of the description. The same holds for experiences induced by alcohol, mental illness, and sleep deprivation. In our world, then, the psychological hypothesis is the best explanation of these experiences.

Religious experiences are like those induced by drugs, alcohol, mental illness, and sleep deprivation: They tell no uniform or coherent story, and there is no plausible theory to account for discrepancies among them. Again the situation could be different. Imagine a possible world where part of reality can only be known through religious experiences. There religious experiences would tend to tell a coherent story. Not only would the descriptions of each religious experience be coherent, but the descriptions of the experiences of different people would tend to be consistent with one another. Indeed, a religious experience in one culture would generally corroborate a religious experience in another culture. When there was a lack of corroboration, there would be a plausible explanation for the discrepancy. For example, it might be known that the experiences of a person who had not performed certain spiritual exercises for at least three months would be untrustworthy. Moreover, if first-hand descriptions of religious experience made no sense, there would be a ready explanation. For instance, the person might not be properly trained to describe such experiences but, once trained, would be able to provide coherent descriptions. Indeed, there might be independent reason to suppose that the incoherent descriptions could be translated into coherent terms. In this possible world the external cause hypothesis might well be the best explanation of religious experiences.

Once again, this possible world is not ours. In our world, descriptions of religious experience sometimes make no sense, yet we have no ready explanation of this incoherence and no reason to suppose that some suggested coherent translation captures the meaning of the description. Furthermore, religious experiences in one culture often conflict with those in another. One cannot accept all of them as veridical, yet there does not seem to be any way to separate the veridical experiences from the rest. With the possible exception of mystical experiences in our world, the psychological hypothesis is therefore the best explanation of these experiences. In a moment I will take up the claim made by some scholars that mystical experience is uniform over cultures and time. Even if it is correct, other types of religious experience of nonpublic objects tell no uniform or coherent story.

But is there really no way to determine which religious experiences should be considered trustworthy and which should be rejected? St. Teresa suggested several ways of ruling out deceptive religious experiences. These techniques have been adopted by other religious believers,[9] and two of them are especially important. If the content of a religious experience is incompatible with Scripture, she says, it should be considered nonveridical. She also maintained that if a religious experience has a bad effect on one—for example, if a person becomes less humble or loving or fervent in faith after the experience—then the experience is deceptive.

Unfortunately, these tests for separating deceptive from trustworthy religious experiences will not do. Since the test of scriptural compatibility already presumes that the Bible is the revealed word of God and therefore that the Christian God exists, it cannot be used to support an argument from religious experience for the existence of God. Further, it would hardly be surprising on the psychological hypothesis (H_2) that people raised in the Christian tradition should tend to have religious experiences that are compatible with Christian Scripture. This hypothesis, combined with plausible auxiliary hypotheses such as that people's delusions tend to be strongly influenced by their training and culture, predicts that in general people raised in a certain religious tradition tend to have religious experiences compatible with the religious literature of this tradition. This is exactly what one finds. Divergences from this prediction are rare and in any case can be accounted for in terms of individual psychological factors and the influence of other traditions.

Unless we grant large and dubious assumptions about the relations between religious experience and conduct, St. Teresa's test of conduct will not work either. Why should one assume that a vision of ultimate reality will always or even usually make a person better? One could have a vision of God and yet, on account of weakness of will or the overpowering and dreadful nature of the vision, degenerate morally. Furthermore, there is no *a priori* reason why a person might not show moral improvement after an illusory religious experience. It might just be the catalyst needed to change the person's life. St. Teresa wrongly seemed to think that the only deception possible in a religious experience is brought about by the devil. But the deceptive nature of such experience could have purely psychological causes, and the moral improvement that results could have such causes as well. In addition to these problems, the test of conduct surely proves too much. Since religious experiences occur in the context of different religions, it would not be surprising to discover that, for example, Christian, Islamic, and Hindu religious experiences have all resulted in improved conduct. However, since they seem to be incompatible, it can hardly be claimed that all these experiences are trustworthy. I must conclude, therefore, that St. Teresa's tests of veridical religious experience are unsatisfactory.

As we have seen, two kinds of religious experience, type 1 and type 2, are of public objects. Could these provide the corroboration needed to claim that some religious experience is trustworthy? Although this is possible in principle, as a matter of fact the ingredients necessary for the experience of a public object are missing. Consider, for example, a type 1 experience of a black cat as the devil. We have here the same problem as in the case of nonpublic objects. There is no agreement among observers and no plausible theory to explain disagreement. To be sure, there is agreement among observers that a black cat is seen. However, there is no agreement that the devil is seen and no plausible theory to account for discrepancies. Because of this, the experience of seeing the black cat as the devil is better explained by the psychological hypothesis (H_2) than by the external cause hypothesis (H_1).

Consider a case in which there is a plausible theory to account for discrepancies and where (H_2) would not be appropriate. To an anthropologist, a person in another culture jumping up and down around a fire might be experienced as a medicine man doing a rain dance, but this phenomenon would not be so experienced by an ordinary observer. We do not discount the experience as unreliable, for we understand that the anthropologist is experiencing the jumping up and down in terms of an extensive theoretical background and training. We know that from studying this culture the anthropologist may have learned to experience such situations like a native. Indeed, we can verify that these interpretations are usually correct by asking native informants and other anthropologists who have studied the culture.

In the case of religious experience there are no analogous ways of certifying that people who experience ordinary objects as religious entities know what they are talking about. One can imagine a situation in which there was a way of checking up on someone who experienced a black cat as the devil. Consider a possible world where it is commonly known that the devil takes the form of a black cat. In this world there are subtle behavorial differences between ordinary black cats and those that are the devil incarnate. A person trained in black magic can discern these subtle differences. Moreover, one can check up on whether someone is an expert in devil detection by seeing if his or her predictions come true. For example, an ordinary black cat would not be adversely affected by being confronted with a cross, whereas the devil-cat would be. Furthermore, there would be wide agreement among devil detectors about what was an ordinary cat and what was not. But this world is not ours. In ours there is no way of checking, no agreement among experts in devil detecting, no plausible theory for explaining discrepancies.

Turning now to experiences of type 2, we must distinguish two different cases. In the first, several people experience some supernatural being at the same time. In the second, some lone individual P experiences a supernatural being, but it is claimed that if other normal people had been with P, they would have experienced what P did. Since the second case can for all practical purposes be treated as a type 3 experience, it can be ignored here.

The first kind of type 2 experience seems important, however. For it may be maintained that if there were clear and uncontroversial cases of type 2 religious experiences, there would be strong evidence for the existence of God. Furthermore, it might be claimed by religious believers that there have been such cases. One example that could be cited is the appearance of Jesus to several of his disciples after his resurrection. It could be maintained that Jesus was a public object capable of being observed by all normal observers. Furthermore, he was surely a supernatural being, since he arose from the dead. Moreover, religious believers could claim that this case provides evidence for the existence of God, since Jesus' appearance after his resurrection is best explained by the hypothesis that he was God incarnate.

But have there been clear and uncontroversial cases of type 2 religious experience? Certainly the case of Jesus' alleged resurrection is not one of them. Indeed, there is little reason to accept this story as true. The accounts of Jesus' resurrection in different gospels contradict each other;[10] the story is not supported by Paul's letters, which many scholars believe were written earlier;[11] and the story is not supported by Jewish and Roman sources.[12] Furthermore, I know of no clear and uncontroversial cases of type 2 religious experiences.

However, suppose that there were good grounds to suppose that Jesus appeared to several of his disciples after his death on the cross. Would this be strong evidence that God, an all-powerful, all-knowing, all-good being, exists? This would, indeed, be strong evidence that Jesus was a supernatural being, but it would not be strong evidence for the existence of an all-good all-powerful, all-knowing being. This is because Jesus' appearance is compatible with many different supernatural explanations. For example, Jesus may have been the incarnation of a finite god or one of many gods or even of the devil. This is a basic problem in appealing to any religious experience—even type 2 religious experiences—as evidence for the existence of God. Even if one has good grounds for supposing a religious experience cannot be explained by (H_2) and must be explained by (H_1), this is compatible with various alternative supernatural explanations.

So although type 2 religious experiences could in principle provide support for belief in *some* supernatural being, in fact it remains to be shown that they do. And in any case it remains dubious that, even if such experience supported the belief that some supernatural being exists, it could provide more support for the existence of an all-good, all-powerful, all-knowing God than for the existence of some other supernatural being.

Mystical Experience

Mystical experiences are typically type 4 religious experiences in which a person has sensations that are not describable by our normal vocabulary. Some scholars of mysticism maintain that there is a common core of mysticism. They maintain that, although there are cultural differences among mystics, mystical experiences in different times and in different religions have important and fundamental similarities. If these scholars are correct, then perhaps these similarities provide the basis for a sound argument from mystical experiences to the existence of God.

Consider the following argument:

(1) All mystical experiences are basically the same.
(2) This similarity is better explained in terms of the external cause hypothesis (H_1) than of the psychological hypothesis (H_2).
(3) The most adequate version of (H_1) is that God causes the mystical experience (H_1').

---

(4) Therefore, mystical experiences provide inductive support for (H_1').

Walter Stace has argued for premise (1). According to Stace, all mystical experiences "involve the apprehension of *an ultimate nonsensuous unity of all things*, a oneness or a One to which neither the senses or the reason can penetrate."[13] He distinguishes two kinds of mysticism: extrovertive and introvertive. In extrovertive mysticism the mystic "looks outward and through the physical sense into the external world and finds the One there. The introvertive way turns inward, introspectively, and finds the One at the bottom of the self, at the bottom of the human personality." Elsewhere Stace characterizes the two types of mysticism in more detail as follows:[14]

Characteristics of Extrovertive Mystical Experience
(1) The Unifying Vision—all things are one
(2) The more concrete apprehension of the One as intersubjectivity, or life, in all things
(3) Sense of objectivity or reality

(4) Blessedness, peace, etc.
(5) Feeling of the holy, sacred, or divine
(6) Paradoxicality
(7) Alleged by mystics to be ineffable

Characteristics of Introvertive Mystical Experience
(1) The Unitary Consciousness: the One, the Void; pure consciousness
(2) Nonspatial, nontemporal
(3) Sense of objectivity or reality
(4) Blessedness, peace, etc.
(5) Feeling of the holy, sacred, or divine
(6) Paradoxicality
(7) Alleged by mystics to be ineffable

Stace concludes that "characteristics 3, 4, 5, 6, 7 are identical in the two lists and are, therefore, *universal common characteristics of mysticism in all cultures, ages, religions and civilizations of the world.*"[15]

Stace's view is not shared by all scholars of mysticism. For example, Steven Katz maintains that there is no clear way of distinguishing the mystical experience itself from the interpretation of it.[16] Consequently, the meaning of the experience and even the meaning of the language used to describe the experience vary from context to context. For example, Katz argues that although all mystics claim that they experience a sense of objective reality (characteristic 3), what they mean differs radically from context to context and, indeed, their interpretations are often mutually incompatible. Katz puts it this way:

> While objectivity or reality (Reality) in Plato or Neoplatonism is found in "the world of ideas," these characteristics are found in God in Jewish mysticism and again in the *Tao, nirvana,* and Nature in Taoism, Buddhism, and Richard Jefferies respectively. It seems clear that these respective mystics do not experience the same Reality or objectivity, and, therefore, it is not reasonable to posit that their respective experiences of Reality are similar.[17]

Fortunately, we do not have to settle the debate between Stace and his defenders on the one hand[18] and his critics on the other, for whether the critics are correct or not, the argument fails. Suppose that critics such as Steven Katz are correct that mystics in different religious traditions experience different realities. Then the first premise of the above argument fails, and in order to argue from mystical experiences to the existence of God, a new one would have to be constructed. Suppose now that Stace's critics are mistaken and that mystical experiences in different religious traditions show significant similarities. Then premise (1) would be true. What about premise (2)? It is possible that the similarity of mystical experience in different religious traditions can be explained in terms of the psychological hypothesis. There have been attempts, for example, to explain mystical experiences in terms of sexual repression and to show that mystical experiences are similar to ones that are caused by psychedelic drugs.[19] But even if these explanations are valid, given the alleged striking similarity of all mystical experiences, the external cause hypothesis is not ruled out. Sexual repression may be necessary if certain individuals are to have access to ultimate reality; and psychedelic drugs, as we have already argued, may provide this access.

The problem with the external cause hypothesis in the case of mystical experiences, and the reason for preferring the psychological hypothesis over the external cause hypothesis, is the difficulty of making sense of these experiences. As we have seen, for the external cause hypothesis to apply, not only must the experiences of different people usually cohere with one another, and not only must there be a plausible theory to explain cases where there are discrepancies, but the individual experiences themselves must be coherent or else there must be some plausible way to account for the incoherence. According to Stace, mystics claim that their experience is ineffable (characteristic 7) and yet describe it (characteristics 3, 4, 5, 6). So his characteristics of mystical experience seem prima facie contradictory. Further, according to Stace, the mystical experience itself has paradoxicality (characteristic 6). By this he means that many mystics describe their experience in seemingly paradoxical language. For example, Dionysius the Aeropagite described his experience of God as "the dazzling obscurity of the Secret Silence, outshining all brilliance with the intensity of their darkness."[20] Taken literally, descriptions of this sort are nonsense. The mystic who gives them cannot be interpreted as making any factual claims.[21] Further, there is no widely accepted theory to account for the incoherences[22] and no objective way of translating such nonsensical statements into statements that are not. Without such a theory and method of translation, the external cause hypothesis is not to be preferred to the psychological hypothesis.

However, let us suppose that there is some good reason to prefer the external cause hypothesis to the psychological hypothesis. This would establish premise (2) in the above argument but not premise (3) (the most adequate version of (H_1) is that God causes the mystical experience (H_1')). However, it is difficult to see why God should be postulated as the external cause rather than the Tao, nirvana, or nature.[23] Indeed, if the paradoxical language of mystical experience points beyond itself to some external cause, this external cause would have to be very obscure and difficult to understand. To suppose that this external cause is God, an all-good, all-powerful, all-knowing being, is surely unwarranted. Thus there seems to be no good reason to suppose that (H_1') is the most plausible version of (H_1). Consequently, even if the argument is successful in providing evidence for an external cause of mystical experience, it fails as an argument for God.

Swinburne's Principle of Credulity and Religious Experience

So far I have raised objections to the argument from religious experience, considered in general terms. Perhaps the most sophisticated and extended defense of this argument to have been presented in recent years is that of Richard Swinburne.[24] If there are serious problems with Swinburne's argument, it is likely that there will be serious problems with other defenses of this argument. The argument from religious experience is of crucial importance to Swinburne's entire philosophical theology, for the combined weight of the other arguments he considers, such as the teleological, the cosmological, and the argument from miracles, does not render the theistic hypothesis very probable. He argues, however, that when these other arguments are combined with the argument from religious experience, theism is made more probable than its rivals.[25]

In his argument from religious experience Swinburne makes use of what he calls the principle of credulity, which allows one to infer from the fact that it seems to a person that something is present to the probability that it is present. Let us evaluate this principle and the use Swinburne makes of it.

THE PRINCIPLE OF CREDULITY AND ITS LIMITATIONS

Traditionally, critics of the argument from religious experience have maintained that it is a fallacy to argue from a psychological experience of x to x—for example, from the fact that it appears to you that God is present to the probability that God is present.[26] Maintaining, however, that the way things seem is indeed good grounds for belief about the way things are, Swinburne calls the general principle that guides our inferences the principle of credulity. It can be formulated as follows:

> (PC) If it seems (epistemically) to a subject S that x is present, then probably x is present.

By the expression "seems (epistemically)" Swinburne means that the subject S is inclined to believe what appears to S on the basis of his or her present sensory experience. Swinburne contrasts this sense of "seems" with the comparative sense in which one compares the way an object looks with the way other objects normally look. Thus when S says, "It seemed that the Virgin Mary was talking to me," S is using "seemed" epistemically. But if S says, "The figure seemed like a beautiful lady bathed in a white light," S is using "seemed" comparatively.

Swinburne gives two basic reasons for advocating (PC). The first one is that without such a means of arguing, we would land in a "skeptical bog."[27] Unfortunately, he does not expand on this reason, but one can assume he means something like this: Without (PC) we would be unable ever to get outside our own experiences and make justified judgments about how things really are; we would be restricted to how things appear to us. However, if we are restricted to how things appear to us, skepticism about the world is the only justified position to take. But with (PC) we can say how things really are and avoid skepticism.

The second reason Swinburne gives for advocating (PC) is that the attempt to restrict it so that it does not apply to religious experience is arbitrary. He considers only two attempts to restrict the range of application. First one might argue that (PC) is not an ultimate principle of rationality but must itself be justified on inductive grounds; in other words, by showing that appearances have in general proved reliable in the past. But, the argument continues, although this reliability has been demonstrated in the case of the appearance of ordinary things, it has not been in the case of religious experience. So (PC) should be restricted to ordinary appearances. Swinburne rejects this restriction on two grounds. He maintains that people are justified in taking what looks like a table to be a table "even if they do not recall their past experience with tables,"[28] and in any case this attempt to restrict the range of application would not allow us to deal with cases where the subject has no experience of x's but does have experiences of the properties in terms of which x is defined.

Another objection is the use of (PC) with respect to religious experiences that Swinburne discusses is based on the distinction between experience and the interpretation of experience. One might argue, he says, that (PC) should be used only when one is experiencing certain properties—for example, the so-called sensible properties of red, brown, soft, hard, left, right—but that it should not be used when one makes interpretations. Thus if it seems that x is red, one can infer that probably it is red since the inference entails no interpretation. But if it seems x is a Russian ship, then one cannot infer that it probably is since one is interpreting. Using this argument one could argue that (PC) cannot be used to infer from the appearance of God that probably God exists, since interpretation is involved. Swinburne rejects this line of argument, maintaining that it rests on the dubious distinction between experience and interpretation. There is no way, he claims, of making this distinction without being arbitrary.

Swinburne of course believes that (PC) is limited in its application by some special considerations. On his view there are in fact four special considerations that limit (PC). First, one can show that the subject S was unreliable or that the experience occurred under conditions that in the past have been unreliable. For example, if S was subject to hallucinations or delusions or was under the influence of a drug such as LSD, this would limit the application of (PC). Second, one can show that the perceptual claim was to have perceived an object of a certain kind in circumstances where similar perceptual claims have proved false. For example, one might show that the perceiver did not have the experience necessary to make reliable perceptual claims in these circumstances. Swinburne argues, however, that what experiences are necessary in order to recognize something is often unclear, and in any case the ability to recognize something, given certain experiences, varies widely from person to person. A variation of this would be to show that many perceptual claims made in particular contexts are in conflict. Clearly if they are, (PC) cannot be used, for its use would lead to incompatible claims about what really exists.

A third circumstance in which (PC) would be limited is one in which there was strong evidence that x did not exist. Because he believes that S's experience has a very strong evidential force, Swinburne emphasizes that this evidence would have to be very, very strong. Finally, a fourth way to limit (PC) would be to show that although x is present, the appearance of x can be accounted for in other ways.

Swinburne believes that these four special considerations do not apply to religious experiences. Although the first special consideration may rule out some religious experience, most religious experiences are not affected, he says. Thus most people who claim that they have had a religious experience are not subject to hallucinations or delusions and are not on drugs such as LSD. Swinburne also argues that the second special consideration does not apply. He maintains that one cannot argue that someone who claims to experience God could not recognize God; nor can one argue that many religious experiences are incompatible. For example, it may be argued that in order to recognize God one would have to have previously perceived God or been given a detailed description of Him. But since people have not previously experienced God and do not have a detailed description of Him, they could not recognize Him. Swinburne rejects this contention and argues that the description of God as an omnipotent, omniscient, and perfectly free person may be sufficient for S to recognize God "by hearing his voice, or feeling his presence, or seeing his handiwork or by some sixth sense."[29]

He goes on to say, "Even if some of us are not very good at recognizing power or knowledge or freedom in the human persons we meet, we might well be able to recognize extreme degrees of these qualities when we cannot recognize lesser degrees." However, Swinburne admits, "Great power, knowledge, or freedom are not characteristics which we easily learn to recognize by hearing a voice or seeing some object which might be an agent's handiwork or by feeling. And *some* mild suspicion is cast on a subject's claim to have recognized an agent with these qualities by the qualitative remoteness of his previous experience from what he claims to have detected—but for the reasons which I have given, only *some* mild suspicion."[30]

Swinburne has a number of objections to the thesis that many religious experiences are incompatible. First, he argues that an apparent conflict may be the result of using different names to refer to the same entity. Thus God may be called by different names in different cultures. But there may be no genuine conflict in the different religious experiences in which these different names are used. Moreover, even if there are some conflicts, this does not show that religious experience in general is unreliable. It only shows that some particular claim must be withdrawn or at least modified. Instead of claiming that one experienced Dionysus, one might claim only that one experienced some supernatural being. After all, says Swinburne, there are conflicts in perceptual claims in astronomical observations, and no one thinks that this should lead to general skepticism about the reliability of such observations.

Of course, Swinburne maintains that if a substantial number of religious experiences were in conflict, this would cast doubt on the reliability of religious experiences. But he says, "Religious experiences in non-Christian traditions are experiences apparently of beings who are supposed to have similar properties to those of God, or experiences of a lesser being, or experiences apparently of states of affairs, but hardly experiences of any person or state whose existence is incompatible with that of God."[31] Swinburne maintains that if there were many religious experiences of an omnipotent devil, then religious experience would indeed be unreliable, since the existence of such a being would be incompatible with God. But, he says, there are no such experiences. Although Swinburne does not say this explicitly, he apparently believes that there is no incompatibility in a Christian's religious experience of the Virgin Mary and a Hindu's religious experience of Kali.

The third special consideration would apply only if one had very strong evidence that God did not exist. The burden of proof would be on atheists to supply the evidence, and Swinburne believes that this burden cannot be borne. The fourth way to limit (PC) does not apply in the context of religious experiences. In this case one would show that, although God exists, God was not the cause of the religious experience. But according to Swinburne, if God exists, He at least indirectly causes everything. Thus this limitation could not be applied.

THE NEGATIVE PRINCIPLE OF CREDULITY

One obvious critical question that can be raised about Swinburne's argument is this: Since experiences of God are good grounds for the existence of God, are not experiences of the absence of God good grounds for the nonexistence of God? After all, many people have tried to experience God and have failed. Cannot these experiences of the absence of God be used by atheists to counter the theistic argument based on experience of the presence of God? Swinburne thinks they cannot be so used.

In ordinary life we suppose that the experience of a chair is a good ground for believing that the chair is present. But we also believe that the experience of the absence of a chair is a good ground for supposing that a chair is absent. If Swinburne is correct that the way things appear is good ground for the way they are, then surely the way things do not seem is good ground for the way they are not. Indeed, if (PC) is a legitimate principle of inference, then one would suppose that there is a negative principle of credulity that can be formulated as follows:

(NPC) If it seems (epistemically) to a subject S that x is absent, then probably x is absent.

One might suppose that (NPC) would be governed by limitations similar to those specified for (PC). If S is on drugs or is otherwise mentally abnormal, if S does not have the requisite experience to recognize x, if there is strong evidence to suppose that x was present, if x was not present but S's perceptual claim could be attributed to something else, then (NPC) would not apply. None of these four limitations seems to apply in the typical case of someone who tries to experience God and fails to do so. Typically the person is not on drugs or otherwise mentally abnormal. There is no reason to suppose that he or she lacks the requisite enabling experience or descriptions of God (or at least no more reason to suppose it in this case than in the case where the person does experience God). It would be difficult to show that God's existence is very, very probable and show that it was very, very probable that God was present.[32] In any case, the burden of proof would be on the theist. (The fourth type of limitation of (PC) would hardly apply, since one would already have to assume that God did not exist.)

Swinburne does not explicitly formulate a negative credulity principle. Whether he would be opposed to one as such or merely to the applications I have made of it is unclear. But let us try to understand his objection to the use of (NPC) to argue that probably God does not exist.

His objection to the use of (NPC) in showing the nonexistence of God based on the experience of God's absence turns on the alleged disanalogy between ordinary perceptual claims that can legitimately be made about the absence of something, such as the absence of a chair, and a perceptual claim in the context of religion that cannot be made, such as the absence of God. Swinburne sees the difference in this way: In the case of a chair one can know under what conditions one would see a chair if a chair was there. But in the case of God one cannot know under what conditions one would see God if God existed. Swinburne seems to believe that since we do not know under what conditions God would appear if He existed, experience of the absence of God cannot be used as evidence that God does not exist. But he maintains that this lack of knowledge only "*somewhat lessens*" the evidential value of perceptual claims of God's presence.[33]

It is difficult to understand why, if there were this difference, it would affect the evidential value of perceptual claims in religious contexts in the way Swinburne says. One would suppose that if one did not know under what conditions a subject could expect to see x if x existed, this would affect both the evidential value of S's claim that it seemed that x is present and S's claim that it seemed that x is not present, and to the same extent. Yet Swinburne maintains that since we do not know under what conditions someone would see God if God existed, this only somewhat lessens the evidential value of a perceptual claim that it seems to S that God is present, but it completely negates the evidential value of the perceptual claim that it seems to S that God is not present. Perceptual judgments of both the absence and the presence of God seem equally suspect, yet Swinburne finds a great disanalogy.

In order to become clearer on the logic of the situation, let us introduce the following notation. Let T be the hypothesis that there is a table in front of me; let C_1 be a certain perceptual condition and A_1 be the perceptual statement that a table appears to S. Now suppose

(1) If T and C_1, then A_1.

Then given $\sim A_1$ and C_1, one can infer $\sim T$. In the case of tables one can often know what C_1 is and whether it holds in a given context.

Swinburne says the situation in the case of God is not analogous. Let G be the hypothesis that God exists. Let C_2 be certain perceptual conditions and A_2 be the perceptual statement that God appears to S. Then:

(2) If G and C_2, then A_2.

Suppose that $\sim A_2$. One cannot infer $\sim G$, since one does not know whether C_2 holds in this situation. In fact, one does not even know what C_2 is.

But if this is true, surely it will affect our ability to infer G inductively from A_2. Let us go back to the case of the table. Suppose it appears to S that a table is in front of him. That is, let us suppose:

(3) A_1.

The inference from (1) and (3) to

(4) T

is a very weak inductive inference. It becomes strong[34] only if we can assume

(5) If $\sim T$ and C_1, then probably $\sim A_1$

and

(6) C_1.

Thus if one can assume that if a table is not present and perceptual condition C_2 is present, then probably a table will not appear to me; and if perceptual condition C_1 is present, then one can infer that there probably is a table in front of me on the basis of the appearance of a table. Surely the same logic will hold for religious experience. Let us suppose that God appeared to S; that is, let us suppose;

(7) A_2.

Then the inference from (2) to (7) to

(8) G

would be a very weak inductive inference unless one assumed:

(9) If $\sim G$ and C_2, then probably $\sim A_2$

and

(10) C_2.

That is, unless one can suppose that if God does exist and condition C_2 holds, then probably it would not appear to S that God is present; and if C_2 does hold, it would not be probable that God exists on the basis of God's appearance. But C_2 is not something one can know, according to Swinburne. So the inference from religious experience to God becomes as problematic as the inference from the appearance of the absence of God to the nonexistence of God, and for the same reason. We do not know what C_2 is and whether it holds in the case of religious experience.

The problem becomes even more acute when one realizes that religious experiences can occur if God does not exist so long as certain perceptual conditions occur. Let C_3 be some of those conditions that result in the appearance of God when God does not exist. Thus

(11) If $\sim G$ and C_3, then A_2.

Then if one could assume

(12) If G and C_3, then probably $\sim A_2$

and

(13) C_3

one could infer that probably

(14) $\sim$G

given

(15) A_2.

Thus the appearance of God can be evidence under some conditions that God does not exist. Whether it is or not depends on what perceptual conditions hold. According to Swinburne, since one cannot know those conditions under which God will appear to people if He exists, it seems unlikely that one can know all those conditions under which He will appear if He does not exist. In our ignorance it surely seems illegitimate to suppose that an appearance of God would be grounds for supposing God exists.

Indeed, the above considerations suggest that perhaps a particular condition should be made an explicit part of the special considerations under which (PC) and (NPC) do not apply. That is, perhaps neither (PC) nor (NPC) should apply unless one has a right to assume that perceptual conditions hold under which the entity at issue is likely to appear to an observer if the entity is present. This right may be justified on inductive grounds, by one's background theory, or in other ways. Whether this should actually be made a condition of application is not clear.[35] But in any case what one cannot do, and what Swinburne apparently tries to do, is to assume this right in perceptual claims about the appearance of God and not assume it in cases of the appearance of the absence of God. Stacking the deck in favor of theism, such a procedure is arbitrary.

Swinburne has attempted to answer this criticism in the following way.[36] He maintains that if it seems to 50 people that there are no dodos, this is not good grounds for supposing that there are no dodos. But if it seems to 50 people that there are dodos, this is good grounds for supposing that there are. The difference, he says, is that in the positive case we have a plausible theory as to how, if things are as they seem, they cause it to be so to us. He says that we apply this theory in the case of material objects that operate on us by means of light rays as well as in the case of God, who cause us directly to have the experience in question. Swinburne argues, however, that with negative cases when the claim is not spatially limited (that is, has the form "There is no x," not "There is no x at place p"), there is no plausible theory. He argues that if there are no dodos anywhere in the world, this general state is not going to operate on observers to cause them to have dodo-absent experiences. Similarly for the absence of God. If there is no God, this general state of the universe is not going to cause us to have God-absent experiences. Some more local mundane cause is what is at work. On the other hand, Swinburne says, if there is God, we can certainly be sure that He is the cause of our experience.

Swinburne is wise to emphasize the importance of background theories in evaluating the relevance of religious experience to the existence of God. However, the situation is not as clear-cut as he supposes. Indeed, the similarities between seeming to see the presence of God and seeming to see the absence of God are closer than he thinks. The circumstances under which some people report having experienced the presence of God do not seem to be different from the circumstances under which other people report having an experience of His absence. For example, some religious people seem to experience God when they pray or meditate or perform various spiritual exercises. But other people do the same thing and experience the absence of God. Unlike our experience of material objects, we have no plausible theory to account for this. Indeed, if God exists, we have no idea under what circumstances He would be experienced and under what circumstances He would not be. In a similar way, if God does not exist, we have no plausible theory of when people would have an experience of God and when they would not. By way of contrast, if 50 people experienced the absence of dodos in certain locations on the island of Mauritius, this would indeed be evidence of their absence on this island and elsewhere, since on our background theory these locations are the only places where dodos have been found. On the other hand, if 50 people reported seeing dodos in the middle of winter in Alaska, this would not be taken seriously, given our background knowledge. Given our lack of background knowledge of when God will be experienced if He exists and when people have experiences of God if He does not exist, no inferences can be made concerning His existence or lack of existence from our experiences of the presence or the absence of God.

I conclude that Swinburne has not answered our criticism.

THE ADEQUACY OF SWINBURNE'S PRINCIPLE OF CREDULITY

So far we have seen that Swinburne has not given any good reason why there is no NPC if there is a (PC). Conclusions that could be derived from this negative principle and the experiences of the absence of God would tend to cancel out the conclusions derived from (PC) and the experiences of the presence of God. But one may well wonder if (PC) is adequate.

Perhaps further restrictions are needed on its use. I have already considered one possible restriction without making any final determination of whether it is acceptable. Let us consider another.

Swinburne seems to assume that if (PC) applies, then we have very strong ground for belief unless one of the four limitations on its application applies. Gary Gutting brings up an example that tends to show Swinburne's assumption is wrong:

> Suppose, for example, I walk into my study one afternoon and seem to see, clearly and distinctly, my recently deceased aunt, sitting in my chair. We may assume that the conditions of this experience (my mental state, the lighting of the room, etc.) are not ones that we have reason to think produce unreliable perceptions. Thus, the first of Swinburne's defeating conditions does not hold. Nor, given normal circumstances, does the second condition hold. Most likely, I have no knowledge at all of circumstances in which experiences of the dead by apparently normal persons have turned out to be nonveridical. (We may even assume that I have never heard of anyone I regard as at all reliable reporting such an experience.) Further, knowing nothing at all about the habits or powers of the dead, I have no reason to think that my aunt could not now be in my study or, if present, could not be seen by me. So Swinburne's third and fourth conditions do not hold for this case. But, although none of the four defeating conditions Swinburne recognizes apply, it is obvious that I am not entitled, without further information, to believe that I have seen my aunt.[37]

Gutting goes on to argue that in order to be entitled to believe he saw his aunt, much more evidence would be needed. If, for example, he had numerous repetitions of the experience, other people had the same experience, he had a long visit in which the appearance behaved in ways characteristic of his aunt, he had information from the appearance that only his aunt had access to, and so on, then, Gutting says, he would be justified in believing he saw his aunt. Without this further evidence, he says, the appearance of his aunt provides only some slight support for the claim that his aunt was in his study.

In general, Gutting argues, an X-experience provides strong evidence for the existence of X only when this experience is supplemented by additional corroborating experience. However, he says:

> In cases of kinds of objects of which we have frequently had veridical experience, we can of course rightly believe that they exist, without further corroboration beyond our seeming to see them. But this is because we have good inductive reason to expect that further corroboration will be forthcoming. With relatively unfamiliar objects—from elves to deceased aunts to divine beings—this sort of inductive reason is not available; and warranted assent must await further corroboration.[38]

Gutting's limitations on the application of (PC) are well taken and, indeed, show that Swinburne's are incomplete as they stand. The question can be raised, however, whether, given this new limitation, an experience of God can receive the further corroboration that Gutting demands. Gutting believes it can. He argues that if a religious experience is veridical, one should expect the occurrence of confirmatory experiences. In particular, he argues that if a religious experience of a very good and very powerful being is veridical, then those who have the experience would be likely to have more of the same again, other individuals will be found with similar experiences, and those having the experiences "will find themselves aided in their endeavors to lead morally better lives."[39]

One problem with Gutting's thesis is that he also argues that we lack knowledge of God's particular intentions because He is all-knowing; consequently, we have no reason to suppose that God "will act in any specific way."[40] Given this lack of knowledge, one wonders how one can possibly predict that someone who has had a veridical experience will have such an experience again. Surely this presumes a knowledge of God's specific intentions that, according to Gutting, we cannot have. After all, God may have a good reason that we do not know for revealing Himself only once to many people. In the case of St. Teresa we have already seen the problems involved in using moral criteria for the veridical nature of religious experience. However, Gutting's thesis that we cannot know God's specific intentions suggests further problems. Perhaps God has good but unknown reasons for not wanting some people to improve morally after veridical religious experiences and good but unknown reasons for wanting other people to improve after nonveridical experiences.

Gutting attempts to solve the problem by arguing that religious experiences usually are not of an all-knowing, all-powerful, and all-good being but simply of a very wise, powerful, and good being.[41] Consequently, one may be able to have knowledge of the specific intentions of the being that one encounters in a religious experience. However, Gutting cites little evidence to support his view that religious experiences in our culture are usually not of the theistic God. Furthermore, it is completely unclear why one should be able to know the specific intentions of a being who knows vastly more than any human being and yet not be able to know the specific intentions of a being who is all-knowing. Small children frequently do not know the specific intentions of their parents although the parents are not all-knowing. By analogy one might expect God's children to lack knowledge of God's specific intentions even if God is not all-knowing. In addition, Gutting provides no evidence that people having an experience of a very wise, powerful, and good being are more aided in their endeavors to lead morally better lives than anyone else. Do those who experience a very wise, powerful, and good being tend to live better lives than those who do not believe in God or have never had a religious experience? I am not aware of any evidence that supports a positive answer to this question, and Gutting provides none.

Nevertheless, Gutting maintains that people sometimes have religious experiences of, for example, an all-knowing being and that one can confirm that the being encountered is all-knowing by subsequent experience of its great knowledge, such as "its predicting unexpected events or revealing profound truths about human nature that we were unlikely to have discovered ourselves."[42] However, it is unclear why such confirmed predictions would support the hypothesis that the being is *all*-knowing rather than the hypothesis that the being has vastly more knowledge than we do. Moreover, even if such a confirmed prediction could confirm in principle the hypothesis of an all-knowing being, Gutting cites no predictions that have been confirmed. But even if he did, there are surely predictions that have been generated from religious experience of an all-knowing being that have proved to be inaccurate. On what basis do we say that the accurate predictions confirm the existence of an all-knowing being and not say that inaccurate predictions disconfirm the existence of such a being? Gutting provides no answer.

In any case, Gutting's criteria cannot deal with the issue of conflicting religious experience. He only considers type 5 religious experience, but there are different type 5 religious experiences in different religious traditions that seem in conflict, and, as we shall see shortly, the ways of reconciling this conflict do not seem promising.

THE RELIABILITY OF RELIGIOUS EXPERIENCES

As I have indicated, Swinburne does not believe it possible to show that religious experience is unreliable by arguing that different religious experiences are incompatible. He maintains that religious experiences stemming from non-Christian traditions are of a being who is supposed to have "similar properties to those of God" or "experiences of apparently lesser beings."[43] Swinburne admits that if there were religious experiences of an all-powerful devil, they would conflict with religious experiences of God. But he argues that no such experiences exist.

However, it is not necessary to have experiences of an all-powerful devil to claim that religious experiences are systematically incompatible. Swinburne must do more than argue that the beings described in the religious experience of non-Western cultures have properties similar to those of God in the Western tradition in order to show no incompatibility. He must show that these beings do not have *any* properties that are incompatible with properties of God.

Prime facie there does seem to be a remarkable incompatibility between the concept of God in the Western tradition and the concept of

Brahma, the absolute, and so on in Eastern thought. In the Western tradition, God is a person distinct from the world and from His creatures. Not surprisingly, many religious experiences within the Western tradition, especially nonmystical ones such as the experience of God speaking to someone and giving advice and counsel, convey this idea of God. On the other hand, mystical religious experience within the Eastern tradition tends to convey a pantheistic and impersonal God. The experience of God in this tradition typically is not that of a caring, loving person but of an impersonal absolute and ultimate reality. To be sure, this difference is not uniform: There are theistic trends in Hinduism and pantheistic trends in Christianity. But the differences between East and West are sufficiently widespread to be noted by scholars,[44] and they certainly seem incompatible. A God that transcends the world seemingly cannot be identical with the world; a God that is a person can apparently not be impersonal. Indeed, Christians who have held pantheistic and impersonal views about God have typically been thought to be heretics by Christian orthodoxy. So there do seem to be incompatible differences in the religious experiences of different cultures.[45]

I can see only three ways in which Swinburne can avoid these apparent incompatibilities, but none of them seems very promising.

First, he can argue that one must distinguish between religious experience and the interpretation of it and maintain that the experiences themselves are compatible while the interpretations are not. Since he rejects the distinction between interpretation and experience in religious experiences, however, this option seems closed to him.[46]

Second, Swinburne can argue that the properties of pantheism and theism, personal and impersonal, are not really incompatible. But on the ordinary understanding of these terms, if God is transcendent, He cannot be identical with the world, and if God is a person, He is necessarily not an impersonal absolute. So one and the same entity could not be both transcendent and identical with the universe, both personal and impersonal. Perhaps it could be argued that "God" is being used ambiguously to refer to two different entities that could both exist; that "God" in the Western tradition is being used to refer to a transcendent personal being (call this God$_1$), whereas in the Eastern tradition it is being used to refer to an impersonal being identical with the universe (call this God$_2$). It may be suggested that both entities could exist. But it is difficult to see how this could be, if for no other reason than that in the Western tradition the universe is supposed to be created by God, and this would mean that God$_1$ created God$_2$. This seems to conflict with much of Eastern thought, including that reflected in Eastern religious experiences, which makes God uncreated.

Finally, Swinburne can use a distinction suggested by Stace. After rejecting Stace's attempt to distinguish between interpretation and experience in mystical experience, Swinburne says in a footnote that the natural way to interpret Stace's claim is as a claim that all subjects have in essence the same kinds of sensory experiences, i.e., the same kinds of experience described comparatively which give rise to different kinds of experiences described epistemically, i.e., lead the subjects to hold different beliefs."[47] But this distinction does not help and does not seem to apply very well to the cases we have in mind.

It does not help, since Swinburne defines religious experience in terms of the epistemic sense of "seems," not the comparative sense. Thus religious experiences are incompatible if different subjects tend to believe they are experiencing incompatible beings. The distinction does not apply very well, since it is implausible to suppose that a Christian who says it seems to him that God is speaking and an Eastern mystic who says it seems to him that he has merged with Brahma would describe their experiences comparatively in the same way, so that the experience would be of compatible beings. A Christian might say comparatively, "It seems as if I was hearing the voice of a wise, powerful father"; the Eastern mystic might say comparatively, "It seems as if I was merging with a warm, infinite, milky sea."

Swinburne is correct that religious experiences of "lesser beings" in different religious traditions are strictly speaking not incompatible. Thus the celestial Virgin Mary and the Hindu goddess Kali are not per se incompatible entities. But to consider these entities in isolation from the religious tradition of which they are a part seems a very limited way to view the problem. One could just as well argue that the medieval force of impetus is compatible with the various subatomic particles postulated by the modern physical sciences. So it is, in the sense that a description of these entities and a description of medieval impetus do not entail a contradiction. But they belong to incompatible world views. In a similar way, if one considers them in isolation, the Virgin Mary and Kali are compatible entities. But the world views of which they are a part are not compatible. Kali, the goddess of death and destruction, is portrayed as "a black female figure, with bloodshot eyes, tongue thrust out and teeth like fangs, blood on her face and bosom, hair matted in horrible clusters. Around her neck hangs a chain of skulls, corpses form her earrings and her waist is girdled with skulls. She is dancing on a prostrate corpse."[48] Surely there is great difficulty in fitting such an entity into the Christian world view, even if populated with angels and a devil, for Kali is also the goddess of creation and fertility.

One can define two senses in which religious experiences are incompatible. In the direct sense, religious experiences E_1 and E_2 are incompatible if and only if E_1 is about being B_1 and E_2 is about being B_2, and the existence of B_1 is incompatible with the existence of B_2. It is in this sense that I have argued that religious experiences typical of the Western tradition of a personal God are incompatible with religious experiences typical of the Eastern tradition of an impersonal pantheistic God. In the indirect sense of incompatible, religious experiences E_1 and E_2 are incompatible if and only if E_1 and E_2 are not directly incompatible, E_1 is about being B_1 and E_2 is about being B_2, B_1 is part of religious tradition T_1 and B_2 is part of religious tradition T_2, and the world views of T_1 and T_2 are inconsistent. It is in this sense that the religious experience of the Virgin Mary and the religious experience of Kali are incompatible.

This point can be put in a different way. As in science, a religious belief is part of a system of beliefs. Thus support for a religious belief indirectly supports the system of beliefs of which it is part. If religious experience provides support for beliefs about the existence of certain entities, it provides support for the system to which these beliefs belong. The problem is that it provides support for incompatible systems. Indirectly, then, the appeal to religious experience results in inductive inconsistency.

In a reply to the above criticisms, Swinburne says we have exaggerated the incompatibilities between states that are purportedly experienced in different religious traditions.[49] However, he also says he may have underestimated the extent to which theory is needed to sort out such claims. By "theory" in the present case he means the theory of theism, which he believes has a much greater probability than rival metaphysical theories. He points out that well-supported theories are used to sort out competing perceptual claims in other fields, such as in detective work and in history, and maintains that while most of such claims are preserved, a few are ruled out as mistaken by well-supported theories accepted in the field.

Since Swinburne does not say in what way we have exaggerated the incompatibilities between states that are purportedly experienced in different religious traditions, it is impossible to answer this charge. I can agree that a well-supported theory might be helpful in sorting out conflicting perceptual reports from different religious traditions and that well-supported theories are indeed used in other fields to sort out conflicting perceptual claims. However, it is difficult to see how theism could be such a theory. Swinburne has admitted that he has not shown, using the standard arguments for the existence of God, that theism is very probable. He believes that *only* when these arguments are combined with the argument from religious experience does it become very probable. Clearly, then, he cannot use a well-supported theory of theism to sort out conflicting claims of religious experiences without begging the question as to which claims of religious experience are veridical, since it is only by using religious experience that the theory of theism becomes well supported. However, if he uses the theory of theism without the support of religious experience, this theory, by his own admission, is not well supported and cannot be used to sort out which of conflicting religious experiences should be taken seriously.

I conclude that Swinburne has not answered my criticisms.[50]

THE DIFFICULTY OF RECOGNIZING GOD

Swinburne says that the remoteness from the subject's experience of these infinite attributes casts only "mild suspicion" on the subject's claim to have recognized an omnipotent, omniscient, completely free being by hearing the being's voice, or by feeling its presence, or by seeing its handiwork, or by some sixth sense. However, it may seem to many thoughtful readers that he is overly sanguine.

In ordinary life, perceptual recognition claims are open to challenge and should be treated with skepticism when they transcend what can reasonably be expected to be known on their basis or when they themselves are based on untried sense modalities. Consider recognition claims made on the basis of a voice. Suppose you claim that the person you spoke to on the phone, a man you never spoke to before, seemed to be the strongest man in County Cork. I may well wonder how, merely by hearing this man's voice, you could recognize him as the strongest man in County Cork. If you convince me that you are an expert in Irish accents (an Irish Professor Higgins) part of my skepticism will be allayed, but the question will remain as to how you could possibly know from his voice that he is the strongest man in his county. Perhaps you could, but surely your remarkable skill would have to be demonstrated under controlled conditions before any reasonable person would take your claims seriously, since, normally, a person's strength cannot be known from the sound of his or her voice.

In religious contexts the same problem occurs. You say it seems to you that God spoke to you. But how can you tell from the voice alone that the being you heard was omnipotent, omniscient, and completely free? How can you distinguish the voice from that of an enormously powerful but finite being—a being with, say, powers $10^{20,000}$ times greater than any human? How can you tell by just the voice that it is not an infinitely powerful but evil being? Surely, any reasonable person would want answers to these questions. It is difficult, however, to see how any satisfactory ones could be given. Answers in terms of the pitch, volume, intensity, and other typical qualities of voices would hardly be adequate.

Moreover, an answer in terms of some indescribable quality of the voice would produce skepticism unless the perceiver could demonstrate an ability to recognize this quality by picking out, for example, an infinite being's voice from a finite but very powerful being's voice. Such a test seems difficult to devise. One would have to hear both kinds of voices and be able to differentiate the qualities that belong to an infinite being from those that belong to a finite but very powerful being. However, this experience is precisely what people with religious experiences do not have: They have not heard the voices of infinitely powerful and finite but enormously powerful beings.

Consider now perceptual claims made on the basis of someone's handiwork. These are also subject to challenge and warrant skepticism if they transcend what one could reasonably expect to know. If you say it seems to you that the painting before you was done by a female artist from Perth, Australia, I will legitimately challenge your claim, for it goes beyond what one can reasonably expect an ordinary viewer of paintings to see. Such a claim would be different from the claim that the painting was done by Van Gogh, whose style is distinctive and well known. A single course in the history of art might well give someone the necessary experience to say with some confidence that a painting appears to be a Van Gogh. But even here one's claim could be challenged if, for example, Van Gogh's style was frequently imitated and if, in fact, only experts could tell the difference. You might say that you can tell from the delicate brush strokes that the artist is a woman and can tell that she is from Perth by her use of the Perthian style, characterized by pastel colors and dynamic themes. But these claims are subject to further challenge. Is it really true that female artists use a more delicate brush stroke than males? Is there a distinct Perthian style? Is not this style characteristic of many artists from Australia and not just from Perth? And so on. Until these questions are answered, your claim should and normally would be treated with skepticism—unless, of course, you have a justified reputation for accurate judgments about the sex and place of origin of artists from viewing their paintings, a skill that other viewers do not have and the basis of which is a mystery.

The same point holds for religious experience. If merely seeing some entity that is supposed to be His handiwork is the basis for your claim that God seems to be present, one can legitimately wonder how you can tell the object is the handiwork of God rather than of a very powerful but finite being or an omnipotent devil. Many of the various problems connected with the teleological argument seem to reappear. Any object, including the universe itself, seems to be compatible with various kinds of supernatural beings. One might have the ability to pick out the handiwork of God from the handiwork of other beings by simply viewing it, but surely this would have to be shown. It would be irrational for us to accept the perceiver's claim without such a demonstration.

Swinburne talks about feeling the presence of an entity or knowing that an entity is present by some sixth sense. Suppose you claim to know by some sixth sense that Jones stole your brother's watch. Or you claim that whenever Jones is around, you feel the presence of the thief. Normally your claim would be dismissed, as it should be unless you had made similar claims in the past that had proved to be accurate. Without such evidence, a sixth sense or feeling should have no credibility. Similarly, one should dismiss your claim that you perceive the presence of God by means of a sixth sense unless there is good reason to suppose your sixth sense is accurate. The reason is obvious. Unlike ordinary perceptual claims based on ordinary sense modalities, the reliability of a sixth sense is untried and unproven. To our knowledge, people with religious experiences who rely on a sixth sense have not demonstrated its trustworthiness.

Swinburne attempts to answer the above criticism as follows.[51] He denies that one can challenge someone's claim to have experienced God by arguing that the person does not have the requisite experience to make that claim. This challenge, he says, would only be possible if one has an established theory about the kind of experience necessary to make claims about experiencing God. In some areas, he says, we do have such a theory. However, he maintains that in the case of religious experience we do not have this sort of theory. Nor can we show by arguments from analogy that the same considerations are relevant as in areas where we do have established theories. Since the mechanism causing an experience of God is different from that causing our ordinary perceptual experience, Swinburne says, we cannot readily carry over theories about the kind of prior experience necessary to make a kind of claim. He admits that since there is some slight analogy between the case of religious perceptual experience and ordinary perceptual experience there is some slight carry-over. Using the example cited above, he says that by the principle of simplicity, having the experience of a being with only $10^{20,000}$ the power of a human being is less likely than having the experience of an omnipotent being. He argues that we should take the following attitude toward any new sense purporting to give us access to objects and properties unobservable by the other senses. In order to determine how this sense works and what its limits are, one must first assume that, by and large, in respect to this sense things are what they seem. Otherwise, unless we have access to the same kind of objects by some other sense, the process of establishing limits could not get started.

How can this rebuttal be answered? One problem with it is that Swinburne advises us when considering a new sense to assume first that by and large things are what they seem. However, as I have already argued, this initial assumption must be quickly abandoned in the case of religious experiences. Religious experiences are often conflicting, and thus things *cannot* be what they seem. We must distinguish what is veridical and what is not, and there is at present no non-question-begging theory that enables us to do this. In particular, we cannot use the theory of theism to distinguish what is veridical from what is not. Given the unavailability of any theory developed within the context of religious experience itself, we must import theories from the outside. Swinburne says that such importation is illegitimate. If so, then he must give up any claim to the veridical nature of some religious experiences. He forbids any imported theories and yet provides no plausible nonimported theory for distinguishing veridical from nonveridical religious experience. I do not see how Swinburne can have it both ways and yet claim that some religious experience is trustworthy.

Moreover, Swinburne is not completely consistent in his rejection of the use of imported theories to rule out nonveridical religious experience. He seems to believe that if a person is subject to delusions or is on drugs, his or her reports of religious experiences should not be taken seriously. But if the causal mechanism is completely different in the case of religious experiences, it is difficult to see how we can rule out, as nonveridical, religious experiences that are associated with drug taking. What is the justification for carrying over theories concerning the influence of drugs from nonreligious contexts to religious contexts and not carrying over other theories? Thus Swinburne seems to maintain that we should not trust our senses if, for example, we take LSD and experience the Virgin Mary. On the other hand, if we do not take drugs and see a beautiful lady bathed in white light and recognize her instantly without prior experience as the Virgin Mary, he seems to assume that we should trust our senses. Presumably, in the LSD case we are not justified in trusting our senses because we know that such drugs cause hallucination. But in the instant recognition case, Swinburne would say, we are justified in trusting our senses since in the context of religious experience previous experience has not been shown to be relevant to instant recognition. One could just as well argue that taking drugs has not been shown to be relevant to the trustworthiness of our experience in religious contexts. Of course, such a position seems implausible. Yet without further argument, so does the position that earlier experience is irrelevant to recognition in the context of religious experience.

As I have argued, Swinburne's appeal to the principle of simplicity is suspect in arguing that the hypothesis of an all-powerful, all-knowing, all-good God is *a priori* more probable than the hypothesis of a finite god. It is no less suspect in the special case of the most adequate explanation of religious experience. First, it is unclear why the hypothesis that one is experiencing an extremely powerful but not all-powerful being is less simple than the hypothesis that one is experiencing an all-powerful being.

Second, even if the hypothesis that one is experiencing an all-powerful being is simpler than the hypothesis that one is experiencing an extremely powerful but not all-powerful being, it is dubious that the former hypothesis is more *a priori* probable than the latter hypothesis.

I must conclude that Swinburne has not adequately answered our criticism.

SKEPTICISM AND GULLIBILISM

Swinburne says that if (PC) and its limitations are rejected, one will land in a "skeptical bog," and that if it is permissible to use (PC) with respect to some experiences, one must have good arguments to show that it is not permissible to use (PC) with respect to religious experiences. I have already suggested some reasons why it is not permissible to use (PC) with respect to religious experiences. It would be well to review these and show that they do not lead to skepticism—indeed, that without these restrictions, (PC) leads to gullibilism.

We saw first of all that in the case of religious experience we do not know under what conditions God, if He exists, will appear to humans. Far from affecting the evidential value of religious experience only slightly, this affects it profoundly. The lack of knowledge affects equally profoundly the evidential value of perceptual claims about the absence of God. (Swinburne provides no principled reason why (NPC) should not be used to argue for the nonexistence of God that does not apply to the use of (PC) to argue for the existence of God.) As we have seen, whether we should restrict the application of (PC) and (NPC) to cases where we have knowledge of the conditions under which objects will appear is an open question. If we did, however, this would not result in skepticism about ordinary objects. For example, knowledge is available about when chairs will appear if they exist. Moreover, Gutting's suggestions for further restrictions on the application of (PC) would not result in skepticism. We have good inductive evidence that our experience of a chair will receive further corroboration in our experience; consequently, our belief in chairs is justified.

We have also seen that perpetual claims about God are subject to challenge. So are all claims about perception insofar as they transcend what one could reasonably expect to perceive, for example, by hearing a person's voice or seeing the person's handiwork, or when appeal is made to a sense modality that is not tested. Although such challenges are sometimes capable of being met in ordinary cases, in religious contexts they have not been met. (Indeed, it is not clear that they could be.) However, this problem does not lead to a general skepticism. In the first place, perceptual claims about ordinary things often do not transcend what one could reasonably expect to know on the basis of what is seen. In the second place, even when they do and are subject to challenge, there are various way in which the challenge can be met and the skeptical questions silenced.

So general skepticism does not seem to be a worry if one restricts the use of (PC) to prevent religious experience from being used to argue from the experience of God to the existence of God. Further, unless these restrictions are made, it would seem that one must assume that the universe is populated by all manner of strange entities—that one has landed in the swamp of gullibilism. The universe becomes populated with the various lesser beings of different religious traditions, from the Virgin Mary to Kali, from Satan to Apollo. It becomes populated with all the lesser beings that religious believers have claimed, down through the ages, to have religious experiences of. The only way to rule out any of these entities would be to show that one or more of the four restrictions apply. It is possible that this could be done in some cases, but one suspects that many hundreds of lesser beings would still remain.

But more is yet to come. Not only would many lesser beings of various world religions now become part of the furniture of the universe, but so also would many creatures of legend and myth: fairies, wood elves, brownies, goblins, water nymphs. Numerous perceptual reports of fairies were made during the years 1917–1920.[52] It seems unlikely that all of them could be ruled out by the four special conditions formulated by Swinburne. So one could use (PC) to argue that fairies probably exist. However, with further restrictions on (PC) neither fairies nor the lesser beings of various religious traditions need be part of our ontology. People's experiences of such beings are not corroborated in the appropriate ways.

Conclusion

I do not wish to deny that (PC) operates in ordinary life and science. But there are more limitations on its use than Swinburne imagines, and they need to be more tightly drawn. If without PC we might land in a skeptical bog, without tighter restrictions on (PC) we would find ourselves in a cluttered ontological landscape. Given Swinburne's version of (PC), there would indeed be more things in heaven and earth than are dreamt of in anyone's philosophy.

With these necessary restrictions, religious experiences provide no evidence for the existence of God. If Swinburne is right about the weakness of the other arguments for the existence of God, this means that the theistic hypothesis is not probable in light of the total evidence available. This does not mean, of course, that theism is improbable. Whether it is will depend on the strength of arguments purporting to show that God does not exist.

CHAPTER 7

The Argument from Miracles

The Argument in General

The literature of religious traditions is filled with stories of strange and mysterious events. Christian literature is abundantly supplied with such stories. According to the Bible, Jesus was born of a virgin, turned water to wine, walked on water, healed the sick, raised the dead, and was resurrected.[1] Moreover, within the Christian tradition, accounts of these sorts of events have continued down through the centuries. There have been stories of wondrous cures, of bleeding religious statues, of stigmata, and of visitations of the Virgin Mary.[2] For example, in Zeitoun, Egypt, from 1968 to 1970, thousands of people observed what seemed to be a luminous figure of the Virgin Mary walking on the central dome of the Coptic church known as St. Mary's Church of Zeitoun and occasionally hovering above it.[3] In Lourdes, France, many unexplained cures have been reported. After having been investigated by the Catholic Church, some of them have been declared to be miraculous. Strange and mysterious events have also been reported in the context of other religious traditions, such as the levitation of Hindu yogis.[4]

It seems that these reports, if accepted as accurate, cannot be explained in either commonsense or scientific terms. For example, there appears to be no ordinary way of explaining how Jesus raised the dead or turned water into wine, no scientific explanation of the luminous figure on the dome of St. Mary's Church of Zeitoun or of the cures at Lourdes, no known ordinary way to account for the levitation of yogis.

An argument for the existence of God that is based on evidence of such unexplained events proceeds as follows. Since these events cannot be explained in ordinary terms, they are miracles. Miracles by definition can only be explained in terms of some supernatural power. The most plausible supernatural explanation of miracles is that God caused them to occur. Hence it is probable that God exists.

Some form of the argument from miracles has been used by philosophers and theologians down through the ages either to prove the existence of God or more commonly to support the truth of some particular religion. For example, both Augustine and Aquinas[5] in the Christian tradition, Philo Judaeus[6] in the Jewish tradition, and Avicenna[7] in the Islamic tradition appealed to miracles. Indeed, the belief that the truth of the Christian religion can be proved on the basis of miracles has been a dogma of the Catholic Church since the third session of the First Vatican Council in 1870.[8] Although belief in the existence of miracles has been deemphasized in recent years by sophisticated Christian theologians,[9] even today most Christian theologians have not given up the belief that Jesus was miraculously resurrected.[10] Further, there are still philosophers of religion who believe that the argument provides some support for theism. Thus Richard Swinburne in *The Existence of God*[11] maintains that it provides support for the hypothesis that God exists, and Richard Purtill in *Thinking About Religion: A Philosophical Introduction to Religion* argues for a limited use of the argument.[12]

The Concept of Miracles

Before we attempt to evaluate the argument from miracles, it is important to be clear on what a miracle is and what it is not. A miracle is not simply an unusual event. There are many unusual events that are not considered miracles; for example, snow flurries in July in Boston and a newborn baby weighing more than 11 pounds. Nor is a miracle just an event that cannot be explained by currently known scientific laws. After all, among the many such events that are not considered miracles are the occurrences of cancer and birth defects.

What then is a miracle? Traditionally it is defined as a violation of a law of nature.[13] However, this traditional account has a serious problem that precludes its being adopted here. Consider a possible world where a god brings about some event, such as a cure of someone's cancer, that cannot be explained by any law yet known to science. However, suppose that in this world the god's action is governed by a law that governs the powers of gods. We could say that in this world a miracle had occurred but there was no violation of any law in that the god's actions are themselves governed by laws.

It is for this reason that I provisionally define a miracle as an event brought about by the exercise of a supernatural power.[14] This definition is compatible with a miracle violating no law. But what is a supernatural power? It is one that is markedly superior to those powers possessed by humans. Supernatural powers are possessed by supernatural beings: gods, angels, Superman, devils.[15] If supernatural beings exist, the powers they possess need not be in violation of the laws of nature. Indeed, one could imagine these abilities being governed by causal laws. As philosophers of science have commonly understood such laws, they are true universal statements that support counterfactual inferences and perhaps meet other technical requirements such as substitutivity. There is no reason why there could not be true generalities about supernatural beings and their powers that fulfill these conditions.

One can think of the situation in this way.[16] Nature in its broadest sense, nature$_b$, includes all entities (supernatural and natural) and their activities (determined by natural and supernatural powers). Thus nature$_b$ comprises the sum total of entities and their causal interactions. The only things not included in nature$_b$ are entities that are incapable of any causal interaction, such as numbers or sets. All entities and their causal interactions in nature$_b$ are governed by causal laws.

Nature in a narrow sense, nature$_n$, consists of the realm of human and subhuman entities and their powers. Nature$_n$ is part of nature$_b$ and, if there are no supernatural entities or powers, is identical with it. Miracles, on this view, do not go beyond nature$_b$; they go beyond nature$_n$. Or, to put it in a different way, miracles cannot be explained by laws governing nature$_n$; they might be explained by laws governing nature$_b$. If there are laws governing nature$_b$ that go beyond nature$_n$, these laws are not investigated by science.

Now, it may be objected that if supernatural beings such as a theistic God exist, their powers are not governed by causal laws. If this were so, our definition would not be affected. We could still say that it is not part of the *meaning* of "miracle," that it is a violation of a law of nature. After all, there could be supernatural beings who perform miracles whose actions are governed by causal laws. If God's actions are not governed by laws, then miracles would violate laws of nature$_n$, and nature$_b$ would not be governed by causal laws. But this would not mean that by definition miracles were violations of natural laws.

On the traditional view, miracles are nonrepeatable as well as being violations of natural law,[17] but I reject this characterization too. On my definition there is no *a priori* reason why a miracle cannot be repeated numerous times.[18] For example, it is not logically impossible for a miracle worker to bring many people back to life. Indeed, so-called faith healers such as W. V. Grant and Oral Roberts have allegedly brought about numerous miracles of the same type. One might question the truth of these claims,[19] but there is nothing incoherent in the stories. One cannot say that the stories are false simply because the "miracle" was repeated. But if nonrepeatability is part of the definition of a miracle, one could.

The Probability That God Exists, Given the Existence of Miracles

We are now ready to begin an evaluation of the argument from miracles. The first thing to be considered is whether the existence of miracles would in fact support the hypothesis that God exists. Let us suppose that miracles in the sense defined above—that is, events brought about by the exercise of a supernatural power—do occur. Would this be good evidence for the existence of God? To state my answer briefly, it would not be, since miracles might be the result of the actions of other supernatural beings besides God.

The question must be considered more carefully, however. By "evidence for the existence of God" is meant inductive evidence in the sense that was characterized earlier. Let us consider whether H_1 (= God exists) is inductively supported by E (=Miracles have occurred). Following Swinburne,[20] let us distinguish two types of inductive arguments for miracles: C-inductive arguments and P-inductive arguments. In a good C-inductive argument,

(1) $P(H_1/E\&K) > P(H_1/K)$

where K is the background knowledge and $P(p/q)$ means that p is probable relative to q. In a good P-inductive argument,

(2) $P(H_1/E\&K) > P(\sim H_1/E\&K)$.

Now, (1) is true if and only if

(3) $P(E/H\&K) > P(E/K)$

so long as $P(H/K) \neq 0$. In turn, (3) is equivalent to

(4) $P(E/H_1\&K) > P(E/\sim H_1\&K)$.

One can immediately see a problem with (4). It is completely unclear why one should suppose that (4) is true. After all, $\sim H_1$ can be interpreted as a disjunction of hypotheses consisting of H_1's rivals. Included in this disjunction would be hypotheses that postulate finite but very powerful beings that have as their basic motive the desire to work miracles. The probability of E relative to these hypotheses about finite miracle workers would be one. The probability of E relative to other members of this disjunction would vary from zero to near one. There is no *a priori* reason to suppose that the probability of E relative to the entire disjunction would be less than the probability of E relative to H_1. It is important to see that:

$P(E/H_1\&K) \neq 1$.

That is, the hypothesis of theism does not entail the existence of miracles. Swinburne, for example, maintains only that miracles are probable given God's existence—how probable is unclear. The crucial question is whether miracles are more probable if theism is false. In his analysis Swinburne wrongly seems to suppose that the only rival to theism is naturalism. But there are numerous rival supernatural hypotheses that would explain the existence of miracles.[21]

Furthermore, some of the miracles that are reported in the Christian tradition seem to be better explained by non-Christian supernatural hypotheses. Some of the miracles performed by Christ, such as driving the demons into the Gadarene swine and cursing the fig tree, seem difficult to reconcile with belief in a kind and merciful God.[22] Moreover, a miracle by definition cannot be explained by any law governing nature$_n$. As such, the existence of miracles cannot be explained by science and indeed is an impediment to a scientific understanding of the world. Furthermore, there are great difficulties and controversies in identifying miracles. Thus whatever good effects miracles might have, they also impede, mislead, and confuse. A benevolent and all-powerful God would seemingly be able to achieve His purposes in ways that do not have these unfortunate effects. Moreover, some miracles seem to happen capriciously (for example, some people are cured and some are not), while other miracles seem trivial and unimportant (for example, bleeding statues and stigmata). They are not what one would have antecedently expected from a completely just and all-powerful being.[23]

So even if the existence of miracles is taken for granted, a good C-inductive argument for H_1 remains uncertain.[24] Thus even if one assumes that miracles exist, it is unclear whether this would support the hypothesis that God exists more than its negation.

Naturalism versus Supernaturalism and the Existence of Miracles

Is there any reason to suppose that miracles do exist? And can we answer this question without a prior commitment to a general metaphysical position? C. S. Lewis, a well known Christian writer, maintains in *Miracles* that in order to assess whether miracles exist, it is first necessary to decide between naturalism and supernaturalism. He argues:

> It by no means follows from Supernaturalism that Miracles of any sort

do in fact occur. God (the primary thing) may never in fact interfere with the natural system He has created. . . . If we decide that Nature is not the only thing there is, then we cannot say in advance whether she is safe from miracles or not. . . . But if Naturalism is true, then we know in advance that miracles are impossible: nothing can come into Nature from the outside because there is nothing outside to come in, Nature being everything. . . . Our first choice, therefore, must be between Naturalism and Supernaturalism.[25]

His argument can perhaps be reconstructed as follows. Appeal to neither historical evidence nor personal experience will prove that miracles exist if we have already decided that miracles are *a priori* impossible or unlikely. One can decide that they are *a priori* impossible or unlikely only if one has decided that naturalism is correct. On the other hand, if one maintains that miracles are *a priori* possible or at least not *a priori* improbable, one has accepted supernaturalism.

If Lewis is correct, then the evidence of miracles could not provide any independent support for supernaturalism, since in order to establish the existence of miracles one would already have to assume supernaturalism. Lewis's position, if accepted, would perhaps do more to undermine the argument from miracles than any naturalistic critique of this argument. But should it be accepted?

Lewis is certainly right to suppose that in considering the question of whether miracles exist there is a danger that one will appeal to *a priori* arguments and assumptions. But the solution to this problem is not to decide on naturalism or supernaturalism beforehand. Rather, one must attempt to reject the *a priori* arguments and instead base one's position on inductive considerations. Lewis has not shown that this is impossible. Thus he has not shown that one must choose between naturalism and supernaturalism before investigating the possibility of miracles.

Moreover, when Lewis attempts to provide reasons for choosing supernaturalism over naturalism (N) he fails miserably. He defines N as the view that all events occurring in space and time are caused by earlier events, and this causal process is "going on, *of its own accord*";[26] that is, there is nothing outside this causal system or whole that intervenes or interrupts the causal process.[27] N is incompatible with both rational reasoning[28] and ethical ideals and judgments, he maintains.[29] If N is true, no one could argue for its truth and no naturalist has any business advocating ethical principles. Thus N is self-refuting, and naturalists are inconsistent.

However, Lewis's arguments for these remarkable theses are either very weak or nonexistent. His argument for the first claim can be reconstructed in this way:[30]

(1) If N is true, all our thinking must be explicated in terms of cause and effect.

(2) If all our thinking must be explicated in terms of cause and effect, then N can give no account of rational inference.

(3) If N can give no account of rational inference, then a naturalist cannot know that N is true.

(4) If a naturalist cannot know that N is true, there can be no justification for believing N.

(5) Therefore, if N is true, there can be no justification for believing N.

The crucial premise is (1), and it is difficult to understand why Lewis holds it. For some reason Lewis seems to suppose that naturalists must distinguish different kinds of thinking (for example, rational and irrational) in *completely* causal terms. But they do not. There is no reason why naturalists cannot use terms such as truth, validity, and probability to explicate rational thinking. Indeed, this is precisely what recent naturalists have done.[31]

The argument for the second claim follows similar lines and is really a special case of the first argument.

(1') If N is true, then all moral judgments are unjustified.

(2') If all moral judgments are unjustified, good and evil are illusions.

(3') If good and evil are illusions, then naturalists are inconsistent when they advocate the good of humanity as an ethical ideal.

(4') Therefore, if N is true, then naturalists are inconsistent when they advocate the good of humanity as an ethical ideal.

Here again the problem is premise (1'), for there is no reason to suppose that it is true. It seems to rest either on the first argument that N cannot give an account of reasoning (hence naturalists can give no account of moral reasoning) and/or on a mistaken view of what ethical naturalists hold. Most ethical naturalists simply do not believe the view that there is no such thing as right or wrong, as Lewis seems to claim.[32] It is significant that Lewis does not cite *one* naturalist who holds the view he attributes to N.

I conclude that it is not necessary to choose between naturalism and supernaturalism prior to answering the question as to whether miracles exist. Moreover, supposing it is necessary, Lewis's arguments for rejecting naturalism are unsound.

The Difficulty of Showing the Existence of Miracles

Having considered the question of whether God's existence is inductively supported by the existence of miracles, I remain skeptical. Furthermore,

Lewis's argument that one must decide between supernaturalism and naturalism before one can decide whether miracles exist is not compelling. The question remains, however, whether there is any reason to suppose that miracles do in fact exist.

David Hume gave a general argument against the existence of miracles in "Of Miracles."[33] According to one standard interpretation, Hume does not attempt to show that miracles are *a priori* impossible but rather that it is *a priori* impossible to have strong evidence for their existence. What does Hume mean by a miracle? On his view a miracle is a violation of a law of nature. Consequently, someone who argues that event E is a miracle has two burdens that are impossible to meet simultaneously:[34] to show that E has taken place *and* that E violates a law of nature. Consider the assumed law of nature L*:

(L*) No person has been brought back to life.

(L*) has been confirmed by the deaths of billions of people; the evidence is overwhelming. Now consider the hypothesis (H*):

(H*) Some people have been brought back to life.

If we had good evidence for (H*), this would disconfirm (L*). But we cannot have such evidence. The evidence that could support (H*) is based on human testimony, but even at its best it is subject to error. Thus there is no uniform relation in our experience between human testimony that something is so and its being so. However, our evidence for (L*) must be stronger than this. Since (L*) is a law of nature, there is a uniform relation in our experience between a person's dying and this person's not returning to life. Consequently, in terms of our experience the probability of (L*) must be greater than the probability of (H*). The low probability of (H*) relative to (L*) may be argued for in another way. On some interpretations of Hume, this violation is by definition nonrepeatable.[35] If miracles are nonrepeatable, there could at most be one confirmatory instance of (H*). However, there are billions of confirmatory instances of (L*). Again, the probability of (L*) must be higher than the probability of (H*).

There is much that is wrong with this argument. It assumes that our evidence for the laws of nature is based not on testimony but on personal experience. But it is not. For example, our knowledge of the truth of (L*) rests in large part on the testimony of others. Indeed, most of us have little direct experience of dead people. Our limited direct experience is supplemented and expanded by fallible human testimony. However, if we understand experience to include not just an individual's direct experience of no dead person's coming back to life but the combined experience of civilization that is based in part on testimony, then the argument seems to beg the question against (H*). After all, there have been a few reports of people coming back to life. How can we know *a priori* that their probability is low?

Moreover, if Hume's argument assumes the nonrepeatability of miracles, then the argument is further weakened. There is no reason why (H*) could not be confirmed by many instances. However, there is no reason why (H*) must be confirmed by many instances for (H*) to be probable. One confirmatory instance is enough. Suppose there were reports of Gandhi's being brought back to life (E). If the evidence for E was extremely good, there would be excellent grounds for thinking that (H*) was true and (L*) was false. For example, if the witnesses to E were extremely numerous, independent, and reliable, if there was excellent physical evidence of Gandhi's being brought back to life—video pictures, EEG records that brain death had actually occurred, and so on—this might be enough to reject (L*) as a law of nature.[36]

This Humean argument fails to show that there is any *a priori* reason to suppose that it is impossible to have strong evidence for the existence of miracles. But there are excellent *a posteriori* reasons, suggested by Hume and others,[37] to suppose that the evidence is not good.[38] Indeed, anyone who would argue for the existence of miracles must overcome at least three *a posteriori* obstacles.

The believer in miracles must give reasons to suppose that the event E, the alleged miracle, will probably not be explained by any unknown scientific laws that govern nature$_n$. Since presumably not all the laws that govern nature$_n$ have been discovered, this seems difficult to do. The advocates of the miracle hypothesis must argue the probability that E will not be explained by future science, utilizing heretofore undiscovered laws that govern nature$_n$. Given the scientific progress of the last two centuries, such a prediction seems rash and unjustified.[39] In medicine, for example, diseases that were considered mysterious are now understood without appeal to supernatural powers. Further progress seems extremely likely; indeed, many so-called miracle cures of the past may one day be understood, as some have already been, in terms of psychosomatic medicine. Whether other mysterious phenomena will be explained by future scientific investigation is less certain, but the possibility cannot be ruled out. The luminous figure on the dome of St. Mary's Church of Zeitoun may be explained in the future by parapsychology. For example, D. Scott Rogo has suggested that the luminous figure can be explained in terms of the psychic energy generated by the Zeitounians' expectation of the visitation of the Virgin Mary.[40] At the present time Rogo's theory is pure speculation, and there are no known laws connected with the manifestations of psychic energy. But the believer in miracles must suppose that probably no laws about psychic energy *or any other laws* of nature$_n$ will be discovered that could explain the luminous figure.

Believers in miracles may argue that some events not only are unexplained in terms of laws governing nature$_n$ but are in conflict with them. Someone who walks on water has done something that not only is not explained by the laws governing nature$_n$ but is in conflict with those laws. But then, in order to explain the event, it is necessary to appeal to the laws governing nature$_b$. The ability to walk on water indicates the causal influences of a supernatural power that goes beyond the working of nature$_n$.

The difficulty here is to know whether the conflict is genuine or is merely apparent. This is the second great obstacle for believers in miracles. They must argue that the conflict is more probably genuine than apparent, but this is difficult to argue, for there are many ways that appearances can mislead and deceive in cases of this sort.

One way in which an apparent conflict can arise is by means of deception, fraud, or trickery. The difficulties of ruling out hoax, fraud, or deception are legend. We have excellent reason today to believe that some contemporary faith healers use fraud and deceit to make it seem that they have paranormal powers and are getting miracle cures.[41] These men have little trouble in duping a public that is surely no less sophisticated than that of biblical times. Even in modern parapsychology, where laboratory controls are used, there is great difficulty in ruling out explanations of the results in terms of fraud. By various tricks, trained experimenters in ESP research have been deceived into thinking that genuine paranormal events have occurred.[42] Parapsychologists themselves have resorted to fraud—so-called experimenter fraud—to manufacture evidence favorable to the reality of ESP. It takes the most stringent controls, the use of experts such as magicians trained in detecting fakery, and insistence on independent investigators in order to have confidence that the positive results in ESP research are not based upon deceit. Thus when eyewitnesses report that they have seen yogis levitating, even when these reports are accompanied by photographs, they must be treated with skepticism unless there is excellent reason to rule out the possibility of fraud and hoax on the part of the yogi as well as of the witness to the event.

If it takes control and precaution today in scientific laboratories in order to eliminate fraud and deceit, what credence should we give to reports of miracles made in biblical times by less educated and less sophisticated people without systematic controls against fraud?[43] The plausible reply would be: "Very little." One surely must ask: Did Jesus really walk on water or only appear to because he was walking on rocks below the surface?[44] Did Jesus turn the water into wine, or did he only appear to because he had substituted wine for water by some clever trick? The hypothesis that Jesus was a magician has been seriously considered by some biblical scholars.[45] The success of some contemporary faith healers and psychic wonders in convincing the public by the use of deception and fraud indicates that it was possible for Jesus, if he was a magician, to do the same.

Further, alleged miracles may not be due to some trick or fraud but to a misperception based on religious bias. People full of religious zeal may see what they want to see, not what is really there. We know from empirical studies that people's beliefs and prejudices influence what they see and report.[46] It would not then be surprising that religious people who report seeing a miraculous event have projected their biases onto the actual event. Did Jesus still the storm (Matt. 8.23–27), or did the storm by coincidence happen to stop when "he rose and rebuked the wind and the sea"? And did witnesses in their religious zeal "see" him stilling the storm?

In addition, religious attitudes often foster uncritical belief and acceptance. Indeed, in a religious context uncritical belief is often thought to be a value, doubt and skepticism a vice. Thus a belief arising in a religious context and held at first with only modest conviction may tend to reinforce itself and develop into an unshakable conviction. It would hardly be surprising, then, if in this context some ordinary natural event were seen as a miracle.

For another thing, an event that is not a miracle may appear like one if the observer has incomplete knowledge of the law governing nature$_n$ that appears to be violated. A scientific law holds only in a known range of conditions, not in all conditions. Thus Boyle's law holds only for gases in a specific temperature range; Newton's laws only correctly predict the mass of a body at accelerations not close to the speed of light. Often the range of application of a law becomes known with precision only years after the law itself is first formulated. Thus consider some physiological and psychological laws governing sight that seem to conflict with the apparent miracle of a faith healer's restoring someone's sight. This law may hold only in a fixed range of applications, and in special circumstances other laws governing nature$_n$ that explain the restoration of sight may hold. Both sorts of laws may be derivable from a comprehensive, but as yet unknown, theory. The advocates of miracles must maintain that an explanation of the event in terms of such a theory is less likely than an explanation by some supernatural power.

However, even if one shows it is more likely than not that some event is in conflict with deterministic scientific laws governing nature$_n$, this would not mean it is more likely than not that the event is a miracle. In other words, it would not show that the event could only be explained by the laws governing nature$_b$.

This brings us to the third great obstacle: What we thought were strictly deterministic laws may in fact be statistical laws. Since statistical laws are compatible with rare occurrences of uncaused events, the events designated as miracles may be wrongly designated since they may be uncaused—that is, they may be neither naturally nor supernaturally determined. Advocates of the miracle hypothesis, then, must show that the existence of miracles is more probable than the existence of uncaused events.

In sum, the advocates of the hypothesis that event E is a miracle (H_m) must show that H_m is more probable than the following:

(H_s) Event E will be explained by future scientific progress when more laws governing nature$_n$ are discovered.

(H_g) Event E seems incompatible with laws that govern nature$_n$ but it is not.

(H_u) Event E is uncaused.

There is no easy way to assess the comparative probabilities that are involved. However, as we have already seen, the progress of science, the history of deception and fraud connected with miracles and the paranormal, and the history of gullibility and misperception all strongly suggest that (H_s) and (H_g) are better supported than (H_m).

It is less clear what one should say about the comparative probability of (H_m) and (H_u). Both seem unlikely in the light of the evidence. But it is certainly not clear that (H_u) is less likely than (H_m). On the one hand, science already allows indeterminacy on the micro level—for example, in quantum theory. On the other hand, macro indeterminacy, the sort of indeterminacy that would be relevant to explaining miracles, is no less incompatible with the present scientific world view than it is with (H_m). At the very least one can say that there is no reason to prefer (H_m) over (H_u) on probabilistic grounds.

Evidence of Miracles in One Religion as Evidence Against Contrary Religions

In a well-known passage in the *Inquiry*, David Hume says:

Let us consider, that, in matters of religion, whatever is different is contrary; and that it is impossible the religions of ancient Rome, of Turkey, of Siam, and of China should, all of them, be established on any solid foundation. Every miracle, therefore, pretended to have been wrought in any of these religions (and all of them abound in miracles), as its direct scope is to establish the particular system to which it is attributed, so has it the same force, though more indirectly, to overthrow every other system. In destroying a rival system, it likewise destroys the credit of those miracles, on which that system is established; so that all the prodigies of different religions are to be regarded as contrary facts, and the evidence of these prodigies, whether strong or weak, as opposite to each other.[47]

Hume has been interpreted as claiming in this argument that every alleged miracle whose occurrence would be evidence in favor of a given religion is such that its occurrence would be evidence against any religion contrary to the first. He has also been interpreted as arguing that the evidence in favor of the existence of a miracle (which would constitute evidence for one religion) would be evidence against the occurrence of any miracle (which would constitute evidence in favor of a contrary religion).

Put more formally, it has been argued that Hume is maintaining the validity of two arguments.[48] The first argument is as follows:

(1) E_1 increases the probability of H_1 more than H_2.
(2) H_1 and H_2 are contraries.

(3) Therefore, E_1 decreases the probability of H_2.

The second argument is as follows:

(1') E_1 is evidence for H_1 and against H_2.
(2') E_2 is evidence for H_2 and against H_1.
(3') H_1 and H_2 are contraries.

(4') Therefore, E_1 is evidence against E_2 and conversely.

However, both of these arguments are invalid.

Consider the following counterexample to the first argument form. Suppose that the fact that a .45 caliber gun was used to murder Smith (E) is evidence that Evans is the murderer (H_1). (We suppose Evans is a suspect and always uses a .45 caliber gun.) Suppose further that H_2 (Jones is the murderer) is a contrary to H_1. Evidence E may still support H_2 although not as strongly. (We know that Jones uses a .45 caliber only 80 percent of the time.)

Consider the following counterexample to the second argument form. Let H_1 and H_2 represent what they did in the preceding example. Evans's fingerprints on the gun are evidence for H_2 and against H_1. Jones's footprints at the scene of the crime are evidence for H_2 and against H_1. But the one piece of evidence is not evidence against the other piece of evidence.

In the religious context, Jesus' walking on water (E_1) may be evidence for the truth of Christianity (H_1) but also for the truth of Hinduism (H_2), since Hindus might consider Jesus a manifestation of the absolute, not an incarnation of a personal God. A Baal priest curing a blind man (E_2), itself evidence for the hypothesis (H_3) that Baal is the supreme god, may support the fact that a priest of Zeus could cure a blind man, since we now have evidence that priests sometimes cure blind men. This in turn would be indirect evidence that the report that a priest of Zeus cured a blind man was true (E_3), which in turn would be evidence that Zeus was the supreme god (H_4).

When it is interpreted in the above way, Hume's two-part argument is invalid, but according to a different interpretation at least the first part of the argument is valid.[49] In the passage cited above, Hume's words suggest not just that the miracles of one religion make that religion more probable than it was before the occurrence of the miracles, but that the miracles make the religion more probable than not. Recall that he says it is impossible that rival religions should be "established on any solid foundation" by the evidence from miracles. Construed in this way, his argument becomes:

(1) Miracles M_1, M_2, . . . M_n occurring in the context of religion R_1 provide evidence that R_1 is more probable than not. [$P(R_1, M_1, M_2, . . . M_n) > 0.5$]
(2) Religion R_1 and religion R_2 are contraries.

---

(3) Therefore, R_2 is less probable than not. [$P(R_2, M_1, M_2, . . . M_n) < 0.5$]

However, a similar argument could be used to show that R_1 is less probable than not by citing other miracles that occur within the context of R_2. Hume was therefore correct to suppose that the miracles of one system can "destroy" rival systems. Of course, one could escape from Hume's argument by maintaining that the evidence of the miracles of one religion does not make it more probable than not but only more probable than it was without this evidence. However, Hume was no doubt correct to suppose that at least in his day the existence of the miracles of one religion was often supposed to make that religion more probable than not—that is, to use his words, to establish that religion on a solid foundation. What advocates of this way of arguing overlooked was that it could also be used to establish rival systems and thus indirectly "destroy" their own system.

What about the second part of Hume's argument: that the evidence of the miracles of one religion destroys the credibility of the evidence of miracles in another religion? Here Hume was clearly wrong, and I know no way of revising Hume's argument that is in keeping with its spirit. This is not to say that one cannot argue from the problematic nature of miracles in the context of one religion to their problematic nature in another. But what Hume was apparently trying to do was to argue thus: If evidence E_1 in religion R_1 allows us to show that R_1 is more probable than not, and if evidence E_1 in religion R_2 allows us to show that R_2 is more probable than not, then E_1 makes E_2 improbable and E_2 makes E_1 improbable. This inference is wrong. But it would not be wrong to argue that since the evidence of alleged miracles associated with, say, the Christian religion is weak, then probably the evidence for miracles in other religions is also weak. This would be a straightforward inductive argument, and its strength would be a function of the representative nature of evidence for Christian miracles. If such evidence is not atypical of miracles in other religions and the evidence is weak, then one is justified in making such an inference. Unfortunately, in the above-quoted passage Hume does not seem to be giving this completely sound argument.

Miracles at Lourdes

So far we have considered in a general way the difficulty in determining whether an event is a miracle. It would be useful now to relate the problems just outlined to a concrete case. In modern times the most famous occurrences of alleged miracles have been at Lourdes in France. These are probably the best documented and most carefully considered in history. If these alleged miracles are suspect, we would have good ground for maintaining that other claims of miracles—in more distant times, when superstition prevailed and objective documentation was either nonexistent or at least much less in evidence—should not be taken seriously.

It all began in February 1858, when a 14-year-old uneducated girl named Bernadette Soubirous, while collecting wood near the grotto of Massabielle in Lourdes, allegedly saw a beautiful lady wearing a white dress with a blue sash, with a yellow rose on each foot and a yellow rosary. Bernadette allegedly saw the Lady of the Grotto 18 times. Speaking the local patois, the Lady told Bernadette to pray for sinners and to tell the priest to have a chapel built. She also said that she wished people to come to the grotto in procession. It was claimed by those in attendance that during one session with the Lady of the Grotto, spring water miraculously came from the ground when Bernadette touched it. In another incident, Bernadette knelt before the Lady of Grotto with her hand cupped around the flame of a candle. Those in attendance claimed that the candle slipped out of place, "causing the flames to dance between Bernadette's fingers for a good ten minutes."[50] Bernadette never flinched, it was said, and the fire did not burn her. On another occasion Bernadette claimed that the Lady said, "I am the Immaculate Conception."

Naturally, Bernadette's claims caused a great stir at the time. She was denounced by skeptics as a fraud, yet many people flocked to the grotto to see her transfixed by her own vision. After a four-year inquiry the Roman Catholic Church declared that Bernadette's vision was the Virgin Mary. Pilgrims, mostly from the surrounding area, began to visit the shrine that had been built there eight years after Bernadette's first vision. By 1947 more than a million people were coming from all parts of France. In 1979, the centennial year of Bernadette's death, about 4.5 million people visited Lourdes—only one-third of them from France. Although the Lady of the Grotto never said to Bernadette that people would be cured at Lourdes, several cures were reported at the very beginning of the pilgrimages to Lourdes: A stone mason with one blind eye applied earth moistened from the spring to his eye, and his sight was restored a few days later; a mother dipped her paralyzed son into the spring, and he was instantly cured.

Lourdes is unique among Catholic shrines where miracles are supposed to occur, for only at Lourdes is there a definite procedure for investigating and recognizing miracles. The procedure is this:[51]

(1) A person whose health is dramatically altered by a trip to Lourdes may come before the medical bureau at Lourdes. The bureau has one full-time physician, who is joined in examining and interrogating the pilgrims by other doctors who happen to be visiting Lourdes at the time.

(2) If a dossier (an official medical file) is to be started, the person alleged to be cured must have a "complete" medical record confirming the nature of the illness and dates of recent treatments. In order to rule out the possibility that the alleged cure was brought about by ordinary medical treatment the pilgrim has undergone, the effectiveness of the treatment must be known.

(3) Special criteria of recovery must be met. The illness must be life-threatening and must be a distinct organic disorder. The recovery must be sudden and unforeseen, and it must occur "without convalescence." There must be "objective evidence"—X-rays, blood tests, biopsies—that the pilgrim had the disease before becoming cured. No disease for which there is effective treatment is considered as a possible miracle. Further, the pilgrim must stay cured and is therefore required to return several times for reexamination.

(4) Cures that meet all these tests are submitted to an international medical committee, appointed by the bishop of the adjacent towns of Tarbes and Lourdes, that meets annually in Paris. The committee votes on one issue: Is the cure medically inexplicable?

(5) If the majority of the committee decides that the cure is inexplicable, the patient's dossier is given to the canonical commission headed by the bishop of the diocese in which the allegedly cured person lives. Only the church can make the final decision as to whether the event is a miracle— that is, whether God has intervened in the natural course of events.

Before we consider the application of this procedure in actual practice, a few points should be noted in the light of previous discussion. First, it is difficult to see how the international committee that meets annually in Paris has the competence to decide if a cure is scientifically inexplicable in any absolute way—that is, in terms of nature$_n$. At best this committee would only have the competence to decide if the cure is scientifically explicable in terms of current knowledge of nature$_n$. This committee does not know what the future development of medical science will be; thus any judgment it makes about the absolute inexplicability of a cure in terms of nature$_n$ can and should have no particular authority.

In order to judge whether the cure is a miracle, one must be justified in believing that it will never and can never be explained in scientific terms—that is, in terms of nature$_n$. But would the committee have the competence to predict that, in the light of the evidence, probably no cure will ever be found? Given the rapid advances in medical knowledge, it is difficult to see that they would. Thus this committee's judgments exceed its scientific competence; indeed, a judgment of the committee *must* exceed its competence in order for it to be relevant to assessing whether a particular cure is a miracle.

Second, even if the international committee's judgment were justified that a particular cure was scientifically inexplicable in some absolute sense, the church seems to have no rational basis for making the final judgment that (a) the cure was a miracle and (b) the miracle was caused by God. As we have already seen, the cure could be uncaused. If so, it would be inexplicable in principle but not a miracle. Further, even if it was caused by some supernatural force or forces, this need not be the Christian God. Church officials who make the final decision about whether a cure is a miracle and, if so, is caused by God apparently ignore these alternatives. As a result, the final decision that the cure is a miracle explained by God's intervention is more like a leap of faith than a rational decision.

So far we have argued that although the doctors on the international committee do not have the competence to decide that a cure is inexplicable in terms of the law of nature$_n$ in some absolute way, they do have the competence to decide if a cure is inexplicable in terms of present scientific knowledge of nature$_n$. However, although they have this competence *in principle*, things may in fact be quite different. The doctors of the international committee may not have adequately applied the procedures specified.

One case in point is that of Serge Perrin, a French accountant, who in 1970 while at Lourdes experienced a sudden recovery from a long illness. After investigation the international committee said that Perrin was suffering from "a case of recurring organic hemiplegia [paralysis of one side of the body] with ocular lesions, due to cerebral circulatory defects."[52] They attempted to substantiate their findings in a 39-page document complete with a medical history of Perrin and his family, a review of the events leading up to his recovery, a detailed discussion of the symptoms of his illness, and supporting evidence including visual field diagrams and X-ray pictures. On the basis of its diagnosis and report, the international committee declared his recovery scientifically inexplicable; the church finally declared Perrin's cure to be a miracle, the 64th and latest official miracle in the history of Lourdes.

But was Perrin's cure inexplicable in terms of current scientific knowledge, let alone inexplicable in some absolute sense? In the light of recent evidence this seems dubious. A small sample of specialists in the United States who independently examined the document produced by the international committee of doctors found the cure of Perrin very suspicious, the data in the document highly problematic, the document obscure and filled with technical verbiage. For example, Donald H. Harter, professor and chairman of the department of neurology at Northwestern University Medical School in Chicago, found "an absence of *objective* neurological abnormalities." Drummond Rennie, associate professor of medicine at Harvard Medical School, maintained that the document presented by the international committee of doctors "was unscientific and totally unconvincing." Robert A. Levine, assistant clinical professor of ophthalmology at the University of Illinois, argued that the visual field diagrams presented in the document are mislabeled and inconsistent with the text of the document. He called the description as a whole "a lot of mumbo jumbo."[53]

The doctors who reviewed the document found a variety of problems. For example, although crucial laboratory tests such as a spinal tap and radioactive brain scan were standard in most hospitals for diagnosing the illness Perrin was said to have, they were not performed. The reviewers also considered the diagnosis of hemiplegia implausible; because he had right leg weakness *and* left visual and motor symptoms, more than one side of Perrin's brain had to be involved. In addition, symptoms of generalized constriction of his visual field and various sensorimotor disturbances suggested hysteria rather than an organic illness. Moreover, the American specialists who reviewed the document maintained that if there was an organic illness at all, multiple sclerosis was the most likely explanation of Perrin's symptoms. However, it is well known that multiple sclerosis has fleeting symptoms with periodic severe flare-ups followed by remissions that are sometimes complete.

There are also problems accepting the 63rd and penultimate official miracle in the history of Lourdes.[54] In this 1963 case, while at Lourdes a 22-year-old Italian, Vittorio Micheli, experienced a sudden recovery from a sarcoma type of tumor on his hip that had destroyed part of the pelvis, iliac, and surrounding muscles. The Lourdes medical bureau said X-rays confirmed that a bone reconstruction had taken place that was unknown in the annals of medicine. In 1976 the church officially recognized Micheli's recovery as a miracle.

However, as James Randi has pointed out in his investigation of this case, spontaneous regression of malignant tumors of the hip are not unknown in the annals of medicine.[55] To be sure, if Micheli's hip had been completely regenerated, this would indeed be unprecedented. But in order to verify that complete regeneration of the bone had taken place, exploratory surgery would have been necessary. X-rays cannot distinguish between a genuine regeneration and a regrowth known as a pseudoarthrosis, which is not unknown in the annals of medicine. But there is no record of any surgical procedure being done to validate Micheli's complete regeneration. Indeed, Randi notes that a case virtually identical to Micheli's was reported in 1978 in the Acta Orthopaedica Scandinavica.[56] In both instances no medical treatment was reported, the recovery took place in the same way, and the results were the same. However, in this latter case no claim was made that a miracle had occurred.

Medical authorities to whom Randi submitted Micheli's dossier for examination were incredulous at the medical treatment Micheli is reported to have received. For example, according to the dossier the hospital waited 36 days before it took an X-ray and 43 days before it performed a biopsy. Moreover, according to the dossier Micheli lived in a military hospital for ten months before he went to Lourdes, during which time he received no medical treatment of any kind except painkillers, tranquilizers, and vitamins. On the other hand, there are hints in the dossier that he did receive drugs and radiation. All this is extremely puzzling and surely casts doubt on the accuracy of the dossier.

The problems with the 1963 Micheli case and the 1970 Perrin case suggest that there is something badly amiss in the application of the procedures used by the Catholic Church for officially declaring something a miracle cure at Lourdes. An apparently questionable diagnosis of Perrin and a unsubstantiated judgment about Micheli's cure were accepted by the Lourdes medical bureau and the international committee.

Furthermore, there is a general problem connected with the procedures at Lourdes that I have not yet mentioned: the expertise of the doctors who first examine a pilgrim at Lourdes who claims to have recovered from an illness. The only qualification needed for a person to join the full-time medical bureau doctor in examining an allegedly cured pilgrim is that the person be a doctor and be visiting the shrine. But one might well question the objectivity of doctors who accompany the sick to

Lourdes or who visit Lourdes for other reasons. For one thing, doctors who visit Lourdes may well get caught up in the awe and excitement of the pilgrimage. For another, doctors who want to visit Lourdes may be initially disposed to accept miracle cures.

Every doctor has of course seen cures and remissions of diseases for which there is no explanation. Some of these diseases are self-limiting; others, like multiple sclerosis, have periods of flare-ups and remissions; still others have hysterical origins. It is difficult to separate hysterical symptoms from organic ones. The problem is made more difficult by the fact that hysterical symptoms may follow and take the place of organic ones. Moreover, in some illnesses, among them multiple sclerosis, physical and hysterical symptoms can exist at the same time. As we have seen, doctors in the United States who reviewed the report of the international committee suggested that Perrin suffered from hysteria or multiple sclerosis; it is conceivable that he had both types of symptoms.

If the alleged miracle cures at Lourdes are merely remissions or are cures based on natural processes that are not understood by the examining physicians at Lourdes, then one would expect that the number of inexplicable cures accepted by the Lourdes medical bureau would decline over the years as medical knowledge and sophistication increased. Indeed, this is precisely what has happened. From 1883 to 1947 nearly 5,000 cures were accepted as inexplicable by the physicians at the Lourdes medical bureau. This is approximately 78 per year. But from 1947 to 1980 only 28 cures were accepted as inexplicable, less than one per year.[57] And we may well expect that there will be further decreases in the "inexplicable" cures as medical knowledge increases. Such evidence surely casts doubt on the 64 officially declared miracles at Lourdes, especially the earlier ones. If the doctors at the Lourdes medical bureau had had the expertise of contemporary doctors, it is doubtful that many of the alleged miracles that occurred before 1947 would have made it through the first screening.

Since the cures at Lourdes are perhaps the best documented of all the so-called miracle cures, and their evidential value seems dubious, one may well have grave doubts about other claims of miracle cures that are less well documented.

Indirect Miracles

Earlier in this chapter I provisionally defined a miracle as an event brought about by the exercise of a supernatural power. However, there is a modern view of miracles that is not captured by this definition,[58] namely that God set up the world in such a way that an unusual event would occur to serve as a sign or message to human beings. Suppose, for example, that God set up the world so that at a certain time in history the Red Sea would part. The parting would be governed by the laws of nature$_n$,—for instance, a freak wind might part the sea. Given the circumstances surrounding the event, this parting would convey a message to religious believers. Although no direct intervention of God would be involved, God would be behind the scenes, setting up the particular working of nature$_n$ so that the Red Sea parted at the exact time needed to save His chosen people.

This view of miracles has become popular in modern philosophy, although it can be traced back at least to Maimonides. To accommodate this sort of case, my provisional definition is revised in the following way: A miracle is an event brought about by the direct or not necessarily direct exercise of a supernatural power to serve as a sign or communicate a message.[59] The second disjunct of the definition is necessary to account for miracles on the modern view (*indirect miracles* let us call them), and the first disjunct accounts for ones on the traditional view (let us call them *direct miracles*).

The difficulties with indirect miracles are apparent. Why believe that an event is a miracle in this indirect sense? Why not suppose that it is merely a coincidence? Moreover, even if one has good reason to suppose that something is an indirect miracle, there is no good reason to believe that God, rather than some other supernatural force, indirectly brought it about.

There is an additional problem. One wonders how much free will is left to humans on this view of miracles. Consider the parting of the Red Sea. If the event had occurred an hour earlier, it would have been of no help; if the event had occurred an hour later, it would have been too late to help the Israelites. This seems to entail that the Israelites, in order to be at the right place at the right time, could not have chosen any differently than they did. For example, if they had decided to rest a little longer along the way, God's plan would have been upset; the sea would have parted before they arrived.

This seems to conflict with the commonly held religious belief that humans have free will and that even God cannot know what they will decide, in that, given the notion of an indirect miracle, it is essential to know what human beings will decide so that the miracle will occur at the right time.[60]

Conclusion

I must conclude that there is no *a priori* reason for there not to be miracles—no reason even for there not to be good evidence for miracles. However, there are difficult *a posteriori* obstacles to surmount before one can claim that miracles have occurred in either the direct or the indirect sense. Furthermore, even if there were good reasons to suppose that miracles existed in either sense, this would not necessarily mean that the existence of miracles provides inductive support for theism. As we have seen, the existence of miracles provides inductive support for theism only if the existence of a miracle is more probable relative to theism and background information than it is relative to the negation of theism and background information. But it is not at all clear that it is. Thus the argument from miracles fails.

CHAPTER 8

Some Minor Evidential Arguments for God

In earlier chapters I critically examined the major arguments for the existence of an all-good, all-powerful, all-knowing God: the ontological argument, the cosmological argument, the teleological argument, the argument from religious experience, and the argument from miracles. In this chapter let us survey some of the less important epistemic arguments for the existence of God, which purport to show that the proposition that God exists is true or probable. Although these arguments do not have the stature of those considered so far, they cannot be ignored, for they are often appealed to by theists to justify their beliefs. It is impossible, of course, to survey all the minor arguments ever given that God exists. However, I will examine what are considered by scholars to be the most important of these.

The Argument from Common Consent

Philosophers and theologians such as Cicero, Seneca, the Cambridge Platonists, Gassendi, and Grotius have appealed to the common consent of humankind (the *consensus gentium*) as support for belief in the existence of God. Such an appeal is usually referred to as the argument from common consent.[1] Religious thinkers such as Rudolf Eisler rank the argument as fifth in importance[2] among the proofs for the existence of God, while John Stuart Mill has maintained that, as far as "the bulk of mankind" is concerned, this argument has had more influence than others with a sounder logical basis.[3] Although few professional philosophers today would advocate this argument, it is still used by popular religious apologists.[4] Let us examine three versions of the argument here.

(1) In the first version it is argued that belief in God is innate or

instinctive. It is then maintained that the best way to account for this fact is to suppose that God made His creatures in such a way that they would not be deceived.[5] There are two basic problems with this version of the argument: For one thing, there is no adequate evidence that the factual premise on which the argument rests is true. For another thing, if the factual premise is true, the existence of God is not thereby shown.

There is no good reason to suppose that belief in God is innate. In one sense of the term, a belief is innate if it is present to the mind at birth. In another sense a belief is innate if there is a disposition to acquire it without instruction, by simply being exposed to such facts as that there is sin.[6] Certainly, belief in God is not innate in the first sense, for there is no reason to think that small children believe in God. Moreover, the theory that belief in God is innate does not account for the presence of millions of atheists. The second interpretation of "innate" has similar problems. There is little reason to suppose that children always acquire their belief in God without instruction or training. Furthermore, the theory that belief in God is innate in the sense that there is a disposition to acquire it without instruction leaves unexplained why there are atheists. People who become atheists have been exposed to the same facts, such as that there is sin, as those who become theists. Yet these atheists did not acquire, or at least did not continue to hold, a belief in God. Either they never became theists or they became theists and later gave up their theistic beliefs.

The second problem with this argument is that even if one accepts the factual premise, it is not clear that the best way to account for the facts is to postulate that God has made humans in this way. One could argue that a much simpler explanation of the facts is to maintain that belief in God has survival value for humans. Thus the disposition to believe in God can be accounted for in terms of evolutionary theory.

(2) Another version of the argument maintains that there is an innate yearning for God,[7] and since our other yearnings have real objects, such as food, there must be a real object for this yearning. Even atheists, it is argued, have a yearning for God, although they cannot bring themselves to believe in God.

The problems with this version of the argument are similar to those with the first version. There is little evidence that people have an innate yearning for God in the same way that babies at birth have a yearning for food. Indeed, it is at least as plausible to suppose that any yearning for God is either acquired by explicit religious training or picked up from the religious society in which people live. Moreover, the theory that there is an innate yearning for God cannot account for those atheists who do not have any such yearning. Furthermore, even if the factual assumption on which the argument rests is accepted, the conclusion that there must be a real object of the yearning is unwarranted. Once again, the yearning for God may have survival value and hence may be explainable in evolutionary terms without any need to postulate a real object of the yearning.

(3) Some advocates of the argument from common consent have not maintained that there is anything innate in believing in God. Rather, they have maintained that the almost universal belief in God has been acquired by the use of reason. If this belief has been acquired by the use of reason and is false, our reason must be untrustworthy. But, the argument proceeds, our reason is basically trustworthy.[8] So belief in God is likely to be true.

One fundamental difficulty with this argument is the assumption that belief in God is almost universal. On the contrary, belief in God varies widely from country to country. For example, recent polls show that the percentage of people who do not believe in God in countries such as Japan, Scandinavia, West Germany, and France is surprisingly high.[9] Another problem with the argument is the assumption that belief in God is acquired by reason. There is good ground to suppose that most religious believers have acquired their convictions through religious indoctrination and socialization.[10] Further, given the assumption that belief in God is acquired by reason, certain facts seem difficult to explain. There are more nonbelievers among outstanding scientists than among the uneducated and scientifically untrained.[11] On the present view, how could this be accounted for? We could suppose that outstanding scientists tend to use their reason in matters of religion less than the scientifically uneducated do. However, this seems implausible.

The Moral Argument

The moral argument for the existence of God is the attempt to argue from human moral experience to the existence of God. Variants of this argument have been proposed by Immanuel Kant, W. R. Sorely, John Henry Newman, and A. E. Taylor.[12] Let us critically consider four versions of the argument.[13]

(1) One popular variant of the argument that is not usually given by professional philosophers but is used by popular apologists for religion begins with the premise that if people did not believe that a theistic God existed, they would not be moral or, at least, they would be less moral than they are now. This allegation is then held to provide an epistemic reason for believing in God. Indeed, it may be maintained that this fact, at least when combined with others, makes the existence of God probable.

The factual premise on which this argument is based is dubious, however. There is no reason to suppose that people would be less moral if they did not believe in God than if they did. As far as can be determined, atheists do not commit more violent crimes than do nonatheists. Nor are there fewer violent crimes in countries where belief in God is more widespread than in countries where it is less widespread. Moreover, even if this premise were true, it is not obvious that *by itself* this would support the conclusion that God exists. For example, it would not seem more likely that atheists would be less moral than theists on the hypothesis that God exists and background knowledge than on the background knowledge alone. Consequently, a C-inductive argument from the fact that atheists tend to be less moral than theists to the existence of God would not be possible. But what if this premise was combined with other premises? It is hard to see what other plausible premises combined with it could provide the conclusion that God exists. For example, one might argue that if a belief B is necessary for some worthwhile social outcome O, it is probably true. Since a belief in God is necessary for the worthwhile social outcome of moral behavior, then it is probably true. However, there does not seem to be adequate evidence for accepting the first premise of the argument.

(2) A more plausible moral argument for the existence of God given by some philosophers maintains that the objectivity of the moral law presumes that God exists. Only if God exists can there be objective and absolute moral truths; thus atheists, whether they realize it or not, have no justification for holding an objective and absolute view of morality. The view that objective moral truth presupposes God is expressed by Hastings Rashdall as follows:

> On a non-theistic view of the Universe . . . the moral law cannot well be thought of as having any actual existence. The objective validity of the moral law can indeed be and no doubt is *asserted*, believed in, and acted upon without reference to any theological creed; but it cannot be defended or fully justified without the presupposition of Theism.[14]

Even some atheists seem partly to agree. J. L. Mackie, for one, has suggested that if ethical properties were objective facts, this would be so strange and puzzling that it would call for a supernatural explanation.[15] Rashdall did not use the idea that the objectivity of morality presupposes the existence of God to demonstrate the existence of an all-good, all-powerful, all-knowing being—he apparently believed that a moral argument could only be used to prove the moral properties of a supernatural being whose existence was known in other ways. But W. R. Sorely uses an argument similar to Rashdall's as a sort of cosmological argument: The cause of objective moral facts must be God.[16] This argument can stated as follows:

(1) If morality is objective and absolute, then God exists.

(2) Morality is objective and absolute.

---

(3) Therefore, God exists.

What can one say about this argument? The first premise is unsupported. Sorely has not shown that ethical statements can only be objective and absolute given the presumption of theism. There have been various attempts to construct a naturalistic foundation of ethics that is both objective and absolute.[17] In order to prove his case, Sorely must show that these attempts are unsuccessful. He has done nothing to show this. Furthermore, Mackie is wrong to suppose that there must be something strange about objective ethical properties. If ethical properties were reducible to objective naturalistic properties, as ethical naturalists have argued, there would be nothing strange or puzzling about them.[18] Finally, even if the objective moral facts would call for *some* supernatural explanation, it would not entail theism. Alternative explanations are possible, including polytheism.

The second premise is not obviously true. Even if Sorely and Mackie are correct about premise (1), an objectivist account of ethics may well be unacceptable. Powerful arguments must be met in order to show that morality is objective and absolute.[19] Moreover, it does not follow from the fact, if it is one, that morality is not objective and absolute that only moral anarchy is warranted, as some theists seem to maintain. Subjectivists like Mackie are far from being moral anarchists.[20] Indeed, moral subjectivism or relativism is compatible with reasoned ethical debate and wide rational agreement.[21]

(3) In a version of the moral argument developed in *The Grammar of Assent*, John Henry Newman argues that our conscience provides us not only with a sense of right and wrong but with a call to duty that enforces our moral sense. When we go against the voice of conscience we feel ashamed and frightened. These emotions cannot be explained by appeal to inanimate things since they are associated with persons.[22] Newman argues:

> "The wicked flees, when no one pursueth"; then why does he flee? whence his terror? who is it that he sees in solitude, in darkness, the hidden chambers of his heart? If the cause of these emotions does not belong to this visible world, the Object to which his perception is directed must be Supernatural and Divine; and thus the phenomena of Conscience, as a dictate, avail to impress the imagination with the picture of a Supreme Governor, a Judge, holy, just, powerful, all-seeing, retributive, and is the creative principle of religion, as the Moral Sense is the principle of ethics.[23]

Thus Newman maintains that in order to explain the phenomena of conscience it is necessary to postulate God.

Two fatal objections can be raised against this argument. First, there are naturalistic explanations of the phenomena of conscience that are more plausible than a theistic one. For example, one obvious alternative explanation is that people internalize the moral precepts of their family or social group. Because of this internalization, when they go against these precepts they feel shame and fear.[24] Second, even if all naturalistic explanations fail, there are alternative supernatural explanations to theism, the most obvious of which is that the phenomena of conscience could equally well be explained by postulating a number of gods. But then, the phenomena of conscience give no unique support to theism over polytheism.

(4) In the version of the moral argument put forth by Kant, it is maintained that the highest good (*summum bonum*) includes moral virtue and happiness as the appropriate reward of virtue. Kant argues that it is our duty to seek to realize the highest good and that, if this is so, then it must be possible to realize it. He maintains, however, that this highest good cannot be realized unless there is "a supreme cause of nature"[25] that has the power to bring about a harmony between happiness and virtue. Thus God is a necessary postulate of practical reason, he argues.

However, it is by no means clear that the highest good is what Kant supposes. For example, one might well argue that being moral is its own reward and that happiness is irrelevant to the highest good. In addition, even if we grant for the sake of argument that Kant is correct about what the highest good is, it may still be possible to achieve the highest good without God. Perhaps it could be achieved by purely human efforts. Why would it not be possible to construct a society in which virtue is always rewarded? And even if this were not possible without supernatural help, it would still not be necessary to posit an all-powerful being, for a very powerful but finite God, or perhaps several finite gods, could do the job. Moreover, it is not necessary that the highest good be completely realizable in order for us to have a duty to seek to realize it. To make sense of the duty to seek to realize the highest good it is only necessary that it be possible to *some* extent to bring it about. It certainly is possible to realize Kant's highest good to some extent without any supernatural help.[26]

The Argument from Reward

It is sometimes argued by popular apologists for religion that people who believe in God and live virtuous lives are happier than people who do not. This can only be explained by supposing that their happiness is God's reward for their faith and virtue.[27]

Perhaps the most basic problem with this argument is that there is no reason to suppose that faithful and virtuous believers are happier than nonbelievers. Indeed, one of the fundamental problems of a religious life is to explain why bad things happen to good, honest, God-fearing people. In a bestselling book Harold Kushner argued:

> The misfortunes of good people are not only a problem to the people who suffer and their family. They are a problem to everyone who wants to believe in a just and fair and livable world. They inevitably raise questions about the goodness, the kindness, and even the existence of God.[28]

Even if religious believers are happier than nonbelievers, there may be an alternative explanation of this fact. As Michael Scriven has pointed out: "It is easy to see that there might be another and more natural explanation for this supposed effect, namely, that the mere belief makes them happier, just as the belief of members of a football team that their team is the best in the country may make them feel and play better even if it does not make the team the best, i.e. even though it is not true."[29] Furthermore, even if there are no alternative naturalistic explanations, there are competing supernatural explanations. The happiness of believers could, for example, be explained by postulating a powerful but finite god or a number of finite gods.

The Argument from Justice

In the argument from reward it was assumed without adequate warrant that virtuous believers are happier than nonbelievers. In the present argument, given by popular apologists for religion, a more realistic assumption is made. It is assumed that in this world the virtuous are not always happy and are not always rewarded for their virtue and, in addition, that wicked people often prosper and go unpunished. It is then argued that the balance of justice must be restored somewhere in the universe. Since clearly this restoration does not occur in this life, there must be another life where virtue is rewarded and evil is punished. There must then be an afterlife in which people are judged and rewarded or punished and a God judges and administers these rewards and punishments.[30] A sophisticated variant of this argument is given by Kant. He maintains that in order to account for our day to seek to realize the highest good—virtue and human happiness as a reward for virtue— there must be an afterlife where the highest good is realized, immortal souls that are capable of infinite progress toward this realization, and a God who is the foundation of the entire process.[31]

There is no reason to suppose, however, that this is the sort of universe where injustice in one part of the universe is balanced by justice in another part. The assumption of a principle of cosmic justice is just as controversial as is the existence of God and can hardly be used in an argument to prove the existence of God. Furthermore, if there is a principle of cosmic justice operating in the universe, there is no necessity that it be controlled by an all-good, all-powerful, all-knowing being who created the universe. Cosmic justice in an afterlife could be administered by many gods who have little control over the rest of the universe. Alternatively, the laws of cosmic justice could operate without the control of any supernatural beings, much as the law of karma in Jainism is said to operate.[32]

Arguments from Scripture

Popular apologists for religion sometimes appeal to claims of the holy books of the major religions to support their views. For example, these apologists may point to the supernatural events reported in these books as evidence for the existence of God or may argue that, since these books claim to reveal God's word and are reliable, it is reasonable to conclude that God exists.

Insofar as such an appeal is meant to express an argument and is not simply an avowal of faith, it is very weak. If it relies on the existence of miracles reported in the holy scripture of different religions, it is heir to all the problems of the argument from miracles. If it relies on a consensus among the holy books of different religions, it also has serious problems. As we have seen, it is not true that all the major holy books claim to reveal God's word; for example, the holy books of Jainism and Buddhism apparently make no such claim. Furthermore, even when they do, the content of what they say differs. For example, both the Bible and the Koran claim to be the revealed word of God, yet they give different messages. Finally, when we confine ourselves to a particular religion such as Christianity and evaluate the evidential grounds for its major claims, there are further problems. For example, the virgin birth and Jesus' resurrection are two of the cornerstones of the Christian faith. Yet different gospels of the New Testament are inconsistent with one another, and there is no independent confirmation of these events in nonscriptural sources.[33]

The Argument from Consciousness

Materialism, the view that only matter exists, is one form of naturalism and is contrasted with theism. According to one popular form of materialism, all phenomena including mental events and mental properties can be accounted for by the laws of physics and chemistry. One way of doing this would be to reduce all mentalistic language to physicalistic language. Another way would be to explain mentalistic phenomena indirectly in

terms of the laws and theories of physics and chemistry by means of
psychophysical laws, which link physical events or processes to mental
events or processes. Some theists have maintained that materialism has
failed to give an adequate account of mental phenomena and that this
failure is indirect evidence for the truth of theism.

One well-known advocate of this position is Richard Swinburne.[34] He
argues that it is impossible to reduce mental events or properties to
physical events or properties and that any attempt to explain mental
events by psychophysical laws has serious problems. In particular, he says
that although there may be psychophysical correlations, they are too
"odd" to be accounted for by scientific laws. Swinburne also rejects dual-
ism, the view that mental and physical events cannot be explained in
terms of one another, as "a very messy world-picture."[35] He concludes
that particular psychophysical correlations must be explained by supposing that God simply chose to have brain states of a certain kind and
mental states of a certain kind correlated. An explanation of this kind in
terms of God's choice is a theological version of what Swinburne calls "a
personal explanation." Personal explanations are commonly used in our
everyday life and, according to Swinburne, are not reducible to scientific
ones. They involve a person's bringing something about through an
intentional act, and they provide a very natural explanatory connection
between the phenomena to be explained and the explanatory hypothesis.
According to Swinburne this is one of the main reasons why a personal
explanation is be preferred to a scientific one in the case of psychophysical
correlations. With a theistic personal explanation of psychophysical correlations there is a natural connection between the kind of brain event
and the kind of mental event specified by the correlation. God's intention
to bring about this correlation "binds" the two kinds of events together.[36]
Thus according to Swinburne, the best explanation of mental phenomena
is the theistic one and, consequently, mental phenomena provide more
inductive support for the theistic hypothesis than for its rivals.

This argument from consciousness has serious problems. First, the
difficulties that Swinburne finds with scientific nomological explanation
of psychophysical correlations either are not as serious as he supposes or
else are based on misunderstandings.[37] For example, the most serious
problem he finds with such explanations is that because of the very
different nature of brain states and mental states, it is difficult to see
how simple scientific laws could explain the diverse correlations between
them. He asks:

> How could brain-states vary except in their chemical composition and the
> speed and direction of their electro-chemical interaction, and how could
> there be a natural connection between variations in these respects and

variations in the kind of respects in which intentions differ—say, the difference between intending to sign a cheque, intending to square a circle, and intending to lecture for a half an hour? There does not seem to be the beginning of a prospect of a simple scientific theory of this kind and so of having established laws of mind–body interaction as opposed to lots of diverse correlations.[38]

Now, by using a parody of this argument one might maintain that it seems impossible to formulate scientific nomological explanations of the correlations between the fall of trees and the damage that results since there seems to be no simple and natural relation between the direction, force of impact, and so on of their fall and the diverse damage such as the killing of animals, the disrupting of electrical circuits, and the blocking of traffic that is brought about. There does not seem to be here "the beginning of a prospect of a simple scientific theory" as opposed to lots of diverse correlations. However, no one doubts that there are nomological explanations of the correlations between falling trees and damage. How can this be?

There is a problem here only if one misunderstands the sort of laws that can be used in such an explanation. It might be supposed, in order to explain the correlations, that there must be particular causal laws explicitly relating falling trees to blocked traffic and disruption of electrical circuits, but this assumption is false. Laws concerning falling bodies can be used to explain the correlation between some of the items covered by the description "disrupted electrical circuit" and some aspects of a tree's fall. Similarly, laws concerning electricity can be used to explain the correlation between the items and the lack of electric power, and so on. In other words, the complex whole can be broken down into component parts, and these can be explained separately.

The same approach can be used to explain mental phenomena. In the explanation of the intention to sign a check we need not expect there to be laws involving concepts such as check signing. Rather, the complex whole that is described by "signing a check" can be broken down into its component parts and explained separately. Once we look at the situation in this way the bulk of the difficulties noted by Swinburne dissolve. Other problems that Swinburne has with accepting the prospects of a successful materialistic explanation of mental phenomena seem to be due to his holding the incorrect belief that a materialist must actually provide a detailed scientific explanation of each mental phenomenon in contrast to simply maintaining that in each case there is such an explanation. Thus a materialist is not committed to some *particular* scientific explanation of mental phenomena but only to the thesis:

> For any mental phenomenon M there is at least one explanation E of M in terms of the laws and theories of physics.

Even if there are residual problems with accepting the thesis that materialistic explanations of mental phenomena can be successful, Swinburne's theistic alternative surely has its own problems. First of all, although personal explanations are familiar and natural in ordinary life, we know that the way one's intention brings about some action has a physiological basis. For example, when I intentionally move my finger it may *seem* that there is a direct connection between the intention and the movement. But we know that this connection is possible only because of a complex physiological causal relation of which I may be unaware between my intention and the movement of my finger. In the case of God there is no such relation. According to Swinburne, the relation between God's intention and the intentional action is direct and unmediated. Given our background knowledge of how personal explanations work in ordinary life, personal explanations of psychophysical correlations in terms of God's intentions seem improbable. All our evidence indicates that intentions do not directly cause physical events. How then can God's intentions adequately explain any correlation between mental events and brain events?

Moreover, even if one accepts theistic personal explanations in general, large questions remain about theistic personal explanations of psychophysical correlations in particular. As Mackie puts it:

> Has God somehow brought it about that material structures do now generate consciousness? But then is this not almost as hard to understand as that material structures do this *of themselves*? Or are we to regard each body–mind connection, for example the supervening of each state of perceptual awareness on the appropriate sensory input and neurophysiological disturbance, as the fulfillment of a fresh divine intention, so that sensory perception is, strictly speaking, an indefinitely repeated miracle so we have an endless series of divine interventions in the natural causal order? But further. . .Could not *omnipotency* superadd a faculty of thinking as easily to a block of wood as to a brain? If materialism has the difficulty in explaining how even the most elaborate neural system can give rise to consciousness, theism, with its personal explanations and direct intention-fulfillments, has at least as great a difficulty in explaining why consciousness is found *only* in them.[39]

In addition to all these problems, a supernatural personal explanation is compatible with the correlations between brain states and mental states being brought about by the intentional action of a finite god or a number of finite gods. Thus the argument from consciousness provides no unique support for an all-good, all-powerful, all-knowing being.

I conclude that Swinburne has not shown that theism is better supported by the fact of mental phenomena than by alternative hypotheses and consequently that the argument from consciousness fails.

The Argument from Providence

Some philosophers and theologians have argued that there is good reason to suppose God exists because ours is the sort of universe that provides for the basic needs of humans and animals. One some accounts, of course, such an argument would be classified as teleological. But not on all accounts. In particular, Swinburne does not consider an argument teleological that is based on the fact that the universe is hospitable to human and animal life. It would be possible to disregard Swinburne's classification, but I choose to follow his own terminology here and call such an argument the argument from providence.[40]

What is Swinburne's argument from providence? He argues that there are many other possible worlds that God *could* have actualized, but these would not have been the sort of world one would have expected God to create. The features of our world suggest that it is a "providential place";[41] in general outline it is just the sort of world one would have predicted that God would actualize. Thus our world is the sort of place where we humans can learn to provide for ourselves. For example, we can learn to use our reason to avoid the disasters that might result from following our unrestrained desires. Our world is also a place where human cooperation is mutually beneficial.

Swinburne has no trouble finding that these general features of our world are good. However, with the possibility of mutual aid comes the possibility of mutual harm. Swinburne also must argue that it is good that our world is a place where humans can harm one another, since if they could not they would have "only very limited responsibility for each other."[42] He considers other possible worlds that God could have actualized, but he finds that in each case our world is better. For example, God could have actualized a world that contains an unchanging set of immortal humanly free agents. The beings and the world would have imperfections, but these could be corrected in a finite amount of time. But after the world had been perfected the "agents would have nothing demanding to do."[43] Consequently, God has more reason to actualize other possible worlds. Another of these is one where humans could go on indefinitely perfecting themselves although they could not create new human beings. But this world would not be as good as one in which humans could "give birth to new agents" and form them "from scratch."[44] God could also have actualized a world where people live forever. Swinburne finds various reasons, however, why such a world would not be as good as one in which we die, the main one being that if humans lived forever, evil and powerful people would be able to make their victims suffer indefinitely. This would be incompatible with a good God, however;[45] there must be some limit to the length of human life in order to prevent infinite human suffering.

The plausibility of some of the key assumptions of this argument depends on an adequate solution to the problem of evil. In a later chapter this problem is considered at length. For now it must suffice to mention briefly a few problems with Swinburne's position. Note that Swinburne assumes that it is a good thing that humans can harm other humans, since if they could not they would have limited responsibility. But, as I argue later, God could actualize a world in which people would have this power (a good thing) and yet never exercise it (a better thing). Alternatively, God could actualize a world in which people would have the power to harm (a good thing), yet it would be much harder—but not impossible—to exercise the power in such a world than in ours, since humans would be less vulnerable to harm there than they are here (a better thing). Moreover, Swinburne says that an all-good God cannot allow even one person to live forever since this might permit powerful people to cause this one person to suffer forever. But the present world allows the descendants of one person to suffer forever for the wrongs of this person. It is difficult to see how an all-good God could allow the one type of indefinite suffering and yet not allow the other type. Unless Swinburne can answer questions of this sort, he cannot claim that this world is a "providential place" and, as such, just the sort of world one would expect there to be if God exists.

The Argument from Cumulative Evidence

A sophisticated religious believer might argue that the case for theism is multidimensional and that no one master argument will prove that God exists. Just as a comprehensive scientific theory is the best explanation for a wide range of experiences, so theism is the best explanation for our experiences in several different domains. On this view, theism is a powerful explanatory hypothesis; it brings together a large and diverse body of evidence from many areas in a coherent scheme and does so better than other theories do.[46] Let us call this the argument from cumulative evidence. In the works of two recent writers, Basil Mitchell[47] and Ian Barbour,[48] such an argument is not explicitly given but is suggested. Both Mitchell and Barbour argue that one can understand religion in quasi-scientific terms.

Although Mitchell does not develop a cumulative case for theism, using Thomas Kuhn's approach to science he suggests how such a case might be developed and how it makes sense of religious data. For example, Kuhn maintains that in scientific debates, schools that hold different paradigms are often slightly at cross-purposes with one another. Mitchell compares this to the debates between atheists and theists. Moreover, according to Kuhn, when a paradigm shift occurs in science there is a radical transformation in how one sees the world that is similar to a religious conversion. Even the language Kuhn uses to describe the experience of someone who undergoes a paradigm shift in science, Mitchell says, is reminiscent of a religious conversion.

Mitchell points out that Kuhn's theory of science has been criticized on the ground that if his account of paradigm shifts is accepted, it would lead to the irrationality of science. Would it not be possible to use the same sort of criticism against a cumulative case for theism interpreted along Kuhnian lines? For example, on one popular interpretation, Kuhn maintains that all criteria used in paradigm evaluation are paradigm-dependent. Thus there are no paradigm-independent criteria that can be used to evaluate competing paradigms. Consequently, one could argue against a Kuhnian interpretation of theism that, although theism may be given high marks as an explanatory theory judged in terms of *its* criteria, this would hardly show that it is a good explanatory theory in terms of neutral and objective criteria.

According to Mitchell, Kuhn does not hold that all criteria for theory evaluation in science are theory-dependent. In particular, Kuhn explicitly argues that criteria such as accuracy, simplicity, scope, and fruitfulness are used by both parties in a paradigm debate.[49] However, says Mitchell, Kuhn does maintain that there are no rules for applying these criteria. So the opposing parties in a paradigm debate may use the same criteria, but come out on different sides of the debate because they apply the criteria differently, and there does not seem to be any rational way (in the sense of the application of some objective rules) to reconcile the difference. Mitchell allows that another notion of rationality may be relevant and that this is implicit in Kuhn's account of the process involved in a scientific community's acceptance of a paradigm. Gary Gutting has characterized this notion of rationality in terms of the informed judgment of the community of trained scientists. This judgment, Gutting says, "is ultimately determined by the carefully nurtured ability of members of the scientific community to assess rationally the overall significance of a wide variety of separately inconclusive lines of argument."[50]

Barbour's views are very similar to Mitchell's. He argues that the epistemology of science and the epistemology of religion have significant similarities and that Kuhn's theory of science is relevant to religion. In particular, he maintains that although there are no rules for the application of criteria of paradigm choice, there are shared criteria[51] and paradigm-independent reasons for paradigm choice and that a cumulative case can be made for both scientific and religious theories.[52] Indeed, he goes beyond Mitchell in applying Kuhn's ideas to religion, maintaining that the notion of paradigm—a tradition transmitted through historical

exemplars—can be applied to religion.[53] According to Barbour this tradition is similar to the scientific world view (basic laws, ontology, methodology, and so forth) that is implicit in some specific scientific achievements
or exemplars (for example, Newton's work in mechanics). Just as a scientific world view that is implicit in its exemplars cannot be formulated in
an explicit set of rules or propositions, the religious world view or tradition that is implicit in its exemplars also cannot be formulated in an
explicit set of rules or propositions. Barbour's account of paradigms is
closely tied to the acceptance of a paradigm by a specific community
and to the acceptance of the paradigm through the recognition of past
achievements as exemplars for the life of the community. Thus both
scientists and religious believers belong to particular communities, and
in both sorts of communities past exemplars play a similar role. In physics,
Newton's work on mechanics has become idealized and embodied in
textbooks, providing a model of scientific practice. In religion, events in
the life of Christ or Moses play a similar role. They become idealized and
embodied in religious accounts, providing a model for religious practices.

What can be said about these attempts to relate Kuhn's view of science
to religion? The first thing to note is that, even if they were successful in
showing close similarities between science and religion, given Kuhn's
interpretation of science this would not show that theism is justified. In
the first place, critics have pointed out serious enough problems with
Kuhn's theory of science to suggest that it is not an accurate account.[54]
If these critics are correct, Kuhn's theory does not provide an acceptable
scheme for understanding religion in terms of science. But even if Kuhn's
theory is an acceptable account of science, neither Mitchell nor Barbour
actually develops a cumulative case for theism along Kuhnian lines. For
example, Mitchell simply suggests how such a case could be developed
along Kuhnian lines, and Barbour seems only to put his approach for-
ward as a way of achieving dialogue between different religious traditions.[55]

It is doubtful that there is as close a similarity as Mitchell and Barbour
suppose between science as interpreted by Kuhn and religion. As Gutting
has argued, both Mitchell and Barbour neglect an essential element of
Kuhn's view of science when they apply his view to religion.[56] According
to Kuhn, the scientific community reaches a consensus about a scientific
paradigm and works within this paradigm in periods of normal science.
Thus Kuhn explicitly rejects the view that his theory applies to social
science, where there is no agreed-upon paradigm. Like social science,
and unlike natural science, there is no agreed-upon paradigm in religion.
Not only are there disagreements within Christianity that prevent us
from speaking of a Christian paradigm, but even when sectarian differences within Christianity are ignored there is no religious paradigm

that embraces such different world religions as Christianity, Buddhism, Islam, and Hinduism. Furthermore, as Gutting points out, Kuhnian paradigms generate problems and solutions, whereas religious world views do not.[57] Thus the alleged close similarity between science and religious thinking from a Kuhnian perspective breaks down.

Given these problems and the arguments for positive atheism presented in this book, it is doubtful that a cumulative case for theism can be developed. As we shall see, both the problem of evil and the atheistic teleological argument show that the existence of God is improbable. In addition, several incoherences in the concept of God show that God could not possibly exist. A cumulative case for theism would at the very least have to dispose of these arguments as unsound. This may be possible, but it would not be easy to do. Further, even if the arguments for positive atheism are shown to be unsound, the major arguments for theism that appeal to experience such as the teleological argument, the argument from religious experience, and the argument from miracles have already been shown to be without merit, as in this chapter have some minor theistic arguments. It is possible, of course, that although all these arguments from experience are without merit when considered individually, a strong case can be made when they are considered together. Without special reasons to suppose otherwise, however, this is to be doubted.

Consider a detective story in which the pieces of evidence have no force when taken individually but do have force when combined. Jones has been murdered. Holmes knows that the murderer is a male athlete under 5 feet 10 inches tall. Holmes suspects that the murderer is a member of an association of former professional basketball players meeting at the hotel where Jones was found dead. Smith is of average height. This bit of information alone is not enough to identify Smith as the murderer, since most people are of average height. Smith is also a former professional basketball player. This bit of information is also not enough to identify Smith as the murderer, since there are thousands of former professional basketball players. Smith did attend the meeting at the hotel, but this bit of information is still not enough to identify Smith as the murderer, since 459 former professional basketball players and their spouses attended that meeting at the hotel. Given all three bits of information, however, the hypothesis that Smith is the murderer becomes more probable since, as Holmes knows, few professional basketball players are of average height and, if the association is representative of the general population of such people, there are likely to be few former players of average height at the meeting. However, in order to infer that the various bits of information taken together make a strong case even though taken individually they do not, Holmes must have specific information about relative frequencies of a certain property that appears in a class. He must know, for example, that few professional basketball players are of average height.

In the case of arguments for theism it is unclear what the analog would be to the information that Holmes possesses. What information do theists have that enables them to argue that evidence E_1 or evidence E_2 or evidence E_3 does not make theism probable when taken in isolation yet makes it probable when combined? This question is hardly ever asked by theists, let alone answered by them.

Two recent accounts of cumulative arguments for theism reinforce one's skepticism about the prospects for such arguments. The most comprehensive attempt in several decades to make a cumulative case for theism has been Swinburne's. He argues that the probability of theism is increased by its ability to explain various phenomena. Yet he maintains in the end that, unless we take religious experience into account, the cumulative support given theism by the various types of evidence that he cites is not strong. He says:

> Theism does not have a probability close either to 1 or to 0, that is, from the evidence considered so far, theism is neither very probable nor very improbable. It does not have a probability close to 1 because it does not have high predictive power. . . . It is compatible with too much. There are many different worlds which a God might have brought about.[58]

In fact the situation is much worse than Swinburne suggests. In earlier chapters we saw that both his cosmological and his teleological arguments have serious problems. In this chapter we saw that other arguments of his also have problems. This surely lowers the probability of theism. Furthermore, as we saw in Chapter 6, although he believes that taking religious experience into account makes the probability of theism high, his argument from religious experience also has serious problems. Thus the probability is still further lowered. Moreover, as we shall soon see, his solution to the problem of evil does not work, and neither do other proposed solutions. And finally, as we shall discover, there are incoherences in the concept of God that Swinburne does not address.[59] For all these reasons, Swinburne's claim that the "probability of theism is not too close to 0"[60] is very dubious.

Gary Gutting also examines the cumulative case for theism,[61] but unlike Swinburne he considers the problems of making such a case only in the most general terms. Gutting defines two ways in which an account (A) explains a fact (F). A explains F in a *strong sense* if, given A and further assumptions that we have good reason to suppose are true, it is reasonable to think that F obtains. A explains F in a *weak sense* if, given A, it is reasonable to think that F obtains only if we add further assumptions that may well be true (that is, there is no reason on balance for supposing the assumptions to be true and no reason for supposing them to be false). Gutting maintains that ordinarily a cumulative case for A requires showing that A strongly explains some facts in its domain. However, a cumulative case for A can be made provided that A is the only explanation of some of the facts it explains, or provided at least that it is the best of the available weak explanations.

There are, according to Gutting, four main sorts of facts that theism purports to explain: cosmological facts, religious facts, moral facts, and personal facts. He maintains that theism does not explain any of these facts in the strong sense. In order for theism to explain some facts strongly, it would be necessary to know what God knows, but this is impossible. For example, Gutting says that in order to explain the existence of seemingly gratuitous evil, the theist must assume that God has relevant knowledge of the situation that we lack. However, the theist who says this in the case of seemingly gratuitous evil must say the same thing in general. Thus the theist must claim that we never have a basis for anticipating God's action since we cannot know what He knows. However, if we never have such a basis, we cannot explain evil or anything else in the strong sense.

Is theism the best of the available weak explanations? Gutting compares it with naturalism, "the most popular generic alternative,"[62] in terms of "four generally accepted criteria of explanatory adequacy: scope, accuracy, fruitfulness, and simplicity,"[63] and finds "that neither theism nor naturalism can be judged superior in the scope of the explanation it offers."[64] With respect to accuracy Gutting argues that naturalism has the edge. For example, naturalistic explanations of religious experience will tend "to point to specific factors in an individual's personality or social background that make it more likely that he or she would have a given sort of experience at a given time. Theism can appropriate this explanatory accuracy only by the *ad hoc* assumption that God is more likely to act through or in accord with our psycho-social natures."[65] The criterion of fruitfulness Gutting deems irrelevant to the choice between theism and naturalism because "an account can be fruitful only to the extent that it is *predictive*: only by making predictions can it make us aware of new phenomena or new interrelations of phenomena."[66] But neither theism nor naturalism is a predictive account. Both make sense of facts that are well known; they do not lead to the experience of new facts. With respect to the criterion of simplicity Gutting argues that naturalism has the edge. Since the theist assumes all the causes that the naturalist does and "adds yet another, the theistic account is less simple in one clear sense."[67]

Gutting concludes: "Even though there is in principle no obstacle to a cumulative case for theism, the case cannot in fact be made, because theism is not superior in scope, accuracy, fruitfulness, or simplicity to the naturalistic alternative."[68] From what Gutting says, it would seem that he should conclude not just that theism is not superior to naturalism but that naturalism is superior to theism. After all, he maintains that the "score" is:

Scope: naturalism and theism are the same.
Accuracy: naturalism is superior.
Fruitfulness: irrelevant.
Simplicity: naturalism is superior.

One would suppose that naturalism is the clear winner. In any case, if the arguments for positive atheism that are given later in this book are correct, one can surely assert that naturalism is superior. The problem of evil and the incoherences in the concept of God indicate that the cumulative case *against* theism is strong.

CHAPTER 9

Beneficial Arguments for God

In this chapter I consider arguments for believing in God that are not based on what the evidence indicates but on the supposed practical results of theistic belief. In Chapter 1, I called such arguments *beneficial*[1] in contrast to *epistemic* ones purporting to show that we should believe in God because the evidence supports such belief. Blaise Pascal and William James have presented the two most famous beneficial arguments for believing in God, and I concentrate here on their arguments. Both Pascal and James maintain that the intellect cannot decide the question of whether God exists, but that nevertheless it is extremely important to decide it. They both conclude that we should believe that God exists since there are good practical reasons to do so. In our terms they are maintaining that although there are no epistemic reasons to believe that God exists, there are good beneficial reasons.

Pascal's Argument

Pascal's approach to religious belief is best understood against a background of Cartesian skepticism. Like Descartes, Pascal was skeptical of our usual claims to knowledge. Descartes believed, however, that one could ultimately achieve knowledge, including knowledge of God, through the clear and distinct intellectual intuitions of one's mind. Pascal rejected Descartes's intellectual and rational answer to skepticism and maintained that skepticism concerning God's existence cannot be answered by demonstrating that God exists since no demonstration is possible:[2] "Know then, proud man, what a paradox you are to yourself. Humble yourself, weak reason. Silence yourself, foolish nature, learn that man infinitely surpasses man, and hear from your master your real state which you do not know. Hear God."[3]

For Pascal the problem of skepticism is solved by religious faith. Only by acceptance of revelation and submission to God, he said, can we achieve knowledge. However, Pascal maintained that there is good reason to have faith in God. Indeed, he argued that the rationality of faith could be shown by a wager.[4] "Let us," said Pascal, "weigh the gain and the loss in wagering that God is. Let us estimate the two choices. If you gain, you gain all; if you lose you lose nothing. Wager then without hesitation that He is."[5]

In what follows I am not concerned with an exegesis of Pascal's thought but with an evaluation of the sort of argument he pursued. The important question for my purposes is not what Pascal meant but whether the line of argument he suggested gives us good beneficial reasons to believe in God.

The Wager in Simple Form

For our purposes Pascal's argument can be put briefly in this way: If one believes in God and God exists, then one gains infinite bliss after life. If one believes in God and God does not exist, one has lost little. If one does not believe in God, and God does exist, one suffers infinite torment in hell after death.[6] But if He does not exist and one does not believe in Him, one has gained little. Clearly one has infinity to gain and little to lose by believing, and infinity to lose and little to gain by not believing. Hence one should believe that God exists.

It is important to have a clear understanding of the status of Pascal's argument. It purports to give a good reason for believing that God exists; in particular it purports to provide a good reason for changing one's belief from agnosticism or atheism to Christian theism. However, the reason that the argument purports to give is not the usual sort. This reason does not make the existence of God any more likely or probable. Thus Pascal's is not an epistemic argument in the sense of this expression introduced earlier. Purporting to show that because it is beneficial to believe in God one should believe in Him is a beneficial argument. Indeed, as we shall see, Pascal's argument can be construed as purporting to show that practically all epistemic reasons for not believing in God are outweighed by beneficial reasons for believing in God.

As many scholars have pointed out, Pascal was not so naive as to suppose that one could believe in God by an act of will.[7] However, he did think that belief could be developed by acting in certain religious ways, such as by attending mass and taking the sacraments. So the two choices of the nonbeliever were really to act or not to act in religious ways. Thus

Pascal's argument purports to provide beneficial reasons for acting in certain religious ways that would indirectly result in religious belief.[8]

THE WAGER AS A PROBLEM IN DECISION THEORY

One way of interpreting Pascal's wager is as a problem in decision theory.[9] Let us suppose for the moment that we do not know the probability of God's existence. So construed, the argument can be put in the matrix shown in Figure 1 (assuming X and Y are finite values).

	God exists	*God does not exist*
Believe in God	$+\infty$	$-X$
Do not believe in God	$-\infty$	$+Y$

FIGURE 1

So construed, Pascal's wager is a problem in decision making under uncertainty, a decision in which the outcome is uncertain and the probabilities of the outcome are unknown. Using either of the two well-known rules of decision making under uncertainty—the maximax or minimax rule—one should believe in God.[10] On the maximax rule one should pick the course of action with an outcome having the most value; on the minimax rule one should pick the course of action with an outcome having the least disvalue.

One can give Pascal's wager a different interpretation. Let us suppose that although one does not know the exact probability, one knows that God's existence has some finite probability p, however small. (Thus one assumes that God's existence is not logically impossible.) Then the problem can be construed in decision theory terms as a decision problem under risk and can be formulated in the matrix shown in Figure 2 (assuming X and Y are finite values).

	God exists	*God does not exist*
Believe in God	$+\infty \times p$	$-X \times (1-p)$
Do not believe in God	$-\infty \times p$	$+Y \times (1-p)$

FIGURE 2

In this case one would follow the Bayesian decision rule: Follow that course of action with the most expected value (value × probability). However, since $(+\infty \times p) + [-X \times (1-p)] = +\infty$ the expected value in believing in God is $+\infty$. Furthermore, since $(-\infty \times p) + [+Y \times (1-p)] = -\infty$ the expected value for not believing in God is $-\infty$.[11]

Thus if Pascal's wager is construed as either a problem in decision making under risk or a problem in decision making under uncertainty, there is a stronger beneficial reason for the belief that God exists than for the belief that God does not exist, despite the fact that the epistemic reasons for believing in God may be less strong than the epistemic reasons for not believing in God. In decision making under risk a higher value is associated with belief than with nonbelief. In this case no probabilities (epistemic reasons) are involved; the higher value provides beneficial reasons for belief rather than for nonbelief. In decision making under uncertainty there is a higher expected value associated with belief than with nonbelief. (This value provides the beneficial reason.) This is true despite the fact that the probability that God exists (the epistemic reason) may be much lower than the probability that God does not exist.

THE WAGER REFUTED

The basic trouble with Pascal's wager is that there are other possibilities that Pascal either did not consider or else supposed were irrelevant to his purposes. Consider the following possibility. Suppose there is a supernatural being—call him the perverse master (PM)—who punishes with infinite torment after death anyone who believes in God or any other supernatural being (including himself) and rewards with infinite bliss after death anyone who believes in no supernatural being. One assumes that since such a being is not logically impossible, his existence is finitely probable. Put in a matrix form as a problem of decision making under risk, the situation would look like Figure 3 (assuming $p_1 + p_2 + p_3 = 1$).

	God exists	PM exists	Neither exists
Believe in God	$+\infty \times p_1$	$-\infty \times p_2$	$-Z \times p_3$
Believe in PM	$-\infty \times p_1$	$-\infty \times p_2$	$-X \times p_3$
Believe in neither	$-\infty \times p_1$	$+\infty \times p_2$	$+Y \times p_3$

FIGURE 3

Now, construed in this way, belief in the perverse master would be the worst choice. The expected value would be $-\infty$. Belief in God would be the next best. The expected value would be $-Z \times p_3$ (where $-Z$ is some finite disutility and p_2 is some finite probability). But believing in neither would be the best choice since the expected value would be $Y \times p_3$ (where there is some finite utility and p_3 is some finite probability).

It should be noted that, given the possibility that another supernatural being exists who gives infinite reward for belief in the perverse master and himself and no reward for anything else, belief in the perverse master would be no worse or better than belief in God. Let us call such a being the anti-perverse master (APM). The matrix is shown in Figure 4 (assuming $p_1 + p_2 + p_3 + p_4 = 1$).

In this case all infinite expected values cancel each other out and the choice turns on the finite expected values in the last column. Since all the

	God exists	PM exists	APM exists	None exists
Believe in God	$+\infty \times p_1$	$-\infty \times p_2$	0	$-Y \times p_4$
Believe in PM	$-\infty \times p_1$	$-\infty \times p_2$	$+\infty \times p_3$	$-X \times p_4$
Believe in APM	$-\infty \times p_1$	$-\infty \times p_2$	$+\infty \times p_3$	$-W \times p_4$
Believe in none	$-\infty \times p_1$	$+\infty \times p_2$	0	$+Z \times p_4$

FIGURE 4

values are negative except belief in one of the possible supernatural beings, the best choice is belief in none of the supernatural beings.

It should be clear that these considerations not only refute Pascal's argument but provide reasons for believing neither in God nor in the perverse master nor in the anti-perverse master. The strategy in our argument can be generalized, and the results remain the same. No matter what other logical possibilities one can conceive of in terms of supernatural beings with infinite rewards and punishments, another supernatural being can be conceived of with infinite rewards and punishments that tend to cancel out the rewards and punishments of the other.

Thus suppose it to be possible that there is a supernatural being who gives an infinite reward to everyone after death no matter what they believe. Then presumably there is also the possibility of a supernatural being who inflicts an infinite punishment on everyone after death no matter what they believe. Put in matrix form, the infinite rewards and punishments cancel each other out and the decision turns on the finite utilities involved when no supernatural being exists. Thus given all the possibilities for various supernatural beings with infinite rewards and punishments and the canceling-out effect, the matrix is reduced to the form shown in Figure 5.

	Either *supernatural being$_1$ exists* *or* *supernatural being$_2$ exists* *or* *...* *or* *supernatural being$_n$ exists*	*No* *supernatural being* *exists*
Believe in supernatural being$_1$	0	$-X_1 \times p$
Believe in supernatural being$_2$	0	$-X_2 \times p$
Believe in supernatural being$_n$	0	$-X_n \times p$
Believe in none	0	$Y \times p$

FIGURE 5

The result is that, for any matrix in which the expected value of belief in some supernatural being is infinite, there exists a more inclusive matrix in which the infinite values cancel out. In this more inclusive matrix, the only remaining values are the finite values involved in believing or not believing the supernatural beings do not exist. In this case, nonbelief has the greatest utility. Consequently, in terms of beneficial reasons, one should not believe that God exists or, indeed, that any other supernatural being exists.

OBJECTIONS ANSWERED

(1) It may be objected that our argument against Pascal's wager as well as our argument that Pascal's wager could be used to provide beneficial reasons for not believing in God miss the point of his wager, since they presuppose that people will accept the possibility of strange alternative conceptions of supernatural beings such as the anti-perverse master. This, it may be claimed, is a dubious assumption. Nicholas Rescher, for example, maintains that Pascal's wager "is addressed only to people who have a very definite sort of view of what God (should he exist) would be like—to the person who is committed to the Christian *idea* of God but hesitates about believing in him."[12] He goes on to maintain that "we are no more at liberty to adopt a God-concept at variance with that of our circumambient tradition than we are to adopt one of a terrier or an elm tree."[13] Further, Rescher says, "if (like most of us) one is prepared to set the probability of strange gods at zero, the argument cannot point one in their direction."[14] Consequently, he would undoubtedly maintain that the possibilities presented above are not "*real* possibilities" and are "simply excluded from the range of the practicable."[15]

This dismissal of the criticism of the wager and of the atheistic counter-argument will not work. First, as far as the validity of the argument is concerned, whom it was *originally* addressed to and for what purposes are irrelevant. The question is whether it can now be addressed to other people and adapted to other purposes. Nothing Rescher says shows that it cannot be. Second, people have in fact adopted concepts of God at variance with their cultural traditions. For example, within the last two decades many people in Western cultures have taken up the teachings of Eastern religions. In any case, for our critique to work it is not necessary that people adopt different concepts of God in the sense of believing that these different Gods exist. All they need do is acknowledge that it is logically possible that certain supernatural beings exist.

Third, if people are prepared to "set the probability of strange gods at zero," they had better have good reason for doing so; otherwise, their action can only be interpreted as arbitrary and irrational. What would be the basis, for example, for supposing that the probability of the perverse master is zero? The only rational basis would seem to be that the concept of the perverse master is inconsistent. However, in order to suppose that the concept of the perverse master is inconsistent, one has to have grounds for supposing that the perverse master has inconsistent properties. Only if the properties of the perverse master are inconsistent could one assume *a priori* that the probability of its existing is zero. However, I know of no reason to think that the perverse master or indeed any of the strange supernatural beings considered above have inconsistent properties. Finally, it is true that the various supernatural beings introduced above are not real possibilities, either in the sense that they are seriously considered by religious believers or in the sense that their objective probability is high. But it would be question-begging to argue that they do not matter practically and can be ignored. The whole point of this discussion is to show that they should be considered and that, despite the low probabilities involved, they are very relevant. Taking these possibilities into account has extremely important practical implications. Indeed, it shows that one should be a nonbeliever. So the possibilities are very much in the range of the practical.

(2) It may be objected that I am making an assumption in my critique of Pascal's wager that is not obviously true. I am assuming that if no supernatural being exists, it is better to believe that no supernatural being exists than that some supernatural being exists. Unless I make this assumption I would not be able to claim, where the wager is construed as a problem of decision making under risk, that the expected value of not believing in God if He did exist was greater than the expected value of believing in God if He did not exist. However, it may be argued that this assumption is false since it may be the case that some people would be better off believing that God exists even if He does not. Such belief may, for example, give them hope in times of crisis.

However, if we take the utilities as given in the original argument, this objection does not hold. As Pascal constructed the problem, there is more to be lost than gained in believing in God if He does not exist. The extension of Pascal's argument to other supernatural beings would not change matters. Further, the utilities involved in believing in some possible supernatural beings seem clearly negative. Suppose there is a supernatural being who is believed to harm rather than help people in times of crisis. Belief in such a being in times of crisis would be cold comfort. At best, belief in some supernatural being—for example, the Christian God or a god who helped anyone who believed in any god—would give comfort. But this comfort, considered as a positive value, would have to be weighed against negative values—for example, the effort and trouble involved in worshipping this being. When translated into actual religious practice, worship can be time-consuming, expensive, and troublesome. The long hours spent in religious ritual, the extreme penance required by some sects, the tithe required by some churches, and the asceticism required by others are some of the more obvious examples of the negative value of religious worship. When the negative values of belief are weighed against the positive values of belief, it is certainly not obvious that Pascal was wrong to suppose that belief in a supernatural being such as God has a negative value if the being does not exist.

Pascal's construal aside, one may grant for the sake of argument that belief in a supernatural being has some positive utility even if this being does not exist. The crucial question is whether the positive utilities of not believing in any supernatural being outweigh this value in case no supernatural being exists. Put in the terms I introduced earlier: Are there better beneficial reasons for believing that no supernatural being exists, if none do in fact exist, than for believing that some exist, if none do in fact exist. The answer, we believe, is yes.

There is practical value in not believing. As atheists and humanists have often pointed out, belief that God and other supernatural beings do not exist puts responsibility for humanity's problems on humans, forcing them to come to grips with their own problems. There is also psychological value in not believing, in that the hope that God or some other supernatural being will help people is immature and childish. Insofar as there is epistemic value in not believing a falsehood, if these beings do not exist, there is epistemic value in not believing in supernatural beings.[16] And finally, belief in a supernatural being may give some comfort in times of crisis, but if no supernatural being exists, such comfort must be short-lived for perceptive believers. Their hopes will be frustrated, their expectations disappointed. These believers, at least, will be unhappy and feel forsaken in the long run.

But what about a supernatural being who people believe does not help them in times of crisis but who in fact wants his creatures to be self-reliant? Belief in this being, if he did not exist, would not have either the practical or the psychological disvalue mentioned above, but there would still be epistemic disvalue. Further, no comfort would be gained by relying on such a being in times of crisis. The advantage would still be with the nonbeliever. The same thing could be said about belief in a God who helps only those who help themselves. Belief in such a being if he did not exist would have epistemic disvalue.

It might be argued that the expected value of believing that no supernatural being does exist would be very small, given the very low probability that no supernatural being exists. But in the first place, whether the expected value is low or not, the crucial question is whether the expected value of not believing is higher than the expected value of believing if no supernatural being exists. No matter how small p is, so long as it is not zero, if the values associated with nonbelief are greater than those associated with belief if no supernatural being exists, then the expected value of nonbelief is greater. In the second place, as I argue later on in this book, there is good reason to believe that putative statements that assert the existence of God are improbable.

(3) Another objection that may be raised is this: I have shown that, given any matrix specifying infinite expected values associated with the existence of supernatural being A, a more inclusive matrix can be constructed specifying infinite values associated with the existence of supernatural being B. The values of this matrix cancel out the expected values associated with the matrix of A. But it may be maintained that the above argument cuts both ways, because a still more inclusive matrix can be postulated with a supernatural being C where not all values are canceled. Thus the victory for the nonbeliever is short-lived.

There are two responses to this objection. First, if one admits a potential infinity of possible supernatural beings, the above maneuver would provide no comfort for the believer. His or her advantage would be canceled out in the next step by the nonbeliever. It does seem possible to go on forever constructing larger and larger matrices in which values that are associated with possible supernatural beings are continually canceled by values associated with other possible supernatural beings. In such a potentially infinite matrix, the expected value of believing in some supernatural being would depend on the expected value associated with there being no supernatural beings, since overall the values would cancel out in the long run.

Second, even if the potential infinity of possible supernatural beings is denied, the argument still has a dialectical point. Any Pascalian type of argument can be used dialectically to establish the superiority of nonbelief if the nonbeliever gets the believer to admit the existence of a possible supernatural being having certain expected value associated with its existence. The believer is trapped by his or her own argument. If the believer has the ingenuity to come back with a further move, this ingenious nonbeliever can counter by getting the believer to admit the possibility of still another supernatural being with the requisite expected value associated with its existence. The argument in this dialectic model is won by the person who fails to convince the other that a particular supernatural being is finitely probable.

Although this dialectical use of the argument by the believer is possible, it is hard to see that it would have much use except as a way to block the nonbeliever's arguments. The believer is interested in giving beneficial reasons for believing in one particular supernatural being, most probably God. Postulating some strange supernatural being to counter the nonbeliever's argument would have little appeal.

CONCLUSION

We have seen not only that Pascal's wager is a bad beneficial argument for belief in God but that once the argument is filled in, it can be turned against the theist and used as a beneficial argument for nonbelief. However, this use of the argument has limitations in terms of the general restraints that need to be placed on the beneficial arguments. I argued in Chapter 1 both for *the presumption of the primacy of epistemic reasons* and for *the presumption of the purely supplementary role of beneficial reasons.* Beneficial reasons, I concluded, should normally be used only when there are inadequate epistemic arguments to believe one way or the other, and should be allowed to override epistemic arguments only in very special circumstances. If the epistemic arguments of this book are correct, a beneficial argument for nonbelief would prima facie have no role to play, since there are good epistemic reasons for nonbelief. Of course, in a particular context the general epistemic and beneficial reasons for nonbelief might be outweighed by specific beneficial reasons. A case in point is the hypothetical example considered in Chapter 1 of the dying Mrs. Smith, the 89-year-old former Catholic. According to our argument, although on general epistemic and even beneficial grounds people should not believe in God, in Mrs. Smith's *particular* circumstances it might be better to believe.

William James and the Will to Believe

Another attempt to base religious belief on a beneficial argument is that of William James in his widely cited essay "The Will to Believe." James's general strategy is to maintain that under certain conditions, if the intellect cannot decide some issue, we have the right to believe on nonintellectual grounds. In terms of the distinction introduced above, James maintains that under certain conditions we should believe on the basis of beneficial, not epistemic, reasons.

JAMES'S ARGUMENT

James defines a hypothesis as "anything that may be proposed to our belief."[17] A choice between hypotheses James calls an option, and an option is considered to be genuine if it is live, forced, and momentous. A choice between hypotheses both of which appeal to an individual as real possibilities is a live option, and one that does not involve two appealing hypotheses is a dead option. For example, for the average person living in the United States, a choice between belief in Buddhism and belief in Hinduism would be a dead option, whereas a choice between belief in Christianity and being an agnostic would be a live option. He calls an option forced if there is no alternative but to choose one hypothesis or the other. If there is an alternative, an option is avoidable. For example, according to James, "Either call my theory true or call it false" presents an avoidable option, since one may choose to call it neither. However, he says, "Either accept this truth or go without it" presents a forced option, since "there is no standing place outside of the alternative."[18] An option is momentous, according to James, when the opportunity is unique, the stakes involved are insignificant, or the choice is irreversible "if it later proves to be unwise";[19] if a choice is not momentous, James calls it trivial.

James maintains that not only does our passionate nature in fact influence our decisions as to what to do and what hypothesis to accept but when the option is genuine it should. In other words, when it is real, forced, and momentous *and* the decision cannot by its nature be decided on intellectual grounds, it should be influenced by our passionate nature. To leave the question open is, according to James, itself a "passional decision" and "is attended with the same risk of losing the truth."[20] By "the same risk of losing the truth" James means that if one does not choose between the two hypotheses and leaves the question open, one cannot gain any benefit that might be involved in having a true belief. Although James agrees that we should avoid error, he maintains that sometimes the possible gain of achieving truth outweighs the risk of falling into error.

One context where there is a genuine option and thus where our passionate nature should decide is religion. Further, it seems clear to James that our choice should be what he calls the religious hypothesis. According to James, religion says essentially two things:

> First, she says that the best things are the more eternal things, the overlapping things, the things in the universe that throw the last stone, so to speak, and say the final word. "Perfection is eternal"—the phrase of Charles Secrétan seems a good way of putting this first affirmation of religion, an affirmation which obviously cannot yet be verified scientifically at all.
>
> The second affirmation of religion is that we are better off even now if we believe her first affirmation to be true.[21]

According to James, the option to believe the religious hypothesis is genuine. (He believes that for some people the religious hypothesis could not be true and thus could not be a live option, but he is not speaking to them.) The option is momentous since even now we gain a vital good by belief and lose this good by nonbelief. Further, the option is forced so far as this good is concerned, for if we do not believe, we will lose this vital good. To James what we should do is clear. "To preach skepticism to us as a duty until 'sufficient evidence' for religion be found," James argues, "is tantamount. . .to telling us, when in the presence of the religious hypothesis, that to yield to our fear of its being in error is wiser and better than to yield to our hope that it may be true."[22] But it is not wiser, since we would lose the vital good involved in believing the religious hypothesis.

James points out a further reason why religious skepticism would be unwise. He says that "the more perfect and more eternal aspects of the universe are represented in our religions as having a personal form. The universe is no longer a mere *It* to us, but a *Thou* if we are religious."[23] According to James, if this interpretation of the religious hypothesis is true, unless "we met the hypothesis half way," evidence may "be forever withheld from us."[24] But what does James mean by meeting the hypothesis half way? On one plausible reading of James, he is maintaining that unless we believe that some personal ultimate reality exists, we will not be able to confirm the existence of this reality in our experience.[25] Consequently, on this interpretation, the verification of the religious hypothesis in experience (where this hypothesis postulates a personal being) may either presuppose belief in this being or at least be facilitated by such belief.

It is not exactly clear how this epistemological consideration is related to James's point that "we are better off even now if we believe" the first affirmation of religion, namely that "the best things are the more eternal things." The problem is that James never really comes out and says exactly how we would be better off even now. Perhaps his epistemological consideration is merely an example of how we would be better off even now if we could believe the best things are the most eternal, on the presupposition that the eternal things are personal in form; that is, the eternal is God. We would be better off even now since we would be better able with this belief than without it to confirm whether God exists. Thus a belief in God would give us an *epistemological* advantage over our having a skeptical attitude toward God.

However, many commentators on James mention only nonepistemological advantages. For example, Rescher has suggested that James held a view similar to Jules Lachelier's that "there is a deep *need* on man's part for God to exist. Without this belief human life would be empty and meaningless."[26] And Wallace Matson maintains that James thought religious belief made people happier in this life than did nonbelief.[27]

Evaluation of James's Argument

One important thing to notice about James's argument is his subjective and relativistic definition of a live option. For James a live option to person P is simply one that appeals to P as a real possibility. But what appeals to a person as a real possibility may have nothing to do with what the evidence indicates and may be completely irrational. Indeed, certain options that appeal to a person as real possibilities may in fact be impossible, while ones that do not appeal as real possibilities may in the light of the evidence be at least as plausible as, or even more plausible than, the ones the person considers to be real possibilities. For example, granted that Buddhism would not appeal to an average American as a real possibility while Christianity would, it is hard to see why this is a reason for excluding Buddhism from serious consideration when this person is choosing a religion. Perhaps objective investigation would show that Christianity rests on historically dubious evidence and an incoherent ontology and that Buddhism does not suffer from these problems.

I suggest that James should have said that a live option is one that is not improbable in the light of the available evidence. Let us understand "live option" in this new sense, and let us assume with James that in matters of religion, options are live, forced, momentous, and not capable of intellectual resolution. On these assumptions there may be many more genuine options than James ever imagined. For example, Buddhism, Christianity, Islam, Judaism, and Hinduism would become genuine options for every person living in this country. Not only would there be the genuine options of the various living world religions but there would also be the genuine options of various concepts of gods or God within those religions. How is one to choose between them? By hypothesis epistemic arguments cannot help, and it is unclear how beneficial reasons can give a clear answer. How can one tell if one would be better off in this life believing that Christianity or Buddhism is true? And if one makes a choice, which form of Christianity or Buddhism is justified on beneficial grounds?

The second thing to notice is that although James uses rather specific examples (Christianity vs. agnosticism) to illustrate what a live option in the choice of religious hypothesis is, his actual statement of the religious hypothesis is extremely vague and unclear. Recall that the first part of James's religious hypothesis says that "the best things are the more eternal things, the overlapping things, the things in the universe that throw the last stone, so to speak, and say the final word," and the second part says that "we are better off even now if we believe" the first part of the hypothesis. This statement has prompted one commentator on James's work to remark:

> "Best" is vague, and "more eternal" comes close to being nonsense: either something is eternal or it is not. To add that the best things are "the overlapping things" and "throw the last stone, so to speak" only adds further mystification. Is James referring to God but embarrassed to say so?[28]

In any case, taken at their face value both parts of the religious hypothesis are normative statements.[29] They seem to have no obvious metaphysical implication. The first part says, in effect, for any X and for any Y, if X is eternal and Y is not, X is better than Y. Let us call this statement B. The second part has the form, it is better to believe B than not to. But unless more is said, there is surely little warrant for either judgment. Mathematical entities such as numbers, at least on a Platonic view of such entities, are eternal. They are timeless and unchanging. But why are numbers better than all noneternal things? One would have thought it at least prima facie debatable that the set of all primes was better than a millennium of world peace and love.

If we give James's religious hypothesis a more specific religious meaning, the first part can perhaps be stated as follows: For any X and for any Y, if X is a perfect and eternal being and Y is neither, X is better than Y. The second part of the hypothesis is that it is better to believe this than not to. On one interpretation the first part of the hypothesis is true by definition. A perfect being is surely better—that is, more perfect—than a less than perfect being. But on other interpretations the religious hypothesis is not true. The expression "is better" is usually used contextually. Something is better for some purposes but not for others. For example, a hammer is better than a pencil for driving a nail, but not for signing one's name. Surely, in this contextual sense, a perfect and eternal being is not always better than some noneternal and less than perfect being. For example, a hammer is better than God if one wants to drive a nail.

But let us concentrate on the sense of "better" that would make the first part of the religious hypothesis true by definition. Given this understanding of the first part of the religious hypothesis, atheists could accept the second part. Atheists could well admit that it is better to believe that an eternal and perfect being is more perfect than a noneternal and nonperfect being, since such a statement is trivially true and it is better to believe that trivially true statements are true than to believe that they are false. It does not follow from this admission that this being actually exists.

However, let us give the religious hypothesis a more metaphysical interpretation. Despite what his words suggest, let us understand James to mean that the religious hypothesis asserts two things:

(1) There exists a perfect and eternal being: God.
(2) It is better in this life to believe that (1) than not to.

One could approach the justification of (2) in a spirit similar to that of Pascal's wager. One might argue that if God exists, then believing in God will result in a better life in this world than not believing. If God does not exist, then believing in God will still bring about a better life in this world than not believing. So in any case it is better to believe in God. Why would one be better off in this life by believing in God than by not believing in God if God exists? Two reasons come to mind. First, if God exists and one believes in Him, He may tend to make one's life better than if one does not believe. On this intervention interpretation, God intervenes in the natural course of events and rewards the faithful. Second, it may just be true, given human nature and the way society is structured, that theists tend to live happier, healthier, and more rewarding lives than nontheists. Let us call this the natural law interpretation. On either the intervention interpretation or the natural law interpretation, belief in God, if God exists, would be preferable. Let us assume further that if God did not exist, given human nature and the way society is structured, theists would tend to live happier, healthier, and more rewarding lives than nontheists. The situation, then, would look like Figure 6,

	God exists	*God does not exist*
Believe in God	X_1	X_2
Do not believe in God	Y_1	Y_2

FIGURE 6

where X_1, X_2, Y_1, and Y_2 are finite values found in this life, such that $X_1 > Y_1$ and $X_2 > Y_2$.

The trouble with James's argument, interpreted in this way, is that there is little empirical reason to suppose that theists are happier and healthier, lead more rewarding lives, and so on than nontheists. It certainly seems to be true that nontheists are capable of living lives with as great an amount of happiness, self-fulfillment, and the like as theists. Nor does it seem to be true that if one is a theist it is more likely that one will achieve happiness and so on in this life than if one is a nontheist. Indeed, an argument could be given for just the opposite conclusion. For example, suppose one picked two children at random, one from a nontheistic family and one from a theistic family in the United States. Which one is more likely to live a healthy and productive life while growing up? From what we know of religious belief and its relation to education, health care, social class, economic level, and the like, the best guess is that the child from the theistic family is more likely to be ill, to have less education, and to end up in some unsatisfying job than the child from a family of nonbelievers. Insofar as health and happiness and a satisfying job are correlated (which seems likely), the child from the nonreligious family is likely to be happier than the child from the religious family as an adult. Further, if we consider two children picked at random from the world at large and not just from the United States, one from a religious family and one from a nonreligious family, the chances surely would improve that the child from a religious family will be worse off than the child from a nonreligious family. The reason is simple. Poverty, ignorance, and sickness are more prevalent in the world at large than in the United States, and we know that religious belief is associated with poverty and lack of education, as well as that poverty and ignorance are associated with disease. Thus one might say that if one had a choice and was interested in staying healthy, getting an education, and getting a challenging job, one should choose not to be born into a religious family.

It still might be maintained that, although theists are less likely to live productive and healthy lives than nontheists, theists are capable of a higher quality of happiness. For example, theists are capable of achieving a state of spiritual tranquility and serenity while nontheists are not, and this state is qualitatively better than any state of happiness that a nontheist can reach. In reply, the following points can be made. First, it is not clear that tranquility and serenity are better than, say, the satisfaction of a challenging job. Why should we consider tranquility and serenity a higher sort of happiness? Recall that tranquility and serenity of a sort can be achieved by means of drugs and frontal lobotomies, yet such a state is not particularly desirable. What makes the tranquility and serenity that are achieved by religious means so valuable? Second, even if tranquility and serenity achieved through spiritual insights are so valuable, it is not clear that nontheists cannot achieve them. Surely, this state of mind is not uniquely associated with belief in God. Certain sects of Buddhism, on most interpretations a nontheistic religion, aim to achieve this state of mind, and transcendental meditation claims great success in achieving tranquility and serenity although it makes no assumption about God in the theistic sense.

Let us admit for the sake of argument that theists are capable of achieving a higher degree of happiness, self-fulfillment, and the like than nontheists. It is still not clear that theism would be the best choice. For despite James's neglect of probabilities, they must be taken into account. Although a theist may be able to achieve a higher degree of happiness, and so on, in this life than a nontheist can, the probability of his or her doing so may be lower than that of a nontheist's achieving a more modest degree of happiness. If we compute the expected value, nontheists may be better off. For example, suppose the probability p_1 of achieving the sort of life that theists are capable of is 0.4 while the probability of achieving the sort of life nontheists are capable of is 0.7. Suppose further that the value of happiness that a theist can achieve is 500 while the value of happiness a nontheist can achieve is 300. Then the expected value EV of theistic belief is $0.4 \times 500 = 200$ while the EV of nontheistic belief is

0.7 × 300 = 210. Thus with these values and probabilities, nontheism would still be preferable to theism despite the assumption that a higher level of happiness is associated with theism. However, we have seen no reason to suppose that this assumption is true.

Further, as I argued above against Pascal's wager, there are certain values associated with nonbelief that have nothing to do with happiness and the like. Once we bring these values into the computation of EV, we seem to tip the scales toward nonbelief even if belief is associated with more happiness. The possibility of less happiness and the like may be offset by these other values. As pointed out above, nonbelief puts responsibility for humanity's problems on humans. There is a certain value in self-reliance that may go far in outweighing the value of any happiness and the like that belief in God may produce. Thus it is by no means clear that we are better off even now in believing that God exists. Indeed, nonbelief seems preferable when all the relevant values are taken into account.

Moreover, as we have seen, even on a generous interpretation of James, he seems to suppose that believing that the religious hypothesis is true involves accepting some undifferentiated theism. But as many religious scholars have noted, one does not have religious belief in the abstract; it is always relative to a certain religious tradition. For example, one does not believe in God per se but rather in the God of the Catholic Church or of Islam. Belief in these different Gods leads to very different ways of life, since different ritual, ethical codes, and religious practices are associated with different concepts of God in different religions. Oddly enough, when James discusses live and dead religious options he seems to be aware of the nature of religious belief, but he forgets this when he specifies the content of the religious hypothesis. Furthermore, there are religions in which belief in God, as we understand it, has no important role.

What would be the effect of bringing specific religious beliefs into James's scheme? For one thing, it would complicate the question of whether it would be better to believe the religious hypothesis even now. For there would not be a single religious hypothesis. The question would become whether it would be better even now to embrace religion R_1 or R_2 or R_3 and so on or to embrace none. There would be no *a priori* reason to suppose that in terms of conduciveness to happiness, health, or whatever, the preferred religion would be theistic or that, on the basis of such values, would be preferred to no religion at all.

So far we have not considered James's claim that there is an epistemological advantage in religious belief. Recall that James can be interpreted as saying at one point that the verification of God's existence in one's experience is facilitated by belief in God. Does this provide a beneficial reason to believe in God?

To see that it is not obvious that it does, recall first that this would be simply one advantage that would have to be weighed against possible disadvantages. Second, on a more plausible conception of live option, any option is live if it is not improbable in the light of the evidence. Therefore, there are surely live religious options where religious belief would not have this epistemological advantage and, indeed, where it would have a disadvantage. Consider a god who reveals himself to his believers less often than to people who are skeptical. After all, he might reason, his followers do not need convincing, whereas skeptics do. Belief in such a god would have a decided epistemological disadvantage. Further, there does not seem to be any more epistemic reason to believe in this god than in the sort of god that James has in mind. Indeed, James's God seems vindictive and ungenerous to withhold evidence from skeptics who may simply be more cautious than believers are. Why should going beyond what the evidence indicates be rewarded even when the reward is new evidence that vindicates the incautious attitude?

In addition to these problems, religious experience varies from one religious tradition to another, and it is often in conflict. If belief in the god of religion R_1 results in the confirmation of R_1, then would belief in the god of religion R_2 result in the confirmation of R_2? If so, since R_1 and R_2 may be incompatible with one another, beliefs in different gods may result in the confirmation of incompatible hypotheses.

Finally, James talks as if believing in God and seeing whether the hypothesis that God exists is confirmed in one's experience is like an experiment. But his procedure lacks an essential element of standard experimental procedure: he does not seem to allow for the *disconfirmation* of the hypothesis by the results of the experiment.[30] Suppose one believes in some god and yet no evidence of his existence is revealed in one's experience. James does not entertain the possibility that this failure would count against the hypothesis that this god exists. Our critique of Swinburne in Chapter 6 indicated some of the problems with this view.

James's Argument Reduced to Pascal's Wager

James's argument is very different from Pascal's wager. In the first place, James appeals only to the advantages of religious belief even now, not in the afterlife, where Pascal's argument stressed the advantages of religious belief, should God exist, in an afterlife. In the second place, James, unlike Pascal, does not consider the probabilities in assessing the advantages of belief over nonbelief. For example, he does not try to estimate the expected value EV of religious belief in this life by multiplying the probability p of achieving a certain value V for believing in God by the value itself—that is, by estimating the value of EV where EV = p × V. As we have seen, estimates of EV are crucial in Pascal's argument when his argument is interpreted as a problem of decision making under risk.

These differences do not indicate that James's theory is to be preferred over Pascal's. Indeed, these differences pose a problem for James that, if corrected, reduces his theory to Pascal's. As we have seen, it is necessary to bring in probabilities in estimating the advantage of belief over nonbelief. Even if the life of a believer has possible advantages over the life of a nonbeliever, the crucial question is: What is the relative probability of these advantages? Once the probabilities are introduced, we begin to approach the structure of Pascal's wager, interpreted as a problem in decision making under risk.

In addition, James gives no good reason why only the advantages of belief in this life need be considered. James was certainly aware that traditionally a large part of the appeal of religions was the reward of heaven and the punishment of hell. Although belief in the afterlife was not explicit in James's vague statement of the religious hypothesis, such belief was explicit in what was, according to James, a live option for most people in this country: Christianity. Christianity has the prize of heaven as one of its attractions, and many Christian sects still hold the punishment of hell as one of its major threats.

If one brings the infinite rewards of Heaven for belief and the infinite punishment of hell for nonbelief into James's argument as well as probability considerations, the expected value for belief would be $+\infty$ and the expected value for disbelief would be $-\infty$. It would be quite irrelevant whether we would be better off in believing in Christianity even now. The expected values of the infinite rewards and punishments of the afterlife would swamp all finite values, including the finite values in this life of believing in the Christian God. Thus it would seem that James stressed the wrong thing in saying that we would be better off even now to believe in God. The important point is that even if we would *not* be better off even now, the logic of his argument, once it is understood in Pascal's terms, should force him to say that we would be better off in the long run.

However, as we should now know from our examination of Pascal's wager, if James's argument is reducible to Pascal's, it has serious problems. The possibility of various supernatural beings with various rewards and punishments means that the expected values involved in believing in them cancel each other out, and the only relevant expected values are the ones associated with there being no supernatural being. James does not provide any reason to suppose that if there were no supernatural being, we would still be better off to believe that there is. As I have already argued, the argument from happiness is very risky, since it can be turned against theists and, in addition, there seem to be other values besides happiness. Once these values are taken into account, nonbelief has the clear edge.

Conclusion

I have found reason to reject the claim that there are general beneficial arguments for belief in God. Both Pascal's and James's arguments fail, and to my knowledge these are surely the best ones available. This is not to say that in no conceivable circumstances can beneficial reasons for believing in God be used. I have argued that there is a presumption to use only epistemic reasons to justify belief, and there is a further presumption that when beneficial reasons are used they should be used in a supplemental role. But given the strong epistemic arguments that are presented later in this book *against* the existence of God, beneficial arguments cannot have this supplemental role. I have argued further that Pascal's and James's arguments can be turned against the theists and used to provide beneficial reasons for not believing in the existence of God. However, given the presumption against the use of beneficial arguments and the strong epistemic arguments for nonbelief, these beneficial arguments for nonbelief play no role in my defense of atheism. There may be special factors in some special contexts, however, that defeat this presumption and justify belief in God for beneficial reasons. As is argued in Chapter 1, this admission is not damaging to my thesis.

CHAPTER 10

Faith and Foundationalism

We have seen in the previous chapters that both epistemic and beneficial arguments for the existence of God fail. But do religious beliefs need to be based on reason? In this chapter I consider attempts to argue that they do not. Some religious thinkers have maintained that religious belief should be based on faith and that, under certain circumstances, faith is completely rational; some that religious faith should not be rational and that the use of evidence and arguments to support faith is a perversion of it; some that the religious way of life is governed by its own rules and logic and that, in the context of this way of life, religious faith is rational; and some that religious beliefs are basic beliefs, hence by definition do not rest on evidence or argument. We shall see that all these arguments fail. In the process of discussing them I also consider the seemingly paradoxical suggestions that avowals of religious faith are neither true nor false and that atheists could have faith in God.

A Traditional Concept of Religious Faith

According to a conception of religious faith developed by Aquinas,[1] religious truths are divided into those of reason and those of faith. Truths of reason, including the propositions that God exists and that He is all-powerful and all-good, can be demonstrated by rational argument. Certain particular Christian doctrines—for instance, the propositions that there are three persons in one God and that the Eucharist is Christ's body and blood—cannot be known by reason. Nevertheless, these truths can be known, since they are revealed by God to human beings through such means as the Bible or the church.

On this view, faith is intellectual, opaque, rational, free, gratuitous, and certain.[2] It is intellectual in the sense that it is capable of being articulated in language; opaque in the sense that the truths of faith are incapable of being shown to be true by rational processes; rational in the sense that there is good reason to believe that God did reveal these truths to human beings; free in the sense that there is nothing in logic or human nature that forces one to believe; gratuitous in the sense that faith is a gift from God; and certain in the sense that a true believer holds an article of faith without reserve and without doubt.

It is important to see than on Aquinas's view, although a truth of faith P is not capable of rational demonstration, the proposition Q—God has revealed P—is capable of such demonstration, at least of a probabilistic kind.[3] Aquinas appeals to three kinds of considerations to show that Q is true: scriptural prophesies have been fulfilled; the Christian church has succeeded without any promise of carnal pleasure in an afterlife or without any resort to violence in this life; miracles have occurred within the Christian tradition.[4] In addition, on this view of faith one must assume that God exists. Otherwise it would make no sense to suppose that God revealed truths through the Bible or through the church. Belief in God is not based on faith, therefore, but is a *precondition* of faith in particular Christian doctrines, such as that there are three persons in one God and that the Eucharist is Christ's body and blood.[5]

Because there is an attempt to guide faith by reason, this view of faith has decided advantages over some more recent ones. Indeed, on Aquinas's theory a Christian who believes, for example, in the Trinity has good reason to suppose that belief is true. Nevertheless, Aquinas's view is unacceptable.

In the first place, as we have seen in Chapter 4, there is no reason to accept the precondition of Aquinas's conception of faith, namely that God exists. But even if the existence of God is assumed, the reasons that Aquinas gives to suppose that God revealed certain truths through the Bible and the church have little merit. As we have seen, Aquinas appeals to the existence of miracles within the Christian tradition as support for his view that it is rational to believe that God revealed particular Christian doctrines. As I have argued in chapter 7, difficult obstacles must be surmounted for anyone who claims that a miracle has occurred, and these obstacles have not been surmounted in the standard defense of miracles.

Aquinas also appeals to the success of the Christian church to justify his belief in the rationality of Christian revelation. However, many churches or church equivalents inside and outside the Christian tradition have been successful in the way Aquinas specifies.[6] If this sort of success shows that God revealed truths in the religious traditions dominated by these churches or their equivalents, then conflicting truths were revealed. But conflicting propositions cannot both be true.

There is a further problem. As we have seen, the truths of faith are certain; they are supposed to be believed without any doubt. But not all the historical events that are supposed to provide the evidence for God's revelation can be known with certainty. This is not to say that no historical event can be known with certainty or even that no historical event connected with the Bible can be known with certainty. For example, unless we give the term "certainty" some technical meaning, one can know with certainty that there was a Civil War in the United States over a century ago. Although some biblical scholars have argued that no major historical claim of Christianity is well supported by the evidence,[7] let us suppose for the sake of argument that there may indeed be *some* historical events connected with the story of the New Testament that can be known with the same degree of confidence with which one can know there was a Civil War in the United States over a century ago. Still, it would be extremely rash to claim that all the major historical events of the New Testament can be known with this degree of confidence. For example, even if stories of Christ's having performed miracles are probable in the light of the evidence, they are hardly as probable as the proposition that there was a Civil War in the United States over a century ago. Thus these stories are not certain in the light of the evidence; at best they possess only a fair degree of probability. It is difficult to see how one can claim certainty for revelations based on historical events that are not known with certainty, however. Yet the existence of Christian miracles is cited by Aquinas as grounds for supposing that God revealed certain truths to humans. But then, how can the degree of belief necessary for faith—that is, certainty—be justified? Such a high degree of belief seems irrational in the light of the historical evidence.

Existential Faith

Aquinas's concept of faith is guided by reason, but some religious thinkers have maintained that faith needs no rational guidance, indeed, that there is great merit in belief that not only goes beyond the evidence but may even go against the evidence.[8] Søren Kierkegaard, for example, argued that religious faith was more important than reason in achieving human happiness.[9]

Religious faith, as Kierkegaard conceives it, is a total and passionate commitment to God. It is the result of an act of will, as it were, or a decision, and the person with this faith completely disregards any doubts. This is not to say that the person with faith or, as Kierkegaard puts it, the knight of faith, is unaware of the possibility of error in such a commitment or is not anxious because of this possibility. The knight of faith keeps well in mind that according to objective reasoning—that is, reasoning that would be accepted by virtually all persons who are sufficiently intelligent, fair-minded, and informed to have established its conclusion as true or probably true—his belief in God is not justified. Nevertheless, it is precisely because it is not based on objective reasoning that faith is the highest virtue. Faith is not and should not be objectively certain; that is, it is not and should not be certain on the basis of objective reasoning. Kierkegaard maintains that with objective certainty comes lack of personal growth and spiritual stagnation. But with faith there is risk, danger, and adventure—all essential for spiritual growth and transcendence. Kierkegaard argues that, even when the Christian God seems paradoxical and absurd, even without adequate evidence for such commitment, total and passionate commitment to God is necessary for salvation and ultimately for happiness. Thus he rejects as irrelevant to Christian faith not only any appeal to the traditional arguments for the existence of God but any recourse to historical evidence to substantiate the claims of Scripture.

What can be said in a general way about such a conception of religious faith? First of all, religious faith as Kierkegaard conceives of it can be condemned on ethical grounds. There is no doubt that for many people there is something appealing about having faith in someone or something despite negative evidence. For example, one may admire faith in a friend's innocence in the light of evidence indicating guilt and be stirred by a superpatriot who remains loyal despite a country's apparently questionable moral practices. But our admiration ought to turn to condemnation as the evidence mounts and guilt becomes uncontroversial. In our reflective moments we all recognize that some faith and loyalty can be misplaced.[10] Surely this is because we realize that it is dangerous to be guided by blind, passionate faith. Yet this is precisely what Kierkegaard recommends.

His knight of faith is a fanatic. Indeed, his model of a knight of faith is Abraham, who is willing to sacrifice his son, Isaac.[11] We know from history the incalculable harm that can be done by fanaticism. Indeed, Walter Kaufmann is certainly correct when he calls fanaticism "one of the scourges of humanity."[12] Since its furtherance tends to result in great social harm, faith as Kierkegaard conceives of it is not a virtue but a vice.

Moreover, it is unclear how Kierkegaard's view of faith can be reconciled with a view of an all-good God.[13] How could an all-good God want his creatures to have blind faith in him without adequate evidence, let alone with negative evidence? Surely an all-good God would not want his creatures to be fanatics, especially when there is good reason to suppose that fanaticism leads to great human suffering. It would seem that if God is good in any sense of the term that is analogous to our standard sense, Kierkegaard's model of faith would not be something that God could desire and reward.

There is another reason why God would not want his creatures to have faith in Kierkegaard's sense. According to Kierkegaard, since one should have faith in improbabilities and absurdities, and since Christianity is absurd and paradoxical, one should have faith in the Christian God. But there may well be other religious beliefs that are even *more* absurd and improbable than Christianity. Some scholars have suggested that some teachings of the Koran are more absurd than some teachings of Christianity and that the claim that Nero is God incarnate is more absurd than the same claim about Jesus.[14] Even if these comparative assessments are mistaken, one could conceive of religious doctrines that called for belief in explicit contradictions or in the existence of gods who took the form of, say, purple giraffes. Following Kierkegaard's recommendation concerning faith, belief in such absurdities rather than in Christian doctrine would result. Surely a Christian God would not approve.

Not all Christian philosophers have embraced Kierkegaard's view. Analyzing the arguments Kierkegaard uses in attempting to show that objective reasoning is completely misguided in the context of religious faith, Robert Merrihew Adams[15] finds them unacceptable. It is useful to consider Adams's analysis here, for his critique not only gives us an idea of what some Christian philosophers have said about Kierkegaard's view of faith but also illustrates the problems involved in constructing an alternative view.

Adams calls Kierkegaard's first argument the approximation argument. It can be stated as follows:[16]

(1) All historical inquiry gives, at best, only approximate results.
(2) Approximate results are inadequate for religious faith, which demands certainty.

(3) Therefore, all historical inquiry is inadequate for religious faith.

Adams accepts premise (1) but rejects premise (2) of this argument. He maintains that historical inquiry could be adequate for religious faith if historical inquiry could give us a very high probability that some historical fact on which our faith rests is correct. This would in some circumstances provide sufficient ground for disregarding possible error. Although in any historical inquiry there is always the possibility of error in some cases, says Adams, the risk of not disregarding the error is greater than the risk of disregarding it. He uses the following example to illustrate his point. Suppose that historical inquiry can establish with a probability of 99 percent the proposition that Jesus declared Peter and his episcopal successors to be infallible in matters of religious doctrine (P). Suppose further that it is of infinite importance to you to have a true belief concerning (P). According to Adams, objective reasoning can establish that you ought to commit yourself to the most probable opinion and disregard the small risk of error in such a commitment. Thus objective reasoning can establish that you ought to commit yourself to (P) and disregard the 1 percent risk of error.

Adams is careful to note that Kierkegaard was not arguing that historical propositions about Christianity such as (P) cannot be established with a high degree of probability by objective reasoning. In turn, Adams is not arguing that they can be. Rather, Kierkegaard was arguing that objective reasoning cannot establish that one ought to commit oneself to certain historical propositions about Christianity even if they are highly probable, and Adams is arguing that it can.

The second argument Adams considers is one he calls the postponement argument. Consider:

(1') One cannot have an authentic religious faith without being totally committed to the belief in question.

(2') One cannot be totally committed to any belief based on an inquiry in which one recognizes the possibility of a future need to revise the results.

(3') Therefore, authentic religious faith cannot be based on any inquiry in which one recognizes the possibility of a future need to revise the results.

(4') Since all rational inquiry recognizes the contingency of future revision, no authentic religious faith can be based on it.

Adams questions the first premise of the argument, saying:

It has commonly been thought to be an important part of religious ethics that one ought to be humble, teachable, open to correction, new inspiration, and growth of insight, even (and perhaps especially) in important religious beliefs. This view would have to be discarded if we were to concede to Kierkegaard that the heart of commitment in religion is an unconditional determination not to change in one's important religious beliefs.[17]

The third argument of Kierkegaard that Adams considers is the one Adams calls the passion argument. It can be stated as follows:

(1") The most essential and valuable trait of religious faith is passion, a passion of the greatest possible intensity.

(2") An infinite passion requires objective improbability.

(3″) Therefore, that which is most essential and valuable in religious faith requires objective improbability.

Why does Kierkegaard hold premise (2″), Adams asks? Kierkegaard requires that some religious beliefs be objectively improbable because he believes that without these there is no risk, and without risk there is no passion. Indeed, according to Adams, Kierkegaard holds that the degree of risk one is willing to take is in part a measure of one's passion.

However, Adams questions premise (1″), not premise (2″). Kierkegaard's ideal of infinite passion is impossible, he says, since "I doubt that any human being could have a passion of this sort, because I doubt that one could make a sacrifice so great that a greater could not be made or have a (nonzero) chance of success so small that a smaller could not be had."[18] Furthermore, Adams is skeptical that infinite passion should even be a goal that one should try to approximate. For example, if one should increase the cost and risk of a religious life, then it would seem by the logic of Kierkegaard's argument that one should exchange "the pursuit of truth, beauty, and satisfying relationships for the self-flagellating pursuit of pain."[19] Adams finds this conception of the religious life "demonic," and he urges that "some way must be found to conceive of religious interest as inclusive rather than exclusive of the best of other interests—including. . .the interest in having well-grounded beliefs."[20]

Adams's critique of Kierkegaard's concept is useful in showing that Kierkegaard is unsuccessful in arguing that religious faith should not be guided by reason, that it ideally should be a commitment to improbable beliefs. But Adams does not show, nor does he purport to show, that religious faith is guided by reason or that it is not committed to improbable doctrines. As Adams well knows, the example mentioned above— the 99 percent probability that Jesus declared Peter and his episcopal successors to be infallible in matters of religious doctrine—is purely hypothetical. There is little evidence that this or many of the other major events described in Scripture actually occurred; indeed, in many cases there is excellent reason to suppose that these events could *not* have occurred as portrayed, since they are portrayed in conflicting ways in different biblical accounts.[21] For example, one of the key events in the Christian story is Christ's death and resurrection. Yet this story is different in different Gospels. A Christian who holds to one version of the story can be contradicted by someone else citing Scripture. Thus Christian belief must go beyond the evidence. Indeed, in some cases it is at least arguable that it not only must go beyond the evidence but must go *against* the historical evidence. And, barring a breakthrough in biblical scholarship, Christians must hold some improbable beliefs. For example, recent historical scholarship makes a plausible case that Jesus did not exist.[22]

Adams is surely correct to say that religious believers should be "open to corrections, new inspiration, growth and insight." Yet he gives no indication of how this is possible without construing religious propositions as testable and how, if religious propositions are testable, they can be adequate for the religious life.

I conclude that Kierkegaard's account of religious faith provides no basis for belief in God, that in fact it counsels fanaticism and irrationality, that it is incompatible with Christian belief, and that Adams in his critique of Kierkegaard provides no plausible alternative view of religious belief.

Wittgensteinian Fideism

Just as Kierkegaard and his followers have strongly influenced one important conception of religious faith, so Ludwig Wittgenstein and his followers have strongly influenced one important conception of the nature of religious discourse. Wittgenstein[23] gave hints of a concept of religious discourse in *Lectures and Conversations on Aesthetics, Psychology and Religious Belief* that have been developed by followers[24] such as Norman Malcolm, D. Z. Phillips, and Peter Winch into an approach to religion called Wittgensteinian fideism.

According to Wittgensteinian fideism,[25] religious discourse is embedded in a form of life and has its own rules and logic. It can only be understood and evaluated in its own terms, and any attempt to impose standards on such discourse from the outside—for example, from science—is quite inappropriate. Since religious discourse is a separate unique language game different from that of science, religious statements, unlike scientific ones, are not empirically testable. To demand that they be is a serious misunderstanding of that form of discourse. On this view of the language game of religion, religious discourse is rational and intelligible when judged in its own terms, which are the only appropriate ones. Because the meaning of a term varies from one language game to another, to understand religious language one must see it from within the religious language game itself. In general, a philosopher's task is not to criticize a form of life or its language but to describe both and, where necessary, to eliminate philosophical puzzlement concerning the operation of the language. In particular, a philosopher of religion's job is to describe the use of religious discourse and eliminate any perplexities that may result from it.

Now, there are some aspects of the Wittgensteinian point of view with which even its severest critics can sympathize; for example, that it is important to get inside a religious practice to understand it. But from this admission the major and most controversial views of Wittgensteinian fideism do not follow.

First of all, the basis for distinguishing one form of life from another, one language game from another, is unclear. For example, consider the practices of astrology and fortunetelling by reading palms, tea leaves, and so on. Do these constitute forms of life with their own language games? What about political practices? Does each political group and its practice constitute a different form of life with its own language game? Did the Nazis have their own form of life with its own language game? In the case of religion, is there only one religious language game, or are there many? Is there one for each religion? One for each denomination or sect within each religion? The differences between Buddhism and Christianity are so vast that one strongly suspects that the Wittgensteinian fideist would have to say that these constitute different forms of life involving different language games. But if this is granted, must one not also admit that the practices of different Christian denominations differ in fundamental ways? Consider, for example, Roman Catholicism, Mormonism, and Christian Science. Would not a Wittgensteinian fideist have to say that in these cases there are different religious forms of life involving different language games? But if one goes this far, would not one have to say that different Protestant denominations such as the Methodist and the Baptist, and even different sects within each, having different religious language games? Yet since for Wittgensteinian fideism the same terms in different language games have different meanings, this seems to have the absurd consequence that members of one Baptist sect would not be able to understand members of another Baptist sect.

Second, since each form of life is governed by its own standards, there could be no external criticism. Yet this has unacceptable consequences. Suppose that astrology and fortunetelling by reading palms or tea leaves constitute separate forms of life. It would follow that these practices must not be judged by outside standards despite the fact that they seem to be based on false or at least dubious assumptions. Suppose that each political practice constitutes a separate form of life. If so, external criticism of a practice such as Nazism would be impossible.

Suppose each religious form of life is governed by its own standards. Then there could be no external standards that could be used in criticizing a religious form of life. However, this has unfortunate consequences. Some religious denominations practice sexual and racial discrimination; for instance, the Mormon church excluded blacks from positions in the church hierarchy, and it still excludes women. It is not implausible to suppose that most enlightened people today believe that this practice and the beliefs on which it rests are wrong. Yet if Mormonism is a separate form of life, there can be no external criticism of its practices.

Despite what Wittgensteinian fideists say, external criticism is not only possible but essential. If Wittgensteinian fideists are correct, there would

be something contradictory or incoherent in the claim, "This is an ongoing religious form of life that is irrational." But there is not. Indeed, even
participants in a religion sometimes find its doctrines incoherent, its
major arguments resting on dubious premises, and some of its practices
morally questionable. In fact, there seems to be no good reason why a
religious form of life or, for that matter, any form of life could not be
evaluated externally and found wanting. Although insight into a form
of life may be gained by taking the participants' perspective, one cannot
rest content with this, for the participants may be blind to the problems
with their own practices and beliefs, and the perspective of an outsider
may be necessary if these are to be detected.

Wittgensteinian fideism also has paradoxical implications concerning
the truth of religious utterances within a language game. If Jones says
"There is no God" within the Buddhist's language game, and Smith says
"There is a God" within the Christian language game, the Wittgensteinian
fideist would seem to be holding that both statements are true. Since
they seem to contradict one another, how can that be? The answer a
Wittgensteinian fideist would give is that the meaning of a religious
utterance is relative to the language game to which it belongs. So despite
appearances to the contrary, what Jones denies in our example is not
what Smith affirms. The Wittgensteinian fideist seems committed to
believing it is an illusion that a Roman Catholic who says the pope is
infallible contradicts a Baptist who says the pope is not infallible. One
tends to think otherwise because one does not realize that the meanings
of religious utterances are relative to different language games.

Why should we accept the view of language and meaning presupposed
by this view? There seems to be no good reason for the thesis that the
meaning of language is radically contextual and that it is impossible to
communicate across practices or ways of life. Indeed, it makes nonsense
of the debates not only between Christians and non-Christians, but between defenders of different Christian denominations. For on this view,
despite the long and bitter arguments, there is no real disagreement; the
debating parties are on different tracks talking past one another. Such a
view, although perhaps not impossible, seems highly unlikely.

Surely a more plausible view of these examples is that the Christian and
non-Christian are really disagreeing and that the Catholic and Baptist are
talking about the same thing; in other words, that there are a common
language and common categories. As Kai Nielsen has argued:

> There is no "religious language" and "scientific language." There is
> rather the international notation of mathematics and logic; and English,
> French, Spanish and the like. In short, "religious discourse" and "scientific
> discourse" are part of the same overall conceptual structure. Moreover, in
> that conceptual structure there is a large amount of discourse, which is

neither religious nor scientific, that is constantly being utilized by both the religious man and the scientist when they make religious and scientific claims. In short, they share a number of key categories.[26]

What Nielsen says about the scientist and the religious person can be said with equal validity about the Christian and non-Christian, the Catholic and Baptist. Religious language is not completely compartmentalized from other languages, and the language of one religion, denomination, or sect is not completely compartmentalized from the languages of others.

Norman Malcolm's approach to religious faith is a typical example of Wittgensteinian fideism. A pupil of Wittgenstein and one of his most sensitive commentators, Malcolm argues in "The Groundlessness of Belief" that many of our fundamental beliefs are merely the framework within which questions are posed and our inquiries are carried out. For example, the belief that "material things (watches, shoes, chairs) do not cease to exist without some physical explanation" is a groundless belief that provides part of the framework of our entire system of beliefs.[27] Suppose one's keys are lost. According to Malcolm, no one in our society would seriously consider that the keys vanished into thin air, but one could imagine a society in which people did believe that. In such a society, Malcolm says, science, people's attitudes toward money, and many other things would differ from ours. People would have a different framework. However, Malcolm insists that our belief that material things do not vanish into thin air is not based on better evidence than the contrary belief of people in that other society. We are not even willing to consider the suggestion that something just ceased to exist, he says. The belief that things do not cease to exist without physical cause "is an unreflective part of the framework within which physical investigations are made and physical explanations arrived at."[28]

Malcolm maintains that religious belief is groundless in the same way. Both it and religious practice are embedded in a form of life in which, because of common training, there is wide agreement. Within the religious language game there is justification, evidence, and proof, but there is no justification of the language game itself. As Malcolm puts it, when pressed for a justification of the religious language game we can only say, "This is what we do. This is how we are."[29] Malcolm is opposed to the common belief that unless one can give a rational proof for the existence of God, a belief in God is irrational. This is as much a misunderstanding as is the supposition that one must have a rational proof in order to have a justified belief that things don't vanish into thin air. According to Malcolm, people's belief in God and the actions that accompany it, such as praying for help or forgiveness and complying with divine commandments, are simply what religious people do, and they need no more justification than does the scientific form of life.

Malcolm's defense of religious faith is unacceptable. The analogy he draws between belief in God (G) and belief that material objects do not vanish into thin air (M) is not compelling. First of all, there are in our society no sane people, other than professional philosophical skeptics, who question M, and it is in fact hard to see how they could. What kind of reason could they give? But there are many people who do question G and give plausible reasons for their disbelief. Further, some people who now question G at one time did not. Even some people who accept G find it problematic and difficult to defend. It is significant that only professional philosophers attempted to defend M in the light of skeptical arguments and that even philosophical skeptics do not seriously question M in their everyday life. But it is not only professional philosophical skeptics who question G. Many ordinary people have either given up their belief in God or believe with difficulty.

In fact, one may agree with Malcolm that we have certain groundless beliefs that provide a framework for questions and inquiries and yet deny that any religious beliefs are groundless, for a particular mode of justification that is embedded within some language game may itself need justification in terms of some more basic mode of justification. For example, it is common practice to appeal to the authority of a dictionary to settle questions about the meaning of a word. However, this practice itself needs justification—for example, justification based on inductive evidence of the reliability of lexicographers in determining the meaning of words. Malcolm must show that the religious mode is autonomous, that it does not need to be justified by some more fundamental mode of justification. To do this would require his giving an adequate account of religious language.[30] This he has not done.

Moreover, despite what Malcolm says, there does seem to be better evidence for M than for ~M. Consequently, there is good reason to suppose that M is not a groundless belief. There is good inductive evidence for M of the following kind. In the vast majority of cases where things have seemed to disappear into thin air—the vanished cards of the magician, the ships and planes missing in the so-called Bermuda triangle—either we know what happened or we have plausible explanations. But what about the small number of cases for which we have no plausible explanations? Aside from their not yet having been explained, these cases do not seem to be significantly different from those that initially seemed unexplainable but now have an explanation. It is therefore a reasonable inductive conclusion that these cases also have an explanation, although it is as yet unknown. However, if M is not groundless, the analogy between the groundlessness of M and the groundlessness of G collapses.

Malcolm seems to assume that people in our culture believe M and people in other cultures believe ~M without good reason. I have just suggested that there are inductive reasons for preferring M over ~M. However, even if there were no inductive reasons for preferring M over ~M, the choice would not be arbitrary. There is good reason to reject ~M, for its acceptance as a working hypothesis would prevent us from ever discovering an explanation if one is available. Thus working on the assumption that there is always an explanation for apparent disappearance into thin air does not block inquiry, whereas working on the assumption that sometimes there is no explanation would block inquiry. Consequently, rejecting ~M and accepting M is vindicated on practical grounds.

As we have seen, Malcolm seems to reject all grounds for belief in God.[31] On the other hand, he does say that *within* a language game there is justification, evidence, and proof. But it is unclear how this suggestion is to be understood and how it relates to the thesis that belief in God is groundless. On one interpretation, Malcolm can be taken to be suggesting that belief in God and perhaps other religious beliefs as well are groundless within the religious language game, while other religious beliefs are proved or justified in terms of these groundless beliefs. On this reading, his position is a type of religious foundationalism: Some basic beliefs are not based on any other beliefs, and all other beliefs are based on these. On a second interpretation, Malcolm can be understood as suggesting that some of the standard arguments for the existence of God—for example, the teleological argument—are sound *within* the religious language game but not when external standards are applied. On a third interpretation, he can be taken as suggesting that proofs very different from the standard ones have a special relevance within certain religious language games but not within others. For example, in some fundamentalist Christian language games a proof consists in simply citing Scripture; in others a proof consists in citing the pronouncements of some religious leader.

The problems with the first interpretation need not detain us here, since religious foundationalism is considered in detail below. It is difficult to understand the second interpretation, since it is not clear how an argument could be both sound and unsound. This view may, however, rest on an assumption we have already rejected: that the meaning of religious language is radically contextual and compartmentalized. The third interpretation has many problems, not the least of which is that the use of scriptural citation as proof allows conflicting religious theses to be proved, as does appeal to different religious leaders.

I must conclude that as an approach to religious faith, Wittgensteinian fideism is no more successful than traditional and existential ones.

Are Avowals of Religious Faith True or False?

So far we have been assuming that when a religious believer avows faith in God or in some particular religious creed, the avowal is true or false. For example, when a Christian avows faith by saying, "Christ became man and redeemed the world," this statement is either true or false.

J. S. Clegg has presented the most powerful argument I know of that avowals of faith are neither true nor false. Here I have been arguing that in many cases there is good reason to suppose that statements expressing faith are probably false, or at least that the degree of belief the religious person has in the statements goes beyond anything warranted by the evidence. If Clegg's position is correct, however, such statements need no evidence or argument to support them.[32] It is important, therefore, to determine whether what Clegg maintains is true. Clegg argues:

> Genuine avowals of faith reveal states of mind. They are most accurately read as symptomatic displays that may be judged as sincere or insincere, but not as true or false. Being that, they require no warrant from an argument—no more than a doubt-excluding moan requires a justifying line of reasoning.[33]

According to Clegg, expressions of faith, although propositional in form, are like symptoms. Just as it would be inappropriate to interpret a fearful airplane passenger's "We are all going to die in a crash" as a prediction of what will happen, it would be inappropriate to interpret a religious believer's "We will all meet in Heaven" as a prediction. In the case of the passenger, the remark is a symptom of terror. In the case of the religious believer, the statement is a symptom of the inverse of terror—namely, a strong hope or powerful trust.

Clegg holds that although arguments and evidence may weaken or bolster faith just as they may weaken or bolster terror, faith is "not made believable, rendered dubious or disproved" by evidence or arguments. He says that what is made believable, rendered dubious, or disproved by evidence and argument is not faith but "the substratum of faith." By this we can take him to mean the beliefs and assumptions that give rise to the symptomatic expression of trust. For example, given what we think or know about the situation, we may be justified in dismissing or being dismayed by a wife's faith in her husband's safe return, but we could not say that her faith was irrational or poorly reasoned.

But what about religious faith? According to Clegg, it is not irrational or poorly reasoned either. The major difference between faith in religious and nonreligious contexts is that in the former there are no good grounds for dismissing a person's faith. He maintains: "The simple fact in need of acknowledgment is that what we call religious faith rests on belief at the borders of what we know. Declaring their truth warrants a charge of dogmatism; declaring their falsity does so as well."[34] We are not justified in dismissing a person's religious faith, presumably, because one does not know whether the substratum of a person's faith is true or false.

Clegg is not saying that religious faith is intellectually autonomous, that canons of evidence and arguments from outside religion are irrelevant to religious faith. He rejects the position of Wittgensteinian fideism that the religious language game is governed by its own rules and logic. According to Clegg, religious faith can be affected by scientific evidence in the sense that the substratum of faith can be supported or undermined by it. Indeed, new knowledge can shake, dash, or even crush religious faith. But he insists that new knowledge cannot falsify such faith.

There is much that one can accept in Clegg's account. What is particularly agreeable about his position is his insistence that faith is not intellectually autonomous and that the usual canons of evidence and argument apply to its substratum. It is difficult to accept or even understand his claim that one is being dogmatic if one maintains that the substratum of some religious faith is false, however. How can Clegg maintain *both* that it is dogmatic to suppose that the substratum of faith is false and that the ordinary canons of evidence and argument can undermine this substratum? Surely it is uncontroversial that in some cases this substratum has been undermined by scientific evidence. Consider, for example, the Christian fundamentalist's faith, in whose substratum belongs the belief that the earth is only several thousand years old. It is hard to see how one who claims that this underlying belief is false is being dogmatic. This belief is hardly on the borders of what we know.

The most important aspect of Clegg's thesis is that avowals of faith are symptomatic of a person's state of mind. However, Clegg goes too far when he maintains that avowals of faith are neither true or false. For not only does it fail to follow from this claim that they are symptomatic of states of mind, but it seems implausible on its own grounds. Consider his example of the frightened airplane passenger. It might be *insensitive* to say to the terrified passenger who expects to die in a crash, "You are mistaken; all the evidence suggests that we will land safely in a few minutes," but this would be a perfectly meaningful and justified thing to say. What Clegg does not consider is that a statement can be true or false yet symptomatic of the state of mind of the person who makes it. A hearer can believe with perfect consistency *both* that the statement is true (or false) and that it reveals some particular state of mind of the speaker.

Surely this is true for religious faith as well. It might be insensitive to say to a Christian who believes that Christ became man and redeemed the world, "The best historical scholarship indicates that Jesus, if he existed at all, was a mere man." But it would be perfectly meaningful and justifiable to do so. The Christian would be saying something that was probably false and yet revealing his or her state of mind. That one would normally not say something like this is not evidence of the statement's truth or falsity.

Until more persuasive arguments are given than those presented by Clegg, one is justified in continuing to hold the common view that avowals of faith are true or false, rational or irrational, well or ill supported.

Could an Atheist Have Faith in God?

So far I have assumed that if X has faith in God, then X believes that God exists. This is certainly the usual way in which faith is understood. To be sure, faith in God has often been thought to involve *more* than the belief that God exists. For example, on Aquinas's view, faith in God involves the belief that particular Christian doctrines are true, the belief that these were revealed by God, and perhaps even public confession of one's belief. On the Lutheran view, faith involves the belief that God exists, something like public confession, and trust in God.[35] Would it be possible, however, for X to have faith in God yet not believe that God exists? If so, could an atheist have faith in God?

In a recent paper Louis Pojman has argued that propositional belief—that is, belief that something is the case—is not necessary for religious faith and that religious faith can be founded on hope.[36] If Pojman's thesis is correct, perhaps a person who does not believe in God but who nevertheless hopes that God exists could still have faith in God's existence.

Pojman maintains that in many nonreligious contexts, in order to act rationally it is not necessary that the evidence be sufficient to justify positive belief. We may be guided by a weak probability or even the bare possibility that something is true. In such a case we may be guided by hope and not belief. What does hope involve? According to Pojman, to hope for something, one must believe that although it is not certain it is possible. Moreover, hope entails desire for the state of affairs hoped for and a disposition to do what one can to bring about this state of affairs. According to Pojman a hope can be irrational—for example, when what is hoped for is nearly impossible. Furthermore, the object hoped for need not be something that one believes exists. For example, he says that one may have deep faith that a race horse will win yet not believe strongly that it exists.

Pojman claims that his analysis of profound hope is relevant to the context of religious faith. To have faith in God, he says, is not necessarily to believe that God exists. Faith in God can be what he calls experimental faith. Such a faith is open to new evidence that would confirm or disconfirm the hypothesis on which the hope is based. Although faith in God does not entail the belief that God exists, it does entail belief in the possibility that God exists and commitment to living *as if* God exists. Pojman maintains that whether it is rational to have faith in God in this sense "depends on the outcome of an analysis of comparative values in relationship to probable outcomes. It is the sort of assessment that goes on in any cost-benefit analysis."[37]

As a consequence of his analysis Pojman maintains that agnosticism and "even an interested type of atheism" are possible religious positions.[38] The atheist, he says, might find the proposition "God exists" genuinely possible and might decide to live by it. Whether Pojman is correct depends on the status of the concept of God and of religious language. An atheist could have faith in God in Pojman's sense only if the existence of God is not impossible and the statement "God exists" is either true or false. As we saw in Chapter 2, there is some reason to believe that religious language is meaningless. As we will see in Chapter 12, even if religious language is not meaningless, there is good reason to believe that the concept of God is incoherent. But if the arguments in either of these chapters are successful, then any hope that God exists is excluded. If the proposition "God exists" is meaningless, then one could not hope that this proposition is true, for meaningless propositions cannot be true or false. If the concept of God is incoherent, one could not hope that He exists, since the proposition "God exists" would be necessarily false.

Further, even if the concept of God is coherent and religious language is not meaningful, a difficult problem confronts an atheist who wants to have faith in God in Pojman's sense. For Pojman's faith in God entails acting *as if* one believes that God exists. However, the way one acts if one believes that God exists depends on one's other beliefs and ultimately on the religion and even the religious denomination or sect that one adopts. There is no acting as if one believes that God exists in general. The way one acts depends on the particular rituals, customs, ceremonies, and moral code of one's particular religion, denomination, or sect. Consider the differences between being an orthodox Jew and being a Roman Catholic. Pojman makes it seem that acting as if one has faith in God entails some unique and agreed-on set of practices. In fact, there are as many sets of behaviors that might be referred to "as acting as if one believes in God" as there are theistic religions, denominations, and sects.

Which of these should be the choice of the atheist who wants to have faith in God in a sense that does not entail belief? As we have seen, Pojman says that whether it is rational to have faith in God "depends on . . . the sort of assessment that goes on in any cost-benefit analysis." But if there is no faith in God in general on Pojman's account of faith, his point might have to be restated. The question of whether it is rational to have faith in God would amount to whether it would be more rational to act as if one was or was not a follower of some theistic religion, denomination, or sect. But once this question was settled, another crucial question would remain. What would be the most rational choice among theistic religions, denominations, and sects? To act as if one was a Catholic? A Mormon? An Orthodox Jew? Needless to say, this would be a difficult choice given the large number of theistic religions, denominations, and sects.

It may be suggested that Pojman's idea of experimental faith could be helpful in making this choice. A defender of Pojman might suggest that one might try some religion, denomination, or sect for a while and then, in light of new evidence, change one's allegiances to a different one. But Pojman's idea of experimental faith has problems of its own. His characterization of such faith makes it sound as if a religious proposition is like a working scientific hypothesis that is confirmed or disconfirmed in the light of new evidence. He gives no clue as to what such evidence could be, however. As we have seen, many religious thinkers have maintained that religious statements are not confirmable or disconfirmable by empirical evidence. The problem is especially acute because, as we have suggested, the choice is not just between faith in God in general and no faith in God but between faith in the God of one or another theistic religion, denomination, and sect. It is far from obvious what sort of evidence would be relevant in making a choice between the Methodist and the Baptist faith, for example. If one starts to act as if one is a believer in Methodism, what possible evidence would induce one to stop acting in this way and start acting as if one is a Baptist? Until this sort of question is answered, Pojman's talk of experimental faith is unwarranted.

Religious Beliefs and Basic Beliefs

One recent attempt to justify religious beliefs argues that some religious beliefs—for example, the belief that God exists—should be considered as basic beliefs that form the foundations of all other beliefs. The best-known advocate of this position is Alvin Plantinga,[39] whose theory is based on a critique of classical foundationalism.

FOUNDATIONALISM

Foundationalism was once a widely accepted view in epistemology; and although it has undergone modifications, it still has many advocates. The motivation for the view seems compelling. If we try to justify all our beliefs in terms of other beliefs, the justification generates an infinite regress or vicious circularity. Therefore, there must be some beliefs that do not need to be justified by other beliefs. Because they form the foundation of all knowledge, these are called basic beliefs, and the statements expressing them are called basic statements.

Foundationalism is usually considered a normative theory. It sets standards of what are properly basic beliefs and standards of how nonbasic beliefs are to be related to basic ones.[40] Not every belief could be basic, and not every relation could link nonbasic beliefs to basic ones. According to the classical normative account of foundationalism, if one believes that a self-evident statement P is true because of the statement's self-evidence, then P is a properly basic one. According to this view, if a statement is self-evident, no conscious inference or calculation is required to determine its truth; one can merely look at it and know immediately that it is true. For example, certain simple and true statements of mathematics ($2 + 2 = 4$) and logic (Either p or $\sim$p) are self-evidently true to almost everyone, while some more complex statements of mathematics and logic are self-evidently true only to some. Consequently, statements such as $2 + 2 = 4$ are considered basic statements for almost everyone while the more complex statements are basic only to some.

In addition to self-evident statements, classical foundationalists held that beliefs based on direct perception are properly basic and the statements expressing such beliefs—sometimes called statements that are evident to the senses—were considered basic statements. Some foundationalists included, in the class of statements that are evident to the senses, ones about observed physical objects (There is a blue bird in the tree). However, in modern times it has been more common for foundationalists to restrict statements that are evident to the senses to ones about immediate sense impressions (I seem to see a blue bird in the tree, or I am being appeared to bluely, or perhaps, Here now blue sense datum). According to the classical foundationalist account, statements that are evident to the senses are incorrigible; that is, one can decide not to believe such statements and be mistaken.

Denying that any statement is incorrigible, many contemporary epistemologists, although sympathetic with the foundationalist program, have maintained that statements that are evident to the senses are either initially credible[41] or self-warranted.[42] Moreover, some contemporary foundationalists have argued that memory statements, such as "I remember having breakfast ten minutes ago" should be included in the class of properly basic statements.[43] Classical foundationalism also maintained that nonbasic beliefs had to be justified in terms of basic beliefs. Thus in order for a person P's nonbasic statement NS_1 (Other people have minds) to be justified, it would either have to follow logically from P's set of basic statements BS_1 & BS_2 & . . . BS_n or be probable relative to that set of statements. However, those contemporary foundationalists who maintain that properly basic statements are only initially credible allow that it is possible that a person P's basic statements BS_1 could be shown to be false if it conflicted with many of the well-supported nonbasic statements NS_1 & NS_2 & . . . NS_n of P. In addition, some have argued that deductive and inductive principles of inference must be supplemented with other principles of derivation.[44] Consequently, a person P's nonbasic statement NS_1 is justified only if it follows from P's set of basic statements or is probable relative to this set or is justified relative to this set by means of certain special epistemic principles.

PLANTINGA'S CRITIQUE OF FOUNDATIONALISM

Plantinga characterizes foundationalism as follows:

> Ancient and medieval foundationalism tended to hold that a proposition is properly basic for a person only if it is either self-evident or evident to the senses; modern foundationalism—Descartes, Locke, and Leibniz, and the like—tended to hold that a proposition is properly basic for S only if either self-evident or incorrigible for S. . . . Let us now say that a *classical foundationalist* is anyone who is either an ancient and medieval or a modern foundationalist.[45]

He defines properly basic statements in terms of this understanding of foundationalism. Consider:

(1) A proposition p is properly basic for a person S if and only if p is self-evident to S, or incorrigible, or evident to the senses.

Plantinga gives two basic arguments against foundationalism so understood. (a) He maintains that many of the statements we know to be true cannot be justified in foundationalist terms. These statements are not properly basic according to the definition given above, nor can they be justified by either deductive or inductive inference from properly basic statements. As examples of such statements Plantinga cites "Other people have minds" and "The world existed five minutes ago." To be sure, he says, such statements are basic for most people in a descriptive sense. According to classical foundationalists, however, they should not be, since they are not self-evident, not incorrigible, and not evident to the senses. According to Plantinga, examples such as these show that there is something very wrong with classical foundationalism.

(b) Plantinga argues also that foundationalists are unable to justify (1) in their own terms; that is, they have not shown that (1) follows from properly basic statements or is probable relative to these. Moreover, (1) is not itself self-evident or incorrigible or evident to the senses. Consequently, he argues, a foundationalist who accepts (1) is being "self-referentially inconsistent"; such a person accepts a statement that does not meet the person's own conditions for being properly basic. Thus he concludes that classical foundationalism is "bankrupt."

BELIEF IN GOD AS PROPERLY BASIC

Following a long line of reformed thinkers—that is, thinkers influenced by the doctrines of John Calvin, Plantinga contends that traditional arguments for the existence of God are not needed for rational belief. He cites with approval Calvin's claim that God created humans in such a way that they have a strong tendency to believe in God. According to Plantinga, Calvin maintained:

> Were it not for the existence of sin in the world human beings would believe in God to the same degree and with the same natural spontaneity that we believe in the existence of other persons, an external world, or the past. This is a natural human condition; it is because of our presently unnatural sinful condition that many of us find belief in God difficult or absurd. The fact is, Calvin thinks, one who does not believe in God is in an epistemically substandard position—rather like a man who does not believe that his wife exists, or thinks that she is like a cleverly constructed robot and has no thoughts, feelings, or consciousness.[46]

Although this natural tendency to believe in God may be partially suppressed, Plantinga argues, it is triggered by "a widely realizable condition."[47] For example, it may be triggered "in beholding the starry heavens, or the splendid majesty of the mountains, or the intricate, articulate beauty of a tiny flower."[48] This natural tendency to accept God in these circumstances is perfectly rational. No argument for God is needed. Plantinga maintains that the best interpretation of Calvin's views, as well as those of the other reformed thinkers he cites, is that they rejected classical foundationalism and maintained that belief in God can itself be a properly basic belief.

Surprisingly, Plantinga insists that although belief in God and belief about God's attributes and actions are properly basic, for reformed epistemologists this does not mean that there are no justifying circumstances or that they are without grounds. The circumstances that trigger the natural tendency to believe in God and to believe certain things about God provide the justifying circumstances for belief. So although beliefs about God are properly basic, they are not groundless.[49]

How can we understand this? Plantinga draws an analogy between basic statements of religion and basic statements of perceptual belief and memory. A perceptual belief, he says, is taken as properly basic only under certain circumstances. For example, if I know that I am wearing rose-tinted glasses, then I am not justified in saying that the statement "I see a rose-colored wall before me" is properly basic; and if I know that my memory is unreliable, I am not justified in saying that the statement "I remember that I had breakfast" is properly basic. Although Plantinga admits that these conditions may be hard to specify, he maintains that their presence is necessary in order to claim that a perceptual or memory statement is basic. Similarly, he maintains that not every statement about God that is not based on argument or evidence should be considered properly basic. A statement is properly basic only in the right circumstances. What circumstances are right? Plantinga gives no general account, but in addition to the triggering conditions mentioned above, the right conditions include reading the Bible, having done something wrong, and being in grave danger. Thus if one is reading the Bible and believes that God is speaking to one, then the belief is properly basic.

Furthermore, Plantinga insists that although reformed epistemologists allow belief in God as a properly basic belief, this does not mean they must allow that anything at all can be a basic belief. To be sure, he admits that he and other reformed epistemologists have not supplied us with any criterion of what is properly basic. He argues, however, that this is not necessary. One can know that some beliefs in some circumstances are not properly basic without having an explicitly formulated criterion of basicness. Thus Plantinga says that reformed epistemologists can correctly maintain that belief in voodoo or astrology or the Great Pumpkin is not a basic belief.

How is one to arrive at a criterion for being properly basic? According to Plantinga the route is "broadly speaking, *inductive*." He adds, "We must assemble examples of beliefs and conditions such that the former are obviously properly basic in the latter. . . . We must frame hypotheses as to the necessary and sufficient conditions of proper basicality and test these hypotheses by reference to these examples."[50]

He argues that, using this procedure,

> the Christian will of course suppose that belief in God is entirely proper and rational; if he does not accept this belief on the basis of other propositions, he will conclude that it is basic for him and quite properly so. Followers of Russell and Madelyn Murray O'Hare [*sic*] may disagree; but how is that relevant? Must my criteria, or those of the Christian community, conform to their examples? Surely not. The Christian community is responsible to *its* set of examples, not to theirs.[51]

EVALUATION OF PLANTINGA'S CRITIQUE OF FOUNDATIONALISM

Recall that Plantinga argues that classical foundationalists are being self-referentially inconsistent. But as James Tomberlin has pointed out, since what is self-evident is relative to persons, a classical foundationalist (CF) could argue that (1) is self-evident and that if Plantinga were sufficiently attentive, the truth of (1) would become clear to him.[52] Tomberlin argues that this response is similar to Calvin's view that in beholding the starry heavens, the properly attuned theist senses the existence of God. As Tomberlin puts it: "If the theist may be so attuned, why can't the classical foundationalist enjoy a similar relation to (1)? No, I do not think that Plantinga has precluded CF's rejoinder; and consequently he has not proved that (1) fails to be self-evident to the classical foundationalist."[53]

However, even if Plantinga can show that (1) is not self-evident for classical foundationalists, he has not shown that (1) could not be deductively or inductively inferred from statements that are self-evident or incorrigible or evident to the senses. As Philip Quinn has argued, the classical foundationalist can use the broadly inductive procedures suggested by Plantinga to arrive at (1). Since the community of classical foundationalists is responsible for its own set of examples of properly basic beliefs and the conditions that justify them, it would not be surprising that the hypothesis they came up with in order to account for their examples would be (1).[54]

Furthermore, even if Plantinga has refuted classical foundationalism, this would hardly dispose of foundationalism. Contemporary foundationalism has seriously modified the classical theory,[55] and it is not at all clear that in the light of these modifications, Plantinga's critique could be sustained. Recall that one of his criticisms was that a statement such as "The world existed five minutes ago" could not be justified on classical foundationalist grounds. Since contemporary foundationalists include memory statements in the class of basic statements, there would not seem to be any particular problem in justifying such a statement, for "I remember having my breakfast ten minutes ago" can be a properly basic statement. Furthermore, if basic statements only have to be initially credible and not self-evident or incorrigible or evident to the senses, the criticism of self-referential inconsistency is much easier to meet. It is not at all implausible to suppose that a criterion of basicality in term of initial credibility is itself either initially credible or based on statements that are.

Plantinga is aware that there is more to foundationalism than the classical formulation of it. He says:

> Of course the evidentialist objection *need* not presuppose classical foundationalism; someone who accepted a different version of foundationalism could no doubt urge this objection. But in order to evaluate it, we should have to see what criterion of properly basic was being invoked. In the absence of such specification the objection remains at best a promissory note. So far as the present discussion goes, then, the next move is up to the evidential objector.[56]

Many contemporary foundationalist theories have been constructed on nonclassical lines.[57] Indeed, it may be safe to say that few contemporary foundationalists accept the classical view or even take it seriously. Moreover, these contemporary versions are hardly promissory notes, as Plantinga must be aware. Indeed, his refutation of classical foundationalism has just about as much relevance for contemporary foundationalism as a refutation of the emotive theory in ethics has for contemporary ethical noncognitivism. The next move, therefore, does not seem to be up to contemporary foundationalists. Plantinga must go on to show that his critique has relevance to the contemporary foundationalist program and that, given the best contemporary formulations of foundationalism, beliefs about God can be basic statements. This he has yet to do.

THE TROUBLE WITH REFORMED FOUNDATIONALISM

What can one say about Plantinga's ingenious attempt to save theism from the charge of irrationality by making beliefs about God basic?

(1) Plantinga's claim that his proposal would not allow just any belief to become a basic belief is misleading. It is true that it would not allow just any belief to become a basic belief *from the point of view of Reformed epistemologists*. However it would seem to allow any belief at all to become basic from the point of view of *some* community.[58] Although reformed epistemologists would not have to accept voodoo beliefs as rational, voodoo followers would be able to claim that insofar as they are basic in the voodoo community they are rational and, moreover, that reformed thought was irrational in this community. Indeed, Plantinga's proposal would generate many different communities that could *legitimately* claim that their basic beliefs are rational and that these beliefs conflict with basic beliefs of other communities.[59] Among the communities generated might be devil worshipers, flat earthers, and believers in fairies just so long as belief in the devil, the flatness of the earth, and fairies was basic in the respective communities.

(2) On this view the rationality of any belief is absurdly easy to obtain. The cherished belief that is held without reason by *any* group could be considered properly basic by the group's members. There would be no way to make a critical evaluation of any beliefs so considered. The community's most cherished beliefs and the conditions that, according to the community, correctly trigger such beliefs would be accepted uncritically by the members of the community as just so many more examples of basic beliefs and justifying conditions. The more philosophical members of the community could go on to propose hypotheses as to the necessary and sufficient conditions for inclusion in this set. Perhaps, using this inductive procedure, a criterion could be formulated. However, what

examples the hypotheses must account for would be decided by the community. As Plantinga says, each community would be responsible only to its own set of examples in formulating a criterion, and each would decide what is to be included in this set.

(3) Plantinga seems to suppose that there is a consensus in the Christian community about what beliefs are basic and what conditions justify these beliefs. But this is not so. Some Christians believe in God on the basis of the traditional arguments or on the basis of religious experiences; their belief in God is not basic. There would, then, certainly be no agreement in the Christian community over whether belief in God is basic or nonbasic. More important, there would be no agreement on whether doctrinal beliefs concerning the authority of the pope, the make-up of the Trinity, the nature of Christ, the means of salvation, and so on were true, let alone basic. Some Christian sects would hold certain doctrinal beliefs to be basic and rational; others would hold the same beliefs to be irrational and, indeed, the gravest of heresies. Moreover, there would be no agreement over the conditions for basic belief. Some Christians might believe that a belief is properly basic when it is triggered by listening to the pope. Others would violently disagree. Even where there was agreement over the right conditions, these would seem to justify conflicting basic beliefs and, consequently, conflicting religious sects founded on them. For example, a woman named Jones, the founder of sect S_1, might read the Bible and be impressed that God is speaking to her and telling her that p. A man named Smith, the founder of sect S_2, might read the Bible and be impressed that God is speaking to him and telling him that ~p. So Jones's belief that p and Smith's belief that ~p would both be properly basic. One might wonder how this differs from the doctrinal disputes that have gone on for centuries among Christian sects and persist to this day. The difference is that on Plantinga's proposal each sect could *justifiably* claim that its belief, for which there might be no evidence or argument, was completely rational.

(4) So long as belief that there is no God was basic for them, atheists could also justify the claim that belief in God is irrational relative to their basic beliefs and the conditions that trigger them without critically evaluating any of the usual reasons for believing in God. Just as theistic belief might be triggered by viewing the starry heavens above and reading the Bible, so atheistic beliefs might be triggered by viewing the massacre of innocent children below and reading the writings of Robert Ingersoll. Theists may disagree, but is that relevant? To paraphrase Plantinga: Must atheists' criteria conform to the Christian communities' criteria? Surely not. The atheistic community is responsible to *its* set of examples, not to theirs.

(5) There may not at present be any clear criterion for what can be a

basic belief, but belief in God seems peculiarly inappropriate for inclusion in the class since there are clear disanalogies between it and the basic beliefs allowable by classical foundationalism. For example, in his critique of classical foundationalism, Plantinga has suggested that belief in other minds and the external world should be considered basic. There are many plausible alternatives to belief in an all-good, all-powerful, all-knowing God, but there are few, if any, plausible alternatives to belief in other minds and the external world. Moreover, even if one disagrees with these arguments that seem to provide evidence against the existence of God, surely one must attempt to meet them.[60] Although there are many skeptical arguments against belief in other minds and the external world, there are in contrast no seriously accepted arguments purporting to show that there are no other minds or no external world. In this world, atheism and agnosticism are live options for many intelligent people; solipsism is an option only for the mentally ill.

(6) As we have seen, Plantinga, following Calvin, says that some conditions that trigger belief in God or particular beliefs about God also justify these beliefs and that, although these beliefs concerning God are basic; they are not groundless. Although Plantinga gave no general account of what these justifying conditions are, he presented some examples of what he meant[61] and likened these justifying conditions to those of properly basic perceptual and memory statements. The problem here is the weakness of the analogy. As Plantinga points out, before we take a perceptual or memory belief as properly basic we must have evidence that our perception or memory is not faulty. Part of the justification for believing that our perception or memory is not faulty is that in general it agrees with the perception or memory of our epistemological peers—that is, our equals in intelligence, perspicacity, honesty, thoroughness, and other relevant epistemic virtues,[62] as well as with our other experiences.[63] For example, unless my perceptions generally agreed with other perceivers with normal eyesight in normal circumstances and with my nonvisual experience—for example, that I feel something solid when I reach out—there would be no justification for supposing that my belief that I see a rose-colored wall in front of me is properly basic. Plantinga admits that if I know my memory is unreliable, my belief that I had breakfast should not be taken as properly basic. However, one knows that one's memory is reliable by determining whether it coheres with the memory reports of other people whose memory is normal and with one's other experiences.

As we have already seen, lack of agreement is commonplace in religious contexts. Different beliefs are triggered in different people when they behold the starry heavens or when they read the Bible. Beholding the starry heavens can trigger a pantheistic belief or a purely aesthetic response without any religious component. Sometimes no particular response or belief at all is triggered. From what we know about the variations of religious belief, it is likely that people would not have theistic beliefs when they beheld the starry heavens if they had been raised in nontheistic environments. Similarly, a variety of beliefs and responses are triggered when the Bible is read. Some people are puzzled and confused by the contradictions, others become skeptical of the biblical stories, others believe that God is speaking to them and has appointed them as his spokesperson, others believe God is speaking to them but has appointed no one as His spokesperson. In short, there is no consensus in the Christian community, let alone among Bible readers generally. So unlike perception and memory, there are no grounds for claiming that a belief in God is properly basic since the conditions that trigger it yield widespread disagreement among epistemological peers.[64]

(7) Part of the trouble with Plantinga's account of basic belief is the assumption he makes concerning what it means to say that a person accepts one proposition on the basis of accepting another. According to Michael Levine, Plantinga understands the relation in this way:[65]

(A) For any person S, and distinct propositions p and q, S believes q on the basis of p only if S entertains p, S accepts p, S infers q from p, and S accepts q.

Contemporary foundationalists do not accept (A) as a correct account of the relation of accepting one proposition on the basis of another. The following seems more in accord with contemporary understanding:

(B) For any person S and distinct propositions p and q, if S believes q, and S would cite p if queried under optional conditions about his reasons for believing in q, then S believes q on the basis of p.

On (B) it seems unlikely that any nonepistemologically deficient person— for example, a normal adult—would be unable to cite any reason for believing in God if this person did believe in God. Consequently, Plantinga's claim that "the mature theist does not typically accept belief in God. . .as a conclusion from other things that he believes"[66] is irrelevant if his claim is understood in terms of (A) and probably false if understood in terms of (B).[67]

(8) Finally, to consider belief in God as a basic belief seems completely out of keeping with the spirit and intention of foundationalism. Whatever else it was and whatever its problems, foundationalism was an attempt to provide critical tools for objectively appraising knowledge claims and

provide a nonrelativistic basis for knowledge. Plantinga's foundationalism is radically relativistic and puts any belief beyond rational appraisal
once it is declared basic.

THE TROUBLE WITH FOUNDATIONALISM

So far in my critique of Plantinga's attempt to incorporate beliefs in or
about God into the set of properly basic beliefs that form the foundation
of knowledge, I have uncritically accepted the idea that the structure of
knowledge must have a foundation in terms of basic beliefs. But, as
Laurence BonJour has recently shown, there is a serious problem with
any foundationalist account of knowledge.[68]

According to all foundationalist accounts, basic statements are justified
noninferentially. For example, contemporary foundationalists who hold
a moderate position maintain that properly basic statements, although
not incorrigible or self-evident, are highly justified without inductive or
deductive support. But, it may be asked, where does this justification
come from? As BonJour argues, a basic constraint on any standards of
justification for empirical knowledge is that there is a good reason for
thinking that those standards lead to truth. So if basic beliefs are to
provide a foundation for knowledge for the moderate foundationalist,
then whatever the criterion for being properly basic, it must provide a
good reason for supposing that basic beliefs are true. Further, such a
criterion must provide grounds for the person who holds a basic belief
to suppose that it is true. Thus moderate foundationalism must hold that
for any person P, basic belief B, and criterion of being properly basic ϕ,
in order for P to be justified in holding properly basic belief B, P must
be justified in believing the premises of the following justifying argument:

(1) B has feature ϕ.
(2) Beliefs having feature ϕ are likely to be true.

---

(3) Therefore, B is highly likely to be true.

Although, as BonJour argues, it might be possible that one of the two
premises in the above argument could be known to be true on an *a priori*
basis, it does not seem possible that both premises could be known *a
priori*. Once this is granted, it follows that B is not basic after all, since B's
justification would depend on some other empirical belief. But if B is
properly basic, its justification cannot depend on any other empirical
belief. BonJour goes on to meet objections to his argument, showing
that a coherent account of the structure of empirical knowledge can be
developed to overcome this problem of foundationalism and that the
objections usually raised against the coherence theory can be answered.
Surely any defender of foundationalism must meet BonJour's challenge.

As we have seen, when Plantinga proposes that belief about God can be considered properly basic, he admits that he did not have any criterion for being properly basic. But BonJour's argument tends to show that whatever criterion Plantinga might offer, there will be a problem for reformed foundationalism. If BonJour is correct, whatever this criterion is, it will have to provide a good reason for supposing that properly basic beliefs are true, and this will involve knowledge of further empirical beliefs.[69] In order to defend his position, Plantinga must refute BonJour's argument.

Conclusion

In Chapter 1 it was argued that there was a strong presumption that belief in God should be based on epistemic reasons. Some theists disagree, maintaining that religious belief is basic or should be based on faith. The conclusion here is that this argument fails. Although not all theories of faith have been examined here, the ones that were are representative enough to give us confidence that all such arguments will fail.

In a way Aquinas seems to agree with our position. He maintains that belief in the existence of God should be based on epistemic reasons; and, as we shall see in Chapter 14, he believed the arguments he produced provided such reasons. However, he believed that certain Christian dogmas were not provable by means of argument and must be based on faith. But even here he thought that one could have good epistemic reason to believe that these dogmas were revealed by God. He was wrong, however, to suppose that they were. Kierkegaard's view that faith in God should be based on absurdities and improbabilities was rejected, since the arguments he used to support this view were unsound and, in any case, his view led to fanaticism. Wittgensteinian fideism was also rejected, since it led to absurdities and presupposed an indefensible view of meaning and language.

Plantinga's reformed foundationalism has some interesting similarities to the doctrine that belief in God should be based on faith, but should not be identified with it.[70] To be sure, his view is similar to that of Aquinas, who maintains that particular Christian doctrines, although not themselves based on reason, are rational. The basic difference between the Aquinas and Plantinga positions is that Aquinas attempts to provide epistemic reasons that would persuade all rational beings to accept certain propositions as revealed truths. Plantinga provides no such reasons other than the argument that belief in God is basic and some such beliefs, including belief in God, are completely rational. Thus Plantinga's views differ markedly from those of Kierkegaard, who forsook any appeal to rationality in justifying religious belief. Plantinga's views also differ in important respects from Wittgensteinian fideism. While Wittgensteinian fideism appeals to ordinary religious practice and language to justify belief in God, Plantinga appeals to theoretical considerations from epistemology. Nevertheless, Plantinga's reformed foundationalism should be rejected since his arguments against classical foundationalism are weak, the logic of his position leads to a radical and absurd relativism, and foundationalism in general has serious problems.

PART II

Positive Atheism

CHAPTER 11

The Justification of Positive Atheism: Some Preliminaries

In Part I I argued for negative atheism with respect to the Christian–Hebraic God—that is, for the view that one is justified in not believing that there exists an all-powerful, all-knowing, all-good being who created the universe. The question remains whether positive atheism is justified—whether one is justified in disbelieving that such a being exists. In this chapter let us consider the relevance of the case for negative atheism to the case for positive atheism in order to set the stage for the arguments in the chapters that follow.

The Justification of Negative Atheism as a Justification of Positive Atheism

Michael Scriven has argued that in certain widely prevailing circumstances, successfully refuting all the arguments for the existence of God would establish positive as well as negative atheism.[1] If he is correct, then a justification of negative atheism is a justification for positive atheism. But then, the arguments presented in Part I of this volume would suffice to establish the conclusion at which Part II aims. Scriven maintains:

> if we take arguments for the existence of something to include all the evidence which supports the existence claim to any significant degree, i.e. makes it at all probable, then the absence of such evidence means there is *no* likelihood of the existence of the entity. And this, of course, is a complete justification for the claim that the entity does not exist, provided that the entity is not one which might leave no traces (a God who is impotent or who does not care for us) and provided we have comprehensively examined the area where evidence would appear if there were any.[2]

Let us formulate a principle of justified belief called *the Scriven principle* (SP):

> (SP) A person is justified in believing that X does not exist if (1) all the available evidence used to support the view that X exists is shown to be inadequate; and (2) X is the sort of entity that, if X existed, there would be available evidence that would be adequate to support the view that X exists; and (3) the area where evidence would appear, if there were any, has been comprehensively examined.[3]

Now, Scriven seems to be assuming that the only reasons relevant to the justification of belief are epistemic ones. Yet although we have seen that there is a presumption that only epistemic reasons are relevant, this is merely a presumption. Consequently, (SP) cannot be accepted as it stands. The following revision corrects the problem:

> (SP') A person is justified in believing that X does not exist if (1) all the available evidence used to support the view that X exists is shown to be inadequate; and (2) X is the sort of entity that, if X existed, there would be available evidence that would be adequate to support the view that X exists; and (3) the area where evidence would appear, if there were any, has been comprehensively examined; and (4) there are no acceptable beneficial reasons to believe that X exists.

Assuming that condition (4) is fulfilled, the crucial question in the application of (SP') to the case where X is an all-good, all-powerful, and all-knowing God is whether condition (2) holds. Is God the sort of entity that, if He exists, there would be reasons adequate to suppose that He does exist? As we know, many philosophers and theologians have thought that God is such an entity and have tried to show that God's existence is clearly evidenced.[4] The argument from design, for example, assumes that God's existence can be inferred from the make-up of the world. However, religious thinkers such as Karl Barth and Emil Brunner, stressing the transcendence of God, have argued that He is remote from the world and human affairs. On such a view of God, condition (2) is not met.

It is unclear how popular this view of God is today. However, there is a strong presumption that if an all-good, all-powerful, and all-knowing being exists, we would have good reason to suppose that He does. Why is there a strong presumption? If God is all-powerful, it seems that He could provide His creatures with good reason for knowing that He exists. If God is all-good, it would seem that He would want His creatures to know He exists so that they could worship Him and follow His commands. Consequently, He would provide them with good reason for believing in

Him. If this is so, there should be adequate evidence for believing in Him. If there is not, this indicates that an all-good, all-powerful, and all-knowing being does not exist.

Of course, the arguments of some theologians purport to defeat the strong presumption mentioned above. God has His reasons, they say, for not providing His creatures with adequate justification for believing in Him. John Hick has constructed perhaps the best-known and most sophisticated explanation of why God does not provide us with good reason for believing in Him. According to Hick, God has good reason to create "an epistemic distance" between Himself and His creatures.[5] Although the argument of theologians such as Hick, if adequate, would defeat the presumptive grounds for disbelief in God, I show in Chapter 17 that Hick's account has serious problems. So unless a more adequate account of the lack of evidence for God's existence is given, and to my knowledge none has been, SP' applies. Consequently, the presumptive ground for disbelief has not been defeated. Incorporating the idea that the application of SP' is only presumptive and could be defeated, we get *the Scriven principle extension* (SP'E):

> (SP'E) A person is justified in believing that X does not exist if (1) all the available evidence used to support the view that X exists is shown to be inadequate; and (2) X is the sort of entity that, if X exists, then there is a presumption that would be evidence adequate to support the view that X exists; and (3) this presumption has not been defeated although serious efforts have been made to do so; and (4) the area where evidence would appear, if there were any, has been comprehensively examined; and (5) there are no acceptable beneficial reasons to believe that X exists.

(SP'E) seems to be justified in terms of our ordinary and scientific practice. Consider the following example. A man dies, apparently leaving no will. One normally supposes that a person's will is the sort of entity that would be discovered through investigation if it existed. So there is a presumption that if a will exists, there should be evidence of its existence. Although the man's son claims that there is a will, none of the available evidence gives support to the hypothesis that a will exists. For example, the man had said he would not make a will, and all his records have been comprehensively examined without one's being found. However, the son insists that a will exists but there are good reasons why it has not been found. He claims that his father had good reasons for saying he would not make a will and that there are good reasons why there is no evidence of a will among his father's records. Thus the son attempts to defeat the presumptive grounds for disbelief in the existence of his father's will. However, the reasons the son gives for his contention are inadequate, and so are the reasons given by the best legal and psychological experts he can hire. The presumptive grounds, then, are not defeated. Unless there were acceptable beneficial reasons for not disbelieving, we would surely be justified in this case not only in having no belief that a will exists but also in disbelieving that a will exists.[6]

This example and others that could be given indicate that (SP'E) is an accepted principle of justification in ordinary life and science. It would be quite arbitrary not to use (SP'E) in the context of religion. So used, (SP'E) gives us good grounds to disbelieve that God exists. For even if there is no positive direct evidence that God does not exist, (SP'E) combined with our conclusions in Part I supplies us with a good reason for positive atheism—that is, with grounds for disbelief in God.

The Strength of the Case Needed for *A Posteriori* Arguments

Even if one rejects (SP'E), the conclusions of Part I are still relevant to the case for positive atheism. The arguments presented in Chapters 13 to 18 are basically *a posteriori* and, like all such arguments, are nondemonstrative in that they show on the basis of certain evidence that belief in God is improbable. Unless the arguments given for believing in God are refuted, the ones for disbelief may not outweigh those for belief. Furthermore, if we refute all the arguments for the existence of God, the positive case against God does not have to be as strong as it would otherwise. Refuting the arguments for God will show that there is no powerful case for theism that atheists need to overcome.

To illustrate this point, consider the following example. Suppose there is strong inductive evidence that Jones stole an expensive watch out of your desk, and suppose you confront Jones with the evidence. Jones will have to produce a very strong case for her innocence before you are warranted in believing her. However, if the evidence for Jones's guilt is not strong, then she should not have to produce as strong a case in order to convince you.

Now, in Part I we saw that the case for belief in God based on the arguments that are usually given is not strong; indeed, these arguments taken by themselves are not strong enough to persuade a rational person to believe in God. In order now to establish positive atheism, it should not be necessary for us to produce as strong an *a posteriori* argument to make our case as it would be otherwise. In fact, however, *a posteriori* arguments can be made that are more than strong enough to establish positive atheism.

The *A Priori* Arguments and the Possibility of Rebuttal

There is a final way that the refutation of the arguments for the existence of God in Part I is relevant to my case for positive atheism. In Chapter 12, assuming that the concept of God is meaningful, I show that the concept of God is inconsistent. If any of my arguments in Chapter 12 are successful, then God, as He has often been characterized, could not possibly exist. If this is so, one might well ask why I have bothered to refute the many arguments for the existence of God in Part I and why I am taking the trouble to give *a posteriori* arguments for the nonexistence of God in Part II. The answer is that I must be cautious. My *a priori* arguments might be refuted, and if they are, I have the *a posteriori* arguments to rely on. And, as we have seen, the *a posteriori* arguments for the nonexistence of God presume that there are no strong *a priori* or *a posteriori* arguments for the existence of God. Thus my work in Part I provides an essential part of the alternative *a posteriori* refutation of the *a priori* refutations attempted in Part II.

CHAPTER 12

Divine Attributes and Incoherence

The standard concept of God is that of a disembodied person who is omniscient, omnipotent, morally perfect, and completely free. Is this concept consistent? In this chapter I show that there are at least three inconsistencies in the concept of God: one connected with God's omniscience, another with His freedom, and still another with His omnipotence.

A problem in showing that the concept of God is inconsistent should be mentioned before I begin my argument. As Richard Swinburne has pointed out in *The Coherence of Theism*, in order to convince a person P that p is an inconsistent sentence, one must get P to accept that p entails a contradiction.[1] This is because by definition p is inconsistent if and only if p entails a contradiction. However, it is difficult to get a person P to accept that p entails a contradiction if p is "God exists," since P will do so only if P accepts some controversial analyses of the attributes of God. But P might refuse to accept such analyses.

This problem certainly affects the present attempt to show that the concept of God is inconsistent, for it too requires analyses of such attributes of God as omniscience, omnipotence, moral perfection, and freedom. Since there are different accounts of these concepts and little agreement even among theists, they cannot all be considered here. However, I examine some of the most sophisticated accounts and where necessary supply my own. Of course, theists can challenge this project by rejecting the analyses that I adopt.[2] If they do, however, the onus is clearly on them to supply ones that do not have similar problems. As I proceed I sometimes point out strategies for avoiding my conclusions. But, as I also argue, such avoidance comes at a price.

Omniscience

OMNISCIENCE AS HAVING ALL KNOWLEDGE

One of the defining properties of God is omniscience. What does this mean? In one important sense, to say that God is omniscient is to say that God is all-knowing. To say that God is all-knowing entails that He have all the knowledge there is.

Now, philosophers have usually distinguished three kinds of knowledge: propositional and procedural knowledge and knowledge by acquaintance. Briefly, propositional or factual knowledge is knowledge that something is the case and is analyzable as true belief of a certain kind. In contrast, procedural knowledge or knowledge-how is a type of skill and is not reducible to propositional knowledge.[3] Finally, knowledge by acquaintance is direct acquaintance with some object, person, or phenomenon.[4] For example, to say "I know Smith" implies that one has not only detailed propositional knowledge about Smith but also direct acquaintance with Smith. Similarly, to say "I know war" implies that besides detailed propositional knowledge of war, one has some direct experience of it.

Consider now the following definition of omniscience:

(1) A person P is omniscient = If K is knowledge, then P has K

where K includes propositional knowledge, procedural knowledge, and knowledge by acquaintance. It clearly will not do. For one thing, since there are no restrictions on what P can believe, definition (1) allows P to have false beliefs.[5] But if P has some false belief that $\sim$ B, since propositional knowledge consists of true beliefs, P would by definition (1) also believe that B. Thus definition (1) allows P to have inconsistent beliefs.

One must qualify definition (1) to rule out the possibility of inconsistent beliefs. But there is still another problem, for knowledge-how comes in various degrees. For example, one can have only a minimal knowledge of how to solve certain math problems. Definition (1) is compatible with an omniscient being having only minimal knowledge-how, but surely this is an intolerable state for an omniscient being. An all-knowing being must have knowledge-how in the highest degree.

Definition (1) is also compatible with an omniscient being having only superficial knowledge by acquaintance, and again this seems intolerable. An omniscient being must have knowledge by acquaintance of the most detailed kind; it must have direct acquaintance with all aspects of everything.

The following definition avoids these problems:

(2) A person P is omniscient = For every true proposition p, P
believes that p and P believes that p IFF P knows that p, and
for every sort of knowledge-how H, P has H to the highest
degree, and for every aspect A of every entity O, P has direct
acquaintance of A.

The implications of this account for the existence of God have usually
not been noticed. God's omniscience conflicts with His disembodiedness.
If God is omniscient, then on this definition He would have all knowledge
including that of how to do gymnastics exercises on the parallel bars, and
He would have this knowledge to the highest degree. Yet only a being
with a body can have such knowledge, and by definition God does not
have a body. Therefore, God's attributes of being disembodied and of
being omniscient are in conflict. Thus if God is both omniscient and
disembodied, He does not exist. Since God is both omniscient and disembodied, He does not exist.

The property of being all-knowing conflicts not only with the property
of being disembodied but also with certain moral attributes usually attributed to God. By definition (2), if God is omniscient He has knowledge
by acquaintance of all aspects of lust and envy. One aspect of lust and
envy is the feeling of lust and envy. However, part of the concept of God
is that He is morally perfect, and being morally perfect excludes these
feelings. Consequently, there is a contradiction in the concept of God.
God, because He is omniscient, must experience feelings of lust and envy.
But God, because He is morally perfect, is excluded from doing so.
Consequently, God does not exist.[6]

It is important to see that in both of the above arguments it is not
necessary to rely on God's omniscience in the sense of definition (2) to
derive a contradiction. Indeed, one only needs to assume a concept of
God in which God has as much knowledge as some human beings. In the
first argument one need merely assume that God knows how to do certain
gymnastic exercises; if He does, He cannot exist, since a disembodied
spirit cannot know how to do these exercises. In the second argument, it
is not necessary to maintain that God is morally perfect, let alone that
God is omniscient. If God knows as much as some humans who know
lust and envy, and if God, although not morally perfect, could not have
the feelings of lust and envy, God could not exist.

In addition, definition (2) conflicts with God's omnipotence. Since God
is omnipotent He cannot experience fear, frustration, and despair.[7] For
in order to have these experiences one must believe that one is limited
in power. But since God is all-knowing and all-powerful, He knows that
He is not limited in power. Consequently, He cannot have complete

knowledge by acquaintance of all aspects of fear, frustration, and despair. On the other hand, since God is omniscient He must have this knowledge.

Various objections to these three arguments can of course be imagined. First, it might be objected that definition (2) is inaccurate. This definition entails that God have all knowledge by acquaintance and all knowledge-how, and it can be argued that this is a mistaken view of God's omniscience. It can be argued that it is not logically possible for God to have all knowledge by acquaintance and all knowledge-how. For God to be omniscient, it is enough that He have in His possession all knowledge that it is logically possible for God to have.[8] This suggests the following definition:

(3) Person P is omniscient = For any true proposition p, if it is logically possible that P could believe that p, then P believes that p, and P believes that p IFF P knows that p, and for any sort of knowledge-how H that it is logically possible for P to have, P has H to the highest degree, and for every aspect A of every entity O that it is logically possible for P to be directly acquainted with, P is directly acquainted with A.

It might be argued that the three arguments given above collapse in the light of this modification of the definition of omniscience. One can admit that God is omniscient and yet, without contradiction, maintain that there is certain knowledge He could not have. The trouble with this reply, however, is that it is logically impossible that God can have knowledge that it is logically possible for humans to have. The result is paradoxical, to say the least. One normally supposes that the following is true:

(a) If person P is omniscient, then P has knowledge that any nonomniscient being has.

Furthermore, omniscience aside, one normally supposes that the following is true:

(b) If God exists, God has all knowledge that humans have.

But both (a) and (b) are false, given definition (3). The definition conflicts with what is normally meant by "omniscient" and, bracketing omniscience, what one means by "God."

In addition, definition (3) does not seem to capture what is meant by omniscience. Consider a being called McNose.[9] His knowledge is of the highest degree, but McNose only knows how to scratch his nose and only has direct experience of all aspects of his nose's itching and being scratched. Let us further suppose that all McNose's beliefs are about his nose's itching and being scratched and that these beliefs constitute knowledge. Absurdly, McNose is omniscient on definition (3).

The problem posed by the example of McNose suggests another modification of the definition of omniscience. McNose's gross lack of knowledge means that he is not epistemologically perfect, whereas an omniscient being must be such. Perhaps then, the concept of epistemological perfection needs to be built into the definition of omniscience. Consider the following:

(4) Person P is omniscient = For any true proposition p, if P's believing that p would increase P's epistemological perfection, then P believes p; and P believes that p IFF P knows that p; and for any piece of knowledge-how H that would increase P's epistemological perfection, then P has H to the highest degree; and for every aspect A of every entity O, if being directly acquainted with A would increase P's epistemological perfection, then P is directly acquainted with A.

One problem with this new account of omniscience is that the notion of epistemological perfection is no clearer than the notion of omniscience. It would seem that unless a being has the knowledge that humans have, it does not have the property of epistemological perfection. But on this interpretation, God does not have epistemological perfection, for, as we have already seen, humans can have certain knowledge-how and knowledge by acquaintance that He cannot have. On the other hand, if one allows God to have the knowledge that humans have, this will conflict with some of God's other characteristics. One can of course define epistemological perfection in such a way that these problems are avoided—for example, by excluding the knowledge-how and knowledge by acquaintance that conflict with God's other attributes. But then "epistemological perfection" will have become a term of art introduced to avoid the problems posed, and the claim that God has epistemological perfection will be trivial.

Another way to deal with the problem of God's seeming not to know what humans know is to argue that God, if He chose, could know how, for example, to do exercises on the parallel bars, for if God chose, He could become incarnate and thus have the requisite skill. Even if one supposes, however, that it makes sense to assume that God can become incarnate, this does not solve the problem. Even if God has the potential to possess this knowledge, He does not have it now. He now lacks some knowledge that some human beings have. Furthermore, if God is omniscient, He is actually, not potentially, omniscient. However, on this account God would merely be potentially omniscient. Moreover, it is not completely clear that it makes sense to suppose that an infinite being can become incarnate.

In addition to these problems, the supposition that God could become incarnate would not solve the problem of knowledge by acquaintance mentioned above. Assuming God became incarnate, as on certain interpretations of Christianity He is supposed to have done, it would still seem that He could not be directly acquainted with lust and envy and yet be the moral ideal of Christians. On the other hand, unless He was directly acquainted with feelings of lust and envy, He would know less than ordinary men, since ordinary men are so acquainted. The teaching of the New Testament on whether Christ was directly acquainted with lust and envy is unclear. This Bible certainly teaches that Christ was tempted by the devil but resisted him. Whether this means that Christ did have feelings of lust and envy but resisted the devil or whether, despite the devil, He did not have feelings of lust and envy is unclear. In any case, whatever Christianity teaches, the problem still comes down to this: If Christ did have feelings of lust and envy, His status as a moral ideal is adversely affected; if He did not, His status as an epistemological ideal is adversely affected.

It might be argued, of course, that God's moral goodness does not concern His feelings but His actions and the principles on which they rest. So the fact that He knows lust and envy does not affect the Christian moral ideal. Now, it is true that in judging the moral quality of a person one sometimes takes into account only the actions and the principles on which they rest. Thus one who did good deeds and acted on moral principles throughout life would normally be considered a good person. Still, we would not consider a person morally *perfect*, despite a life of good action, if there was envy and lust in the person's heart. Freedom from such feelings as lust and envy is precisely what religious believers expect of a saint, and it is inconceivable that God would be less morally perfect than a saint.

Various objections might be raised to the argument that there is an inconsistency between omnipotence and omniscience.[10] First, it might be objected that there is no experience of fear or frustration distinct from complex dispositions to behave in certain ways. Consequently, God could have knowledge by acquaintance of fear simply by having knowledge by acquaintance of certain behavior. Obviously, God cannot have knowledge by acquaintance of His own behavior, since He does not have a body. But he can have knowledge by acquaintance of someone else's body. However, if fear is merely a complex behavioral disposition, then belief must be as well. Indeed, the state of fear involves certain beliefs. But then, although God would not have to have a body in order to have knowledge by acquaintance of fear, He would have to have a body in order to have any belief *about* someone else's fear. Since, by definition, God is a pure spirit without a body, He cannot exist if He has any beliefs. But God must have certain beliefs in order to be omniscient.

It might also be objected that, despite the fact that God is omnipotent, He can experience fear and frustration. After all, even humans sometimes experience fear when they know they have nothing to fear. If humans can do this, given their limitations, surely without these limitations God can do so as well. He can experience fear although He knows He has absolutely nothing to fear. However, although in ordinary life we are afraid when we know we having nothing to fear, we *also* have a belief, perhaps an unconscious one, that there *is* something to fear. Indeed, if we did not have such a belief, it would be incorrect to speak of our state as one of fear. Because it is part of the meaning of "P is experiencing fear" that "P believes that P has something to fear," even God must believe He has something to fear if He experiences fear. But He cannot believe H has something to fear if He is omniscient. Furthermore, if someone experiences fear knowing that there is nothing to fear, this fear is by definition irrational. By definition God cannot be irrational.

Finally, it might be argued that God could experience fear by becoming incarnate, as He did in Jesus Christ. However, this solution to the problem will not do. First, there is the general difficulty of understanding how an infinite God could become incarnate in a human being. Even if this idea does make sense, are we to suppose that Jesus Christ was not all-powerful and not all-knowing? If Christ was all-powerful and all-knowing, the same problem would arise for him. How could an incarnate all-powerful being experience fear? If He could not, then how could He be all-knowing? If He could experience fear, how could He be all-powerful? If He was not all-powerful and all-knowing, how could Christ be God incarnate? Further, if in order to know fear, God had to become incarnate, then before His incarnation He was not omniscient. But by definition God is *necessarily* omniscient. Hence if He exists, He has always been omniscient.

I must conclude that God's omniscience conflicts with His disembodiedness, His moral perfection, and His omnipotence.

OMNISCIENCE AS HAVING ALL FACTUAL KNOWLEDGE

The only solution to the problems posed above is to reject the idea that God is omniscient in the sense of having all three kinds of knowledge. However, to restrict His knowledge to knowledge-that or factual knowledge, as do defenders of theism such as Swinburne, is to pay a great price.[11] In the first place, this restriction has the paradoxical implication that humans have kinds of knowledge that God cannot have. Second, it attributes to God purely intellectual knowledge, and only of a certain kind at that. Granted, this conception of God's knowledge may cohere well with the view of God put forth by certain philosophers and theologians, but it does not accord with the ordinary religious believer's view of God. People tend to think of God as a superperson who has many of the characteristics of ordinary people but to a greater degree. However, one characteristic of ordinary people is that of having knowledge-how and knowledge by acquaintance. Thus the price that the believer pays for avoiding contradiction is paradoxical or is a purely intellectual view of God that is not in keeping with the ordinary believer's.

But let us consider this intellectual view of omniscience on its own merits. How could an omniscient being of this limited sort be defined? One suggestion is this:[12]

(5) Person P is omniscient = For any true proposition p, P believes that p and believes that p IFF P knows that p.

Unfortunately, this account leads to incoherence. In fact, three separate arguments can be adduced to show that it is logically impossible for God to be omniscient in this sense. Defenders of theism can escape from these arguments, I argue, only by making implausible assumptions or accepting paradoxes.

The Argument from Essential Indexicals

One recent attempt to show that omniscience is impossible in the sense of definition (5) is due to Patrick Grim.[13] Grim maintains that indexical expressions like "I" are essential and therefore cannot be replaced by nonindexical ones such as proper names. He argues that what I know when I know

(1) I spilled my soup

can be known only by me. Consequently, God as an omniscient being cannot exist, since God could not know what I know in knowing (1).

Grim's argument proceeds as follows. One might suppose that the proposition expressed by (1) is the same as the proposition expressed by

(2) Martin spilled his soup.

But according to Grim, this identity cannot be maintained. When I realize that I spilled my soup, my knowledge is not the impersonal kind expressed by (2). I am ashamed and feel guilty about *my* spilling my soup. However, this is the knowledge expressed by (1), not (2). My friends and relatives may be embarrassed about Martin's spilling his soup. But only *I* can feel ashamed and guilty, since the clumsiness was *mine*.

Furthermore, Grim argues that when I start to clean up after my mishap, this can be fully explained by saying I realize that I spilled my soup. But it cannot be fully explained by saying I realize that Michael Martin spilled his soup unless I know I am Michael Martin. However, this would reintroduce the indexical "I." Thus God or some other being could know what is expressed by (2), but not even God could know what is expressed by (1). Consequently, God cannot be omniscient. So God as a being that is necessarily omniscient cannot exist.

Faced with this problem defenders of theism have two options. First, the knowledge I have when I know that (1)—so-called indexical knowledge—can be classified as nonpropositional. God could exist and still be omniscient. The trouble with this reply is similar to the trouble with a reply criticized above: One is committed to paradoxes. First, an omniscient being is supposed to have all knowledge that nonomniscient beings have. But on this account, I have knowledge that an omniscient being does not have. Second, God is supposed to have at least all knowledge that humans have. But on this account, I have knowledge that God could not have.

The second option is to admit that indexical knowledge is propositional but to argue that a being is omniscient so long as it knows all propositional knowledge that it is logically possible for such a being to know. Since it would not be logically possible for such a being to know what I know when I know that (1), God could be omniscient and yet not know what I know when I know that (1). The problem with this solution, however, is that of the last. It is paradoxical to suppose it to be logically impossible for God to have knowledge that it is logically possible for some humans to have; it is paradoxical to suppose it to be logically impossible for an omniscient being to have knowledge that it is logically possible for a human to have.

Thus one can save the coherence of an omniscient being only by recourse to implausible assumptions or to paradoxes.

The Argument from Negative Unrestricted Existential Statements

Another attempt to show that the concept of omniscience in the sense of having all factual knowledge is self-contradictory has been produced by Roland Puccetti.[14] The argument proceeds as follows.

If P is omniscient, then P would have knowledge of all facts about the world. Let us call this totality of facts Y. If P is omniscient, then P knows Y. One of the facts included in Y is that P is omniscient. But in order to know that P is omniscient, P would have to know something besides Y. P would have to know:

(Z) There are no facts unknown to P.

How can (Z) be known? Puccetti argues that (Z) cannot be known, since

(Z) is an unrestricted negative existential statement. He admits that it is possible to know the truth about negative existential statements that are restricted temporally or spatially. But (Z) is completely uncircumscribed. Knowing (Z), Puccetti says, would be like knowing it is true that no centaurs exist anywhere at any time.

But why could not God, with his infinite power, search all space and time and conclude that there are no centaurs? Similarly, why could not God search all space and time and conclude that there is no more factual knowledge that He can acquire? Puccetti is not as clear as he might be, but one can assume he would answer this question by saying God could not exhaustively search space and time because they are both infinite. No matter how much God searched, there would be more space and time to search. Consequently, it is possible that there are facts He does not know. Thus for God to know that He knows all the facts located in space and time is impossible, and since omniscience entails such knowledge, omniscience is impossible.

Now, it may be objected that God will know that (Z) because He is the sole creator of the totality of facts (other than himself). But this reply begs the question. How could God know that He is the sole creator of the totality of facts unless He also knew (Z)? But since (Z) cannot be known, God cannot know He is the sole creator of the totality of facts.

This reconstruction of Puccetti's argument turns on the factual assumption that space and time are infinite, but some scientists have claimed that space is finite but unbounded. At most, then, the argument proves that *if* space and time are infinite, *then* God is omniscient. But since by definition God is omniscient, He cannot exist if space and time are infinite.

There is one realm that is uncontroversially infinite. If God is omniscient, He must know all mathematical facts and know that there are no mathematical facts He does not know. In order to know all mathematical facts, however, it would be necessary to investigate all mathematical entities and the relations between and among them. But the number of mathematical entities and relations is infinite.[15] So even God could not complete such an investigation.

We can conclude, then, that given the existence of infinite realms of space, time, and mathematical entities, God is not omniscient; hence if omniscience is a necessary attribute of God, He does not exist. Since omniscience is a necessary attribute of God, He does not exist.

The Impossibility of There Being a Set of All Truths

Puccetti's argument seems to assume that there is a set of all truths for God to know. The problem is that, since this set is infinite, God cannot know that He knows all the truths in such a set. But a recent argument by Grim[16] utilizing Cantor's work shows that there is no set of all truths. Consequently, God's inability to know the set of all truths is not merely an epistemological impossibility. A much more basic assumption of omniscience is mistaken—namely, there is not a set of all truths to know.

Suppose there is a set of all truths T. Then

$$T = \{T_1, T_2, T_3 \ldots\}$$

where T_1, T_2, T_3, and so on are all the truths there are. There is a power set PT of T, the set of all subsets of T. The elements of PT are:

$\emptyset$

$\{T_1\}$

$\{T_2\}$

$\{T_3\}$

.

.

.

$\{T_1, T_2\}$

.

.

.

$\{T_1, T_2, T_3\}$

etc.

Corresponding to each element of PT will be a truth. For example, T_1 will or will not be a member of each of the elements of PT. Thus all the following are truths:

T_1 is not a member of $\emptyset$.

T_1 is a member of $\{T_1\}$.

T_1 is not a member of $\{T_2\}$.

T_1 is a member of $\{T_1, T_2\}$.

There will be at least as many truths as there are elements of PT, since a distinct truth corresponds to each element of PT. However, as Cantor has shown, the power set of all sets will be larger than the original set. Thus there will be more truths than there are members of T. But since

T is supposed to be the set of *all* truths, there cannot be a set of all truths. Consequently, an omniscient being that knows the set of all truths is impossible. Since an omniscient being must surely know the set of all truths, God as an omniscient being cannot exist.[17]

Divine Freedom

We have seen that the concept of God as an omniscient being is incoherent. Depending on how this concept is defined, either it is internally incoherent or it conflicts with God's moral attributes or His omnipotence. We shall now see whether combining God's omniscience with the attribute of divine freedom makes more incoherences appear.

FREEDOM AND OMNISCIENCE

On one common view, God is completely free. Unlike finite beings, He is not restrained by anything except logic. Human freedom is restricted by the environment and the causal laws operating in it. Even defenders of contracausal freedom admit that to some extent human beings are influenced in their decisions by their culture and their heredity. Swinburne, whose discussion of divine freedom is one of the most developed and sophisticated in recent literature, maintains that God is free in the sense that no agent or natural law or state of the world or other causal factor in any way influences Him to have the intentions on which to act.[18] Given this account of divine freedom, however, God cannot be omniscient in the usual sense. Recall definition (5):

(5) Person P is omniscient = For any true proposition p, P believes that p and believes that p IFF P knows that p.

There are true propositions about the future that God cannot now know. Swinburne argues that if some of God's creatures are free in the contracausal sense, if their choices are not caused, then God cannot know now what they will do in the future. Of course, if God's creatures are not contracausally free, He will know what they will do in the future. However, most theists maintain that humans are contracausally free at least some of the time. Moreover, whatever the case with His creatures, God Himself is completely free in the contracausal sense.[19] Because of this, Swinburne admits that in the usual sense of omniscience, God cannot be omniscient and free since God cannot know what some of His future actions will be.[20] Consequently, a person who is omniscient in the sense specified in definition (5) and free cannot exist.

Although Swinburne is thus committed to the view that because God is free He cannot know certain true propositions, he still chooses to refer to God as omniscient. However, it is clear that his sense of omniscience is weaker than that of definition (5). Swinburne defines "omniscience" as follows:

> A person P is omniscient at time t IFF P knows, of every true proposition about t or an earlier time, that it is true; *and* P also knows, of every true proposition about a time later than t such that what it reports is physically necessary as a result of some cause at t or earlier, that it is true.

For the reasons cited above, this definition must be modified in the following way:

> (6) A person P is omniscient at time t = For any true proposition p about t or an earlier time, P believes that p at t and believes that p at t IFF P knows that p at t, *and* for any true proposition about a time later than t, such that what it reports is physically necessary as a result of some cause at t or earlier, P believes p at t and P believes that p at t IFF P knows p at t.

Let us call one who is omniscient in this sense a person with *limited omniscience* and one who is omniscient in the sense of definition (5) a person with *unlimited omniscience*. On definition (6), God would know about everything "except those future states and their consequences which are not physically necessitated by anything in the past; and if he knows that he does not know about those future states."[21] So according to Swinburne, although God's perfect freedom is incompatible with unlimited omniscience, it is compatible with limited omniscience.

However, Swinburne is mistaken in supposing that God's perfect freedom is compatible with limited omniscience, for God always has the option of intervening in any natural event and performing a miracle. Swinburne should have said that God can know that some event in the future, necessitated by physical laws, will occur *only if* He knows that He will not intervene and perform a miracle. But by Swinburne's own admission, God cannot know now that He will or will not intervene in some future event. Consequently, He cannot know now whether *any* particular event will occur in the future. He cannot know what the future actions of His creatures will be; He cannot know what His own future actions will be; He cannot know if any event governed by natural laws will occur, since He cannot know now if He will intervene in the natural course of events. This seems to cover all possible future events.

God's perfect freedom is thus incompatible with both unlimited and limited omniscience. A being that by definition has both attributes cannot exist. To be sure, one can give a still weaker definition of omniscience to eliminate the incompatibility. However, this move has its price. It seems to conflict radically with both what is usually meant by "omniscience" and what is usually meant by "God."

OMNISCIENCE, FREEDOM, AND MORAL PERFECTION

There is a further implication of the view that God has limited omniscience and complete freedom. Given that He cannot know whether any particular future event will occur, it follows that God cannot know whether His past actions have been moral. This is because the morality of His past actions and forbearances depends in part on what will happen in the future, which He cannot know. In order to know, for example, whether His past decision not to intervene and perform some miracle at some past time t_1 was a correct moral decision, He would have to know what would have happened after t_1 if He had intervened. In particular, He would have to know what would have been the long-range consequences if He had intervened.

This is not something that God with His complete freedom can know, for such knowledge depends on knowledge of His creatures' future decisions, which certainly will depend on His own future decisions. But this knowledge He cannot have. God can know, of course, that if His past action or forbearance were to have consequences X, it would be moral. But He cannot know if it will have these consequences, since whether it does or not will depend on His creatures' as yet unknown free choices and His own as yet unknown interventions or forbearances.

The argument to this point suggests one more incoherence in the concept of God. Consider that God is by definition morally perfect. What is meant by "morally perfect"? A typical account of moral perfection is offered by Swinburne. According to him,[22] to say that God is morally perfect is to say that God never takes any actions that are morally wrong.

> (M) Person P is morally perfect IFF P never does anything morally wrong.

However, as we have just seen, God cannot know whether His past actions or forbearances are morally correct. On (M) this would *not* mean that God could not be morally perfect. It would mean, however, that if God's actions were never morally wrong, it would be by accident. The morally correct outcome would be completely unrelated to God's knowledge. But this suggests that there is something wrong with (M) as an analysis of moral perfection, for a person cannot be morally perfect by accident; the outcome of a morally perfect person's action must be based on the person's knowledge. So although God can be both morally perfect in terms of (M) and completely free, the definition of morally perfect is incorrect.

What happens if we attempt to improve (M) to meet the problem? Consider the following revision of (M):

> (M') Person P is morally perfect IFF P never does anything wrong and P's never doing anything wrong is not accidental.

However, on (M') God cannot be morally perfect and completely free. This is because, as we have seen, complete freedom limits God's knowledge in a most radical way, and one cannot be morally perfect and completely ignorant if one is doing what is morally correct. Consequently, God's moral perfection is in conflict with His perfect freedom. Hence God cannot exist.

One can put this point in a slightly different way. God can know that (M') is true since (M') is an analytic truth. But He cannot know that He is morally perfect since He cannot know that He never does anything wrong, let alone if He does, it is not accidental. But God must have knowledge that He is morally perfect to be God. However, this is knowledge that He cannot have. Hence God cannot exist.

The various objections that can be made to the above arguments can all be met. It might be objected that, in our argument that God's freedom is incompatible with His moral perfection, I am assuming some utilitarian theory of morality. It may be said that I must assume that God must know the future consequences of His actions in order to know whether His actions are moral. But it may be maintained that God need not be a utilitarian and, in any case, that utilitarianism is an implausible theory of morality.

My argument does not assume what utilitarianism assumes—namely, that *only* the consequences of one's actions are morally relevant. It simply assumes that the consequences of one's actions are morally relevant and leaves open the question as to whether other factors are also morally relevant. The only moral theory excluded by this argument is an extreme deontological theory such as Kant's, in which the consequences of an action are totally irrelevant to deciding its morality. But this sort of moral theory is almost universally recognized as inadequate.

A critic might also maintain that although God cannot have complete knowledge about the future, He can have probabilistic knowledge. He can know it is unlikely that He will intervene in the working of natural law by performing miracles because He has seldom done so in the past. Given this probabilistic knowledge, God can have probabilistic knowledge as to whether His actions are moral and consequently whether He is morally perfect.

However, inductive inferences about the future presuppose the uniformity of nature, and this in turn assumes not only that nature is governed by natural laws but that these laws are seldom violated by God's intervention. But whether natural laws will continue to operate without God's frequent intervention is precisely what is at issue. Hence this cannot be assumed without begging the question. Furthermore, to suppose that God is likely to continue to intervene infrequently in the workings of natural law seems to limit His freedom. If God is completely free, He is not restrained by this probability. Moreover, even if one could establish that God would seldom intervene to perform miracles without begging the question or limiting His freedom, this would not show that His infrequent intervention in the past was morally justified. Insofar as God's claim to probabilistic knowledge of the morality of His future actions is based on knowledge of His past moral actions, it begs the question of the morality of these past actions. The crucial issue is, can God know whether His past actions are moral? This objection seems to assume in advance that the question has been answered.

One might argue that the logical impossibility that God can know some future events is no limitation on His knowledge. God can be all-knowing in any sense that matters and yet not know the future. In particular, God can be all-knowing and yet not know whether His past actions are moral and, consequently, whether He is morally perfect.

However, the objection seems to assume wrongly that to say some entity is all-knowing means it knows everything that it is logically possible for it to know. However, given that there could be some entity such that it is logically impossible for it to know everything, it would be all-knowing on the account of all-knowing assumed by the objection. But this is absurd. On a more adequate definition of all-knowing—the unlimited sense of omniscience discussed above—an all-knowing being knows all truths and has no false beliefs. Now, as we have seen, God cannot be all-knowing in this sense for several reasons. Nor can God be all-knowing in the more limited sense suggested by Swinburne. In what sense of all-knowing *is* God supposed to be all knowing then?

A critic might maintain that God could be completely free and yet know what His future actions would be. Consequently, He could know that He is morally perfect since He could know if His actions are moral. This contention would seem to be supported by the following argument and the analogy to the problem of free will. A person P is said to be free to do A; if P chooses to do A, P will be successful. In this sense of "free," human action can be both free and determined. But if a future human action is determined, it can be known in advance. And if a human action can be free and predictable, then surely God's action can be as well. Hence God can know what his future actions will be and yet be completely free.

Theists have said this is not an adequate account of human freedom, let alone of divine freedom. Their standard argument against this goes as follows: If a person P's choice to do A is determined, P could not have done otherwise than A. If, on the other hand, P's choice not to do A is determined, P could not have done otherwise than not to do A. In either case, the argument goes, P could not have done otherwise than P did. It is irrelevant that if P had chosen to do A, P would have been successful.

Even if this were an adequate account of human freedom, it does not seem at all plausible as an account of divine freedom. If human action is determined and predictable, this is because it is part of the nexus of natural law. But God is supposed to have created that nexus and to transcend it. He is certainly not supposed to be *part* of the nexus He created.

I must conclude that a common traditional concept of God is incoherent and thus that God in the sense of a morally perfect, omniscient, omnipotent, and completely free being cannot exist. I have not shown, of course, that God in other senses is incoherent. However, the concept of God that I have shown to be incoherent is so widespread and plays such a central role in Western theological thinking that it can be fairly said that the most common and widely accepted concept of God is incoherent.

Omnipotence

A third divine attribute is omnipotence. Philosophers have long been concerned with certain paradoxes connected with omnipotence, and it is controversial, to say the least, whether plausible solutions to them can be constructed. The paradox of the stone is an example. This paradox, generated by the question "Can God make a stone He cannot lift?" has produced a considerable literature. If the answer to the question is yes, then God is not omnipotent since there is something He cannot do. But if the answer is no, then there is also something He cannot do.[23]

Once again the crucial question is, what is the meaning of omnipotence? Unless we are clear on what omnipotence means, we will not know whether the paradoxes can be generated or, if they can be, how they can be solved. But an adequate account is not easy to come by. Further, once we are clear on what is meant by omnipotence, we might ask whether an omnipotent being can have other divine attributes—whether, for example, omnipotence is compatible with moral perfection. Thus it might be argued that if God is morally perfect, He cannot do evil. But if He is omnipotent, He can.

In what follows I consider four recent sophisticated attempts by Richard Swinburne, George Mavrodes, Charles Taliaferro, and Jerome Gellman to define omnipotence, and I argue that all these are plagued by serious problems. If omnipotence is defined in the way suggested, then a being that is omnipotent cannot possess other attributes associated with

God. But since God is supposed to have these other attributes, God cannot exist. To be sure, other attempts at definition that I am unaware of might succeed where these have failed. But the sophistication of these attempts, building as they do on the failures of earlier attempts, suggests that this is unlikely.[24] In any case, the failure of these attempts puts the burden of providing an alternative analysis squarely on the theists.

SWINBURNE'S DEFINITION

After rejecting several provisional attempts to define omnipotence, Richard Swinburne[25] comes up with the following definition:

(E) A person P is omnipotent at time t IFF P is able to bring about the existence of any logically contingent state of affairs x after t, the description of the occurrence of which does not entail that P did not bring it about at t, given that P does not believe that P has overriding reasons for refraining from bringing about x.

This definition, according to Swinburne, solves the problems of his earlier provisional definitions and is free of problems of its own. Unfortunately, however, even if this definition avoids the problems of his earlier provisional ones, Swinburne's definition (E) is not free of problems.

In order to understand (E) and its problems it is necessary to consider its elements as well as Swinburne's rationale for stating the definition as he does.

(1) The first thing to be noted about (E) is that omnipotence is defined in terms of what a being can bring about, not what a being can do. According to Swinburne, a definition in terms of being able to take any logical possible action runs immediately into the problem that certain actions can only be taken by certain kinds of beings. For example, only an embodied being can sit down. So a definition of omnipotence in terms of being able to perform any logically possible action would mean that a disembodied being would not be omnipotent; consequently, God, a disembodied omnipotent being, could not exist.

(2) The temporal qualifications in (E) are introduced to solve another problem. Without such qualifications a being who is omnipotent at t would have to be able to bring about an event *before* t. But according to Swinburne, it is logically impossible to bring abut events in the past. Since it is no limitation on an omnipotent being that it cannot bring about what is logically impossible, a temporal qualification is necessary.

(3) (E) requires that the logically possible states of affairs that an omnipotent being brings about be logically contingent. Without this requirement, (E) would entail that P could bring about a logically necessary state of affairs, something that no being can bring about.

(4) The qualification that "the occurrence of which does not entail that P did not bring it about at t" is inserted because otherwise a state of affairs could be described as uncaused or not caused by P. But this description would make it logically impossible for P to bring about the state of affairs. It is no limitation that an omnipotent being cannot bring about a state of affairs that it is logically impossible for it to bring about.

(5) The last qualification, that "P does not believe that P has overriding reasons for refraining from bringing about x," is put in to make omnipotence compatible with being perfectly free. According to Swinburne, a perfectly free being "can only perform an action if he believes that there is no overriding reason for refraining from doing it."[26] If a person had an overriding reason for not performing an action and still performed it, he would be influenced by nonrational factors and consequently not be completely free. Swinburne admits that (E) defines a narrower sense of omnipotence than is sometimes used, but he argues that this limitation is not important. If a being is unable to exercise its power because it judges that, on balance, to do so would be irrational, he says, this does not make the being less worthy of worship.

Thus Swinburne admits that God could *not* be omnipotent in the sense in which the term has often been understood and, consequently, that God, as He is commonly understood, not only does not exist but could not exist. By Swinburne's own admission, then, a common notion of God is incoherent. Swinburne rejects the idea that a different term be used— for example, "almighty"—and insists on using "omnipotent" in a narrower sense than it is often understood. But his use should not induce us to suppose he has shown that the common concept of God is coherent. Indeed, just the opposite is true.

He defends himself by saying that theism often understands omnipotence in this narrower sense, although he does not cite any evidence for this contention, and that a being that is omnipotent in this sense is no less worthy of worship. What does he mean by this? Swinburne says that in order to worship a person legitimately, one must show respect toward the person *and* acknowledge this person "as *de facto* and *de iure* lord of all."[27] What properties would a being need to have in order to have lordship of this kind? He says:

> First, in order to be supremely great and the ultimate source of our well-being, he must be perfectly free, for if he is in any way pushed into exercising his power, sovereignty is not fully his. But given this, there must be no limits to his power other than those of logic; otherwise his lordship would not be supreme. This means he must be omnipotent in my sense [E].[28]

The trouble with this justification is that, according to Swinburne's definition (E), there *are* limits to God's power besides logic. Now, as we have seen, in (E) God's power is limited by His freedom. Swinburne is thus incorrect to suppose that if God is omnipotent as defined by (E), He is worthy of worship. In order to be worthy of worship, God must be omnipotent in a stronger sense than (E). For example, if God is omnipotent in the following sense, He is worthy of worship:

(D) A person P is omnipotent at time t IFF P is able to bring about the existence of any logically contingent state of affairs x after t, the description of the occurrence of which does not entail that P did not bring it about at t.

This sense of omnipotence was rejected by Swinburne as incompatible with God's complete freedom. Indeed, sense (E) was generated from sense (D) in order to make God's omnipotence compatible with His complete freedom by adding the qualification "given that P does not believe that P has overriding reasons for refraining from bringing about x." So it would seem that if God is omnipotent in sense (D), He could not exist and be completely free. However, if God is omnipotent in sense (E), He could not exist and be worthy of worship.

There are other problems with Swinburne's definition as well. Richard La Croix has shown that, on Swinburne's definition of omnipotence, God's omnipotence conflicts with God's omniscience.[29] Consider the state of affairs S_1, which has the property of being brought about by a being that has never been omniscient. (E) would seem to entail that in order for P to be omnipotent at t, P would have to be able to bring about S_1 after t. Then the ability of P to bring about S_1 at t entails that P is not omniscient, because it entails that P never had the property of being omniscient. Since Swinburne's definition holds for all existing beings, it holds for God. It follows that if God is omnipotent, He is not omniscient.

A similar argument could be used to show that God is not disembodied, not unchanging, not simple, and so on. In order to avoid these implications one would have to deny that S_1 is a logically contingent state of affairs after t or say the description of S_1 entails that P did not bring about S_1 at t.

With respect to the first defense, S_1 certainly seems like a logically possible state of affairs in the sense that Swinburne intends: S_1 and not S_1 are both logically possible states of affairs, and S_1 is a state of affairs compatible with everything that happened after t or before t. With respect to the second defense, the description of S_1 would not entail that P did not bring about S_1 if P was omniscient. One might suppose that this entailment would hold if "God" was substituted for P. However, if "God" is understood as a proper name, such an entailment would not hold. In particular, "God" used as a proper name does not entail that someone with this name is omniscient.

But let us suppose that "God" is not understood as a proper name. Let us suppose rather that "God" is a short form for a definite description: the being that is omniscient, omnipotent, and all-good. In this case, of course, the entailment would hold and the defense would work. Unfortunately, allowing "God" to be a short form for this definite description raises another problem. If we allow "God" to be so understood, consider the expression "McEar." Let us understand this expression not as a proper name, but as a short form for a definite description: the man capable only of scratching his ear. La Croix points out that on (E) McEar is omnipotent. This is because the only states of affairs whose occurrences after t do not entail McEar's having brought them about are the scratchings of the ear of McEar. Other states of affairs, such as the scratchings of McEar's nose, would entail that McEar did not bring about these states of affairs. Thus, absurdly, McEar is omnipotent on (E).

One objection to La Croix's argument is that God could bring about state of affairs S_1.[30] Let us suppose that S_1 consists of Hidden Valley's being flooded. Suppose this state has been brought about by some being—say, a beaver—that has never been omniscient. It can be argued that an omniscient and powerful being could bring about S_1 indirectly by causing the beaver to build a dam and flood the valley. In order to eliminate this problem, S_1 would have to be stated differently. We would have to say that S_1 is a state of affairs that has the property of not being brought about *directly or indirectly* by an omniscient being. With this small amendment, La Croix's argument is sound; for it is certainly the case that if an omniscient being caused the beaver to build a dam, such a being would indirectly have caused the valley to be flooded.

I must conclude that if God is omnipotent, then He is neither omniscient nor all-good nor disembodied, or else, absurdly, that McEar is also omnipotent. Thus Swinburne's definition fails. However, even if La Croix's argument is wrong, there is our earlier argument, that Swinburne's definition of omnipotence is incompatible with his own account of being worthy of worship.

MAVRODES'S DEFINITION

George Mavrodes[31] suggests the following definition of omnipotence:

(F) For any agent n, n is omnipotent IFF for any proposition p that meets conditions (C_1) and (C_2), n is able to bring about some state of affairs that satisfies p.

Mavrodes characterizes (C_1) and (C_2) in the following way:

(C₁) There is some possible state of affairs S that satisfies p, and such that it is not a necessary truth that no agent has brought it about that S obtains.

(C₂) If p entails that some proposition q is satisfied, and if it is not a necessary truth that no agent can have brought about the satisfaction of q, then p does not exclude any agent, or class of agents, from among those that may have brought about the satisfaction of q.

A few words of explanation are necessary here. Mavrodes speaks of a state of affairs "satisfying" a proposition. He defines this idea as follows:

A state of affairs S satisfies proposition p IFF p could not fail to be true if S were actually to obtain.

The rationale for (C₁) seems clear. An omnipotent being should not be required to bring about either a logically impossible state of affairs or a state of affairs such that it is a necessary truth that no agent brought it about. For example, an omnipotent being should not be required to bring about a state of affairs consisting of a round square or consisting of the contracausal free action of some person.

(C₂) is used by Mavrodes to eliminate more complicated problems. Consider the following conjunctive proposition:

(p) A nonomnipotent being brings it about that Hidden Valley is flooded, and no omnipotent being brings it about that Hidden Valley is flooded.

Mavrodes argues that even if (p) meets condition (C₁), it does not meet (C₂). For although (p) entails that q is satisfied (where q = that Hidden Valley is flooded), and it not a necessary truth that no agent can bring about the satisfaction of q, (p) does exclude some agents, or a class of agents, who may have brought about the satisfaction of q. Proposition (p) excludes the class of omnipotent beings and thus does not meet the condition (C₂).

However, as Joshua Hoffman has shown,[32] Mavrodes's definition is inadequate since other propositions that fail to meet (C₂) are excluded, and these are such that an omnipotent being should be able to bring about a state of affairs that satisfies them. Consider, for example:

(r) A spoon falls off the table, and Jones does not bring it about that a spoon falls off the table.

Since (r) entails that q′ is satisfied (where q′ = that a spoon falls off the table), and it is not a necessary truth that no agent can have brought about the satisfaction of q′, and (r) does exclude an agent, Jones, from among those who may have brought about the satisfaction of q', proposition (r) would not meet condition (C_2), and consequently an omnipotent agent could bring about a state of affairs that satisfies (r). But this is mistaken. An omnipotent agent could surely cause a spoon to fall off the table and prevent Jones from doing so. Not only should an omnipotent agent be able to do this, but it seems clear that many nonomnipotent agents can do this.

What would happen if we eliminated (C_2) from (F)? This would solve the problem just mentioned, but it would seem to generate another. Consider:

(m) A being that has never been omniscient either directly or indirectly flooded Hidden Valley.

Presumably (m) would only be satisfied by the state of affairs q'' (where q'' = that Hidden Valley's being flooded is brought about directly or indirectly by a being that has never been omniscient) or any states of affairs that entailed q''. Proposition m would seem to meet condition (C_1). It would seem that q'' is a possible state of affairs and that it is not a necessary truth that no agent has brought about q''. Presumably, q'' could be brought about by an omnipotent but not an omniscient being. This means q'' could not be brought about by God. Consequently, God cannot be omnipotent since there is a proposition, namely (m), that meets (C_1), such that God is not able to bring about a state of affairs that satisfies (m). But since by definition God is omnipotent, God does not exist. Similar arguments could be constructed to show that God's omnipotence conflicts with His omnipresence, His infinite goodness, and His other attributes, but we will not pursue these here.

The only way I can see of solving this problem is to argue that a being that is omnipotent must by necessity be omniscient. If this were true, then it would be impossible for q'' to be brought about by an omnipotent being, and consequently, (C_1) would not be satisfied. This view seems extremely implausible. Omnipotence involves bringing about states of affairs. Although it may take some knowledge to bring about any state of affairs S, it would not be necessary to have all possible knowledge of S. Furthermore, there are many states of affairs that an omnipotent being cannot bring about but an omniscient being can have knowledge of. For example, an omniscient being can know all about an inconsistent state of affairs and yet an omnipotent being cannot bring this state of affairs about. Indeed, it would seem that the omnipotent being would need to know very little about such a state of affairs in order to be omnipotent. I conclude without further argument that this way out of the problem will not work.

Thus either Mavrodes's definition entails that God's omnipotent conflicts with His omniscience or it is inadequate as a definition of omnipotence, since clearly nonomnipotent beings are omnipotent on this definition.

Taliaferro's Definition

Charles Taliaferro proposes the following definition of omnipotent:[33]

(G) X is omnipotent = The scope of X's power is such that it is metaphysically impossible for there to be any being Y that has a greater scope of power.

Taliaferro maintains that although comparing the scope of power of very powerful nonomnipotent beings can be problematic, it is not unclear how to compare the scope of power of different ostensibly omnipotent beings. For example, if there is one being B_1 that can bring an infinite number of rocks into existence but no tables, and another being B_2 that can bring an infinite number of tables into existence but no rocks, it may be difficult to say which is more powerful. But if there is a being B_3 that can bring an infinite number of rocks *and* tables into existence, then a comparison of B_1 and B_2 would not be relevant to our purpose. We should know that B_1 and B_2 are not as powerful as B_3, and that is all we would need to know about B_1 and B_2 in order to rule them out as omnipotent beings.

Consider, however, the following problem. Suppose there are two ostensibly omnipotent beings B_4 and B_5, indistinguishable except for the fact that one is essentially omniscient and the other is not. Suppose B_4 could bring about some state of affairs q'' (where q'' = that Hidden Valley's being flooded is brought about directly or indirectly by a being that has never been omniscient) while B_5 could not. However, B_5 could bring about some state of affairs q''' (where q''' = that Hidden Valley's being flooded is brought about directly or indirectly by a being that is essentially omniscient) that B_4 could not.[34] Taliaferro argues that q'' and q''' cancel each other out and hence that B_4 and B_5 would tie for the title of omnipotent being. However, he believes there is independent reason to suppose that there is at most one omnipotent being.[35]

Does Taliaferro's account show that the property of omnipotence is consistent with the other properties associated with God? No, it does not. He seems to admit that his account of omnipotence entails that if God is omnipotent, He is not triune, not the three persons of the Trinity. This is because if God is omnipotent, He could bring about state t (where t = that Hidden Valley's being flooded is brought about directly or indirectly by a being that has never been triune). For suppose God is not able to bring about t. Then presumably there is a being B_6 that is otherwise indistinguishable from God that can bring about t. Consequently, B_6 has a larger scope of power than God, and God is by definition not omnipotent. However, the attribute of being triune and the attribute of being omnipotent are essential attributes of the Christian God. So on Taliaferro's definition, the Christian God could not exist.

Could it not also be argued that God's omnipotence conflicts with some of His other attributes, such as His omniscience and omnipresence? For example, could one not maintain that an omnipotent being could bring about the state of affairs q'' (where q'' = that Hidden Valley's being flooded is brought about directly or indirectly by a being that has never been omniscient)? In this case, omnipotence and omniscience would seem to be in conflict. It would also seem that a similar argument could be given to show that other divine attributes, such as omnipresence, are in conflict with omnipotence. However, Taliaferro says that such conflicts are problematic. Citing Thomas Reid's argument that an omnipotent being must also be omniscient, he maintains also that it has been argued, although he does not say by whom,[36] that omnipresence can be analyzed as a function of omnipotence and omniscience. He says that "if these arguments are successful, an ostensibly 'bare' omnipotent being also has theologically interesting attributes such as omniscience and omnipresence."[37] Consequently, he concludes, omnipotence may well be compatible with omniscience and omnipresence.

The "if" in this quotation is a big one. As we have seen, the thesis that omnipotence entails omniscience is implausible on its face. Not surprisingly, the recent sophisticated attempts of Richard Swinburne[38] to analyze omnipotence and omniscience do not attempt to derive omniscience from omnipotence.[39] Furthermore, since it is implausible that omnipotence entails omniscience, and since, according to Taliaferro, omnipresence is a function of omnipotence and omniscience, it is implausible that omnipotence entails omnipresence. Consequently, unless better reasons are offered by Taliaferro, there is a strong *prima facie* case to suppose on his definition, as on the definitions of Swinburne and Mavrodes, that if God is omnipotent, He could not have the other attributes associated with God. In particular, God could not be omniscient and omnipotent.

What about the compatibility of God's omnipotence with His infinite goodness? Could not one argue that an omnipotent being could bring about state of affairs v (where v = that Hidden Valley's being flooded is brought about directly or indirectly by a being that has never been infinitely good)? If the answer is yes, this would seem to show that an omnipotent being could not be infinitely good. Since God has always been infinitely good, He could not bring about v. But if the answer is no, then how could the being be omnipotent? There would be something He could not do that could be done by a more powerful being.

In response to this sort of problem, Taliaferro might maintain that

God is able to bring about v but chooses not to.[40] Whether this is an adequate response is unclear but, even if it is, surely the example can be modified to undercut this reply. One could now ask whether an omnipotent being could bring about state of affairs v' (where v' = that Hidden Valley's being flooded is brought about directly or indirectly by a being that has never been infinitely good and could not choose to bring about v'). It would seem that the answer is yes, for if one answered no, one could imagine a being B' that has all the power of the alleged omnipotent being B but could bring about v'. Hence B' would have a larger scope of power than B, and by definition B would not be omnipotent.

I must conclude that on Taliaferro's definition, several of God's attributes are in conflict. Consequently, if his definition is acceptable, God does not exist.

GELLMAN'S DEFINITION

Jerome Gellman[41] defines omnipotence in the following way:

(H)   P is omnipotent IFF (1) P can bring about any state of affairs that is logically possible for P to bring about where (2) there is no state of affairs, S, such that (a) it is logically possible for P to bring about S and (b) the bringing about of S by *any* agent y entails an imperfection in y and (3) there is no state of affairs, S, such that (a) it is logically impossible for P to bring about S and (b) its being logically impossible for P to bring about S entails that there is an imperfection in P.

Conditions (2) and (3) are needed, according to Gellman, for the following reasons. Without condition (2) one would be forced into saying that because God cannot sin He is not omnipotent. But according to Gellman, God's lack of the ability to sin does not entail any imperfection in God. On the contrary, the ability to sin would entail an imperfection. Further, although Gellman does not explicitly deal with this problem, condition (3) seems to rule out the McEar case discussed above. Thus the logical impossibility of McEar's being able to do many things would entail an imperfection in McEar. Consequently, McEar could not be said to be omnipotent.

Although Gellman does not explicitly argue this, his condition (2) seems to rule out one sort of problem that our other definitions of omnipotence confront. For example, let S be the state of affairs brought about either directly or indirectly by a being that was never omniscient. Although bringing about this state of affairs would be logically possible, it would mean that any being that brought about S would have an imperfection—namely, the lack of omniscience. So it would seem that omnipotence could not conflict with omniscience. A similar argument could

be constructed to show that omnipotence does not conflict with other
attributes of God that are considered to be perfections.

What attributes of God are considered to be perfections? Being triune?
Being the God of the Jews? Being the God revealed in the Book of
Mormon? Attributes such as these are usually not cited by theologians
when they consider the perfections of God. If any of these attributes is
not considered a perfection of God, then an omnipotent being could
bring about a state of affairs that is brought about either directly or
indirectly by a being that has never had these attributes. Suppose being
revealed in the Book of Mormon is not considered a perfection of God.
Then one could show that God could not be omnipotent and be the God
revealed in the Book of Mormon. Let S = that Hidden Valley's being
flooded is brought about directly or indirectly by a being that has never
been revealed in the Book of Mormon. Then on Gellman's definition, an
omnipotent being and a being revealed in the Book of Mormon are
incompatible, and God could not exist and be revealed in the Book of
Mormon. Similar arguments could be given for other attributes not
considered to be perfections. Although this may not show that the concept of God is incoherent per se, it does show that the existence of God
is incompatible with a wide variety of beliefs held by millions of religious
believers.

Gellman admits that there are difficulties in the concept of perfection
that plays a large role in his account, but he maintains that they should
not be exaggerated. In the religious sense, perfection "has to do with
being worthy of worship, and the perfect possible being represents the
maximally possible case of worshipfulness."[42] Gellman does not give any
analysis whatsoever of what it means to say that a being is worthy of
worship, however, and, as we saw in our examination of Swinburne's
account of omnipotence, recourse to worthiness of worship may not help
here, for this concept may itself be incoherent.

In addition, Gellman seems to assume that what is worshipfulness is
agreed on. Although this might be clear in some contexts, in many
religious contexts there seems to be wide disagreement. Religious people
worship many entities with very different properties. Some sects worship
Satan, the prince of darkness; the ancient Greeks worshiped gods that
had bodily forms; some illiterate people worship idols. The objects of
worship of many people of the world are finite and limited and contrast
sharply with the infinite beings proposed as objects of worship by philosophers and theologians. Indeed, for many people the idea that the true
object of worship is an infinite being, all-good, omnipotent, omniscient,
disembodied, and so on, is unintelligible. Without some explicit analysis
of worthiness of worship, the relativity of worshipfulness in actual religious practice precludes its being a guide to the explication of perfection

in the way that Gellman intends. Thus appeal to this notion is of no help in understanding the concept of perfection.

Furthermore, to go directly to the concept of perfection is unavailing. What is considered a property that would increase the perfection of one type of entity would not be considered a property that would increase the perfection of another type.[43] An island resort's perfection would be affected by the number of palm trees and the number of days of sunshine, but these properties would not be relevant to the perfection of a game of chess or a military campaign. Even a sentient being's perfection varies according to the sort of sentient being it is. A logician's perfection would be affected by properties that might not be relevant to an artist's perfection. Indeed, the properties that would increase the perfection of the logician might be incompatible with the properties that would increase the perfection of the artist.

Theologians who construct the idea of a perfect being, a being that is all-powerful, all-knowing, all-good, disembodied, unchanging, and so on, do so in a rarefied atmosphere that has little to do with what we call perfection in other contexts. For example, God, the perfect being, cannot have a perfect physique since God has no body at all. Is this a limitation of God? The usual reply given by philosophers and theologians is that it is not, since God's inability to win a physique contest does not affect his worshipfulness. But now we can see the problem with Gellman's answer, for lack of a body may well affect whether God could be worshiped by people for whom the body has a special religious significance. Further, the claim that God's lack of a body does not adversely affect His perfection turns out to be trivially true: The way philosophers and theologians have characterized God's perfection, He must be disembodied to be perfect. God's perfection has been defined for technical purposes and certain very restricted contexts. In contexts such as athletic contests, lack of a body, far from adding to the perfection of a being, would be an imperfection.

But are not some of the attributes of God's perfection relevant to any context? Surely, it will be said that God's inability to sin is. However, a little reflection shows that even this is not the case. For example, in the context of moral education a person who did not have the ability to sin would not be a perfect role model. In this case one needs a person who can and even does sin *sometimes*, yet usually triumphs over temptation. A person who could never sin would be so distant as to seem out of reach and nonmotivating.

Similar remarks apply to other divine attributes. Infinite knowledge would hardly be a property of the perfect explorer. Since a primary purpose of exploring is to find things out, having the property of omniscience would make exploring pointless. A necessary condition for a perfect explorer is the strong desire to find out certain things that are not known. This necessary condition would be undercut if the explorer is omniscient.

One would suppose that omnipotence would in any context be a property that would add to the perfection of the person who has it, but this is not so. An omnipotent competitive athlete is not a perfect competitive athlete at all. Such a person could break all records and defeat all comers who were not omnipotent. But whatever else competitive athletics involves, it involves struggle, overcoming hardships, and striving to achieve feats of excellence. Being an omnipotent competitive athlete would entail none of this.

With these ideas firmly in mind, let us return to (H). Consider condition (2), which says there is no state of affairs, S, such that (a) it is logically possible for P to bring about S and (b) the bringing about of S by *any* agent y entails an imperfection in y. As we have seen, if, for example, y is an athlete and P is God, then there are states of affairs that it is logically impossible for P to bring about, and if y could bring them about, this would cause an imperfection in y. Thus God is not omnipotent on condition (2).

Consider condition (3), which says there is no state of affairs, S, such that (a) it is logically impossible for P to bring about S and (b) its being logically impossible for P to bring about S entails that there is an imperfection in P. But it is logically impossible for God to win a physique contest, and in some contexts this inability would be an imperfection in God. It is only because of the technical meaning of "perfection" used by philosophers and theologians that this has not been seen. Perfection, then, in the context of theological discussions, is a term of art; it has a special technical meaning. With this in mind, one can restate Gellman's definition:

> (H')   P is omnipotent IFF (1) P can bring about any state of affairs that it is logically possible for P to bring about, where (2) there is no state of affairs, S, such that (a) it is logically possible for P to bring about S, and (b) the bringing about of S by *any* agent y entails that y is less than all-good, omnipotent, omniscient, disembodied, and so on, and (3) there is no state of affairs, S, such that (a) it is possible for P to bring about S, and (b) its being logically impossible for P to bring about S entails that P is less than all-good, omnipotent, omniscient, disembodied, and so on.

Given this understanding of omnipotence, it is of course impossible that God's omnipotence could conflict with His omniscience, goodness, disembodiedness, and so on. Incompatibility is ruled out by definition.

However, (H') is not what is normally meant by omnipotence. Omnipotence has been given a technical meaning in order to avoid the sort of problems we have been considering. On the other hand, as we have seen, given a less technical understanding of perfection, God could not be said to be omnipotent.

I conclude that on Gellman's account, either God is not omnipotent and hence does not exist, or else the sense in which He is omnipotent is a technical one that seems far removed from what is normally meant.

Conclusion

We have seen that there is very good reason to suppose that the traditional concept of God is incoherent and, consequently, that God does not exist. Therefore, positive atheism in the sense of disbelief in a being who is omniscient, omnipotent, morally perfect, and completely free is indeed justified. As I have suggested, there are ways of escaping from this conclusion, but these are purchased at a great price. My argument turns, of course, on analyses of the traditional attributes of God such an omniscience, omnipotence, moral perfection, and freedom, which might be rejected by theists. If they do reject my analyses, then the onus is on them to supply an analysis that does not have similar problems.

Suppose theists accept the challenge. As Swinburne points out, there are grave difficulties in proving that any sentence p is consistent.[44] No matter how many consistent statements p entails, there may still be a contradiction that p entails that has not yet been brought to light. This problem is approached by Swinburne in the following way. First, he maintains that a statement p is proved consistent if it is entailed by a statement r that is assumed to be consistent. The problem now is how one can know that r is consistent. In order to convince a critic that p is consistent, one must get the critic to agree that sentence r, which entails p, is consistent. But this may be difficult or impossible. In particular, it is difficult to see what sentence r that entails "God exists" would be more clearly consistent to critics than "God exists." Second, Swinburne suggests that inductively successful *a posteriori* arguments for the truth of p could indirectly show that p is consistent. Thus if we had factual evidence that inductively supported the hypothesis that God exists, then this would be some reason to suppose that "God exists" is true and, consequently, some reason to suppose that "God exists" is consistent.[45] However, the trouble with this indirect inductive proof of consistency with respect to the sentence "God exists" is that, as we have seen in Part I, there is no strong inductive reason to believe that God exists. Thus this way of establishing the consistency of theism has been ruled out by our earlier criticisms of the theistic arguments.[46]

Suppose my arguments fail and theists show, despite the problems considered in this chapter, that the concept of God is consistent. This would not show that the concept of God has any application to the real world. Consistency does not entail truth, although it is a necessary condition of truth. After all, many statements embodying consistent concepts are false. Indeed, as I show in Chapters 13 to 18, there are good reasons to suppose that even if the concept of God is consistent, God does not exist.

CHAPTER 13

Atheistic Teleological Arguments

As we saw in Chapter 5, the traditional teleological argument and its various modern formulations are not sound arguments for the existence of God. However, what has not been fully appreciated is that the sort of criticisms of the traditional teleological argument developed by Hume can be used *against* the existence of all-knowing, all-powerful, and all-good God. That is to say, Hume's arguments, if properly understood, can be used to support positive atheism in the narrow sense. In other words, they can be used to support disbelief in the existence of a theistic God. In this chapter I develop and defend arguments of this sort. I call them atheistic teleological arguments.

Salmon's Argument

Recall that Philo in Hume's *Three Dialogues Concerning Natural Religion* maintained that there is no strong argument from analogy from our experience to the conclusion that the universe was created out of nothing by an infinite disembodied being. A stronger argument from analogy, he says, is from our experience to the conclusion that the universe was created from preexisting material by a plurality of finite embodied gods. If we take Philo's argument seriously, it suggests that the *nonexistence* of a theistic God is supported by analogical arguments from experience.

A recent argument by Wesley Salmon can be understood as building upon this insight. Salmon uses probabilistic considerations derived from a reformulation of Philo's argument to show that the existence of God is improbable.[1] Salmon estimates these probabilities: (1) that an entity created by an intelligent agency exhibits order, (2) that an entity that is not created by an intelligent agency does not exhibit order, (3) that an entity is created by an intelligent agency, (4) that an entity is not so created, (5) that an entity exhibits order, and (6) than an entity does not. Given these estimates and Bayes's theorem, he argues that it is much more probable that an entity such as the universe whose origin is unknown was not created by intelligent agency than that it was.

The argument, stated more formally and in greater detail, is this: Let D designate the class of objects created by an intelligent agency. Let O refer to the class of objects that exhibit order. Then

$P(D,O)$ = the probability that an object created by an intelligent agency exhibits order.

$P(\sim D,O)$ = the probability that an object not created by an intelligent agency exhibits order.

$P(D)$ = the probability of an object created by an intelligent agency.

$P(O)$ = the probability of an object exhibiting order.

$(P\sim D)$ = the probability of an object not created by an intelligent agency.

$P(O,D)$ = the probability that an object exhibiting order is created by an intelligent agency.

$P(O,\sim D)$ = the probability that an object exhibiting order is not created by an intelligent agency.

According to Bayes's theorem:

$P(O,D) = [P(D,O) \times P(D)]/P(O)$
$P(O,\sim D) = [P(\sim D,O) \times P(\sim D)]/P(O)$

Salmon attempts to assess the various probabilities involved in this theorem. He maintains that given the incredibly large number of entities in our universe that are not the result of intelligence—galaxies, planets, atoms, molecules—$P(D)$ is very low whereas $P(\sim D)$ is very high. Further, he maintains that although $P(D,O)$ is high, it may not be near unity. This is because intelligent design may in fact produce chaos such as one finds in war. He maintains that $P(\sim D,O)$ is not negligible since biological generation and mechanical causation often produce order. Salmon argues that given this assessment, "we are in a position to say, quite confidently," that $P(O,D)$ is very low for any unspecified entity.[2]

But Salmon maintains that this does not settle the matter in the case of the creation of the universe, since we are dealing with a single unique event. Where a unique event is at issue one should refer the case to the broadest homogeneous reference class—that is, to the broadest class that cannot be relevantly subdivided. When this is applied to the design argument, Salmon says, one must take into account the type of order that the universe exhibits and the sort of intelligent creator that theists believe the teleological argument proves. Following Philo's argument, he maintains that if one takes these considerations into account, far from improving the probability of the theists' conclusion, the situation is worsened.

For example, the creator of the universe is regarded as pure spirit, a disembodied intelligence. But in no instance in our experience has a disembodied intelligence produced order. Thus where D_i is the class of disembodied intelligences, $P(D_i) = 0$. Further, as far as our experience is concerned, order of a large magnitude is never produced by a single designer. Thus if D_s is the class of single designers and O_m is the class of extremely large objects, $P(D_s,O_m) = 0$. Since the universe is an entity with a large magnitude it is improbable that it was created by a single designer. Thus when one takes into account the particular attributes involved in the unique case of the creation of the universe, the probability that the universe was created by an intelligent being comes vanishingly small.

CARTWRIGHT'S CRITIQUE

Nancy Cartwright maintains that Salmon has begged the question in supposing that galaxies, planets, atoms, molecules, and so on are not the result of design.[3] Consequently, he cannot assume that $P(D)$ is very low whereas $P(\sim D)$ is very high. She argues that in fact it is very hard to assess these probabilities inductively since there are few cases on whose origin the theist and the atheist agree. Therefore, to determine the frequency at which ordered objects arise from a random process, she suggests a controlled experiment. For example, she suggests that we might put the parts of a watch in a box and shake the box. The probability of getting the watch together in this way is, according to Cartwright, "as near to zero as can be."[4] As Cartwright points out, atheists may argue that given billions of years there is a great likelihood that the watch would come together in this random way. But there is no way of knowing this with any confidence, she says, and it is best to use experimental results. On the basis of these results, and contrary to Salmon's claim, $P(D,O)$, is much higher than $P(\sim D,O)$.

SALMON'S RETORT

In a reply[5] to Cartwright, Salmon maintains that the proposed experiment is irrelevant. He never supposed, he argues, that watches and other human artifacts could result from unintelligent causes: "I rested my case on things like atoms and molecules, stars and galaxies."[6] Salmon says that on the best cosmological knowledge, "everything from atoms to galaxies" was formed without intelligent design. Although cosmology is not an experimental science, Salmon adds, "it is built upon physical disciplines, such as thermodynamics and quantum mechanics, which are extensively supported by experimental evidence."[7]

ASSESSMENT OF THE DEBATE

Has Salmon answered Cartwright's charge that he has begged the question? What does it mean to beg the question? As this expression is usually understood, to beg the question is to assume what one is supposed to prove. Salmon was out to show that it is probable that the universe was not designed by an intelligent being, and he assumed in his premises that atoms, molecules, and galaxies were not the result of intelligent design. This is not what he was out to prove unless one supposes that the universe is nothing more than atoms, molecules, and galaxies. But it is not clear that Salmon assumes this. At the very least, Cartwright's criticism is mislabeled. Cartwright can be understood, however, as simply saying that some of Salmon's premises are now unjustified and could only be justified by experimental evidence that is all but impossible to acquire. But Salmon provides indirect experimental evidence from scientific cosmology to support the premises that Cartwright questioned. Unless Cartwright finds problems with this evidence it would seem not only that no question has obviously been begged but that the disputed premises have a good degree of empirical support.[8] Given these premises, it is improbable that the universe was created by an intelligent being.

Furthermore, even if Salmon has begged the question in assuming that atoms, molecules, and galaxies are not the result of an intelligent agency, or if at least he has not provided enough support for this assumption, his arguments that turn on the special properties of the universe and the alleged creator of this universe would not be affected. Recall that he maintained:

$$P(D_i) = 0$$
$$P(D_s, O_m) = 0$$

It is difficult to see that any question has been begged or why these propositions are not justified by our experience. Experience surely teaches that there are no disembodied beings. As Salmon puts it: "In no instance within our experience . . . has a disembodied intellect produced any kind of artifact, whether or not it might have exhibited order. Indeed, since disembodied intelligence has never operated in any fashion, to the best of our knowledge, we must conclude from experience that for such an intelligence," $P(D_i) = 0$, and $P(D_iO)$ is simply undefined.[9] Furthermore, experience teaches that the agency of a single being does not produce extremely large objects with order; that is, $P(D_s, O_m) = 0$. Substituting in Bayes's theorem we obtain the following results: $P(O, D_i)$ is undefined and $P(O_m,D_s) = 0$. In terms of our experience, then, the probability that a unique disembodied being created the universe is "as near to zero as can be." $P(O_m,D_s) = 0$ yields this result when substituted in Bayes's theorem, and $P(D_i) = 0$ yields this directly without need of substitution.

I conclude, therefore, that unless a better refutation is offered, Salmon's argument gives good grounds for supposing that God did not create the universe.

Expansion of the Argument

If Salmon's arguments concerning the unique properties of God are restated and expanded, they provide a powerful inductive case for positive atheism in the narrow sense.[10] The theistic God is an all-powerful, all-knowing, all-good, disembodied person who created the universe out of nothing. If it can be shown that, in the light of the evidence, such a being is improbable, then disbelief that the theistic God exists is justified. Consequently, positive atheism in the narrow sense is justified.

The general form an expanded argument takes is this:

(1) In terms of our experience, created entities of kind K that have been examined are always (or almost always, or usually) created by a being (or beings) with property P.

(2) The universe is a created entity.

(2a) If the universe is a created entity, it is of kind K.

[Probably]

(3) The universe was created by a being with property P.

(4) If the theistic God exists, then the universe was not created by a being with property P.

(5) Therefore, the theistic God does not exist.

The first part of the argument takes the form of an acceptable inductive argument. The inference from premises (1), (2), and (2a) to the conclusion (3)—sometimes called a predictive inference—moves from a property shared by all or most of the examined members of a class to some unexamined member that has this property. Premises (1), (2), and (2a) do not entail (3), they only make (3) probable. On the other hand, (3) and (4) do entail (5). Nevertheless, since (3) is only probable and it is one of the premises used in the derivation of (5), (5) is not established with certainty. Premise (1) is established by empirical observation. That is, in all cases that we have observed, created entities of a certain kind are created by a being or beings with certain properties. Premise (2) is assumed by theists. Premise (2a) is justified unless we have independent evidence to suppose that the universe should not be classified as an entity of type K. Premise (4) is an analytic truth; given our usual understanding of "God," it is true by definition. Let us now consider some instantiations of this argument.

THE ARGUMENT FROM EMBODIEDNESS

As we have seen, theists believe that God is a disembodied person and that He created the universe.[11] Some people have questioned whether the concept of a disembodied person is meaningful and, if it is, whether it is coherent. In the present argument I assume that the concept is both meaningful and coherent. It maintains that it is unlikely that a being who is disembodied created the universe, and since this is unlikely, it is unlikely that God exists.

The argument proceeds as follows:

(1)   In terms of our experience, all created entities of the kinds that we have so far examined are created by one or more beings with bodies. [Empirical evidence]

(2)   The universe is a created entity. [Supposition]

(2a) If the universe is a created entity, then it is of the same kind as the created entities we have so far examined. [Empirical evidence]

[Probably]

(3)   The universe was created by one or more beings with bodies. [From (1), (2), and (2a) by predictive inference]

(4)   If the theistic God exists, then the universe was not created by a being with a body. [Analytic truth]

---

(5)   Therefore, the theistic God does not exist. [From (3) and (4) by *modus tollens*]

Since premises (2) and (4) seem unproblematic and the deductive inference from (3) and (4) to (5) seems uncontroversial, let us concentrate on premises (1) and (2a) and the inference from (1), (2), and (2a) to (3).

Consider premise (1). What possible objections could there be to this premise? One objection that could be raised is that premise (1) begs the question against theism by assuming what needs to be proved: that if the universe was created, it was not created by a being without a body. It may be said that this is already assumed in premise (1), for it is assumed that all created entities are created by one or more beings with bodies. However, this objection is mistaken. Premise (1) does not assume that all created entities are created by one or more beings with bodies. It simply says that, as far as we can tell from our experience, all created entities of the kinds we have so far examined are created by one or more beings with bodies.

There might be cases for which there is no evidence as to whether some entity is created by some being or beings. Perhaps in the case of living organisms we do not have this kind of evidence. Perhaps this is also true in the case of stars and atoms. Then again, taking into account Salmon's retort to Cartwright, perhaps we do. For the purpose of the argument this need not be decided. What *is* clear is that in all uncontroversial cases of created objects, these were created by one or more beings with bodies. Or to put it in a slightly different way, we know of no cases where an entity is created by one or more beings without bodies.

Our experience does not rule out the possibility of an entity created by a disembodied being. Indeed, some of the entities we see every day may be of that sort. But we have no experience to support the belief that there are such entities. We have seen created entities that are large, old, complex, and so on that are created by one or more beings with bodies. We have not seen any created entities that are large, beautiful, difficult to understand, and so on that are created by a disembodied entity or entities. The universe is large, old, complex, and so on. We cannot observe whether it is created by one or more beings with or without bodies. But from the evidence we do have, we can infer that if it was created, it was probably created by one or more beings with bodies. Thus there is no reason to suppose that the question has been begged. We do not *assume* that the universe was created by one or more beings with bodies. We *infer* this from the available evidence.

It may also be objected that premise (2a) is dubious, and therefore the argument fails. The universe, it is said, is unique; it is one of a kind. Consequently, it is a mistake to put it in the same class as other created objects. For example, the universe is infinitely larger, older, and more complex than any created object we have ever experienced. Because of these differences, we have no right to assimilate the universe to the kind of created object that we normally experience.

What reason is there to suppose that the vase size, age, or complexity of the universe is relevant? There does not seem to be any evidence supporting this view. For example, as we examine larger and larger entities that we know are created, we do *not* find that more and more of them are created by beings that are disembodied. In fact, as far as our evidence is concerned, the size of the created object is irrelevant. All created objects from the smallest (a pinhead) to the largest (a battleship or a city) are created by beings with bodies. Similar points can be made about age and complexity. As far as our experience is concerned, neither the age nor the complexity of a created object is relevant to whether it is created by a being that is disembodied. Indeed, as far as our experience is concerned, no property of a created thing is relevant to whether it is created by a disembodied entity. No matter what kinds of things known to be created we have examined, none of them is known to be created by a disembodied entity. We must conclude that this objection does not show that (2a) is a dubious premise.

Finally, it may be argued that the inductive inference from (1), (2), and (2a) to (3) is weak in that the sample on which it is based is relatively small. For most of the objects we experience in our lives, we do not know if they are created or not. For all we know, atoms, molecules, stars, living organisms, and grains of sand may be created objects. Relative to this class, the class of objects that we know to be created is small. Yet it is this latter class that our inference is based on. If, for example, we had knowledge of whether atoms, molecules, stars, living organisms, and grains of sand were created, our sample might well give us good grounds for concluding that the universe is a created object. But we do not.

As Salmon has argued, scientific theory and evidence strongly support the view that entities such as stars and molecules are not created. But let us suppose that such evidence and theory do not exist. We must base our rational beliefs on the available evidence, which indicates that in all noncontroversial cases of objects known to be created, these objects were created by beings with a body. Our sample would be changed if new evidence came to light, and our present belief would not be rational in relation to this enlarged sample. Yet this is irrelevant to our present situation. Our sample as it stands is large and varied. It consists of literally billions of known created entities that have not been created by a disembodied being or beings and contain no known created entity that has been created by a disembodied being or beings. Furthermore, it contains evidence of all the various kinds of known created entities. It is surely irrelevant that the sample would be larger or more varied if, for example, we knew that atoms, molecules, stars, living organisms, and grains of sand were created and if these were included in it. The larger sample might give us more confidence in any inference made on its basis, but it would not show that an inference made on the basis of a smaller and less varied sample was unreliable.

Since the argument from embodiedness has the form of a strong inductive argument, the premises are well supported, and objections to it can be met, we conclude that it is a strong argument for the nonexistence of the theistic God.

THE ARGUMENT FROM MULTIPLE CREATORS

Theism is a monistic view in that God and not a plurality of supernatural beings is said to have created the universe. Yet our experience indicates that all large and complex entities are created by a group of beings working together. Although we have no direct experience of the universe's being created by a group of beings, from our experience one should infer inductively that if the universe is a created entity, it was created by a group of beings. But if so, then the existence of a theistic God is unlikely. The argument can be stated more formally as follows:

(1) In terms of our experience, all large and complex created entities of the kinds that we have so far examined are created by a group of beings working together. [Empirical evidence]
(2) The universe is a created entity. [Supposition]
(2a) If the universe is a created entity, then it is a large and complex created entity of the same kind as some of the created large and complex entities we have so far examined. [Empirical evidence]

[Probably]
(3) The universe was created by a group of beings working together. [From (1), (2), and (2a) by predictive inference]
(4) If the theistic God exists, then the universe was not created by a group of beings working together. [Analytic truth]

---

(5) Therefore, the theistic God does not exist. [From (3) and (4) by *modus tollens*]

Presumably the same sort of objections that just were discussed in relation to the argument from embodiedness could be raised against this argument, and they can be disposed of in exactly the same way. For example, it may be argued that the universe is unique; it is infinitely larger and more complex than any known created object. Consequently, it cannot be classified with the known created entities that are large and complex. But why should the universe's infinitely greater size and complexity make any difference? Indeed, as far as experience is concerned, the larger and more complex a created entity becomes the greater the likelihood that it was created by a group of beings working together. The largest and most complex created entities—cities, battleships, hydroelectric plants, interstate highway systems—are in all cases created by many individuals working together. In general, the larger and more complex the entity, the more beings are involved in its creation. Thus the vastness and complexity of the universe would show not the inappropriateness of the argument from multiple creators but that its conclusion is even better supported than one might have supposed. This conclusion about the number of entities involved in the creation of large and complex entities is supported also by a large and varied sample. We have found that large and complex created objects are created by multiple entities in numerous cases and in a wide variety of circumstances—for example, the pyramids and Hoover Dam. It seems to be true no matter what the object is made of, no matter what the moral views of the partici- pants, no matter what the technology of the creators.

We must conclude, then, that there is strong inductive reason to sup- pose that if the universe was created, it was created by multiple beings and, consequently, that the theistic God does not exist.

THE ARGUMENT FROM APPARENT FALLIBILITY

In our observation of created objects we sometimes notice what appear to be mistakes and errors. It usually turns out that these are the result of the fallibility of the creator or creators. The universe also appears to have mistakes and errors. If it is a created object, chances are that any and all of its creators are fallible. But if the creator of the universe is fallible, then God does not exist, since God is infallible and the creator of the universe. The argument, stated more formally, is as follows:

(1)   In terms of our experience, most seeming errors or mistakes in the kinds of created entities we have so far examined are the result of the fallibility of one or more creators of the entities. [Empirical evidence]
(2)   The universe is a created entity. [Supposition]
(2a) If the universe is a created entity, then it is an entity of a kind we have so far examined, with seeming errors or mistakes. [Empirical evidence]

[Probably]
(3)   The seeming errors or mistakes in the universe are the result of the actions of a fallible being or beings. [From (1), (2), and (2a) by predictive inference]
(4)   If the theistic God exists, then the seeming errors or mistakes in the universe are the results of the actions of a being who is infallible. [Analytic truth]

---

(5)   Therefore, the theistic God does not exist. [From (3) and (4) by *modus tollens*]

Consider premise (1). This is well confirmed by our experience. For example, we are told that a recently constructed building has poor ventila- tion; we notice that getting the spare tire out of the trunk in our new car is awkward because of the way the trunk is constructed; we read about a new city in Brazil that has been constructed with inadequate sanitation facilities for the estimated population.

Sometimes, of course, we are mistaken in our judgments about what is an error. The evidence of poor ventilation may stem from our failure to understand how the new system works. The city in Brazil may have adequate sanitation facilities despite reports. Our mistaken suppositions about errors are usually corrected as we become acquainted with the created objects. Indeed, it would be most unusual if the misapprehension persisted after a few years of acquaintance. Moreover, whatever the problems with the created entity, we usually discover that they result from the fallibility of the creator or creators. For example, the failure of the architects of the building to anticipate certain factors resulted in poor circulation of air; the automotive engineers did not forsee that building the trunk in a certain way would make it awkward to remove the spare tire; the city planners made errors in their calculations.

Sometimes, of course, we find that the problem was anticipated, yet there was a compelling reason for creating the object in that way. For example, the automotive engineers built the trunk in a certain way, knowing it would be awkward to remove a tire, because it was much cheaper to do so. If this is not so, we can usually tell. For example, we reason that if the trunk was built in this way to save money, we can expect that other design aspects of the automobile will reflect similar attempts at economy. But we may not find other attempts at economy. Moreover, there may be other reasons to suppose that economy was not an issue. For example, we may also estimate that getting a tire out of the trunk could have been made much easier without any more expense by raising one part of the trunk and lowering another. We could be wrong in our reasoning, but experience teaches that we usually are not. What appear to be mistakes because of the fallibility of the creators of objects are usually just that.

If the universe is a created entity, it contains what appear to be errors or mistakes of its creator or creators. For example, there appear to be great inefficiencies in the process of evolution: some of the organs of animals have no apparent function; some organisms seem to have no function in the ecological whole. There are apparent errors also in the genetic endowment of certain organisms: for example, because of genetic deficiencies, children are born blind and crippled. Our experience indicates that in most of the cases we have examined when a created entity seems to have some mistakes, the mistakes are due to the fallibility of the creator or creators. So it is probable that this is true of the apparent errors or mistakes found in the universe; the creator or creators of the universe are fallible. However, since God is supposed to be infallible and the creator of the universe, God does not exist.

The same sort of objections can be raised against this argument as against the argument from embodiedness and the argument from multiple creators, and they can be handled in exactly the same way. However, a new objection can be raised against this argument. It can be maintained that, to the eye of the believer, the universe does not seem as if it contains errors or mistakes. It may be said that what the nonbeliever sees as the uselessness of certain organs and organisms, a theist sees as God's mysterious but perfect handiwork.

This objection has no force, however. First, the way the universe appears to the believer is irrelevant. The question is how it appears to those who have not made up their minds and are basing their beliefs on the evidence. Second, very often the universe appears to theists to contain mistakes and errors of creation. They attempt to explain these appearances away by assumptions such as that God cannot logically create a better universe. The force of the present argument is that all these ways of explaining away the appearance of error fly in the face of the evidence. If we remain true to the evidence, we must suppose, if the universe was created at all, that what seems like an error is just that and is based on what most apparent errors are based on: the fallibility of the creator or creators.

We must therefore conclude that there is good reason to suppose that the theistic God does not exist.

THE ARGUMENT FROM FINITENESS

Our experience with entities known to be created is that they are created by beings with finite power. No matter what the object—be it small or large, old or new, simple or complex—if we know that it was created, we have found that it was created by a being or beings with finite power. If the universe is a created object, then probably it was created by a being or beings with finite power. However, since the theistic God has unlimited power and is supposed to be the creator of the universe, the theistic God does not exist. More formally, the argument can be stated in this way:

(1)   In terms of our experience, all created entities of the kinds that we have so far examined were created by a being or beings with finite power. [Empirical evidence]

(2)   The universe is a created entity. [Supposition]

(2a) If the universe is a created entity, then it is of the same kind as some of the created entities we have so far examined. [Empirical evidence]

[Probably]

(3)   The universe was created by a being or beings with finite power. [From (1), (2), and (2a) by predictive inference]

(4)   If the theistic God exists, then the universe was not created by a being with finite power. [Analytic truth]

(5) Therefore, the theistic God does not exist. [From (3) and (4) by *modus tollens*]

The same sort of objections can be raised against this argument as against the preceding ones, and they can be handled in exactly the same way. Again, however, a new objection can be raised. It can be maintained that the vast size and complexity of the universe suggest that the creator or creators of the universe would have to have infinite power. If we extrapolate to the universe from the amount of power it takes to produce the things we know are created, we can reasonably infer that the universe, if it was created, was created by a being or beings with unlimited power.

This argument is not warranted by our experience, however. Of course, one could imagine a world in which experience supports to some extent the extrapolation assumed in the argument. But even in that case it is unclear that an inference to an infinitely powerful being would be warranted. Consider a world in which the larger and more complex the entities known to have been created, the larger and more powerful the beings who created the objects. For example, in this world there might be a series of progressively larger giants. If an object of x size and complexity were found, we would discover that it was created by 20-foot-tall giants; if an object of x^2 size and complexity were found, we would discover that it was created by 200-foot-tall giants. And so on. In this world we might infer that if galaxies were created, they were created by giants of truly enormous size and power. In this world we also might infer that if the universe was created at all, then it was created by giants of even greater size and power than those that created the galaxies. However, it is unclear that we would be justified in inferring that the universe was created by giants of infinite size and power.

In any case, the world is not our world. In our world all known created objects are created by finite beings. The size of the beings seems to be roughly the same; the power of the beings is increased only through technological means. If modern creators have more power than the ancients, it is only because of advanced technology. The ancients were able to compensate for inferior technology by the use of mass labor. Given this experience we may infer that if the world was created, it was created by finite beings, perhaps with their power greatly enhanced through superadvanced technology. Any inference that goes beyond this is simply flying in the face of the evidence.

We again must conclude that if the universe was created, it was probably created by a being or beings with finite power. Consequently, the theistic God does not exist.

THE ARGUMENT FROM PREEXISTING MATERIAL

In all cases of created objects that have been investigated, the created object was created on the basis of preexisting material. This is true of all the various kinds of created objects we know, small and large, old and new, complex and simple, useful and useless. We can infer, then that the universe, if it was created, was probably created on the basis of preexisting material. However, although creation *ex nihilo* is perhaps not an essential tenet of theism, it has been claimed to be a distinctive feature of Christianity.[12] If it is, we can infer that the Christian God does not exist. The argument, stated more formally, is this:

(1) In terms of our experience, all created entities of the kinds that we have so far examined are created from preexisting material. [Empirical evidence]

(2) The universe is a created entity. [Supposition]

(2a) If the universe is a created entity, it is of the same kind as some of the created entities we have so far examined. [Empirical evidence]

[Probably]

(3) The universe was created from preexisting material. [From (1), (2), and (2a) by predictive inference]

(4) If the Christian God exists, then the universe was not created from preexisting material. [Analytic truth]

---

(5) Therefore, the Christian God does not exist. [From (3) and (4) by *modus tollens*]

The same sort of objections can be raised against this argument as against the preceding ones, and they can be handled in exactly the same way. So again we must conclude that there are good inductive reasons to suppose that the Christian God does not exist.

The Universe as a Created Object

In all the arguments considered above I have supposed for the sake of argument that the universe is a created object. I have shown that if it is, then it probably was not created by the theistic God. But is there any reason to believe that the universe is a created entity? There is Salmon's argument against this. It may be possible, moreover, to develop an argument similar to his that does not make any assumptions about the size of the relative classes of created and noncreated objects. Recall that in Chapter 5 on the teleological argument, I cited Wallace Matson's critique of the analogical version of the argument. He maintained that both proponents and critics of the argument assume that "the properties according to which we judge whether or not some object is an artifact, are accurate adjustments of parts and the curious adapting of means to ends."[13] However, Matson argues that this assumption is false. In actual practice an artifact is distinguished from a natural object by the evidence of machinery and the material from which the object was made.

Matson's insight can be developed in the following way. Let T be the tests that anthropologists and other scientists use to determine whether some item is a created object. We know that almost always when an object meets test T it turns out to be a created object. For example, we know almost always that when an object has certain peculiar marks on it, these have been left by a flaking tool and, consequently, that the object was created. We also know that usually when an object does not meet test T it is not a created object. As Matson points out, the tests actually used by anthropologists and other scientists are not aimed at determining whether the object serves some purpose—that is, whether it shows a fine adjustment of parts and a curious adaptation of means to ends. To illustrate his point, Matson suggests the thought experiment of separating into two piles a heap of created and noncreated objects that one has not seen before:

> Let us put in the heap a number of "gismos"—objects especially constructed for the test by common methods of manufacture, i.e., metallic, plastic, painted, machined, welded, but such that the subject of the test has never seen such things before, and they do not in fact display any "accurate adjustment of parts" or "curious adaptation of means to ends." Put into the heap also a number of natural objects which the subject has never seen. Will he have any more difficulty [in separating the objects into two piles]? He will not. The gismos go into one pile, the platypuses and tektites into the other, quite automatically.
>
> Of course one might conceivably make mistakes in this sorting procedure. And it is perhaps hazardous to predict that human visitors to another planet would be entirely and immediately successful in determining, from an inventory of random objects found on its surface, whether it was or had been the abode of intelligent beings. But space explorers would not be at a loss as to how to proceed in the investigation. They would look for evidence of machining, materials that do not exist in nature, regular markings, and the like. Presence of some of these things would be taken as evidence, though perhaps not conclusive, of artifice.[14]

Let us call the argument for the nonexistence of God developed on the basis of Matson's insight the argument from the tests of artifice and state it more formally as follows:

(1) In almost all the cases examined so far, if an object does not meet test T, it is not created. [Empirical observation]

(2) The universe does not meet test T. [Empirical observation]

[Probably]
(3) The universe is not created. [From (1) and (2) by predictive inference]
(4) If the theistic God exists, then the universe is created. [Analytic truth]

(5) Therefore, the theistic God does not exist. [From (3) and (4) by *modus tollens*]

This argument may be criticized in much the same way as the other ones considered here, and these criticisms can be just as easily answered. First, it may be maintained that it begs the question of whether the universe is created. But no question has been begged. I have not assumed that the universe is not created; I inferred this from the evidence. Second, it may be argued that premise (1) is not established. But it has been established in the same way that Salmon's assumption was established that planets, atoms, and galaxies are not created objects. According to the best scientific theory and evidence we have, if some object is not made of certain material, does not have certain markings, and so on, it is usually not a created object. Such evidence and theory could be mistaken, but it is the best we have to go on.

Third, it may be objected that the universe is unique and should not be judged by the same tests we use to judge other objects. Although it may be true that the universe is unique, there is no reason to suppose, in the light of our present evidence, that this is relevant in judging whether it is created or not. We have no reason to suppose it cannot be judged by the same criteria we use to judge whether planets, rocks, and gismos are created. Fourth, it may be urged that as our technology advances, we may be able to create objects that resemble more and more the natural objects we find in the universe. If so, then test T will no longer be a reliable method of distinguishing some created objects from noncreated objects. Whether our technology will ever advance to a stage where it would be possible to distinguish by any conceivable test, for example, a created platypus from a noncreated one seems unlikely. Of course, it is certainly likely that our technology will advance to a stage where it would be impossible to tell a created object from a noncreated one by test T. But there is every reason to suppose that our tests for an artifice will improve with our technology and that a new test will be devised that will be able to distinguish the created from the uncreated. In any case, the argument from the tests of artifice is based on our *present* evidence and may have to be given up as new evidence is gathered. This possibility does not affect the present force of the argument.

We can conclude that there is good reason to suppose that the universe is not created and, consequently, that the theistic God does not exist.

Conclusion

I have shown that if we take seriously the evidence at our disposal, we can infer that the theistic God does not exist. If we assume that the universe is a created object, the creator is probably not the theistic God. However, if we use the criteria for creation that are used by scientists, it is probable that the universe is not created and consequently that the theistic God does not exist.

CHAPTER 14

The Argument from Evil

In the last two chapters I considered two arguments that can be used to establish positive atheism in the sense of disbelief in an all-knowing, all-powerful, all-good, completely free, disembodied being. In Chapter 12 I attempted to show that the concept of a theistic God is inconsistent, and in Chapter 13 I argued that Hume's critique of the teleological argument can be used to show that the existence of a theistic God is unlikely. If either of these arguments is successful, positive atheism in the sense of disbelief in an all-knowing, all-powerful, all-good, completely free, disembodied being is justified.

However, suppose these arguments are not successful. Do atheists have any other arguments that justify disbelief in God? They do. Historically, perhaps the most important one is the argument from evil. The problem that generates the argument was apparently first formulated by Epicurus (341–270 B.C.).

> God either wishes to take away evil, and is unable, or He is able, and unwilling; or He is neither willing nor able, or He is both willing and able. If He is willing and is unable, He is feeble, which is not in accordance with the character of God; if He is able and unwilling, He is envious, which is equally at variance with God; if He is neither willing nor able, He is both envious and feeble, and therefore not God; if He is both willing and able, which alone is suitable to God, from what source then are evils? or why does He not remove them?[1]

Both believers and nonbelievers have taken this problem seriously. On the one hand, theologians from Augustine to John Hick have grappled with it and produced what they believe to be adequate solutions to Epicurus's problem. The proposed solutions range from the suggestion that evil is an illusion to the one that evil is the result of free will. On the other hand, atheologians from Hume to J. L. Mackie have maintained that the problem can be used to support disbelief in God. They have argued that the existence of evil cannot be reconciled with belief in God and that the proposed solutions offered by theologians are inadequate.

The argument for positive atheism in the sense of disbelief in an all-knowing, all-powerful, all-good, completely free, disembodied being based on Epicurus's problem can be stated very simply: God is by definition all-powerful, all-knowing, and all-good. If God is all-powerful, He can prevent evil. If God is all-knowing and can prevent evil, He knows how to prevent it. If God is all-good, He wants to prevent evil. But since there is evil, God cannot exist.

Atheologians have usually construed this as a deductive argument. They have, in other words, attempted to show that the conjunction of the following statements is inconsistent:

(1) God is all-powerful and all-knowing.
(2) God is all-good.
(3) Evil exists.

However, this approach has generally been regarded as unsuccessful. The logical compatibility of (1), (2), and (3) is suggested by the following considerations.[2] (1) entails

(1') God could prevent evil unless evil was logically necessary.

and (2) entails

(2') God would prevent evil unless God had a morally sufficient reason to allow it.

(1') and (2') combined entail

(3') Evil exists only if either God has a morally sufficient reason to allow it or it is logically necessary.

(3') does not conflict with (1) and (2).

Because of the failure of deductive arguments from evil, atheologians have developed inductive or probabilistic arguments from evil for the nonexistence of God. In this chapter I distinguish, explicate, and defend two types of such arguments.

A Direct Inductive Argument from Evil

A contemporary philosopher, William Rowe, has defended what he calls an empirical argument from evil, in which, on the basis of evil, one infers that it is unlikely that God exists.[3] Since Rowe's argument from evil is one of most sophisticated and well argued in the literature, I present it in some detail. In what I call a *direct inductive argument from evil,* he argues directly from the existence of evil, and refutations of theodicies play no role in his argument. Rowe considers only one type of evil: human and animal suffering caused by natural forces. It is not important for our purposes here whether Rowe's argument would hold for other types of evil, since if it is successful with regard to human and animal suffering, we would have good grounds for nonbelief. Following Rowe, let O represent an omnipotent, omniscient, wholly good being. Standard theism, Rowe says, maintains that O exists. Two claims are essential to Rowe's version of the argument.

(1) There exist evils that O could have prevented, and had O prevented them, the world as a whole would be a better place.

(2) O would have prevented the occurrence of any evil O could prevent, such that had O prevented it, the world as a whole would have been better.

Rowe argues that since (1) and (2) entail

(3) O does not exist

if (1) is probable and (2) is true, then it is probable that theism is false.

However, Rowe maintains that the evidential argument from evil is not the inference from (1) and (2) to (3) but the argument that seeks to provide a good reason for thinking that (1) is more probable than not, that (2) is true and, therefore, that (3) is probably true.[4] Rowe takes it for granted that (2) or "something quite like it is true"[5] and concentrates his efforts on showing that (1) is probably true.

He admits that it is extremely difficult to *know* that (1) is true because one would have to know that if some great evil such as the suffering caused by the Lisbon earthquake had been prevented by O, either a greater evil would not have occurred or a greater good would not have been prevented from occurring. Such knowledge is, according to Rowe, difficult if not impossible to come by. Nevertheless, he argues that we have good grounds for thinking that (1) is true: first, our knowledge of the vast amount of human and animal suffering that occurs daily in our world; second, our understanding of the goods that do exist and that we can imagine coming into existence; third, our reasonable judgment of what an omnipotent being can do; and, fourth, our reasonable judgment of what an omniscient and wholly good being would endeavor to accomplish with respect to human and animal good and evil in the universe.

To illustrate his thesis Rowe presents the example of the suffering of a fawn that is badly burned in a forest fire caused by lightning. In this case, he argues, as far as we can determine the suffering "serves no greater good at all, let alone one that is otherwise unobtainable by an omnipotent being."[6] Rowe admits that, appearances to the contrary notwithstanding, this suffering may be necessary either for some larger good or to prevent some larger evil. But he says it is incredible that "all instances of suffering that served no greater good we know or can think of should nevertheless be such that none could have been prevented by an omnipotent being without loss of greater good."[7]

Although Rowe does not put his argument in terms of the superiority of the predictive power of alternative accounts over theism, it may be useful to construe it in these terms. Consider two alternative hypotheses:

(H_1) O exists.

(H_2) No supernatural beings exist that are concerned with the welfare of humans or other sentient beings.

Let e be the existence of the apparently pointless suffering of the fawn. Let K be background knowledge, which includes our knowledge about what an omnipotent being can accomplish, what goods exist or can be imagined to exist, and what a morally perfect and all-knowing being would attempt to bring about with respect to human and animal good and evil. Rowe may be interpreted as arguing that e is more likely on (H_2) and K than on (H_1) and K.

Rowe defends his argument against two objections, the first of them put forth by Stephen Wykstra.[8] Rowe interprets Wykstra's objection as claiming that Rowe is committed to the following:

(4) It appears that the fawn's suffering is pointless; that is, it appears that the fawn's suffering does not serve an outweighing[9] good otherwise unobtainable by an omnipotent, omniscient being.

But according to Wykstra, Rowe can claim (4) only if

(5) We have no reason to think that were O to exist, things would strike us in pretty much the same way.

However, Wykstra argues that (5) is false in that the outweighing good in relation to which O must permit the fawn's suffering is probably beyond our ken. For example, suppose the outweighing good is occurring in an afterlife, or suppose the outweighing good is currently existing but we cannot discern it with any of our senses. In this case, the suffering of the fawn would still strike us as pointless even if O existed.

Put in terms of the comparative predictive power of rival accounts, Wykstra can be interpreted as saying either that K should include the information that the outweighing good is beyond our ken—let us call K with this added information K'—or that H_1 should be modified to read:

(H₁') O exists and there are goods that outweigh the fawn's suffering that are beyond our ken but not beyond God's.

Given these modifications, it may be argued that e is no more likely on (H_2) and K' than on (H_1) and K' or, alternatively, that e is no more likely on (H_2) and K than on (H_1') and K.

Rowe counters this argument by maintaining that, although God *may* indeed grasp goods beyond our ken, it does not follow that the outweighing goods probably have not yet occurred or, if they have occurred, that they are beyond our grasp. Indeed, he argues that even if O exists, the likelihood of the existence of such ungraspable goods would not follow. So there would be no justification for changing K to K'. But what about modifying (H_1) to (H_1')? Rowe's answer deserves close study.

He admits that on some versions of what he calls *expanded theism* the likelihood of ungraspable goods would follow. Expanded theism is the hypothesis that O exists conjoined with certain other significant religious claims—for example, about sin, a future life, a last judgment. Orthodox Christianity is a version of expanded theism and (H_1') is another. Rowe denies, however, that this follows from *restricted theism*—the claim that O exists *without* this being conjoined to other theses.

But does not Rowe's admission give theists an easy reply to his argument? It would seem that, to their belief that O exists, they need only add certain other religious claims that make the existence of ungraspable goods likely. For example, (H_1') does precisely this. However, Rowe argues that this reply has a price. The existence of suffering will not disconfirm expanded theism as it does restricted theism. But since expanded theism entails restricted theism, the probability of the former can be no greater than that of the latter when it was disconfirmed by the existence of this suffering. Consequently, if restricted theism (H_1) is less probable than not on the basis of apparently pointless suffering, expanded theism (H_1') cannot be more probable than restricted theism. Rowe concludes that "there is not much to be gained by retreating to" expanded theism.[10]

In terms of our example, although (H_1') and K may have the same predictive value as (H_2) and K with respect to e, (H_1') would have no higher probability in the light of e and K than does H_1. Such a result should not be surprising. In science and in ordinary life it is quite common for two hypotheses to have the same predictive value with respect to the evidence e and yet for one of them to be better supported by e and the background knowledge. For example, suppose our evidence e is that Evans's fingerprints are on the murder weapon and we have two rival hypotheses: Evans is the murderer (H_3) and Jones is the murderer (H_4). Let us suppose that the predictive value of (H_3) is higher than that of (H_4) relative to E. That is, E is less surprising relative to (H_3) and the detective's background knowledge K than it is relative to (H_4) and K. Let us suppose further that in the light of the evidence E and our background evidence K, (H_3) is more probable relative to E and K than is (H_4). Let us suppose further that the detective attempts to expand (H_4) to better account for E. She postulates that Jones is the murderer, that he wore gloves, and that after he killed his victim he hypnotized Evans and made him hold the gun (H_4*). Suppose that with this expansion (H_4*) and (H_3) have the same predictive value with respect to E. That is, the fact that Evans's fingerprints are on the murder weapon is no less surprising on (H_3) and K than on (H_4*) and K. Despite this, since (H_4*) entails (H_4), the probability of (H_4*) relative to E and K cannot be more than the probability of (H_4) relative to E and K.

Rowe also attempts to meet an objection raised by Delmas Lewis[11] that he argues fallaciously from the claim

(6) There are instances of apparently pointless evil

to

(7) There are instances of pointless evil.[12]

According to Rowe, Lewis wrongly demands that before (6) can be accepted as a good reason for (7), Rowe must *show* that (6) is a good reason for accepting (7). Rowe says that Lewis is "demanding too much"[13] since the project was simply to give a good reason for the following:

(1) There exist evils that O could have prevented, and had O prevented them, the world as a whole would be a better place.

It is *another* project, says Rowe, to show why a good reason for (1) is a good reason, adding that although he has completed his own project he may not convince some people of this unless he completes this other one as well.

Lewis argues that Rowe would be justified in inferring (7) from (6) if we knew that the following principle is true:

(8) If there were goods for whose sake O must permit instances of intense human and animal suffering, we would know or be able to imagine these goods and understand why O must permit the suffering in order to obtain them.

However, Lewis says that we cannot know (8). Although Rowe admits that we cannot establish (8) with certainty, he maintains that we do not need to. He says, "That things appear to us to be a certain way is itself justification for thinking things are this way. Of course, this justification may be defeated. But apart from such defeat, the fact that things appear to us to be a certain way renders us rationally justified in believing that they are that way."[14]

Although Rowe does not explicitly formulate his argument, it seems to be this:

(a) If, in the light of the evidence, X appears to be Y and there is no positive reason to suppose that X's appearance is misleading, then it is reasonable to suppose that X is Y.
(b) In the light of the evidence, the fawn's suffering appears to be pointless.
(c) There is no positive reason to suppose that it is not.

(d) Therefore, it is reasonable to suppose that the fawn's suffering is pointless.

Now, if there were positive evidence for God's existence, or if one had positive reason to suppose there were goods beyond our ken that the fawn's sufferings would be needed to achieve, then (c) would be false. But this is precisely the sort of evidence we do not have.

Rowe also argues that there are some considerations that speak in (8)'s favor. Unless we are "excessively utilitarian,"[15] it is reasonable to suppose that the goods for whose sake O permits human and animal suffering either are or include good experiences for the humans or animals that endure the suffering. This is because we normally regard it to be morally impermissible to cause some person great involuntary suffering in order to achieve some greater good unless this person would "figure significantly in the good."[16] Further, we have reason to believe that the goods for which humans suffer are conscious experiences that are themselves good. However, the conscious experiences of others are among the things we do know, and we also know the humans and animals that now suffer and have suffered in the past. Yet as far as we can tell, these humans and animals do not and did not have good conscious experiences that outweighed the evil of their sufferings.

However, it may be argued that these goods will be experienced in the future by the creatures that suffered in the past or are suffering now. Rowe admits that some of these experiences may only be achieved in the distant future. But, "in the absence of any reason to expect that O would need to postpone these good experiences, we have reason to expect that many of these goods would occur in the world we know."[17] This gives us some reason to believe that (8) is true.

Rowe is aware that even if evil does tend to disconfirm theism, arguments for the existence of God may tend to confirm theism more than evil disconfirms it. For this reason, an essential part of any argument for the nonexistence of God is the refutation of arguments for the existence of God. Unless these arguments are shown to be worthless, the theist may well accept the fact that evil, taken in isolation from other evidence, tends to disconfirm theism without rejecting theism. So if Rowe's argument is to be used to establish the nonexistence of God, it is important to combine it with refutations of the arguments for the existence of God.

One might also think it important to combine his argument with refutations of the standard theodicies, the traditional solutions to the problem of evil. However, although Rowe does not explicitly say so, it is likely that he believes he does not need to consider standard theodicies of natural evil, since his basic argument is directed at restricted theism. Theodicies, he might say, would be relevant only when expanded theism is considered. Indeed, each theodicy for theism can be considered a different version of expanded theism. Recall that expanded theism is the claim that O exists conjoined with other significant religious claims. Given this understanding of a theodicy, Rowe could maintain that he does not need to refute theodicies of natural evil, since he has shown by his previous argument that no form of expanded theism could be any more probable than restricted theism. Since restricted theism is rendered improbable by Rowe's argument from the existence of natural evil, theodicies of natural evil can be ignored.

An Indirect Inductive Argument from Evil

The Argument Stated

Although Rowe does not develop the inductive argument from evil in terms of the failure of known theodicies to solve the problem of evil, it is possible to do so. The general strategy would be to maintain that since no known theodicy is successful, probably no theodicy will be successful. And since probably no theodicy will be successful, there is probably no explanation for evil. However, there must be such an explanation if God exists. So it is likely that He does not exist. I call such an argument an *indirect inductive argument from evil*.

In a previous paper[18] I suggested developing an indirect inductive argument from evil by considering the implications of the problems involved in showing that the existence of evil is inconsistent with the existence of God. As we have seen above, conjunction of the following three statements is *not* inconsistent.

(1) God is all-powerful and all-knowing.
(2) God is all-good.
(3) Evil exists.

This is not changed if, instead of considering evil in general, we consider the sort of evil considered by Rowe: apparently pointless or gratuitous evil. Let us understand apparently pointless or gratuitous evil to be evil such that if God exists, He could apparently prevent it, and if God had prevented it, then the world as a whole would apparently be a better place. The following conjunction is also not inconsistent:

(1) God is all-powerful and all-knowing.
(2) God is all-good.
(3') Apparently pointless evil exists.

But suppose one also assumes:

(4) The existence of apparently pointless evil is not logically necessary, and there is no morally sufficient reason for God to allow it.

Then (1), (2), and (4) entail

~(3) Apparently pointless evil exists

which conflicts with (3).

This by itself does not give one any deductive or inductive reasons for disbelieving in God unless one also has good reason to suppose that premise (4) is true. There is no *a priori* way to demonstrate the truth of (4). However, suppose all attempts down through the ages have failed to specify a sufficient moral reason for the existence of what seems like pointless or gratuitous evil; that is, suppose they have failed to explain away the appearances by showing that there is in fact a sufficient moral reason for such evil. Furthermore, suppose all attempts have failed to show that what seems like pointless evil is really not pointless, since it is logically necessary. If this failure did occur, it should give us some confidence in (4). For if every attempt to specify a needed explanation fails over a long period of time, this gives us good grounds for supposing that an explanation is impossible. In the present case this means, if theodicies have failed, we would have good reason to suppose that evil that seems pointless *is* in fact pointless.

Even if this failure would provide inductive support for (4) and consequently provide indirect evidence for the nonexistence of God, this evidence would not necessarily outweigh evidence for the existence of God. Given some positive evidence, disbelief in God would on balance not be rational. However, as we have seen, the traditional arguments for the existence of God are bankrupt. We have also seen that nontraditional arguments are no better. Thus there is no positive reason for belief in God that could outweigh any possible negative evidence. A more formal statement of the argument is this:

(a) If (i) there is no positive evidence that P; and
   (ii) unless one makes assumption A, evidence E would falsify that P; and
   (iii) despite repeated attempts, no good reason has been given for believing A;
   then on rational grounds one should believe that P is false.
(b) There is no positive reason that God exists.
(c) The existence of apparently pointless evil would falsify the existence of God unless one assumes either that God has morally sufficient reason for allowing the existence of such evil or that it is logically necessary.
(d) Despite repeated attempts to do so, no one has provided a good reason to believe either that God has morally sufficient reasons to allow such evil to exist or that it is logically necessary.

(e) Therefore, on rational grounds one should believe that God does not exist.

Although this is formulated as a deductive argument, it is not a demonstrative argument that God does not exist; it only purports to show that on rational grounds one ought not to believe that God exists. The argument can in fact be recast as a straightforward inductive argument rather than a deductive argument with a conclusion about what one should believe. The general form of the argument is:

(a') Evidence E falsifies H unless A.
(b') Repeated attempts to establish A have failed.
(c') There is no positive evidence that H.

(d') ~H.

~H is not established by but is made probable relative to (a'), (b'), (c'). The atheist argument from evil is achieved by substituting in the obvious variables.

The Argument Defended

This argument has been criticized by Robert Pargetter in the following ways. First, he argues that the above inductive version of the argument is valid, but unlike deductive arguments, inductive arguments must meet the requirement of total evidence.[19] An inductive argument establishes nothing if a known piece of evidence is not included. Pargetter claims that the above argument does not include a relevant piece of evidence, namely:

(5) If God exists, then necessary evil exists, and necessarily God has sufficient reason for the evil or it is logically necessary, and necessarily any attempt to show that God didn't have such reasons would fail.

One assumes that the evil specified in (5) includes all apparently pointless evil, since even an atheist can admit that if God exists, then *some* evil may well be necessary. One problem with this objection is that either (5) is a necessary truth or it is not. If it is a necessary truth, as Pargetter seems to assume, its addition as a premise to an inductively strong argument should make no difference to the strength of support that the premises give the conclusion. Adding a necessary truth to the premises of an inductive argument no more affects the support the premises give the conclusion than it affects the support the premises give a deductive argument. On the other hand, if (5) is not a necessary truth, one must ask what justification there is for assuming it to be true. If it is not a necessary truth, its inclusion as a premise in the above argument is simply gratuitous. Indeed, if one interpreted evil in (5) to include apparently pointless evil, then (5) would be unacceptable even to many thoughtful theists, for it entails that

(5′) If God exists, then necessarily apparently pointless evil exists.

However, many theists have been puzzled about why there is such evil if God exists. Their puzzlement would be completely unintelligible if (5′) were true.

In addition, Pargetter seems to be confused on what I attempt to show. His objections seem to assume that since if God exists, He necessarily has sufficient reasons for allowing apparently pointless evil, my inductive argument attempting to show that there are no sufficient moral reasons must fail. However, the argument does not attempt to show that God, assuming He exists, has no sufficient reason for apparently pointless evil. This would indeed be impossible. It shows that probably there are no such reasons; and since, if God exists, there must be such reasons, God probably does not exist.

A related objection raised by Pargetter is based on the same confusion. He maintains that the statement that God has a morally sufficient reason for evil or that evil is logically necessary "is not a simple empirical statement" and "we do not usually regard" failure to establish the truth of such a statement as evidence for its falsehood. He argues further that the argument begs the question in assuming that repeated failure to establish the truth of such a statement is evidence against the statement in a situation "where it is agreed that there *could* be such a reason, a reason for God not only allowing abundant evil but also for the world being exactly as it is."[20]

However, consider

(6) If God exists, then either there is sufficient moral reason for the existence of apparently pointless evil, or such evil is logically necessary.

Although this may not be a simple empirical statement, and the failure to establish the truth of (6) should not be taken as establishing its falsehood, this is irrelevant to the argument. No attempt is made to argue that failure to establish (6) tends to establish its falsehood. Indeed, the argument *assumes* that (6) is true. The argument is that there are inductive reasons to suppose that the *consequence* of (6) is false—that the failure to establish the truth of this consequence tends to establish the falsehood of the consequence of (6), not of (6) itself. But if this consequence is probably false and (6) is true, then the antecedent of (6) is probably false.

Obviously, theists would want to claim that the above argument does not apply to theism. However, those like Pargetter who would reject this argument must have reasons for their rejection that are not ad hoc and arbitrary. It is easy enough to treat statements about God differently from analogous statements without providing any reason for this different treatment. Consider the following hypothetical case.

Jones is dead, and some of his friends suspect foul play. Let us suppose that the available evidence E would falsify the foul play hypothesis H unless the police are involved in a coverup R. However, although Jones's friends are skillful and dedicated, they try without success to establish R. Furthermore, there is no independent evidence for H. Surely in this case the above inductive argument applies; it would constitute an inductive argument for ~H. No question has been begged. It is irrelevant that there *could have been* a coverup. Obviously there could have been, but the question is, was there? Clearly this is an empirical issue, and the failure to establish any coverup after diligent and skillful effort does provide good, although not conclusive, evidence that there is no coverup. Furthermore, the lack of positive evidence for the foul play hypothesis reinforces this conclusion. For if there was positive evidence of foul play, this might indirectly support the coverup theory given certain background knowledge, such as that foul play is often associated with a police coverup.

Countless other examples of the same mode of inference can be found in everyday life and in science. Critics of our argument may be correct that when this mode of inference is applied to the existence of God, religious people reject it. The crucial question, however, is whether there is any *good* reason for treating this mode of inference differently in the context of religion. So far, no reasons have been supplied. Are there any?

One reason that might be given is that, in the context of religion, one knows or has justification for believing that there must be a reason for evil in the world since God is all-good and all-powerful. Of course, if one had independent reason to suppose that God does exist, then this would indeed provide justification for believing that there was a reason. But this evidence is precisely what one does not have. As the argument is stated above, there is no independent reason for supposing that God exists, since there is no positive reason for His existence. The situation is no different in ordinary life and in science. In the case of Jones, if one had independent reason for supposing that Jones's death was the result of foul play, one might have reason to suppose that despite the failure to turn up a police coverup, there was one. But in this example there was no such evidence.

Another reason that might be given is that the reasons God might have for creating a world with so much evil are so profound and difficult that they cannot be understood by mere mortals. Small wonder, then, that no reason for the existence of apparently pointless evil has ever been satisfactorily stated. However, what is the independent evidence that this is true? If one had independent reason to suppose that God exists and works in strange and deep ways, there might be justification for believing that there is some reason for the existence of apparently pointless evil that humans have not thought of or even never will think of. But there is no positive evidence to suggest that God exists, let alone that the reasons for evil are beyond human comprehension. Indeed, the idea that God's reasons for evil are comprehensible has been widely accepted by theologians from St. Augustine to Hick, who have attempted to specify what those reasons might be. Every attempt to formulate a systematic theodicy confirms the view that it is commonly accepted that it is possible to understand why, if God exists, there is evil. Naturally, the failure of all such attempts might have driven theists to claim that the reasons are beyond human comprehension. But without independent support, such a claim rings hollow. For example, Jones's friends could claim that despite their repeated failures to expose a police coverup, there is one nonetheless. They could say the police are so clever and cunning that exposing such a coverup is all but impossible. But without independent evidence, this charge is ad hoc and arbitrary. The same is true in the context of the problem of evil.

But does not the mere fact that God is omniscient create a presumption that He has knowledge about certain goods and evils as well as about certain connections between goods that humans do not have? It does create such a presumption, and if God exists, it is quite certain that God has such knowledge. The question is whether this admission by itself makes the existence of evil less surprising than it is on rival accounts— for example, than on the hypothesis that God does not exist. Why should we suppose that if God has such knowledge, this does not make it more likely that evil exists than if He does not exist? Although God might have reasons that are unknown or even unknowable to us for permitting evil, He might have reasons that are unknown or unknowable to us for preventing such evil. Further, since He is omnipotent, He may know means that we cannot understand to obtain certain goods without the evils that we find in the world. Thus the mere fact that, if God exists, He has knowledge we cannot have does not explain the existence of evil as well as rival hypotheses do. For example, the hypothesis that God exists and has knowledge of good and evil that we cannot have does not enable us to predict that there will be seemingly pointless evil as well as the rival hypothesis (H_2) specified above—namely, that neither the nature nor the condition of sentient beings on earth is the result of actions performed by benevolent or malevolent nonhuman persons.[21]

At least two further considerations strengthen the claim that failure to find a morally sufficient reason for evil is evidence that there is no reason. First, the various unsuccessful attempts down through the ages have not basically changed. As Hare and Madden point out: "The repeated failure, the recurrence and clustering of criticisms, the permutations of basic moves which have been found wanting, and the slight variations of old favourites is evidence that counts heavily against the likelihood of eventual success."[22] One might understand these philosophers to be saying there is inductive evidence that, if an inquiry results in variations of past unsuccessful explanations, it is unlikely to produce a satisfactory explanation. This claim is well supported in the history of science and in the history of many fields of inquiry.

It might be objected that this may be a strong inductive inference for the conclusion that success in finding a satisfactory explanation is unlikely, but this inference does not inductively support the conclusion that no correct theistic explanation is to be had. However, Hare and Madden's argument can be expanded and strengthened. The first thing to note is that there are successful explanations of apparently pointless evil from a naturalistic viewpoint. Indeed, naturalism has no general problem in explaining apparently pointless evil. Natural evil can be explained in terms of certain natural laws. For example, the birth of a defective baby can be explained in terms of genetics. Moral evil can be explained in terms of certain psychological or sociological theories. For example, the murder of an innocent bystander can be explained in terms of the motives and beliefs of the police. There might of course be a problem with some naturalistic explanations. Some might be inadequate. But there is no general problem like that of reconciling apparently pointless evil with belief in God.[23]

Hare and Madden's claim can be seen against the above background.

There is inductive evidence that if explanations of a particular phenomenon P made from a particular theoretical perspective T_1 not only continue to be unsuccessful but are simply variants of earlier ones, and if there is another theoretical perspective T_2 that generates successful explanations, then it is unlikely that there are successful explanations from T_1. Such an inductive inference becomes even stronger when there is no positive evidence for T_1. This sort of inference is used frequently both in everyday life and in science, and it would be arbitrary and ad hoc not to use it in the context of religion.

To illustrate, let us suppose that various advocates of the occult have put forth unsuccessful explanations of Uri Geller's feats and that these explanations are simply variants of past occult explanations. Suppose further that nonoccult explanations have been successful, and there is no positive evidence for the occult theoretical framework that the unsuccessful explanations assume. Surely, in this case one would be justified in inductively inferring not only that explanations will be no more successful in the future than they have been in the past, but also that there are no correct occult explanations of Geller's success. This situation is precisely analogous to the situation concerning the argument from evil. If one accepts the argument as it is used in this example, it would be arbitrary and ad hoc to reject it when it is applied to the problem of evil.

Another point that strengthens Hare and Madden's claim is "the fact that the riddle of God and evil involves the ordinary meaning of moral terms and that the structure of deliberate argumentation about God and evil has never been shown to be dissimilar to arguments in ordinary contexts about excusing or defeating evil."[24] Hare and Madden are here saying that, had the meaning of moral terms or the structure of argumentation been different from the ordinary, the failure to find sufficient moral reason for evil might not provide evidence that there is none to be found. But the meaning of the terms and the structure of the argumentation are the same.

Once again to illustrate, suppose there are fragmentary historical data concerning a group of people living in Central Africa who in the second century A.D. experienced great suffering. Some scholars who study the data postulate that there was a king named X who had a morally sufficient reason for inflicting great suffering on his subjects. Let us suppose that although many explanations of the data have been suggested through the years, none provides a satisfactory, morally sufficient reason why King X made his people suffer. Surely, in such a case one would have inductive justification for supposing that there is no morally sufficient reason for the king's action. This conclusion would be strengthened if the explanations offered over the years were simply variants of ones previously given and if there were no independent reason to believe that this king even existed or, if he did exist, that he was a moral person.

This argument and the indirect argument from evil to the nonexistence of God are closely analogous. There are some differences, of course. In the case of God, if there were independent evidence for His existence, then there would be evidence that He was moral, since God is by definition completely good. But since there is no independent reason for the existence of either God or the king, the arguments are strengthened. Furthermore, when we examine some of the proposed solutions to the problem of evil, in the argument from evil we shall see that certain explanations are ruled out *a priori*. One may be able to justify the actions of the postulated King X by his lack of knowledge or his lack of power, but this option is not open with respect to God. Thus in some respects it would seem easier to justify X's action than God's. In short, there are no significant differences between the structure of the argument from evil and the structure of prima facie arguments whereby relevant inductive evidence would lessen the force of the argument from evil.

It may be claimed that although the indirect inductive argument from evil is very similar to arguments in ordinary life, the meaning of the terms is different. For example, God is not good in the same sense as human beings are and consequently cannot be held to the same standards. But if this were true, it would completely change believers' view of God. God is supposed to be an object of worship and a moral ideal. Why would anyone worship God or consider Him to be a moral ideal unless He were good in *our* sense of the term?

Criticisms of a Probabilistic Argument from Evil

Various criticisms have been leveled against probabilistic or inductive arguments from evil. Do they affect the particular version of the argument given above? Do they have problems in their own right?

Although in *The Nature of Necessity*[25] Alvin Plantinga devotes only a little over two pages to attempting to refute what he takes to be a probabilistic argument from evil, he is perhaps the best known critic of such an argument. Plantinga defines confirmation and disconfirmation as follows:

p *confirms* q if q is more probable than ~q with respect to what we know if p is the only thing we know that is relevant to q.

p *disconfirms* q if p confirms ~q.

Given these definitions, Plantinga argues, "it is evident that"[26]

(40) There are 10^{13} turps of evil (the amount of evil that exists in the world)

does not disconfirm either

(37) All the evil in the world is broadly moral evil; and every world that God could have actualized, and that contains as much evil as the actual world displays, contains at least 10^{13} turps of evil

or

(39) Every world that God could have actualized, and that contains less than 10^{13} turps of evil, contains less broadly moral good and a less favorable overall balance of good and evil than the actual world contains.

He also maintains that (40) does not disconfirm either

(41) God is the omnipotent, omniscient, and morally perfect creator of the world; all the evil in the world is broadly moral evil; and every world that God could have actualized, and that contains as much evil as the actual world displays, contains at least 10^{13} turps of evil

or

(42) God is the omnipotent, omniscient, and morally perfect creator of the world; and every world that God could have actualized, and that contains less than 10^{13} turps of evil, contains less broadly moral good and a less favorable overall balance of good and evil than the actual world contains.

Plantinga argues that since (40) does not disconfirm either (41) or (42), and since these statements entail:

(G) God is omnipotent, omniscient, and wholly good

they do not disconfirm (G). He admits there may be other evidence making (41) or (42) improbable. But he says:

> I cannot see that our total evidence disconfirms the idea that natural evil results from the activity of rational and significantly free creatures. Of course our total evidence is vast and amorphous; its bearing on the idea in question is not easy to assess. So I conclude, not that our total evidence does not disconfirm (41), but that I have no reason to suppose that it does.[27]

Plantinga goes on to say the same thing about (42). However, he does not even consider, let alone refute, the indirect inductive argument from evil that was presented above, an argument based on the failure of previous attempts to solve the problem of evil. Thus Plantinga's argument in *The Nature of Necessity* is irrelevant to refuting the indirect inductive argument from evil just given.

But what about the direct inductive argument from evil formulated by Rowe? It appears that Plantinga has confused restricted theism and expanded theism. The crucial question is whether (40) disconfirms (G) without any embellishments of a theodicy. (G) is a statement of restricted theism. That (40) does not disconfirm (41) and (42) is irrelevant to Rowe's argument. Both (41) and (42) are statements of expanded theism—that is, (G) with other statements conjoined that specify a theodicy. As Rowe has shown, if the probability of (40) on (G) is less than 0.5, the probability of (41) or (42) on (G) cannot be any more, since (41) and (42) entail (G). Plantinga does nothing to show that (G) is not disconfirmed by (40).

Furthermore, Plantinga's refutation of the argument from evil that he does consider has problems of its own.[28] First, in order that (40) not disconfirm (37), one of two things must be true. The first is that (37) does not disconfirm (40) because no probability function is defined for the case where p is identical to (37) and q is identical to (40). But this is certainly not evident, and to establish it would take a serious argument that Plantinga does not give. The second is that (37) does not disconfirm (40) because the probability of (37), given (40), is at least 0.5. But this is not even plausible, let alone evident, since (37) entails:

(37′) All the natural evil in the world is the result of the activity of rational and free creatures, that is, fallen angels.

And if the probability of (37) is at least 0.5, then the probability of what it entails must be at least 0.5. So Plantinga seems to be claiming that it is evident that the probability of (37′) must be at least 0.5. Notice that Plantinga must claim not merely that it is logically possible that (37′) is true (the sort of claim he often makes in his writing), but that it is evident that there is at least an even chance that (37′) is true.

In addition to this problem, Plantinga assumes without explicit argument that since (40) does not disconfirm (37), it does not disconfirm (41). Since (41) is a conjunction of (G) and (37) and entails (40), which Plantinga says does not disconfirm (37), perhaps a tacit argument can be reconstructed along the following lines.

(40) does not disconfirm (37).

(G) combined with (37) entails (40).

Therefore, (40) does not disconfirm the conjunction of (G) and (37), that is, (41).

However, as Michael Tooley has pointed out, this pattern is fallacious,[29] for the following argument schema is invalid:

p does not disconfirm q.

(q and r) entails p.

Therefore, p does not disconfirm (q and r).

In Plantinga's reply to Tooley he admits that this inference schema is "*obviously* invalid" and maintains that he did not depend on it in undermining the inductive argument from evil in *The Nature of Necessity*.[30] He says that what he intended was that since (37) entails (G) and (G) entails (37), then (37) is equivalent in the broad logical sense to its conjunction with (G), that is, with (41). It follows by the probability calculus, Plantinga says, that if (40) does not disconfirm (37), then (40) does not disconfirm (41).

However, it is hard to see either that (37) entails (G) or that (G) entails (37). How can (G) entail that all evil is broadly moral, since many theists believe that (G) and deny that all evil is broadly moral? On Plantinga's account, such theists would be inconsistent. Moreover, surely one could maintain that (37) is true and deny (G). There are other concepts of God besides the one embodied in (G). One would not contradict oneself by accepting (37) and denying (G).

If Plantinga's argument against the argument from evil in *The Nature of Necessity* is too brief, he makes up for it in his 53-page paper, "The Probabilistic Argument from Evil" (1979).[31] Fortunately, for our purposes, the major thesis of the paper can be briefly summarized.

Plantinga holds that the atheologian is committed to the thesis that

(12*) God is omnipotent, omniscient, and wholly good, and God could not have actualized a world as good as the actual world but containing less evil than the 10^{13} turps of evil the world actually contains.

This is improbable on

(E) There are 10^{13} turps of evil

since (12*) entails

(G) God is omnipotent, omniscient, and wholly good.

However, (G) is improbable on (E) only if (12*) is.

According to Bayes's theorem, where T is any tautology,

(13) $P[(12^*)/E\&T] = P(12^*/T) \times P(E/12^*\&T)/[P(E/T)]$.

Since any proposition is logically equivalent to its conjunction with a tautology, E&T is equivalent to E and (12*)&T is equivalent to (12*). And since (12*) entails E, P(E/(12*)) = 1. It follows, then, that (13) reduces to:

(15) P[(12*)/E] = P(12*)/T/[P(E/T)].

The probability of a proposition with respect to a tautology is called the *a priori* probability. So according to (15), P[(12*)/E] is equal to the *a priori* probability of (12*) divided by the *a priori* probability of (E). According to Plantinga, the atheologian's claim that P(G/E) <0.5 is true only if the *a priori* probability of (12*) is less than 0.5 the *a priori* probability of E.

Since it is difficult to make sense of an *a priori* probability in general, Plantinga devotes most of his paper to reviewing the three most important interpretations of the probability calculus (the logical, the frequency, and the personalist interpretations) in order to see if any of these can provide an interpretation of an *a priori* probability that justifies what the atheologian needs to justify—that the *a priori* probability of (12*) is less than 0.5 the *a priori* probability of (E).

Plantinga argues that the personalistic and logical interpretations are inadequate to the task. Since on the former interpretation probability is a measure of a person's degree of coherent belief—that is, belief that conforms with the probability calculus—whether the *a priori* probability of (12*) would be less than half the *a priori* probability of (D) would vary from person to person. In particular, it would vary from the atheist to the theist and thus could provide no objective justification for the atheologian's claim. On the latter interpretation, probability is an objective logical relation holding between propositions. It may be thought of as partial entailment, with entailment considered as a limiting case where P(A/B) = 1. Plantinga maintains that this interpretation "confronts enormous difficulties"[32] because there is no reason to think that contingent propositions have *a priori* probabilities and there seems to be no plausible function to assign *a priori* probabilities. He concludes:

> It is therefore hard to see how the atheologian could work out his atheological argument employing the logical interpretation of the probability calculus. Of course, even if this interpretation is in fact correct and (12*), G and E have *a priori* probabilities, there isn't the slightest reason to think that the *a priori* probability of (12*) is less than that of E; hence there isn't the slightest reason to think that E disconfirms G.[33]

On the frequency interpretation, probability is interpreted as the limit of the relative frequency of an attribute in an infinite sequence of events. For example, to say that the probability of getting heads in a toss of a coin is 0.5 is to say that the limit of the relative frequency of heads in an infinite sequence of tosses is 0.5. Plantinga finds many problems with this interpretation. First, he maintains that it is difficult to see how it could apply to the atheologian's claim that P(G/E) < 0.5. On the one construal of the frequency interpretation, the atheologian could be claiming that the limit of relative frequency of possible worlds created by God (G-worlds) among possible worlds that contain 10^{13} turps of evil (E-worlds) is less than 0.5. Since probability is defined in terms of sequences, Plantinga argues that in order for this to make sense, the number of possible E-worlds would have to be a countable infinity. But for all we know, the number of possible E-worlds might be uncountable. In addition, Plantinga says that even if the number of E-worlds is a countable infinity, there is the problem of choosing a particular infinite sequence of E-worlds. As different sequences of infinite tosses of a coin result in different limits of relative frequency, different sequences of E-worlds would result in different limits of relative frequency. A choice in terms of a temporally ordered sequence—the natural choice in the case of coin tosses—seems out of the question in the case of possible E-worlds.

Plantinga rejects Wesley Salmon's construal of the frequency interpretation of probability that uses Bayes's theorem. Claiming that Salmon's own statement of the use of Bayes's theorem with the frequency interpretation is unintelligible, Plantinga suggests an alternative reading. Bayes's theorem can be stated as follows:

$$P(H/E) = [P(H) \times P(E/H)]/P(E)$$

Where H is the hypothesis under consideration and E is the evidence. The theorem says that the probability of the hypothesis on the evidence is equal to the *a priori* probability of the hypothesis, times the probability of the evidence on the hypothesis, divided by the *a priori* probability of the evidence. In the case where H entails E, the theorem reduces to

$$P(H/E) = P(H)/P(E).$$

Following Salmon's lead, Plantinga suggests that the *a priori* probabilities of H and E can be understood as the frequency of truth among propositions like H(H-like propositions) and like E(E-like propositions). Bayes's theorem applied to the problem of evil would be:

$$P(12*)/E = P(12*)/P(E)$$

which says that the probability of (12*) [God is omnipotent, omniscient, and wholly good and God could not have actualized a world as good as the actual world but containing less evil than the 10^{13} turps of evil the world actually contains] on (E) [there are 10^{13} turps of evil] is equal to the *a priori* probability of (12*) divided by the *a priori* probability of (E).

The atheologian, according to Plantinga, is committed to the claim that the relative frequency of truth among propositions like (12*) is less than half the relative frequency of truth among propositions like (E). However, Plantinga argues that (12*) and (E) are members of many different classes of propositions. How, then, is one to pick the appropriate reference class? He finds many problems with Salmon's suggestion that one should choose the broadest homogeneous reference class. One such problem is that in using this criterion, the notion of a homogeneous reference class must be relativized to persons.

Plantinga concludes his critique of the inductive argument from evil by saying that what one takes to be the probability of (12*) or (G) or (E) will depend on one's *noetic structure*—in other words, the set of propositions one believes "together with various logical and epistemic relations among these propositions."[34] In terms of Bayes's theorem, the theist will choose the class of true propositions as the broadest homogeneous reference class, while the atheist will choose the class of false propositions. As a result, the *a priori* probability of (G) [God is omnipotent, omniscient, and wholly good] will be one for the theist and zero for the atheist.

We have already seen that Plantinga's critique in *The Nature of Necessity* of what he takes to be the probabilistic argument from evil, even if sound, is irrelevant to the indirect inductive argument from evil presented here. So too is Plantinga's longer critique. Despite its length he makes no attempt in "The Probabilistic Argument from Evil" to evaluate an inductive argument based on the long history of failed theodicies. So his critique is irrelevant to the indirect inductive argument from evil. Furthermore, it seems irrelevant also to the direct argument from evil developed by Rowe, who does not use Bayes's theorem and does not seem to be committed to *a priori* probabilities. In addition, Plantinga's critique has basic problems of its own.

Plantinga's critique is based on the difficulties involved in making sense of inductive inference, given the probability calculus and standard interpretations of it. These problems are quite general and apply to a wide variety of inductive inferences having nothing to do with the existence of God or the problem of evil. Thus if his argument is successful, it should also be successful in refuting inductive arguments for the nonexistence of many things that we know, on the basis of inductive evidence, do not exist. This strongly suggests that something is seriously wrong either with Plantinga's construal of the inductive argument from evil or with his critique of it.

Consider fairies, those tiny magical woodland creatures of myth and legend. It seems clear that one could construct both a probabilistic argument against the existence of fairies and a critique of this argument along Plantinga's lines. The critic of fairy existence is committed to the thesis that

(M) Fairies, tiny woodland creatures with magical powers, exist and make it appear that they do not exist except to those who are pure of heart

is improbable on V, the evidence that is usually cited against the existence of fairies, such as the failure to see them dancing on moonbeams. Since (M) entails

(F) Fairies, tiny magical woodland creatures, exist

(F) is improbable on V only if (M) is. Using Bayes's theorem, the probability of (M), given V, can be expressed as

(15′) $P(M/V) = P(M/T)/P(V/T)$

The probabilistic argument against fairies comes down to the claim that the probability of (M) on V < 0.5, and this would be true only if the *a priori* probability of (M) is less than 0.5 the *a priori* probability of V. Since it is difficult to make sense of *a priori* probabilities in general, one can review the three most important interpretations of the probability calculus and find the same sort of problems that Plantinga found with them.

The personalistic interpretation would be rejected, for whether or not the *a priori* probability of (M) would be less than 0.5 the *a priori* probability of V would vary from person to person. In particular, it would vary from those who believe in fairies to those who do not. Thus it could provide no objective justification for the claims of disbelievers in fairies. The logical interpretation would again "confront enormous difficulties" and could not be used as the basis for making sense out of $P(M/T)/P(V/T)$. It is difficult to see how (M) and V could have *a priori* probabilities. And even if they could, "there isn't the slightest reason to think" that the *a priori* probability of (M) is less than that of V.

The frequency interpretation of probability would also confront great difficulties. On one construal of it, the critic of the existence of fairies might argue that the frequency of possible worlds in which fairies exist (F-worlds) among possible worlds that contain the sort of evidence specified by V (V-worlds) is less than 0.5. But the same problems of interpretation would arise. The number of possible V-worlds might be uncountable; and, in any case, there is the problem of deciding which infinite sequence of V-worlds to choose.

Nor would Salmon's account of the frequency interpretation of probability be helpful to the critic of fairy existence. Salmon's own statement of the frequency theory interpretation of Bayes's theorem would still be found unintelligible, and Plantinga's reading of Salmon would have the same problems. The problem of the reference class would remain, and Salmon's suggestion that the broadest homogeneous reference class should be chosen would have the same difficulties. For example, the broadest homogeneous reference class must be relativized to persons. The defender of fairy existence could conclude by arguing that what one takes to be the *a priori* probability of (F) or V will depend on one's noetic structure. In terms of Bayes's theorem the defender of fairy existence will choose the class of true propositions as the broadest homogeneous reference class, while the critic of their existence will choose the class of false propositions. As a result the *a priori* probability of F will be one for the defender of fairy existence and zero for the defender of their nonexistence.

It should be clear that similar arguments could be given against inductive arguments for the nonexistence of gremlins, leprechauns, brownies, Santa Claus, and assorted other creatures generally thought by educated people to be nonexistent. Yet surely we *do* have inductive evidence that such creatures do not exist. Insofar as Plantinga's mode of argument appears to refute inductive arguments against the existence of such creatures, this strongly suggests that something is basically wrong with either his construal of the inductive argument from evil or his critique of it.

Does Plantinga take into account this objection? The closest he comes is in the conclusion of his paper, where he denies that he is exploiting "the difficulties inherent in the current analyses of probability to urge a sort of skepticism about probability claims."[35] Indeed, he says he has no quarrel with the personalist's account or with Salmon's attempt to apply the frequency theory to "probability relations as it holds between propositions." He maintains that he "wouldn't dream of denying" there are cases where one proposition is improbable with respect to our total evidence. But he says that "the present discussion" is not about one of these cases. There are contexts, he says, "where arguments formally similar to the atheological probabilistic argument from evil are entirely in order." These have a "basic body B of knowledge or belief accepted by all parties to the discussion" and an agreement that "the acceptability of a given proposition A depends on its relationship to B—perhaps its probability with respect to B, or perhaps its capacity to explain some significant segment of B."[36] Plantinga says that cases like these sometimes occur in everyday life, in relatively uncontroversial areas of well-established science, and in courts of law.

He concludes his paper with the tentative suggestion, developed at greater length elsewhere, that the theist's belief that God exists be considered a basic belief, one that is not supported by other beliefs.[37] Construed in this way, belief in God would be rational and yet not based on any evidence or arguments. The atheistic argument from evil would be irrelevant to a theist with a basic belief in God.

But this reply to the atheistic argument is inadequate. First of all, Plantinga's attempt to argue that some probabilistic arguments are safe from his critical attack will not work. Many of Plantinga's criticisms are so general that they do not turn on the issue of whether there was agreement either on some body B of knowledge or belief or on whether the acceptability of proposition A depends on its relationship to B. For example, his argument based on the uncountability of possible worlds does not depend on the lack of this sort of agreement. Indeed, it is difficult to see how *any* probabilistic argument would be acceptable if one took all of Plantinga's arguments seriously. That Plantinga accepts some probabilistic arguments suggests either that he does not take all his own criticisms seriously or that he does not want to face up to the implications of them.

Moreover, the scope of the sort of agreement Plantinga seems to have in mind may be vanishingly small. As a result, the area where Plantinga would allow probabilistic arguments may be virtually nonexistent. The idea made popular by Thomas Kuhn that there is an aspect of science (normal science) characterized by wide agreement about fundamental concepts and modes of procedure is thought by many historians of science to be a myth. Law cases very often involve challenges to what has to be proved and what evidence is relevant to the proof. There is controversy lurking everywhere in our everyday life; that it may seem to be otherwise is due to the superficiality of our understanding of everyday arguments and experience.

Further, Plantinga's attempt to answer the objection that he is exploiting the difficulties of current analyses of probability does not address the absurd implications of his theory. Since there is controversy over the existence of beings such as fairies, gremlins, leprechauns, brownies, and the like, the implication of his theory is that there cannot be a legitimate probabilistic argument against the existence of these creatures. But the belief of educated people that such creatures do not exist does seem to be based on inductive probabilistic reasoning.

Finally, Plantinga's suggestion that belief in God be considered basic has its own serious problems, as we have already seen. We can therefore conclude, that his long criticism of the argument from evil is no more successful than his earlier, shorter one.

Bruce Reichenbach is perhaps the second-best-known critic of the inductive argument from evil.[38] Like Plantinga, he approaches his task by construing the argument as using Bayes's theorem. Bayes's theorem on Reichenbach's formulation is this:

$$P(G/N\&E) = \frac{P(G/N) \times P(E/N\&G)}{[P(G/N) \times P(E/N\&G) + P(\sim G/N) \times P(E/N\&\sim G)]}$$

where

P(G/N) = the probability that a personal, loving, omnipotent, omniscient, perfectly good God exists, given the furniture and structure of the world, including sentient creatures, insentient creatures, physical objects, and laws of nature, but *excluding* any morally sufficient reason, defense, or theodicy for evil, any construed evidence for God's existence, or evil.

P(~G/N) = the probability that a personal, loving, omnipotent, omniscient, perfectly good God does not exist, given the furniture and structure of the world.

P(E/N&G) = the probability of there being 10^6 turps of natural evil (the amount of evil that exists in the world), given that the world described above obtains and the God described above exists.

P(E/N~G) = the probability of there being 10^6 turps of natural evil (the amount of evil that exists in the world), given that the world described above obtains and the God described above does not exist.

P(G/N&E) = the probability that God as described above exists, given that the world described above obtains and there are 10^6 turps of natural evil in the world.

According to Reichenbach, given this interpretation of Bayes's theorem, the atheologian might argue that since there is no agreement over the prior probabilities—that is, over P(G/N) and P(~G/N)—one should assign each of these probabilities the value of 0.5. Given this assignment, the value of P(G/N&E) will depend on the relation between P(E/N&G) and P(E/N~G). In particular, if P(E/N&G)<P(E/N~G), then P(G/N&E)<0.5 and the atheologian has a prima facie case against natural evil. Reichenbach says that the atheologian would go on to argue that P(E/N&G)<P(E/N~G) on the ground that one would expect that if God existed, there would be less natural evil than there is.

Reichenbach maintains that the argument from evil, construed in this way, has serious problems. First, theists would object to the way the prior probabilities are interpreted on the ground that not all relevant evidence is being considered. For example, theists might say that theistic arguments and proofs for the existence of God have been excluded, yet these are relevant to P(G/N). In addition, he objects that the assignment of a prior probability of 0.5 to P(G/N) in cases of disagreement is an unsatisfactory procedure for settling disputes.

Reichenbach also maintains that the atheologian does not have any good reason to assume that P(E/N&G)<P(E/N~G). It might be the case that

(T) God eliminates all the evil He can without losing a greater good
     or producing an equal or greater evil.

(T) is compatible with the falsehood of P(E/N&G)<P(E/N~G). Furthermore, Reichenbach argues that although it may be unreasonable for
theists to believe (T), it does not follow that it is reasonable to believe that
(~T)—in other words, that God does *not* eliminate all the evil He can
without losing a greater good or producing an equal or greater evil.

Reichenbach concludes that the atheologian gets nowhere by presenting cases of seemingly gratuitous evil. What the atheologian is required
to do "at minimum" is to "show the proposed theodicies and defenses
are unsound if he is to make his case for the truth of" P(E/N&G)<P(E/
N~G).[39] But if the atheologian were to refute all extant theodicies and
defenses, even this would not be enough for Reichenbach, since God may
have reasons for not eliminating more evil that have not been suggested in
any known theodicy. Reichenbach says that he "does not know how the
atheologian would propose to show" that there are no such reasons.
However, he says he does not think "the theist can comfortably rest
content with this defense"—that is, with simply arguing that there could
be reasons for the existence of evil that we do not know. Presumably, the
theist should actually present good reasons.[40]

Even if one agreed with much of Reichenbach's critique, it is clearly
irrelevant to the indirect inductive argument from evil presented here.
Only at the end of his attempt to refute the inductive argument from
evil does he come close to considering the evidential relevance of failed
extant theodicies. And even then he misses the *inductive* relevances of
these failures. He seems to conclude that since there could be a morally
sufficient reason for the existence of evil that it is not presented in any
extant refuted theodicy, the atheologian's case has not been proved. This
belief is correct if the atheologian was attempting to give a demonstrative
and conclusive argument. But if the atheologian is concerned with giving
an inductive argument, the failure of all known theodicies, combined
with the lack of positive evidence for the existence of God, provides
inductive support for the nonexistence of God. Reichenbach is surely
right that theists cannot rest content with pointing out that there might
be some unknown reason that justifies God's ways to humans. But the
explanation has escaped his notice—namely, that as more and more
theodicies are refuted, it becomes less and less likely that any reason
exists.

Reichenbach's critique is irrelevant to the indirect argument from evil
and also to the direct argument given by Rowe. Reichenbach assumes
that an argument from evil must use Bayes's theorem. But as Rowe's
work makes clear, this is not so.

Besides the irrelevance of Reichenbach's critique to both direct and indirect inductive arguments from evil, there are other problems with his argument. Just as Plantinga's critique can be used against inductive arguments against fairies, gremlins, and other clearly fictional creatures, so can Reichenbach's. Once more it provides a *reductio* of this critique.[41]

Conclusion

In sum, the two forms of an inductive argument from evil are formally sound and can be defended against criticism. Furthermore, the best known attempts to refute an inductive argument from evil are irrelevant to both versions of such an argument used here and, in any case, have absurd implications.[42]

Although I have argued that an indirect version of the inductive argument from evil is sound in the sense that it has the form of a strong inductive argument, more needs to be done. It particular, this argument assumes that theodicies produced today and in the past do not work and that there is no positive evidence for the existence of God. In earlier chapters we saw that there is none. In the chapters to follow I critically consider all major and most minor theodicies produced by theists, concentrating on those theodicies that play the most important role in current debates. This strategy is justified. In the first place, because excellent critical reviews of past theodicies are already available, they need not be repeated here.[43] Moreover, although the latest is not always the best, theistic philosophers, like everyone else, learn from their mistakes. Thus there is a presumption that recent work constitutes the most sophisticated and best effort to date to justify God's ways to humans and to demonstrate His existence. If the most recent versions of theodicies produced by the best philosophical minds of our time in response to the problems of earlier versions can be refuted, one can have confidence that earlier versions fail as well. In addition, each refutation of a new theodicy or of a new version of an old theodicy increases support for the conclusion. The greater the number of theodicies that are refuted, the more confidence one should have that none will be successful and that none can be successful.

CHAPTER 15

The Free Will Defense

Perhaps the most popular theistic response to the argument from evil is the free will defense (FWD), which can be traced back at least as far as St. Augustine (354–430) and has in recent years been developed and refined by philosophers such as John Hick, Alvin Plantinga, and Richard Swinburne. As it is usually formulated, the FWD purports to be an explanation of *moral evil,* not *natural evil*—that is, evil intentionally and deliberately brought about by human action—the torture of a small child, for example, as opposed to the child's death from cancer.

The FWD in its simplest form can be stated as follows. Moral evil cannot be blamed on God, since it is the result of free human choice; consequently, human beings are responsible for moral evil. Despite the possibility of misuse, God gave humans the ability to make choices because a world with free choice is more desirable than a world without it. On the one hand, advocates of the FWD maintain that it undermines any argument from moral evil. Indeed, some, like Plantinga, believe that the FWD can be extended to all arguments from natural evil, since that could be the result of the free choice of fallen angels such as Satan. On the other hand, atheists like Antony Flew and J. L. Mackie have challenged various aspects of the FWD, maintaining, for example, that humans do not have free will in the sense required by the argument, or that God could have created human beings who have free will in the required sense yet never do anything wrong, or that God, despite human free will, is still indirectly responsible for the moral evil that results directly from His creatures' actions.

In this chapter I consider the FWD against the argument from moral evil. In the next chapter Plantinga's extension of the defense is discussed.

Background

To understand the FWD, it is helpful to set it in the context of a broader theodicy. Although the one presented here may not be representative of all uses of the FWD, it illustrates the major problems in practically all contexts.

Theists have argued that evils such as pain, suffering, and disease make possible certain goods—that in fact sympathy, kindness, generosity, heroism, are parasitic on such evils. They argue, for example, that if there were no pain or suffering or disease, there could be no sympathy or kindness, that if there were no evils in the world, there would be no heroic acts to overcome them. Let us call evils such as suffering and disease first-order evils.[1] These are to be contrasted with first-order goods such as pleasure and happiness. The goods that emerge as responses to first-order evils—for example, kindness and sympathy—are then second-order goods.[2] According to theists, a whole that contains both first-order evils and second-order goods is better than a whole that contains merely first-order goods. Thus although God *could* eliminate first-order evils, He allows them to exist so that the overall good of the whole is increased. In this way, first-order evil is explained and justified.

J. L. Mackie calls evils that are justified in this way absorbed evils.[3] The crucial question is whether all evils that appear in the world are absorbed evils. The answer seems to be no. Some first-order evils are not responded to with kindness, sympathy, and so on. There are also second-order evils—that is, responses to first-order evils, such as cruelty and cowardice. However, theists have argued that unabsorbed evils are not the responsibility of God but of His creatures who misuse their free will. That some of His creatures do not respond to suffering with kindness and sympathy is not God's fault; that God's creatures develop into cruel instead of kind persons is not God's responsibility. The misuse of free will by God's creatures, then, not only explains the existence of unabsorbed evil but relieves God of responsibility for the existence of evil.

Notice that advocates of the FWD must maintain that the unabsorbed evil is somehow justified on a higher level. After all, why did God give free will to His creatures when He knew they would—or at least might— misuse it? The answer theists give is that free will is a third-order good. Thus the whole that contains this third-order good, with all its potential for misuse, is better than one that lacks this good. And so unabsorbed evils, although unjustified at one level, are justified at a higher level.

When placed in this context, the FWD can be seen to consist in the justification of the second premise of the following argument:

(1) Although some first-order evils are explained by second-order

goods, other first-order evils and all second-order evils are not
explained by second-order goods.

(2) But a third-order good, namely free will, explains first-order
evils that are not explained by second-order goods and explains
all second-order evils.

(3) Therefore, all evil that is not explained by second-order goods
is explained by a third-order good.

The Justification in General

The theistic defense of premise (2) is made up of three steps. The first
is to maintain that free will is a very important good. Thus premise (2)
assumes that the third-order good of free will outweighs those first-order
evils that are not explained by second-order goods as well as any second-
order evil. The second step is to maintain that free will is purchased at
a price. Thus premise 2 assumes that the exercise of free will does result
or may result in second-order evils and also some first-order ones that
are not explained by second-order goods. The third step is to argue that
these unabsorbed evils cannot be blamed on God, since He did not bring
them about. The blame for evil is on the creatures with free will created
by God. Thus premise (2) assumes that God cannot be held responsible
either for first-order evils not explained by the second-order goods or
for second-order evils.

Each one of these steps can be challenged. It can be argued that given
the possible disastrous results of granting free will, the price of free will
is too great. It can also be held that an all-powerful, all-knowing, and all-
good being could have created human beings with free will who never
do wrong. Finally, it can be maintained that despite the gift of free
will to humans, God is still in some sense responsible and therefore
blameworthy.

Although the challenge to and justification of the second step of the
FWD has preoccupied theologians and philosophers of religion, the first
and third steps in the argument are equally important.

The Assumption of the Importance of Freedom

In *God, Freedom, and Evil*, Plantinga states a key premise in the first step
of the FWD:

(P_1) A world containing creatures who are significantly free is more
valuable, all else being equal, than a world containing no free
creatures at all.[4]

By "significantly free" he means free with respect to morally significant action.

But is it true that all else is equal? Because of the possibility of misusing free will, all else might not be equal, since free creatures could cause so much evil that it could outweigh any value of free will. Furthermore, the way things have in fact turned out, all things are not equal. Indeed, it would seem that advocates of the FWD must assume a stronger premise than Plantinga does. Consider:

(P₂) A world containing creatures who are significantly free is more valuable than a world containing no free creatures, even though the free creatures might perform many evil actions and nonfree creatures would perform no evil actions.

If, however, we suppose as Plantinga does that God knows what humans beings will do, given their gift of freedom, then it would seem that advocates of the FWD would have to maintain an even stronger premise:

(P₃) A world containing creatures who are significantly free is more valuable than a world containing no free creatures, even though the free creatures will in fact perform many evil actions and nonfree creatures would perform no evil actions.

Indeed, perhaps an even stronger premise would be necessary, given the actual course of human events. For it might be argued that the evil brought about by free will is greater than the good brought about by free will. Thus a defender of the FWD would have to claim:

(P₄) A world containing creatures who are significantly free is more valuable than a world containing no free creatures, even though the free creatures might perform more evil actions than good actions and nonfree creatures would perform no evil actions.

If on the other hand we suppose, pace Plantinga, that God does not know what humans will do because of His gift of freedom, it would seem that a defender of the FWD would have to assume a very strong premise:

(P₅) A world containing creatures who are significantly free is more valuable than a world containing no free creatures, even though the free creatures might perform only evil actions and nonfree creatures would perform no evil actions.

Clearly anyone maintaining (P₁)–(P₅) is committed to the view that significant human freedom is very valuable. For example, in (P₅) the value of freedom would outweigh *any* possible evil that might result from its misuse. Since the evil that could result from the misuse of freedom is potentially unlimited, freedom would have to be considered virtually of infinite value.

What is this freedom that is supposed to be so valuable? Plantinga maintains that whatever it is (he provides no explicit analysis), it is incompatible with causal determinism. When someone is free in the sense of having free will, he says, the person's behavior is not caused by antecedent factors.[5] Many other advocates of the FWD such as Richard Swinburne,[6] and C. A. Campbell[7] have assumed such an account of freedom. Let us call the sense of freedom championed by Plantinga and other advocates of the FWD *contracausal freedom*. Although they reject any analysis that makes freedom compatible with causal determinism, they reject explicitly the following compatibilist analysis:

X is free to do action A = If X had chosen to do action A, then X would have succeeded

as capturing what is usually meant by free.

Critics of what is usually called contracausal freedom point out that a compatibilist sense of freedom captures quite well what people usually mean by saying that someone is not free.[8] Thus we say that a person P is not free to do Y when P's choice is restrained by external factors or psychological blockages, and that P is free when P's choice is not so restrained. These ideas, Plantinga's critics urge, are captured well by the compatibilist's sense of freedom. However, Plantinga does not rest his case on the issue of whether contracausal freedom captures what is usually meant by freedom, for he is willing to stipulate that "free" or "freedom" be used in the contracausal sense or else a different term be used. For example, he suggests that the free will defender may say that God made human beings so that some of their actions are unfettered, where an action is unfettered if is is free in the compatibilist sense *and* not causally determined.

The initial plausibility of the FWD is partly the result of the intuition that freedom is an important value and that one may have to sacrifice other things for it. The idea that God made a correct choice in creating our world seems initially in accord with our reflective moral judgments. Yet it is not the case that in making reflective moral judgments, freedom is always given the highest priority. We sometimes think that freedom must be sacrificed for other values.

Part of the difficulty with assessing the value of contracausal freedom is that, unlike political freedom, there is no practical difference between having it and not having it. If one lacks freedom of speech, this fact is usually readily apparent. But if one lacks contracausal freedom, no one is the wiser. Thus as far as human experience is concerned, living with contracausal freedom is indistinguishable from living without it. People would not feel less free with no contracausal freedom. They do not seem to behave any differently if they believe they have or do not have contracausal freedom. Thus from a pragmatic point of view there seems to be no choice between a life with contracausal freedom and a life with compatibilist freedom. Any value connected with contracausal freedom must be of a purely nonpractical nature.

Keeping this point in mind, one can pose a question: Which of the following two worlds, World* and World$_1$, is the more valuable, other things being roughly equal?

W* A world with the same amount of pain and suffering as our world where God's creatures have contracausal freedom.

W$_1$ A world with much less pain and suffering than our world where God's creatures have only compatibilist freedom.

It is by no means clear that reflective people would choose W* over W$_1$ given that a person's experience in W* would be identical with that in W$_1$. It is not clear that reflective people so value contracausal freedom that they would agree with God's choice of W* over W$_1$. Indeed, many reflective people would surely choose W$_1$ over W*. Furthermore, the choice is not just between W$_1$ and W*.

As Plantinga sets up the problem, it looks as if there are only two options: Either there are creatures who have contracausal freedom or there are no creatures who do. The hypothetical choice situation just outlined also presupposes this. But once we analyze the situation in more detail we find more possibilities.

First of all, contracausal freedom is supposed to be possessed by few if any nonhuman animals. Plantinga, for instance, believes there may be other beings—for example, fallen angels, if any exist—who have contracausal freedom. Most humans supposedly have it. Presumably, small children and severely mentally retarded people do not have such freedom, however. Given these factors, many possibilities are open to God. God could have created a world where only fallen angels have contracausal freedom or where only a few human beings have contracausal freedom or where many nonhuman animals have contracausal freedom. God could have created a world in which the creatures who now have contracausal freedom in our world have this freedom relative to some but not all significant actions. For example, they might only have contracausal freedom with respect to actions that do not potentially involve great suffering or death.

Once we consider these various factors, God's options are not merely W* and W$_1$. Consider another possible world, W$_2$. In this world the only humans who have contracausal freedom for all significant choices are those who have undergone moral and spiritual training. All other people have contracausal freedom only where their choices could not result in great suffering and death. Let us assume that in W_2 there is no devil or cohorts of the devil and that the overall amount of suffering and pain is significantly less than in W*. Let us assume further that in W_2, although some humans in some of their significant moral decisions have contracausal freedom, they have compatibilist freedom in all their significant moral decisions.

We can now ask if world W* is more valuable overall than W_2, other things being equal. To morally sensitive people it is certainly not obvious that the answer is yes. Thus it is not clear that they would agree with God's choice of W* over W_2. Indeed, for most morally sensitive people the choice of W_2 over W* would surely be clear.

If it is dubious that morally sensitive people would approve of God's choice, what follows? One might argue that nothing of importance does, since morally sensitive people can be wrong. But in order for people to judge that God is good, in our sense of good, it is essential that there not be deep disparities between God's choice and that of morally sensitive persons. The seeming conflict between these choices suggests that the FWD only works if it is assumed that the goodness of God is not in conflict with a human concept of good. But since the major point of the FWD is to show that evil in the world is consistent with the existence of an all-good, all-powerful, all-knowing God (where an all-good God is good in the human meaning of good), the FWD fails.

Free Will and Contracausal Freedom

I have argued so far that it is dubious that sensitive moral persons would prefer our world with all its evil and allegedly contracausal freedom to other worlds with less evil and less contracausal freedom. It is now time to explore the problems surrounding contracausal freedom.

The first problem with contracausal freedom is an empirical one. Advocates of the FWD who rely on contracausal freedom are not just saying that some of the significant moral choices of *some* rational human beings are not caused. They maintain that *all* significant moral choices of *all* rational human beings are uncaused. Their thesis is a sweeping one. Any evidence tending to show that some moral choices of some humans are caused would tend to refute the thesis.

The social sciences are increasingly able to predict such human action as delinquent behavior.[9] Surely such ability makes it likely that the choice of young people to engage in criminal behavior is caused. Plantinga, for one, would disagree. He argues that predictability is not to be confused with lack of contracausal freedom. He admits that one might be able to predict a person's actions if one knew the person well. But, he says, it does not follow from this that the person is not free in the contracausal freedom sense of free.[10]

This is true. For example, to say that Jones's voting behavior is predictable by those who know him well is not *logically* equivalent to saying that Jones's voting behavior is caused by outside influences on him. However, although predictability and causal determinism are logically distinct notions, they are much more closely related than Plantinga and other defenders of the FWD are willing to admit. As we learn more and more about the causal factors operating upon a person in certain circumstances, we are better able to predict the person's behavior. Conversely, when we are able to predict Jones's behavior because we know him well, this is surely because we know to some extent (at least tacitly) the causal influences operating on Jones and his reaction to them. Indeed, if human choice were completely uncaused, as Plantinga says, it is difficult to see how knowing Jones well or knowing what happened to Jones in the past would be at all helpful in predicting his behavior. Thus although Plantinga is correct that predictability and causal determinism are not logically equivalent, they are factually connected, and the predictability of human behavior can be most plausibly explained by assuming that it is caused.

Further, most advocates of contracausal freedom seem to want to limit such freedom to rational human choice. Thus they seem to exclude severely mentally retarded children and higher primates from having contracausal freedom. But the evidence suggests that there is no sharp break between the physical and mental workings of normal adult human beings and the classes being excluded. There is no reason to suppose that the decisions made by chimps and mentally retarded people are caused while the decisions of rational humans are not. The weight of the evidence indicates that similar causal processes are at work. The differences are of degree and not of kind. But if the advocates of contracausal freedom are correct, then it would seem that there must be a sharp break between the mental and physical workings of normal human beings and those of chimps and mentally retarded humans.

On the other hand, empirical evidence from the social sciences has done nothing to undermine our belief that humans are often free in the compatibilist sense. For even if *every* human choice is caused, human choice is often not coerced; it is often not restrained by external obstacles and psychological blockages. Indeed, in the very ordinary and normal sense of free captured by the compatibilist sense, the freedom of human action is quite independent of whether the action is caused.

Second, in addition to the empirical problem already mentioned, there is a theological one. If human moral choice is free in the contracausal freedom sense, then God could not be the sustaining cause of all creation, since His creation would contain uncaused causes. Such a notion of God would be quite unacceptable to such great philosophers and theologians of the past as Leibniz, Descartes, Aquinas, and Luther.[11] As Flew has pointed out and Plantinga fails to mention, the compatibilist concept of freedom was assumed by all these philosophers and theologians. Indeed, Plantinga ignores the problem of reconciling contracausal freedom with the traditional concept of God as a sustaining cause of all creation.[12]

Third, there is the analytic problem of what exactly contracausal freedom is. Plantinga strongly denies that if someone is contracausally free, that person's decision to do this or that is a random event. However, he has supplied no alternative analysis, and I am not aware of anyone else who has clearly said what it is.[13] This is not to deny that an alternative analysis is possible, but until one is supplied it is difficult to know what to make of it. Plantinga points out that if God exists, His decisions are not caused, and yet they are not random events.[14] This hardly dispels the mystery. Moreover, the mystery is compounded when human beings are involved. How can human beings who have bodies and brains and operate within the causal nexus of the world make moral decisions that are not caused and yet are not random?

Fourth, there is a moral question that is closely related to the analytic one. Without a clear analysis of what contracausal freedom means, it is not obvious why we should hold people responsible for what they do. A person's decisions would be causally untraceable to thought processes, past character development, or anything else. Advocates of contracausal freedom believe it enables people to be held responsible for what they do, since it entails that their decisions are not inevitable. Still, it is unclear why it does not show that it would be unjust to hold them responsible, since their actions would be causally unrelated to their character, thoughts, and so on. Indeed, it has seemed to many that a god who punished his creatures for making wrong decisions that are uncaused would be unfair and unjust. Such an appearance might be dispelled with some plausible account of contracausal freedom. But none is available.

We have already seen one reason why it is dubious that morally sensitive people would prefer our world with allegedly contracausal freedom and much evil to another world with less contracausal freedom and less evil. Other reasons now emerge. Since the meaning of contracausal freedom is unclear and might prevent people from being held accountable for their decisions, its value is further decreased. In addition, anyone advocating contracausal freedom would have to advocate it in the light of mounting evidence that such freedom, on the large scale assumed by advocates of the FWD, is nonexistent; they would also have to suppose that God is not omnipotent. Surely such factors would further discount the value of contracausal freedom.

Contracausal Freedom and Statistical Laws

There is still another problem with the assumption that God created His creatures with contracausal freedom. It is logically possible that humans have contracausal freedom—in other words, that their choices are not determined by causal laws and yet that they have a strong tendency to perform morally correct actions. In some logically possible worlds, human choice would be controlled by statistical laws. If so, although there would be no causal necessity for humans to choose one way rather than another, it would be unlikely that they would choose to do what is morally wrong. Such a world would seem to have great advantages from a theist's point of view, for it would have contracausal freedom and yet few moral evils. It would seem that an all-good, all-powerful God would want to and could actualize such a possible world. The question is, then, why our actual world is not this possible one in which there is a strong tendency for God's creatures to do good.

One answer has been given by Bruce Reichenbach.[15] He argues first that it may make no sense to say that humans have an "inbuilt desire to do good," since the desire to do good can be "learned and developed only through human experience."[16] But it does not seem to be part of what one means by "doing good" that it can be learned and developed. If God is all-powerful, surely He could create humans with a built-in desire to do good. One need not follow Reichenbach and be limited to human psychology as it is now constituted. Furthermore, it is not obvious that in order to have a world in which people possess a tendency to do good, there must be an innate desire to do good. Surely an all-powerful God could have actualized a possible world in which people have a strong tendency to do good that is not innate but learned and developed.

Reichenbach maintains that if it does make sense to suggest that there could be built-in desire to do good, it could be the case that there was such a tendency in human beings in our distant history. Following the Augustinian tradition, he imagines the first human beings having a tendency to do good but freely choosing to do evil. This tendency to good became weakened "as a result of the evil actions of the first and succeeding members of human species,"[17] and evil became widespread.

However, Reichenbach's speculations have serious problems. He provides no historical evidence that human beings in our distant past had such a tendency, although in the light of the evidence, the Augustinian story is most implausible. Moreover, if such a tendency was really innate, it is hard to see how it could have become weakened by doing evil actions. In any case, if God is all-powerful, He could have created human beings who have a tendency to do good that could not have become so weakened. Such a world would seem to be better than the one we now have.

Compatibilism and World Preference

Heretofore I have assumed that insofar as one is concerned with freedom in the compatibilist scene, there would no be problem in creating a world in which humans were free and yet never did anything wrong. Indeed, it is surely because of the apparent compatibility of freedom in this sense and the lack of moral wrongdoing that theists have been driven to suppose that humans have contracausal freedom. Only with contracausal freedom can the FWD possibly succeed against the argument from evil.

However, Robert Young has maintained that although a world in which humans never do wrong and yet are free in the compatibilist sense is logically possible, it is not clearly more desirable than our present world.[18] Although such a world would have no murder, robbery, rape, or war, it would involve radical changes in human character and society that may be judged less desirable overall than the moral evils of our present world. Initially, such a claim surely seems implausible. The prospect of a large-scale nuclear war in our world is *extremely* undesirable. It is difficult to imagine another world without this prospect but with human character and society so radically changed that we would judge it worse than our world with this prospect.

Let us, however, consider some of the changes that would supposedly come about in a world, W_p, where humans were free in the compatibilist sense and yet never did anything wrong. Would they actually have to occur, and if they did, would they be so undesirable? According to Young, human beings in W_p would be regarded as "conformists, sycophantic and repressed."[19] But it is difficult to see why this is so. A person is said to be a conformist only if he or she does what is considered morally correct according to the popular morality and not out of genuine duty. But in W_p, people would always do their genuine duty and there would be no popular morality different from one's genuine duty. Indeed, in this world the concept of conformity in the usual sense would have no application. A sycophant is a self-serving servile flatterer, and it seems plausible to suppose that acting in this way is morally wrong. But since people in W_p would never do what is morally wrong, how could they be sycophantic?

Would people in W_p be repressed? In the usual meaning of the term, a repressed person is one who does not express emotion and who lacks warmth and spontaneity. But people in W_p need not be repressed in this sense. They could express emotion as long as doing so was not harmful.

There would be nothing to prevent them from being warm and acting with spontaneity so long as this did not result in something morally wrong. Granted, to act in this way would take a certain amount of training and practice and perhaps even innate psychological abilities different from those that most people now possess. But it seems quite possible. Even people in our world who are considered warm, emotional, and spontaneous do not usually display such traits in all social contexts. They learn when and where they can let themselves go. One can imagine that people in W_p would have developed this ability to a high degree. Of course, they would be repressed in another sense. They would never give way to destructive emotions and, in fact, would keep such emotions under tight control. But if this is repression, it is no bad thing and cannot be used as evidence of the undesirability of W_p.

Young also claims that in a world such as W_p there would be less freedom,[20] presumably of the legal or social sort. But it is hard to understand why this would be so. Consider legal freedom, which is the ability to do or refrain from doing something that is not forbidden by law. Since people in W_p would never do what is morally wrong, it would not be necessary to control their behavior by means of the segment of the criminal or civil law that now embodies moral principles. If people would do what is morally correct without the law's coercive force, they would have *more* legal freedom in W_p than in our present world. The same can be said with respect to social freedom, which is the ability to do or to refrain from doing something without social coercion or punishment. Human beings could be constructed so that they need no social coercion to do what is morally correct. Consequently, social mechanisms that limit social freedom, such as peer pressure, ridicule, and economic sanctions, would have no point and could be expected to play a smaller role in W_p than in our world. Then social freedom would be increased, not decreased in W_p.

Without better counterarguments it is reasonable to suppose that a world with compatibilist freedom and no moral evil is to be preferred to our world. Although such a world might well be very different from ours, there is no reason to suppose that the differences would be so profound or undesirable as to outweigh the great advantages of there being none of the war, murder, rape, and so on that result from human choice and are so common an occurrence in our world.

Free Will and Evil

As we have seen, according to the FWD free will is purchased at a price. God's creatures not only could but did misuse the gift God gave them and have brought about much evil. They have murdered, raped, robbed, plundered. Millions have been killed and mutilated in wars, massacres, concentration camps. According to FWD these great evils are worth the price of freedom. There is reason to doubt, however, that most morally sensitive people would agree.

But there is another issue. Critics of the FWD have argued that there is a logically possible world in which God's creatures have free will in the contracausal sense and yet never do what is evil. If God is omnipotent, He could have actualized any logically possible world, so He could have actualized this world. J. L. Mackie, one of the strongest advocates of this position, then concludes that since God has not created this world, God does not exist.[21]

Defenders of the FWD might argue against Mackie that it is incoherent for God to make creatures with free will and then make them do good. However, Mackie's thesis does not entail that God make people good. Rather, it holds that there is a logically possible world in which people with free will always do good, and God could have actualized this world. In this logically possible world it is not the case that God's creatures cannot do evil; it just so happens that they never do so.

FWD's defenders might also object that the beings in this logically possible world who never do wrong must be beings who, unlike us, are free from the temptation to do evil. They must have, in Kant's phrase, a holy will. But a world with such beings, it may be objected, lacks the value of having beings who resist temptation, control their bad tendencies, and act from a sense of duty. Mackie's thesis does not, however, presume a world of beings with holy wills. Mackie can claim that there is a world in which God's creatures have good and bad inclinations and yet always act out of duty. If such a world is better than the one in which God's creatures always do good because of their holy will, so be it. Yet God did not create this possible world where God's creatures always do good despite the fact they do not have holy wills. Mackie's thesis remains unscathed.

Plantinga has argued that it is possible that God cannot actualize all logically possible worlds. So although Mackie's thesis is correct in one respect, it is wrong in claiming that, since there is a logically possible world where free creatures always do good, God can actualize such a world. Since this appears to be a serious challenge to Mackie's thesis, it is important to consider it in some detail.

In *God, Freedom, and Evil* Plantinga argues that Leibniz was wrong to suppose that God could actualize all logically possible worlds He is part of. Calling this Leibniz's lapse,[22] he says it is a mistake to suppose that God could actualize a logically possible world in which there are creatures with free will who never do wrong. Plantinga considers the hypothetical case of Boston mayor Curley Smith, who is offered a bribe. Let S be all the conditions that obtain at the time the bribe is offered excluding

Smith's acceptance or rejection of the bribe. Then there is a possible world W_1 in which

(1) S obtains
(2) Smith accepts

and a possible world W_2 in which

(1) S obtains
(3) Smith refuses

are true. But Plantinga argues that it may be possible for God to actualize both these worlds. He maintains that one and only one of the following statements is true:

(4) If S were to obtain, then Smith would have accepted.
(5) If S were to obtain, then Smith would have refused.

So although both W_1 and W_2 are possible worlds, God could not actualize both. Supposing (4) is true, then it would be impossible for God to actualize the possible world where Smith refused the bribe; that is, it would be impossible for God to actualize W_2.

Plantinga generalizes this argument, saying there might be a possible world in which Smith never does anything wrong and Smith has free will but which God could not actualize. That is, in any world God could actualize where Smith is free, there is at least one wrong action performed by Smith. If so, Curley Smith suffers from what Plantinga calls transworld depravity, which he defines as follows:

TWD = A person P suffers from transworld depravity IFF the following holds: For every world W, such that P is significantly free in W and P does only what is right in W, there is an action A and a maximal world segment S' such that

    (a) S' includes A's being morally significant for P
    (b) S' includes P's being free with respect to A
    (c) S' is included in W and includes neither P's performing A nor P's refraining from performing A
    (d) If S' were actual, P would go wrong with respect to A

where a maximal world segment S' is a complex state of affairs, such that when any state of affairs is added to S', S' becomes a possible world.

Now, counterfactuals such as (4) and (5) above have been called counterfactuals of freedom. They are contingently true or false. According to Plantinga, God knew these counterfactuals in advance of the actualization of any world. To say that some person P suffers from transworld depravity, then, is to assert that a number of such counterfactuals are true of P. Consequently, transworld depravity is a contingent property, not a necessary property, of those creatures who are afflicted with it.[23] According to Plantinga it is possible that every possible person suffers from transworld depravity. If so, God could not have actualized any world with free creatures that do no wrong. What can be said against this ingenious attempt to answer Mackie's thesis?

Because Plantinga sharply distinguishes between a theodicy and a defense, he argues that it is only necessary for him to show that it is logically possible for a possible person to suffer from transworld depravity. It is not necessary for him to show that this assumption is probable or even plausible. In a defense of the problem of evil one need simply show that evil is logically compatible with the existence of God; in a theodicy one must explain how evil is compatible with the existence of God. His efforts in the FWD, he insists, are a contribution to a defense and not a theodicy.

In the preceding chapter I acknowledged that the existence of evil and the existence of God are logically compatible. Here the crucial question is whether Plantinga has provided an adequate theodicy. Therefore, despite his disclaimers, I examine Plantinga's FWD not merely as a defense in his sense but as a theodicy.

One problem Plantinga's theory faces concerns the counterfactuals of freedom.[24] How is one to understand what it means for a counterfactual of freedom to be true? Ordinary counterfactuals, like those used in science, are true because there is a causal, or at least a nomological, connection between the event specified in the antecedent and the event specified in the consequent. But clearly this cannot be the case in counterfactuals of freedom like (4), for then the choice of Smith would be causally determined and not free. Furthermore, it cannot merely be the case that if S were to obtain, then Smith would probably accept the bribe. For according to Plantinga, if S were to be actualized, then Smith would definitely accept the bribe.

The obscurity of contracausal freedom is compounded rather than clarified by the introduction of the counterfactuals of freedom. Although Smith's choice is not random, it is not caused, and yet (4) is true of Smith. However, it is hard to see how Smith can be free in the sense desired by Plantinga and (4) be true of Smith. Above all, Plantinga wants Smith to be free in the sense of having the ability to choose otherwise than he did. But how can this be?

Following Plantinga, let us refer to our actual world as Kronos. As we have seen, although Plantinga argues that there are possible worlds in which God's creatures are contracausally free and never do wrong, these worlds cannot be actualized. Furthermore, Plantinga maintains that some of God's creatures in Kronos are contracausally free. However, although

God's creatures in Kronos may be contracausally free in that their decisions are not *causally* determined, they do not seem to be free in the sense desired by Plantinga. How could they act otherwise than they do? Consider Curley Smith. He is contracausally free and does not accept the bribe in World$_2$. But if (4) is true in Kronos, then W$_2$ could not be actualized. In Kronos he would accept the bribe; indeed, his acceptance of the bribe would seem to be just as inevitable as if it had been causally determined. It would not be true to say that in Kronos he could not have done otherwise. However, it is important to recall that Plantinga rejected the compatibilist view of freedom and opted for contracausal freedom because the former view did not, and the latter view did, permit us to claim that people could do otherwise. Recall:

(4) If S were to obtain, then Smith would accept the bribe.

Given (4), Smith is not free in the required sense either to accept or to refuse the bribe in Kronos. Thus (4) seems to have the force of a nomological conditional. Given the truth of (4) in Kronos, it would be impossible in some strong sense for S to obtain in Kronos and for Smith to refuse the bribe in Kronos. Although Smith's decisions may not be strictly speaking *causally* determined, the difference hardly seems to matter.

The argument can be generalized. Transworld depravity depends on counterfactuals of freedom being true in Kronos—see condition (d) in the definition of transworld depravity—so transworld depravity is incompatible with being able to choose otherwise than one does in moral situations in Kronos. It would seem that the only way Plantinga can allow for freedom, in the sense of being able to choose otherwise than one does in Kronos, would be to maintain that counterfactuals of freedom are neither true nor false in Kronos. However, in this case Plantinga's argument that God cannot actualize a world where no one does wrong and is contracausally free seems to collapse. For such an argument turns explicitly on counterfactuals of freedom being true in Kronos.[25] Furthermore, as we shall see, the thesis that counterfactuals of freedom are neither true nor false has problems of its own.

Another problem Plantinga's argument faces is that, supposing counterfactuals of freedom to be either true or false and not reducible to causal or nomological counterfactuals, it is not clear what makes them true. Proposition (4) is not made true because of what Smith does, since Smith does not exist prior to God's creation. In any case, God would have to know the truth of (4) prior to creating the creature it is true of. Why could it not be the case that God made counterfactuals of freedom true? After all, such counterfactuals are contingent, and God is all-powerful. If God could make counterfactuals of freedom true, then He could have made counterfactuals of freedom true in which His creatures always do the morally correct thing. Since the transworld depravity of a person P is a function of the sorts of counterfactuals of freedom that are true of P, it is unclear why God could not have created P without this property or, what amounts to same thing, made different counterfactuals of freedom true of P so that P freely always did the right thing in Kronos.

Now, it may be argued that if God had made different counterfactuals true of P, He would be causing P to do the right thing; consequently, the counterfactual would not be a counterfactual of *freedom*. Although it is tempting to argue in this way, the argument is dubious. If God made (5) true, it is difficult to see why (5) would not still be a counterfactual of freedom. Why, if (5) was caused to be true by God, would Smith not still choose freely in the elusive sense of "freely" that is never explained by Plantinga? God's making (5) true would not mean that (5) is a causal or nomological conditional and that there is a causal relation between the event specified by the antecedent and the event specified by the consequent. To be sure, if God caused (5) to be true, there would be a causal relationship between God's action and the proposition referred to by (5). But from this, nothing follows about whether the action described in (5) is causally determined. Indeed, the causal origin of (5) is irrelevant to the question of whether the action specified by (5) is causally determined.

Can it not be argued that if (5), a counterfactual of freedom, was caused by God to be true, Smith's action would be determined in some noncausal sense? For it may be said that if God caused (5) to be true and actualized the antecedent of (5), then Smith's choice would be determined, at least in the sense that Smith could not have done otherwise than refuse the bribe.[26] However, even if God did not cause (5) to be true and (5) just happened to be true, if God actualized the antecedent of (5), Smith's choice would be determined in the sense that Smith could not but refuse the bribe. It is hard to see any significant difference.

I must conclude that, taken by themselves, the problems involved in the use of counterfactuals of freedom prevents Plantinga's FWD from being a plausible theodicy. Moreover, there are further problems with Plantinga's position.

As we have seen, according to Plantinga there are possible worlds that God cannot actualize that are better than this world, yet the worlds that God cannot actualize are logically possible worlds. But a logically possible world is presumably by definition a world that *could* be actual. It is difficult to make sense of a possible world such that it would be logically impossible for it to be actual. It follows that the worlds that God could not actualize could be actual. But how could possible worlds that God could not actualize be actual without God's actualizing them? Let us recall that some world must be actual. If God did not actualize some world, there would be some world nonetheless. Consequently, God has it in His power to *indirectly* bring a world about by not actualizing any of the worlds that He can actualize through directly causing them to become actual.

According to Plantinga, some of the possible worlds that God cannot actualize are better than our actual ones. The question naturally arises as to why God did not indirectly bring about a better world than the present one by not actualizing any of the worlds that he could directly cause to become actual. Let W_4, W_5, and W_6 be the worlds that God cannot actualize but that may nevertheless be actual. One and only one of these would be actual if God did not actualize any of the worlds that He could directly cause to be actual. So God could have indirectly brought about exactly one of these worlds by refraining from taking any direct action. However, it may be objected that the world that God could indirectly bring into existence in this way need not be better than our present world. For example, suppose W_5 is better than Kronos while W_4 and W_6 are not. Suppose further that if God refrains from any action, then W_6 and not W_5 will be actual. Since this is logically possible, it may be argued, it is logically possible that God could not indirectly bring about a better world by refraining from any direct action.

Unfortunately, this objection will not work, for there is only one possible world that God can indirectly bring about by refraining from taking direct action.[27] Suppose God had chosen not to actualize the worlds it is in His power to actualize. What would have happened? Consider these three claims.

(a) Had God not actualized one of the worlds it is in His power to actualize, W_4 would have been actual.
(b) Had God not actualized one of the worlds it is in His power to actualize, W_5 would have been actual.
(c) Had God not actualized one of the worlds it is in His power to actualize, W_6 would have been actual.

Surely *at least* one of these claims must be true if God had not actualized a world that it is in His power to actualize. However, it seems clear that *at most* one of these claims would be true. Suppose (a) is true. In that case W_5 and W_6 are not possible worlds, for there are only two logical possibilities. Either God actualizes what is in His power or He does not. If He did, neither (b) nor (c) would be true. But if He did and (a) is true, then again neither (b) nor (c) would be true. Consequently, neither W_5 nor W_6 could have been actual. Since the same argument applies if we were to assume that either (a) or (b) is true, there must be only one logically possible world that God could not actualize. Let us call this W_a.

Plantinga says there is a logically possible world, better than our world, that God cannot actualize by direct action; that is, by causing this world to be actual. Let us call this W_0. Since W_0 is logically possible, it must be capable of being actual. And since it cannot be made actual by direct action of God, and since W_a is the only world that can be actual without direct action from God, $W_a = W_0$. It follows that God can bring about a better world than this one by refraining from actualizing any world through directly causing the world to be actual. The question is why He did not.[28]

So far, two problems with Plantinga's version of the FWD have been raised. First, it is hard to see how, given Plantinga's notion of counterfactuals of freedom, God's creatures could be free in Kronos in the sense he desires. Second, Plantinga has not shown that either directly or indirectly God could not bring about all logically possible worlds. In particular he has not shown that, by not actualizing any world, God could indirectly bring about a world in which people are free and always do the right thing.

There is one final problem with Plantinga's general argument. Once it is made explicit, it is formally invalid.[29] In a section of *God, Freedom, and Evil* Plantinga says he has shown that

(1) God is omnipotent, omniscient, and wholly good

is consistent with

(3) There is evil.

in the following way:

What we have just seen is that

(35) It was not within God's powers to create a world containing moral good but no moral evil.

is possible and consistent with God's omnipotence and omniscience. But then it is clearly consistent with (1). So we can use it to show that (1) is consistent with (3). For consider

(1) God is omnipotent, omniscient, and wholly good.
(35) It was not within God's powers to create a world containing moral good without creating one containing moral evil.

and

(36) God created a world containing moral good.

These propositions are evidently consistent—i.e., their conjunction is a possible proposition. But taken together they entail

(3) There is evil.[30]

Using Plantinga's notion of consistency as truth in some possible world, which we symbolize by ◊, and symbolizing entailment by →, his argument can be reconstructed more formally. Consider:

(A₁) If ◊(P&R)&(P&R→Q), then ◊(P&Q)

This statement is an uncontroversial theorem of modal logic. It says that if two propositions P and R are consistent and entail Q, then P and Q are consistent.

Now consider:

(A₂) ◊[(God is omnipotent and omniscient)&(35)]

This says that (35) is consistent with God's omnipotence and omniscience. Let us grant for the sake of argument that Plantinga has established this.

It seems as if Plantinga attempts to derive

(A₃) ◊[(1)&(35)]

from (A₂). (A₃) says that God's goodness, omnipotence, and omniscience are consistent with (35). To quote Plantinga: "But then it [(35)] is clearly consistent with (1)."

(A₄) ◊[(1)&(35)&(36)]

says that (1) and (35) and (36) are consistent. It is unclear if Plantinga thinks (A₄) follows from (A₃) or if he thinks (A₄) is trivially true. He says: "These propositions are evidently consistent i.e. their conjunction is a possible proposition."

(A₅) ◊[(1)&{(35)&(36)}]

This is a trivial step justified by the associative law of conjunction.

(A₆) [(1)&{(35)&(36)}]→(3)

This premise says that there must be evil given (1) and {(35)&(36)}; it is basically what transworld depravity comes to.

(A₇) ◊[(1)&(3)]

This says that the existence of an all-good, all-powerful, all-knowing being is consistent with evil. It follows from (A₁), (A₅), and (A₆).

The questionable steps in the argument are from (A₂) to (A₃) and from (A₃) to (A₄). Clearly the step from (A₂) to (A₃) is formally invalid: it is fallacious to argue from ◊(P&Q) to ◊(P&Q&R) since either P or Q might entail ~R. This would be a valid step only if the following suppressed premise were true:

(A₂.₁) ◊[God is all-good &(35)]

But the truth of this premise is by no means obvious. (35) contains the

evaluative terms "moral good" and "moral evil," and these may conflict
with (1), which is about God's goodness. Unless Plantinga establishes
$(A_{2.1})$, the FWD fails, and he makes no attempt to do so. But even if $(A_{2.1})$
were established, this would not be enough, for $\Diamond(P\&Q)\&\Diamond(R\&Q)$ does
not entail that $\Diamond(P\&R\&Q)$. Thus (A_2) and $(A_{2.1})$ do not entail (A_3).

The step from (A_3) to (A_4) is also invalid, for it also moves fallaciously
from $\Diamond(P\&Q)$ to $\Diamond(P\&Q\&R)$. One would have to assume that (1) and
(35) do not entail $\sim$(36). But one might argue that if in fact an all-good
God must create evil in any possible world He actualizes, He would not
create any world at all.

So even if there were no other problems with Plantinga's FWD, the
fallacies in the argument and his assumptions of unwarranted premises
show that the defense fails.

Possible Worlds and God's Ignorance

So far, in presenting Plantinga's FWD we have assumed that in any
possible world in which Curley Smith is offered a bribe, God knows
whether Smith will freely accept it. In order for God to have such knowledge, it is necessary to assume that the counterfactuals of freedom are
either true or false, and Plantinga does assume that one or the other of
the following statements is true:

(4) If S were to obtain, then Smith would have accepted.
(5) If S were to obtain, then Smith would have refused.

However, Bruce Reichenbach has recently argued that this is an assumption one cannot make. Reichenbach maintains that counterfactual
statements about what free agents would do in possible worlds are neither
true nor false.[31] So God could not know whether Curley Smith would
freely accept a bribe if he were offered one. Reichenbach concludes
that because of the indeterminacy of the truth value of counterfactuals,
Mackie's thesis fails: God could not bring about a possible world in which
His creatures are free but always do what is correct, since He could not
know in advance what this world would be.

If Reichenbach is right about counterfactual conditionals, then Mackie's thesis does seem to be undermined, but the price is great. As Mackie
points out, if God does not know what free choices human beings will
make, then God knows little more than we do now about what will happen
in the next 20 years and in 1935 knew little more than we did then about
what would happen in the next 20 years. Such a limitation on God's
knowledge, Mackie says, "carries with it a serious effective limitation of
his power."[32]

The rejection of counterfactuals of freedom has even wider implications than Mackie and other commentators have realized.[33] God would not only be ignorant about all future human choices in this world but also about *His own* future choices. God could not know now whether tomorrow He would intervene in the natural course of events. According to most accounts, God always has the option of intervening in any natural course of events and performing a miracle. Given any future event governed by natural laws, God could not know in advance whether He would perform a miracle and prevent an event from occurring. It follows, then, that God could not know *anything* about the future. He could not know the future decisions of human beings, who, according to the contracausal account of free will, are not governed by natural laws. He could not know whether events that are governed by natural law will occur since He cannot know whether He would intervene and prevent the events from occurring. Given Reichenbach's account, God's ignorance of all future contingencies is complete.

But there is more. Unless one adopts an extreme deontological theory of ethics, the moral correctness of God's actions is determined *at least in part* by the long-range consequences of His actions. Consequently, it would be impossible for anyone, including God, to tell if God's present and past decisions were morally correct. Even God would not know if He was doing the morally correct thing. His ignorance, moreover, would not seem to be correctable, given an indefinitely long future. No matter the consequences of one of His past decisions D up to the present, God could not know there might be some relevant moral consequences of D yet to come.

This idea of a God who does not know whether His moral decisions are correct is surely not one most theists hold and may even be incoherent.[34] A being who is ignorant about whether he is doing the morally correct thing can hardly be called God, for God is usually understood as a being who is not only morally perfect but knows that He is. I must conclude that, although Reichenbach's argument, if valid, would undermine Mackie's thesis, it would result at least in a concept of God that few theists would accept and at worst in a concept of God that makes nonsense of what we normally understand by "God."

The Responsibility of God

In the third step of the FWD it is maintained that God is not responsible for the evil that results from the actions of God's creatures, since they and not God are the cause of the actions that result in evil.

Does Omnipotence Entail Universal Agency?

One crucial question to ask is whether it can be consistently maintained that although God is omnipotent, He does not bring about the action of His creatures. In other words, can God's omnipotence be maintained without maintaining that God is a universal agent? Intuitively one assumes that such a supposition is consistent. But our intuitions may be wrong. A recent theorem of Frederic Fitch suggests that on this matter they indeed are.[35]

Let us sketch Fitch's proof that if an omnipotent agent can personally bring about any state of affairs, then the agent does personally bring about the state of affairs.[36] This proof, if valid, would entail that omnipotence entails universal agency. But first, some preliminary terminology.

A class of propositions is said to be closed with respect to conjunctive elimination if (necessarily), whenever the conjunction of two propositions is in a class, so are the two propositions themselves. For example, for the class of operators δ that obtains between an agent and a state of affairs, δ is closed with respect to conjunctive elimination where

$$\delta(p\&q)\rightarrow(\delta p\&\delta q)$$

Such operators might be believing, doing, justifying, and so on. For example, when Bp means the agent A personally brings about that p obtains, then

$$B(p\&q)\rightarrow(Bp\&Bq)$$

is true if B is closed with respect to eliminative conjunction. Fitch plausibly assumes that B is closed with respect to conjunctive elimination. Fitch also assumes that B is truth-entailing. That is, he assumes:

$$Bp\rightarrow p$$

This says: if an agent brings about the proposition p, then p is true.

Fitch postulates that a class of propositions is said to be a *truth class* if (necessarily) every member of it is true. Thus if δ is a truth class

$$\delta p\rightarrow p$$

B is a truth class since, as we have seen:

$$Bp\rightarrow p$$

Fitch's proof can be sketched as follows (where $\Diamond$ means "It is possible that"):

(1) $\sim\Diamond B(p\&\sim Bp)$

where this reads: It is not possible that an agent personally brings it about that the following proposition is true: p obtains and p is not personally brought about by B.

The proof of this step is as follows: Suppose that (p&~Bp) was something that B could bring about. Then, since B is closed with respect to conjunctive elimination, p&~(Bp) must both be propositions that the agent A can bring about. Thus Bp and B[~(Bp)] must be true. Since B is a truth class and has ~(Bp) as a member, we can infer that ~(Bp) is true. But this contradicts the result that (Bp) is true. Consequently, it is impossible that B[p&~(Bp)].

The second step in the argument is to establish that

(2) $\sim Bp^t \rightarrow \sim \Diamond B[p\&\sim(Bp)]^t$

which says that if it is not the case that agent A personally brings about the true proposition p, then it is impossible that agent A can bring it about that the true proposition p obtains, and it is not the case that A personally brings p about. The proof is this: Disregarding the claim that the consequence is true, the consequence of (2) follows since it is an instance of (1). That the part of the consequences within the brackets is true follows from the antecedent. Obviously, ~Bp follows from ~Bp and from ~Bp^t, p follows.

The third step in the argument results in the derivation of:

(3) $\Diamond(Bp)^t \rightarrow Bp^t$

The proof is this: Suppose it is possible that agent A personally can bring about all true propositions, but there are some true propositions that A personally does not bring about. In other words, suppose ~Bp^t. But from step (2) and this supposition we can derive $\sim \Diamond B[p\&\sim(Bp)]^t$, which contradicts the supposition that A can bring about all true propositions. Consequently, if agent A is all-powerful—in other words, $\Diamond(Bp)^t$—then Bp^t. Thus omnipotence entails universal agency.

Further, Douglas Walton has shown that an even stronger result is possible.[37] Since physical possibility entails logical possibility, one can show that if it is physically possible for an agent to bring about personally every actual state of affairs, then the agent has brought about every actual state of affairs.

If Fitch's theorem and Walton's extension of this theorem are valid, it would seem to show that the third step in the FWD is in serious trouble. If God could have brought about evil, then He did. He personally brought about the evil that advocates of FWD tend to attribute to God's creatures.

Is there any way of avoiding the implications of Fitch's theorem? Clearly one way will not work. It might be maintained that God's omnipotence does not consist in being able to bring about personally every logically possible state of affairs. God, who is all-good, for example, cannot bring about evil states of affairs although these are logically possible. However, it might be said that this is no limitation on God, since this inability adds to His perfection rather than subtracting from it. However, as we saw in Chapter 12, this answer is problematic in that this account of omnipotence conflicts with what is usually meant by the term.

The intuitive implausibility of Fitch's theorem remains, but this perhaps can be attenuated by considerations suggested by Mackie. He argues that the commonsense distinction between bringing something about and merely letting it happen when one could have prevented it does not hold for beings of unlimited power and knowledge.[38] Mackie suggests that this everyday distinction rests on two basic considerations. First, if we bring something about we exert effort, but if we allow it to happen we do not. Second, letting something happen is associated with some degree of inadvertence, whereas bringing something about usually involves conscious attention.

Mackie argues that both these distinctions "fade out" as one's power and knowledge "increase without limit," and for a being with "unlimited power and unlimited vision," these distinctions "would not hold at all."[39] Thus an omnipotent and omniscient being does everything. This does not mean that his creatures do nothing. But, as Mackie argues, if God is all-powerful and all-knowing, He is in full control of people's choices. As Mackie sees it, the only way that God cannot be made the author of human sin is to maintain that God cannot control the free choices of humans, not merely that He can control them but does not. But this limitation of God's power would conflict with our ordinary understanding of God's omnipotence.

THE LEGAL CASE AGAINST GOD

Let us admit for the sake of argument that, despite Fitch's theorem, God is not a universal agent. This, by itself, does not mean that God should not be held responsible for moral evil. After all, God created human beings and according to some accounts could have foreseen that His creatures would do evil acts. Yet He went ahead. Under these circumstances could He not still be held responsible? Let us consider God's responsibility from both a legal and a moral perspective.

Suppose God was being tried in a court for an offense under tort law. Would he be held responsible for the harmful results of the actions of His creatures? Let us quickly sketch in the sort of case that could be made for God's responsibility.

In some tort liability cases a preliminary test "but for" must be passed. That is, it must be established that but for the defendant's action, the harm would not have resulted.[40] This test of actual causation must be passed before legal causation can be assessed in negligence cases, and surely in the case of God's action in creating creatures with free will, this test is passed. According to the religious account, but for God's action there would be no free creatures and consequently no harmful actions.

In addition to establishing actual causation, one must establish legal causation. A widely accepted test of legal causation in negligence cases is that the harm must have been foreseen; in particular, it must be shown that it was reasonable to expect the actual harm that occurred. For example, if a defendant carelessly placed a can of poison on a shelf of food and the can explodes, causing injury to the plaintiff, the defendant is not liable, since the harm was not within the scope of what could reasonably have been expected in this case.[41] In the case of God, it is often claimed that God completely foresaw the harm that would result from his creatures' actions. For example, according to Plantinga, since God knows whether counterfactuals of freedom are true or false, He foresees what harm His creatures will do. But if so, this harm was surely within the scope of what God could reasonably have expected. Indeed, it was precisely the sort of harm God knew would occur. Thus in a civil court God would surely be held negligent.

But the situation can be looked at differently. Since humans are often considered servants of God, one could consider God to be vicariously liable for their actions so long as they were acting in the scope of His service.[42] In this case it would not have to be assumed that God actually foresaw the results of human action. The question is what would be considered as acting within the scope of the service of God. On a strict interpretation, it would be acting only under God's explicit orders. The trouble here is that it is difficult, if not impossible, to determine what these orders are and hence when they are being acted on. But in any event, it is not unreasonable to suppose that humans might cause great harm, even if they were acting under God's orders, since these orders might be difficult to carry out and mistakes might be made. So even on this strict interpretation, God could be held vicariously responsible for at least some evil. On a less strict interpretation, to act within the scope of God's service would be to perform any of the normal activities of daily living: working, raising children, playing, and so on. As we know, humans commit many harmful actions in doing these. So God would be vicariously responsible for this evil.

Another way of viewing the situation would be to consider God as strictly liable for the actions of His creatures. In English and American tort law, owners are held strictly liable for the harm caused by dangerous animals in their care, and manufacturers are held liable for the harm that might result from dangerous products such as dynamite. It is not necessary to show that the owners or manufacturers are at fault.[43] It can be argued that the creatures created by God are no less dangerous than wild animals and dangerous products. Indeed, humans constitute the most dangerous class of entities ever made, and their creator, it can be argued, should be held responsible for their actions.

THE MORAL CASE AGAINST GOD

Talk of vicarious liability and strict liability is perhaps beside the point since their rationale in the law is mainly economic, a consideration that hardly applies in the present context. One can be held vicariously liable and strictly liable without being morally blameworthy. However, the judgment of negligence does carry with it the taint of moral blame, and the fact that God may be negligent is relevant in the present context.

The moral principle that seems to be operating is what I call the first principle of creator responsibility:

(CR$_1$) If X creates Z, and X foresees that Z will cause harm H, and H occurs in the way that X foresaw, then X is directly to blame for H.

(CR$_1$) accounts for a wide range of our intuitions about blame and holds even if the behavior of Z is not governed by causal law.

Consider the following hypothetical example. Suppose Dr. Jones creates a device emitting deadly rays at random times that are not causally determined, and suppose he places this device in Times Square, knowing that it will probably cause many people to die. Suppose Dr. Jones is able to stop the device, yet he does not. Surely, we would hold him responsible for the harm caused by the device. The relevance of (CR$_1$) to God's creation of human beings should be obvious. God created human beings who He knew would cause great harm. Because of the gift of contracausal freedom, His creatures' choices are not caused. Yet like Dr. Jones, He could have prevented the harm, and He did not. Surely, He is to blame. Indeed, Dr. Jones seems less responsible that God does, since God knew on some accounts when and to whom the harm would result, and Jones did not.

Would the situation change if Dr. Jones did not foresee that the device would cause great harm but only knew that it was capable of causing great harm? In this case, Dr. Jones would not be directly to blame for the harm the device might cause, but he would still be guilty of gross negligence or recklessness if he took no precautions. This suggests a second principle of creator responsibility:

(CR$_2$) If X creates Z, and X knows that Z might produce great harm H, and H occurs in the way X thought it might occur, and X takes no precautions to prevent H, then X is guilty of recklessness.

The relevance of (CR$_2$) to the FWD is obvious. Even if Plantinga is wrong and Reichenbach is correct that God does not foresee that His creatures will misuse their free will, (CR$_2$) still applies. God can still be accused of recklessness unless He took precautions to prevent harm. However, there is no evidence that God took any precautions. One can imagine, for example, that the laws of nature would be very different if God were concerned that His creatures might abuse their free will and He wanted to take precautions against the harm that would result from some misuse. For example, wounds would heal more rapidly than they do now and human skin would offer more protection from lethal weapons than our skin does.

GOD IS NO GOOD SAMARITAN

Even if there is some unknown reason why God did not create natural laws that afforded His creatures more protection than they have now from the possible abuses of free will, this would not explain why God does not come to the aid of His creatures who are in danger or are injured because of the misuse of free will. It is well known that in common law countries such as England and the United States there is no general duty to come to the rescue of a stranger. There is a duty only if the person in need of rescue has a particular relation to the potential rescuer. Thus if one's own child is in distress, one does have a duty to provide aid if one can do so without harming oneself.[44]

Many morally sensitive people believe that the good samaritan laws in common law countries are too harsh and are out of keeping with most people's moral sentiments. Critics of the common law point to civil law countries, where there is a duty to come to the aid of a stranger so long as the aid can be rendered without danger to the person who attempts the rescue. These laws are often considered more morally enlightened and progressive than ours.

Now, sometimes when people are in distress no human can or will come to their aid. Given His unlimited powers, in these cases God is certainly able to come to their aid without danger to Himself. In many civil law countries, if God were a human being, He would be doing something illegal. But a strong case can be made that the same thing would be true in common law countries. As I have noted, in common law countries one can be held legally responsible for not going to the aid of another person whom one stands in a special relation to. Humans are often considered God's children; they are not strangers to God. They *do* stand in a special relation to God, as required by tort law in common law countries. Thus if God were a human being, His failure to come to the aid of people in distress would probably be considered a tort even in common law countries.

Further, even if it were not illegal, His failure would be immoral. This is shown by the almost universal acknowledgment of the following moral principle, which I call the good samaritan principle:

(GS) If X can come to Z's aid and by so doing prevent Z's death or serious injury, and X can do so without risk to X, and there is no other person who will come to Z's aid, and X knows this, then X has an obligation either to come to Z's aid directly or to persuade someone else to come to Z's aid.

God's behavior does not seem to live up to this principle.

It may be objected that if God were a good samaritan, either we would no longer have free will or our world would no longer be governed by causal laws. On the one hand, if causal laws were arranged by God so that no harm could come to us, this would take away our free choice of causing harm. On the other hand, if God intervened in the natural course of events to rescue people in trouble, our world would be chaotic and not governed by natural law. As we shall soon see, the first objection presumes a questionable notion of the nature of free will. Whether the second objection has any weight is discussed in detail in the next chapter. For now it is sufficient to point out that when millions of lives are at stake, God could perform rescue missions without intervening constantly in the course of events. He could, for example, have intervened to save the Jews from the Holocaust without always intervening to rescue drowning kittens. Thus God's good samaritan intervention to save millions of lives is compatible with natural laws that pertain on a wide scale.

Is the Free Will Defense Relevant to the Problem of Moral Evil?

So far we have assumed that the FWD, although seriously flawed, is at least relevant to the problem of moral evil. Is this assumption justified? Certainly, Plantinga and other defenders of the defense suppose this. As we have seen, Plantinga defended the view that it is logically impossible that God could actualize a world in which people are free in the contra-causal sense and in which they do no moral evil. But what does it mean to say that people do no moral evil? Does it mean that they are morally perfect in the sense that they always make the morally correct choice or that they perform no actions having morally objectionable consequences? Plantinga seems to mean that it would be logically impossible for God to actualize a world in which people always make the correct moral choice.

Let us suppose that Plantinga is correct. It would not follow that God could not actualize a world in which there are no actions that have morally objectionable consequences. A moral agent could be less than morally

perfect and yet never do anything with morally objectionable consequences. Presumably, God could have constructed natural laws in such
a way that any attempt by a moral agent to do some morally objectionable
act would end in failure; that is, the consequences of the act would not
be morally objectionable. In this world a Hitler would choose to kill
millions, but he would be unsuccessful.

However, in a world where agents could choose in the contracausal
sense to do evil, there would be free will. Recall that free will in the
contracausal sense exists when one's moral choices are not causally determined. It follows that free will in the contracausal sense is compatible
with no action ever having morally objectionable consequences. In particular, to revert back to why God is not a good samaritan, He could be a
good samaritan in the sense of making natural laws that never allow
people to come to harm as a result of morally objectionable human
choices, yet not prevent humans from making morally objectionable
human choices.

Even if it were free from the other problems outlined above, the FWD
does not seem to account for evil that results from human free choice.[45]
Perhaps in order to account for such evil the arguments that are used to
defend natural evil are more relevant.

Conclusion

The FWD fails. In the first place, in order to be successful the defense
must presume contracausal freedom. But the price of this sort of freedom
is too great. Not only has contracausal freedom resulted in great evil, but
the value of having it is discounted by other considerations. For one
thing, it is unclear what it means to be contracausally free and how, if
one is, one can be held morally responsible for one's actions, for another
thing, the hypothesis that all significant moral actions are contracausally
free is in conflict with the findings of science. For yet another thing, the
traditional concept of God is incompatible with contracausal freedom.
Finally, there are no practical differences between contracausal freedom
and freedom in the compatibilist sense. In the second place, it is possible
for God to have created human beings with contracausal freedom who
never do wrong. Recent attempts to argue against this possibility assume
the obscure notion of counterfactuals of freedom and have other problems as well. In the third place, despite the gift of free will to humans,
God is still in some sense responsible and therefore morally blameworthy
for moral evil. In the fourth place, even if the other problems with the
FWD are put aside, it fails to explain why God does not allow humans to
make morally incorrect decisions and then prevent these decisions from
having harmful consequences.

CHAPTER 16

Natural Evil

The free will defense is usually put forth as a solution to the problem of moral evil. Even if it is successful, the problem of *natural* evil remains. This kind of evil is not just brought about by disease, earthquakes, and other so-called natural processes. It can also be produced accidentally, unintentionally, and negligently by human action and inaction.

It is not implausible to suppose that most of the evil in the world is natural in this sense of the term. A significant portion of the world's harmful events are brought about by human actors who either did not know the consequences of their actions or did not believe that what they were doing was wrong. Thus misplaced idealism, ignorance, shortsightedness, and circumstances that induce people to act cruelly to one another out of what seem to be commendable motives surely account for many of the horrors of the past and present. Add to these wrongs disease and natural disasters such as earthquakes, famine, drought, and tidal waves, and the large majority of the bad things in the world are probably accounted for. So any attempts to solve the problem of evil must provide an adequate account of natural evil as well as moral evil.

As I have already argued, the failure of theodicies can provide an inductive justification for disbelief in God. We have already seen that the FWD is an inadequate explanation of moral evil, but even if my arguments against the FWD are rejected, theists must still provide an adequate explanation of natural evil. If they do not, one would then have inductive grounds for disbelief. Have theists provided an adequate explanation?

Three Contemporary Attempts to Solve the Problem of Natural Evil

Theists from Augustine to Karl Barth have attempted to explain why, if God is all-good, all-powerful, and morally perfect, natural evil exists. They have suggested a variety of explanations, among them that there is such evil because this is the best of all possible worlds; that natural evil is necessary for the development of moral character; that it is necessary as a warning for potential evil-doers. Since the explanation that evil is necessary for the development of moral character—the so-called soul making theodicy—raises special problems, it is considered separately in the next chapter. Some of the other explanations are of such minor importance that they are best treated briefly with other minor theodicies, and still other explanations have been so thoroughly examined in standard works in the field that it would be repetitious to discuss them here.[1] The contemporary attempts of Plantinga, Swinburne, and Reichenbach to solve the problem of natural evil deserve special attention, however. Since the are three of the best known contemporary philosophical theists, we can be reasonably confident that if their solutions are inadequate, no better ones exist.

PLANTINGA'S SOLUTION

In *God, Freedom, and Evil* Plantinga's solution to the problem of evil takes the form of an application of the FWD to natural evil.[2] Its adequacy therefore depends on the adequacy or inadequacy of the FWD itself. When applied to natural evil, however, features of this defense merit special consideration.

Plantinga maintains that natural evil could possibly be the result of actions of Satan and other fallen angels.[3] For example, Satan and his cohorts could cause disease, earthquakes, and other natural disasters and even presumably bring it about that human actions sometimes result in evil that is not intended by the human actor. The freedom of Satan and his cohorts is a higher good that outweighs any resulting evil. It should be recalled that with respect to moral evil, Plantinga's FWD was that such evil was not inconsistent with the existence of an all-powerful, all-knowing, all-good God because He could not have created humans with free will who never perform morally wrong actions. A world with humans who have free will was a higher-order good, something that God would want to create despite the possibility that humans would deliberately use their freedom in evil ways. Plantinga simply extends this line of reasoning to the problem of natural evil. As in his FWD of moral evil, Plantinga does not maintain that the existence of Satan is probable but only that it is not improbable. Thus he maintains that the existence of Satan, who causes natural evil, is not inconsistent with the existence of God and that there is no evidence against the hypothesis that Satan exists.

This defense inherits all the problems that plague the free will defense of moral evil, and it has additional problems as well. Let us grant that it is logically *possible* that Satan and his cohorts are the cause of natural evil. The key question is how *probable* this supposition is. There are several reasons for supposing that it is improbable.

(1) The Satan hypothesis is about the actions of disembodied conscious beings. Although Satan and his cohorts are thought to take on bodily form sometimes, the consciousness of fallen, no less than of ordinary, angels is independent of any physical causality. But our experience is that consciousness is causally dependent on physical organisms. This does not show that consciousness could not be independent of bodily processes, but it does render such an idea unlikely.[4] Thus we have inductive evidence against the Satan hypothesis.

(2) Although Satan and his cohorts are basically disembodied, they have been portrayed in Scripture and in popular myth as taking bodily form. But if they do take on bodily form, one would expect that there would be reliable eyewitness reports of Satanic creatures with superhuman powers. That no such reports seem to exist provides some evidence against the Satan hypothesis.

(3) Plantinga seems to admit that the hypothesis (H_1) that natural evil has natural causes is well supported. He also admits that Satan and his cohorts are not natural causes of natural evil. He denies, however, that if (H_1) is well supported, this is evidence against

(H_2) Natural evil is caused by Satan.

Natural evil, says Plantinga, could be caused by both natural and supernatural causes. Thus the truth of (H_1) is compatible with

(H_3) Natural evil is caused by both natural causes and Satan.

Presumably Plantinga does not mean that natural evil is overdetermined, that it has two independent causes, each sufficient to bring it about. Two other interpretations of his position seem more plausible than this one. Plantinga might mean that if one traces the chain of causality from some natural evil back into the past, one will find not physical events, but events in the mind of a disembodied fallen angel. In contrast to this historical origin thesis, Plantinga may mean that Satan and his cohorts have simply created natural laws with evil effects. On this natural law interpretation, natural evil has no empirically traceable historical origin in the mind of disembodied fallen angels.

Now, the historical origin hypothesis is disconfirmed by historical evidence. As Michael Tooley has argued:

> Observation of present occurrences surely supports the hypothesis that all physical events are caused by other physical events or, possibly, are events in the brain of some organism which are caused by events in the organism's mind. And a straightforward generalization of this hypothesis from the present to the past leads to the conclusion that it is unlikely that if one were to trace back the causal chain from diseases and natural disasters, one would always eventually come upon physical events caused by a nonembodied person.[5]

The natural law interpretation also has problems. If Satan and his cohorts create natural evil by creating natural laws with evil consequences, one would expect other evidence to be found. But one does not find this evidence. This suggests that (H_3) is improbable. In order for Satan and his followers to create natural evil by means of natural law, they must have incredible power and intelligence. Given this power and intelligence and the evil nature of Satan, one would expect natural laws to bring about much more evil than they do. Consider cancer. On the present interpretation, we are not to understand that the growth of a cancer is a miraculous event produced by Satan but rather that it is an event governed by natural law which Satan has devised to bring about pain and suffering to humans. One wonders why, if such laws were really consciously designed to bring about suffering to humankind, they could not have been designed with greater effectiveness. It would seem that any being that would create laws governing cancer, and any being that really was evil, would have created laws making cancer lead more often to pain and suffering than it does now and making it even more often untreatable. Given Plantinga's account, the mystery is why things are not much worse.

The most plausible solution that comes to mind is that Satan does not have enough power to create laws or manipulate laws so as to have worse consequences. But it is difficult to see why it takes any more power to create laws that affect more people in more severe ways than to create laws in the first place. Indeed, since the time will shortly come when humans will have the power by means of genetic engineering to create more severe forms of cancer and other deadly diseases than exist at present, it is implausible to suppose that Satan does not have that power now.

(4) The hypothesis of Satan fails to explain why good people are not afflicted with more evil than bad people. One would expect that if certain laws of nature were designed by Satan to bring about evil, human beings who were morally good would be struck down more than those who were not. Satan is portrayed as giving certain privileges to those who follow

his evil ideals, but no such pattern is discernible. Evil people are no better rewarded than good people by natural catastrophes.

It might be argued that natural laws could not be devised by Satan so that evil people were rewarded and good people punished, since human choice is free and unpredictable. But Satan would not have to know in advance what people would choose in order to set up laws that would reward evil. There would only need to be laws that governed what would happen to a person who chose in a certain way. Similarly, it cannot be argued that what would happen to someone who chose in a certain way could not be specified in advance, since that would be determined by the free choices of other people. There could, for example, be statistical laws making evil people more resistant to infection than good people. This would be tantamount to rewarding evil action and punishing good action, and it would not be closely related to the choice of other free human agents.

(5) Another problem with the Satan hypothesis is that one would have expected Satan to perform miracles, to interfere in the natural course of events in order to perform evil works. There are many incidents in the history of the human race in which stopping some human action would have left the human race worse off. Suppose Dr. Salk, who developed the serum to prevent infantile paralysis, had been struck down by some satanic intervention before he completed his work. The human race would surely have been worse off than it is. Yet there was no satanic intervention. Certainly Satan has the power to intervene, since any being that can make laws governing disease and tidal waves could strike down a scientific researcher on the verge of a breakthrough.

(6) Several of the above objections to Plantinga's solutions to the problem of natural evil assume that if (H_3) is true, there should be independent support for it. But since this support is not found in our experience, (H_3) is improbable in the light of the evidence. Consequently, (H_3) cannot be used to solve the problem of natural evil. This assumption seems justified in the light of scientific practice and the sort of inferences we make in ordinary life. Consider the following example. Suppose Jones is accused of the murder of Evans. All the available evidence points to Jones: fingerprints, footprints, and so on. There is no evidence that Jones was induced to commit the murder by someone else. But it is logically possible that Smith, a person whom no one has ever seen or heard of, somehow induced Jones to kill Evans. However, there is no independent evidence of this: no record of anyone named Smith talking to Jones, no evidence of anyone named Smith or anyone else hypnotizing Jones, and so on. In such a case, the hypothesis that Jones performed the murder while being controlled by Smith is less likely than not. One assumes here that if Smith were controlling Jones, there would probably be evidence of certain kinds. But there is not. So we conclude that probably Smith did not

control Jones. Surely one can assume something similar about Satan. If Satan were indirectly responsible for natural evil, there would be independent evidence of his existence. But there is not. So the hypothesis (H₃) is less likely than not.

Plantinga may of course argue that as he understands Satan, there is no reason to suppose that there would be independent evidence for his existence. So it could not be argued that the lack of such evidence gives any ground for supposing that Satan is not the cause of natural evil. However, as Swinburne and Mackie argue against Plantinga, if there is no independent evidence for (H₃), (H₃) would add to the complexity of the hypothesis that God exists. In order to save theism from falsification, (H₃) would have the status of an ad hoc hypothesis, and as such it would decrease the prior probability of the hypothesis that Plantinga attempts to save from falsification. Thus Swinburne argues that "an ad hoc hypothesis added to the theory complicates the theory and for that reason decreases its prior probability and so its posterior probability."[6] So the use of (H₃) without independent evidence to save theism from falsification would tend to decrease the probability that there is a God. However, as Swinburne points out, this would not necessarily mean that theism would be less probable than not. Whether or not it would, depends on other evidence for the existence of God. However, the failure of the traditional arguments for the existence of God as well as the arguments against God presented in Chapters 12 and 13 give us little reason to hope that, on balance, theism would be more probable than not.

(7) There are certain natural evils that we have every reason to suppose are not caused by Satan. There are evils caused by free human actions that are based on nonculpable ignorance rather than on evil intent. Since they are the result of free human action, they are not caused by Satan; since they are the result of nonculpable ignorance, they cannot be blamed on human beings. Now, it may be suggested that Satan is the underlying cause of evils that result from human ignorance since Satan is the cause of humans' acting in ignorance. However, if one assumes, as Plantinga does, the contracausal sense of freedom, then there is no cause of a person's *free* action even if he or she acts in ignorance.

(8) Plantinga points out that many people find the idea of Satan preposterous and that theologians in particular find it repugnant to "man come of age" and "to modern habits of thought."[7] He insists, however, that this does not constitute evidence against the hypothesis but is at best an interesting sociological datum. If our evidence merely consisted in the fact that belief in Satan is now repudiated by many people including most theologians, Plantinga would be correct. However, one must ask who tends to repudiate this belief and who does not. There is good reason to suppose the belief in Satan tends to be repudiated by the people who are the best

educated and the most intelligent, and it tends to be held by people who are less well educated and less intelligent. We know that people who are religious conservatives tend to believe in Satan more than those who are religious liberals; for example, if one person is a Baptist or a member of a Pentecostal sect and another is a Methodist or a Unitarian, the former is more likely to believe in Satan than the latter.[8] But we also have good reason to suppose that there is an inverse correlation between degree of religious conservatism and level of education and intelligence.[9] Furthermore, since education and scientific sophistication are highly correlated, one can infer that there is probably an inverse correlation between degree of belief in Satan and level of scientific education.[10]

But is there a correlation between educated and scientific opinion and truth? Although educated and scientific opinion has not been infallible, most religious believers would now maintain that there are good historical reasons to suppose that in such fields as medicine and technology it has been a better guide to truth than uneducated and unscientific opinion. On inductive grounds one should then expect that it will continue to be a better guide in these areas. But why should we suppose that educated and scientific opinion will be a better guide to truth in fields outside of medicine and technology? In particular, why should we expect it to be a better guide to truth in the field of religion?

One very good reason is that in cases *where scientific investigation of religious claims is possible*, scientific and educated opinion has been a better guide to truth than unscientific and uneducated opinion. For example, even many religious believers would now admit that traditional religious claims about the age of the earth and the nonevolutionary origins of human beings were in error and that educated and scientific opinion was correct. Indeed, much of our intellectual history has consisted in conflict between science and traditional religion, with the latter retreating in the light of new advances of the former.[11] Thus there is good reason to suppose that science has been correct about religious claims more often than traditional religion has been, where these claims have been capable of being investigated by science. It is surely for this reason that many contemporary religious apologists have argued that religious beliefs, correctly understood, are about a transcendent realm that is incapable in principle of scientific investigation and consequently that religious believers are wrongly intruding in areas reserved for science when they make claims that are capable of scientific confirmation or disconfirmation.

But what about religious beliefs that cannot be investigated by science? In particular, what about belief in Satan? First of all, it is at least debatable whether the Satan hypothesis is incapable of indirect scientific investigation. As I have already suggested, many religious believers have argued that although Satan is usually disembodied, there are cases where he takes on a bodily form. But as we have seen, there is inductive evidence against the hypothesis of the disembodied existence of Satan or any other conscious being. Furthermore, the lack of reliable evidence of cases where Satan is embodied should also be taken as indirect negative evidence against the hypothesis.

Suppose, however, that indirect evidence of this sort is ruled out. There is still good reason to follow educated and scientific opinion, for it is a reasonable inductive generalization that unless there is good reason to think otherwise, what is true of the examined members of a sample is also true of the unexamined members, even if these are incapable in principle of being examined. If all examined ravens are black, this is surely good grounds for supposing that all ravens are black—even those that might be incapable in principle of being examined—unless we have good grounds to suppose that those ravens incapable of being examined are unrepresentative of the population as a whole with respect to color. Since in cases where scientific investigation of religious claims is possible, scientific and educated opinion is a better guide to truth than unscientific and uneducated opinion, unless we have good reason to suppose otherwise we should infer on inductive grounds that it is a better guide to truth even in cases where scientific investigation is impossible.

Are there any good grounds to suppose otherwise? It is difficult to see what they could be. They would presumably have to be based on religious premises that are as unjustified as the Satan hypothesis itself. But in any case, without an articulation and defense of such grounds we are justified in thinking that the tendency of scientifically trained people to repudiate the Satan hypothesis and the tendency of the uneducated to accept it are good reason to suppose that the hypothesis is false.

(9) Even if one grants that the existence of Satan is not an improbable hypothesis, one wonders why God does not help the victims of natural disaster—that is, the victims of Satan's indirect action. Since often these victims are unable to help themselves, one would have thought that a loving God would help them if He could. Indeed, even other human beings would seem to have an obligation to help if they can. That a person is not responsible for some evil does not free that person of responsibility to aid the victims of the evil. Yet God does not aid the victims of natural disaster, some of whom die in horrible ways in great agony and suffering. He seems then to be immoral or less powerful than those human beings who do aid the victims.

So even if Plantinga is correct that God could not have actualized a world in which Satan and other fallen angels would never do wrong, he gives no reason why God does not aid the victims of natural disasters caused by Satan. God has the power, the goodness, and the knowledge. Presumably God could aid the victims of Satan's powers in at least two ways. He could perform miracles: For example, victims of tidal waves could be saved by being miraculously plucked out of the water and set down on shore; drowning victims could be miraculously restored to life. Or else God could have arranged natural laws in such a way that victims of Satan were aided by the natural course of events or would be less likely to be affected by the actions of Satan than in fact they are. For example, humans could have been constructed so that it would be harder for them to drown. In the wake of tidal waves, schools of dolphins could come to the aid of the victims, gently pushing them to shore. It takes only a little imagination to see how God could have helped the victims of natural disasters, the victims of Satan.

Indeed, one does not even have to suppose that God is all-powerful, for even a finite God could help the victims. Suppose a very small child who is lost in the woods is dying of hunger and cold. Suppose that the child's being lost is not the result of any human action but is indirectly brought about by the action of Satan. God does not help the child, and the child dies. A loving older child who knew the whereabouts of the smaller one could have led the rescuers to the lost child. Or an older child who was in the woods and knew the way out could have led the small child to safety. Here God's failure to aid the child cannot be attributed to a lack of power or knowledge, unless God has less power and knowledge than a ten-year-old child.[12] Nor can God's failure be attributed to His unwillingness to block Satan's free will, for God allowed Satan to cause the child to become lost and to suffer; and after Satan had acted, God could have prevented the child from dying.

I conclude that the attempt to solve the problem of natural evil by an extension of the FWD in conjunction with the hypothesis of Satan's existence is not successful. Satan's existence is improbable in the light of the evidence, it does not explain God's failure to come to the aid of victims, and in any case the FWD, as we have seen in Chapter 15, has serious problems even without Plantinga's extension.

SWINBURNE'S SOLUTION

Richard Swinburne in *The Existence of God* also presents a solution to the problem of evil.[13] According to Swinburne: "It is not the fact of evil or the kinds of evil which are the real threat to theism, it is the quantity of evil." This, he says, is "the crux of the problem."[14]

Swinburne's solution to the problem of natural evil as he sees it is basically that the amount of evil in the world is necessary for humans to have "*knowledge* of how to bring about evil or prevent its occurrence."[15] This knowledge is necessary if human agents are to make moral choices and become responsible for their own development. Swinburne maintains that our knowledge of the consequences of our actions is established inductively from experience. The more data our inductive inferences are based on, the better established they are. Further, inductive inferences are the most reliable insofar as they are part of one's own experience rather than based on the experience of others. Swinburne argues that it is good that humans make informed moral choices and become responsible for what they do. So an all-good God would want humans to make moral choices and become responsible. Consequently, God would want humans to have reliable knowledge connected with making moral choices; thus God creates abundant natural evil to provide the data for this knowledge.

In order to know the consequences of my choices in a most reliable way, I must have direct experience of the good and evil consequences of my action, and these experiences must be abundant. If this direct experience is unavailable, I must base my inferences on the experience of others. For example, in order for us to know the effects of rabies, it is necessary that people die of rabies. Their deaths provide data for our inductive evidence. With this knowledge we have the choice of preventing such deaths, or negligently allowing rabies to occur, or even deliberately causing rabies. The data on which we base our inductive inferences about the effects of rabies must be extensive if the inferences are to be reliable. Consequently, the number of deaths from rabies should not be negligible if our inductive knowledge of the effects of rabies is to be reliable.

There are several difficulties with this solution to the problem of natural evil.

(1) An obvious one is that if God has created natural evil in order to provide data for reliable inductive inferences, He has not done a good job. Because of the occurrence of certain kinds of evil—for example, certain very rare diseases—scientists are not able to study them and reliable knowledge is therefore unavailable. One wonders why God has not increased the incidence of such diseases so that inferences can be made.

(2) On the other hand, some evils are so common that we understand their workings in great detail. Since our knowledge of them has already reached practical certainty, it would not be increased by further instances of evils. From the point of view of increasing the degree of confirmation of hypotheses about the workings of these evils, their occurrence thus has only marginal significance. Yet such evils continue. We must ask why.

(3) God, being all-powerful, does not need to have humans learn about the consequences of their actions through inductive inferences, for God could have created a variety of other ways to inform His creatures. Swinburne considers and rejects the possibility that God could have told humans what the consequences of their actions would be. If God had done this, says Swinburne, His existence would become common knowledge. But, according to Swinburne, if God's existence became known,

then given His omniscience, omnipotence, and infinite justice, humans would expect punishment for every evil action. This, in turn, would eliminate our temptation to do evil, and consequently our moral responsibility would be eliminated.

However, God need not tell us in advance the consequences of our actions. He could simply have created people with this knowledge stored in their memories.[16] This knowledge would not preclude free choice, for there need be no innate directive for any particular action. The knowledge would simply be of the form, "If you do action A, then X will happen." Moreover, people with this innate knowledge would not necessarily infer that a God exists who punishes their transgressions. In giving people this innate knowledge, God would not have to reveal its source.

(4) Moreover, why would people necessarily infer that the knowledge they received about the consequences of their actions came from God? Swinburne apparently envisages situations in which God says aloud such things as: "If you want to kill your neighbor, cyanide is very effective." But so long as the voice does not tell people what they should do, doubts as to the moral attributes of the entity behind the voice would remain. Furthermore, the knowledge provided by God need not be transmitted by a voice from on high. God could provide the necessary knowledge by such means as oracles, books, tablets, or ouija boards, leaving ambiguous the ultimate source of information.

Finally, if people did know that God exists because of the way the information is conveyed, it is difficult to see why this would preclude their making moral choices and being responsible for their own destinies.[17] After all, some Christians today claim with absolute certainty that God exists, and they do not believe that this certainty precludes the making of moral choices. Their claim to knowing God's will with certainty is not thought to be inconsistent with their claim to having chosen freely.

(5) There is also the problem of whether God has the right to inflict harm on a human being for some greater good. According to Swinburne's solution, natural evil is created to provide knowledge for making moral choices. In order to establish the inductive data base of this knowledge, innocent people must suffer. This suffering is justified, according to Swinburne, because of the greater good.

However, as Swinburne points out, we normally suppose that no one has the right to inflict harm on an agent, for the greater good of another, without the agent's consent. He says: "We judge that doctors who use people as involuntary guinea pigs for medical experiments are doing something wrong."[18] Does this moral insight not apply to God? Swinburne thinks there are three crucial differences between the doctors and God, indicating that God has the right to make choices for humans that they do not have the right to make for each other.

First, God, unlike a doctor, could not have asked for the consent of the person affected. His choice is not about how to use already existing agents but about the sort of agents to make and the sort of world to put them in. Second, God "as the author of our being" has rights over us that we do not have over strangers.[19] Swinburne makes an analogy here to illustrate his point. Although I have no right to let some stranger X suffer for some other stranger Y, says Swinburne, I do have some right of this kind in respect to my own children. For example, I may let my younger son suffer *somewhat* for the good of his older brother's soul. So *a fortiori* "a God who is, *ex hypothesi*, so much more the author of our being than our parents, has so many more rights in this respect."[20] Third, God knows exactly how much humans will suffer. Swinburne maintains that one reason we hesitate to inflict suffering on one person for the good of others is because of our ignorance of what, and how extensive, the suffering will be.

However, none of Swinburne's crucial differences seems to have much force.

(a) In response to the first it need only be pointed out that if the existence of a soul is possible after death, the existence of a soul is possible before birth. But surely then, God could have created pre-birth-existing souls and could have determined whether these souls wished to have pain inflicted on them in a bodily existence for some greater good.

In addition, the fact that one cannot ask people whether they want pain inflicted on them because they have not yet been created hardly justifies such infliction. Suppose that human scientists are able to create a new intelligent species using the techniques of genetic engineering and that the scientists deem it good that this new species will suffer great pain for some higher purpose. Suppose, for example, that the plan is to create intelligent beings with eyes that are very sensitive to light, that this sensitivity will cause the beings great pain, and that this experiment in genetic engineering is intended to improve our understanding of certain diseases of the human eye. In this case, where it would be impossible to ask members of the new species for permission since they would not exist prior to their creation, most morally sensitive people would surely say the experiment was morally impermissible.

(b) Swinburne's view that a parent has a right to let a younger son suffer "somewhat" for the sake of the older brother's soul is one that many morally sensitive parents would have difficulty in accepting. But in any case, this hardly justifies the right of God to cause the enormous amount of suffering involved. Even if God has more rights than parents over their children because of His greater creative role, this hardly justifies supposing that He has absolute rights over His creatures in terms of the pain and suffering that He can inflict. It is significant that Swinburne specifies no limit to what God can do with respect to the infliction of pain and suffering on humans. Since we are given no clue as to what it would be like for God to go beyond His right to inflict pain for the greater good, one must assume that for Swinburne there is no limit. Besides being morally intolerable, this shows that Swinburne's analogy to parents' rights to inflict suffering on their children has no force at all in justifying God's right to inflict suffering on humans.

(c) Swinburne's last difference seems to point in the opposite direction from that which he intends. According to Swinburne, when inflicting suffering on nonconsenting humans, a crucial difference between God and a doctor is that God knows the result with certainty and the doctor does not. But one would have thought that God's certain knowledge that humans will suffer would provide less, not more, justification than the doctor's less-than-certain knowledge. Doctors who use humans as if they were guinea pigs surely become more reprehensible as the probability increases that their subjects will suffer.

REICHENBACH'S SOLUTION

Reichenbach maintains that natural evil is the "outworking upon sentient creatures of the natural laws according to which God's creation operates."[21] God created a world operating according to natural law in order that human beings could make free choices concerning good and evil. A world in which humans can make free choices, according to Reichenbach, is better than one in which free choices cannot operate. In a world operating according to natural law, natural evil can occur. Although Reichenbach rejects the traditional argument that natural evil is necessary for the greater good, he maintains that the *possibility* of natural evil is necessary for this good.

Now, it might be argued that God could have created a world run entirely by miracles instead of law. In such a world, by direct intervention, God would prevent all natural evil from occurring. Reichenbach rejects this possibility as a viable option for God, however, on the grounds that in a world operated by miracles, God would be constantly intervening in human affairs in order to prevent natural evil. As a result of this intervention, events would be unpredictable; and, consequently, rational choices would be impossible. Humans could not make significant moral choices, and thus God would not be able to fulfill His purpose of creating a world where human beings could make free choices.

The problems with this theodicy are many. Consider first Reichenbach's claim that in a world operated only by miracles there would be no possibility of rational choice. He argues that humans could not be rational moral agents since they could not calculate the outcome of their choices. This is because nothing would happen according to any regular sequence.

All outcomes of human choice would depend on how and in what way God intervened. Sometimes if a moral agent P did A, X would result, sometimes Y would result. P could never know in advance whether X or Y would result and consequently could not decide on a rational basis what to do.

There are two problems with this argument. First, a world operating according to miracles does not necessarily operate without regularities. Reichenbach supposes otherwise, perhaps because he defines "miracle" as "a special act of God whereby for a moral or spiritual purpose he produces in nature a new being or mode of being."[22] On an obvious interpretation of this definition, God could never perform the same miracle twice, since on the second time around He would not be creating a *new* being or mode of being. Naturally then, given this definition, in a world of miracles there could be no regularities since every miracle would be unique. However, this is an inadequate definition of "miracle," for, as we saw in Chapter 7, there seems to be no *a priori* reason why God could not perform the same miracle any number of times.

Let us adopt a more adequate definition of "miracle" along the lines developed in Chapter 7—namely, an event that can be explained by a direct act of God. We may wish to add "for a moral or spiritual purpose" although, given the nature of God, this seems redundant. On this definition, in a world of miracles God can intervene in human affairs according to regular patterns. Indeed, it is plausible to suppose that in such a world God's actions in performing miracles would be based on a grand scheme and would have a definite purpose and point that would result in regular patterns. To be sure, such patterns might not be completely discernible to finite minds. Whether or not they would be discernible would depend on the complexity of the patterns and other factors.

The second problem Reichenbach's argument confronts is that even if the patterns are not discernible to finite minds, God could choose to reveal, if not his overall scheme, at least what His intervention will be if certain choices are made. Such revelations would give humans the needed knowledge to make rational moral decisions. To use Reichenbach's example of Samson and Delilah,[23] God could tell Delilah what He would do if she acted in certain ways. His notification would be hypothetical—perhaps in the form of golden letters written in the sky or soft words spoken in Delilah's ear. For example: "If you cut Samson's hair and Z occurs, I will do Y." The occurrence of Z could be due to the decisions of other free moral agents. Given this notification, Delilah would have enough knowledge to make a rational choice and could operate as a free moral agent.[24] A world of miracles is therefore compatible with rational decisions and free moral choice.

But even if Reichenbach is correct that a world run completely by miracles is not a viable option for God, could there not be a world in which natural laws operated and God intervened in the natural course of events in order to eliminate natural evil? After all, the world view that most theists hold is one in which natural laws operate and miracles occur. The atheologian need only argue that in order to eliminate natural evils, God could perform more miracles than He has in our world.

Reichenbach responds to this objection by arguing that if events sometimes followed a regular pattern and sometimes not, "there would be no natural laws regarding that particular event."[25] This is because natural laws "assert universal and necessary connections between phenomena."[26] Furthermore, "if this absence of universal and necessary connections is widespread, as would seem to be required in order to prevent all natural evil," human beings would be unable to make rational predictions and consequently would not be able to make rational choices and be free moral agents.[27]

Reichenbach's first objection seems to rule out miracles a priori, although this hardly seems to be a tack that a theist would want to take. In any case it is unwarranted. As has been pointed out, to say that a generalization of the form "All A's are B" is a universal law is to say that being A physically necessitates B so that any A will be B—apart from exceptions that are the result of interventions from outside the system. One may think of the natural laws operating in our world as for the most part a closed system, and one may think of God's action "as something that intrudes into that system from outside the natural world as a whole."[28] Given this understanding of natural law, miracles are not a priori impossible. In any given case where there is a prima facie counterexample to an alleged natural law, one must decide if the alleged law has been falsified or if there has been an intervention from outside the system; that is, one must decide whether a miracle has occurred.

Reichenbach's second objection overlooks the possibility that God could notify humans of his interventions in the natural course of events, thus enabling them to anticipate what will occur. For example, God could cause it to become known that "heavy snowfall in the mountains and collapse of snow walls will cause an avalanche to proceed down the mountain slope according to the law of gravity when no sentient creature is in its path" but that if a climber is in the avalanche's path it "will swerve around the climber or halt at his feet."[29] Given enough cases of avalanches swerving around climbers or halting at their feet that cannot be explained by natural law, humans might well discern the pattern of God's intervention in avalanches without any special revelation from God. With this empirical inductively based knowledge or else knowledge resulting from special revelation, humans would be able to predict what will occur as well as they do now. Thus a mixed world of natural law and God's intervention need not detract from moral agents' ability to choose good and evil rationally.

Furthermore, even if for some reason humans were unable to have detailed knowledge of God's interventions and as a consequence were not able to make rational moral choices, this would not explain why God did not intervene before humans appeared on the earth. For millions of years before the coming of *Homo sapiens*, many sentient creatures experienced great suffering as a result of disease and natural calamities. Presumably, God could have intervened in order to prevent this suffering and then, after humans developed and were capable of making rational moral choices, He could have stopped His interventions. God's interventions prior to the coming of humans would have had no effect on their future ability to predict the course of events by means of natural law. Indeed, God could have let it be known that this is what He had done. By a special revelation He could have proclaimed: For millions of years I have intervened in the course of natural events in order to prevent pain to the nonhuman beings I have created. Now that humans inhabit the earth and have the ability to make free moral choices, I will cease this intervention so as to better enable them to know the outcomes of their choices and to make free and informed moral decisions. Given this revelation, humans could make rational moral choices in the future and also be able to understand paleontological evidence from the past, such as evidence suggesting that before the coming of *Homo sapiens*, animals were spared pain and suffering by events unexplainable in terms of natural laws.

Another possibility considered and rejected by Reichenbach is that God could have created a world that operated only with statistical laws. In such a world, it may be argued, humans could predict what would happen on the basis of their knowledge of these laws, and at the same time God could intervene in the natural course of events to prevent natural evil without violating any general laws. God's intervention would, as it were, take up some of the slack in the statistical laws. For example, if a statistical law stated that 90 percent of As are B, God's intervention to prevent natural evil would cause at most 10 percent of As not to be B.

Reichenbach maintains that a world operating only with statistical laws is impossible because statistical frequency "is itself based on the assumption that there are universal and necessary natural laws, that there is uniformity."[30] Furthermore, he holds that the atheologian who claims that prediction by statistical law is possible cannot have it both ways. On the one hand, if prediction by statistical laws is possible, then the frequency of natural evil cannot be high. But the atheologian who argues against the existence of God from natural evil maintains that the frequency is significant. If, on the other hand, the atheologian maintains that the frequency of natural evil is not high, then although prediction by statistical law would be possible, the argument against the existence of God based on the high frequency of natural evil collapses.

Reichenbach's claim that statistical laws are based on the assumption of universal laws is ambiguous in that it could be either an epistemological or an ontological thesis. He could be claiming that knowledge of statistical laws is based on knowledge of universal laws or that it would be impossible for statistical laws to exist without universal laws. The epistemological thesis is surely mistaken. For centuries before the development of modern science, humans used rough statistical regularities to predict the future. Even today most people predict the future on the basis of their knowledge of statistical correlations without any knowledge of universal laws.

Reichenbach's ontological thesis is not well supported either. True, in our world scientific inquiry assumes that, in general, statistical laws are based on universal laws. For example, the rough statistical law L_{S1} that most people who fall from the top of a three-story building either die or are very badly injured is assumed to be true because of the existence of universal law L_{U1}, exact content as yet unknown, which says in effect that all people who fall from the top of a three-story building under condition X either die or are very badly injured. Proceeding on this assumption, scientific inquiry attempts to determine condition X. It tries, as it were, to take up the slack and transform the statistical law into a universal one. But this assumption can be understood as a special case of a methodological maxim stating, in effect, that science should not rest content with statistical laws but should endeavor to replace them with universal laws. This maxim, justified by its usefulness in furthering inquiry and in making important scientific discoveries, is not an ontological truth. Given a completely statistical world, for instance, a different maxim might be more useful in furthering inquiry.

Even in our world, empirical and theoretical considerations have induced scientists to operate on the assumption that in some areas of inquiry, only statistical laws hold. Thus modern physics assumes that only statistical laws hold on a subatomic level. Although it may be true, as Reichenbach points out,[31] that such statistical laws hold universally within a set range of limits, this should not obscure the fact that in terms of present physical theory, some fundamental laws are statistical. That is to say, they are irreplaceable in principle by universal laws that result from taking up the slack in statistical laws. Reichenbach gives little reason to suppose that there is no possible world in which all fundamental laws are statistical—even laws operating on the macro-level—and in which intelligent creatures living in this world could use these laws as the basis for rational prediction.

Is the atheologian inconsistent to maintain that fundamental statistical laws could be used for rational prediction and that God would intervene to eliminate the widespread natural evil in the world? Could there be statistical laws stating high correlations and no natural evil? To see that there could be, it is necessary to draw certain distinctions not made by Reichenbach. First, it is necessary to distinguish the frequency of a property's occurrence in different reference classes. To use Reichenbach's avalanche example, the frequency of avalanches swerving in order to avoid a climber relative to the number of avalanches may be very small even in the statistical world under consideration, a world in which God intervenes to prevent natural evil. In this world, as in ours, there are no climbers in the path of most avalanches. (But the frequency of such swervings relative to the class of avalanches that have a climber in their direct path could be extremely high.) A rational person in this statistical world could use the rough statistical law that almost all avalanches go directly down the mountain to make predictions. The fact that God intervenes to save climbers on every occasion when a climber is in the path of an avalanche would not affect the high statistical correlation.

Moreover, let us suppose that in such a world, unlike ours, the number of climbers who would die without this intervention is very large relative to some suitable reference class. One can imagine a snowy mountainous world where, without God's intervention, avalanches would be the largest single cause of accidental death, yet where they seldom result in death. In the same world but with God's intervention, although the leading cause of accidental death would be eliminated, rational beings would know on the basis of statistical laws what would happen in the vast majority of avalanches.

A distinction also needs to be made between basic and derived statistical laws. Consider the rough statistical law L_{S1} that most people who fall from atop a three-story building either die or are very badly injured. Presumably L_{S1} is derived from a more basic law of physics that does not mention people or even living organisms. This law, whose exact contents are unclear, would state in effect that almost all objects with a certain structure that fall from a certain height are damaged in certain ways. Let us call this more basic law L_{S2}. Now, in a world in which God intervenes to prevent natural evil one could expect that L_{S1} would no longer hold. But this would not mean that L_{S2} would not hold. Relative to the number of falling bodies with a certain structure that would be damaged in a fall from a certain height, the number of human falling bodies or indeed the number of sentient falling bodies that would be damaged might be insignificant. Thus rational agents could still use L_{S2} to predict the future. Despite this, the number of people dying from falling out of upper-story windows might be significant relative to some other reference class. For example, falling from an upper story might be a leading cause of accidental death in infants. Once the proper distinctions are made, it would seem that the atheologian's claim that God could eliminate significant natural evil and have a world where rational agents could predict the future by statistical laws is not inconsistent or unreasonable.

In addition, in a world where God intervenes to prevent natural evil, rational agents would not be able to predict by means of L_{S1} that a human being who fell from atop a three-story building would be likely to be injured or to die. This would not mean that they could not rationally predict what would happen in case of such a fall. As we have already seen, rational agents could come to know, by induction from observation or from special revelation, when and in what way God would intervene. In either of these two ways, rational agents could come to know that a human who fell from a three-story building would not be badly hurt. This knowledge, combined with L_{S2}, would enable rational agents to predict the future with an accuracy that would not be significantly different from what is now possible.

We conclude that not only is a statistical world possible but it is compatible with rational human prediction and the elimination, or at least the vast reduction, of natural evil.

After rejecting the alternative that God could have prevented natural evil by creating a world of miracles, Reichenbach turns to the alternative of God's creating a world governed by natural laws. He argues that in such a world the *possibility* of natural evil is necessary for a greater good— a world in which rational agents can make moral choices. We have already seen that Reichenbach's rejection of the alternative of God's creating a world of miracles is unwarranted: A world of miracles is compatible with rational predictions and moral choices. This is all that need be shown in order to refute Reichenbach's theodicy, but more can be shown.

Reichenbach argues in great detail that a theodicy that attempts to justify all natural evils by maintaining that they are necessary for the greater good is inadequate. He concludes that although this theodicy accounts for some natural evil, it fails to account for "the diseases, calamities, or debilitating conditions which cause the pain."[32] Using Rowe's example of a fawn that is suffering in a forest fire,[33] he maintains that the fawn's suffering is gratuitous; that is, it is neither logically nor causally necessary for the greater good. Nevertheless, Reichenbach argues: "The suffering of the fawn may be pointless or gratuitous, but the possibility of it is a necessary condition of there being that greater good."[34] Thus he maintains:

(1) It is not the case that existing natural evils E are necessary for the greater good.

However, he argues:

(2) The possibility of existing natural evils E is necessary for the greater good.

This argument does not seem to answer the question of why there is *actual* natural evil E in this world. Explaining why existing natural evil E is possible, given God's purpose, it does not say why natural evil E exists, given this purpose. The atheologian may well grant that the *possibility* of existing natural evil E is compatible with an all-good, all-powerful God. After all, there may be a possible world in which in order to achieve the greater good, God creates the very natural evil that exists in this world. But since (1) is true, there must be a possible world in which God can bring about His purposes without natural evil. If so, then the crucial question is why God has actualized a world that has this evil, since there is another possible world in which God achieves the greater good and there is no natural evil. In short, (1) and (2) are not only compatible with but seem to imply the following:

(3) It is possible that the greater good exists and there are no existing natural evils E.

If (3) is true, then why has God not actualized this possibility? According to Reichenbach, God is omnipotent in the sense that He can bring about any contingent state of affairs whose description does not entail a contradiction and does not exclude or entail the exclusion of God or any omnipotent agent from among those that may have brought about this state of affairs.[35] Given this account of omnipotence, it is difficult to see why God could not have actualized a world in which His purpose is achieved and there is no natural evil. By Reichenbach's own admission, such a possible world seems to exist since he grants (1), and (1) seems to assume the existence of such a world. According to Reichenbach's own presupposition,[36] since God could have created a world in which the greater good was achieved and there was no natural evil, He can be held responsible for not creating such a world.

At one point Reichenbach says that "what the atheologian has to show is that pointless suffering is not such that its possibility is necessary for there being the greater good—a tall order indeed."[37] Showing this may indeed be a tall order, but the atheologian need not show this to refute Reichenbach. The atheologian needs to show first that the greater good and the absence of pointless suffering are possible in combination, that there is a possible world where they both exist. However, this seems already to have been granted by Reichenbach when he held that pointless suffering is not logically necessary for the greater good—that is, when he granted (1). If pointless suffering is not logically necessary to the greater good, then there must be at least one possible world in which the greater good is realized and there is no pointless suffering. The atheologian must then point out that no sufficient moral reason has been given why this possible world was not actualized. The tall order is really Reichenbach's. He is obliged to explain how he can admit that natural evil is not necessary to the greater good and yet apparently deny the possibility that the greater good could exist without natural evil. If he does not deny this possibility, he faces another tall order: to give a sufficient moral reason why God did not actualize this possibility. This he has not done.

I conclude that Reichenbach's appeal to the operation of natural law has failed to offer an adequate theodicy and, consequently, that he has not provided a morally sufficient reason for natural evil. However, even if I am wrong on this particular point, the arguments developed earlier criticizing his rejection of the alternative of a world of miracles shows that, despite Reichenbach's efforts, the problem of evil remains unsolved. For, as I have shown, God had other alternatives than to actualize a world that operates by natural law and has no miracles. He could have created a world with miracles in which the greater good is achieved and natural evil is nonexistent. Reichenbach has provided no morally sufficient reason why God actualized a world that operates by natural law rather than one that operates in these other ways.

Conclusion

None of the three attempts to solve the problem of natural evil considered here is successful. Since these are among the most widely cited and respected theodicies of natural evil in contemporary philosophical theology, their failure provides evidence that no solutions that are more adequate can be found in contemporary philosophical theology. Furthermore, since these attempts are among the most sophisticated ever produced, and since they have been formulated in full awareness of the failures of theodicies of the past, their failure provides some grounds for supposing that no better solutions have ever been produced. This conclusion is confirmed in the chapters to follow, as other attempts to solve the problem of natural evil are shown to be inadequate. As I argued in Chapter 14, the continued failure of theodicies provides inductive evidence that no explanation of evil is possible. Thus the failure of the theodicies considered in this chapter, combined with the failure of other theodicies, provides inductive evidence that no adequate theodicy of natural evil is possible.

CHAPTER 17

Soul Making Theodicy

Next in importance to the free will defense (FWD) against the argument from evil is the soul making defense (SMD). The basic idea of this defense can be stated simply. In creating the world, God did not create a hedonistic paradise but a place to make souls. Rational agents freely choose to develop certain valuable moral traits of character and to know and love God. In order to do this they must be free to make mistakes and consequently to cause evil. This freedom accounts for the moral evil in the world. Moreover, in order to develop moral and spiritual character there must be a struggle and obstacles to surmount. In a world without suffering, natural calamities, disease, and the like, there would be no obstacles and no struggle. Consequently, there would be no soul making. This account, then, also explains natural evil. Since soul making is of unsurpassed value, it outweighs any moral or natural evil that results from or is a necessary means to it. Thus SMD purports to justify both moral and natural evil and in the process utilizes insights and arguments from both the FWD and some of the defenses of natural evil that have already been discussed.

In this chapter I evaluate the SMD. With a history going back at least to Irenaeus (c.130–c.202), in modern times it was adopted by F. W. Schleiermacher.[1] In contemporary thought the most comprehensive account of it is presented by John Hick.[2] Since Hick's SMD is generally regarded as the best available I concentrate on it here, for if it fails, the likelihood is that all SMDs will fail.

Some General Problems with the Soul Making Defense

Before considering Hick's particular version of the SMD it is useful to highlight some general problems about the SMD by critically evaluating one key premise of an argument developed in Chapter 15:

(1) Although some first-order evils are explained by second-order goods, other first-order evils and all second-order evils are not explained by second-order goods.
(2) But a third-order good, free will, explains first-order evils that are not explained by second-order goods and explains all second-order evils.

---

(3) Therefore, all evil that is not explained by second-order goods is explained by a third-order good.

Consider premise (1). The assumption that a first-order evil such as pain is explained by second-order goods such as sympathy and courage is made by advocates of the SMD. They maintain that in order to develop valuable traits of character (second-order goods), it is necessary to overcome suffering, natural disasters, disease, and the like (first-order goods). Thus in order to have kindness and sympathy there must be pain and suffering, for which kindness and sympathy can be offered; in order to have generosity, there must be a lack of material goods—privation. In a world of complete abundance there could be no generosity. In order to have heroic acts there must be danger for people to face.

It is important to stress that advocates of this line of argument must maintain that the dependence of certain second-order goods on first-order evils cannot be merely contingent or empirical. It must be necessary. If the dependence were merely contingent, then God, an all-powerful being, could arrange things in such a way that people could become kind without there being first-order evils. Surely an all-good God would want to arrange things so that there would be less total evil. However, if the dependence is logical, then even an all-powerful God could not create a world in which people are kind, generous, and brave and there are no deadly diseases, great natural disasters, floods, hurricanes, famines, and the like. To put it a different way, defenders of premise (1) seem to be committed to the following thesis:

(A) There is no possible world where God's creatures have second-order goods and where there are no first-order evils such as deadly diseases, great natural disasters, floods, hurricanes, and famines.

But is (A) true? Surely not. There can be acts of kindness, generosity, sympathy, and bravery without there being first-order evils of the kind one finds in our world. Surely kindness, generosity, sympathy, bravery can be manifested in response to other situations. Physical bravery and courage can be manifested in sports, for example, moral and intellectual courage can be manifested in scientific inquiry. Generosity can be manifested in situations of economic plenty; for instance, teachers can be generous with their time, mothers with their care, and so on. People can be sympathetic when there is no disease, no famine, no great physical pain. Parents can be sympathetic to their children's concerns, and people can be sympathetic to their friends' worries. Kindness and love can be manifested in a mother's care of her infant without the infant's having a disease or being deformed. The idea that the world has to be filled with misery and pain in order to have the manifestations of the dispositions that make up second-order goods is based on too limited a view of how and in what respect these dispositions can be manifested.

The proponents of the argument may argue as follows: It is possible that kindness, generosity, and so on will be manifested without there being great pain and suffering, but the *greatest* acts of kindness can occur only in relation to great pain and suffering. Thus in order for the dispositions that make up second-order goods to be manifested in their most extreme form, great suffering is necessary. But this does not seem to be true. A mother's kindness and love toward her infant is not necessarily less because the child is not diseased or deformed or undergoing great suffering. An aging sports figure's comeback need be no less courageous than a soldier's action in the heat of battle.

But let us suppose what does not seem to be true, that only the appearance of great suffering and tragedy can bring about the most extreme manifestations of the dispositions that make up second-order values. There is nothing *logically necessary* about this. God could have made things differently. He could have made the laws of human psychology such that the most extreme manifestations of second-order goods could be brought about by other events besides war, disease, famine, and the rest.

Moreover, even if it were logically necessary that sympathy, kindness, bravery, and so on, in their highest forms could be acquired only in response to apparent extreme suffering, it still does not follow that there must be great suffering. There need only be the *appearance* of such suffering. Suppose I hypnotize Jones and make him believe that I am undergoing great suffering and hardship. Then Jones, in his hypnotic state, could be extremely kind and sympathetic although I am in fact not suffering at all. One can imagine a world free of disease and physical suffering in which people are given drugs during regularly performed ceremonies that induce them to believe that their friends are suffering. Because of their training, people in this world perform great acts of kindness and sympathy during these ceremonies. It might be argued that at least one great evil is introduced in this world: deception. But the deception by hypothesis is short-lived and strictly regulated in the sense that it is voluntary. People taking the drugs in the ceremony know the consequence. Thus the deception involved in the ceremony seems a small

evil indeed in comparison with the suffering and pain found in our
world.

I must stress that strictly speaking this last argument is not necessary.
It should not be thought that our argument crucially depends on it.
Given the present laws of human psychology, recourse to deception
would be necessary only if the laws did not allow for the fullest manifestation of second-order goods. But there is no reason to think that these
laws of human psychology are restricted in such a way or, if they are,
that they could not be changed.

There is a further point. I have assumed so far that the virtues of
kindness, sympathy, and courage must be manifested. For example, I
have assumed that in order to be kind one must act kindly. However, it
is plausible to analyze the virtues of kindness, sympathy, and courage as
dispositions or propensities to respond in certain ways to certain situations. Although people who have these dispositions in our world usually
manifest them, it is *logically possible* that these dispositions could be possessed by someone without ever being manifested. Thus it is logically
possible that someone could have the disposition to do kind acts without
ever doing a kind act. Since this is true for the other so-called second-
order virtues, it seems logically possible for people to be kind, and so on,
without there being pain and suffering in the world.

This does not end the matter. A defender of premise (1) might maintain that moral virtues such as kindness and sympathy are valuable only
because they are acquired through moral training, and the only way they
could be so acquired is by being manifested in response to pain and
suffering. However, it can be argued that in the possible world that I
envisage these virtues would have to be innate. This would mean that
God would have to create human beings with them. But in this case they
would lose their value.

However, this is mistaken. Surely, if God was all-powerful, He could
have created humans with the ability to acquire moral virtues in many
ways. One way for humans to acquire traits such as kindness and sympathy would be through the reading of imaginative literature. One can
imagine a logical possible world with no actual pain and suffering but
with a tradition of imaginative literature about pain and suffering,
through which people learn to be kind and sympathetic. One must of
course assume that in this world, humans have a well-developed power
of empathy; that is, they can empathize with the characters depicted in
this literature. Although the people in this world would have no actual
experience of what the characters in the literature were feeling, they
could imagine this. One must also assume that some people in this world
have well-developed powers of creative imagination so that they can write
such literature. One must also assume that the people in this world want

to teach their young such moral virtues as kindness. Given the laws operating in this world, there is no reason to suppose that people's kindness is different or less well developed there than in our world.

It might be maintained that although the dispositions that constitute second-order goods can exist without there being first-order evils, they cannot be manifested without these evils. Thus although one can be a sympathetic person without there being pain and suffering to be sympathetic toward, one cannot manifest this emotion except in the face of suffering and pain. Moreover, it might be maintained that it is more valuable for the disposition that makes up the second-order goods to be actualized than not to be—that, for example, having the disposition to be sympathetic but never having the opportunity to be so would be like having an artistic disposition but never being able to exercise the talent. The artistic person would remain unfulfilled, and the sympathetic person would remain unfulfilled too.

Certainly some of the dispositions that make up second-order goods could be manifested even if there were no first-order evils. For example, it is logically possible that one could feel sympathetic toward suffering characters in literature even if there were no suffering in the real world. Sympathy need not be felt toward actual people. However, it can be argued that one cannot actually perform an act of kindness or sympathy if there is no actual pain or suffering. But as we have already argued, there can be acts of kindness, generosity, sympathy, and bravery without there being first-order evils of the kind one finds in our world.

I conclude that thesis (A) is not true. It can be argued that even if there are possible worlds where there are second-order goods and none of the first-order evils that are characteristic of our world, these possible worlds would not be as valuable as ours. But this seems dubious. It is not at all clear that reflective moral people would prefer world W_1 over world W_2 where these are described as follows:

W_1: There are many acts of kindness, generosity, and bravery in response to great suffering, privation, and extreme danger.

W_2: Many people are kind, generous, and brave in the dispositional sense but do not perform kind, generous, or brave acts because there is no suffering, privation, or extreme danger to respond to.

Even if there is agreement among morally sensitive people that W_1 is preferable to W_2, there may well be no agreement as to whether W_1 is preferable to W_3. Consider:

W_3: People are kind, generous, and brave in the dispositional sense; and having voluntarily agreed to be deceived, they do perform

> kind, generous, and brave acts in respect to what they mistak-
> enly believe are cases of suffering, privation, and extreme
> danger although there are no actual cases of suffering, priva-
> tion, and extreme danger.

It was suggested earlier that if the disposition of sympathy is unactualized, something valuable is lost. But the analogy drawn between an artistic
and a sympathetic disposition is faulty. The artistic person usually has a
desire to create works of art. Sympathetic persons do not have a desire
to be confronted with great suffering. In addition, the actualization of
the artistic disposition does not involve the pain or suffering of another
person, whereas the actualization of a sympathetic disposition, according
to the present argument, necessarily involves this. Thus one can with
perfect consistency argue that an unactualized artistic disposition is a
shame whereas an unactualized sympathetic disposition is a blessing, if
great misery is a necessary condition of actualizing it.

However, as we have seen, great misery and suffering are not logically
necessary for actualizing the dispositions that make up second-order
goods. The choice confronting an all-good God is not between actualizing
W_1 or W_2 or W_3, for there could be a world with great acts of kindness,
generosity, bravery, and so on in which there is no great suffering,
disease, or famine, and where people are not deceived.

I conclude that premise (1) is questionable. Second-order goods do
not seem to explain any first-order evil. Thus there are general considerations that tell against one of the major assumptions of SMD. Let us
proceed now to Hick's particular version of this defense.

Hick's Soul Making Theodicy Explained

In reviewing the history of attempts to solve the problem of evil, Hick
distinguishes two distinct theoretical approaches, the Augustinian and
the Irenaean.[3] On the one hand, the Augustinian tradition attempts to
relieve God of responsibility for evil by placing the blame on God's
creatures who have misused their freedom. This tradition also tends to
look to the past, when angels and humans fell from God's grace. Hick
would undoubtedly place Alvin Plantinga in this tradition since, as we
have seen, Plantinga attempts to account for both moral and natural evil
in terms of the misuse of free will by humans or by fallen angels.[4] On
the other hand, the Irenaean tradition accepts God's responsibility and
attempts to show why God created a universe where evil was inevitable.
This tradition tends to look toward the future, not the past. It holds that
it is part of God's plan in the fullness of time to bring about an infinite
good: the creation of beings that freely love and obey God.

Hick sees himself as working within the Irenaean tradition. Indeed, he regards as a myth the Augustinian picture of a historical rebellion of humans and angels bringing about sin that affected the whole human race and that could be atoned for only through faith in Christ. Although this myth may be useful for certain purposes, says Hick, it fails to solve the problem of evil. In addition, it is incoherent because one can only explain why God's "finitely perfect" creatures rebelled against God by supposing that they were predestined to rebel.[5] Hick asserts: "Its original intention was to blame evil upon the misuse of creaturely free will. But now this misuse is itself said to fall under the divine predestinating decrees."[6]

According to Hick, there is "another and better way" than the incoherent myth inherited from the Augustinian tradition.[7] Instead of thinking of humans as created by God in a finished state, one can think of God's creatures as incomplete beings in the process of developing. In the first stage of development, God's creatures evolved into *Homo sapiens* to a point where they were capable of having a personal relationship with their creator. The second stage of development is not brought about by God, however. He can merely create the opportunity for growth. The choice is up to His creatures.

For Hick the ideal relationship between God and humans is the relationship between God and Jesus, who lived in perfect obedience to God. All other humans, even those who believe in God, are egotistically motivated at least some of the time, and most human beings are so motivated most of the time. The basis of sin, then, is that we treat ourselves as the center of the universe instead of living in perfect obedience to God. This disorientation in our vertical relationship with God adversely affects our horizontal relationship with other human beings and thus results in the production of the vast amount of moral evil we find in the world.[8]

Hick rejects the FWD as it has usually been presented, apparently believing that Mackie's and Flew's critiques of it are correct, at least up to a point. Claiming that Plantinga's attempt to meet Mackie's argument fails,[9] Hick argues that the FWD can be reinterpreted to avoid this criticism. He agrees with Mackie that it would be possible for God to make human beings who always choose freely to do good. He notes, however, that they would be free only *relative to other human beings* and insists that there is a religious as well as a moral dimension to God's purpose. It would be logically impossible, he says, for God to create human beings who always freely respond *to Him* with love and faith.

To make this claim possible, Hick presents the analogy of a patient who is given a posthypnotic suggestion to follow certain instructions. According to the compatibilist account of freedom, the actions of the patient who follows the posthypnotic suggestion are free: the actions are not externally compelled but flow from the character of the actor. However, Hick argues, this simply shows that there is something wrong with this account of freedom. He insists that if one takes the wider context into account, the patient is not free. In particular, the patient is not free *in relation to the hypnotist* but is in fact a puppet of the hypnotist. In a similar way, if God had fashioned human beings such that they always did what was correct, then they might be free relative to other humans, but they would not be free relative to God. They would be God's puppets.[10]

Hick agrees with Flew that the contracausal sense of freedom is inadequate, for this is "to equate freedom with randomness of behaviour." He says that it "is very difficult to see how concepts of responsibility and obligation could have any application if human volition occurred at random."[11] There is a third concept of freedom that he advocates, although he admits that it is not easily defined. Hick calls this concept freedom as limited creativity. He maintains that it involves an element of unpredictability. While "a free action arises out of the agent's character it does not arise in a fully determined and predictable way. It is largely but not fully prefigured in the previous state of the agent. For the character is itself partially formed and sometimes partially re-formed in the very moment of free decision."[12]

Although Hick believes that the challenges of Mackie and Flew can be met, he maintains that traditional theodicy "contains within itself tensions and pressures which it cannot withstand."[13] What are these tensions? If humans were living face to face with God, an infinite being, there would be no temptation to sin. They would be in a state of *non posse peccare*— not able to sin. On the other hand, if God's presence is not clearly revealed to His creatures, "the situation is now weighted against" the creatures. Hick says: "If God has elected not to make Himself initially evident to His creatures, can the latter be altogether to blame if he fails to worship his Maker with his whole being?" So the fall of humankind is either impossible or else "so very possible as to be excusable."[14]

According to Hick, God has created the world so it appears to humans as if there were no God. In this way humans are set at an "epistemic distance" from God, and although God's presence is not evident, we can "expect the reality of God to become evident to men in so far as they are willing to live as creatures in the presence of an infinitely perfect Being whose very existence sets them under a sovereign claim to worship and obedience."[15] This epistemic distance makes it "virtually inevitable that man will organize his life apart from God and in self-centered competition with his fellows."[16] It also makes it possible for humans "to freely accept God's gracious invitation and to come to Him in uncompelled faith and love."[17]

Hick attempts to account for pain and suffering in terms of this framework of soul making and epistemic distance. The physical sensation of pain finds its justification, he says, in its biological utility. Pain serves not only as a warning system for disease but, more important, as a way for healthy organisms to learn to cope with danger in their external environment. Pain teaches organisms self-preservation. Hick admits that it would be possible for someone to learn to avoid danger without the sensation of pain but he argues that this knowledge would be indirectly based on normal organisms' pain sensations. For example, an organism O who had no sensation of pain could learn to avoid fire by watching the reaction of organisms with pain sensations who come into contact with fire. But in order for O to do this, there would have to be normal organisms who experienced pain and, because of this, avoided fire.

Hick admits it would be possible for God to have created a world "in which pain-producing situations would be systematically prevented by special adjustments to the course of nature. Causal regularities could be temporally suspended so that the pain mechanism of sentient creatures would never have occasion to be activated."[18] This sort of world would have far-reaching implications. There would be no science, since there would be "no enduring world structure to investigate."[19] Humans would not have to earn their living by the sweat of their brows or the ingenuity of their brains. There would be no need for exertion, no challenge, no problems to overcome. This would be "a soft, unchallenging world" inhabited by a "soft, unchallenged race of men."[20] Such a world, Hick says, would not be a place to build souls.

Attempting to explain pain in lower animals in terms of his general framework, Hick says that, as in humans, it has survival value. It teaches them to avoid danger. But it may still be asked why, given God's purpose of soul making, there are any lower animals at all. Since these creatures cannot make moral choices or come to love God, Hick's answer seems to be that the existence of the lower animals is part of God's plan to create an epistemic distance between humans and God. If humans see themselves as related to animals, they will be placed in a situation in which the awareness of God is not forced on them. Thus the existence of animals when conjoined with the pain that animals must feel in order to survive contributes to epistemic distance and ultimately to soul making.

Hick distinguishes between pain, a physical sensation with physiological causes, and suffering, "the state of mind in which we wish violently or obsessively that our situation were otherwise."[21] The state of suffering may be "as complex as human life itself."[22] Although pain is sometimes a cause of suffering, often many other complex factors enter the picture: remorse, shame, anguish, rage, disappointment, anxiety, fear, despair.

According to Hick, suffering is a function of sin. If we were fully conscious of God and His purpose, we would accept our lot and not wish it
were otherwise.

Just as Hick believes that a world free from pain would not be conducive to soul making, so he believes that a world free from suffering would
not be conducive to this end. In a world custom-made to avoid suffering
there would be neither morally wrong acts nor morally right acts. There
would be no need for self-sacrifice, care for others, courage, honesty, or
other virtues. Indeed, there would be no love in such a paradise, since
love presupposes a real life in which obstacles are surmounted and problems are solved.

The question still remains as to why there is so much suffering. Surely
suffering could serve the purpose of soul making without being so excessive. As Hick points out, sometimes, instead of making souls, suffering
crushes and destroys them. Instead of acting as a constructive force in
creating character, suffering is "distributed in random and meaningless
ways."[23] He admits that at present he does not have "any rational or
ethical way to explain why men suffer as they do."[24] But he does suggest
one reason why some suffering seems so pointless. If it did not seem
pointless, he says, people would not be sympathetic and would not sacrifice. Thus the mystery of why there is seemingly pointless suffering is
used by Hick as further support for his SMD. Without apparently excessive and pointless suffering, souls would not develop.

There is a further aspect of Hick's theodicy. If we look around the
world, Hick says, we see that suffering does not always result in spiritual
growth and God's creatures coming to God. If God's purpose of soul
making is to be fulfilled, one must suppose that the opportunity of
spiritual growth continues after death. Since in hell God's creatures suffer
for eternity without chance of redemption, Hick rejects the idea of hell
as incompatible with soul making and God's ultimate purpose.[25] However, he accepts the idea of an intermediate state between our mundane
and heavenly existence similar to the Catholic idea of purgatory, in which
God's creatures are further perfected through suffering. Although Hick
argues that it is not logically necessary that all God's creatures love and
have faith in God, he says there is a practical certainty that in time they
will.[26]

Hick maintains that we cannot know what our existence will be once
we reach spiritual perfection in the afterlife. Since he argues that certain
virtues would not be possible without hardships to overcome, one wonders if in order to have these virtues in heaven, despite popular belief to
the contrary, it would be a place of pain and hardships. According to
Hick this is only one of several possibilities. For example, he suggests:
"Perhaps these earthly virtues will become heavenly qualities analogous

to courage, perseverance, truthfulness, etc. These analogues would no longer presuppose evil to overcome and temptations to resist, but nevertheless they would be such that they could have been arrived at only via their corresponding earthly virtues."[27]

Hick's Soul Making Theodicy Evaluated

What can one say of this comprehensive scheme that purports to justify evil both moral and natural? Although Hick's scheme is an impressive effort, it fails in several ways.

The Problem of Excessive Evil

According to Hick, the major justification of natural evil is that it provides obstacles and hardships conducive to soul making. But there are plenty of evils to overcome in this world without there being floods, disease, and other natural disasters. Since the evil deliberately brought about by human beings—moral evil—provides abundant material for soul making, natural evil seems largely redundant and unnecessary if one's purpose is to make souls. Hick supposes that in a world free from disease and most other natural evils, humans would live soft lives and develop into morally weak creatures. But surely a large part of our everyday problems and hardships are brought about by other humans; and insofar as hardships contribute to spiritual and moral growth, overcoming moral evil seems to provide a sufficient challenge.

Even if one admits that some natural evil is needed to build character, it is not necessary that there be disease, earthquakes, droughts, and other natural disasters. The arguments to this effect given above need not be repeated here but it is instructive to consider some of the related criticisms of this theory.[28]

Roland Puccetti maintains that Hick uses "the all-or-nothing gambit,"[29] by which he means that Hick sets up the choices open to God as "between a completely painless world and the actual world." He argues that although suffering may be necessary for soul making, a large part of the natural evil in the world is unnecessary for this purpose and God could have actualized other worlds in which souls were developed but there was not so much evil. G. Stanley Kane argues, in turn, that one can develop character through such things as helping one's spouse complete a doctoral dissertation or taking part in competitive sports.[30]

Hick's reply to Puccetti, as I understand it, is that if there were not apparently excessive evils, deep sympathy and compassion would be impossible. He argues that unless human suffering seemed pointless there would be no "organized relief and sacrificial help and service."[31]

Against Kane, Hick argues that in the doctoral dissertation case, if one takes into account the larger context, the character-building potential is not innocuous. In this context there can be great anxiety, pressure, academic failure, and relative poverty. He argues also that in competitive sports there is the possibility of serious injury and death and that taking away this possibility would be taking away possibility of character building.

But this answer is not adequate. Let us grant that in order to build character, there must be the real possibility of problems and difficulties in the context. Surely Kane's point, like Puccetti's, is that these problems and difficulties need not be as great as those in life. Character building is possible with many fewer problems than one finds in the actual world. For example, although serious injury and death are real possibilities in sports such as parachuting, they are quite rare in sports such as tennis. There does not seem to be any reason to suppose that less character is built in less dangerous sports or indeed that less character is built in sports than in many everyday life situations where the danger and suffering are greater.

To answer Kane, Hick must use the same argument he used against Puccetti, that without excessive evil there could be no great sympathy and compassion. Is this reply adequate? The first thing to notice is that it appears to be a factual claim. Hick seems to be saying that as a matter of fact, human beings cannot show great sympathy or compassion for someone who is suffering unless they believe that the suffering is not necessary to build character. But surely there is much evidence against this claim. For example, parents often feel great compassion for their child's suffering even though they believe the suffering is necessary to correct misconduct and indirectly character. It is certainly unclear that all parents would show less compassion for their child's suffering, other things being equal, if they believed that the suffering was not necessary to character building. Furthermore, if one includes suffering that is justified not just in terms of character development but in terms of larger purposes, compassion abounds. For example, nurses often show great sympathy for patients who are suffering because of operations that were absolutely necessary to restore their health. I am not aware that nurses always show more compassion for patients whose suffering is for no good purpose. But even if the factual thesis were true, there is no necessity in this. At best this is only a contingent fact of human nature. If God had wished, He could have chosen to create human beings in such a way that they showed compassion for all suffering, whether they believe it to be character building or not.

Perhaps Hick is making a normative point misleadingly expressed as an actual one. Perhaps this point is that although humans sometimes show great compassion for suffering that is necessary for character building, their compassion should never be as great as it would be in cases where the suffering is not necessary. Yet why should one accept this normative claim? It is easy here to confuse two things. One might argue against showing great compassion for the suffering of people who bring it on themselves, or for the suffering that results from a just punishment. This may or may not be true. But given our present laws of nature, the suffering that might be necessary for soul making need not be brought on by the person who is suffering, and it certainly need not be the result of a just punishment.

Consider one case in which a woman's suffering is not brought on herself and yet is necessary to building character. Let us suppose that Jones would never have developed the discipline to become a great writer if she had not been confined to her bed for many years with a heart ailment and that having this ailment and the suffering that resulted from it was not something she had brought on herself. Why should our compassion be less for Jones's suffering than for that of Smith, a woman whose ailment and suffering were similar but whose character was unaffected by them? Indeed, at the time of the suffering we may not know if the outcome will have any particular effect on the characters of these two women. It seems implausible that such knowledge should have affected our attitude. If we had been the nurse for both women and could have seen into the future, should we have given less care to Jones than to Smith? This certainly seems wrong.

Even if Hick is correct that some excessive evil is necessary to develop compassion, Puccetti and Kane seem to have an obvious reply to Hick, in keeping with their general criticism. They could simply maintain that some excessive evil is necessary to develop compassion, but not the amount that exists. Much less excessive evil would have accomplished the same goal. Perhaps Evans would never have shown great compassion for his aunt had he not believed that her heart disease was pointless and that it had no effect on her character development or on anyone else's. But why is it necessary that his aunt also have other diseases? Evans could be equally compassionate toward his aunt whether she had one disease or many.

There is a final reply to Hick's claim that great compassion and sympathy could only or should only be manifested in the face of pointless and excessive evil. If this is true of humans, why would it not be true of God? From God's vantage point, given Hick's SMD, no human suffering would be pointless, since God views human suffering as necessary for soul making. Could not or should not God feel great compassion for human suffering that He knows is not pointless? If He could, why could not His creatures? To suppose that He could not would seem to put a limitation on His power, for such compassion does not seem logically impossible. To suppose that He should not would seem to impugn His goodness, since great compassion for all suffering is a mark of the highest morality. If He should, why should not His creatures? Shouldn't they follow His example? If He could, then feeling such compassion would not be logically impossible. His creatures would be able do the same with modifications in the laws governing human nature.

So far we have accepted the assumption that some suffering and hardships are necessary for building certain moral traits of character. However, as I have already argued, it is possible to have the various virtues associated with a high moral character without undergoing any suffering or hardships. Indeed, Hick himself seems to allow for just this in the afterlife. Recall that he suggested that in heaven there could be qualities that were analogous to earthly virtues yet would "no longer presuppose evils to overcome and temptations to be resisted, but nevertheless they would be such that they could have been arrived at only via their corresponding earthly virtues."[32] But if it is possible for there to be such heavenly virtues, why could there not be earthly virtues that do not presuppose evil to overcome and temptations to resist? The heavenly virtues that are analogues to earthly virtues, Hick says, could only be arrived at by means of their corresponding earthly virtues. But there does not seem to be anything *logically* necessary about this. At most, God chose to make the earthly and heavenly realms related in this way. If He had wished, He could have made the earthly realm such that humans develop qualities that are analogous to moral traits but do not presuppose evil to be overcome and temptations to be resisted and do not depend on previously acquiring moral traits. Since the heavenly analogues are of utmost value, why not the earthly analogues as well?

Hick would no doubt argue that traits directly or indirectly acquired without suffering could not be of great value. However, the truth of this value judgment is not obvious. Surely most sensitive moral observers see traits such as honesty, sympathy, and compassion as valuable whether they were acquired from reading literature or from undergoing torture. Why is compassion acquired by undergoing great suffering more valuable than compassion acquired by reading great literature and empathizing with the suffering of the characters?

PAIN-FREE ORGANISMS AND SURVIVAL

Even if suffering is necessary for character building, is the sensation of pain? Hick maintains that pain is justified as a means of survival because pain teaches organisms to avoid danger. Although he acknowledges that an organism without the ability to feel pain could learn to avoid danger by watching the avoidance behavior of organisms that do feel pain, he insists that organisms could not survive if they all lacked the ability to experience pain.

With natural laws operating as they do now, Hick is perhaps correct. But he tends to forget here, as elsewhere in his SMD, that at issue are the options open to an omnipotent being.[33] There is no need for God to operate according to present laws. All logical possibilities are open to Him. Thus He could have constructed organisms having innate knowledge of dangerous situations. He could have constructed organisms that sense danger without feeling pain. There are other options too, none of which seem logically impossible.

Hick cannot argue that pain is necessary to build souls, for, as we have seen, he distinguishes between pain and suffering, and suffering seems quite sufficient to build character. Indeed, it could be that many of the character traits of great value in this world are built through surmounting obstacles that do not involve suffering, let alone pain. Consider the typical projects of ordinary life that one strives to accomplish. What must usually be overcome is boredom, conflicting desires, mental fatigue, and external and internal distractions. Not all these obstacles should be considered instances of suffering, let alone of pain. The overcoming of pain is usually not crucial to the process. Indeed, even the overcoming of many natural disasters (which we may concede, for the sake of argument, to be necessary for soul making) does not necessarily involve pain. For example, overcoming the effects of a tornado may involve a great deal of hardship and sacrifice but little actual physical pain.

If pain if not necessary to survival or to soul making, why, since it is surely an evil, does it exist? At this point in his argument, Hick might fall back on his ace in the hole: the notion of epistemic distance. He might argue that the existence of pain is conducive to creating epistemic distance between God and His creatures; this apparent needlessness of pain makes it seem that God does not exist and consequently allows God's creatures freely to love and obey God. Clearly, such a defense assumes that the notion of epistemic distance is free from problems of its own. However, this assumption is dubious.

THE NOTION OF EPISTEMIC DISTANCE

Although the notion of epistemic distance plays a large role in Hick's theodicy, it is an extremely unclear and ambiguous idea. One unclarity is this. If a state of epistemic distance exists in the world, are human beings justified, in the light of the evidence, in being negative or even positive atheists? Many of the things Hick says certainly suggest that the answer to this question is yes. He says that in a state of epistemic distance the world must seem *"etsi deus non daretur,* 'as if there is no God.' "[34] He speaks of the human environment as having an "apparently atheous character."[35] He says the epistemic distance "makes it virtually inevitable that man will organize his life apart from God."[36] Let us call this *the strong interpretation of epistemic distance.*

However, at other times, what Hick suggests has a weaker interpretation. The condition that is contrasted with epistemic distance has "created beings living face to face with infinite plenitude of being, limitlessly dynamic life and power, and unfathomable goodness and love,"[37] and God's presence "automatically and undeniably evident to us."[38] Clearly, there are many epistemic positions besides atheism that are compatible with this condition's not existing. One position might be that on balance the evidence supports theism more than any rival positions, although it would not be "automatic and undeniable to us" that God exists. Let us call this *the weak interpretation of epistemic distance.* The only thing that would be ruled out by the weak interpretation is that God's existence is obvious and evident to human beings.

Other things Hick says suggest a still different interpretation. He says that the implications of the Irenaean conception "for the character of our present world are that it should be religiously ambiguous."[39] This suggests that in a state of epistemic distance the available evidence is evenly balanced between theism and atheism. The choice between belief and disbelief is a matter of faith and not reason. Let us call this *the neutral interpretation of epistemic distance.*

There are serious problems with all these interpretations. The strong interpretation of epistemic distance has ethically unacceptable implications. As we have seen, Hick admits that epistemic distance makes the imperfection of humankind at least in this lifetime nearly a foregone conclusion. Humans who have not accepted God in this life will be further perfected by suffering in a purgatorial state in an afterlife. However, it is unfair that God should require people who have rationally rejected God in this life to undergo further suffering in a future state. Further, it would follow absurdly that, given Hick's assumption that only with epistemic distance can people freely choose God, atheists alone could so choose.

Now, it may be objected that if one starts to come to God, His presence will become clear. As Hick puts it, we can "expect the reality of God to become evident to men in so far as they are willing to live as creatures in the presence of an infinitely perfect Being whose very existence sets them under a sovereign claim to worship and obedience."[40] But why should humans be willing to live as His creatures when, as far as the evidence is concerned, the world is only a natural order? Epistemic distance in the strong sense creates a situation where any attempt to come to God would be *initially* epistemologically unjustified. Thus the act of starting to live as God's creature would be irrational. Yet this irrational act is the one that makes entrance into heaven possible, and the rejection of this act will result in great suffering in the afterlife. Morally sensitive people would surely maintain that a being that creates the world in this way cannot be morally good.

The weak interpretation of epistemic distance does not explain why the available evidence does not seem to support an inductive argument for God. As we have seen, such support is compatible with this weak interpretation. Thus on this interpretation there can be epistemic distance and free choice of God. Since God's existence is not obvious and evident to human beings, they can still freely reject or accept Him. But if there are inductive grounds for belief in God, then, although the choice of God is not obvious, it is not a difficult one for a rational person. The apparent lack of inductive evidence for God makes the choice of God by His creatures harder than necessary. The choice of God, if not an irrational act, is certainly not a rational one, although there is no reason why it could not be. If, however, one argues that the existence of God is very probable in the light of the evidence, then one wonders why freedom to choose God is to some extent not compromised. After all, if atheism and agnosticism are believed to be irrational choices, there is great pressure not to make them.

The neutral interpretation has the paradoxical implication that the free choice of God would have been impossible for people raised in deeply religious traditions, for in these traditions there may be belief that the evidence is evenly balance between theism and its rivals. Indeed, it would seem to follow that only agnostics could freely choose God. For centuries most humans, at least in the Western cultural tradition, saw the world as if it were part of God's handiwork. For the educated and ignorant alike the universe was seen to be the creation of a superior being. It was a world where people believed in miracles, signs from heaven, and intelligent design and where many people believed that they were blessed with a vision of, or at least a message from, their creator. It is only in modern times, with the general acceptance of the scientific world view, that our vision of reality has changed and that for a large portion of the population the existence of God is problematic. Thus the neutral interpretation of epistemic distance may capture the religious phenomenology of many typical modern believers but it fails to capture the religious phenomenology of past ages.

What difference does this make? Could not Hick maintain that he only intended his notion of epistemic distance to apply to modern times? He could not, for on the neutral interpretation of epistemic distance it is only when the world appears religiously ambiguous that the free acceptance of

God is possible. Yet it did not so appear to people for centuries. Either this interpretation of epistemic distance must be rejected or one must suppose that the typical religious believer of the past did not freely accept God. This latter option does not seem very appealing, for some of the world's allegedly greatest religious souls were found in times when the world did not appear religiously ambiguous to the typical person. One would be forced into saying that these great souls did not freely accept God.

Another unclarity in the notion of epistemic distance is how human beings overcome epistemic distance and what happens when they do. According to Hick, "we should expect the reality of God to become evident to men in so far as they are willing to live as creatures in the presence of an infinitely perfect Being." And given this willingness we should expect that "we become able to recognize all around us the signs of divine presence."[41] But what exactly do human beings have to do in order to recognize these signs? It is an experience common to many deeply religious people that, although they devoutly wish for some sign from heaven, none comes. And so, despite their faith, it seems as if there is no God. In any case, what are these signs? Does Hick mean religious experiences and alleged miracles? Or does he mean that ordinary experiences—a sunset, for example—take on new religious significance when one has faith in God? And whatever is meant, why should these signs be given a theistic interpretation? Why, for example, should a person give religious experiences any more epistemic weight after being converted to belief in God than before?

THE MYTH OF NON POSSE PECCARE

Let us assume for the sake of argument that epistemic distance is not problematic. Does it explain what it is supposed to explain? Hick introduced the notion of epistemic distance in order to explain why God does not reveal Himself. According to Hick, if God did reveal Himself, humans would be in a state of *non posse peccare*—not able to sin. Humans could not, Hick says, reject an omnipotent being of which they were "overwhelmingly conscious."[42] Consequently, their choice to love and obey God would not be free. Hick gives no argument to support this thesis, and, moreover, there are arguments that tell against it.

One would expect that if Hick's thesis is true, then religious believers who have had a powerful and moving religious experience in which they claim to be conscious of God would become completely free from sin. But this expectation is surely proved false in our experience. Moreover, by analogy one would expect that if Hick's thesis is true that people would not reject an omnipotent being of which they were conscious, they would tend not to reject an extremely powerful secular authority of which they were conscious. But people who are completely aware of what a great and powerful secular authority such as their king or leader commands have sometimes disobeyed this authority even when they believed the commands to be correct. In addition, if Hick's thesis is true, one would expect that if people knew what is morally correct, they would invariably do what is correct. However, it is a common human experience to know what is correct and yet, because of weakness of the will, not be able to *do* it.[43]

Hick may object that in none of these cases is the person continuously aware of an infinite being. For example, the person who has the powerful religious experience can sin, but only after the religious experience is finished. However, it is difficult to see why the continuous awareness of God's presence should cure weakness of the will. The continuous awareness of the desire of a powerful secular leader does not have this curative power, and by analogy one would expect that it would if Hick's thesis were correct.

EPISTEMIC DISTANCE AND THE AFTERLIFE

If Hick has a problem with holding both the belief in epistemic distance and the belief in the goodness of God, he also has a problem in holding both the belief in epistemic distance and the belief in the intermediate purgatorial state found in the afterlife. Recall that Hick postulates an intermediate state between earthly existence and heaven where there is further suffering and soul making. In this state, those of God's creatures who have not developed sufficiently to go to heaven are further perfected. However, it is no less important in this state than in their earthly existence that God's creatures freely choose to obey God. In terms of Hick's ideas, then, epistemic distance must be maintained in the intermediate state as well as in our earthly state.

The problem is how this is to be done. Presumably, in this intermediate state one will have memories of one's past earthly existence. However, in one's past earthly existence an afterlife is clearly associated with God. Hick seems to admit that if one is awakened after death to another existence, even if one was not directly confronted by God's infinite presence, it would not take a great deal of insight to conclude that the naturalistic view of the world was incorrect and that some supernatural one was correct.[44] Further, a follower of Hick would have to admit that given the nature of one's companions and their suffering, one might well be led to infer that one was in some sort of purgatorial state. But then, on this view one might reasonably conclude, if one had been an atheist or skeptic in one's earthly existence, that one had been seriously wrong and that God does indeed exist. If so, epistemic distance at least in the neutral sense considered above would have been compromised. On the one hand, one would have good grounds for believing in God's existence since it could be plausibly argued that the existence of God was a good explanation of one's post-mortem existence. Thus it seems hard to understand how, if free choice presupposes epistemic distance in the neutral sense, post-mortem beings could come freely to God. On the other hand, if free choice does not presuppose epistemic distance in the neutral sense in the afterlife, it is difficult to see why it does in our earthly existence.

Moreover, as Kane has argued,[45] if all God's creatures are to be saved, as Hick believes they will be, it would seem to be imperative that epistemic distance be reduced in the afterlife. For given the numerous failures to make souls in this life, if the same degree of epistemic distance is maintained in the afterlife, one would have no good reason to suppose that universal salvation would be achieved. But the reduction of epistemic distance in the afterlife causes problems. On the one hand, if epistemic distance is relaxed in the afterlife so that, for example, strong inductive arguments are available for the existence of God, how can one freely choose God? Atheism would be irrational and there would be strong pressure to reject it. On the other hand, if in the afterlife one *could* have free choice either to accept or to reject God *and* know strong inductive arguments for God's existence, why could one not have both in this life?

HICK'S ANALYSIS OF THE FREE WILL DEFENSE AND FREE WILL

Hick maintains that although Plantinga's version of the FWD fails, it can be construed in such a way that it is a successful defense against Mackie's thesis that God could have created a world in which humans, although free, never do wrong. Hick's argument is that although God could have accomplished this relative to human beings, He could not have created a world in which God's creatures were free and never did wrong relative to Him. To do so, Hick argues, God would have to manipulate or create His creatures so that they were bound to love and obey Him. But then their love and obedience would not be free. Recall that he presents this point by way of analogy. If God created a world in which His creatures must always love and obey Him, then they would be like patients in a posthypnotic state and God would be like the hypnotist: they would seem to be free but would in fact be under God's control.

What could Mackie say in response to this argument? He could point out that he is not suggesting that God could program human beings or perform miraculous psychological manipulations on them such that they loved and obeyed God and yet were free. The question for Mackie is whether there is a logically possible world in which humans always do what is right and always love and trust God *without* such programming and manipulation. If the answer is yes, and God could have actualized this world, why didn't He? If the answer is no, why not? It certainly seems as if there is a logically possible world in which people could of their own free will choose to do right and love and obey God. In any case, Hick does nothing to show that there is no such logically possible world.

Now, perhaps Hick's thesis is that although there may be such a logically possible world, God could not know in advance what it would be. Consequently, He could not actualize such a world and know in advance that people in it would always love and obey God. This idea would tie in with Hick's third concept of freedom, in which freedom is understood as limited creativity. With this concept of freedom, we have learned, free actions, although arising out of the agent's character, do "not arise in a fully determined and predictable way."[46] One natural reading of Hick is that even God could not know completely and in advance if one of His creatures will freely obey Him. On this view, free choice is in principle partially unpredictable.

Hick does not wish to embrace the contracausal freedom concept in its most radical form. But without a more careful account of what limited creativity means, his suggestions can hardly get over the problems with the notion of contracausal freedom that I outlined in Chapter 15. The findings of science give no support to the thesis that our actions are in principle only partially determined and predictable. Furthermore, if there is only partial determination of our actions, it is difficult to see how humans can be held *fully* responsible for them. Any aspect or part of a human decision that is not determined must arise spontaneously.[47] Although Hick rejects any analysis that equates freedom with randomness, it is difficult to see how, given his own view, he can completely escape the idea that freedom and randomness are closely linked.

But if Hick's brief remarks on freedom as limited creativity flirt with contracausal freedom and its problems, remarks elsewhere in his writings come dangerously close to advocating a position on the opposite end of the spectrum with problems of its own.[48] Although Hick admits the logical possibility that some of God's creatures will never accept God, he believes for two reasons that all God's creatures will come in the fullness of time to accept God. First, he maintains that we are created with an innate longing or desire to accept God. To use Hick's words: "Man has been created by God for God." Second, he argues that God actively seeks to draw us to Him. With these two powerful forces operating on human decision making—one an internal push and the other an external push—one may well wonder in what sense the decision to accept God is free. Hick says, of course, that He is actively trying "to save us by every means compatible with our existence as free personal beings." However, the question remains as to how a finite human being B, who by hypothesis is predisposed to accept the efforts of an infinite being X to draw B to X, can resist those efforts even if the infinite being is supposed to respect B's freedom. Given the pushes and pulls operating in the context, the area that is left open for free choice seems vanishingly small. Given these conditions it is little wonder that Hick can feel confident that there will be universal salvation. One mystery is why it takes so long and why, in particular, the process of soul making needs to be continued into an afterlife. The other mystery is why humans can be held responsible for their acceptance of God.

Consider the following analogy. Suppose the Federal Trade Commission allowed the Coca Cola Company to inoculate all people with a drug that predisposed them to drink Coke for the rest of their lives and did not grant this privilege to other soft drink companies. Suppose further that, short of coercion, the FTC allowed the Coca Cola Company to use all the most powerful techniques of modern advertising to get people to buy Coke and that the company threw all its extensive resources into converting the country to Coke. Let us suppose too that the advertising resources of Coca Cola are 10,000 times more extensive than those of its nearest competitor, that the government promised to give a plush condominium on retirement to each person who converted to Coke, and that it offered no incentives to other soft drink users. One may well wonder in what nontrivial sense people would be free to buy Pepsi and other rival soft drinks. In the actual situation characterized by Hick, free choice seems even further compromised since finite humans are not being influenced by a powerful company but by an infinite being and the incentive is not a plush condo but eternal happiness in the afterlife.

If we understand Hick's notion of freedom as limited creativity where unpredictability and indetermination are stressed, he cannot give a plausible account of human responsibility. But if his notion of freedom is set in the context of his views on universal salvation where God and human nature contrive for our ultimate salvation, he cannot give a plausible account of human responsibility either. Choice is too undetermined or else is too determined for humans to be blamed.

One might suppose that these problems could be overcome if Hick used the notion of epistemic distance. But they cannot be. On the other hand, if Jones's choice not to accept God in the light of ambiguous evidence for His existence is partially undetermined, how can she be held fully responsible? On the other hand, if she does accept God, how can she be held fully responsible? According to Hick she has a innate desire to accept God and He is using all His noncoercive power to get her to accept Him. Thus recourse to epistemic distance does not solve the problem.

THE PARADOX OF EPISTEMIC DISTANCE AND HICK'S THEODICY

If the notion of epistemic distance has problems of its own and does not in any case solve the problem of freedom in Hick's theodicy, it also seems to generate a curious paradox.[49] Assuming that epistemic distance is what Hick claims, should Hick have published *Evil and the God of Love*, in which this idea is revealed, as well as other books in which the notion of an afterlife is argued? He maintains that epistemic distance is of utmost importance since it is necessary for human free choice and salvation. Although Hick does not make this clear, the perception, if not the state, of epistemic distance seems a fragile one. Human perception of epistemic distance in both the strong and the neutral sense could be undermined if people ceased believing that the world is only a natural order and started believing it likely that the world is a place for soul making.[50] But it may be argued, if people read and believe Hick's books, they will believe that our world is a place for soul making. Will this not tend to undermine God's purpose? Indeed, it may be urged that the more persuasive Hick's arguments are, the more they would tend to undermine God's purpose.

Hick would of course argue that this is a misunderstanding. He would say that his work, far from being in conflict with God's purpose, furthers His purpose since it gives people the intellectual tools to break away from the prevailing view that the world is merely a natural order or is religiously ambiguous and to accept another view of the world. But this response is plausible only if the major theses of his book do not become widely accepted and obvious. Surely if they did, epistemic distance in both the strong and the neutral senses would no longer exist.

Given this worry one can only wonder why Hick published his work. Perhaps he was reasonably certain on the basis of similar publications that wide acceptance of his work was not likely even if his arguments were very strong. Nevertheless, one might think that, although the likelihood of wide acceptance was not great, the negative value of wide acceptance would be so great that it would not be worth the gamble. But even if it was not widely accepted, he may have supposed that some people would have their perception of epistemic distance changed by reading it and, consequently, Hick's book would be indirectly responsible for their suffering in the afterlife.

CHAPTER 18

Some Minor Theodicies

In previous chapters I critically evaluated the two most important defenses, the FWD and the SMD, that theists have developed against the argument from evil, as well as three of the most sophisticated solutions to the problem of natural evil in contemporary philosophy. In this chapter let us consider some relatively minor attempts to justify the existence of evil. By relatively minor I mean, first, that sophisticated philosophical theists have not used these defenses as much as some of the accounts already discussed to justify God's ways to His creatures and, second, that these defenses do not seem as convincing. For these reasons I do not discuss them in as great detail as the theodicies that were covered in previous chapters. Some have been used by popular apologists for theism rather than by theologians or philosophers of religion, others are of historical interest, and still others raise interesting philosophical questions. There are so many minor theodicies I cannot examine all of them here, and any selection is to some extent arbitrary. I examine those that strike me as having the greatest historical importance, as philosophically interesting, or as most often used by popular apologists.

The Finite God Theodicy

One attempt to justify the existence of evil, given the existence of an all-good God, is to maintain that God is not all-powerful. Although He wants to prevent evil, because He is not all-powerful He cannot do so. Hence evil exists despite the existence of God.[1]

This view has recently been advocated in the bestselling *When Bad Things Happen to Good People*, by Rabbi Harold Kushner.[2] Kushner, whose son, Aaron, died of rapid aging, rejects many of the usual theodicies as completely implausible. Indeed, he suggests that some of the bad things that happen to good people are random events—that is, they are un-caused. He puts it this way:

> Can you accept the idea that some things happen for no reason, that there is randomness in the Universe? Some people cannot handle that idea. They look for connections, striving desperately to make sense of all that happens. They convince themselves that God is cruel, or that they are sinners, rather than accept randomness. . . . Why must everything happen for a specific reason? Why can't we let the universe have a few rough edges?[3]

Kushner goes on to say that God did not complete the creation of the universe and even now is attempting to replace chaos—that is, random-ness—with order. So while this process of creation is going on, "every now and then, things happen not contrary to those laws [of nature] but outside them."[4]

However, uncaused events are not, according to Kushner, the only source of evil. Evil is sometimes the result of the workings of natural law rather than of events outside natural law. But natural laws do not "make exceptions for good people."[5] Good and bad people get sick, they die by natural disaster, and this happens according to natural law. Kushner seems to believe that God could neither intervene and prevent these things from happening nor create different laws that would bring about less pain and suffering.

Kushner's theodicy is best understood to be a finite God solution to the problem of evil for the following reasons. He never indicates that there could not be a more powerful being that could have brought order out of the chaos all at once and could have immediately created a world without random events. Nor does he indicate that there could not be a more powerful being that could intervene to present some evil or that could create natural laws that would bring about less pain and suffering. He apparently assumes that God must work with some preexisting mate-rial rather than create the universe out of nothing, although presumably an all-powerful God would not be limited by such material. We must assume that, according to Kushner, God's inability to create the world out of nothing, create laws that could bring about less pain, and so on reflects His lack of power, since other logically possible supernatural beings would be able to do what Kushner says God cannot do.[6]

This theodicy has serious problems. First of all, Kushner gives no examples of evils that have occurred as a consequence of uncaused events. The typical evils he cites in his book are sickness, disease, and natural disasters that occur to good people and innocent children. But no one supposes that these are random events—that is, events that have no causes. Indeed, no one supposes that the death of his son was a random event in this sense. Thus it is difficult to know exactly what Kushner is referring to. Furthermore, if one takes seriously his view that God is continuing to create order out of chaos, it would have certain verifiable results. One would expect scientists to discover that some natural laws have come into existence only recently, others some time ago, and still others much farther back in time, and that the amount of the evil that is based on randomness would have decreased as randomness was continually being eliminated by God. But scientists do not believe that the laws of the universe have come into existence at different times. Since Kushner does not specify what evils are based upon random evils, it is impossible to tell whether such evil has decreased. However, there is certainly no reason to suppose that there has been a decrease in the overall amount of evil.

Second, Kushner gives no reason to suppose that *if God was powerful enough to make laws at all,* He could not have made laws with fewer evil consequences than there are now. Of course, one can imagine a finite supernatural being incapable of creating laws. Some of the gods of Greek mythology are perhaps of this kind. However, it is difficult to imagine a finite but very powerful being capable of fashioning the laws that govern the vast regions of galactic space and the wondrous workings of living organisms yet incapable of fashioning laws that result in less apparently pointless evil. Kushner admits that he has no answer to the question of "why our bodies had to be made vulnerable to germs and viruses and malignant tumors."[7] He does not realize that it is unlikely that a completely good being, powerful enough to do what Kushner claims He has done, could not also create laws in which, for example, people would not be so vulnerable to germs and viruses and malignant tumors as they are now.

Even if Kushner were able to explain why God could not create such laws, there would still be the problem of why He does not intervene to prevent harm from coming to some of His creatures. Suppose a 3-year-old girl is lost in the woods, and if she is not rescued, she will die. God would not have to have great powers to achieve a rescue. No new laws would have to be created, no old laws would have to be transgressed. Indeed, someone with the powers of a ten-year-old child could rescue the little girl if the person knew where she was. In fact, the young girl's sister, a ten-year-old, *would* rescue her if she knew where to find her. But God does not act, nor does He give the older sister the necessary information to act. To make sense of the death of the child by exposure, we seem to be forced into assuming something that is absurd. We must suppose that God does not have the power of a ten-year-old or the knowledge that a ten-year-old could obtain.[8]

Michael Burke has argued that a finite God might have had the power to eliminate an evil that has been eliminated by human beings, such as smallpox, and yet have failed to do so "because all of his vast but finite power was required for the elimination or the prevention of *greater* evils." It may be suggested that "our galaxy is but one of hundred millions with intelligent life, that God can attend to only a dozen galaxies at a time and that our galaxy is not among those most urgently in need of his attention."[9] Thus although He has the power to save a lost child from death, God may be occupied with eliminating greater evils that tax to the limit His great but finite powers.

There are some problems with this reply, however. In the case of the lost child, as in the case of smallpox, God need not actually eliminate the evil Himself; He need only convey certain information to scientists in the case of smallpox and to the sister in the case of the lost child. Presumably God could accomplish this in microseconds. The reply would thus have us suppose something that seems incredible—namely, that more serious problems occupy God's attention every microsecond. Moreover, if we accept the standard view according to Scripture that God created all the universe at the same time, it is difficult to understand how any god that is capable of *creating* a hundred million galaxies simultaneously cannot *attend* to them simultaneously. On the other hand, if we assume that God created different galaxies at different times, since He did not have the power to create them at the same time, then He may not be able to attend to them at the same time. However, in this case God would have to know that He would not be able (or might not be able) to attend to them at the same time and eliminate evil in all of them. But a god that would create millions of galaxies knowing that He might not be able to attend to them and eliminate evil in them would surely be considered irresponsible. Furthermore, whether God created all of the universe at the same time or at different times, the question remains as to why He would create any galaxy that contained any evil in the first place.

The only way around these problems is to suppose that although God does have the power to eliminate evil in all existing galaxies, He does not exercise it because His actions will bring about more evil than good or His not acting is necessary for bringing about a greater good. However, this defense of God's ways to man has nothing to do with His limited power. Indeed, as we have seen, it has been used for traditional theists postulating an omnipotent God. Thus any *unique* contribution a finite God theodicy such as Kushner's makes to this problem must suppose that God wants to save the child or eliminate smallpox because it would be the best thing to do but that He is unable to do so because of His limited power. But as we have just noted, this has the absurd implication that God has less power than do those of His creatures who could prevent the evil.

Although Kushner's finite God solution to the problem is less philosophically sophisticated than many other treatments that use the notion of a finite God,[10] those others have similar problems.[11] In view of the fact that the finite power that is attributed to God seems quite adequate to prevent many of the world's evils, it is improbable that a god who has this much power *and* is completely good can exist.

The Best of All Possible Worlds Theodicy

One traditional theodicy maintains that this is the best of all possible worlds[12]—that although our world contains evil, any other possible world would be worse overall in that it would contain more evil or less good than ours. God in his infinite knowledge surveyed all the possible worlds and, according to this theodicy, in His infinite goodness chose the best of all possible worlds and made it actual. Consequently, the evil in our world is necessary. Although an omnipotent being, God could do no better.

The thesis that this is the best of all possible worlds has seemed patently absurd to many people and has been ridiculed in story and song.[13] It is extremely improbable in the light of our evidence that no improvement could be made in our world without the situation's becoming worse overall. In Chapter 14 this issue was pursued at length.[14] However, there is an even more fundamental problem with this theodicy than its improbability. The concept of the best of all possible worlds is incoherent and cannot, therefore, be used to justify the existence of evil.

Consider first the argument of Alvin Plantinga against the coherence of the best possible world.[15] He argues that the concept of the largest number is incoherent, since no matter how large a number one picks, there is always another number that is larger. He maintains that the concept of the best of all possible worlds is like the concept of the largest number, since no matter how good a world one picks out from all the possible worlds, there is always another possible world that is better.[16] Consequently, he argues, the concept of the best possible world is incoherent. Unlike his argument against the coherence of the best of all possible islands, this argument seems sound.[17]

However, Patrick Grim offers a more powerful argument showing that the concept of the best possible world is incoherent.[18] One can argue that if God exists, this cannot be the best of all possible worlds, since all possible worlds are equally good. To say that this is the best of all possible worlds presumably implies that there are possible worlds that are worse than this. But how can it be shown that all possible worlds are equally good?

Possible worlds are by definition worlds that could be actual. There are two ways that a possible world could become actual. (1) Some possible words can be actualized by God's directly causing them to be actual. (2)

Some possible worlds cannot become actual by God's directly causing them to become actual but can become actual in some other way. Let us assume that (1) is true. Then if there were possible worlds worse than ours, this would mean that they could be actualized by God. But by definition God is morally perfect. However, if He is morally perfect, He will necessarily not pursue a morally inferior course of action. Thus on (1) God is incapable of actualizing any world that is morally inferior to any other world. Hence there could not be a possible world that is worse than this one.[19]

Assume now that (2) is true. How could the possible worlds become actual that God could not actualize by directly causing them to be actual? Some possible world must be actual. Consequently, God could indirectly bring about some world that He could not directly cause to be actual by not actualizing any world. Could the world that God brought about by refraining from directly causing any world be better than this world? No, it could not. For the same argument can be used to show that all these possible worlds are no better than this world. Suppose for simplicity that W_1, W_2, and W_3 are the only worlds that God can bring about by directly causing them to be actual. Suppose that W_4, W_5 and W_6 are worlds that God cannot actualize but that might be actual. Now, although God could not bring about W_4 or W_5 or W_6 directly by causing them to be actual, He could bring one and only one of them into being indirectly by simply not actualizing W_1 or W_2 or W_3.[20] Whichever world this is, it could not be worse than the world that God has actualized, and for the reason already given. Since God is morally perfect He is incapable of directly or indirectly actualizing a world that is inferior to the actual one. Thus on the supposition that the best possible world implies that there are morally inferior possible worlds, the concept of the best possible world makes no sense. Consequently, although there may be other possible worlds, there are no worse ones than this world.[21]

Grim has pointed out the rather startling implications of the thesis that all possible worlds are equally good. First, there is presumably a possible world in which only God exists. If there were not such a world, God would lack certain attributes that He is usually thought to have, such as self-sufficiency and completeness. However, if there is such a world, it is just as good as ours with its large amount of evil. This seems to imply that all that exists in our world is as perfect as God himself. Second, the view implicates ethical fatalism. Since no world could be any better than this one, there would be no use in trying to improve things. No matter what one would do, there would be no overall improvement. Third, certain counterfactual statements that we normally take to be in conflict would not conflict, while other counterfactual statements that we take to be false would be true. For example, normally we take "Had things been worse overall, I would have resigned" to conflict with "Had things been worse overall, I would not have resigned." But on both Lewis's and Stalnaker's semantics for counterfactuals, if the antecedent is impossible, the counterfactual is true. Since the antecedents in both these counterfactuals are false, both are true. Further, we would normally take the counterfactual "Had the USSR and the United States engaged in an all-out nuclear war, things would have been worse overall" to be true. On both Lewis's and Stalnaker's semantics for counterfactuals, if the consequent of a counterfactual is impossible, the counterfactual is false.[22] Since the consequence is logically impossible, the statement is false. However, this is absurd.

I conclude that the defense that this is the best of all possible worlds is either improbable or incoherent.

The Original Sin Theodicy

One of the most popular defenses of evil in Christian thought has been to maintain that evil came into the world through original sin. This theodicy is closely connected to a particular story of how God's creatures fell from grace and how God, through Christ's death and resurrection, atoned for human sin. John Hick characterizes this traditional view as follows:

> In this great amalgam of Jewish and Christian themes, God created spiritual beings, the angels and archangels, to be His subjects and to love and serve Him in the heavenly spheres. But a minority of them revolted against God in envy of His supremacy, and were defeated and cast into an abode suited to their now irreconcilably evil natures. Either to replenish the citizenry of heaven thus depleted by the expulsion of Satan and his followers, or as an independent venture of creation, God made our world, and mankind within it consisting initially of a single human pair. This first man and woman, living in the direct knowledge of God, were good, happy, and immortal, and would in due course have populated the earth with descendants like themselves. But Satan, in wicked spite, successfully tempted them to disobey their Creator, who then expelled them from this paradisal existence into a new situation of hardship, danger, disease and inevitable death. This was the fall of man, and as a result of it the succeeding members of the human race have been born as fallen creatures in a fallen world, participating in the effects of their first parents' rebellion against their Maker. But God in Christ has made the atonement for man's sin that His own eternal justice required and has offered free forgiveness to as many as will commit themselves to Christ as their Saviour. At the last judgement, when faith and life alike will be tested, many will enter into eternal life whilst others, preferring their own darkness to God's light, will linger in a perpetual living death.[23]

Hick points out that we know from science that the conditions and causes of human hardship, disease, death, and other natural evils existed *before* the emergence of human beings, hence before human beings first sinned.[24] However, according to this theodicy, human disease, death, and other natural disasters came into the world only after human beings sinned. Since this view has verifiable consequences that have been disconfirmed, to save it from refutation one must reject the findings of science. In addition, Hick notes that this theodicy has unacceptable moral implications. It is grossly unjust to punish the descendants of the first pair of human beings because this pair sinned against God. If God did this, then He must be unjust. But God by definition is completely just. Moreover, there is a fatal incoherence in the story. God created creatures (humans and angels) who were free and finitely perfect and who lived in a completely good world. Yet they inexplicably rebelled against them. How could such creatures in such circumstances have sinned? Apparently, evil was created *ex nihilo*. It is undoubtedly for these reasons that sophisticated Christian theologians such as Hick refer to this theodicy as a myth and rely on other theodicies in their own work.

The Ultimate Harmony Theodicy

Popular apologists for theism have sometimes maintained that what seems like evil is justified because it is not really evil when seen from the perspective of God or that what seems like evil is evil but is justified in terms of its good long-range consequences. These two distinct defenses have been ambiguously called the ultimate harmony solution. Since they raise different questions, following Madden and Hare I refer to the former as the all's well in God's view solution and the latter as the all's well that ends well solution.[25]

There are several serious problems with the all's well in God's view solution. In the first place, if evil is only an illusion from our limited perspective, then acting to change something that appears evil to something that appears good will make no moral difference in the ultimate scheme of things. Thus this view has disastrous consequences for the practical moral life. It entails moral fatalism.[26]

In addition, this solution seems to entail that God's morality is completely different from that of His creatures. Perhaps the greatest moral evil of the twentieth century was the Holocaust. Yet according to the present view, from the perspective of God the Holocaust was not really evil. If this is so, then God has a completely different morality from His creatures. But given such a morality, it is impossible to see how He can be an object of worship or moral guidance to us. Why should we worship or follow the commands of a being who does not think the Holocaust evil?

The all's well that ends well solution also has problems.[27] First, although it may be true that some present or past evil may generate great good in the long run, this does not explain why an omnipotent God finds it necessary to have even short-term evils of the kind we find in our world. If God achieves end E by means M_1, and if M_1 is evil and E is good, and if E outweighs M_1, why cannot God bring about E by M_2 where M_2 is less evil than M_1? The theist must maintain that even an omnipotent God could not bring about E or something as good without bringing about M_1 or something worse. As we have seen in the other chapters, although this is possible it is very unlikely in the light of our evidence.

Furthermore, even if it was the case that God could not fulfill his purposes without bringing about the amount of evil we have in our world, one can ask if E is worth the price. What ultimate end is worth the price of the Holocaust? Would any sensitive moral person judge that anything is worth this price? Insofar as God thinks the Holocaust was worth the price, we again face the problem of God's morality radically conflicting with ours. Any god who believed that the Holocaust is justified in terms of long-range consequences is not a being who should be worshiped or from whom we can take moral guidance. Not only is he not a morally perfect being in terms of our concept of morality; he is not even a being for whom we can have great respect.

A special case of the all's well that ends well solution is the use of heaven as a justification for all the evil that occurs in this life. On this view anything bad that happens to a person in this life is far outweighed by the life of eternal bliss that will be led in a heavenly paradise. Consequently, the evil that is experienced in this life is justified by what will happen in the next. The trouble with this solution is that it is morally just to compensate persons for the suffering and other evils that have been inflicted on them, but this does not make the act of inflicting suffering and other evils morally permissible. A parent who neglects a child, causing it pain and suffering, has a moral duty to compensate the child in some way. But this compensation is hardly moral justification for the neglect. If God permits evil to occur to His creatures simply on the ground that He will make it up to them in Heaven, then He is not moral and does not deserve to be worshipped.

I must conclude that both versions of the ultimate harmony solutions to the problem of evil fail.

The Degree of Desirability of a Conscious State Theodicy

George Schlesinger has suggested an interesting new theodicy that turns on the concept of the degree of desirability of a conscious state (DDS) of one of God's creatures.[28] According to Schlesinger, DDS is a function not just of the degree to which the creature's wants are satisfied but also of the potential of the creature to experience certain qualities of pleasure, satisfaction, and happiness. However, the potential of one of God's creatures to experience such things is dependent on the kind of creature it is. A human being has the potential for experiencing higher qualities of pleasure, satisfaction, and happiness than an animal, and perhaps some human beings have the potential for experiencing higher qualities of pleasure, satisfaction, and happiness than others. There may, moreover, be some beings in our world that have the potential for experiencing higher pleasure, satisfaction, and happiness than the most intelligent and aesthetically sensitive humans. Even if there are not, there is such a being in some possible world.

According to Schlesinger, one of the universal rules of ethics is:

(R) If everything else is equal, increase DDS as much as possible!

Schlesinger maintains that human beings have an obligation to follow R, since they can. However, a human being usually has a limited ability to increase other people's potential for pleasure, satisfaction, and happiness. For example, one cannot make into a Socrates a person P who is incapable of experiencing higher intellectual satisfactions; indeed, one may only have a limited ability to increase the experience of satisfaction and pleasure that P is capable of. But such limitations, Schlesinger says, are not found in God.

Suppose that Socrates' DDS is x. God has the ability to create a type of being B_1 whose DDS is x^2. He also has the ability to create a being B_2 whose DDS is x^3. And so on. Indeed, there is no limit to the DDS of beings that it is possible for God to create. There is in fact an infinite hierarchy of possible beings with higher and higher DDS. Schlesinger points out, however, that if this is so, then God, unlike humans, has no obligation to follow R. He does not because He logically cannot follow it. He can no more follow R than someone could follow the rule: State the largest number possible.

Now, if this is granted, Schlesinger argues, then "the problem of evil vanishes."[29] God has no moral obligation to increase DDS and consequently no moral obligation to improve the world. Evil is compatible with an all-good and all-powerful God who follows all the moral obligations that it is logically possible for Him to follow.

Does the problem of evil vanish on Schlesinger's theory? It is difficult to see that it does. First of all, one may question whether R is really a universal rule of ethics. Consider the following hypothetical example, a variant of one used by Schlesinger. Suppose I have a girl under my care who has an above-average potential for the appreciation of fine music and art. I am assured by the best medical authorities that a minor operation would raise her aesthetic appreciation to a level beyond that of any human being. Unfortunately, however, after this operation she would be very dissatisfied with almost all artistic performances she hears or sees and almost all objects of art she encounters. Of course, on those rare occasions when she was satisfied, her satisfaction would be at a level well beyond what she would achieve without the operation, when she would enjoy and appreciate most of the performances and objects of art she encountered. Suppose further that she is now indifferent to whether the operation should be performed but that, because of her age, her preference or rather her lack of it cannot be considered informed. Should I, the girl's guardian, have the operation performed on her? One supposes that R would entail that I should, but that I should is far from obvious. Although her DDS may be higher with the operation than without it, it is far from clear that in this case we *should* bring about a higher DDS.

Thus the moral validity of R is not as clear as Schlesinger supposes. In addition, one might argue that even if R is not a rule that God can possibly follow, He can and should follow some rule very similar to R that has intuitive appeal. Although it is not possible to follow the rule, "State the largest possible number," it is possible to follow the rules, "Continue to state larger and larger numbers," and "Continue to state larger and larger numbers, such that if you state N, the next number that you state is N^{10}." By analogy, although it is not logically possible for God to follow R, it is logically possible for God to follow:

R': If everything else is equal, continue to increase DDS each second, such that if DDS is x at time t, DDS is x^{10} at t + 1 seconds.

God might never be able to increase DDS as much as possible, but He would be constantly improving DDS and doing so at greater and greater increments each second. However, as far as we can determine, there is no reason to suppose that things are improving with respect to DDS, let alone improving at greater increments each second. Thus the problem of evil has not vanished.

Schlesinger seems to believe that in order for there to be a problem of evil it must be possible for God to increase DDS as much as possible. As we have just seen, given a modified version of R, namely R', the problem of evil can be formulated without making this assumption. Moreover, as Philip Quinn has shown, still another problem of evil can be generated without Schlesinger's assumption.[30] Quinn points out that given the claim that there is no highest DDS, it is consistent to maintain that for any individual that God might create, there is a best state for it.

Of course, the DDS of human beings would be less than the DDS of beings who are superintelligent and aesthetically sensitive.

Following Quinn, let us define a state as having positive desirability for an individual, just in case it would be better for that individual to be in that state than never to have existed. Quinn argues that there is at least one possible world W where two conditions hold:

(1) Every individual in W occupies a state at least as desirable as it would have occupied in any other world where it could have existed.

(2) Every individual in W occupies one of its states of positive desirability.

Any possible world in which conditions (1) and (2) hold, Quinn calls *maximally desirable relative to its denizens*. Any possible world that satisfies (2) but not (1) he calls *good for its denizens*. Quinn argues that the existence of what seems to be pointless suffering in our world suggests that our world is neither maximally desirable relative to its denizens nor good for its denizens. Yet an all-good, all-powerful God would actualize at least a world good for its denizens and even perhaps a world that is maximally desirable to its denizens if He actualizes any world at all. Quinn concludes that although there may be some solution to the problem of evil, the problem has not vanished as Schlesinger claimed.

In addition to these problems, Schlesinger's solutions entail giving up a traditional view of God.[31] He must assume that God experiences no satisfactions or pleasure, for if God did experience these, then Schlesinger's argument could be used to show that the concept of God is incoherent. Since God is perfect, if He had satisfactions and pleasure, He would have the greatest possible DDS. But Schlesinger has shown that the greatest possible DDS is logically impossible. So God cannot have satisfactions and pleasure. However, on the traditional view God does have satisfactions and pleasure. Consequently, either the concept of God is incoherent or it is not in keeping with what most theists have understood "God" to mean.

I conclude that Schlesinger's DDS theodicy fails.

The Reincarnation Theodicy

Some religious believers have argued that the evils that afflict human beings in their present lives are a result of their evil deeds in past incarnations. This view is characteristic of Eastern religious thought and is by no means confined to theistic religions. For example, Jainism and Buddhism accept the doctrine of reincarnation and the law of Karma, which governs

its operation.[32] Belief in reincarnation and the law of Karma is not confined to Eastern religions, however; indeed, there have been Christian
reincarnationists.[33] Advocates of reincarnation and the law of Karma,
whether Western or Eastern, theistic or nontheistic, must assume certain
controversial views about the relation between body and mind. They
must hold not only that the mind is not identical with the body, but that
a mind does not require the particular body with which it is connected
in this life. A believer in reincarnation must believe that a person is
identified with a mind or soul and has been born countless times in
various bodies.

Although a clear statement of the law of Karma governing rebirth is
difficult to find, what it entails can be simply stated: The world is completely just, since anything good that happens to a person in some life,
such as the present one, is a reward for good actions in an earlier life,
and anything bad that happens to a person is a punishment for bad
actions in an earlier life. The reincarnationist admits that the world
contains what seem like injustices. People are born with physical and
mental handicaps, they suffer from sickness, disease, and natural disasters, they suffer because of the evil inflicted on them by other human
beings. However, the reincarnationist maintains that despite appearances, all these seeming injustices are just. They are punishments for evil
deeds done by the person in some past incarnation.

This theory has a number of serious problems that prevent it from
being an acceptable solution to the problem of evil.

(1) One obvious problem is that its implications are not only absurd
but morally appalling. Paul Edwards has put this objection well:

> It follows from [the law of Karma] that Abraham Lincoln, Jean Jaurès, the
> two Kennedy brothers, and Martin Luther King got no more than they
> deserved when they were assassinated. It equally follows that six million
> Jews exterminated by the Nazis deserved their fate. I will add one more
> outrageous consequence of Karma. Contrary to what almost everyone
> believed and believes, the seven *Challenger* astronauts who perished earlier
> this year were entirely responsible for their own death, and the grief felt
> by millions of people all over the world was quite out of place.[34]

(2) The theory of reincarnation combined with Karma is also morally
empty. No matter what we do, we will have done the morally correct
thing. If we do not help people who are in trouble and they suffer, this
is just. They deserve to suffer because of their bad deeds in a former
incarnation. But if we do help people who are in trouble and they do not
suffer as much as they would have done otherwise, then they did not
deserve to suffer as much as they would have if we had not intervened.[35]

(3) Many believers in the law of Karma do not believe in God, but

even those who do maintain that the law of Karma operates autonomously. This raises the problem of how Karma is administered. How is it decided who is to be punished and who is to be rewarded, and how much? How is it decided who is to be reincarnated and in which body? How are all these decisions coordinated in a large-scale disaster such as the Lisbon earthquake, where thousands died and others benefited? Advocates of reincarnation do not give adequate answers to these questions, although they believe that no mistakes are ever made in the administration of Karma.[36]

(4) It is difficult to see how reincarnation theodicy can be compatible with the findings of science. Reincarnationists often postulate a series of incarnations in human bodies stretching backward forever in time. However, science teaches that human life came into existence relatively recently. Even if one postulates, as some reincarnationists do, that souls can inhabit the bodies of animals or plants, there is still a problem, for science teaches that life came into existence and has not existed forever. Further, reincarnationists who do believe that souls can be reincarnated in animals do not believe that the sequence of biological evolution parallels reincarnation. For example, a person's soul might have been incarnated millions of years ago as a dog and reincarnated only recently as a bird.[37] Moreover, it is difficult to see how the widely accepted scientific belief that animals came before humans in the evolutionary scale can be reconciled with the retributive punishment dispensed by the law of Karma. It would seem grossly unjust to punish Jones, a human being, for the actions of a carnivorous dinosaur millions of years ago when Jones's soul inhabited the dinosaur's body. We ordinarily suppose that animals cannot be blamed and punished for what they do. Reincarnation combined with biological evolution suggests that they can and should be.

(5) Reincarnationists who believe in God have a problem explaining the origin of evil. If people's present suffering is the result of their evil deeds in earlier incarnations, why did God allow the past evil deeds for which they are now being punished?[38] At this point the reincarnationist may fall back on another theodicy, perhaps the free will defense. If so, however, the reincarnationist theodicy will possess all the problems associated with reincarnation and the law of Karma as well as the problems connected with the free will defense.

(6) If free will is assumed and if we understand it in the contracausal sense, another problem arises. Freedom of the will of the contracausal variety makes it even more difficult to understand how the law of Karma is administered. A person exercising free will would seem able to contradict the law of Karma. Suppose that Evans was a saint in a past incarnation. Following the law of Karma, Evans is born into excellent circumstances in this present incarnation. Her body is strong and healthy; her

intelligence is sharp and keen; her disposition is gentle and warm. But Smith, by exercising his free will, can torture Evans and inflict undeserved pain and suffering on her. Thus it is difficult to see how free will, in the sense usually understood by theists, is compatible with the law of Karma. Without freedom of the will, however, it is difficult to see how in past incarnations evil ever originated.

I conclude that the reincarnation theodicy has far too many problems to be taken seriously.

The Contrast Theodicy

Sometimes popular apologists for theism argue that evil is needed in the world as a contrast with good. Without evil, people would have no appreciation or understanding of good. Just as one learns what night is by contrasting it with day, so one learns what good is by contrasting it with bad.

Again there are several problems with this solution. Suppose we grant the need to contrast good with evil in order to understand good. If God is all-powerful, it would seem that He could create us in such a way that we could appreciate and understand good to a high degree without *actually* experiencing evil. If a contrast with evil is necessary, it is not necessary to have knowledge by acquaintance of evil, such as the suffering of a person being tortured. Vicarious and empathic acquaintance is enough.[39] Even now, people with extremely sensitive empathic ability can understand and appreciate the suffering that a torture victim feels, without actually undergoing torture. Thus they can understand and appreciate the good of not being tortured without actually having been tortured. God could have created *all* humans with a high degree of empathic ability. God has already created some humans with the ability to produce imaginative art and literature that depicts evil. By viewing art and reading literature about evil, people created with highly sensitive empathic ability could empathically experience what is depicted and thus learn to appreciate good without experiencing evil.

Even if God could not have accomplished this and had to have humans experience evil to appreciate good, it was not necessary that there be as much evil as we find in the world. For contrast purposes, evil could be on a much smaller scale.

I conclude that contrast theodicy fails.

The Warning Theodicy

Another popular justification of evil is that it is God's method of warning humans to mend their sinful ways. God causes evils such as earthquakes, tidal waves, and hurricanes as a display of his awesome power in order to shock His creatures into following the path of righteousness. It seems that this solution at best would solve the problem of natural evil, not of moral evil. On the most popular defense of moral evil, the free will defense, God does not bring about moral evil; rather, it is due to the misuse of human free will, which God permits for some higher good. But then, it is difficult to see how its existence could be a warning from God.

Is the warning theodicy a plausible solution to the problem of natural evil? One crucial criticism it does not address is that God could warn human beings without causing them harm. We would not think much of a father who warned his children to be good by killing or torturing a few of them if he could warn them in other ways. An all-powerful God could warn people by writing in gold letters in the sky, for instance, that if they do not change their ways, such and such will happen to them. Unlike natural disasters, this sort of warning would be unambiguous in intent, and at the same time it would not harm anyone. Given that He could warn people without harming them, warning them by causing natural disasters seems morally wrong.

The Bible teaches that God sometimes issued verbal warnings before He inflicted great suffering. However, at other times He punished His creatures simply for doing what He had not explicitly commanded. For example, Nadab and Abihu "offered unholy fire before the Lord such as he had not commanded them. And fire came forth and devoured them and they died before the Lord" (Lev. x 1, 2). The Bible does not say that the Lord commanded them *not* to offer unholy fire; it says that He did not command them to do so. Surely an all-powerful God could have warned them that they would die by fire if they offered unholy fire; one would suppose that a completely just God should have done so. In many other places in Scripture, God gives no verbal warning although it would have been easy to do so. Thus He was unhappy with the "wickedness of man" and was sorry He "had ever made man on earth," and because of this He destroyed all life except Noah and his family and the creatures on the ark (Gen. 6). Yet He did not warn people with such words as "I will destroy you all unless you change your wicked ways." Surely He could and should have done so.

Furthermore, even if God has to harm some of His creatures in order to warn them all, it certainly seems likely that an all-powerful God could do so with less disastrous results than we have now. For example, He could bring about a violent hurricane in which only a few people are hurt and, immediately afterward, write in gold letters in the sky that people should reform. Finally, it seems extremely implausible that all natural evils could constitute warnings to human beings. Animals underwent

enormous suffering long before humans existed. Clearly, it could not
have been a warning to them, since they could not have understood
what was happening to them. Further, some human suffering occurs in
relatively private circumstances. Who is warned by the suffering of the
patient slowly dying of cancer in a private hospital room? The doctors
or nurses at the hospital? But they see suffering daily. The family? The
patient may have none. Thus it is difficult in some cases to see who the
recipient of the warning could be.

I conclude that the warning theodicy is inadequate.

Conclusion

The minor theodicies examined in this chapter all have serious problems
and therefore cannot be accepted as adequate solutions to the problem
of evil. Although I have not attempted to cover all the existing minor
theodicies, this work has been done by other critics with the same results.[40]
In earlier chapters I considered the major theodicies and showed that
they were inadequate solutions to the problem of evil. Thus both major
and minor theodicies fail. As I have stressed, these theodicies are the best
efforts that the best theistic minds have been able to develop over the
centuries. Although it would be rash to rule out completely the possibility
that an adequate solution will be discovered in the future, this seems
extremely unlikely.

Conclusion

In Chapters 1 to 10 I maintained that belief in an all-knowing, all-powerful, all-good being who created the universe is not justified. Of course, if the thesis of Chapter 2 that religious language is cognitively meaningless were to be accepted, this book would be much shorter. I could simply have concluded that one is justified not to believe in God but that one is not justified to disbelieve in Him. That is, I could have concluded that negative atheism is justified but positive atheism is not. However, knowing the controversial nature of this thesis, I did not stop. Instead, I assumed for the sake of argument that religious language is not cognitively meaningless. I argued for not believing in God on independent grounds, and in Chapters 11 to 18 I went on to argue for disbelief in God. In brief, then, the conclusion of this book is this: If religious language is cognitively meaningless, not believing in god is justified. There is good reason to think it is meaningless. So not believing in God is justified. However, supposing it is not, then not believing in God is still justified and, in addition, so is disbelief in God.

What follows from this conclusion? If one should not believe that the theistic God exists but perhaps should believe that He does not exist, what does this mean for our society and our way of life? Does it entail radical change for our social world?

To answer this question, it must be clarified. If it is taken to be asking what would happen if my argument is correct but few believe it, of course nothing much would change. Presumably, however, the intent of the question is to ask: What would follow if the thesis of this book became widely accepted? This question is not easy to answer, since the way most people in our society would act if they did not hold theistic beliefs is by no means clear. Human behavior is surely a function of many factors, only one of which is religious conviction. If belief in God were eliminated but other factors came to the fore, things could well be unchanged. It is much easier to say what would *not* happen, or at least what *need* not happen, if the thesis of this book were to become widely accepted.

As argued in the Introduction, there would not necessarily be any deterioration of moral standards. There is no reason to think that atheists and nonbelievers have a lower moral character than believers. Indeed, if there were to be moral deterioration in a population that became atheistic, it could not without further investigation be attributed to a conversion to atheism, for the deterioration might be due to factors having nothing to do with atheistic belief. As we saw in the Introduction, there is no reason to suppose that either moral anarchy or moral relativism would be justified if atheism were accepted. This is not to say that such positions might not become dominant in an atheistic society. But if they did, it would not be because they were necessitated by atheism.

Should one anticipate a decline in religion or church attendance in an atheistic society? Certainly. But the extent to be expected is not clear. Religion is possible without belief in God, even with disbelief in God. If atheism became widespread in our society, new atheistic religions might arise to fill the gap in people's lives, or old atheistic religions such as Jainism might gain converts. Moreover, it is not only possible but likely that some people would continue to attend theistic religious services and to be members of theistic churches even if they did not believe. To some people church membership meets an important social need, and to other people religious ceremonies have significant aesthetic value. The teachings of theistic religions can provide moral insights to atheistic participants.

One might worry that in a society dominated by atheists there would be diminished freedom of religion for theists. Would not atheists control the seats of power and try to prevent the theistic minority from practicing their religion? Although this unfortunate situation could come to pass in an atheistic society, there is no necessity that it would. There can be complete religious freedom for theists in an atheistic society—one in which the vast majority of people are atheists and atheists hold political and social power. Even positive atheism is compatible with religious tolerance, for to be tolerant of someone's beliefs does not mean that one thinks they are true or even possibly true.[1] Indeed, atheists can believe that theists hold views that are not only false but necessarily false, and they can be perfectly tolerant of theistic religious practices in the sense of never interfering with them. An atheistic society with religious tolerance and freedom could have no laws against theistic practices. Indeed, it could forbid discrimination based on theistic beliefs and could rigorously enforce such prohibitions while promoting harmonious social relations between atheists and theists.

Thus an atheistic society need not be similar to that of the USSR. According to unofficial estimates, only about 10 percent of the Soviet people have some religion, the largest proportion being members of the Russian Orthodox Church. In the USSR, so-called scientific atheism has been officially sanctioned by the government and has become the functional equivalent of a state religion. The Institute for Scientific Atheism, a division of the Soviet Academy of Social Science whose headquarters are in Moscow, is a thinktank of 40 scholars. It carries on research, coordinates the activities of 51 local Houses of Scientific Atheism, publishes a learned journal and a popular magazine, and designs the curricula for required university courses on scientific atheism. Although Russian scientific atheism maintains no shrines, conducts no services, and has no priesthood, a church of sorts seems to have developed. For example, marriages are performed in state-run wedding palaces by specially trained officials who function as a sort of secular clergy. There are also state-administered ceremonies at baby palaces, crematoria, and schools. These rites of passage seem to have taken the place of religious ceremonies performed in churches.

Although according to the constitution of the USSR there is complete freedom of religion, the teachings of scientific atheism are broadcast on state-controlled television and radio, whereas the teachings of religions are not. Moreover, churches operate under strict governmental control and there is evidence of severe persecution of minority religions, such as Jehovah's Witnesses and Seventh-Day Adventists. It is also well documented that Jews have been discriminated against by the government. However, despite several anti-religious campaigns directed against the Russian Orthodox Church and the confiscation of many of its properties, it seems to have occupied a privileged position in the USSR since World War II, when Stalin made a truce with its leaders in order to further national unity.[2]

When atheists are the vast majority in a society, they need not have their views sanctioned by the state. There need be no institutes of atheism sponsored by the government and no secular clergy to perform ceremonies. Religious teachings need not be kept off the airwaves by the government. Religious minorities need not be persecuted. In short, a society of atheists is quite compatible with the separation of church—even an atheistic church—and state as well as with religious freedom.

There is indeed theoretical backing for allowing freedom of religion to theists in an atheistic society. Consider, for example, John Rawls's scheme in *A Theory of Justice*.[3] Rawls attempts to derive general principles of justice by arguing that people in the "original position" would choose them. This derivation, if successful, provides a justification for these principles, since the conditions defining the original position are supposed to be fair and reasonable. Rawls argues that, assuming that economic development and standards of living meet a minimum level, parties in the original position would choose the following principles:[4]

First principle: Each person is to have an equal right to the most
   extensive total system of equal liberty compatible with a similar
   system for all.
Second principle: Social and economic inequalities are to be arranged
   so that they are both:
   (a) reasonably expected to be to everyone's advantage; and
   (b) attached to positions and offices open to all.

Rawls says that these principles of justice would be chosen by people
in a particular hypothetical circumstance. We are to imagine a group of
rational people who are concerned to advance their own interests and
who must agree on a set of moral principles to govern their society.
However, we must imagine that they make their decision behind a veil
of ignorance; that is to say, while ignorant of their social position, wealth,
age, sex, race, concept of good, and the particular circumstances of their
society. Under these circumstances, Rawls argues, they would choose the
two principles of justice listed above if the only alternatives available to
them were these and other standard ethical principles—for example,
utilitarian ones.

Although Rawls is not explicitly concerned with religious freedom,[5] his
scheme allows for it. One must assume that behind the veil of ignorance,
parties in the original position would not know their own religious beliefs.
Nor would they know the number of atheists and theists in their society.
Such ignorance would prevent parties to the original position from choosing principles of justice that gave unfair advantage to atheists in an
atheistic society.[6] Presumably, then, the first principle of justice would
include extensive religious liberty for everyone, even if the society turned
out to be dominated by atheism. This is not to say that religious intoler-
ance would not be a problem in such a society. Atheists, no less than
theists, might want to suppress what they did not believe was true or what
they thought was dangerous. However, there is no necessity for this
suppression, and there are good moral reasons for avoiding it.

So far I have said what would not, or at least need not, be the case if
atheism became widespread. But what would likely be some of the actual
changes? Although I offer the following predictions, they must remain
tentative and speculative. Superficially, I would expect some of the more
obvious symbols and trappings of our present theistic society to fade and
disappear. For example, I would expect that our currency would no
longer be imprinted with "In God we trust," that Christmas and Easter
would not longer be national holidays, that a prayer would no longer be
offered at presidential inaugural ceremonies, that blue laws would become a thing of the past, and that prayers in public schools would no
longer be a serious issue. As for the public media and the popular culture,

I would also expect to see changes. I would expect TV evangelism and the billion-dollar industry it has spawned to disappear and the Sunday religious services broadcast nationally and locally on TV and radio to diminish. I would anticipate that the Pope or Mother Teresa would no longer be front-page news, that many religious bookstores would close, that Bibles would no longer be found in hotel rooms, that expressions such as "God bless you" and expletives such as "God damn it" would disappear from our language.

On a less superficial level, surely the political power of traditional churches and of the religious right would be greatly reduced. With this would come more liberalized laws concerning abortion, divorce, homosexuality, and birth control. Theism-based morality would have few adherents, and this in turn would affect our view on moral education. Although the Bible would be the source of some moral guidance, it would be read critically and would no longer be thought of as divinely inspired. Theistic religious leaders would no longer be looked to for moral guidance unless their moral insights did not purport to be based on revelation.

If atheism became the dominant view throughout the world, one would anticipate vast changes in many areas. For example, there would probably be fewer wars and less violence than there is now. In many places in the world today, such as Northern Ireland and the Middle East, war and violence are at least partially based on religious bigotry and hatred.[7] The birth rate would also drop in many countries, since religious objections to contraception would no longer prevail. Further, if atheism was widely held throughout the world, one would anticipate the secularization even of societies where religious fundamentalism is now a way of life. Church and state would probably become separate in countries in which they have traditionally been interwoven, not because of any constitutional guarantees but because of diminished Church power. This in turn would bring about profound political changes. However, there is also the danger that if atheism became widespread, as it has in the Soviet Union and in other countries of the world,[8] it would become the functional equivalent of a state religion with suppression of theistic minorities. As I argued above, this is not a necessary consequence of widespread atheism; but it is of course a possibility.

However, I do not anticipate the spread of atheism in the immediate future. Indeed, there is good reason to suppose that theistic religions, especially of the fundamentalist variety, are gaining ground not only in the United States but throughout the world.[9] The reasons for this are not completely clear. Paul Kurtz, in an interesting article, discusses what he calls a transcendental temptation, "a tendency to believe in a unseen, hidden, supernormal world that transcends the natural world of science and controls our destinies."[10] Kurtz suggests that this temptation is "both biological and social in origin and function" and maintains that it can be overcome by scientific investigation and critical skeptical rationality. Consequently, he concludes that this temptation is not deterministically genetic.[11]

I venture to hope that this volume will make a small contribution in combating the transcendental temptation, if it exists, and in helping to stem the tide of theistic religion. However, as I stressed in the Introduction, my aim—not a practical one—is merely to provide good reasons for being an atheist—that is, to show that atheism is a rational position and belief in God is not.

Appendix

Atheism Defined and Contrasted

Atheism Defined

In the first part of this appendix I define atheism and in the second I contrast atheism with other 'isms' and movements that are sometimes associated with it.

ATHEISM POSITIVE AND NEGATIVE

If you look up "atheism" in a dictionary, you will probably find it defined as the belief that there is no God. Certainly many people understand atheism in this way. Yet many atheists do not, and this is not what the term means if one considers it from the point of view of its Greek roots. In Greek "a" means "without" or "not" and "theos" means "god."[1] From this standpoint an atheist would simply be someone without a belief in God, not necessarily someone who believes that God does not exist. According to its Greek roots, then, atheism is a negative view, characterized by the absence of belief in God.[2]

Well-known atheists of the past such as Baron d'Holbach (1770), Richard Carlile (1826), Charles Southwell (1842), Charles Bradlaugh (1876), and Anne Besant (1877) have assumed or have explicitly characterized atheism in the negative sense of absence of belief in God.[3] Furthermore, in the twentieth century George H. Smith, in *Atheism: The Case Against God* (1979), maintains, "An atheist is not primarily a person who *believes* that god does *not* exist; rather he does *not believe* in the existence of god."[4] Antony Flew, in "The Presumption of Atheism" (1972), understands an atheist as someone who is not a theist.[5] Gordon Stein, in *An Anthology of Atheism and Rationalism* (1980), says an atheist "is a person *without* a belief in God."[6] A recent pamphlet entitled "American Atheists: An Introduction" says an atheist "has no belief system" concerning supernatural agencies.[7] Another recent pamphlet entitled "American Atheists: A History" defines American atheism as "the philosophy of persons who are free from theism."[8]

Still there is a popular meaning of "atheism" according to which an atheist not simply holds no belief in the existence of a god or gods but believes that there is no god or gods. This use of the term should not be overlooked. To avoid confusion, let us call this *positive atheism,* and the type of atheism derived from the Greek root and held by the atheistic thinkers surveyed above let us call *negative atheism.* Clearly, positive atheism is a special case of negative atheism: Someone who is a positive atheist is by necessity a negative atheist, but not conversely.

In my usage, positive atheism is positive only in the sense that it refers to a positive belief—the belief that there is no god or gods. It is positive in contrast to negative atheism, which has no such positive belief. Of course, in another sense that is not relevant here, what I have called positive atheism is more negative than what I have called negative atheism. Positive atheism denies that one or more gods exist; negative atheism does not.

Atheism Broad and Narrow

If positive atheists disbelieve in god or gods and negative atheists have no belief in a god or gods, what it is that they either disbelieve or have no belief about? No general definition of god is attempted here,[9] but it is useful to distinguish different concepts of god that have played a role in the traditional controversies and debates. In modern times, theism has for the most part come to mean a belief in a personal god who takes an active interest in the world and has given a special revelation to humans. So understood, theism is contrasted with deism, the belief in a god that is not based on revelation but on evidence from nature. Deism has also come to be associated with belief in a god that is remote from the world and not intimately involved with its concerns. Theism is also contrasted with polytheism, the belief in more than one god, and with pantheism, the belief that God is identical with nature.

A negative atheist, if we understand theism in the way it has been understood in modern times, would simply be a person without a belief in a personal god. Atheism, so understood, would be compatible with deism, polytheism, and pantheism. However, this construction of atheism seems to conflict not only with the original Greek meaning, but also with what past and present professed atheists have meant. Consequently, I use "negative atheism" in its most fundamental sense to mean an absence of belief in any god or gods, not just the absence of belief in a personal god. Let us call this *the broad sense of negative atheism.*[10]

Although this broad sense is what most atheists have meant by atheism, many philosophical debates between atheists and nonatheists in Western society have been over the question of whether the Hebrew–Christian God exists. In particular, the debates have been over whether there is a personal being who is omniscient, omnipotent, and completely good and who created heaven and earth. Thus although the broad sense seems to capture what atheists have usually intended by atheism, it does not capture well what the traditional debate has been about. For this it is necessary to distinguish a *narrow sense of negative atheism,* according to which an atheist is without a belief in a personal being who is omniscient, omnipotent, and completely good and who created heaven and earth.

This distinction between a broad and narrow sense of atheism can be applied to positive as well as negative atheism. A *positive atheist in the broad sense* is a person who disbelieves that there is any god or gods and a *positive atheist in the narrow sense* is a person who disbelieves that there is a personal being who is omniscient, omnipotent, and completely good and who created heaven and earth.

In a way, the above characterization of atheism is misleading since it masks the complexity and variety of positions an atheist can hold. A person can hold different atheistic positions with respect to different concepts of God—for example, an anthropomorphic finite god and a nonanthropomorphic infinite god. Thus a person might maintain that there is good reason to suppose that anthropomorphic gods such as Zeus do not exist and thus be a positive atheist with respect to Zeus and similar gods. However, this person could maintain that Paul Tillich's concept of God is meaningless and thus be a negative atheist only with respect to Tillich's God.[11]

In addition, people can and often do hold different atheistic positions with respect to different conceptions of a theistic God. For example, an atheist might disbelieve that the theistic God of Aquinas exists and yet maintain that with respect to the theistic God of some Christian mystics such as St. Teresa, the sentence "God exists" is meaningless. Such a person would be a positive atheist with respect to Aquinas's God and only a negative atheist with respect St. Teresa's God.

ATHEISM AND ALIENATED THEISM

Atheism, whether positive or negative, broad or narrow, should be clearly distinguished from another view that is sometimes confused with it. Some people have rejected the moral authority associated with a god or gods, or perhaps have rejected a god or gods as objects of worship, admiration, and the like. Consider Ivan Karamazov's conversation with his younger brother Alyosha in *The Brothers Karamazov*. In discussing the suffering of children being reconciled in a higher harmony, Ivan says:

> I don't want harmony. From the love of humanity I don't want it. I would rather be left with the unavenged suffering. I would rather remain with my unavenged suffering and unsatisfied indignation, *even if I were wrong*. Besides, too high a price is asked for harmony; it's beyond our means to pay so much to enter on it. And so I hasten to give back my entrance ticket, and if I am an honest man I am bound to give it back as soon as possible. And that I am doing. It's not God that I don't accept, Alyosha, only I most respectfully return Him the ticket.[12]

Some existential philosophers have proposed views that come close to this rejection of a god's or gods' moral authority. For instance, Sartre, a professed atheist, suggested at times that even if God exists, the only thing that matters is for people to acknowledge their total freedom; humans are beings, according to Sartre, who in every circumstance will their total freedom. God is irrelevant to moral choice and its attendant anguish.[13] Thus in Sartre's play *The Flies*, Orestes says to Jupiter: "What have I to do with you or you with me? We shall glide past each other, like ships in a river without touching. You are God and I am free, each of us is alone, and our anguish is akin."[14]

Whether Orestes' position should be called atheism is doubtful. Perhaps a better name for his position and Ivan Karamazov's is *alienated theism*.[15] They both believe in God but reject part of the moral authority that usually goes with such a belief.[16]

Atheism Distinguished and Contrasted

How is atheism related to isms often contrasted or associated with it? How is it related to agnosticism? humanism? communism? naturalism? rationalism? positivism? How is atheism related to movements such as ethical culture and freethought? In any careful justification and defense of atheism it is necessary to answer these questions.

ATHEISM AND AGNOSTICISM

In common understanding, agnosticism is contrasted with atheism. In the popular sense an agnostic neither believes nor disbelieves that God exists, while an atheist disbelieves that God exists. However, this common contrast of agnosticism with atheism will hold only if one assumes that atheism means positive atheism. In the popular sense, agnosticism is compatible with negative atheism. Since negative atheism by definition simply means not holding any concept of God, it is compatible with neither believing nor disbelieving in God.

Putting aside the current popular sense of the term, "agnosticism" was coined by T. H. Huxley in 1869. According to Huxley, "Agnosticism is not a creed but a method, the essence of which lies in the vigorous application of a single principle. Positively the principle may be expressed as, in matters of the intellect, follow your reason as far as it can carry you without other considerations. And negatively, in matters of the intellect, do not pretend the conclusions are certain that are not demonstrated or demonstrable. It is wrong for a man to say he is certain of the objective truth of a proposition unless he can produce evidence which logically justifies that certainty."[17]

It should be clear that agnosticism understood in this way does not entail atheism even of a negative sort, although it is compatible with it. Indeed, it could be compatible with theism, since some theists have argued that one can demonstrate the existence of God. Huxley's agnosticism would entail negative atheism only if the existence or nonexistence of God was not capable of proof and it was assumed that one should not believe or disbelieve something unless it was capable of proof or disproof.

Certainly some agnostics have intended more by agnosticism than simply a methodology. On this view an agnostic is someone who neither believes nor disbelieves that a god or gods exist since their existence or nonexistence cannot be proved by reason. Agnosticism so understood is identical with one type of rationalism considered below[18] and is compatible with a negative atheism in which belief or disbelief in God should be based on reason.

According to some dictionary definitions, an agnostic is a person who claims one cannot know whether god exists or not. This view is compatible with theism, since a theist need not base this belief on knowledge. Belief may be based on a leap of faith. So unless one assumes that one ought not to believe something unless one can have knowledge of it, agnosticism in this sense is compatible with either theism or positive atheism.

ATHEISM AND SKEPTICISM

In one sense of the term a skeptic is someone who questions whether one can have knowledge of anything. A religious skeptic, in particular, questions whether one can have knowledge about religious claims such as that God exists.[19] Understood in this way, skepticism is compatible with theism and does not entail negative atheism. For theists might not claim to have knowledge that God exists; they might say only that they have faith that God exists.

However, sometimes "religious skepticism" is used in a narrower sense to mean not only that knowledge of the existence of God is impossible but also that one ought to suspend one's belief concerning the existence of God because of this lack of knowledge. Skepticism so understood entails negative atheism and is identical with one type of agnosticism considered above.

ATHEISM AND RATIONALISM

The term "rationalism" has been used over the years to refer to several outlooks and systems of ideas.[20] In philosophy it is often contrasted with empiricism. In this usage it refers to a philosophical outlook that stresses the power of *a priori* reason to arrive at truth about the world.[21] This sense of rationalism has little historical connection to atheism, if only because the famous philosophical rationalists—Descartes, Spinoza, and Leibniz—believed in God and thought they could prove the existence of God by reason. To be sure, Spinoza can be classified as an atheist in the narrow sense defined above, but Descartes and Leibniz cannot.

Rationalism in theology, in contrast to philosophy, is used to refer to rational criticism directed against the allegedly revealed truth of the Bible. In particular the term refers to the doctrine of a 1740–1840 school of German theologians that had an important influence on biblical criticism.[22] The connection is certainly closer between this sort of rationalism and atheism than between philosophical rationalism and atheism, but it is by no means a necessary one. Criticism of the Bible as the revealed word of God can lead to at least the negative variety of atheism, but it need not, for theologians can criticize and reject Scripture and yet continue to believe in God on nonscriptural grounds.

Perhaps the best known use of "rationalism" is as a popular rather than a technical term. In this sense it stands for an anti-religious and anti-clerical movement that stressed historical and scientific arguments against theism.[23] It is in this sense that various atheist societies and presses use the term. For example, the Rationalist Press Association defines "rationalism" as "the mental attitude which unreservedly accepts the supremacy of reason and aims at establishing a system of philosophy and ethics verifiable by experience and independent of all arbitrary assumptions or authority."[24] It is noteworthy that the Rationalist Press Association does not mean by "reason" what philosophical rationalists do: It is contrasting reason and revelation or reason and appeal to authority, not reason and experience.

Still, this use of "rationalism" leaves open the question as to whether a rationalist is an atheist, for a deist is a rationalist in this sense of the term. To be sure, the societies and presses that have used "rationalist" in their titles have in general been atheist at least in the negative sense of the term specified above. They have not only believed that reason should be used (in contrast to revelation and authority) in religious contexts but they have also thought that if reason was used, it would not establish that any gods exist.

This is made clear, for example, in the writings of Charles Watts, former publisher of the Rationalist Press Association. In a chapter of his *Collected Works* entitled "The Meaning of Rationalism," Watts says, "The Rationalist does not deny the existence of God or a future life. Upon such hope it is not thought rational to dogmatise. Where knowledge is absent, to either affirm or deny is sheer presumption."[25] Thus Watts maintains that by the use of reason one cannot conclude that God either does or does not exist. On this interpretation a rationalist is a person who believes that only reason (in contrast to revelation) should be used to establish belief about a god or gods but that reason cannot determine whether a god or gods do exist. In short, Watts believes that the use of reason leads to negative atheism in the broad sense. Thus rationalism in this usage has a methodological and a substantive component.

ATHEISM AND NATURALISM

According to Arthur Danto, naturalism is a "species of philosophical monism, according to which, whatever exists or happens is *natural* in the sense of being susceptible to explanation through methods which, although paradigmatically exemplified in the natural sciences, are continuous from domain to domain of objects and events. Hence, naturalism is polemically defined as repudiating the view that there exists or could exist any entities or events which lie, in principle, beyond the scope of scientific explanation."[26]

Naturalism is compatible with materialism but should not be confused with it. According to Danto, naturalism is compatible with a variety of rival ontologies, and a heterogeneous group of thinkers identify themselves as naturalists: dualists, idealists, materialists, atheists, and non-atheists.

Now, in order not to be at least a negative atheist and yet to be a naturalist, a person would have to believe in the existence of a god or gods that can be explained by the methods of science. Such a god or gods would be a part or the whole of the natural order. Certainly this view is not common today. Most religious thinkers suppose that God is a supernatural being transcending the natural order.

Yet such a naturalistic view of a god or gods has been advocated. John Dewey, for example, defines God as "the unity of all ideal ends arousing us to desire and action."[27] Such a unity is surely explainable by scientific method and is part of the natural order. Auguste Comte developed an organized religion, completely within a naturalistic framework, in which the object of worship was humanity. Comte sometimes referred to humanity as the supreme being.[28] Again, such a notion of God or a supreme being is compatible with naturalism. Other philosophers, among them Spinoza, identified God with nature itself. Such pantheistic views may well be compatible with naturalism insofar as nature itself is explainable by scientific method. Thus the acceptance of naturalism does not exclude belief in a god or gods, interpreted in a nonsupernatural way.

However, belief in a god or gods is usually given a supernatural interpretation. Most of the famous atheists of history could well believe that God exists if God only meant what Dewey meant by this term. This suggests that great confusion would result by defining God along Deweyian or other naturalistic lines. So it may be maintained that Danto's claim that naturalism is compatible with nonatheism is true only if "god" is understood in a most peculiar and misleading way.

In any case, atheism does not entail naturalism. Certain Eastern religions such as Jainism are atheistic in the sense that they do not assume the existence of an all-knowing, all-powerful, all-good God, and yet the world view presented in these religions is not clearly naturalistic. In Jainism the law of Karma plays an important role. It is far from clear that such a law can be considered to be explainable by scientific method.

ATHEISM AND POSITIVISM

Positivism, a doctrine associated with Auguste Comte (1798–1857), maintains that the highest form of knowledge is the mere description of observable phenomena. Comte based this doctrine on the evolutionary "law of three stages." In this scheme the history of each science goes through three inevitable and irreversible stages. In the theological stage everything is explained in terms of a will and a purpose similar to human will and purpose. At first, humans believed that each object has a will of its own (animism). Later they believed that gods imposed their wills on objects (polytheism). In the most advanced phase of theological thinking they believed that one God imposed His will on objects (monotheism). In the metaphysical stage, things were explained by things-in-themselves and by impersonal forces that operated behind appearances. Explanations in terms of will and purpose play no role. However, in the positivistic stage science forsakes all explanatory schemes that appeal to unobservable entities. The object of scientific inquiry is simply the study of the laws of succession and resemblance.[29]

The view of science developed in Comte's positivistic stage of science was elaborated and defended by Ernst Mach (1838–1916), an Austrian physicist and philosopher of science. Mach argued that science aims at the most economical descriptions of appearance; no hidden entities or causes are postulated. Atoms and other seemingly unobservable entities are treated as mere *façons de parler*.[30]

Clearly such views would entail at least negative atheism unless God was treated as Mach treated atoms, as a mere *façon de parler*. However, atheism certainly does not entail positivism. Of the atheists who have rejected positivistic restrictions on scientific explanations, one contemporary example is Michael Scriven, who has vigorously defended atheism as well as the explanatory value of unobservable entities.[31] Further, some atheistic religions are not positivistic. For example, metaphysical entities such as souls are postulated in Jainism.

Logical positivism is a philosophical movement primarily associated with the Vienna Circle of the 1920s, whose most famous members were Moritz Schlick, Rudolf Carnap, Otto Neurath, and Friedrich Waismann. Carl G. Hempel and Hans Reichenbach in Berlin and later A. J. Ayer in England also came to be identified with the movement.[32] The basic tenet of logical positivism was that a statement was meaningful if and only if it was one of logic or mathematics or was verifiable by the empirical methods of science. Given this criterion of meaningfulness, all statements of metaphysics and theology were declared to be meaningless. In particular, both the statements "God exists" and "God does not exist" were deemed meaningless. Consequently, it follows that logical positivists were negative but not positive atheists.

Logical positivists tended to give a noncognitive account of ethical statements. They argued that statements such as "One ought to be kind to people" were neither true nor false and were not used to state facts; ethical language had another function or use. On one account, for example, ethical sentences were used to express emotions and influence others to adopt one's point of view. Some philosophers sympathetic to the tenets of logical positivism attempted to give an account of religious discourse along similar lines; that is, they have argued that statements about God do not assert any fact but have another function. Richard Braithwaite, for example, has maintained that religious statements should be interpreted as expressing a commitment to a certain moral way of life that is associated with certain parables and stories.[33] This attempt to make religious discourse acceptable to the tenets of logical positivism closely parallels Dewey's attempt to make religion compatible with naturalism, and it has similar problems: The interpretation distorts religion discourse and may be more confusing than helpful. However, there is a crucial difference between Dewey's naturalistic reinterpretation of religion and Braithwaite's noncognitive interpretation of religious discourse. A Deweyian naturalist could believe that God exists if God were understood along the lines Dewey suggests. Braithwaite's reinterpretation does not allow logical positivists to have a belief about God, however. It simply allows logical positivists to use religious language.

ATHEISM AND HUMANISM

The term "humanism" refers to a number of different movements of thought. In general it refers to any view in which interest in human welfare is central. It is thus opposed to views that emphasize otherworldly concerns and deemphasize secular problems. Certainly, in this general sense one could be a humanist and yet not be an atheist. Deists, for example, may well stress human welfare over otherworldly considerations.

More narrowly, humanism refers to the revival of classical learning in the Renaissance as opposed to merely ecclesiastical studies.[34] Representing a break with an authoritarian, sterile intellectual method and a turning to Greek and Latin writers as a source of inspiration and guidance, humanism has sometimes been considered just a chapter in the history of literature, but it was an attempt to find a more important place for humanity in the secular world. Since many of the most famous humanists in this movement were Christians, humanism in this sense cannot be considered atheistic.

Humanism also refers to a modern literary movement, led in America by Irving Babbitt, Paul Elmer More, and Norman Foerster, which opposed the extreme emphasis on vocational education and recommended a return to classical liberal education in the humanities.[35] Clearly, a humanist in this sense may or may not be an atheist.

Religious humanism is a modern movement that maintains that the religious way of life should be understood purely in terms of human purposes and goals. Otherworldly considerations are completely excluded. This movement of thought has been associated with naturalism and with the importance of scientific method in human affairs. Indeed, some scholars have argued that one cannot be a humanist without being a naturalist. However, other writers have maintained that being a humanist only excludes being a theist.[36]

In their attempt to found a religion on human purposes and goals, humanists such as Comte have suggested elaborate humanistic ceremonies and rituals. Others, such as Dewey, have stressed the importance of reinterpreting the religious dimension of life in naturalistic terms. Some of these latter have redefined God in naturalistic terms, while other humanists have avoided this sort of redefinition.[37]

In a 1983 announcement, the Academy of Humanism said "humanism" refers to "a point of view that rejects supernatural and occult explanations of the Universe and focuses on the use of reason and science in life and seeks to encourage the moral growth and ethical development of the individual, based on experience."[38] On this recent account, being a humanist seems to entail being an atheist unless a naturalistic interpretation of "God" *à la* Dewey is given. However, leading members of the academy have denied that humanism so construed is a religion.[39]

Other humanists have viewed humanism as a religion, but they have not been atheistic, at least in the broad sense. These thinkers have argued that belief in a god is not vital to religion. Thus the 1933 Humanist Manifesto, representing the views of a group of left-wing Unitarian ministers and university professors, maintained that religion "consists of those actions, purposes, and experiences which are humanly significant."[40] One could be a nonatheist, at least in the broad sense of the term, and uphold the 15 tenets of humanism specified in this manifesto.

In a recent statement put out by the American Humanist Association entitled "What Is Humanism?" nothing is said explicitly about not believing in God, but humanists are said to make no claims about transcendent knowledge, to reject arbitrary faith, revelation, and altered states of consciousness, and to recognize that there is no compelling evidence for a separable soul. This view may or may not be compatible with belief in God. On the other hand, in "The Humanist Philosophy in Perspective," published in *The Humanist,* the official publication of the American Humanist Association, Frederick Edwards, the organization's national administrator, maintains that in the light of the findings of astronomy, "we find it curious that, in the absence of direct evidence, religious thinkers can conclude that the universe or some creative power beyond the universe is concerned with our well-being or future. From all appearances, it seems more logical to conclude that it is only we who are concerned for our well-being and future."[41]

Just as one can be a religious humanist without being an atheist, one can be an atheist without being a religious humanist. As I have mentioned, there are atheistic religions. Some of these religions could hardly be called humanistic in the sense that they stress secular problems and social reforms. For example, the supreme object in Jainism is to escape from the fetters of Karma, which means, in effect, for the soul to escape from the body and the cycle of birth and rebirth, and to reach salvation or Nirvana. Nothing could be farther, it would seem, from the spirit of the Humanist Manifesto or other modern statements of humanists.

ATHEISM AND COMMUNISM

In its most general sense, communism is a system in which land, buildings, implements, and goods are held in common. There is no private property; property is owned by the community.[42] Given this understanding of communism, there is no necessary connection between atheism and communism. Indeed, many proposed communist societies have been based on theistic views of the world. For example, the Apostolic Brethren of the fourteenth century were communists. Further, there have been atheists who were vigorously anti-communist. For example, in contemporary times the libertarian thinker Ayn Rand has expounded atheism as well as militant capitalism.[43]

Perhaps the close connection between atheism and communism in popular thought is based on a confusion between the Marx–Engels brand of communism and communism in general. Marx and Engels were indeed atheists—positive atheists—and their anti-religious views were an important part of their revolutionary program. Religion, according to Marx, distorted people's self-awareness, because their self-awareness was based on a view of society that was itself distorted. Religion was the opium—the painkiller—of the suffering masses. The cure was for people to free themselves from the life that made them crave this opium. The way to free themselves was to uproot the organization of society by social revolution.[44]

Millions of people today claim to be Marxists and yet believe in God. Whether they are, strictly speaking, correct is not clear. Much depends on what one means by "being a Marxist." If being a Marxist entails embracing all of Marx and Engels's views, one cannot be a Marxist without being an atheist. But there are many schools of Marxist thought, and it might well be possible to accept a large part of Marx and Engels's doctrine without accepting their analysis of religion. If accepting a large part of their doctrine makes one a Marxist, one could indeed be a Marxist and yet not be an atheist.

Furthermore, even if one accepts all of Marx and Engels' views, it would be possible to interpret religion and the concept of God along naturalistic lines, making belief in God compatible with Marx and Engels' analysis. After all, Marx and Engels understood belief in God in a traditional supernatural way. If one followed the naturalistic lines suggested by Comte and Dewey, and identified God with the final stage of communism, the classless society, belief in God might be a stimulus to social revolution instead of an opium. As far as I know, no Marxist has attempted to reinterpret religion along these Deweyian or Comtian lines. The problem with this sort of naturalistic reinterpretation of God has already been mentioned: the use of the term "God" may be more misleading than helpful.

ATHEISM AND THE FREETHOUGHT MOVEMENT

A freethinker is generally understood to be a person who arrives at conclusions, especially in religious matters, by reason and not by authority. Although it had been used before,[45] the term "freethinker" came into general use after the publication in 1713 of Anthony Collins's *Discourse of Freethinking Occasioned by the Rise and Growth of a Sect Called Freethinkers.* Associations of freethinkers took different forms in different countries. In England the association was closely linked to deism but did not break completely with Christianity. In other countries the break was more extreme. Voltaire, a freethinker, broke all connections with Christianity; the encyclopedists, also considered freethinkers, broke with all religion. In the United States the term "freethinkers" came to be associated with organizations such as the American Association for the Advancement of Atheism, American Atheists, Freedom from Religion Foundation, and United Secularists of America.[46]

In general the term "freethinker" is very close, if not identical, in meaning to one of the senses of "rationalist" defined above. Thus being a freethinker does not entail being an atheist even in the negative sense. In can be and historically has been compatible with deism.

ATHEISM AND THE ETHICAL CULTURE MOVEMENT

The Society for Ethical Culture was started in 1876 by Felix Adler. Based on the conviction that morality need not rest on religious dogma, the new movement adopted the motto "deed rather than creed" and at once undertook practical and philanthropic work such as free kindergartens and tenement house reforms. Maintaining that Judaism and Christianity were wrong to make ethics dependent on religious dogma, Adler based the organization on Immanuel Kant's ethical principle that human beings are ends-in-themselves. He proposed three goals for the society: (1) sexual purity, (2) devoting surplus income to the improvement of the working class, and (3) continued intellectual development. Although the movement spread from New York to other major cities in the United States and to other parts of the world, in terms of the number of members it was never a large movement. Even at the peak of its popularity the society never had more than about 6,000 members in the United States.[47]

Adler intended to found a religion based on fervent devotion to the highest moral ideals. The society conducted Sunday services as well as marriage and funeral ceremonies. However, it remained neutral toward the existence of a god or gods. Thus membership in the society was not contingent on being an atheist even in the negative sense. Although undoubtedly there were many in the ranks of the Society for Ethical Culture, there were nonatheists as well. There is, then, no necessary relation between atheism and the ethical culture movement.

Conclusion

I have distinguished several varieties of atheism and have distinguished atheism in its various forms from other isms that have tended to be associated with it. Since this is a book on atheism, I have not been concerned with these other isms. But what senses of atheism were most important for our purpose? In view of the fact that the controversy between atheists and nonatheists in Western society has usually been about the question of whether an all-good, all-knowing, all-powerful being exists, there was good reason to limit the discussion to atheism in the narrow sense. In addition, it is impossible to criticize in one volume all the views of God that people have held. There are so many different senses of "god" that a detailed appraisal of the disbelief or nonbelief in God in all these senses would fill volumes.

Notes
and
Index

NOTES

Introduction

1. See, for example, James Thrower, *A Short History of Western Atheism* (Buffalo, N.Y.: Prometheus Books, 1971); J. M. Robertson, *A History of Free Thought, Ancient and Modern, to the Period of the French Revolution,* 2 vols. (London: Watts, 1936); J. M. Robertson, *A History of Free Thought in the Nineteenth Century,* 2 vols. (London: Watts, 1929); David Tribe, *100 Years of Free Thought* (London: Elek Books, 1967); Edward Royle, *Radicals, Secularists and Republicans: Popular Freethought in Britain 1866–1915* (Manchester: Manchester University Press, 1980); Samuel P. Putnam, *Four Hundred Years of Freethought* (New York: Truth Seeker, 1894); John Edwin McGee, *A History of the British Secular Movement* (Girard, Kans.: Haldeman-Julius Publications, 1948).

2. Angelo Juffras, "Unbelief in the Ancient World," *The Encyclopedia of Unbelief,* ed. Gordon Stein (Buffalo, N.Y.: Prometheus Books, 1985), vol. 1, pp. 16–25; Thrower, *Short History of Western Atheism,* chaps. 2 and 3.

3. David Berman, "Unbelief During the Enlightenment," *Encyclopedia of Unbelief,* vol. 1, pp. 164–169; Thrower, *Short History of Western Atheism,* chap. 8.

4. Thrower, *Short History of Western Atheism,* chap. 6.

5. See, for example, the articles on unbelief in literature in *Encyclopedia of Unbelief.*

6. See, for example, the articles on unbelief in various countries of the world in *Encyclopedia of Unbelief.*

7. *The World Christian Encyclopedia,* ed. David Barrett (New York: Oxford University Press, 1982), p. 6. More recent evidence suggests that this estimate is a little too low. *The Britannica Book of the Year, 1987* estimated that there were then approximately 220 million atheists and 805 million agnostics in the world. Cited in *1988 Information Please Almanac* (Boston: Houghton Mifflin, 1988), p. 400.

8. *World Christian Encyclopedia*, pt. 3.

9. Conversely, there is social pressure in atheistic countries not to express belief in God. *The World Christian Encyclopedia* in 1982 maintained that by 1985 there would be about 78 million crypto-Christians—that is, Christians who practice their religion in secret.

10. Thomas H. Davenport, "Prevalence of Unbelief," *Encyclopedia of Unbelief*, vol. 2, p. 520.

11. *Ibid.*, p. 519. The source of these figures is the Gallup International Research Institute, 1974 and 1976. The Gallup Cross-National Values Survey of 1981 confirms the extent of nonbelief in many countries, though not the exact figures given in the Gallup polls of 1974 and 1976. To the question: Do you believe in God? the following answers were given:

	Yes, believe	No, don't believe	Don't know
Great Britain	76%	16%	9%
West Germany	72%	16%	12%
Norway	72%	22%	7%
Netherlands	65%	25%	10%
France	62%	29%	9%
Denmark	58%	27%	15%
Sweden	52%	35%	14%

These figures are cited in *Unsecular America*, ed. Richard John Neuhaus (Grand Rapids, Mich.: Eerdmans, 1986), p. 119.

12. Davenport, "Prevalence of Unbelief," pp. 518–524.

13. See William McCready and Andrew Greeley, *The Ultimate Values of the American Population* (Beverly Hills, Calif.: Sage, 1976). Cited in Davenport, "Prevalence of Unbelief," p. 521.

14. For a survey of these, see *Encyclopedia of Unbelief*, vol. 2, pp. 757–799.

15. Richard Bentley, *Eight Sermons* (Cambridge, 1724). Quoted in Paul Edwards, "Atheism," *The Encyclopedia of Philosophy*, ed. Paul Edwards (New York and London: Macmillan and Free Press, 1967), vol. 1, p. 174.

16. John Locke, *A Letter Concerning Tolerance*. Quoted *ibid.*

17. *Ibid.*, p. 175.

18. *The Central Military Tract Railroad Co.* v. *A. Rockafellow*, 17 Ill. 541 (1856). Quoted in Frank Swancara, *Separation of Religion and Government* (New York: Truth Seeker, 1950), p. 136.

19. *Odell* v. *Koppee*, 5 Heisk. (Tenn) 91. Quoted in Swancara, *Separation of Religion and Government*, p. 140.

20. Umakant Premanand Shah, "Jainism," *Encyclopaedia Britannica*, 15th ed., vol. 10, 1984, pp. 8–14; Ninian Smart, "Jainism," *Encyclopedia of Philosophy*, vol. 4, pp. 238–239; E. Royston Pike, *Encyclopaedia of Religion and Religions* (New York: Meridian Books, 1958), pp. 203–205; Herbert Stroup, *Four Religions of Asia* (New York: Harper & Row, 1968), pp. 81–114.

21. Jim Herrick, *Against the Faith* (London: Glover and Blair, 1985), p. 96.

22. Terry L. Meyers, "Percy Bysshe Shelley," *Encyclopedia of Unbelief*, vol. 2, p. 621.

23. Philip M. Smith, "Organized Religion and Criminal Behavior," *Sociology and Social Research*, 33, 1949, pp. 632–637.

24. See, for example, Philip M. Smith, "Role of Church in Delinquency Prevention," *Sociology and Social Research*, 35, 1951, pp. 183–190; Travis Hirschi and Rodney Stark, "Hellfire and Delinquency," *Social Problems*, 17, 1969, pp. 202–213. A more recent study commissioned by the National Catholic Educational Association of 16,000 public and nonpublic high school seniors shows that students in Catholic high schools are more likely to use alcohol, cocaine, and marijuana and more likely to steal. See Edd Doerr, "Bashing Public Education," *Humanist*, July/August 1987, p. 43.

25. Clifford Kirkpatrick, "Religion and Humanitarianism: A Study of Institutional Implications," *Psychological Monographs*, vol. 63, no. 9, 1949. Indeed, Kirkpatrick found a negative relation between religious belief and a humanitarian attitude.

26. Richard L. Gorsuch and Daniel Aleshire, "Christian Faith and Ethnic Prejudice: A Review and Interpretation of Research," *Journal for the Scientific Study of Religion*, 13, 1974, p. 281.

27. See Roderick Firth, "Ethical Absolutism and the Ideal Observer," *Readings in Ethical Theory*, 2d ed., ed. Wilfrid Sellars and John Hospers (Englewood Cliffs, N.J.: Prentice Hall, 1970), p. 201.

28. See Richard B. Brandt, *Ethical Theory* (Englewood Cliffs, N.J.: Prentice Hall, 1959), pp. 272–275.

29. For a detailed critique of this theory, see Kai Nielsen, *Ethics Without God* (Buffalo, N.Y.: Prometheus Books, 1973).

30. For this version of the theory see Philip L. Quinn, *Divine Commands and Moral Requirements* (Oxford: Clarendon Press, 1978).

31. For a criticism of Quinn's defense, see Thomas B. Talbott, "Quinn on Divine Commands and Moral Requirements," *International Journal for the Philosophy of Religion*, 14, 1982, pp. 194–198; and John Chandler, "Is the Divine Command Theory Defensible?" *Religious Studies*, 20, 1984, pp. 443–452.

32. William Frankena, *Ethics*, 2d ed. (Englewood Cliffs, N.J.: Prentice Hall, 1973), p. 110.

33. See Brandt, *Ethical Theory*, p. 175. He maintains in the light of present evidence that a Hopi who used the qualified attitude method would probably not disapprove of certain cruelties to animals although someone from our culture would. As far as we can tell, this is the *only* case cited by Brandt where there is evidence that conflict would occur.

34. *Ibid.*, p. 288.

35. See, for example, *ibid.*; Frankena, *Ethics*; John Rawls, *A Theory of Justice* (Cambridge, Mass.: Harvard University Press, 1971), pp. 48–51; Morton White, *What Is and What Ought to Be Done* (New York: Oxford University Press, 1981).

36. William James, *Varieties of Religious Experience* (1902). Quoted in Edwards, "Atheism," p. 187.

37. G. L. Romanes, *A Candid Examination of Theism* (1878). Quoted *ibid.*

38. Bertrand Russell, "A Free Man's Worship." Quoted in Paul Edwards, "Meaning and Value of Life," *The Meaning of Life*, ed. Steven Sanders and David R. Cheney (Englewood Cliffs, N.J.: Prentice Hall, 1980), p. 89.

39. See Shah, "Jainism;" Smart, "Jainism;" Pike, *Encyclopaedia of Religion and Religions;* Stroup, *Four Religions of Asia.*

40. See, for example, Kurt Baier, "The Meaning of Life," *Meaning of Life,* pp. 50–51; Edwards, "Meaning and Value of Life," p. 94.

41. Albert Camus, *The Myth of Sisyphus and Other Essays,* trans. Justin O'Brien (New York: Knopf, 1955). Relevant selections of this work are reprinted in Sanders and Cheney, *Meaning of Life.* See also Albert Camus, "An Absurd Reasoning," *Meaning of Life,* pp. 65–75.

42. Camus, "Absurd Reasoning," p. 69.

43. Thomas Nagel, "The Absurd," *Meaning of Life,* pp. 155–165.

44. *Ibid.,* p. 157.

45. *Ibid.,* p. 159.

46. *Ibid.,* p. 160.

47. *Ibid.,* p. 165.

48. Cf. Jonathan Glover's review of Thomas Nagel, *The View from Nowhere,* in *New York Review of Books,* April 9, 1987, p. 34.

49. Thus I reject the position that traditional arguments are irrelevant to belief in the existence of God. See, for example, Steven M. Cahn, "The Irrelevance to Religion of Philosophic Proofs for the Existence of God," *Philosophy of Religion,* ed. Steven M. Cahn (New York: Harper & Row, 1970), pp. 239–245. For a defense of theistic proofs against the sort of criticism given by Cahn, see Stephen T. Davis, "What Good Are Theistic Proofs?" *Philosophy of Religion,* ed. Louis P. Pojman (Belmont, Calif.: Wadsworth, 1986), pp. 80–88.

50. See Richard Swinburne, *The Existence of God* (Oxford: Clarendon Press, 1979).

51. Alvin Plantinga, "Is Belief in God Properly Basic?" *Nous,* 15, 1981, pp. 41–51.

52. Alvin Plantinga, *God, Freedom, and Evil* (Grand Rapids, Mich.: Eerdmans, 1974).

53. George H. Smith, *Atheism: The Case Against God* (Buffalo, N.Y.: Prometheus Books, 1979).

54. J. L. Mackie, *The Miracle of Theism* (Oxford: Clarendon Press, 1982). For example, the index (p. 263) indicates that the term "atheism" is not used often in the book.

55. For a discussion of this tradition, see Hazel E. Barnes, "Existentialism and Unbelief," *Encyclopedia of Unbelief,* vol. 1, pp. 211–218.

56. For example, although Sartre, a professed atheistic existentialist, gives arguments for the nonexistence of God, they cannot be easily fitted into the traditional mold. For a brief discussion of Sartre's arguments, see William A. Luijpen and Henry J. Koren, *Religion and Atheism* (Pittsburgh: Duquesne University Press, 1971), pp. 152–154.

57. Thrower, *Short History of Western Atheism,* pp. 120–121. See also James Thrower, *Marxist-Leninist "Scientific Atheism" and the Study of Religion in the USSR* (Berlin and Amsterdam: Mouton Publishers, 1983).

58. Ernest Nagel, "Philosophical Concepts of Atheism," *Critiques of God,* ed. Peter Angeles (Buffalo, N.Y.: Prometheus Books, 1976), p. 6.

59. There are, however, publications that are concerned with these issues, and

interested readers are referred to them. For example, in the United States there are *The American Atheist, The American Rationalist, Atheist, The Humanist, Free Inquiry,* and *Freethought Today.* For a complete list see "Periodicals of Unbelief," *Encyclopedia of Unbelief,* vol. 2, pp. 778–799.

60. Since most contemporary normative ethical theory is secular in its orientation, one can interpret the various contemporary ethical systems as the functional equivalent of atheistic moralities. However, there have been avowed atheists who have developed normative ethical systems. For example, see Michael Scriven, *Primary Philosophy* (New York: McGraw-Hill, 1966); J. L. Mackie, *Ethics: Inventing Right and Wrong* (New York: Penguin Books, 1977); Richard Robinson, *An Atheist's Values* (Oxford: Blackwell, 1964). See also the position developed by avowed secular humanists—for example, Corliss Lamont, *The Philosophy of Humanism* (New York: Frederick Ungar, 1985); Paul Kurtz, *Exuberance: An Affirmative Philosophy of Life* (Buffalo, N.Y.: Prometheus Books, 1977). See also those ethical theorists who have explicitly argued that ethical principles are logically independent of religion and have gone on to develop normative ethical systems without religious foundations—for example, Frankena, *Ethics.*

CHAPTER 1

1. Anthony Flew, "The Presumption of Atheism," *God, Freedom and Immortality* (Buffalo, N.Y.: Prometheus Books, 1984), pp. 13–30.

2. *Ibid.,* p. 22. Anthony Kenny has objected to Flew's use of the term "negative atheism." According to Kenny one could just as well speak in terms of the presumption of negative theism. Kenny defines a negative theist as someone who is not an atheist and does not disbelieve in God. Kenny prefers to say that there is a presumption of agnosticism. By this he means that there is a methodical presumption that we do not know whether God exists or even whether the concept of God is coherent. See Anthony Kenny, *Faith and Reason* (New York: Columbia University Press, 1983), pp. 85–86.

3. This is similar to what Antony Flew calls the principle of agnosticism, except that Flew seems to restrict the reasons to what I call epistemic reasons. See Antony Flew, "The Principle of Agnosticism," *God, Freedom and Immortality,* pp. 30–41. Moreover, it is not completely clear that philosophers like Flew who advocate this general thesis allow that there could be properly basic beliefs that are justified, yet are not completely justified in terms of any reasons or evidence. If there are such beliefs, this general thesis can be understood to mean that without adequate reasons one should not have any *nonbasic* beliefs.

4. William K. Clifford, "The Ethics of Belief," *Philosophy of Religion,* ed. Louis P. Pojman (Belmont, Calif.: Wadsworth, 1987), p. 387.

5. Lorraine Code, *Epistemic Responsibility* (Hanover, N.H.: University Press of New England, 1987), p. 78.

6. Roderick Chisholm, *Perceiving: A Philosophical Study* (Ithaca, N.Y.: Cornell University Press, 1957), p. 9. Actually, Chisholm does not talk about justifying belief in terms of beneficial reasons. His position seems to be that it is permissible to believe that p so long as there is no adequate evidence for ~p, even if there is no reason—beneficial or otherwise—to believe that p. However, this leaves

unclear whether he believes that there is an *epistemic* right to believe p if there is
no adequate evidence for ~p. On this point, see Code, *Epistemic Responsibility*, p.
47.

7. Roderick Firth, "Chisholm and the Ethic of Belief," *Philosophical Review*,
68, 1959, pp. 496–497.

8. Gary Gutting, like Chisholm, has argued that if a person P believes p, and
p is epistemologically indeterminate for P, then P is entitled to believe p where
a proposition is epistemologically indeterminate for P, just in case the evidence
P is aware of does not justify P's believing p and does not justify P's believing ~p.
Gutting argues for this position on the ground that most of the propositions one
believes on controversial subjects are based on such scanty information and such
a low level of understanding that experts on these subjects could easily show us
that our reasons for what we believe are woefully inadequate. Consequently,
he concludes that one's beliefs on these subjects are usually epistemologically
indeterminate. However, Gutting argues, one has a right to entertain beliefs
about these subjects. If we did not have this right, then we would be forced into
accepting the strange conclusion that almost all of us would have to give up our
most characteristic and important beliefs. He argues further on what he calls
Millian grounds: The interest of truth would be better served by lively debate
over firmly held beliefs than by "withdrawal from commitment on controversial
issues."

However, Gutting is mistaken to believe that one's beliefs on a controversial
subject are epistemologically indeterminate if they are not backed up by the
reasons that could be mustered by some expert on the subject. Many of our
beliefs on controversial subjects are and should be based on the view of experts
or sources that we have good reason to trust. We may not know very well what
reasons the experts would use to back up their opinions, but nevertheless, on
inductive grounds, we would be justified in believing the experts or sources. In
addition, the reasons and level of understanding that should be demanded for
justified belief are surely contextual. One should not judge that an educated
layperson does not have a justified belief that Freudian theory is not scientific
because he or she does not know Popper's arguments and Grünbaum's rebuttal,
although one would be justified in making this judgment of a graduate student
writing a dissertation on the scientific status of psychoanalysis. Hence Gutting
has provided no reason why there is not a presumption that one should only
believe propositions for which there is adequate evidence, where adequate evidence is understood in a much broader and more contextual way than Gutting
allows. One can accept his Millian argument with the proviso that vigorous debate
is enhanced when the participants have some reason for their belief even if this
reason is only that some expert is usually correct or that it is appropriate to the
context and their level of expertise. See Gary Gutting, *Religious Belief and Religious
Skepticism* (Notre Dame, Ind.: University of Notre Dame Press, 1982), pp. 100–
102.

9. Mackie, for example, has suggested that it is reasonable in science to give
tentative acceptance to a hypothesis that is only plausible and lacks adequate
evidential support, and it is reasonable in social contexts to trust others before
there is adequate evidence that trust is justified, since such trust is necessary for

cooperation. See J. L. Mackie, *The Miracle of Theism* (Oxford: Clarendon Press, 1984), p. 206.

10. See Jonathan L. Kvanvig, "The Evidentialist Objection," *American Philosophical Quarterly*, 20, 1983, pp. 47–55. Although Kvanvig uses this argument against a more rigid position than mine, there seems little doubt that he would say this argument would apply to mine as well.

11. *Ibid.*, p. 48.

12. See, for example, the papers by Peter Unger, James Cargile, Keith Lehrer, and Dan Turner in *Essays on Knowledge and Justification,* ed. George S. Pappas and Marshall Swain, (Ithaca, N.Y.: Cornell University Press, 1978), pp. 317–369. See also O. K. Bousma, "Descartes' Evil Genius," *Philosophical Review*, 58, 1949, pp. 141–145.

13. See Marguerite Foster and Michael Martin, *Probability, Confirmation and Simplicity* (New York: Odyssey Press, 1962), pp. 238–240, for various justifications for the use of simplicity.

14. For this argument, see Laurence BonJour, *The Structure of Empirical Knowledge* (Cambridge, Mass.: Harvard University Press, 1985), p. 185.

15. For an example of this sort of pragmatic argument against the skeptic, see Nicholas Rescher, *Methodological Pragmatism* (New York: New York University Press, 1977), chap. 12.

16. Naturally there are other skeptical hypotheses that I do not explicitly consider here. However, their similarity to the evil demon hypothesis suggests that my arguments against the evil demon hypothesis would hold for them as well.

17. Kvanvig, "Evidentialist Objection," p. 51.

18. Kvanvig speaks sometimes of a general human tendency and sometimes of a natural human tendency. A general human tendency seems compatible with the tendency's being the result of learning; a natural human tendency suggests a tendency that is innate.

19. *Ibid.*

20. According to Kvanvig: "S believes p on e without grounds for doubt = $_{df}$ (i) S bases his belief that p on e; and either (ii) nothing counts against p for S or (iii) what counts against p for S is overriding for S . . . Nothing counts against p for S = $_{df}$ no conjunction i of propositions which S believes or are acceptable for S is such that if i and the tree of justification for each conjunct of i were all that were evident for S, then not-p would have some presumption in its favor for S. . . . T is a tree of justification p for S = $_{df}$ (i) if p is a foundational belief for S, then T = p; and (ii) if p is not a foundational belief for S, then T is composed of levels L_1 . . . , L_n such that (a) L_1 contains propositions e_1 . . . , e_n which are S's epistemic grounds for p, (b) for any L_m where m is less than n, L_{m+1} contains propositions f_1 . . . , f_n which are S's epistemic grounds for the propositions g_1, . . . , g_n of L_m." *Ibid.*, p. 51.

21. For example, according to the Gallup International Research Institute surveys of 1974 and 1976, 56 percent of the people surveyed in Japan answered no when asked whether they believed in God or a universal spirit, while only 2 percent of the people surveyed in India answered no to the same question. See Thomas H. Davenport, "Prevalence of Unbelief," *The Encyclopedia of Unbelief* (Buffalo, N.Y.: Prometheus Books, 1985), vol. 2, p. 519.

22. See David Marks and Richard Kammann, *The Psychology of the Psychic* (Buffalo, N.Y.: Prometheus Books, 1980), pp. 7–11; William Sims Bainbridge and Rodney Stark, "Superstitions: Old and New," *Paranormal Borderlines of Science*, ed. Kendrick Frazier (Buffalo, N.Y.: Prometheus Books, 1981), pp. 46–59.

23. See Frazier, *Paranormal Borderlines of Science*, pp. 111–147.

CHAPTER 2

1. Michael Durrant, *The Logical Status of "God"* (London: Macmillan, 1973), p. 27.

2. David Hume, *An Inquiry Concerning Human Understanding* (New York: Liberal Arts Press, 1955), p. 173.

3. Charles Bradlaugh, *A Plea for Atheism*, reprinted in *An Anthology of Atheism and Rationalism*, ed. Gordon Stein (Buffalo, N.Y.: Prometheus Books, 1980), p. 10.

4. Richard B. Braithwaite, "An Empiricist's View of the Nature of Religious Belief," reprinted in *The Logic of God*, ed. Malcolm L. Diamond and Thomas V. Lizenbury, Jr. (Indianapolis, Ind.: Bobbs-Merrill, 1975), pp. 127–147.

5. J. L. Mackie, *The Miracle of Theism* (Oxford: Clarendon Press, 1985), p. 2.

6. Alvin Plantinga, *God and Other Minds* (Ithaca, N.Y.: Cornell University Press, 1967), pp. 156–168.

7. Alvin Plantinga, *God, Freedom, and Evil* (Grand Rapids, Mich.: Eerdmans, 1974), pp. 65–66.

8. See Kai Nielsen, *Contemporary Critiques of Religion* (New York: Herder and Herder, 1971), *An Introduction to the Philosophy of Religion* (New York: St. Martin's Press, 1982), *Philosophy and Atheism* (Buffalo, N.Y.: Prometheus Books, 1985).

9. Richard Swinburne, *The Coherence of Theism* (Oxford: Clarendon Press, 1977).

10. See note 8, above.

11. Paul Edwards, "Some Notes on Anthropomorphic Theology," in *Religious Experience and Truth*, ed. Sidney Hook (New York: New York University Press, 1961), pp. 244–245.

12. Nielsen, *Introduction to the Philosophy of Religion*, p. 83.

13. *Ibid.*, p. 88.

14. See Nielsen, *Contemporary Critiques of Religion*, pp. 65–67. I interpret Nielsen to be arguing that we need to know what confirms or disconfirms a statement before we can understand it *as* a statement—that is, as something either true or false. As I have argued above, we could understand it in a different way without knowing this.

15. Nielsen, *Introduction to the Philosophy of Religion*, pp. 40–42. This is one good reason why someone could not accept the verifiability theory of meaning but could argue that confirmation meant revelation or being recorded in holy writ. On this construal, religious statements would be factually meaningful and scientific ones would not be. However, this would conflict with religious believers' own intuitions on the matter. Further, such an interpretation would provide no explanation of our pretheoretical judgments about what is factually meaningful and what is not.

16. *Ibid.*, p. 41.

17. See George I. Mavrodes, "God and Verification," *Logic of God*, pp. 227–229.

18. Kai Nielsen, "God and Verification Again," *Logic of God*, p. 236.

19. Antony Flew, "Theology and Falsification," *Logic of God*, pp. 257–259. However, it seems clear that Flew would not be happy with Nielsen's formulation. See Antony Flew, " 'Theology and Falsification' in Retrospect," *Logic of God*, pp. 273–274.

20. Nielsen, *Contemporary Critiques of Religion*, p. 57.

21. See, for example, Alvin Plantinga, "Verificationism," *Logic of God*, pp. 446–455.

22. Nielsen, *Contemporary Critiques of Religion*, p. 63.

23. Cf. Salmon, "Verifiability and Logic," *Logic of God*, p. 472.

24. *Ibid.*, p. 469.

25. Of course, the premises are inconsistent. It would therefore be possible to derive any statement, since an inconsistent set of premises entails any statement. But "God is gluberfied" is not a statement since it is factually meaningless, so it could not be derived even from inconsistent premises.

26. Alonzo Church, review of Ayer's *Language, Truth, and Logic*, in *Journal of Symbolic Logic*, 14, 1949, pp. 52–53. John Foster, in *Ayer* (London: Routledge and Kegal Paul, 1985), pp. 15–38, distinguishes two interpretations of Ayer's principle of verifiability. Foster argues that as originally proposed, Ayer's principle of verifiability said a statement was verifiable if and only if there could be evidence for or against it. Foster calls this the evidence principle. However, Foster maintains that when Ayer goes on to try to clarify the principle of verifiability he reformulates it in a way that gets him into serious trouble, for the reformulation does not exclude any statement from being factually meaningful. This attempt at clarification, Foster argues, was in fact an unsuccessful attempt to formulate the principle of verifiability along lines very different from the principle of evidence. It was an attempt to specify the factual content of a statement entirely in terms of its empirical content. This second formulation Foster calls the content principle. Foster argues that the content principle is much more in keeping with Ayer's phenomenalistic and reductionist tendencies than the evidence principle, which has no reductionistic implications.

It should be clear from what I have argued in this chapter that the principle I am defending is closer to what Foster calls the evidence principle than to the content principle, since I do not see the principle of verifiability as having reductionistic implications. However, I disagree with Foster's assessment of the evidence principle (pp. 28–29). For example, Foster believes we do not consider it a necessary condition for the factual meaningfulness of physical object statements that they be open to indirect empirical verification or refutation by sense experience. Foster argues that if we came to believe with the skeptic that the existence of physical objects is not open to indirect verification, we would still regard statements about physical objects as meaningful. According to Foster we regard the problem raised by the skeptic of physical objects as an epistemological and not as a semantic problem. Foster concludes that unless we accept the content principle, there is no rationale for making openness to observation a requirement for factual meaningfulness.

I disagree. I have already given a rationale for one version of the evidence principle: It provides a criterion that matches our intuitions in clear cases and provides a criterion in more controversial cases. In addition, it is not so obvious as Foster supposes that the questions raised by the skeptic are epistemological and not semantic. To suppose that the questions are purely epistemological is tantamount to begging the question against verificationists.

27. Salmon, "Verifiability and Logic," p. 460.

28. Swinburne, *Coherence of Theism*, pp. 24–25.

29. *Ibid.*, p. 25.

30. *Ibid.*, p. 26.

31. *Ibid.*, p. 27.

32. *Ibid.*

33. *Ibid.*

34. *Ibid.*, p. 28.

35. *Ibid.*

36. *Ibid.*

37. *Ibid.*

38. For example, Michael Tooley and Kai Nielsen argue in this way. See Michael Tooley, "Theological Statements and the Question of an Empiricist Criterion of Cognitive Significance," *Logic of God*, p. 493; and Nielsen, *Contemporary Critiques of Religion*, pp. 66–67.

39. The following discussion on types of observational language is indebted to Tooley's analysis in "Theological Statements," pp. 512–519.

40. *Ibid.*, p. 515.

41. I consider here in a general way the problems of various observational languages. However, certain observational languages raise special problems for the confirmation of theism. For example, if phenomenalistic observational language is allowed, there is still the problem of specifying what observational sentences in this language would confirm theism and not confirm naturalism to the same extent. It is not implausible to suppose that, no matter what might appear to a human or an organism or even to a being that was not a human or an organism, in a religious context it could be accounted for at least as well by some nontheistic hypothesis as by the theistic hypothesis. If so, the appearance would support other hypotheses besides theism. Thus O'_2 and O''_2 would surely confirm certain naturalistic hypotheses as well as theism; O'''_2 would seem to confirm polytheism as well as theism. If this is so, it tends to show that theism and its rivals are equally confirmed by the same evidence. This in turn would indicate that theism is factually meaningless.

Indeed, as we see in Chapter 7, it is certainly unclear whether a sentence such as O_2 construed in physicalistic terms would confirm theism more than naturalism. For one thing, it is not clear that O_2 is more likely on the supposition that theism is true plus background knowledge than on the supposition that it is not true plus background knowledge; hence O_2 would not confirm theism more than its negation. For example, is it more likely that if God exists, He would perform a miracle of raising the dead, or that if naturalism is true, the dead would be raised in accordance with unknown natural laws? The answer, as we shall see, is by no means obvious. Thus it is by no means clear that O_2 confirms theism more that its negation.

42. Tooley, "Theological Statements," pp. 481–524.

43. *Ibid.*, p. 483.

44. In a more recent paper Tooley argues that there is no general problem in confirming infinite attributes. He argues, for example, that in order to confirm that a person has infinite knowledge, one merely confirms that there is nothing that the person does not know. Be that as it may, in the paper under discussion here Tooley's claim is that phenomenalistic language can be used to construct or confirm statements about an infinite being. How statements couched in phenomenalistic language can be used to construct or confirm that someone knows anything, let alone that there is nothing that the person does not know, is certainly not clear. See Michael Tooley, "John Hick and the Concept of Eschatological Verification," *Religious Studies*, 12, 1976, pp. 177–199.

45. Tooley, "Theological Statements," p. 520.

46. John Hick, "Theology and Verification," *Logic of God*, pp. 188–208.

47. *Ibid.*, p. 193.

48. *Ibid.*, p. 201.

49. *Ibid.*, p. 202.

50. *Ibid.*, p. 203.

51. *Ibid.*, p. 206.

52. For further problems with his account, see Tooley, "John Hick and the Concept of Eschatological Verification," pp. 180–181.

53. Kai Nielsen, "Eschatological Verification," *Logic of God*, p. 215.

54. *Ibid.*, p. 216.

55. *Ibid.*

56. *Ibid.*, pp. 217–218.

57. See Tooley, "John Hick and the Concept of Eschatological Verification," for further arguments as to why observational statements couched in nonreligious language cannot confirm a hypothesis about the existence of a transcendent God.

58. John Hick, "Faith and Knowledge," *Logic of God*, pp. 239–243.

59. *Ibid.*, p. 242.

60. *Ibid.*

61. See Nielsen, *Contemporary Critiques of Religion*, pp. 78–79.

62. Gregory S. Kavka, "Eschatological Falsification," *Religious Studies*, 12, 1976, pp. 201–205.

63. *Ibid.*, p. 202.

64. See Alvin Plantinga, *God, Freedom, and Evil* (Grand Rapids, Mich.: Eerdmans, 1974), p. 58.

65. See, for example, G. A. Wells, *The Historical Evidence for Jesus* (Buffalo, N.Y.: Prometheus Books, 1982); Michael Arnheim, *Is Christianity True?* (Buffalo, N.Y.: Prometheus Books, 1984).

66. See *A Handbook of Christian Theology* (New York: Meridian Books, 1958), p. 51.

67. I. M. Crombie, "The Possibility of Theological Statements," *Faith and Logic*, ed. Basil Mitchell (London: Allen and Unwin, 1958), pp. 31–83.

68. *Ibid.*, p. 32.

69. *Ibid.*, p. 40. For further problems with the logical status of the term "God" see Durrant, *Logical Status of "God."*

70. Crombie, "The Possibility of Theological Statements," p. 55.

71. *Ibid.*, p. 56.

72. *Ibid.*, p. 66.

73. *Ibid.*, p. 72.

74. I. M. Crombie, "Theology and Falsification," *Logic of God*, pp. 311–329.

75. *Ibid.*, p. 325.

76. *Ibid.*, p. 326.

77. *Ibid.*, pp. 319–320. Crombie admits that he is using parable in an extended sense.

78. *Ibid.*, p. 327.

79. Cf. Nielsen, *Introduction to the Philosophy of Religion*, p. 163.

80. *Ibid.*, p. 210, n. 46. As Nielsen points out, Crombie only speaks of utterly and irremediably pointless suffering in "The Possibility of Theological Statements" (p. 72), and no mention is made of the eternity of such suffering. But whether this allows his position to be refutable, as Nielsen supposes, is less than clear. In any case, Crombie says that the Christian is committed to believing that there is no utterly and irremediably pointless suffering. Does this mean that there could be no evidence of such suffering or merely that a Christian could not accept such evidence?

81. *Ibid.*, p. 161.

82. *Ibid.*, p. 157.

83. The exceptions are not based on the use of the verifiability theory of meaning. In the Introduction, for example, I question whether it makes sense to assume that God issues commands, since so doing seems to presuppose that God has a body.

CHAPTER 3

1. See Alvin Plantinga (ed.), *The Ontological Argument* (Garden City, N.Y.: Doubleday, 1965), for relevant selections from St. Anselm, Descartes, Leibniz, Kant, Spinoza, and Schopenhauer as well as contemporary philosophers.

2. St. Anselm, *Proslogion*, chap. 2, in Plantinga, *Ontological Argument*, pp. 3–4.

3. For one influential contemporary critique see G. E. Moore, "Is Existence a Predicate?" reprinted in Plantinga, *Ontological Argument*, pp. 71–85.

4. Immanuel Kant, *The Critique of Pure Reason*, trans. Norman Kemp Smith (London: Macmillan, 1929), p. 505, reprinted in Plantinga, *Ontological Argument*, p. 62.

5. Norman Malcolm, "Anselm's Ontological Arguments," reprinted in Plantinga, *Ontological Argument*, p. 139.

6. Cf. David and Marjorie Haight, "An Ontological Argument for the Devil," *Monist*, 54, 1970, pp. 218–220. Richard Swinburne, *The Coherence of Theism* (Oxford: Clarendon Press, 1977), pp. 141–148, argues that the concept of an all-powerful, all-knowing, free, and completely evil being is incoherent. However,

Swinburne is mistaken. See Michael Martin, "The Coherence of the Hypothesis of an Omnipotent, Omniscient, Free and Perfectly Evil Being," *International Journal for the Philosophy of Religion*, 17, 1985, pp. 185–191.

7. Gaunilo, "In Behalf of the Fool," reprinted in Plantinga, *Ontological Argument*, pp. 6–13.

8. St. Anselm "St. Anselm's Reply to Gaunilo," reprinted in Plantinga, *Ontological Argument*, pp. 13–27.

9. Charles Hartshorne, *The Logic of Perfection* (La Salle, Ill.: Open Court, 1962), p. 55.

10. Alvin Plantinga, *God, Freedom, and Evil* (Grand Rapids, Mich.: Eerdmans, 1983), pp. 90–91.

11. See Patrick Grim, "In Behalf of 'In Behalf of the Fool,' " *International Journal for the Philosophy of Religion*, 13, 1982, pp. 33–42.

12. See J. L. Mackie, *The Miracle of Theism* (Oxford: Clarendon Press, 1982), pp. 52–53.

13. A similar point is made in William Rowe, "The Ontological Argument," *Reason and Responsibility*, ed. Joel Feinberg (Belmont, Calif.: Wadsworth, 1985), pp. 14–22. Rowe argues that one can build existence into the definition of a concept. Modifying Rowe's example slightly, one can define a real magician as an existing magician. But it does not follow that there are any real magicians. The only thing that follows is that no nonexisting thing is a real magician. Similarly, if existence is part of the concept of God, the only thing that follows is that no nonexisting thing is God. But what if one supposes that God's existence is possible? Rowe shows that this indeed allows one to infer that God exists only because one has begged the question. In granting that God was possible, one is granting that God exists. In a similar way, if one granted that a real magician is possible, one would be granting that a magician exists.

14. Norman Malcolm, "Anselm's Ontological Arguments," reprinted in Plantinga, *Ontological Argument*, pp. 136–159.

15. *Ibid.*, p. 146.

16. Malcolm rejects Leibniz's proof that since perfections are simple properties, they must be compatible with one another. See *ibid.*, p. 157. Leibniz's argument is reprinted in Plantinga, *Ontological Argument*, p. 56.

17. Malcolm, "Anselm's Ontological Arguments," p. 157.

18. See Grim, "In Behalf of 'In Behalf of the Fool,' " p. 34.

19. Cf. Paul Henle, "Uses of the Ontological Argument," reprinted in Plantinga, *Ontological Argument*, pp. 172–180. Henle by parody of reasoning "proves" the existence of a whole family of necessary beings called Nec, NEc, and NEC.

20. See Alvin Plantinga, "A Valid Ontological Argument?" reprinted in Plantinga, *Ontological Argument*, pp. 160–171.

21. Malcolm, "Anselm's Ontological Arguments," pp. 143–147.

22. See Henle, "Uses of the Ontological Argument," p. 176. Although more than 25 years have passed, he has not clarified his meaning or indeed attempted in any way to answer his many critics. In addition to Plantinga, "Valid Ontological Argument?" and Henle, "Uses of the Ontological Argument," see R. E. Allen, "The Ontological Argument," *Philosophical Review*, 70, 1961, pp. 56–66; Raziel Abelson; "Not Necessarily," *Philosophical Review*, 70, 1961, pp. 67–84; Terrence

Penelhum, "On the Second Ontological Argument," *Philosophical Review*, 70, 1961, pp. 85–92.

23. Hartshorne, *Logic of Perfection*, p. 25.

24. *Ibid.*, p. 51.

25. R. L. Purtill, "Hartshorne's Modal Proof," *Journal of Philosophy*, 63, 1966, p. 408.

26. Hartshorne, *Logic of Perfection*, p. 55.

27. *Ibid.*, pp. 74–75.

28. Charles Hartshorne, "The Necessarily Existent," reprinted in Plantinga, *Ontological Argument*, p. 127.

29. Carl R. Kordig, "A Deontic Argument for God's Existence," *Nous*, 15, 1981, pp. 207–208.

30. Patrick Grim, "Against a Deontic Argument for God's Existence," *Analysis*, 42, 1982, pp. 171–174.

31. Alvin Plantinga, *God, Freedom, and Evil* (Grand Rapids, Mich.: Eerdmans, 1983), pp. 108–112; *The Nature of Necessity* (Oxford: Clarendon Press, 1974), pp. 213–217.

32. Plantinga, *God, Freedom, and Evil*, p. 112.

33. See Mackie, *Miracle of Theism*, pp. 56–57.

34. See Michael Tooley, "Plantinga's Defense of the Ontological Argument," *Mind*, 90, 1981, pp. 426–427.

35. Plantinga, *Nature of Necessity*, pp. 220–221.

36. Peter van Inwagen, "Ontological Arguments," *Nous*, 11, 1977, pp. 388–389.

37. See Patrick Grim, "Plantinga's God and Other Monstrosities," *Religious Studies*, 15, 1979, pp. 91–97; Tooley, "Plantinga's Defense," pp. 422–427.

38. See Grim, "In Behalf of 'In Behalf of the Fool,'" p. 38.

39. Cf. Tooley, "Plantinga's Defense," p. 425.

40. For a milder criticism than the one given here, see William Rowe, "Modal Versions of the Ontological Argument," *Philosophy of Religion*, ed. Louis P. Pojam (Belmont, Calif.: Wadsworth, 1987), pp. 67–74. Rowe argues that the only thing Plantinga has established is that it *may* not be foolish to accept the argument, and he has not established that it is not foolish to accept. However, one would have thought that the various parodies of the argument suggest the folly of accepting the argument. Consequently, Plantinga has not even established this very weak conclusion.

41. Arthur Schopenhauer, *The Fourfold Root of the Principle of Sufficient Reason*, reprinted in Plantinga, *Ontological Argument*, p. 66.

CHAPTER 4

1. Because of this, an argument for a first cause must be supplemented with some other argument that attempts to show that the first cause is God. Indeed, sometimes the cosmological argument is considered to have two parts. In the first part a first cause is established, and in the second part the first cause is identified with God. See William L. Rowe, *The Cosmological Argument* (Princeton, N.J.: Princeton University Press, 1975), p. 5.

2. Because of the failure of Aquinas's ways to provide sound arguments for the existence of God, some theologians have argued that the ways should be given a different interpretation. For a discussion and critique of this different interpretation, see W. E. Kennick, "A New Way with the Five Ways," *Australasian Journal of Philosophy*, 38, 1960, pp. 225–233.

3. *Summa Theologiae*, pt. 1a, quest. 2, art. 3. See the Kenny translation in Anthony Kenny, *The Five Ways*, (New York: Schocken Books, 1969), p. 34.

4. Kenny, *Five Ways*, p. 40.

5. Kenny argues that Aquinas's views on nontemporal causal sequences are closely related to theories of medieval astrology and that his argument that an infinite nontemporal causal series is impossible rests on an equivocation between "first = earlier" and "first = unprecedented." See Kenny, *Five Ways*, p. 44. However, Rowe suggests that Aquinas's views do not rest on medieval astrology but on a metaphysical analysis of existence and causation. Nevertheless, Rowe argues that Aquinas's actual argument is question-begging and tries to reformulate the argument in a way that is not. Rowe's reformulation presupposes the principle of sufficient reason. See Rowe, *Cosmological Argument*, pp. 32–38. As Rowe argues elsewhere, we have no reason to suppose that the principle of sufficient reason is true or that we can assume that it is true. See William Rowe, *An Introduction to the Philosophy of Religion* (Belmont, Calif.: Wadsworth, 1978), pp. 27–29.

6. *Summa Theologiae*, pt. 1a, quest. 2, art. 3 in Kenny, *Five Ways*, p. 46.

7. See, for example, Edward P. Tryon, "Is the Universe a Vacuum Fluctuation?" *Nature*, 246, December 14, 1973, pp. 396–397; Edward P. Tryon, "What Made the World?" *New Scientist*, 8, March 1984, pp. 14–16; Alexander Vilenkin, "Creation of Universes from Nothing," *Physics Letters*, 117B, 1982, pp. 25–28; Alexander Vilenkin, "Birth of Inflationary Universes," *Physical Review*, 27, 1983, pp. 2848–2855; L. P. Grishchuk and Y. B. Zeldovich, "Complete Cosmological Theories," *The Quantum Structure of Space and Time*, ed. M. J. Duff and C. J. Isham (Cambridge: Cambridge University Press, 1982), pp. 409–422; Quentin Smith, "The Uncaused Beginning of the Universe," *Philosophy of Science*, 55, 1988, pp. 39–57.

8. For another evaluation of the argument, see Rowe, *Cosmological Argument*, pp. 39–45.

9. The idea of a necessary being used in premise (14) has been supposed by some philosophers to be suspect conceptually. If by necessary being one means a being whose nonexistence is inconceivable, then it has been argued that any entity one can conceive of as existing, one can conceive of as not existing. The notion of a necessary being is discussed in more detail in the previous chapter. However, it is unlikely that this objection can be used against Aquinas, since by necessary being he seems to mean only a being that cannot cease to exist. See Kenny, *Five Ways*, p. 48; Rowe, *Cosmological Argument*, p. 40.

10. William Lane Craig, *The Kalam Cosmological Argument* (New York: Barnes & Noble, 1979).

11. See G. J. Whitrow, review of Craig, *Kalam Cosmological Argument*, in *British Journal for the Philosophy of Science*, 34, 1980, p. 408.

12. Craig, *Kalam Cosmological Argument*, p. 65.

13. *Ibid.*, p. 83.

14. *Ibid.*, pp. 102–110.

15. *Ibid.*, pp. 111–130.

16. *Ibid.*, pp. 130–140.

17. *Ibid.*, p. 141.

18. *Ibid.*, pp. 172–174.

19. *Ibid.*, pp. 149–150.

20. *Ibid.*, pp. 150–152.

21. *Ibid.*, p. 149.

22. *Ibid.*

23. See William J. Wainwright, review of Craig, *Kalam Cosmological Argument*, in *Nous*, 16, 1982, pp. 328–334; David A. Conway, " 'It Would Have Happened Already': On One Argument for a First Cause," *Analysis*, 44, 1984, pp. 159–166.

24. See Wainwright, review of Craig, *Kalam Cosmological Argument*, p. 331.

25. *Ibid.*, p. 333. See also Conway, "It Would Have Happened Already," for further refutations of Craig's *a priori* arguments.

26. Milton K. Munitz, *The Mystery of Existence: An Essay in Philosophical Cosmology* (New York: Appleton-Century-Crofts, 1965), p. 139.

27. *Ibid.*, p. 141.

28. See note 7 above.

29. Richard Swinburne, *The Existence of God* (Oxford: Clarendon Press, 1979), chap. 7.

30. *Ibid.*, chap. 1.

31. *Ibid.*, chap. 14.

32. See Georg Henrik Von Wright, *A Treatise on Induction and Probability* (Paterson, N.J.: Littlefield Adams, 1960), chap. 4.

33. Henry E. Kyburg, Jr., and Howard E. Smokler, *Studies in Subjective Probability* (New York: Wiley, 1964).

34. Marguerite Foster and Michael Martin (eds.), *Probability, Confirmation and Simplicity* (New York: Odyssey Press, 1966), pp. 17–26.

35. Swinburne, *Existence of God*, pp. 130–131.

36. *Ibid.*, p. 130.

37. The two hypotheses are equally refutable: The same number of observations will refute the one as the other. So in one obvious sense both hypotheses allow the same room for error. See Michael Martin, "The Falsifiability of Curve-Hypotheses," *Philosophical Studies*, 16, 1965, pp. 56–60.

38. See Richard Swinburne, *The Coherence of Theism* (Oxford: Clarendon Press, 1977).

39. Swinburne, *Existence of God*, pp. 129–130.

40. *Ibid.*, p. 131.

41. *Ibid.*

42. Bruce C. Reichenbach, *The Cosmological Argument: A Reassessment* (Springfield, Ill.: Charles C. Thomas, 1972).

43. *Ibid.*, p. 142.

44. *Ibid.*, p. 143.

45. *Ibid.*, p. 61.

46. *Ibid.*

47. *Ibid.*, p. 66.

48. See Houston Craighead, "The Cosmological Argument: Assessment of a Reassessment," *International Journal for the Philosophy of Religion*, 6, 1975, pp. 117–124; William Lane Craig, "A Further Critique of Reichenbach's Cosmological Argument," *International Journal for the Philosophy of Religion*, 9, 1978, pp. 53–60.

49. In a reply to one critic he still seems to beg the question. See Bruce Reichenbach, "The Cosmological Argument and the Causal Principle," *International Journal for the Philosophy of Religion*, 6, 1975, p. 187. On this point, see Craig, "Further Critique," p. 54.

50. Alvin Plantinga, *The Nature of Necessity* (Oxford: Clarendon Press, 1974), p. 61. For more on this point, see Craig, "Further Critique," pp. 56–58.

51. Cf. Timothy W. Bartel, "The Cosmological Argument and the Uniqueness of God," *International Journal for the Philosophy of Religion*, 13, 1982, pp. 23–31.

52. Reichenbach, *The Cosmological Argument*, p. 142.

53. *Ibid.*, pp. 120–121.

54. *Ibid.*, p. 100.

55. *Ibid.*, p. 102.

CHAPTER 5

1. William Paley, *Natural Theology, or Evidences of the Existence and Attributes of the Diety Collected from the Appearances of Nature* (1802). Reprinted in part in Louis P. Pojman, *Philosophy of Religion* (Belmont, Calif.: Wadsworth, 1987), pp. 29–31.

2. David Hume, *Dialogues Concerning Natural Religion* (New York: Hafner, 1957).

3. Paley, *Natural Theology*, p. 31.

4. Hume, *Dialogues Concerning Natural Religion*, p. 17.

5. John Hick, "Frederick Robert Tennant," *The Encyclopedia of Philosophy*, ed. Paul Edwards (New York and London: Macmillan and Free Press, 1967), vol. 8, p. 93.

6. George Schlesinger, *Religion and Scientific Method* (Dordrecht, Holland: D. Reidel, 1982), chap. 23.

7. Richard Swinburne, *The Existence of God* (Oxford: Clarendon Press, 1979), chap. 8.

8. Antony Flew, *God, Freedom and Immortality* (Buffalo, N.Y.: Prometheus Books, 1984), chap. 4.

9. Wallace I. Matson, *The Existence of God* (Ithaca, N.Y.: Cornell University Press, 1965), p. 129.

10. *Ibid.*, p. 130.

11. F. R. Tennant, *Philosophical Theology* (Cambridge: Cambridge University Press, 1930), vol. 2, p. 121.

12. Our summary of Tennant's views is indebted to Hick, "Frederick Robert Tennant," pp. 93–95, and William Alston, "Teleological Argument for the Existence of God," *Encyclopedia of Philosophy*, vol. 7, pp. 84–88.

13. Tennant, *Philosophical Theology*, p. 82.

14. *Ibid.*, p. 85.

15. *Ibid.*, p. 87.

16. *Ibid.*, p. 93.

17. *Ibid.,* p. 103.

18. *Ibid.,* p. 106.

19. *Ibid.,* pp. 113–115.

20. See, for example, C. D. Broad, review of Tennant, *Philosophical Theology,* vol. 2, in *Mind,* 39, 1930, pp. 476–484; Delton L. Scudder, *Tennant's Philosophical Theology* (New Haven, Ct.: Yale University Press, 1940), chap. 2.

21. Tennant, *Philosophical Theology,* p. 88.

22. *Ibid.,* pp. 121–122.

23. *Ibid.,* p. 148.

24. Cf. Broad, review of Tennant, *Philosophical Theology,* p. 481.

25. Tennant, *Philosophical Theology,* p. 129.

26. *Ibid.,* p. 123.

27. *Ibid.,* p. 125.

28. Broad, review of Tennant, *Philosophical Theology,* p. 480.

29. Tennant, *Philosophical Theology,* p. 125.

30. Broad, review of Tennant, *Philosophical Theology,* p. 481.

31. Cf. *ibid.,* p. 482.

32. See Tennant, *Philosophical Theology,* p. 87.

33. Broad, review of Tennant, *Philosophical Theology,* p. 479. For another skeptical argument against the possibility of making *a priori* judgments about the improbability of the universe, see David A. Shotwell, "Is the Universe Improbable?" *Skeptical Inquirer,* 11, Summer 1987, pp. 376–382.

34. Tennant, *Philosophical Theology,* p. 113. Indeed, Tennant may have been the first to use the term "anthropic" in this context, when he speaks of a relation between "the intelligibility of the world to the specifically anthropic intelligence possessed by us, and on the connection between the conditioning of that intelligibility, on the one hand, and the constitution and process of Nature, on the other hand." See also John D. Barrow and Frank J. Tipler, *The Anthropic Cosmological Principle* (Oxford: Clarendon Press, 1986), p. 181.

35. George Gale, "Anthropocentrism Reconsidered," *Human Nature and Natural Knowledge,* ed. A. Donagon, A. N. Perovich, Jr., and M. V. Wedin (Dordrecht, Holland: D. Reidel, 1986), p. 236.

36. *Ibid.* See also John Leslie, "Anthropic Principle, World Ensemble, Design," *American Philosophical Quarterly,* 19, 1982, pp. 141–151.

37. See J. Wheeler, "Genesis of Observership," *Foundational Problems in the Special Sciences,* ed. R. Butts and J. Hintikka (Dordrecht, Holland: D. Reidel, 1977). See also Barrow and Tipler, *Anthropic Cosmological Principle,* pp. 21–22, for a discussion of the strong anthropic principle.

38. Gale, "Anthropocentrism Reconsidered," p. 237.

39. See Barrow and Tipler, *Anthropic Cosmological Principle,* p. 16, for a definition of an uncontroversial and nonspeculative formulation of the anthropic principle (the weak anthropic principle). This says basically that the values of physical and cosmological quantities are restricted by the requirement that there be locations where carbon-based life can evolve and the requirement that the universe be old enough for this life to have already evolved.

40. George Gale, "Whither Cosmology: Anthropic, Anthropocentric, Teleological?" *Current Issues in Teleology,* ed. Nicholas Rescher (Lanham, Md.: University Press of America, 1986), p. 105.

41. See Leslie, "Anthropic Principle, World Ensemble, Design," p. 141.

42. *Ibid.,* pp. 148–150.

43. See, for example, George Gaylord Simpson, *The Meaning of Evolution* (New York: New American Library, 1952).

44. Tennant, *Philosophical Theology,* p. 93.

45. *Ibid.,* p. 114, n.1.

46. *Ibid.,* p. 91.

47. Cf. Broad, review of Tennant, *Philosophical Theology,* p. 480.

48. Cf. Edward H. Madden and Peter H. Hare, *Evil and the Concept of God* (Springfield, Ill.: Charles C. Thomas, 1968), pp. 69–70.

49. Tennant, *Philosophical Theology,* p. 103.

50. Schlesinger, *Religion and Scientific Method,* p. 157.

51. *Ibid.,* p. 182.

52. *Ibid.,* p. 185.

53. Cf. Graham Priest, "The Argument from Design," *Australasian Journal of Philosophy,* 59, 1981, pp. 227.

54. Schlesinger, *Religion and Scientific Method,* p. 182.

55. Swinburne, *Existence of God,* chap. 8.

56. *Ibid.,* p. 142.

57. *Ibid.,* p. 144. K would also include so-called tautological evidence—that is, analytic statements of logic and mathematics.

58. Cf. Priest, "Argument from Design," p. 425.

59. Swinburne, *Existence of God,* p. 147.

60. Cf. Gary Doore, "The Argument from Design: Some Better Reasons for Agreeing with Hume," *Religious Studies,* 16, 1980, pp. 157–160.

61. It may be argued that the uniformity of temporal order in this case is due to technology, and the recording would be uniform even if one person had made it. However, the way our present recording technology functions is that usually many people are involved, and one has good reason to infer, from the temporal uniformity of a recording, that many people were involved in making it.

62. For some further criticisms of Swinburne not considered here, see Doore, "Argument from Design."

63. Richard Taylor, *Metaphysics* (Englewood Cliffs, N.J.: Prentice Hall, 1963), p. 96.

64. *Ibid.,* p. 98.

65. *Ibid.*

66. *Ibid.,* p. 99.

67. *Ibid.,* p. 100.

68. *Ibid.*

69. *Ibid.,* p. 102.

70. Jan Narveson, "On a New Argument from Design," *Journal of Philosophy,* 62, 1965, pp. 223–229. For a similar criticism, see John Hick, *Arguments for the Existence of God* (New York: Herder & Herder, 1974), pp. 21–26.

71. Narveson, "On a New Argument from Design," p. 225.

72. *Ibid.,* pp. 227–228.

73. *Ibid.,* p. 228.

74. *Ibid.,* p. 229.

75. In the 1974 edition of *Metaphysics,* Taylor repeats almost word for word

the argument that appeared in the 1963 edition and does not mention either Narveson's or Hick's criticism, although Narveson's appeared in 1965 and Hick's in 1971.

76. Richard E. Creel, "A Realistic Argument for Belief in the Existence of God," *International Journal for the Philosophy of Religion*, 10, 1979, pp. 223–253.

77. *Ibid.*, p. 246.

78. Taylor, *Metaphysics*, p. 101.

79. See, for example, Philip Kitcher, *Abusing Science* (Cambridge, Mass.: MIT Press, 1982); Douglas J. Futuyman, *Science on Trial: The Case for Evolution* (New York: Pantheon Books, 1983).

80. See Futuyman, *Science on Trial*, chap. 6.

81. See, for example, Abner Shimony, "Perception from an Evolutionary Point of View," *Journal of Philosophy*, 68, 1971, 571–583; F. Dretske, "Perception from an Evolutionary Point of View," *Journal of Philosophy*, 68, 1971, pp. 584–591; W. V. Quine, "Epistemology Naturalized," *Ontological Relativity and Other Essays* (New York: Columbia University Press, 1969); D. T. Campbell, "Evolutionary Epistemology," *The Philosophy of Karl Popper*, ed. P. A. Schilpp (La Salle, Ill.: Open Court, 1974).

CHAPTER 6

1. I am indebted here to William Rowe's illuminating discussion of the meaning of religious experience. See William L. Rowe, *Philosophy of Religion: An Introduction* (Belmont, Calif.: Wadsworth, 1978), pp. 63–64.

2. Cf. R. M. Chisholm, *Perception* (Ithaca, N.Y.: Cornell University Press, 1957), chap. 4.

3. See Richard Swinburne, *The Existence of God* (Oxford: Clarendon Press, 1979), pp. 249–253.

4. Quoted in Paul Kurtz, *The Transcendental Temptation* (Buffalo, N.Y.: Prometheus Books, 1986), p. 237.

5. Quoted from Walter T. Stace, *The Teachings of the Mystics* (New York: New American Library, 1960), p. 137.

6. See also Gary Gutting, *Religious Belief and Religious Skepticism* (Notre Dame, Ind.: University of Notre Dame Press, 1982), chap. 5, for further discussion of this type of experience.

7. St. Teresa, *The Life of Teresa of Jesus*, trans. and ed. by E. Allison Peers (Garden City, N.Y.: Image Books, 1960), p. 249. Quoted by George Mavrodes in "Real v. Deceptive Mystical Experiences," *Mysticism and Philosophical Analysis* (New York: Oxford University Press, 1978), p. 238.

8. See Laurence BonJour, *The Structure of Empirical Knowledge* (Cambridge, Mass.: Harvard University Press, 1985), p. 112.

9. Cf. Mavrodes, "Real v. Deceptive Mystical Experiences."

10. Kurtz, *Transcendental Temptation*, pp. 153–159.

11. G. A. Wells, *The Historical Evidence for Jesus* (Buffalo, N.Y.: Prometheus Books, 1982), pp. 22–25.

12. R. Joseph Hoffman, *Jesus Outside the Gospels* (Buffalo, N.Y.: Prometheus Books, 1984).

13. Stace, *Teachings of the Mystics*, p. 14.

14. Walter T. Stace, *Mysticism and Philosophy* (London: Macmillan, 1961), pp. 131–132.

15. *Ibid.*, p. 132.

16. Steven Katz, "Language, Epistemology and Mysticism," *Mysticism and Philosophical Analysis*, pp. 22–74.

17. *Ibid.*, p. 50.

18. See, for example, Gary E. Kessler and Norman Prigge, "Is Mystical Experience Everywhere the Same?" *Sophia*, 21, 1982, pp. 39–55. They argue against Katz, maintaining that mystical experience is contentless consciousness, and such experience is found in all cases of introvertive mysticism. See also Agehananda Bharati, *The Light at the Center* (Santa Barbara, Calif.: Ross-Erikson, 1976), chap. 2. Bharati maintains that his mystical experience and that of others are a "zero experience," by which he means an experience that has zero cognitive content.

19. See, for example, Kurtz, *Transcendental Temptation*, pp. 97–102.

20. Stace, *Teachings of the Mystics*, p. 135. Whether this means that the experience seems to the mystic to have contradictory features or whether, as Katz has suggested, the paradoxical language cloaks the content, we need not decide here. We are assuming for the sake of argument that the experience seems contradictory. See also Katz, "Language, Epistemology and Mysticism," *Mysticism and Philosophical Analysis*, p. 54.

21. Robert Hoffman, "Logic, Meaning and Mystical Intuition," *Philosophical Studies*, 5, 1960, pp. 65–70.

22. For one interesting attempt to account for the incoherence of the descriptions of mystical experiences, see Paul Henle, "Mysticism and Semantics," *Philosophy and Phenomenological Research*, 9, 1948–1949, pp. 416–422.

23. In *Teachings of the Mystics*, p. 27, Stace admits that mystical experiences can be interpreted in terms of many religious traditions.

24. Swinburne, *Existence of God*, chap. 13.

25. *Ibid.*, pp. 290–291.

26. Indeed, I have argued something similar above: In order to justify my spontaneous perceptual belief, for example, that there is a brown table in front of me, it is necessary to give some sort of argument. Moreover, as my criticism of Swinburne's argument makes clear, I do not believe that the way things appear is *by itself* good grounds for believing how they are. A sound argument is needed that enables one to infer from the appearance of x to x.

27. *Ibid.*, p. 254, n. 1.

28. *Ibid.*, p. 255.

29. *Ibid.*, p. 268.

30. *Ibid.*, pp. 268–269.

31. *Ibid.*, p. 267.

32. As Robert Shope has pointed out to me, if one had warrant for applying PC before NPC, then there may already be good evidence for the existence of God, assuming that there are no further problems with PC. However, I see no reason why PC should be applied first; and, in any case, there *are* further problems.

33. Swinburne, *Existence of God*, p. 263.

34. See Ronald N. Giere, *Understanding Scientific Reasoning* (New York: Holt, Rinehart and Winston, 1979), pp. 88–103.

35. It may be argued that one can only know that these perceptual conditions hold by applying PC. If so, then, it may be argued, this would lead to either an infinite regress or a circularity of justification. However, it is not clear that one could only know that these conditions are present by applying PC. One may know that these conditions hold because their existence is entailed by some well-supported theory. To be sure, this theory may be supported indirectly by applications of PC, and although circular justification may be involved, it is not obvious that the circularity is vicious.

36. Personal correspondence, 19 January 1987.

37. Gutting, *Religious Belief and Religious Skepticism*, pp. 148–149.

38. *Ibid.*, p. 149.

39. *Ibid.*, p. 152.

40. *Ibid.*, p. 129.

41. *Ibid.*, p. 187, n. 9.

42. *Ibid.*, pp. 187–188, n. 9.

43. Swinburne, *Existence of God*, p. 267.

44. See Stace, *Teachings of the Mystics*, p. 126; Katz, "Language, Epistemology and Mysticism," *Mysticism and Philosophical Analysis*, p. 27.

45. There are also differences in the same culture. For example, Meister Eckhart tended to describe his religious experience in pantheistic language; some other Christian mystics did not. See Stace, *Teachings of the Mystics*, p. 139.

46. Swinburne, *Existence of God*, pp. 258–259.

47. *Ibid.*, p. 267, n. 1.

48. E. Royston Pike, *Encyclopedia of Religion and Religions* (New York: Meridian Books, 1958), p. 219.

49. Personal correspondence, 19 January 1987.

50. Gutting also attempts to show that religious experiences are not incompatible. But his efforts are no more successful than Swinburne's. He admits that Hindus do not have religious experiences of the Virgin Mary, and Moslems do not have encounters with the trinity. However, he says that "at best this diversity shows that religious experience does not establish the superiority of one religious tradition over others. The fact remains that in all traditions there are countless experiences of a superhuman loving person concerned with us; and even the otherwise divergent physical and mystical visions share this essential core of content." However, as we have already seen, the thesis that all mystical experiences have a common core has been challenged by religious scholars. Moreover, Gutting's thesis that in *all* religious traditions there are countless experiences of a supernatural loving person concerned with us surely needs documentation that he does not provide. It seems unlikely that people in religious traditions that do not have a creator God, such as Jainism and Theravada Buddhism, would have such experiences. Furthermore, as we have argued, the experience of different deities in different religious traditions is often indirectly incompatible. In addition, Gutting's attempt to explain away the differences between experiences of a personal God and experiences of an impersonal God seems inadequate. Gutting suggests that people's religious experience of a supernatural person could be

partially revelatory of the divine nature or perhaps an experience of a mediator between us and God. However, it is unclear how the experience of a personal God can be partially revelatory of an impersonal God. In any case, usually someone who has an experience of a personal or impersonal supernatural being describes the experience as an experience of God, not as an experience of a mediator between us and God. On what non–ad hoc basis does Gutting reinterpret these experiences? It is clear that given enough ad hoc modifications, any seemingly incompatible experience can be made to seem compatible. See Gutting, *Religious Belief and Religious Skepticism*, p. 170.

51. Personal correspondence, 19 January 1987.

52. Robert Shaeffer, "Do Fairies Exist?" *Skeptical Inquirer*, 2, Fall/Winter 1977, pp. 45–52. See also Sir Arthur Conan Doyle, *The Coming of the Fairies* (New York: Samuel Weiser, 1921).

CHAPTER 7

1. See Alan Richardson, *The Miracle-Stories of the Gospels* (New York: Harper & Brothers, 1941).

2. See D. Scott Rogo, *Miracles* (New York: Dial Press, 1982).

3. *Ibid.*, pp. 250–257.

4. *Ibid.*, pp. 33–34.

5. As we saw in Chapter 4, Aquinas appealed to miracles occurring within the Christian tradition to justify the reliance on Christian revelations.

6. See Harry A. Wolfson, "Philo Judaeus," *The Encyclopedia of Philosophy*, ed. Paul Edwards (New York and London: Macmillan and Free Press, 1967), vol. 6, p. 152.

7. Fazlur Rahman, "Islamic Philosophy," *Encyclopedia of Philosophy*, vol. 4, p. 222.

8. The canon runs as follows: "If anyone shall say that miracles cannot happen . . . or that the divine origin of the Christian religion cannot properly be proved by them: let them be anathema." See H. Denzinger, *Enchiridion Symbolorum*, 29th rev. ed. (Freiburg im Breisgau: Herder, 1953), sec. 1813. Quoted in Antony Flew, *God: A Critical Enquiry*, 2d ed. (La Salle, Ind.: Open Court, 1984), p. 136.

9. For an analysis of some recent views on miracles, see Ernst and Marie-Luise Keller, *Miracles in Dispute* (Philadelphia: Fortress Press, 1969).

10. Flew, *God: A Critical Enquiry*, p. 136.

11. Richard Swinburne, *The Existence of God* (Oxford: Clarendon Press, 1979), chap. 12.

12. Richard L. Purtill, *Thinking About Religion: A Philosophical Introduction to Religion* (Englewood Cliffs, N.J.: Prentice Hall, 1978), pp. 124–134. Reprinted in Louis P. Pojman, *Philosophy of Religion* (Belmont, Calif.: Wadsworth, 1987), pp. 287–289.

13. See, for example, Antony Flew, "Miracles," *Encyclopedia of Philosophy*, vol. 5, p. 346.

14. I am indebted here to Paul Fitzgerald, "Miracles," *Philosophical Forum*, 18, 1985, pp. 48–64. The definition adopted here is compatible with the view that

every event is brought about by some supernatural power. It is also compatible with the view that the world would not exist without the conserving power of some supernatural being. See Alvin Plantinga, "Is Theism Really a Miracle?" *Faith and Philosophy*, 3, 1986, p. 111. Our definition should be compared with Richard Swinburne's in *The Concept of Miracle* (London: Macmillan, 1970), p. 1. Swinburne gives a general definition of a miracle as an event of an extraordinary kind brought about by a god and of religious significance. However, he argues that the word is sometimes used in a narrower or wider sense.

15. Is it logically possible for a human being to have supernatural powers? It may be argued that it is logically possible for humans to have powers of ESP and psychokinesis. These are often called paranormal powers, but the difference between a paranormal and a supernatural power is not completely clear. See Fitzgerald, "Miracles," pp. 50–51; see also Stephen E. Braude, *ESP and Psychokinesis* (Philadelphia: Temple University Press, 1979), pp. 242–263.

16. Fitzgerald, "Miracles," pp. 58–62.

17. See, for example, Swinburne, *Existence of God*, pp. 228–230; see also Swinburne, *Concept of Miracle*, pp. 26–27.

18. For a similar argument, see Andrew Rein, "Repeatable Miracles?" *Analysis*, 46, 1986, pp. 109–112.

19. See the special issue of *Free Inquiry*, 6, Spring 1986, on faith healing.

20. Swinburne, *Existence of God*, chap. 1.

21. See Swinburne, *Concept of Miracle*, chap. 6.

22. Criticisms similar to this were raised by eighteenth-century deists Thomas Woolston and Thomas Chubb. See R. M. Burns, *The Great Debate on Miracles* (Lewisburg, Penna.: Bucknell University Press, 1981), pp. 77–79.

23. This argument from miracles against the existence of God has obvious similarities to the argument from evil against the existence of God, which I consider in Part II. See Christine Overall, "Miracles as Evidence Against the Existence of God," *Southern Journal of Philosophy*, 13, 1985, pp. 347–353.

24. C. S. Lewis, *Miracles* (New York: Macmillan, 1978), chaps. 12–16. Lewis argues at some length that belief in the Christian God is compatible with miracles. This does not seem very controversial. The crucial question is whether the existence of miracles gives more support to theism than to other supernatural theories. Lewis does not address this question.

25. *Ibid.*, pp. 10–11.

26. *Ibid.*, p. 6.

27. It seems clear that Lewis is referring to what above we call nature$_n$.

28. Lewis, *Miracles*, chap. 2.

29. *Ibid.*, chap. 5.

30. *Ibid.*, p. 18.

31. See, for example, D. M. Armstrong, *Belief, Truth, and Knowledge* (London: Cambridge University Press, 1974), chap. 6.

32. Lewis, *Miracles*, p. 36. For example, see Richard Brandt, *Ethical Theory* (Englewood Cliffs, N.J.: Prentice Hall, 1959), chap. 7.

33. See David Hume, *An Inquiry Concerning Human Understanding* (New York: Liberal Arts Press, 1955), sec. 10. Reprinted under the title "Against Miracles," in Pojman, *Philosophy of Religion*, pp. 264–273.

34. Cf. J. L. Mackie, *The Miracle of Theism* (Oxford: Clarendon Press, 1982), pp. 26–29, and Fitzgerald, "Miracles," p. 56.

35. For example, Fitzgerald in "Miracles" clearly interprets Hume in this way. Whether Richard Swinburne "Miracles," *Philosophical Quarterly*, 18, 1968; reprinted under the title "For the Possibility of Miracles," in Pojman, *Philosophy of Religion*, pp. 273–279 so interprets Hume is less clear. Whether Hume actually held that miracles by definition are nonrepeatable is uncertain.

36. Cf. Gary Colwell, "On Defining Away Miracles," *Philosophy*, 57, 1982, pp. 327–336. Notice, however, that this evidence would not be enough to suppose that E was not governed by a law of nature$_n$. Consequently, it would not be enough to suppose that E was a miracle.

37. As Burns has shown, Hume was not the first to propose the sort of *a posteriori* arguments found in "Of Miracles" against the existence of miracles. See Burns, *Great Debate on Miracles*, chaps. 3 and 4.

38. See Mackie, *Miracle of Theism*, pp. 14–16, for a lucid exposition of these arguments.

39. John B. Gill, "Miracles with Method," *Sophia*, 16, 1977, pp. 19–26. Gill has argued that miracle claims are compatible with scientific progress, since such claims may be only tentatively held and are compatible with reconsidering the claims in the light of new evidence. Although it may well be true that such open-mindedness is logically compatible with miracle claims, one wonders if it in fact works this way. Historically it seems clear that belief in miracles has been detrimental to scientific progress; and given the psychology of typical believers, it is likely to remain so. Moreover, even if such claims are put forth tentatively, the question is whether they are justified in the light of the rapid increases in knowledge in such fields as medical science. As we show later, in discussing the cures at Lourdes, as medical knowledge has increased the number of inexplicable cures has decreased. This evidence suggests that miracle claims in the area of medical science, even if tentatively held, may be unjustified in terms of the progress of medicine.

40. Rogo, *Miracles*, p. 256. Oddly enough, Rogo does not even consider the possibility that the luminous figure may have been the result of fraud and deception. The technical capacity to create such a luminous figure certainly existed in the late 1960s, yet Rogo provides no evidence of any attempt to rule out fraud.

41. See James Randi, " 'Be Healed in the Name of God!' An Exposé of the Reverend W. V. Grant," *Free Inquiry*, 6, 1986, pp. 8–19. See also James Randi, *The Faith Healers* (Buffalo, N.Y.: Prometheus Books, 1987).

42. See James Randi, "The Project Alpha Experiment: Part I, The First Two Years," *Skeptical Inquirer*, 7, Summer 1983, pp. 24–33; "Part 2, Beyond the Laboratory," *Skeptical Inquirer*, 8, Fall 1983, pp. 36–45.

43. Cf. Gary G. Colwell, "Miracles and History," *Sophia*, 22, 1983, pp. 9–14. Colwell argues that in the Bible in Lk. 24:1–11 and Jn. 20:24–29 one finds examples of skeptical humanity among Jesus' followers who were forced to accept his miracles from love of truth. But it is unclear why Colwell accepts these biblical stories as true, since there are many inconsistencies in the story of the resurrection, where the examples of skeptical humanity are supposed to be

found. Furthermore, Colwell ignores the independent evidence we have from contemporary faith healers, indicating the difficulty of being skeptical when one is deeply involved in a religious movement. See Paul Kurtz, *The Transcendental Temptation* (Buffalo, N.Y.: Prometheus Books, 1986), pp. 153–160, for an analysis of these inconsistencies; and see Randi, *Faith Healers,* for the lack of skepticism in the context of faith healing.

44. Carl Friedrich Bahrdt, a German theologian of the Enlightenment, suggested that Jesus walked on floating pieces of timber. For a discussion of Bahrdt's views, see Ernst and Marie-Luise Keller, *Miracles in Dispute,* pp. 69–70. The Kellers raise two objections to Bahrdt's explanation. They argue that according to Scripture the boat was not near the shore, and that in any case Jesus' disciples would have noticed the timber. However, it is uncertain whether Scripture is correct about the location of the boat. In any case, if we substitute rocks for timber, the location of the boat according to Scripture can be accepted. Rocks below the surface of the water may extend for many furlongs out to sea. The Kellers mention Bahrdt's not-implausible explanation of the failure of the disciples to notice. "They were 'held prisoner' by the prejudices of their own miracle-believing age—with constantly inflamed imaginations—always saw more in the phenomena than was there in reality" (p. 71.).

45. See Morton Smith, *Jesus the Magician* (New York: Harper & Row, 1978).

46. See, for example, A. Daniel Yarmey, *The Psychology of Eyewitness Testimony* (New York: Free Press, 1979).

47. Hume, *Inquiry Concerning Human Understanding,* pp. 129–130.

48. See Bruce Langtry, "Hume on Miracles and Contrary Religions," *Sophia,* 14, 1975, pp. 29–34.

49. Cf. David A. Conway, "Miracles, Evidence and Contrary Religion," *Sophia,* 22, 1983, pp. 3–14; Bruce Langtry, "Miracles and Rival Systems of Religion," *Sophia,* 24, 1985, pp. 21–31.

50. Ellen Bernstein, "Lourdes," *Encyclopaedia Britannica,* Medical and Health Annual, 1982, p. 130.

51. *Ibid.,* pp. 131–133.

52. *Ibid.,* p. 134.

53. *Ibid.*

54. See Patrick Marnham, *Lourdes: A Modern Pilgrimage* (New York: Coward, McCann and Geoghegan, 1981).

55. Randi, *Faith Healers,* pp. 27–29.

56. *Acta Orthopaedica Scandinavica,* 49, 1978, pp. 49–53. Cited in Randi, *Faith Healers,* pp. 28–29.

57. Bernstein, "Lourdes," p. 139.

58. See Fitzgerald, "Miracles," p. 61.

59. *Ibid.*

60. As we shall see in Chapter 15 on the free will defense, some philosophers have argued that free will in the contracausal sense, in which human decisions are uncaused, is compatible with God's knowing how human beings will decide and how they would decide under certain hypothetical circumstances. However, as I argue, this view is difficult to make sense of.

CHAPTER 8

1. In our treatment of common consent arguments I am deeply indebted to Paul Edwards, "Common Consent Argument for the Existence of God," *The Encyclopedia of Philosophy* (New York and London: Macmillan and Free Press, 1967), vol. 2, pp. 147–155.

2. See Rudolf Eisler, "Consensus Gentium," *Wörterbuch der philosophischen Begriff*, 3 vols., 4th ed. (Berlin, 1930). Cited in Edwards, "Common Consent Argument for the Existence of God," p. 147.

3. See J. S. Mill, *Three Essays on Religion* (London, 1874). Cited in Edwards, "Common Consent Argument for the Existence of God," p. 147.

4. See Edwards, "Common Consent Argument for the Existence of God," p. 154, for a bibliography of popular religious apologists who use the argument.

5. Here I depart somewhat from the formulation suggested by Mill in *Three Essays on Religion*, p. 156. Mill argued that the "belief that the human mind was made by a God who would not deceive his creatures" begs the question. However, one might argue that the hypothesis that God made humans with this innate belief so they would not be deceived is the best explanation of the fact of innateness. Construed as an inference to the best explanation, there is no problem of begging the question. Cf. Edwards, "Common Consent Argument for the Existence of God," p. 149.

6. *Ibid.*, p. 148. According to Edwards, this dispositional version of the argument was used by Charles Hodge in *Systematic Theology* (New York, 1871–1873), vol. 1, p. 199.

7. According to Edwards, "Common Consent Argument for the Existence of God," p. 149, this version of the argument was used by Hodge in *Systematic Theology*, vol. 1, p. 200.

8. Edwards argues that this version of the argument was used by G. H. Joyce in *The Principle of Natural Theology* (London, 1923), p. 179. See Edwards, "Common Consent Argument for the Existence of God," p. 150.

9. According to a poll conducted by the Gallup International Research Institute 56 percent of the Japanese, 35 percent of the Scandinavians, 28 percent of the West Germans, and 28 percent of the French who were polled answered no to the question, "Do you believe in God or a universal spirit?" One would suppose that these figures would rise considerably if the question were posed more specifically—for example: Do you believe in a God who is all-good, all-powerful, and all-knowing and who created the universe? See Thomas H. Davenport, "Prevalence of Unbelief," *The Encyclopedia of Unbelief* (Buffalo, N.Y.: Prometheus Books, 1985), vol. 2, p. 519.

10. See Edwards, "Common Consent Argument for the Existence of God," p. 151.

11. Burnham P. Beckwith, "The Effect of Intelligence on Religious Faith," *Free Inquiry*, 6, Spring 1986, p. 51.

12. See Ronald W. Hepburn, "Moral Arguments for the Existence of God," *Encyclopedia of Philosophy*, vol. 5, pp. 381–385.

13. For a critical analysis of several other versions, see *ibid.*

14. Hastings Rashdall, "God and the Moral Consciousness," *Religious Belief and Philosophical Thought*, ed. William Alston (New York: Harcourt, Brace and World, 1963), p. 92.

15. J. L. Mackie, *The Miracle of Theism* (Oxford: Clarendon Press, 1982), p. 115. See also J. L. Mackie, *Ethics: Inventing Right and Wrong* (New York: Penguin Books, 1977), pp. 38–42. Since Mackie believes that a satisfactory subjectivist account of ethics is possible, he argues that no such explanation is needed.

16. See W. R. Sorely, "The Moral Argument," *Approaches to the Philosophy of Religion*, ed. Daniel J. Bronstein and Harold M. Schulweis, (New York: Prentice Hall, 1954), pp. 171–175.

17. See, for example, Roderick Firth, "Ethical Absolutism and the Ideal Observer," *Philosophy and Phenomenological Research*, 12, 1952, pp. 317–345; Peter Railton, "Moral Realism," *Philosophical Review*, 95, 1986, pp. 163–207.

18. See Railton, "Moral Realism," p. 165.

19. See Richard B. Brandt, *Ethical Theory* (Englewood Cliffs, N.J.: Prentice Hall, 1959), chap. 11; Mackie, *Ethics*, pp. 36–42.

20. See Mackie, *Ethics*.

21. Brandt, *Ethical Theory*, chap. 10.

22. John Henry Newman, "Conscience as the Voice of God," *Approaches to the Philosophy of Religion*, pp. 175–183.

23. *Ibid.*, p. 178.

24. See Mackie, *Miracle of Theism*, p. 105.

25. Immanuel Kant, "God and Immorality as Postulates of Practical Reason," in John Hick, *Classical and Contemporary Readings in the Philosophy of Religion*, 2d ed. (Englewood Cliffs, N.J.: Prentice Hall, 1970), p. 152.

26. Mackie, *Miracle of Theism*, p. 109.

27. Michael Scriven, *Primary Philosophy* (New York: McGraw-Hill, 1966), p. 140.

28. Harold S. Kushner, *When Bad Things Happen to Good People* (New York: Schocken Books, 1981), pp. 6–7.

29. Scriven, *Primary Philosophy*, p. 141.

30. *Ibid.*, p. 131.

31. See Kant, "God and Immorality," p. 150.

32. Cf. Scriven, *Primary Philosophy*, p. 132.

33. See Michael Arnheim, *Is Christianity True?* (Buffalo, N.Y.: Prometheus Books, 1984), chaps. 1 and 4; Paul Kurtz, *The Transcendental Temptation* (Buffalo, N.Y.: Prometheus Books, 1986), pp. 120–125, 151–160; R. Joseph Hoffman, *Jesus Outside the Gospels* (Buffalo, N.Y.: Prometheus Books, 1984).

34. Richard Swinburne, *The Existence of God* (Oxford: Clarendon Press, 1979), chap. 9.

35. *Ibid.*, p. 172.

36. *Ibid.*, p. 173.

37. See Mackie, *Miracle of Theism*, pp. 121–128.

38. Swinburne, *Existence of God*, p. 172.

39. Mackie, *Miracle of Theism*, pp. 130–131.

40. Swinburne, *Existence of God*, chap. 10.

41. *Ibid.*, p. 180.

42. *Ibid.,* p. 189.

43. *Ibid.,* p. 193.

44. *Ibid.*

45. *Ibid.,* p. 194.

46. I am indebted here to the account of this argument by Gary Gutting, *Religious Belief and Religious Skepticism* (Notre Dame, Ind.: University of Notre Dame Press, 1982), chap. 4.

47. Basil Mitchell, *The Justification of Religious Belief* (New York: Seabury, 1973).

48. Ian Barbour, *Myths, Models, and Paradigms* (New York: Harper & Row, 1974).

49. Thomas Kuhn, "Reflections on My Critics," *Criticism and the Growth of Knowledge,* ed. Imre Lakatos and Alan Musgrave (Cambridge, Eng.; Cambridge University Press, 1970), p. 262.

50. Gary Gutting, "Introduction," *Paradigms and Revolutions,* ed. Gary Gutting (Notre Dame, Ind.: University of Notre Dame Press, 1980), p. 8.

51. Barbour, *Myths, Models, and Paradigms,* p. 115.

52. See, for example, *ibid.,* p. 145.

53. As Gutting points out, Barbour's notion of paradigm differs from Kuhn's. Although Kuhn's use of "paradigm" was ambiguous in his original work, he now seems to identify a paradigm with an exemplar—that is, a universally recognized scientific achievement. Barbour identifies a paradigm with the tradition associated with an exemplar. Kuhn now prefers to call this a disciplinary matrix.

54. For some of this criticism, see the papers by Dudley Shapere and Alan Musgrave in *Paradigms and Revolutions.*

55. See Barbour, *Myths, Models, and Paradigms,* p. 179.

56. Gutting, *Religious Belief and Religious Skepticism,* chap. 4.

57. *Ibid.,* p. 126.

58. Swinburne, *Existence of God,* p. 289.

59. Richard Swinburne, *The Coherence of Theism* (Oxford: Clarendon Press, 1977).

60. Swinburne, *Existence of God,* p. 289.

61. Gutting, *Religious Belief and Religious Skepticism,* pp. 127–140.

62. *Ibid.,* p. 131.

63. *Ibid.*

64. *Ibid.,* p. 135.

65. *Ibid.,* p. 136.

66. *Ibid.*

67. *Ibid.,* p. 137.

68. *Ibid.*

CHAPTER 9

1. Arguments of this kind have also been called practical arguments. See Nicholas Rescher, *Pascal's Wager: A Study of Practical Reasoning in Philosophical Theology* (Notre Dame, Ind.: University of Notre Dame Press, 1985).

2. *Ibid.,* p. 4.

3. Quoted in Richard Popkin, "Blaise Pascal," *The Encyclopedia of Philosophy,*

ed. Paul Edwards (New York and London: Macmillan and Free Press, 1967), vol. 6, p. 54.

4. Rescher, *Pascal's Wager*, pp. 3–7.

5. Blaise Pascal, "The Wager," *Philosophy of Religion*, ed. Louis P. Pojman (Belmont, Calif.: Wadsworth, 1987), p. 383.

6. Cf. Blaise Pascal, *Thoughts*, trans. W. F. Trotter (New York: Collier, 1910). Rescher argues that Pascal's wager "seeks to invite belief through the prospect of reward and not by intimidation through the possibility of eternal hellfire." See Rescher, *Pascal's Wager*, p. 91. I do not wish to deny the historical accuracy of Rescher's interpretation. But his point is irrelevant to our purposes here. A God who did punish nonbelievers not only is possible but has been accepted by many Christians past and present. A God who was more tolerant of nonbelief than the God considered here would not affect our argument in any way.

7. See Ian Hacking, "The Logic of Pascal's Wager," *American Philosophical Quarterly*, 4, 1972, pp. 186–192; James Cargile, "Pascal's Wager," *Philosophy*, 41, 1966, pp. 250–257; Michael Martin, "On Four Critiques of Pascal's Wager," *Sophia*, 14, 1975, pp. 1–11.

8. See Antony Duff, "Pascal's Wager and Infinite Utilities," *Analysis*, 46, 1986, pp. 107–109. Duff has argued that given the fact that infinite utilities are involved, it makes no difference what action one takes. This is because no matter what action one takes there is some finite probability that it will lead to belief in God. This finite probability, multiplied by the infinite reward for belief in God, means that the result of every action has an infinite expected utility. Duff concludes that this result suggests that there is something wrong with trying to capture the infinite in a calculus of probabilities.

9. For a more detailed discussion of Pascal's wager from a decision-theory standpoint, see Hacking, "Logic of Pascal's Wager."

10. For a discussion of these and other rules, see D. C. Luce and Howard Raiffa, *Games and Decisions* (New York: Wiley, 1957), chaps. 1–4.

11. Clearly then the view is mistaken that one must assume that the probability is 0.5 that God exists and 0.5 that he does not exist in order to make the argument work. For this mistaken criticism, see Monroe Beardsley and Elizabeth Beardsley, *Philosophical Thinking: An Introduction* (New York: Harcourt, Brace and World, 1965), p. 140. Hacking, "Logic of Pascal's Wager," p. 189, claims that Pascal is committed to this assumption in one formulation of his argument. However, this assumption is not made in the version of the argument considered here.

12. Rescher, *Pascal's Wager*, p. 98.

13. *Ibid.*, p. 99.

14. *Ibid.*, p. 93.

15. *Ibid.*.

16. For a discussion of epistemic values in decision theory, see Isaac Levi, *Gambling with Truth* (New York: Knopf, 1967); Carl Hempel, "Inductive Inconsistencies," *Aspects of Scientific Explanation* (New York: Free Press, 1963), pp. 73–79.

17. William James, "The Will to Believe," *Philosophy of Religion*, p. 388.

18. *Ibid.*

19. *Ibid.*, p. 389.

20. *Ibid.*, p. 391.

21. *Ibid.*, pp. 393–394.

22. *Ibid.*, p. 394.

23. *Ibid.*

24. *Ibid.*

25. See, for example, J. L. Mackie, *The Miracle of Theism* (Oxford: Clarendon Press, 1982), p. 209.

26. Rescher, *Pascal's Wager*, p. 119.

27. Wallace I. Matson, *The Existence of God* (Ithaca, N.Y.: Cornell University Press, 1965), p. 213.

28. Walter Kaufmann, *Critique of Religion and Philosophy* (New York: Harper & Brothers, 1958), p. 85.

29. Cf. Mackie, *Miracle of Theism*, p. 207.

30. *Ibid.*, p. 209.

CHAPTER 10

1. See, for example, *Summa Contra Gentiles*, 1, trans. Vernon J. Bourke (New York: Doubleday, 1953).

2. Anthony Kenny, *Faith and Reason* (New York: Columbia University Press, 1983), p. 70.

3. See William L. Rowe, *Philosophy of Religion* (Belmont, Calif.: Wadsworth, 1978), p. 172.

4. *Summa Contra Gentiles*, bk. 1, chap. 7.

5. Kenny, *Faith and Reason*, p. 75.

6. The only other religious tradition that Aquinas considers is Islam. He dismisses its success as based on promises of carnal pleasure and force of arms. That this is too simple a view of the success of Islam seems clear. Further, Aquinas's thesis that the success of Christianity is a miracle not explainable in naturalistic terms is surely dubious.

7. See, for example, Michael Arnheim, *Is Christianity True?* (Buffalo, N.Y.: Prometheus Books, 1984).

8. Cf. J. Kellenberger, "Three Models of Faith," *International Journal for the Philosophy of Religion*, 12, 1981, p. 219.

9. See Søren Kierkegaard, *Concluding Unscientific Postscript*, trans. David F. Swenson, ed. Walter Lowrie (Princeton, N.J.: Princeton University Press, 1941).

10. Cf. J. L. Mackie, *The Miracle of Theism* (Oxford: Clarendon Press, 1982), pp. 215–216.

11. See Walter Kaufmann, *From Shakespeare to Existentialism* (Garden City, N.Y.: Doubleday, 1959), p. 177.

12. *Ibid.*, p. 178.

13. Mackie, *Miracle of Theism*, p. 216.

14. See Kaufmann, *From Shakespeare to Existentialism*, p. 198.

15. Robert Merrihew Adams, "Kierkegaard's Arguments Against Objective Reasoning in Religion," *Philosophy of Religion*, ed. Louis P. Pojman (Belmont, Calif.: Wadsworth, 1986), pp. 408–417.

16. My statement of Adams's reformulations of Kierkegaard's arguments follows the statement given in Louis P. Pojman, "Fideism: Faith Without/Against Reason," *Philosophy of Religion,* p. 398.

17. Adams, "Kierkegaard's Arguments," p. 413.

18. *Ibid.,* p. 417.

19. *Ibid.*

20. *Ibid.*

21. See, for example, Arnheim, *Is Christianity True?*; Paul Kurtz, *The Transcendental Temptation* (Buffalo, N.Y.: Prometheus Books, 1986); G. A. Wells, *The Historical Evidence for Jesus* (Buffalo, N.Y.: Prometheus Books, 1982).

22. See Arnheim, *Is Christianity True?*; Wells, *Historical Evidence for Jesus.*

23. See Ludwig Wittgenstein, *Lectures and Conversations on Aesthetics, Psychology and Religious Belief,* ed. Cyril Barrett (Oxford: Blackwell, 1966).

24. See, for example, Norman Malcolm, "The Groundlessness of Belief," *Philosophy of Religion,* pp. 422–430. See also D. Z. Phillips, *Concept of Prayer* (London: Routledge and Kegan Paul, 1970); and Peter Winch, *The Idea of a Social Science* (London: Routledge and Kegan Paul, 1958).

25. For an excellent analysis and evaluation of this approach, see Kai Nielsen, *An Introduction to the Philosophy of Religion* (New York: St. Martin's Press, 1982), chaps. 3–5. See also Gary Gutting, *Religious Belief and Religious Skepticism* (Notre Dame, Ind.: University of Notre Dame Press, 1982), chap. 1.

26. Nielsen, *Introduction to the Philosophy of Religion,* p. 83.

27. Malcolm, "Groundlessness of Beliefs," p. 423.

28. *Ibid.,* p. 424.

29. *Ibid.,* p. 427.

30. Gutting, *Religious Belief and Religious Skepticism,* p. 34.

31. For further criticism of Malcolm's view on religious belief found in some of his other papers, see Nielsen, *Introduction to the Philosophy of Religion,* pp. 93–100. For criticism of D. Z. Phillips's Wittgensteinian views, see Gutting, *Religious Belief and Religious Skepticism,* pp. 34–49.

32. J. S. Clegg, "Faith," *American Philosophical Quarterly,* 16, 1979, pp. 225–232.

33. *Ibid.,* p. 229.

34. *Ibid.,* p. 231.

35. See Richard Swinburne, *Faith and Reason* (Oxford: Clarendon Press, 1981), pp. 104–115.

36. Louis Pojman, "Faith Without Belief?" *Faith and Philosophy,* 3, 1986, pp. 157–176.

37. *Ibid.,* p. 170.

38. *Ibid.,* p. 171.

39. See Alvin Plantinga, "Religious Belief Without Evidence," *Philosophy of Religion,* pp. 454–468; Alvin Plantinga, "Is Belief in God Properly Basic?" *Nous,* 15, 1981, pp. 41–51; Alvin Plantinga, "Is Belief in God Rational?" *Rationality and Religious Belief,* ed. C. F. Delaney (Notre Dame, Ind.: University of Notre Dame Press, 1979), pp. 7–27. For a similar position see Nicholas Wolterstorff, "Can Belief in God Be Rational If It Has No Foundations?" *Faith and Rationality,* ed.

Alvin Plantinga and Nicholas Wolterstorff (Notre Dame, Ind.: University of Notre Dame Press, 1983).

40. Foundationalism could be considered a descriptive theory. As such it simply describes the beliefs that are basic for certain cultures or individuals and how nonbasic beliefs are related to the basic ones. It contains no reasons why any belief at all might not be basic for certain groups or for a certain person.

41. See, for example, D. M. Armstrong, *Belief, Truth and Knowledge* (London: Cambridge University Press, 1973), p. 157.

42. Mark Pastin, "Modest Foundationalism and Self-Warrant," *Essays on Knowledge and Justification,* ed. George S. Pappas and Marshall Swain (Ithaca, N.Y.: Cornell University Press, 1978), pp. 279–288.

43. See, for example, Kenny, *Faith and Reason,* pp. 32–33.

44. See Roderick M. Chisholm, *Theory of Knowledge* (Englewood Cliffs, N.J.: Prentice Hall, 1966), chap. 3.

45. Plantinga, "Religious Belief Without Evidence," p. 461.

46. *Ibid.,* p. 464.

47. *Ibid.*

48. *Ibid.,* p. 465.

49. Plantinga, "Is Belief in God Properly Basic?" p. 46.

50. Plantinga, "Religious Belief Without Evidence," p. 468.

51. *Ibid.*

52. James E. Tomberlin, review of Plantinga and Wolterstorff, *Faith and Rationality,* in *Nous,* 20, 1986, p. 405.

53. *Ibid.*

54. Philip Quinn, "In Search of the Foundations of Theism," *Philosophy of Religion,* pp. 472–473. In Plantinga's reply to Quinn he argues that statements of the data to be used in the inductive inference, such as " '2 + 1 = 3' is properly basic in circumstances C," are neither self-evident nor incorrigible. See Alvin Plantinga, "The Foundations of Theism: A Reply," *Faith and Philosophy,* 3, 1986, p. 299. However, Quinn argues that they could be, and there seems to be no clear way of reconciling his disagreement with Plantinga. This seems to be especially true given that what is self-evident is relative to persons. Cf. Tomberlin, review of Plantinga and Wolterstorff, *Faith and Rationality,* p. 405. Furthermore, it is not completely clear why statements such as " '2 + 1 = 3' is properly basic in circumstances C" need be either self-evident or incorrigible. Perhaps such a statement should not be considered as a basic data statement but as an intermediate hypothesis that provides a partial explanation of the basic data, the fact that 2 + 1 = 3. Using such intermediate hypotheses, one inductively generalizes that (1) is true.

55. Cf. Michael P. Levine, review of Plantinga and Wolterstorff, *Faith and Rationality in Philosophia,* 16, 1986, p. 447. See also Julie Gowen, "Foundationalism and the Justification of Religious Belief," *Religious Studies,* 19, 1983, pp. 393–406.

56. Plantinga, "Religious Belief Without Evidence," p. 462.

57. See, for example, Armstrong, *Belief, Truth and Knowledge*; Pastin, "Modest Foundationalism and Self-Warrant"; Kenny, *Faith and Reason*; Anthony Quinton, *The Nature of Things* (London: Routledge and Kegan Paul, 1973); James W.

Corman, "Foundational versus Nonfoundational Theories of Empirical Justification," *Essays on Knowledge and Justification,* ed. George S. Pappas and Marshall Swain (Ithaca, N.Y.: Cornell University Press, 1978), pp. 229–252.

58. Cf. Kenny, *Faith and Reason,* p. 16; William J. Abraham, *An Introduction to the Philosophy of Religion* (Englewood Cliffs, N.J.: Prentice Hall, 1985); pp. 93–96; Quinn, "In Search of the Foundations of Theism," p. 472; Louis Pojman, "Can Religious Belief Be Rational?" *Philosophy of Religion,* p. 481; J. Wesley Robbins, "Is Belief in God Properly Basic?" *International Journal for the Philosophy of Religion,* 14, 1983, pp. 241–248.

59. See Abraham, *Introduction to the Philosophy of Religion,* p. 95.

60. Indeed, as we shall see, Plantinga takes the argument for evil so seriously that he has attempted to answer it in detail.

61. In his latest writings Plantinga has begun to relate epistemic justification to proper cognitive functioning as well as to relate proper cognitive functioning to God's designing human beings in such a way that they tend to have true beliefs under certain circumstances. See Alvin Plantinga, "Epistemic Justification," *Nous,* 20, 1986, p. 15.

62. Cf. Gutting, *Religious Belief and Religious Skepticism,* p. 83.

63. See Richard Grigg, "Theism and Properly Basic: A Response to Plantinga," *International Journal for the Philosophy of Religion,* 14, 1983, p. 126.

64. Further, given Plantinga's latest attempt to relate epistemic justification to God's designing human beings in such a way that they tend to have true beliefs under certain circumstances, a problem for Plantinga is how to account for this lack of uniformity. How can the human cognitive apparatus be working properly in the area of religious belief when there is so little agreement among people about such beliefs? And if this apparatus is not working properly in the area of religious belief, how can one claim that God designed the apparatus?

65. Levine, review of Plantinga and Wolterstorff, *Faith and Rationality,* p. 455.

66. Plantinga, "Is Belief in God Rational?" p. 27.

67. On this point see also Gowen, "Foundationalism and the Justification of Religious Belief," p. 404.

68. Lawrence BonJour, *The Structure of Empirical Knowledge* (Cambridge, Mass.: Harvard University Press, 1985), pp. 31–32.

69. Since in recent writings Plantinga has begun to relate epistemic justification to the creation by God of beings who are designed "to achieve true beliefs with respect to a wide variety of propositions," perhaps a criterion of properly basic belief will soon be forthcoming. See Plantinga, "Epistemic Justification," p. 15. If this idea of proper cognitive functioning is used to formulate a criterion of properly basic, it would seem to follow that a belief is properly basic only if the person who holds the belief has a properly functioning cognitive apparatus for the environment. This would entail that God designed the person in such a way that the basic beliefs tended to be true. If this is so, then it is clear that BonJour's critique holds. To be justified in holding that a belief is basic or that it is likely to be true would involve at least one further empirical belief. In particular, it would entail holding beliefs about the existence of God and what He created.

70. For an interesting attempt to distinguish Plantinga foundationalism from

fideism, see Richard Askew, "On Fideism and Alvin Plantinga," *International Journal for the Philosophy of Religion*, 23, 1988, pp. 3–16.

CHAPTER 11

1. Michael Scriven, *Primary Philosophy* (New York: McGraw-Hill, 1966), p. 102.

2. *Ibid.*

3. These conditions are to be understood as jointly sufficient for disbelief and not as individually necessary.

4. Moreover, it seems to be a dogma of the Catholic Church defined by the First Vatican Council that "the one and true God our creator and lord can be known for certain through the creation by the natural light of human reason." H. Denzinger, *Enchiridion Symbolorum*, 29th rev. ed. (Freiburg im Breisgau: Herder, 1953), sec. 1806. Quoted in Antony Flew, "The Presumption of Atheism," *God, Freedom and Immortality* (Buffalo, N.Y.: Prometheus Books, 1984), p. 16.

5. See John Hick, *Evil and the God of Love*, rev. ed. (New York: Harper & Row, 1977), p. 353.

6. The view presented here appears to be in conflict with an argument of Thomas V. Morris, who maintains that the absence of good grounds for the existence of God would warrant atheism in contrast to agnosticism only if one were in good epistemic position to deny the claim that God exists. For Morris, "being in a good epistemic position relative to a proposition is being in such a position that should there be positive epistemic considerations for the truth of the proposition, one would have them, or most likely have them" (p. 222). Morris argues that since the claim that God exists is a metaphysical existence claim, it is unlikely that one could be in a good epistemic position relative to it without being able to prove or disprove it. However, as I have already argued, there is good prima facie reason to suppose that if God exists, there should be evidence for His existence. Thus there are prima facie grounds for supposing that we are in a good epistemic position with respect to the proposition that God exists. Although these grounds may be defeated, they have not been; and until they are, we are justified in disbelieving in God. See Thomas V. Morris, "Agnosticism," *Analysis*, 45, 1985, pp. 219–224. For a different argument against Morris, see P. J. McGrath, "Atheism or Agnosticism," *Analysis*, 47, 1987, pp. 54–56.

CHAPTER 12

1. Richard Swinburne, *The Coherence of Theism* (Oxford: Clarendon Press, 1977), pp. 38–49.

2. On this point, see Thomas V. Morris, *The Logic of God Incarnate* (Ithaca, N.Y.: Cornell University Press, 1986), pp. 86–87.

3. For an account of these two types of knowledge, see Israel Scheffler, *Conditions of Knowledge* (Chicago: Scott, Foresman, 1965).

4. See D. W. Hamlyn, *The Theory of Knowledge* (Garden City, N.Y.: Doubleday, 1970), pp. 104–106.

5. See Patrick Grim, "Some Neglected Problems of Omniscience," *American Philosophical Quarterly*, 20, 1983, p. 265.

6. This argument was developed in Michael Martin, "A Disproof of the God of the Common Man," *Question*, 7, 1974, 115–124.

7. Cf. David Blumenfeld, "On the Compossibility of the Divine Attributes," *Philosophical Studies*, 34, 1978, pp. 91–103.

8. For example, Morris in *Logic of God Incarnate*, pp. 112–115, has argued that our beliefs about the moral perfection of God can be used to limit what we take to be logically possible. On this approach, since experiencing lust and envy would conflict with God's moral perfection, it would be logically impossible for God to know lust and envy. The problem with this is that it has the paradoxical implication that certain things that it is logically impossible for an omniscient being to know, humans can know.

9. Cf. Richard R. La Croix, "Swinburne on Omnipotence," *International Journal for the Philosophy of Religion*, 6, 1975, pp. 251–255.

10. For a more detailed refutation of these objections, see Blumenfeld, "On the Compossibility of the Divine Attributes."

11. See Swinburne, *Coherence of Theism*, chap. 10.

12. This definition is due to Grim, "Some Neglected Problems of Omniscience." The usual definition of omniscience (X is omniscient = For any true proposition p, p is true IFF X knows that p) is rejected by Grim for the reason given above.

13. *Ibid.* See also Patrick Grim, "Against Omniscience: The Case from Essential Indexicals," *Nous*, 19, 1985, pp. 151–180.

14. Roland Puccetti, "Is Omniscience Possible?" *Australasian Journal of Philosophy*, 41, 1963, pp. 92–93.

15. For more on the problems involved in divine knowledge of mathematical infinity, see Morris Lazerowitz, "On a Property of a Perfect Being," *Mind*, 92, 1983, pp. 257–263.

16. Patrick Grim, "There Is No Set of All Truths," *Analysis*, 44, 1984, pp. 206–208.

17. See also Patrick Grim, "Logic and Limits of Knowledge and Truth," *Nous*, forthcoming.

18. Swinburne, *Coherence of Theism*, p. 145.

19. Swinburne is presumably assuming here that there are no counterfactuals of freedom. It seems correct to assume this, for the idea of counterfactuals of freedom makes little sense. See the discussion of counterfactuals of freedom in Chapter 15.

20. *Ibid.*, p. 172.

21. *Ibid.*, p. 175.

22. *Ibid.*, p. 179.

23. See, for example, I. T. Ramsey, "The Paradox of Omnipotence," *Mind*, 65, 1956, pp. 263–265; Bernard Mayo, "Mr. Keene on Omnipotence," *Mind*, 70, 1961, pp. 249–250; J. L. Cowan, "The Paradox of Omnipotence," *Analysis*, 25, 1963, pp. 102–108; C. Wade Savage, "The Paradox of the Stone," *Philosophical Review*, 76, 1967, pp. 74–79; Julian Wolfe, "Omnipotence," *Canadian Journal of*

Philosophy, 1, 1971, pp. 243–246; J. L. Cowan, "The Paradox of Omnipotence Revisited," *Canadian Journal of Philosophy*, 3, 1974, pp. 435–445.

24. Thomas P. Flint and Alfred J. Freddoso in "Maximal Power," *The Existence and Nature of God*, ed. Alfred J. Freddoso (Notre Dame, Ind.: University of Notre Dame Press, 1983), p. 99, have constructed a complicated technical analysis of omnipotence that also seems vulnerable to the sort of criticism offered here. According to Flint and Freddoso:

(D) S is omnipotent at t in world W IFF for any state of affairs p and world-type-for-S Ls such that p is not a member of Ls, if there is a world W* such that
　(i) Ls is true in both W and W*, and
　(ii) W* shares the same history with W at t, and
　(iii) at t in W* someone actualizes p,
　then S has the power at t in W to actualize p.

Consider the state of affairs p (where p = that Hidden Valley being flooded on Monday is actualized by a being that has never been omniscient and disembodied). This state of affairs does not seem to be excluded by any of the technical qualifications constructed by Flint and Freddoso that are in fact introduced to solve other problems. On the one hand, if S has the power to bring about p, then S could not be God if God is omniscient and disembodied. On the other hand, if S does not have the power to bring about p, then S could not be God if God is omnipotent. Yet God is supposed to be omnipotent, omniscient, and disembodied.

25. Richard Swinburne, *The Coherence of Theism* (Oxford: Clarendon Press, 1977), chap. 9; Richard Swinburne, "Omnipotence," *American Philosophical Quarterly*, 10, 1973, pp. 231–237.

26. Swinburne, *Coherence of Theism*, p. 159.

27. *Ibid.*, p. 288.

28. *Ibid.*

29. La Croix, "Swinburne on Omnipotence." For a different critique of Swinburne's definition see Joshua Hoffman and Gary Rosenkrantz, "Swinburne on Omnipotence," *Sophia*, 23, 1984, pp. 36–40.

30. Cf. George I. Mavrodes, "Defining Omnipotence," *Philosophical Studies*, 32, 1977, pp. 191–202.

31. *Ibid.*

32. Joshua Hoffman, "Mavrodes on Defining Omnipotence," *Philosophical Studies*, 35, 1977, pp. 311–313.

33. Charles Taliaferro, "The Magnitude of Omnipotence," *International Journal for the Philosophy of Religion*, 14, 1983, pp. 99–106.

34. The wording of our examples differs from Taliaferro's, since he assumes that the state of affairs at issue must have a certain property *necessarily*. I believe that if possible it is best to avoid this locution. However, our rationales seem to be the same: to assure that no cause of the state of affairs being brought about is the action of a being of a certain kind.

35. On the question of whether there can be more than one omnipotent being, see Louis Werner, (New York: Oxford University Press, 1978), "Some

Omnipotent Beings," *The Power of God*, ed. Linwood Urban and Douglas N. Walton (New York: Oxford University Press, 1978), pp. 94–106.

36. Swinburne in *Coherence of Theism*, chap. 7, may hold such a position. However, he certainly does not hold that omnipotence entails omniscience.

37. Taliaferro, "Magnitude of Omnipotence," p. 101.

38. Swinburne, *Coherence of Theism*, chaps. 9 and 10.

39. Although Taliaferro claims that Thomas Reid has an argument in which he attempts to derive omniscience from omnipotence, he cites no specific references in his paper and has not so far produced them in personal correspondence.

40. See Taliaferro, "Magnitude of Omnipotence," p. 101.

41. Jerome Gellman, "Omnipotency and Impeccability," *New Scholasticism*, 55, 1977, pp. 21–37.

42. *Ibid.*, p. 37.

43. This criticism based on the contextual nature of the notion of perfection should not be confused with another criticism based on the impossibility of a universal scale of value in which everything is value-commensurable. For an analysis of this latter argument see Morris, *Logic of God Incarnate*, pp. 78–81.

44. Swinburne, *Coherence of Theism*, pp. 38–49.

45. *Ibid.*, p. 49. However, Swinburne argues that the reverse is not true. If we had factual evidence that p is false, this would not show that p is inconsistent.

46. The difficulty of showing that sentences about God are consistent is compounded by another aspect of Swinburne's account. In the first part of his *Coherence of Theism*, Swinburne insists that the terms one uses to describe God are usually used in their ordinary mundane senses and not in senses that are analogous to these senses. Swinburne maintains that there are decided advantages in using terms in their ordinary senses in referring to God, since if these terms are used in senses that are only analogous to the ordinary senses it may be much harder to show inconsistency and consistency (p. 61). For example, once we eliminate some syntactical rules for the use of a term it is less clear than before what follows from a sentence p that contains this term. Once we loosen up the semantic rules, the use of the term that appears in p is also less clear than before whether sentence r that contains the term and that entails p is inconsistent. Indeed, in part 2 of *Coherence of Theism* his defense of the coherence of theism is based on understanding the terms that define technical terms such as "omnipotent" and "omniscient" in their mundane ordinary senses.

Despite these advantages of using terms that refer to God in their ordinary mundane senses, Swinburne finds it necessary in part 3 of *Coherence of Theism* to use some terms in referring to God in senses that are analogous to the ordinary senses. Thus he maintains that although God is a person, He must *necessarily* have attributes such as omnipotence, omniscience, and perfect freedom. God, unlike other persons, could not lack these attributes without loss of self-identity. Consequently, the term "person" when it refers to God is used in such a way as to be analogous to its ordinary use. However, Swinburne also says a change in the meaning of "person" will involve changing the meaning of many other terms that are closely connected with it. Some of these closely related terms are used to define other terms such as "omnipotence," "omniscience," and "perfect freedom" (pp. 272–274). So it would seem that in the end, almost all the terms used to define God must be used in an analogous sense. However, this would seem to adversely affect his defense of the coherence of theism in part 2 of his book. Swinburne says that a theist can play the "analogical card" but that it should not be played too often. Indeed, he calls it a "joker that would be self-defeating to play more than two or three times a game" (p. 272). Yet although he explicitly plays the analogical card only once, he seems to be playing it constantly from the bottom of the deck. As I have already mentioned, all his defense of the coherence of the thesis in part 2 is based on the assumption that the terms used to define terms such as "omnipotence," "omniscience," and "perfect freedom" are used in the ordinary mundane sense. Yet from what he says in part 3, they cannot be so used. Cf. Terrence Penelhum, review of Richard Swinburne's *The Coherence of Theism*, in *Journal of Philosophy*, 71, 1980, p. 507.

CHAPTER 13

1. Wesley C. Salmon, "Religion and Science: A New Look at Hume's *Dialogues*," *Philosophical Studies*, 33, 1978, pp. 143–176.

2. *Ibid.*, p. 151.

3. Nancy Cartwright, "Comments on Wesley Salmon's 'Science and Religion . . . ,'" *Philosophical Studies*, 33, 1978, pp. 177–183.

4. *Ibid.*, p. 182.

5. Wesley Salmon, "Experimental Atheism," *Philosophical Studies*, 35, 1979, pp. 101–104.

6. *Ibid.*, p. 102.

7. *Ibid.*, p. 103.

8. Whether Salmon's arguments would be affected by recent cosmological thinking that is influenced by the anthropic principle is not clear. For a brief discussion of this principle, see Chapter 5.

9. Salmon, "Religion and Science," p. 153.

10. Students of David Hume will recognize that I do little more than expand some of the arguments in *Dialogues Concerning Natural Religion*.

11. In recent literature one theist has gone so far as to argue that God does indeed have a body. God's body is the world. See, for example, Grace Jantzen, *God's World, God's Body* (Philadelphia: Westminster Press, 1984). Apparently, this unorthodox theology is in response to arguments attempting to show that the notion of a disembodied being is incoherent. Whether Jantzen's theology succeeds we need not decide here. The problem with this position, from the perspective of the present argument, is that either the world is created or it is not. If it is created, then it is improbable that God exists, even if we grant that He has a body, since in our experience there have been no cases of beings creating their own bodies. If it is not created, then an essential aspect of theism has been given up. For a discussion of Jantzen's views, see Charles Taliaferro, "The Incorporeality of God," *Modern Theology*, 3:2, 1987, pp. 179–188; Grace Jantzen, "Reply to Taliaferro," *Modern Theology*, 3:2, 1987, pp. 189–192.

12. See Ronald W. Hepburn, "Religious Doctrine of Creation," *The Encyclopedia of Philosophy*, ed. Paul Edwards (New York and London: Macmillan and Free Press, 1967), vol. 2, p. 252.

13. Wallace I. Matson, *The Existence of God* (Ithaca, N.Y.: Cornell University Press, 1965), p. 129.

14. *Ibid.*, pp. 129–130.

CHAPTER 14

1. Quoted by John Hick in *Evil and the God of Love*, rev. ed. (New York: Harper & Row, 1977), p. 5, n. 1.

2. See Michael Martin, "Is Evil Evidence Against the Existence of God?" *Mind*, 87, 1978, pp. 429–432.

3. William L. Rowe, "The Problem of Evil and Some Varieties of Atheism," *American Philosophy Quarterly*, 16, 1979, pp. 335–341; William L. Rowe, "The Empirical Argument from Evil," *Rationality, Religious Belief, and Moral Commitment*, ed. Robert Audi and William J. Wainwright (Ithaca, N.Y.: Cornell University Press, 1986), pp. 227–247.

4. Rowe, "Empirical Argument from Evil," p. 229.

5. *Ibid.*, p. 228, n. 3.

6. *Ibid.*, p. 235.

7. *Ibid.*

8. See Stephen Wykstra, "The Humean Obstacle to Evidential Arguments from Suffering: Avoiding the Evils of 'Appearance,'" *International Journal for the Philosophy of Religion*, 16, 1984, pp. 73–93; William Rowe, "Evil and the Theistic Hypothesis: A Response to Wykstra," *International Journal for the Philosophy of Religion*, 16, 1984, pp. 95–100.

9. According to Rowe, an evil is *outweighed* if and only if there is a good state of affairs G such that the conjunctive state of affairs G and E is a good state of affairs.

10. Rowe, "Empirical Argument from Evil," p. 240.

11. Delmas Lewis, "The Problem with the Problem of Evil," *Sophia*, 22, 1983, 26–35.

12. One of Rowe's critics admits that some suffering is pointless but denies that this counts against the existence of God. See Bruce Reichenbach, *Evil and a Good God* (New York: Fordham University Press, 1982), pp. 37–38. This argument is considered in Chapter 8.

13. Rowe, "Empirical Argument from Evil," p. 242.

14. *Ibid.*, p. 244.

15. *Ibid.*

16. *Ibid.*

17. *Ibid.*, p. 245.

18. Martin, "Is Evil Evidence Against the Existence of God?"

19. Robert Pargetter, "Evil as Evidence," *Sophia*, 21, 1982, pp. 14–15.

20. *Ibid.*, p. 13.

21. Paul Draper, "An Evidential Problem of Evil," unpublished.

22. Peter H. Hare and Edward H. Madden, "Evil and Inconclusiveness," *Sophia*, 11, 1975, p. 9.

23. In "An Evidential Problem of Evil" Draper argues that the hypothesis that neither the nature nor the conditions of sentient human beings result from

actions performed by benevolent or malevolent nonhuman persons has more explanatory value than theism. Draper's hypothesis is compatible with naturalism but not identical with it, since it is compatible with the existence of supernatural beings that have no concern with humans or other sentient creatures.

24. Hare and Madden, "Evil and Inconclusiveness," p. 9.

25. Alvin Plantinga, *The Nature of Necessity* (Oxford: Clarendon Press, 1974), pp. 193–195. I follow Plantinga's numbering in this section.

26. *Ibid.*, p. 194.

27. *Ibid.*, p. 195.

28. I am indebted in what follows to Michael Tooley, "Alvin Plantinga and the Argument from Evil," *Australasian Journal of Philosophy*, 58, 1980, pp. 360–376.

29. *Ibid.* pp. 368–370.

30. Alvin Plantinga, "Tooley and Evil: A Reply," *Australasian Journal of Philosophy*, 60, 1981, p. 75.

31. Alvin Plantinga, "The Probabilistic Argument from Evil," *Philosophical Studies*, 35, 1979, pp. 1–53. Again I follow Plantinga's numbering.

32. *Ibid.*, p. 30.

33. *Ibid.*

34. *Ibid.*, p. 44.

35. *Ibid.*, p. 49.

36. *Ibid.*

37. See Alvin Plantinga, "Is Belief in God Rational?" *Rationality and Belief in God*, ed. C. F. Delaney (Notre Dame, Ind.: University of Notre Dame Press, 1979); Alvin Plantinga, "Is Belief in God Properly Basic?" *Nous*, 15, 1981.

38. Bruce Reichenbach, "The Inductive Argument from Evil," *American Philosophical Quarterly*, 17, 1980, pp. 221–227. See also Bruce Reichenbach, *Evil and a Good God* (New York: Fordham University Press, 1982), chap. 2.

39. Reichenbach, "Inductive Argument from Evil," p. 227.

40. *Ibid.*

41. Consider fairies again. Let:

$P(F/N)$ = The probability that fairies exist, given the furniture and structure of the world (including sentient creatures, insentient creatures, physical objects, and laws of nature, but *excluding* any construed evidence for fairies' existence).

$P(\sim F/N)$ = The probability that fairies do not exist, given the furniture and structure of the world.

A = The usual evidence cited to show that fairies do not exist, such as the failure to observe fairies.

$P(A/N\&F)$ = The probability of A, given that the world described above obtains and that fairies exist.

$P(A/N\&\sim F)$ = The probability of A, given that the world described above obtains and that fairies do not exist.

$P(F/N\&A)$ = The probability that fairies exist, given that the world described above obtains and A is true.

Now, critics of the fairy hypothesis might argue that since there is no agreement over the prior probabilities—that is, over $P(F/N)$ and $P(\sim F/N)$—one should assign each of these probabilities the value of 0.5. Given this assignment, the value of P(F/N&A) will depend on the relation between P(A/N&F) and P(A/N ~F). In particular, if P(A/N&F) < P(A/N ~F), then P(F/N&A) < 0.5 and the critics have a prima facie case against fairies. The critics would go on to argue that P(A/N&F) <P(A/N ~F), since they would say that one would expect that if fairies existed, then A would not be true.

One could maintain that, construed in this way, the argument against fairies has serious problems. First, defenders of the fairy hypothesis might object to the way the prior probabilities are interpreted in the argument on the ground that not all relevant evidence is being considered. Defenders might say, that eyewitness evidence has been excluded, and this is relevant to P(F/N). In fact numerous perceptual reports of fairies were made during the years 1917–1920. See, for example, Robert Shaeffer, "Do Fairies Exist?" *The Skeptical Inquirer*, 2, Fall/Winter 1977, pp. 45–52, and Sir Arthur Conan Doyle, *The Coming of the Fairies* (New York: Samuel Weiser, 1921). In addition, a defender might object that the assignment of a prior probability of 0.5 to P(F/N) in case of a disagreement is an unsatisfactory procedure for settling disputes.

The defender might also maintain that the critics have no good reason to assume that P(A/N&F)<P(A/N ~F). For it might be the case that

(T') Fairies make it appear that they do not exist except to those who believe in them with a pure heart.

(T') is compatible with the falsehood of P(A/N&G)<P(A/N ~G). Furthermore, the defender might argue that although it may be unreasonable for people to believe (T'), it does not follow that it is reasonable to believe that (~T)—in other words, that it is not the case that fairies make it appear that they do not exist except to those who believe in them with a pure heart.

42. Moreover, a recent attempt to present a theistic inductive argument *from* evil to the existence of God is unsuccessful. See Michael Peterson, *Evil and the Christian God* (Grand Rapids, Mich.: Baker Books, 1982), chap. 5, and my criticism in "A Theistic Inductive Argument from Evil?" *International Journal for the Philosophy of Religion*, 22, 1987, pp. 81–87. In addition to the problems with Peterson's argument that I specify in this paper, there is another problem. Peterson argues that the moral evil that results from the exercise of human free will is gratuitous, and yet God cannot eliminate such evil without undermining human free will. Consequently, he maintains, God's existence and gratuitous evil are compatible. He never clearly defines what he means by gratuitous evil, yet it seems clear that on a standard definition of the term, theists cannot maintain that the moral evil resulting from free will is gratuitous. To call something a gratuitous evil normally entails that it can be eliminated and that this can be done without making the world worse. But as we shall see in the next chapter, theists maintain that elimination of free will and the evil produced by its exercise would result in a world that is worse than the present one. Peterson's claim that God's existence and gratuitous evil are compatible must therefore be based on some account of gratuitous evil *different* from the one usually accepted by theists. What this might be remains *completely* obscure.

43. For a long critical survey of arguments for the existence of God, including many of the minor arguments, see Michael Scriven, *Primary Philosophy* (New

York: McGraw-Hill, 1966), chap. 4. For another standard survey of some of the problems with traditional arguments and rationales, see Wallace I. Matson, *The Existence of God* (Ithaca, N.Y.: Cornell University Press, 1965). For the critique of particular arguments for the existence of God, see the articles on each of these arguments in *The Encyclopedia of Philosophy*, ed. Paul Edwards, (New York and London: Macmillan and Free Press, 1967), and *The Encyclopedia of Unbelief*, ed. Gordon Stein (Buffalo, N.Y.: Prometheus Books, 1985). For two recent critiques of the standard arguments and some nonstandard ones, see J. L. Mackie, *The Miracle of Theism* (Oxford: Clarendon Press, 1982) and Anthony O'Hear, *Experience, Explanation and Faith* (London: Routledge and Kegan Paul, 1984). For an extended survey and critique of theodicies old and new, see Edward H. Madden and Peter H. Hare, *Evil and the Concept of God* (Springfield, Ill.: Charles C. Thomas, 1968). See also Mackie, O'Hear, Matson, and the survey of possible solutions in Hare's article "The Problem of Evil," *Encyclopedia of Unbelief*.

CHAPTER 15

1. It should be noted that first-order evils need not be natural evils—in other words, evils that are not the result of intentional human choice. The pain and suffering and so on that are said to be necessary for second-order goods could be the result of intentional human choice.

2. J. L. Mackie, *The Miracle of Theism* (Oxford: Clarendon Press, 1982), p. 154.

3. *Ibid.*

4. Alvin Plantinga, *God, Freedom and Evil* (Grand Rapids, Mich.: Eerdmans, 1977), p. 30.

5. *Ibid.*, p. 29.

6. Richard Swinburne, *The Existence of God* (Oxford: Clarendon Press, 1979), p. 153.

7. C. A. Campbell, *On the Selfhood and Godhood* (London: Allen & Unwin, 1957), pp. 167–178.

8. For a general defense, see Wilfrid Sellars, "Thought and Action," *Freedom and Determinism*, ed. Keith Lehrer (New York: Random House, 1966), pp. 105–140; Wilfrid Sellars, "Fatalism and Determinism," *Freedom and Determinism*, pp. 141–174; Keith Lehrer, "An Empirical Disproof of Determinism?" *Freedom and Determinism*, pp. 175–202. For a defense within the context of the FWD, see Antony Flew, *God, Freedom and Immortality* (Buffalo, N.Y.; Prometheus Books, 1984), pp. 81–99; Mackie, *Miracle of Theism*, pp. 166–172.

9. Don M. Gottfredson, "Assessment Methods," *Crime and Justice*, vol. 3, ed. Sir Leon Radzinowicz and Marvin E. Wolfgang (New York: Basic Books, 1977), pp. 79–110.

10. Plantinga, *God, Freedom, and Evil*, pp. 29–30.

11. Flew, *God, Freedom and Immortality*, pp. 81–99. On this point, also see Wesley Morriston, "Is Plantinga's God Omnipotent?" *Sophia*, 23, 1984, 45–57.

12. See also David Basinger, "Christian Theism and the Free Will Defense," *Sophia*, 19, 1980, pp. 20–33. Basinger argues that the FWD is unsuccessful in establishing the compatibility of moral evil and God's specific sovereignty. God

has specific sovereignty if He can be assured that what He desires in any specific situation will come about. Yet as Basinger shows, Christian thinkers such as Aquinas, Calvin, and Luther have supposed that God has specific sovereignty.

13. One of the most recent and sophisticated accounts is that of John Foster in *Ayer* (London: Routledge and Kegan Paul, 1985), pp. 283–298. He has developed a theory of agent causality, which attempts to account for the contra-causal sense of freedom needed in the FWD and does not entail that decisions are random events. On this view an agent can cause some event such as a decision of the agent, but this decision is not caused by an event or a state of the agent's mind. Foster admits that agent causality is "philosophically perplexing" and attempts to construct an analysis of agent causality. His analysis relies on the notion of an intrinsic autonomous event, defined as an event such that if T is its intrinsic type, then it is *logically impossible* for an event of type T to be causally determined by prior conditions. Foster admits that such events may seem inconceivable. He defends such events by appeal to our intuitions in those cases in which we make decisions, but admits that in other cases our intuitions pull us in another direction. However, the issue here is not generated by intuitions conflicting with one another but by intuitions conflicting with empirical evidence. First, we know from other areas of inquiry that intuitions have often been mistaken. Thus our background knowledge should make us skeptical about relying on intuitions. Second, we have reason to suppose from our background theory that the actions of human beings are part of a causal nexus of events. Our background evidence makes the existence of intrinsic autonomous events improbable. Finally, the view that decisions are such events would exclude *a priori* any empirical investigation into their causal origins in terms of other events and thus would be methodologically inappropriate.

14. See Alvin Plantinga, "Is Theism Really a Miracle?" *Faith and Philosophy*, 3, 1986, p. 125.

15. Bruce Reichenbach, *Evil and a Good God* (New York: Fordham University Press, 1982), pp. 79–82.

16. *Ibid.*, p. 80.

17. *Ibid.*

18. Robert Young, "Omnipotence and Compatibilism," *Philosophia*, 6, 1976, pp. 49–67.

19. *Ibid.*, p. 62.

20. *Ibid.*, p. 61.

21. This thesis was first presented in J. L. Mackie, "Evil and Omnipotence," *Mind*, 64, 1955, pp. 200–212. See also Mackie, *Miracle of Theism*, chap. 9.

22. Plantinga, *God, Freedom, and Evil*, pp. 45–55. See also Alvin Plantinga, *The Nature of Necessity* (Oxford: Clarendon Press, 1974), pp. 174–190. I do not consider here whether in fact Leibniz would have any reply to Plantinga's charge. But there is good reason to suppose a Leibnizian would deny any lapse. See Robert Burch, "Plantinga and Leibniz's Lapse," *Analysis*, 39, 1979, pp. 24–29.

23. Plantinga, "Is Theism Really a Miracle?" p. 126.

24. See Robert Merrihew Adams, "Middle Knowledge and the Problem of Evil," *American Philosophical Quarterly*, 14, 1977, pp. 109–117; Robert M. Adams, "Plantinga on the Problem of Evil," *Alvin Plantinga*, ed. James E. Tomberlin and

Peter Van Inwager (Dordrecht, Holland: D. Reidel, 1985), pp. 225–255. See also Plantinga's reply to Adams in *Alvin Plantinga*, pp. 372–382.

25. In *The Nature of Necessity*, pp. 180–181, Plantinga maintains that his version of the FWD can dispense with the assumption that propositions (4) and (5) are true. However, it seems clear that in his alternative formulation some counterfactual of freedom must be true.

26. Cf. Adams, "Plantinga on the Problem of Evil." See also William Hasker, "A Refutation of Middle Knowledge," *Nous*, 20, 1986, pp. 545–557.

27. I owe this point to Patrick Grim, "Some Problems of Evil," unpublished.

28. There is an even more basic problem. Plantinga has assumed that some possible worlds are worse than others, and among the possible worlds that God can actualize, some are worse than others. I have assumed this as well, but in Chapter 18 we see that from a theistic perspective there is good reason to suppose that all possible worlds are equally good. Briefly the argument developed there is that since God is morally perfect, He is incapable of actualizing any world that is worse than any other. Thus any world that is worse than the present world is not one that God, given His moral perfection, can actualize. Consequently, any world that God can actualize has the same degree of goodness as any other He can actualize.

Given this way of thinking, it also follows that we were wrong to suppose that a possible world that God cannot directly actualize but can bring about by refraining from any direct action is better than Kronos. There may indeed be an actual world W_a that would exist if God did not actualize any world by directly causing it to exist, but W_a would not be any better than Kronos or any other world that God could directly bring about. For given God's moral perfection, God cannot directly or indirectly bring about any world that is worse than any other. Consequently, all logically possible worlds are equally good—the worlds that God can actualize directly and the worlds that he can actualize only indirectly by refraining from causing any world to be actualized. See Grim, "Some Problems of Evil."

29. See Fred Chernoff, "The Obstinance of Evil," *Mind*, 89, 1980, pp. 269–273.

30. Plantinga, *God, Freedom, and Evil*, p. 54.

31. Reichenbach, *Evil and a Good God*, pp. 14–16.

32. Mackie, *Miracle of Theism*, p. 175.

33. See, for example, David Basinger, "Middle Knowledge and Classical Christian Thought," *Religious Studies*, 22, 1986, pp. 407–422. Basinger argues that Christian theism is much more dependent on counterfactuals of freedom than most people have realized. Actually, Christian theism is much more dependent on counterfactuals of freedom than even Basinger realizes.

34. A similar argument is developed at greater length in Chapter 11.

35. Frederic Fitch, "A Logical Analysis of Some Value Concepts," *Journal of Symbolic Logic*, 28, 1963, pp. 135–142.

36. The following sketch is based on Douglas Walton, "Some Theorems of Fitch on Omnipotence," *The Power of God*, ed. Linwood Urban and Douglas N. Walton (New York: Oxford University Press, 1978), pp. 182–191.

37. *Ibid.*

38. Mackie, *Miracle of Theism,* p. 161.

39. *Ibid.*

40. See Page Keeton and Robert E. Keeton, *Cases and Materials on the Law of Torts,* 2d ed. (St. Paul, Minn.: West Publishing, 1977), chap. 8; H. L. A. Hart and A. M. Honoré, *Causality in the Law* (Oxford: Clarendon Press, 1956), chap. 5.

41. See *Larrimore* v. *American National Insurance Co.,* 184 Okl. 614 (1939), 89 P. 2d 340.

42. Keeton and Keeton, *Torts,* chap. 7.

43. *Ibid.,* chap. 12.

44. *Ibid.,* chap. 9.

45. Cf. Steven E. Boer, "The Irrelevance of the Free Will Defense," *Analysis,* 38, 1978, pp. 110–112.

CHAPTER 16

1. See, for example, John Hick's critique of the Augustinian type of theodicy in *Evil and the God of Love,* rev. ed. (New York: Harper & Row, 1977); and Edward H. Madden and Peter H. Hare's detailed evaluation of various solutions in *Evil and the Concept of God* (Springfield, Ill.: Charles C. Thomas, 1968).

2. Alvin C. Plantinga, *God, Freedom, and Evil* (Grand Rapids, Mich.: Eerdmans, 1974), chaps. 10 and 11.

3. *Ibid.,* p. 58.

4. See Chapter 13.

5. Michael Tooley, "Alvin Plantinga and the Argument from Evil," *Australasian Journal of Philosophy,* 58, 1980, p. 372.

6. Richard Swinburne, *The Existence of God* (Oxford: Clarendon Press, 1979), p. 202. See also J. L. Mackie, *The Miracle of Theism* (Oxford: Clarendon Press, 1982), p. 162, n. 12.

7. Plantinga, *God, Freedom, and Evil,* p. 62.

8. Rodney Stark and Charles Y. Glock, *American Piety: The Nature of Religious Commitment* (Berkeley and Los Angeles: University of California Press, 1968), pp. 37–38.

9. Burnham P. Beckwith, "The Effects of Education on Religious Faith," *Free Inquiry,* 2, Winter 1981/82, pp. 26–31; "The Effect of Intelligence on Religious Faith," *Free Inquiry,* 6, Spring 1986, pp. 46–53.

10. See, for example, H. C. Lehman and P. A. Witty, "Scientific Eminence and Church Membership," *Scientific Monthly,* 33, 1931, pp. 545–548; J. A. Chambers, "Creative Scientists of Today," *Science,* 145, 1964, pp. 1203–1205. For further evidence, see Beckwith, "Effect of Intelligence on Religious Faith."

11. Andrew Dickson White, *A History of the Warfare of Science with Theology* (Gloucester, Mass.: Peter Smith, 1978).

12. For a more extended discussion of this point, see Chapter 18.

13. Swinburne, *Existence of God,* chap. 11.

14. *Ibid.,* p. 219.

15. *Ibid.,* p. 202.

16. Cf. David O'Connor, "Swinburne on Natural Evil," *Religious Studies,* 19, 1983, p. 72.

17. *Ibid.*, p. 69.
18. Swinburne, *Existence of God*, p. 216.
19. *Ibid.*, p. 217.
20. *Ibid.*
21. Bruce R. Reichenbach, *Evil and a Good God* (New York: Fordham University Press, 1982), p. 101.
22. *Ibid.*, p. 45.
23. *Ibid.*, pp. 104–105.
24. *Ibid.*, p. 106. Reichenbach also maintains that even if the alternative of a world that operated by miracles were free of other problems he mentions, it would not solve the problem of evil. He argues that what might be good for or bring pleasure to person P_1 might not be good for or bring pleasure to person P_2. Hence it would be logically impossible for God to perform a miracle that was good for or brought pleasure to both P_1 and P_2. But this argument is confused. The problem of natural evil is not the problem of why everyone does not obtain what brings pleasure. What gives someone pleasure may not be good, and its absence may not be evil. Moreover, the atheologian is not asking that God do what is logically impossible. The problem of natural evil is why there is apparently pointless or gratuitous suffering that is not the result of any action for which an actor can be held responsible—suffering that apparently could be eliminated by an all-powerful being without adversely affecting the greater good.
25. *Ibid.*, p. 108.
26. *Ibid.*
27. *Ibid.*
28. Mackie, *Miracle of Theism*, p. 21. See also Swinburne, *Existence of God*, p. 230, for another account of miracles that allows for the violation of natural laws.
29. Reichenbach, *Evil and a Good God*, p. 108.
30. *Ibid.*, p. 109.
31. *Ibid.*
32. *Ibid.*, p. 101.
33. William L. Rowe, *Philosophy of Religion* (Belmont, Calif.: Wadsworth, 1978), p. 88.
34. Reichenbach, *Evil and a Good God*, p. 39.
35. *Ibid.*, p. 44.
36. *Ibid.*, p. 102. According to Reichenbach, no person can be held accountable for an action if it was impossible for the person to have done otherwise.
37. *Ibid.*, p. 39.

CHAPTER 17

1. See John Hick, *Evil and the God of Love*, rev. ed. (New York: Harper & Row, 1977), chaps. 9 and 10.
2. *Ibid.*
3. *Ibid.*, pts. 1 and 2.
4. See Alvin Plantinga, *God, Freedom, and Evil* (Grand Rapids, Mich.: Eerdmans, 1974), pp. 57–59.
5. Hick, *Evil and the God of Love*, p. 250. For further discussion of this point,

see Illtyd Trethowan, "Dr. Hick and the Problem of Evil," *Journal of Theological Studies,* N.S., 18, 1967, pp. 407–416; John Hick, "The Problem of Evil in the First and Last Things," *Journal of Theological Studies,* N.S., 19, 1968, pp. 591–602.

6. Hick, *Evil and the God of Love,* p. 250.

7. *Ibid.,* p. 253.

8. *Ibid.,* p. 264.

9. *Ibid.,* pp. 365–370.

10. *Ibid.,* pp. 266–275.

11. *Ibid.,* p. 276.

12. *Ibid.*

13. *Ibid.,* p. 277.

14. *Ibid.,* p. 280.

15. *Ibid.,* p. 282.

16. *Ibid.,* p. 286.

17. *Ibid.,* p. 287.

18. *Ibid.,* p. 305.

19. *Ibid.,* p. 306.

20. *Ibid.,* p. 307.

21. *Ibid.,* p. 318.

22. *Ibid.*

23. *Ibid.,* p. 333.

24. *Ibid.*

25. See Trethowan, "Dr. Hick and the Problem of Evil," pp. 407–416; Hick, "Problem of Evil in the First and Last Things," pp. 591–602.

26. Hick, *Evil and the God of Love,* pp. 342–343. This view is elaborated in John Hick, *Death and Eternal Life* (New York: Harper & Row, 1976), chap. 13.

27. Hick, *Evil and the God of Love,* p. 351.

28. See Roland Puccetti, "The Loving God—Some Observations on John Hick's *Evil and the God of Love,* in *Religious Studies,* 2, 1967, pp. 255–268; G. Stanley Kane, "The Failure of Soul-Making Theodicy," *International Journal for the Philosophy of Religion,* 6, 1975, pp. 1–22; John Hick, "God, Evil and Mystery," *Religious Studies,* 3, 1968, pp. 539–1546; Hick, *Evil and the God of Love,* pp. 376–386.

29. Puccetti, "Loving God," p. 260.

30. Kane, "Failure of Soul-Making Theodicy."

31. Hick, "God, Evil and Mystery," p. 545.

32. Hick, *Evil and the God of Love,* p. 351.

33. See J. L. Mackie, *The Miracle of Theism* (Oxford: Clarendon Press, 1982), p. 153.

34. Hick, *Evil and the God of Love,* p. 281.

35. *Ibid.*

36. *Ibid.,* p. 286.

37. *Ibid.,* p. 278.

38. *Ibid.,* p. 282.

39. Hick, "God, Evil and Mystery," p. 541.

40. Hick, *Evil and the God of Love,* p. 282.

41. *Ibid.*

42. *Ibid.*, p. 278.

43. Cf. Keith Ward, "Freedom and the Irenaen Theodicy," *Journal of Theological Studies,* N.S., 20, 1969, pp. 249–254.

44. Hick seems to admit that postmortem beings would be able to conclude that they were existing after death. See Hick, *Death and Eternal Life,* chap. 20.

45. G. Stanley Kane, "Soul-Making Theodicy and Eschatology," *Sophia,* 14, 1975, pp. 24–31. Hick mentions this paper in *Evil and the God of Love* and refers the reader to *Death and Eternal Life,* chap. 13 and his replies to Ward and Rist. See John Hick, "Freedom and Irenaean Theodicy Again," *Journal of Theological Studies,* N.S., 21, 1970, pp. 419–422; John Hick, "Coherence and the God of Love Again," *Journal of Theological Studies,* N.S., 24, 1973, pp. 522–528. But I cannot see that he has answered this objection in chapter 13 or in these replies.

46. Hick, *Evil and the God of Love,* p. 276.

47. Cf. Ward, "Freedom and Irenaen Theodicy." Ward finds, as I do, two conflicting notions of freedom in Hick's work. The one is a notion of freedom in which human decisions are *completely* unpredictable. In his reply to Ward (Hick, "Freedom and Irenaean Theodicy Again") Hick rightly rejects this notion as not his. However, Hick does have the notion of human freedom as partially unpredictable, and this may be enough to create a tension in his views. For further discussion of Hick's notion of freedom and human salvation, see John M. Rist, "Coherence and the God of Love," *Journal of Theological Studies,* N.S., 23, 1972, pp. 95–105; Hick, "Coherence and the God of Love Again."

48. Hick, *Death and Eternal Life,* chap. 13.

49. This paradox should be compared with the paradox presented in Kane, "Failure of Soul-Making Theodicy," pp. 15–22. Whether Hick has successfully answered Kane is unclear (Hick, *Evil and the God of Love,* pp. 376–384). However, it seems quite clear that he has not answered the present objection.

50. Kane in "The Failure of Soul-Making Theodicy," p. 16, interprets Hick as saying that epistemic distance is an objective fact about the world and does not change in terms of people's beliefs. I am not sure if this is Hick's view, but it seems to me that even if epistemic distance is an objective fact about the world, what is relevant for free acceptance of God is not the objective fact but people's perception of this fact. If people thought that God's presence was obvious, whatever the objective fact is, Hick would have to say that there is less freedom in the choice of God.

CHAPTER 18

1. Strictly speaking this defense is not open to theists, who, by definition, believe in an all-powerful God. Consequently, atheists in the narrow sense need not take a particular stance on this theodicy. However, the defense is interesting in its own right, and I consider it here although it is not completely relevant to the main purpose in this book.

2. Harold S. Kushner, *When Bad Things Happen to Good People* (New York: Schocken Books, 1981).

3. *Ibid.*, pp. 46–47.

4. *Ibid.*, p. 52.

5. *Ibid.*, p. 58.

6. *Ibid.* I could be wrong in my interpretations of Kushner, since he is not completely clear. It is possible that in a much less sophisticated way than professional philosophers, Kushner is suggesting that it is logically impossible for God to create a world without random evil, or a world with laws with less evil consequences, or a world in which He intervenes and prevents evil. However, if this is Kushner's thesis, his theodicy is similar to Plantinga's and to others that I have already examined and rejected.

7. *Ibid.*, p. 64.

8. For a more formal statement of this argument, see Michael Martin, "The Formalities of Evil and a Finite God—Corrigenda," *Critica*, 10, 1978, pp. 133–135. For a similar argument, see P. J. McGrath, "Evil and the Existence of a Finite God," *Analysis*, 46, 1986, pp. 63–64.

9. Michael B. Burke, "Theodicy with a God of Limited Power: A Reply to McGrath," *Analysis*, 47, 1987, pp. 57–58.

10. See, for example, John Stuart Mill, "A Limited God," in *Philosophical and Religious Issues*, ed. Edward L. Miller (Belmont, Calif: Dickenson, 1971), pp. 266–270. For a bibliography of literature regarding finitist concepts of God, see Edgar S. Brightman, *A Philosophy of Religion* (New York: Prentice Hall, 1940), pp. 286–301; and Peter A. Bertocci, "The Explanation of Excess Evil," in *An Introduction to the Philosophy of Religion* (New York: Prentice Hall, 1951), pp. 420–440.

11. For an extensive critique of Brightman's so-called finite God solution to the problem of evil, see Edward H. Madden and Peter H. Hare, *Evil and the Concept of God* (Springfield, Ill.: Charles C. Thomas, 1968), pp. 107–114. However, it may be misleading to say that Brightman held in any straightforward way a finite concept of God. See John H. Lavely, "Edgar Sheffield Brightman: Good-and-Evil and Finite-Infinite God," *The Boston Personalist Tradition in Philosophy, Social Ethics and Theology*, ed. Paul Deats and Carol Robb (Macon, Ga.: Mercer University Press, 1986), pp. 121–146.

12. This theodicy is usually associated with Gottfried Leibniz.

13. See Voltaire's novel *Candide* and the song "The Best of All Possible Worlds" from the Leonard Bernstein musical *Candide*.

14. See Madden and Hare, *Evil and the Concept of God*, for further criticisms of Leibniz's theodicy.

15. Alvin Plantinga, *God, Freedom, and Evil* (Grand Rapids, Mich.: Eerdmans, 1977), p. 61.

16. See also Peter Forrest, "The Problem of Evil: Two Neglected Defenses," *Sophia*, 20, 1981, pp. 49–54.

17. In rejecting Gaunilo's parody of the ontological argument, Plantinga argued that there could not be an island such that no greater island could be conceived of. He maintained that no matter how good an island is imagined—for example, one with x number of coconut trees—an island with more coconut trees could be imagined. I argue in Chapter 2 that on a perfect island there might be some right number of coconut trees. That this counterargument would hold in the present case is not completely clear. An island is by definition limited in space, and at some point the addition of coconut trees to it would be ecologically undesirable. But a possible world could be unlimited in space. In any case, one

might argue that in the best of all possible worlds, unlike the best of all possible islands, the number of coconut trees is irrelevant. Other attributes mentioned by Plantinga would be more relevant. For example, the number of happy people may be a crucial ingredient in deciding whether it is the best possible world. But if so, no matter how many happy people there are in a given possible world, God could actualize a world with more happy people. Suppose that the quality as well as the quantity of the happiness in a possible world is crucial in deciding if this is the best possible world. It can be argued that no matter how high the quality of the happiness in any given possible world, there is a possible world with a higher quality of happiness. See George Schlesinger, *Religion and Scientific Method* (Dordrecht, Holland: D. Reidel, 1981), pp. 59–63; and Patrick Grim, "Some Problems of Evil," unpublished. I conclude that Plantinga's argument has some initial plausibility, and if it is accepted, it shows that the concept of the best possible world is incoherent.

18. Grim, "Some Problems of Evil."

19. Thomas V. Morris in *The Logic of God Incarnate* (Ithaca: Cornell University Press, 1986), pp. 112–113, suggests that theists may maintain that although no logical possible world is worse than this world, there are at least partially *conceivable* worlds worse than this. He bases this view on a particular interpretation of partially conceivable that in turn is based on an unexplained interpretation of counterfactuals with necessarily false antecedents. He maintains that some worlds are at least partially conceivable that would, if *per impossible* God did not exist, be worse than this world. Morris must maintain that some counterfactuals with logical false antecedents are true while others are false, thus departing from a standard interpretation that assumes that all counterfactuals with logically false antecedents are true. However, Morris provides no grounds for his construal and seems to ignore the difficulties of interpreting counterfactuals in general and counterfactuals with necessarily false antecedents in particular. For example, Morris does not tell us how we can tell which counterfactuals with logically false antecedents are true and which are false.

20. See Chapter 15 for the argument showing that only one of these worlds could be actual.

21. A similar argument has been developed by Lawrence Resnick in "God and the Best Possible World," *American Philosophical Quarterly*, 10, 1973, pp. 313–317. A theist could avoid Resnick's conclusion by denying that God necessarily exists, and many philosophical theists do not believe in what Resnick calls the God of the ontological argument. However, the argument that the concept of the best of all possible worlds is incoherent has been developed, in a way that does not assume this view of God, by Grim in "Some Problems of Evil." I here rely on a simplified version of his argument rather than on Resnick's.

22. Grim, "Some Problems of Evil."

23. John Hick, *Evil and the God of Love* rev. ed. (New York: Harper & Row, 1977), p. 247.

24. *Ibid.*, pp. 249–250. See also Madden and Hare, *Evil and the Concept of God*, pp. 71–73.

25. Madden and Hare, *Evil and the Concept of God*, p. 60.

26. *Ibid.*, p. 61. Madden and Hare argue that if evil is only an illusion from

our limited perspective, then we should not try to change what seems evil to what seems good, and "any efforts to remove *prima facie* evil are morally pernicious." This is not quite correct. They are correct that we should not try to improve things. But this is because our efforts would be futile, not morally pernicious.

27. For further criticisms of this position, see *ibid.*, pp. 64–65.

28. Schlesinger, *Religion and Scientific Method*, chaps. 9 and 10.

29. *Ibid.*, pp. 62–63.

30. Philip L. Quinn, review of Schlesinger, *Religion and Scientific Method*, in *Philosophy of Science*, 46, 1979, pp. 170–171.

31. Peter H. Hare, "The Problem of Evil," *The Encyclopedia of Unbelief* (Buffalo, N.Y.: Prometheus Books, 1985), vol. 1, p. 190.

32. See Paul Edwards, "The Case Against Reincarnation: Part 1," *Free Inquiry*, 6, Fall 1986, pp. 24–34; "Part 2," *Free Inquiry*, 7, Winter 1986/87, pp. 38–43.

33. Edwards, "Case Against Reincarnation: Part 1," p. 27. Edwards cites Dr. Raynor Johnson, former Master of Queen's College, University of Melbourne, as a leading spokesman of Christian reincarnationists.

34. *Ibid.*, pt. 2, p. 42.

35. *Ibid.*, p. 41.

36. *Ibid.*, pp. 40–41.

37. *Ibid.*, p. 43.

38. Madden and Hare, *Evil and the Concept of God*, p. 57.

39. This is compatible with the claim made in Chapter 12 that in order for a being to be all-knowing, it has to have knowledge by acquaintance of all aspects of everything. For example, to be all-knowing one would have to have knowledge by acquaintance of the suffering of a person being tortured.

40. See Madden and Hare, *Evil and the Concept of God*.

Conclusion

1. See Jay Newman, *Foundations of Religious Tolerance* (Toronto: University of Toronto Press, 1982), chap. 1.

2. See the articles on religion and atheism in the Soviet Union in *Humanist*, 47, January/February 1987. I am especially indebted to Robert M. Hemstreet, "Religious Humanism Meets Scientific Atheism," pp. 5–7, 34. See also Dimitry V. Pospielovsky, *A History of Marxist–Leninist Atheism and Soviet Antireligious Policies*, vol. 1 (New York: St. Martin's Press, 1987), for a detailed account of Soviet antireligious policies.

3. John Rawls, *A Theory of Justice* (Cambridge, Mass.; Harvard University Press, 1971), chaps. 2 and 3.

4. These principles are in lexical order; that is, the first principle has precedence over the second principle, and part (a) of the second principle has precedence over part (b).

5. For example, there is no reference to religion in the index to his *Theory of Justice*.

6. This is not to say that Rawls's derivation of the principle of justice is free from problems or that his method has not been criticized. For some of these

criticisms, see Norman Daniels, ed., *Reading Rawls: Critical Studies of A Theory of Justice* (New York: Basic Books, 1975).

7. For an analysis of the relation between war and religion, see Charles W. Sutherland, *Disciples of Destruction: The Religious Origins of War and Terrorism* (Buffalo, N.Y.: Prometheus Books, 1987).

8. *The World Christian Encyclopedia* estimated in 1980 that there were 30 atheistic states in the world and 1,488 million people living under atheistic regimes. See *The World Christian Encyclopedia*, ed. David Barrett (New York: Oxford University Press, 1982), p. 5.

9. See Paul Kurtz, "The Growth of Fundamentalism Worldwide: A Humanist Response," *Free Inquiry*, 7, Winter 1986/87, pp. 18–24.

10. *Ibid.*, p. 22.

11. *Ibid.* See also Paul Kurtz, *The Transcendental Temptation* (Buffalo, N.Y.: Prometheus Books, 1986).

Appendix

1. Gordon Stein, "The Meaning of Atheism and Agnosticism," *An Anthology of Atheism and Rationalism*, ed. Gordon Stein (Buffalo, N.Y.: Prometheus Books, 1980), p. 3.

2. This negative sense of atheism should be distinguished from the sense introduced by Paul Edwards. According to Edwards, an atheist is a person who rejects a belief in God. This rejection may be because the person believes that the statement "God exists" is false, but it may have other reasons. The negative sense of atheism used here is broader than the Edwards definition, since on the present definition someone could be an atheist who had no belief in God, although the lack of belief was not the result of rejection. See Paul Edwards, "Atheism," *The Encyclopedia of Philosophy*, ed. Paul Edwards (New York and London: Macmillan and Free Press, 1967), vol. 1, p. 175.

3. *Ibid.*, p. 4.

4. George H. Smith, *Atheism: The Case Against God* (Buffalo, N.Y.: Prometheus Books, 1979), p. 7.

5. Antony Flew, "The Presumption of Atheism," *Canadian Journal of Philosophy*, 2, 1972, p. 30.

6. Stein, "Meaning of Atheism and Agnosticism," p. 3.

7. "American Atheists: An Introduction," distributed by American Atheists, Massachusetts chapter, P.O. Box 147, E. Walpole, MA 02032.

8. "American Atheists: A History," American Atheists, Massachusetts chapter.

9. See Monroe Beardsley and Elizabeth Beardsley, *Philosophical Thinking: An Introduction* (New York: Harcourt Brace, 1965), pp. 46–50. The definition of god proposed by Beardsley and Beardsley has considerable merit. On their view, for a being to be a god it must meet four criteria: It must have supernatural powers; be free from so many of the natural limitations of inanimate objects, subhuman organisms, and humans that it cannot be classified as belonging to any of these groups; have some kind of mental life; and be regarded as superior to human beings.

10. I owe the distinction between the broad and narrow senses of atheism to William L. Rowe, "The Problem of Evil and Some Varieties of Atheism," *American Philosophical Quarterly*, 16, 1979, pp. 335–341.

11. This seems to be the position of Kai Nielsen. He rejects a nonanthropomorphic god as meaningless and an anthropomorphic god as false. See, for example, Kai Nielsen, "Introduction: How Is Atheism to Be Characterized?" *Philosophy and Atheism* (Buffalo, N.Y.: Prometheus Books, 1985). See also his "Atheism," *Encyclopaedia Britannica*, vol. 2, 1984.

12. Fyodor Dostoyevsky, *The Brothers Karamazov* (New York: Random House Modern Library ed., n.d.), p. 254.

13. Patrick Masterson, *Atheism and Alienation* (Notre Dame, Ind.: University of Notre Dame Press, 1971), p. 133.

14. Quoted *ibid.*, p. 182, n. 6.

15. Cf. Kai Nielsen, "How Is Atheism to Be Characterized?" p. 12.

16. This statement does not, of course, do complete justice to the subtlety of the position of Ivan Karamazov. For a sensitive analysis of this position, see Stewart R. Sutherland, *Atheism and the Rejection of God* (Oxford: Blackwell, 1977), chap. 2. The only problem with Sutherland's analysis is that he insists on calling Ivan Karamazov an atheist. I believe it would be much clearer to use some other term. The position of alienated theism should be distinguished from a position that maintains that one or more gods exist but have nothing to do with salvation. This position, held by Jainists and some Buddhists, has been called soterilogical atheism. See Arvind Sharma, "Buddhism and Atheism," *Sophia*, 16, 1977, p. 29. Again, I think it misleading to use the term "atheism" in this way.

17. Quoted in Stein, *Anthology of Atheism and Rationalism*, p. 5.

18. Cf. Gordon Stein, "Agnosticism," *Encyclopedia of Unbelief*, vol. 1, pp. 3–4.

19. See Richard Popkin, "Skepticism," *Encyclopedia of Unbelief*, vol. 2, pp. 625–633.

20. Lauchlan Chipman, "Rationalism,"*Encyclopedia of Unbelief*, vol. 2, pp. 531–533.

21. A. R. Lacey, *A Dictionary of Philosophy* (New York: Scribner's, 1976), p. 180.

22. Bernard Williams, "Rationalism," *Encyclopedia of Philosophy*, vol. 7, p. 69.

23. *Ibid.*

24. Stein, *Anthology of Atheism and Rationalism*, p. 315.

25. *Ibid.*, p. 24.

26. Arthur Danto, "Naturalism," *Encyclopedia of Philosophy*, vol. 5, p. 448.

27. John Dewey, *A Common Faith* (New Haven, Ct.: Yale University Press, 1934), p. 42.

28. See William Alston, "Natural Reconstructions of Religion," *Encyclopedia of Philosophy*, vol. 7, pp. 145–146; Christopher Kent, "Positivism," *Encyclopedia of Unbelief*, vol. 2, pp. 512–518.

29. Bruce Mazlish, "Auguste Comet," *Encyclopedia of Philosophy*, vol. 2, pp. 173–177; Christopher Kent, "Auguste Comte," *Encyclopedia of Unbelief*, vol. 1, pp. 119–120.

30. Peter Alexander, "Ernst Mach," *Encylopedia of Philosophy*, vol. 5, pp. 115–119.

31. See Michael Scriven, *Primary Philosophy* (New York: McGraw-Hill, 1966),

chap. 4; Michael Scriven, "A Study of Radical Behaviorism," *Minnesota Studies in the Philosophy of Science*, vol. 1, ed. Herbert Feigl and Michael Scriven (Minneapolis: University of Minnesota Press, 1965), pp. 88–130. Thus Ignace Lepp is mistaken when he says that "the 'perfect' atheist would be one who believes in no being or forces that transcend the empirical order." See Ignace Lepp, *Atheism in Our Time* (New York: Macmillan, 1963), p. 5.

32. John Passmore, "Logical Positivism," *Encyclopedia of Philosophy*, vol. 5, pp. 52–57; Paul Edwards, "Logical Positivism and Unbelief," *Encyclopedia of Unbelief*, vol. 2, pp. 422–435.

33. R. B. Braithwaite, *An Empiricist's View of the Nature of Religious Beliefs* (Cambridge: Cambridge University Press, 1955).

34. Nicola Abbagnano, "Humanism," *Encyclopedia of Philosophy*, vol. 4, pp. 69–72; Max Otto; "Humanism," *Colliers Encyclopedia*, vol. 12, 1980, pp. 349–350.

35. Otto, "Humanism," p. 350.

36. Cf. Paul Kurtz, "Humanism," *Encyclopedia of Unbelief*, vol. 1, pp. 328–333; E. Royston Pike, *Encyclopedia of Religion* (New York: Meridian Books, 1958), p. 185.

37. Alston, "Natural Reconstructions of Religion," p. 146.

38. "The Academy of Humanism," *Free Inquiry*, 3, Fall 1983, p. 6. See also Marvin Zimmerman, "Aren't Humanists Really Atheists?" *The Humanist Alternative*, ed. Paul Kurtz (Buffalo, N.Y.: Prometheus Books, 1973), pp. 83–85.

39. See, for example, Paul Kurtz, "On Definition-Mongering," *Free Inquiry*, 6, Fall 1986, p. 54.

40. Reprinted in Corliss Lamont, *The Philosophy of Humanism*, 6th ed. (New York: Frederick Ungar, 1982), p. 287.

41. Frederick Edwords, "The Humanist Philosophy in Perspective," *Humanist*, January/February 1984, pp. 17–20, 42.

42. Neil McInnes, "Communism," *Encyclopedia of Philosophy*, vol. 2, p. 160.

43. See, for example, Ayn Rand, *For the New Intellectual* (New York: Random House, 1961); Ayn Rand, *The Virtues of Selfishness* (New York: New American Library, 1964).

44. See V. G. Kierman, "Religion," *A Dictionary of Marxist Thought*, ed. Tom Bottomore (Cambridge, Mass.: Harvard University Press, 1983), pp. 413–416; George J. Stack, "Karl Marx," *Encyclopedia of Unbelief*, vol. 2, pp. 441–444.

45. See Gordon Stein, "Freethought," *Encyclopedia of Unbelief*, vol. 1, pp. 247–248.

46. *Ibid.* See also "Freethinkers," *The New Columbia Encyclopedia* (New York: Columbia University Press, 1975), p. 1008.

47. Howard B. Radest, "Ethical Culture," *Encyclopedia of Unbelief*, vol. 1, pp. 169–174; Percival Chubb, "Societies for Ethical Culture," *The New Schaff-Herzog Encyclopedia of Religious Knowledge*, ed. Samuel Macauley Jackson (New York and London: Funk & Wagnalls, 1909), vol. 4, pp. 183–184.

INDEX

535